CIVILIZATION IN THE WEST

VOLUME A TO 1500

CIVILIZATION IN THE WEST

VOLUME A TO 1500

MARK KISHLANSKY
University of Chicago

PATRICK GEARY
University of Florida

PATRICIA O'BRIEN
University of California, Irvine

HarperCollins*Publishers*

Executive Editor: Bruce Borland
Development Editor: Betty Slack
Project Coordination: The Wheetley Company, Inc.
Cover Design: Lucy Lesiak Design, Inc.: Lucy Lesiak
Text Design: Debbie Costello
Photo Research: Sandy Schneider
Cartographer: Paul Yatabe. Maps produced by Mapping Specialists, Inc.
Production: Michael Weinstein
Compositor: Dayton Typographic Services
Printer and Binder: R.R. Donnelley & Sons Company
Cover Printer: The Lehigh Press, Inc.

Cover: (background) Detail from the cycle of frescos depicting *The Legend of the True Cross* by Piero della Francesca, c. 1450s. In the church of San Francesco, Arezzo. Courtesy Superintendence of Cultural, Architectural, Asristic and Historical Welfare of Arezzo; (inset) Saracophagus of Larthia Scianti, Etruscan, second century B. C. Hirmer Fotoarchiv, Munich.

Civilization in the West, Volume A To 1500

Library of Congress Cataloging-in-Publication Data
Kishlansky, Mark A.
    Civilization in the West / Mark Kishlansky, Patrick Geary,
  Patricia O'Brien.
        p.   cm.
    Includes bibliographical references and index.
    Contents: v. A. To 1500 -- v. B. 1350-1815 -- v. C. Since 1789.
    ISBN 0-673-46386-9 (v. A). -- ISBN 0-673-46387-7 (v. B). --
  ISBN 0-673-46388-5 (v. C)
    1. Civilization, Occidental--History. I. Geary, Patrick J.,
  1948- . II. O'Brien, Patricia, 1945-   . III. Title.
  CB245.K546 1991c
  909'.09821--dc20   90-23788
                                                        CIP

    91 92 93   9 8 7 6 5 4 3 2

Contents

1 The First Civilizations 1

2 Early Greece 33

Maps

Charts, Tables, and Figures

Preface

We have tried to write a book that students would *want* to read. Throughout three years of planning, writing, revising, rewriting, and numerous meetings together, this was our constant overriding concern. Would students read this? Would it be effective in conveying information while stimulating imagination? Would it work across the variety of Western civilization courses, with the different levels and formats that make up this fundamental course? It was not easy to keep this concern in the forefront through the long months of composition, but it was easy to receive the reactions of scores of reviewers to this single questions: "Would students *want* to read these chapters?" Whenever we received a resounding "no!" we began again—not just rewriting, but rethinking how to present material that might be complex in argument or detail or that might simply seem too remote to engage the contemporary student. Though all three of us were putting in long hours in front of word processors, we quickly learned that we were engaged in a teaching rather than a writing exercise. And though the work was demanding, it was not unrewarding. We hope that you will recognize and come to share with us the excitement and enthusiasm we experienced in creating this text. We have enjoyed writing this book, and we want students to enjoy reading it.

Approach

We made a number of decisions early in the project that we feel contributed to our goal. First, we were *not* writing an encyclopedia of Western civilization. Information was not to be included in a chapter unless it fit within the themes of that chapter. There was to be no information for information's sake, and each of us was called upon to defend the inclusion of names, dates, and events whenever we met to critique our chapters. We found, to our surprise, that by adhering to the principle that information included must contribute to or illustrate a particular point or dominating theme, we provided as much, if not more, material than books that habitually list names, places, and dates without any other context.

Secondly, we were committed to integrating the history of ordinary men and women into our narrative. We believe that isolated sections, placed at the end of chapters, that deal with the experiences of women or minority groups in a particular era profoundly distort historical experience. We called this technique *caboosing*, and whenever we found ourselves segregating women or families or the masses, we stepped back and asked how we might recast our treatment of historical events to account for a diversity of actors. How did ordinary men, women, and children affect the course of world historical events? How did world historical events affect the fabric of daily life for men and women and children from all walks of life? We tried to rethink critical historical problems of civilization as gendered phenomena. To assist us in this endeavor, we engaged two reviewers whose sole responsibility was to evaluate our chapters for the integration of these social groups into the themes of our chapters.

We took the same approach to the coverage of central and eastern Europe that we did to women and minorities. Even before the epochal events of 1989 that returned this region to the forefront of international attention, we realized that in too many textbooks the Slavic world was treated as "marginal" to the history of Western civilization. Thus, with the help of a specialist reviewer, we worked to integrate more of the history of eastern Europe into our text than is found in most others, and to do so in a way that presented these regions, their cultures and their institutions, as integral rather than peripheral to Western civilization.

To construct a book that students would *want* to read, we needed to develop fresh ideas about how to involve them with the material, how to transform them from passive recipients to active participants. We borrowed from computer science both the language and the concept of "user-friendly." We wanted to find ways to stimulate the imagination of the student, and the more we experimented with different techniques, the more we realized that the most effective way to do this was visually. It is not true that contemporary students cannot be taught effectively by the written word; it is only true that they cannot be taught *as* effectively as they can by the combination of words and images. From the beginning, we realized that a text produced in full color was essential to the features we most wanted to use: the pictorial chapter openers; the large number of maps, some inset directly into the text for maximum effectiveness; the geographical tours of Europe with their specially designed maps; and the two-page special feature in each chapter, each with its own illustration.

Features

It is hard to have a new idea when writing a textbook—so many authors have come before, each attempting to do something more effective, more innovative than his or her predecessor. It is probably the case that somewhere there has been a text that has used a chapter-opening feature similar to the one we use here. What we can say with certainty is that nothing else we experimented with, no other technique we attempted, has had such an immediate and positive impact on our readers or has so fulfilled our goal of involving the students in learning as our **pictorial chapter openers**. An illustration—a painting, a photograph, a picture, an artifact, an edifice—appears at the beginning of each chapter, accompanied by text through which we explore the picture, guiding students across a canvas or helping them see in an artifact or a piece of architecture details that are not immediately apparent. It is the direct combination of text and image that allows us to achieve this effect, to "unfold" both an illustration and a theme. In some chapters we highlight details, pulling out a section of the original picture to take a closer look. In others we attempt to shock the viewer into the recognition of horror, or of beauty. Some chapter-opener images are designed to

transport students back into time, to make them ask the question, "What was it like to be there?" All of the opening images have been chosen to illustrate a dominant theme within the chapter, and the dramatic and lingering impression they make helps reinforce that theme.

We have taken a similar image-based approach to our **presentation of geography**. When teachers of Western civilization courses are surveyed, no single area of need is cited more often that geographical knowledge. Students simply have no mental image of Europe, no familiarity with those geophysical features that are a fundamental part of the geopolitical realities of Western history. We realized that maps, carefully planned and skillfully executed, would be an important component of our text. To complement the standard map program of the text, we have added a special geographical feature. Six times throughout the book, we pause in the narrative to take a tour of Europe. Sometimes we follow an emperor as he tours his realm; sometimes we examine the impact of a peace treaty; sometimes we follow the travels of a merchant. Whatever the thematic occasion, our intention is to guide the student around the changing contours of the geography of Western history. In order to do this effectively, we have worked with our cartographer to develop small inset, or thumbnail, maps to complement the overview map that appears at the beginning of each tour section. We know that only the most motivated students will turn back several pages to locate on a map a place mentioned in the text. Using the small inset map allows us to integrate the map directly into the relevant text, thus relieving the student of the sometimes frustrating experience of attempting to locate not only a specific place on a map but perhaps even the relevant map itself. The great number of maps throughout the text, the specially designed tour-of-Europe geographical feature, and the ancillary programs of map transparencies and workbook exercises combine to provide the strongest possible program for teaching historical geography.

The third technique we have employed to engage students with historical subjects is the two-page **special feature** that appears in each chapter. These special features focus on a single event or personality chosen to enhance the student's sense that history is something that is real and alive. These features are written more dramatically or sympathetically or with a greater sense of wonder than would be appropriate in the body of the text. The prose style and the accompanying illustration are designed to captivate the reader. Three of the features concern utopias (Plato's *Republic,* More's *Utopia,* and Orwell's *Animal Farm),* posing questions about the ways in which different societies dream. Three of the features focus on Paris at various points in its history (the medieval period, the early modern age, and the modern era), tracing the development of the quintessential European city over a millennium. Accounts of the discovery of King Tut's tomb, of the fall of Constantinople, or of tsarist cavalry trampling women protesters place the student squarely in the middle of a historical event.

There are many new features in our text, and much that is out of the ordinary. But there are important traditional aspects of the narrative itself that also require mention. **Civilization in the West** is a mainstream text in which most energies have been placed in developing a solid, readable narrative of Western civilization that integrates coverage of women and minorities into the discussion. We have highlighted personalities while identifying trends. We have spotlighted social history, both in sections of chapters and in separate chapters, while maintaining a firm grip on political developments. We hope that there are many things in this book that teachers of Western civilization will find valuable. But we also hope that there are things here with which you will disagree, themes that you can develop better, arguments and ideas that will stimulate you. A textbook is only one part of a course, and it is always less important than a teacher. What we hope is that by doing our job successfully, we have made the teacher's job easier and the student's job more enjoyable.

Mark Kishlansky
Patrick Geary
Patricia O'Brien

Acknowledgments

We want to thank the many conscientious historians who reviewed our manuscript and gave generously of their time and knowledge. Their valuable critiques and suggestions have contributed greatly to the final product. We are grateful to the following:

Meredith L. Adams, *Southwest Missouri State University*
John W. Barker, *University of Wisconsin*
William H. Beik, *Northern Illinois University*
Lenard R. Berlanstein, *University of Virginia*
Raymond Birn, *University of Oregon*
Donna Bohanan, *Auburn University*
Werner Braatz, *University of Wisconsin at Oshkosh*
Thomas A. Brady, Jr., *University of Oregon*
Anthony M. Brescia, *Nassau Community College*
Elaine G. Breslaw, *Morgan State University*
Daniel Patrick Brown, *Moorpark College*
Ronald A. Brown, *Charles County Community College*
Edward J. Champlin, *Princeton University*
Stephanie Evans Christelow, *Western Washington University*
Gary B. Cohen, *University of Oklahoma*
John J. Contreni, *Purdue University*
Samuel E. Dicks, *Emporia State University*
Frederick Dumin, *Washington State University*
Margot C. Finn, *Emory University*
Allan W. Fletcher, *Boise State University*
Elizabeth L. Furdell, *University of North Florida*
Thomas W. Gallant, *University of Florida*
Joseph J. Godson, *Hudson Valley Community College*
Eric Haines, *Bellevue Community College*
David A. Harnett, *University of San Francisco*
Paul B. Harvey, Jr., *Pennsylvania State University*
Daniel W. Hollis, *Jacksonville State University*
Kenneth G. Holum, *University of Maryland*
Charles Ingrao, *Purdue University*
George F. Jewsbury, *Oklahoma State University*
Donald G. Jones, *University of Central Arkansas*
William R. Jones, *University of New Hampshire*
Richard W. Kaeuper, *University of Rochester*
David Kaiser, *Carnegie-Mellon University*
William R. Keylor, *Boston University*

Joseph Kicklighter, *Auburn University*
Charles L. Killinger, III, *Valencia Community College*
David C. Large, *Montana State University*
Roberta T. Manning, *Boston College*
Lyle McAlister, *University of Florida*
Therese M. McBride, *College of the Holy Cross*
Robert Moeller, *University of California at Irvine*
Pierce C. Mullen, *Montana State University*
Thomas F. X. Noble, *University of Virginia*
Dennis H. O'Brien, *West Virginia University*
Peter E. Piccillo, *Rhode Island College*
Marlette Rebhorn, *Austin Community College*
John P. Ryan, *Kansas City Kansas Community College*
Steven Schroeder, *Indiana University of Pennsylvania*
Bonnie Smith, *University of Rochester*
Peter N. Stearns, *Carnegie-Mellon University*
Darryl R. Sycher, *Columbus State Community College*
Steven Vincent, *North Carolina State University*
Richard A. Voeltz, *Cameron University*
Eric Weissman, *Golden West College*

Each author also received invaluable assistance and encouragement from many colleagues, friends, and family members over the years of research, reflection, writing, and revising that went into the making of this text.

Mark Kishlansky wishes to thank Ann Adams, Robert Bartlett, Ray Birn, David Buisseret, Ted Cook, Frank Conaway, Constantine Fasolt, Katherine Haskins, Richard Hellie, Matthew Kishlansky, Donna Marder, Mary Beth Rose, Jeanne Thiel, The Staff of the Joseph Regenstein Library and the Newberry Library.

Patrick Geary wishes to thank Mary Geary, Catherine Geary, and Anne Geary for their patience, support, and encouragement as well as Anne Picard and Dale Scofield for their able assistance throughout the project.

Patricia O'Brien thanks Jon Jacobson for his constant support and for sharing his specialized knowledge and his historical sense. She also wishes to thank Elizabeth Bryant for her encouragement and enthusiasm throughout the project; Robert Moeller for his keen eye for organization and his suggestions for writing a gendered history; and Katherine Turley for her unflagging assistance with bibliographic issues.

All the authors would also like to thank, though words are but a poor expression of our gratitude, Barbara Muller, Bruce Borland, and Betty Slack, the editors of our project. If ever authors have had more felicitous experiences with their editors than we have had with ours, they have been lucky indeed. The authors also extend sincere appreciation to Michael Weinstein, Elizabeth Gabbard, Susan Ritchey, Lucy Lesiak, Sandy Schneider, and Paul Yatabe, who contributed their skills and expertise to the editorial, design, photo research, and cartographic processes involved in the production of this book.

Supplements

The following supplements are available for use in conjunction with this book:

For the Student

Student Study Guide in two volumes. Volume 1 (chapters 1-16) prepared by Steven Schroeder, Indiana University of Pennsylvania, and Volume 2 (chapters 15-30) prepared by Werner Braatz, University of Wisconsin at Oshkosh. Includes learning objectives, an overview of each chapter, glossary terms, and sample study exercises, including identification questions, chronology exercises, multiple-choice questions, and historical thinking/essay questions. Each volume also contains the essay, "Writing About History," a brief guide to writing a history research paper.

Mapping Western Civilization: Student Activities workbook by Gerald Danzer, University of Illinois at Chicago. Features numerous map skill exercises written to enhance students' basic geographical literacy. The exercises provide ample opportunities for interpreting maps and analyzing cartographic materials as historical documents. The instructor is entitled to one free copy of **Mapping Western Civilization: Student Activities** for each copy of the text purchased from HarperCollins.

Sources of the West by Mark Kishlansky, a collection of primary source documents available in two volumes, features a well-balanced selection of constitutional documents, political theory, intellectual history, philosophy, literature, and social description. Review questions follow each selection. Each volume includes the introductory essay, "How to Read a Document," which leads students step by step through the experience of using historical documents.

SuperShell Computerized Tutorial, an interactive program for computer-assisted learning, prepared by Paul A. Bischoff, Oklahoma State University. Features multiple-choice, true-false, and completion quizzes, comprehensive chapter outlines, "Flash Cards" for key terms and concepts, and diagnostic feedback capabilities. Available for IBM computers.

Historical Geography for Western Civilization: Computerized Atlas by William Hamblin, Brigham Young University. Computerized atlas and historical geography tutorial for the Macintosh.

For the Instructor

Instructor's Resource Manual by Margot C. Finn of Emory University. Includes units on Teaching the Western Civilization Course, Teaching with Primary Sources, Teaching Through Film, and Teaching Through Maps as well as a chapter-by-chapter guide to each chapter of the text. The chapter-by-chapter guides contain a chapter synopsis, a list of key terms, and sample questions for class discussion or writing assignments.

Test Bank prepared by Daniel Patrick Brown, Moorpark College, Paul A. Bischoff, Oklahoma State University, and Darryl R. Sycher, Columbus State

Community College. A total of 1500 questions, 50 per text chapter, including both objective and essay questions. Each test item is referenced by topic, type, and text page number. Available in print and computerized format.

TestMaster Computerized Testing System, test-generation software package available for the IBM, Apple, and Macintosh. Allows users to add, edit, and create graphics. Test questions are translatable to word processing software. Available free to adopters.

Visual Archives of Western Civilization—Video Laser Disc includes a "Portrait Gallery" of fine art and photos, over 300 still images and 29 minutes of full-motion film clips. Crisp detail and remote-control access make this supplement especially useful in large lecture halls. An accompanying **Instructor's Guide** contains fully referenced user's notes keyed to the text, a frame-by-frame list of images, and a brief tutorial on using the laser disc in the classroom.

Discovering Western Civilization Through

Maps and Views by Gerald Danzer, University of Illinois at Chicago, and David Buisseret, Newberry Library, Chicago. This set of 100 four-color transparencies from selected sources is bound in a three-ring binder and available free to adopters. Also contains an introduction on teaching history with maps and a detailed commentary on each transparency. The collection includes cartographic and pictorial maps, views, and photos, urban plans, building diagrams, classic maps, and works of art.

The Winner's Circle Video Program, a collection of ten prize-winning films and videos for Western Civilization. Available for loan exclusively to adopters of the text.

The Integrator, a cross-referencing guide to all print, software, and media supplements accompanying the text.

Grades, a grade-keeping and classroom management system maintains date for up to 200 students.

About the Authors

Mark Kishlansky

Recently appointed to the Committee on Social Thought at the University of Chicago, Mark Kishlansky is among today's leading young scholars. After receiving his Ph.D. at Brown University, Professor Kishlansky joined the University of Chicago faculty where he has taught since. A Fellow of the Royal Historical Society, his primary area of expertise is seventeenth-century English political history. Among his main publications are *Parliamentary Selection: Social and Political Choice in Early Modern England* and *The Rise of the New Model Army*. He is the editor of the *Journal of British Studies* and the recipient of the 1989 Most Distinguished Alumnus Award from SUNY Stony Brook.

Patrick Geary

Holding a Ph.D. in Medieval Studies from Yale University, Patrick Geary is both a noted scholar and teacher. Named outstanding undergraduate history teacher for the 1986-87 year at the University of Florida, where he currently teaches, Professor Geary

has also held academic positions at the Ecole des hautes etudes en sciences sociales, Paris, the Universitat Wien, and Princeton University. A member of the Institute for Advanced Study, his many publications include *Readings in Medieval History, Before France and Germany: The Creation and Transformation of the Merovingian World, Aristocracy in Provence: The Rhone Basin at the Dawn of the Carolingian Age,* and *Furta Sacra: Medieval Narratives of Stolen Relics.*

Patricia O'Brien

An Associate Professor at the University of California, Irvine, and Assistant Vice Chancellor in the Office of Research and Graduate Studies, Professor O'Brien holds a Ph.D. from Columbia University in modern European history. Among her many publications are *The Promise of Punishment: Prisons in 19th Century France, l'Embastillement de Paris: The Fortification of Paris During the July Monarchy, Crime and Punishment as Historical Problem,* and Michel Foucault's *History of Culture.*

1

The First
Civilizations

The Idea of Civilization

The West is an idea. It is not visible from space. An astronaut viewing the blue and white terrestrial sphere can make out the forms of Africa, bounded by the Atlantic, the Indian Ocean, the Red Sea, and the Mediterranean. Australia, the Americas, and even Antarctica are distinct patches of blue-green in the darker waters that surround them. But nothing comparable separates Europe from Asia, East from West. Viewed from one hundred miles up, the West itself is invisible. Although astronauts can see the great Eurasian land mass curving around the Northern Hemisphere, the Ural Mountains, the theoretical boundary between East and West, appear but faintly from space. Certainly they are less impressive than the towering Himalaya, the Alps, or even the Caucasus. People, not geology, determined that the Urals should be the arbitrary boundary between Europe and Asia.

Even this determination took centuries. Originally, Europe was a name that referréd only to central Greece. Gradually, Greeks extended it to include the whole Greek mainland and then the landmass to the north. Later, Roman explorers and soldiers carried Europe north and west to its modern boundaries. Asia too grew with time. Initially, Asia was only that small portion of what is today Turkey inland from the Aegean Sea. Gradually, as Greek explorers came to know of lands farther east, north, and south, they expanded their understanding of Asia to include everything east of the Don River to the north and the Red Sea to the south.

Western civilization is as much an idea as is the West itself. Under the right conditions, astronauts can see the Great Wall of China snaking its way from the edge of the Himalaya to the Yellow Sea. No comparable physical legacy of the West is so massive that its details can be discerned from space. Nor are Western achievements rooted forever in one corner of the world. What we call Western civilization belongs to no particular place. Its location has changed since the origins of civilization, that is, the cultural and social traditions characteristic of the *civitas* or city. "Western" cities appeared first outside the "West," in the Tigris and Euphrates river basins in present-day Iraq and Iran, a region we today term the Middle East. These areas have never lost their urban traditions, but in time other cities in North Africa, Greece, and Italy adapted and expanded this heritage. From our modern perspective, the developments in Europe after the birth of Jesus become more significant than those of Egypt and Mesopotamia for understanding our contemporary culture.

Until the sixteenth century after Jesus, the western end of the Eurasian landmass, what we think of as western Europe, was the crucible in which disparate cultural and intellectual traditions of the Near East, the Mediterranean, and the North

were smelted into a new and powerful alloy. Then the "West" expanded beyond the confines of Europe, carried by the ships of merchants and adventurers to India, Africa, China, and the Americas.

Western technology for harnessing nature, Western forms of economic and political organization, Western styles of art and music are—for good or ill—dominant influences in world civilization. Japan is a leading power in the Western traditions of capitalist commerce and technology. China, the most populous country in the world, adheres to Marxist socialist principles—a European political tradition. Millions of people in Africa, Asia, and the Americas follow the religions of Islam and Christianity. Both are monotheistic faiths that developed from Judaism in the cradle of Western civilization.

Many of today's most pressing problems are also part of the legacy of the Western tradition. The remnants of European colonialism have left deep hostilities around the globe. The integration of developing nations into the world economy keeps much of humanity in a seemingly hopeless cycle of poverty as the wealth of poor countries goes to pay interest on loans from Europe and America. Western material goods lure millions of people from their traditional worlds into the sprawl of third world cities. The West itself faces a crisis. Impoverished citizens of former colonies flock to Europe and North America seeking a better life but often finding instead

poverty, hostility, and racism. Finally, the advances of Western civilization endanger our very existence. Technology pollutes the world's air, water, and soil, and the nuclear arms race threatens the destruction of all civilization. And yet these are the same advances that allow us to lengthen life expectancy, harness the forces of nature, and conquer disease. It is the same technology that allows us to view our world from outer space.

How did we get here? In this book we attempt to answer this question. The history of Western civilization is not simply the triumphal story of progress, the creation of a better world. Even in areas in which we can see development, such as technology, communications, and social complexity, change is not always for the better. However, it would be equally inaccurate to view Western civilization as progressive decline from a mythical golden age of the human race. The roughly three hundred generations since the origins of civilization have bequeathed a rich and contradictory heritage to the present. Inherited political and social institutions, cultural forms, and religious and philosophical traditions form the framework within which the future must be created. The past does not determine the future, but it is the raw material from which the future will be made. To use this legacy properly, we must first understand it, not because the past is the key to the future, but because understanding yesterday frees us to create tomorrow.

Before Civilization

The human race was already ancient by the time civilization first appeared around 3500 years before the traditional date of the birth of Jesus. (Such dates are abbreviated B.C. for "before Christ"; A.D., the abbreviation of the Latin for "in the year of the Lord" is used to refer to dates after the birth of Jesus.) The first humanlike creatures whose remains have been discovered date from as long as five million years ago. One of the best-known finds, nicknamed "Lucy" by the scientist who discovered her skeleton in 1974, stood only about four feet tall and lived on the edge of a lake in what is now Ethiopia. Lucy and her band did not have brains that were as well developed as those of modern humans. They did, however, use simple tools such as sticks, bone clubs, and chipped rocks, and they worked together to protect themselves and to find small animals, roots, and berries for food. Lucy lived to a considerable age—she was around twenty when she died. Although small and relatively weak compared with other animals, Lucy's species of creatures—neither fully apes nor human—survived for over four million years.

Varieties of the modern species of humans, *homo sapiens* (thinking human), appeared well over a hundred thousand years ago and spread across the Eurasian landmass and Africa. The earliest *homo sapiens* in Europe, the *Neanderthal*, differed little from us today. Although the term *Neanderthal* has gained a negative image in the popular imagination, these early humans were roughly the same size and had the same cranial capacity as we. They not only survived but even spread throughout much of Africa, Europe, and Asia during the last great ice age. To survive in the harsh tundra landscape, they developed a cultural system that enabled them to modify their environment. They knew how to make and use stone tools and lived in shelters they built from wood. Customs such as the burial of their dead with food offerings indicate that Neanderthals may have developed a belief in an afterlife. Thus they apparently had the capacity for carrying on intellectual activities such as abstract and symbolic thought. Although a bit shorter and heavier than most people today, they were clearly our close cousins.

No one knows why or how the Neanderthals were replaced by our subspecies, *homo sapiens sapiens* (thinking thinking human), around forty thousand years ago. Whatever the reason and whatever the process—extinction, evolution, or extermination—this last arrival on the human scene was universally successful. All humans today, whether blond, blue-eyed Scandinavians, Australian aborigines, Africans, Japanese, or Amerindians, belong to this same subspecies. Differences in skin color, type of hair, or build are minor variations on the same theme. The identification of races, while selectively based on some of these physical variations, is, like civilization itself, a fact not of biology but of culture.

Early *homo sapiens sapiens* lived in small kin groups of twenty or thirty, following game and seeking shelter in tents, lean-tos, and caves. We know little about the organization of this hunter-gatherer society. Although some contemporary historians have suggested that the Paleolithic era

The remains of Lucy, the oldest known australopithecine, were found in East Africa. She is believed to have lived about 4 million years ago.

In this cave painting at Tassili in northern Africa, animal magic evokes help from the spirit world in ensuring the prosperity of the cattle herd. A similar ceremony is still performed by members of the Fulani tribes in the Sahel, on the southern fringe of the Sahara.

(ca. 600,000–10,000 B.C.) was a peaceful "golden age" in which women played a dominant role in social organization, no evidence substantiates this theory. Still, Paleolithic people worked together for hunting and defense and apparently formed emotional bonds based on more than sex or economic necessity. The skeleton of a man found a few years ago in Iraq, for example, suggests that although he was born with only one arm and was crippled further by arthritis, the rest of his community supported him and he lived to adulthood. Clearly his value to his society lay in something more than his ability to make a material contribution to its collective life. But even with this cooperation and socialization, life expectancy was very short. Most people died by age twenty, but even among those who survived into adulthood, most women were dead by thirty and most men by forty.

During the upper or late Paleolithic era (ca. 35,000–10,000 B.C.), *culture*, meaning everything about humans not inherited biologically, was increasingly determinant in human life. Paleolithic people were not on an endless and all-consuming quest to provide for the necessities of life. They spent less time on such things than we do today. Thus they found time to develop speech,

religion, and artistic expression. Wall paintings, small clay and stone figurines of female figures, and finely decorated stone and bone tools indicate not just artistic ability but also abstract and symbolic thought. Presumably such figures had religious functions. Hunters may have painted images of animals to ensure that such species of game would always be plentiful. Figures of women may reflect concerns about human and animal fertility.

The arid wastes of Africa's Sahara Desert may seem an unlikely place to find a continuous record of the civilizing of the West. Yet at the end of the last ice age, around 10,000 B.C., much of North Africa enjoyed a mild, damp climate and supported a diverse population of animals and humans. At Tassili-n-Ajjer in modern Algeria, succeeding generations of inhabitants have left over four thousand paintings on cliff and cave walls that date from ca. 6000 B.C. until the time of Jesus. Like a pictorial time line, these paintings show the gradual transformations of human culture.

The earliest cave paintings were produced by people who, like the inhabitants of Europe and the Near East, lived by hunting game and gathering edible plants, nuts, and fruit. The cave paintings include images of great, now-extinct buffalo and other game animals as well as human figures apparently participating in ritual dances. Through this long period, humans perfected the making of stone tools, learned to work bone, antler, and ivory into weapons and utensils, and organized an increasingly complex society.

Sometime around 5000 B.C., the artists at Tassili-n-Ajjer began to include in their paintings images of domesticated cattle and harnesslike equipment. Such depictions give evidence of the arrival in North Africa of two of the most profound transformations in human history, sedentarization, that is, the adoption of a fixed dwelling place, and the agricultural revolution. These fundamental changes in human culture began independently around the world and continued for roughly five thousand years. They appeared first around 10,000 B.C. in the Near East, then elsewhere in Asia around 8000 B.C. By 5000 B.C., the domestication of plants and animals was under way in Africa and what is today Mexico.

Around 10,000 B.C., many hunter-gatherers living along the coastal plains of what is today Syria and Israel and in the valleys and the hill country near the Zagros Mountains between modern Iran and Iraq began to develop specialized strategies that led, by accident, to a transformation in human culture. Near the Mediterranean coast, the close proximity of varied and productive ecosystems—the sea, coastal plains, hills, and mountains—encouraged people to practice what is called broad-spectrum gathering. That is, rather than constantly traveling in search of food, people stayed put and exploited the various seasonal sources of food, fish, wild grains, fruits, and game. In communities such as Jericho, people built and rebuilt their mud brick and stone huts over generations rather than moving on as had their ancestors. In the Zagros region, sedentary communities focused on single, abundant sources of food at specific seasons, such as wild sheep and goats in the mountains during summer and pigs and cattle in the lower elevations in winter. These people also harvested the wild forms of wheat and barley that grew in upland valleys.

No one really knows why settlement led to agriculture, which is, after all, a riskier venture than hunting and gathering. When humans focused on strains of plants and animals with

This stone quern and round pestle, dated between 7000 and 4000 B.C., were found in Iraq. They are evidence of the beginnings of sedentary life — the quern is too heavy for hunter-gatherers to carry from camp to camp.

naturally occurring recessive genetic traits that were advantageous to humans, they increased the risk that these varieties might be less hardy than others. Specialization in only a few such species of plants or animals could spell starvation if severe weather caused that crop to fail or if disease destroyed herds. Some scholars speculate that the push to take nature in hand came from population growth and the development of a political hierarchy that reduced the natural breaking away of groups when clans or tribes became too large for the natural resources of an area to support. In settled communities, infant mortality decreased and life expectancy rose. In part, these changes occurred because life in a fixed location was less exhausting than constant wandering for the very young and the very old. The killing of infants and the elderly decreased because young and old members of the tribe or community could be useful in simple agricultural tasks rather than the hindrance they might be in a community always on the move. Archaeologists working in Turkey have found the skeleton of an adult who had lived to maturity although his legs were so deformed that he could never have walked. That he was supported and on death buried with respect by his fellows shows that he was valued in spite of his handicap. In a nomadic society, he would never have lived beyond infancy.

As population growth put pressure on the local food supply, gathering activities demanded more formal coordination and organization and led to the development of political leadership. This leadership and the perception of safety in numbers may have prevented the traditional breaking away to form other similar communities in the next valley, as had happened when population growth pressured earlier groups. In any case, settlements began to encourage the growth of plants such as barley and lentils and the domestication of pigs, sheep, and goats. People no longer simply looked for these favored species of plants and animals where they occurred naturally. Now they introduced them into other locations and favored them at the expense of plant and animal species not deemed useful. Agriculture had begun.

The ability to domesticate goats, sheep, pigs, and cattle and to cultivate barley, wheat, and vegetables changed human communities from passive harvesters of nature to active partners with it. The ability to expand the food supply in a limited region allowed the development of sedentary communities of greater size and complexity than those of the late hunter-gatherer period. These peoples of the Neolithic or New Stone Age, approximately 8000–6500 B.C., organized sizable

Sculptured skulls found at Jericho date from between 7000 and 6000 B.C. They are actual human skulls whose faces have been reconstituted with molded and tinted plaster. Pieces of seashells represented the eyes.

villages. Jericho, which had been settled before the agricultural revolution, grew into a fortified town complete with ditch, stone walls, and towers and sheltered perhaps two thousand inhabitants. Catal Hüyük in southern Turkey may have been even larger.

The really revolutionary aspect of agriculture was not simply that it ensured settled communities a food supply. The true innovation was that agriculture was portable. For the first time, rather than looking for a place that provided them with the necessities of life, humans could carry with them what they needed to make a site inhabitable. This portability also meant the rapid spread of agriculture throughout the region. Farmers in Catal Hüyük cultivated varieties of plants that came from hundreds of miles away. In addition, the presence there of tools and statues made from stone not obtainable locally indicates that some trading with distant regions was taking place.

Agricultural societies brought changes in the form and organization of formal religious cults. Elaborate sanctuary rooms decorated with frescoes, bulls' horns, and sculptures of heads of bulls and bears indicate that structured religious rites were important to the inhabitants of Catal Hüyük. At Jericho, human skulls covered with clay, presumably in an attempt to make them look as they had in life, suggest that these early settlers practiced ancestor worship. In these larger communities the bonds of kinship that had united small hunter-gatherer bands were being supplemented by religious organization, which helped control and regulate social behavior. The nature of this religion is a matter of speculation. Images of a female deity, interpreted as a guardian of animals, suggest the religious importance of women and fertility. An echo of these goddesses appears at Tassili-n-Ajjer. On one wall four females and one male appear in a painting with two bulls. The painting may depict a female guardian and her servants or priests.

Around 1500 B.C., a new theme appears on the cliff walls at Tassili-n-Ajjer. Now men herd horses and drive horse-drawn chariots. These innovations had only gradually reached the arid world of North Africa. They had developed over fifteen hundred years before in Mesopotamia (a name that means "between the rivers"), that featureless desert plain stretching to the marshes near the

Before Civilization

ca. 100,000 B.C.	*Homo sapiens*
ca. 40,000 B.C.	*Homo sapiens sapiens*
ca. 35,000–10,000 B.C.	Late Paleolithic era (Old Stone Age)
ca. 8000–6500 B.C.	Neolithic era (New Stone Age)
ca. 3500 B.C.	Civilization begins

mouths of the Tigris and Euphrates rivers. Chariots symbolized a new, dynamic, and expansive phase in Western culture. Constructed of wood and bronze and used for transport and especially for aggressive warfare, they are symbolic of the culture of early river civilizations, the first civilizations in western Eurasia.

Between the Two Rivers

Need drove the inhabitants of Mesopotamia to create a civilization; nature itself offered little for human comfort or prosperity. The upland regions of the north receive most of the rainfall, but the soil is thin and poor. In the south, the soil is fertile but rainfall is almost nonexistent. There the twin rivers provide life-giving water, but also bring destructive floods that normally arrive at harvest time. Thus agriculture is impossible without irrigation. But irrigation systems, if not properly maintained, deposit harsh chemicals called alkaloids on the soil, gradually reducing its fertility. In addition, Mesopotamia's only natural resource is clay. It has no metals, no workable stone, no valuable minerals of use to ancient people. These very obstacles pressed the people to cooperative, innovative, and organized measures for survival. Survival in the region required planning and the mobilization of manpower possible only through centralization. Driven by need, they created a civilization.

Until around 3500 B.C., the inhabitants of the

lower Tigris and Euphrates lived in scattered villages and small towns. Then the population of the region, known as Sumer, began to increase rapidly. Small settlements became increasingly common, then towns such as Eridu and Uruk in modern Iraq began to grow rapidly. These towns developed in part because of the need to concentrate and organize population in order to carry on the extensive irrigation systems necessary to support Mesopotamian agriculture. In most cases, the earlier role of particular villages as important religious centers favored their growth into towns. These towns soon spread their control out to the surrounding cultivated areas, incorporating the small towns and villages of the region. They also fortified themselves against the hostile intentions of their neighbors.

Nomadic peoples inhabited the arid steppes of Mesopotamia, constantly trading with and occasionally threatening settled villages and towns. Their menace was as ever present in Near Eastern history as were drought and flood. But nomads were a minor threat compared with the dangers posed by settled neighbors. As population growth increased pressure on the region's food supply, cities supplemented their resources by raiding their more prosperous neighbors. Victims sought protection within the ramparts of the settlements that had grown up around religious centers. As a result, the population of the towns rose along with their towering temples, largely at the expense of the countryside. Between ca. 3500 and 3000 B.C., the population of Uruk quadrupled, from ten to forty thousand. At the same time, the number of smaller towns and villages in the vicinity decreased rapidly. Other Mesopotamian cities, notably Umma, Eridu, Lagash, and Ur, developed along the same general lines. The growth of these cities established a precedent that would continue throughout history.

As villages disappeared, large areas of agriculture were abandoned. Regions previously irrigated by small natural waterways reverted to desert, while urban centers concentrated water supplies within their districts with artificial canals and dikes. By 3000 B.C., the countryside near the cities was intensively cultivated, while outlying regions slipped back into swampland or steppe. The city had become the dominant force in the organization of economy and society.

The Ancient World

The Ramparts of Uruk

Cities did more than simply concentrate population. Within the walls of the city, men and women developed new technologies and new social and political structures. They created cultural traditions such as writing and literature. The pride of the first city dwellers is captured in a passage from the *Epic of Gilgamesh*, the first great heroic poem, which was composed sometime before 2000 B.C. In the poem, the hero Gilgamesh boasts of the mighty walls he had built to encircle his city, Uruk:

> Go up and walk on the ramparts of Uruk
> Inspect the base terrace, examine the brick
>   work:

> Is not its brickwork of burnt brick?
> Did not the Seven Sages lay its foundations?

Gilgamesh was justly proud of his city. In his day (ca. 2700 B.C.) these walls were marvels of military engineering and even now their ruins remain a tribute to his age. Archaeologists have uncovered the remains of the ramparts of Uruk, which stretched over five miles and were protected by some nine hundred semicircular towers. In size and complexity they surpassed the great medieval walls of Paris, which were built some four thousand years later. These protective walls enclosed about two square miles of houses, palaces, workshops, and temples. For the first time, a true urban environment had appeared in the West, and Uruk was the first city.

Within Uruk's walls, the peculiar circumstances of urban life changed the traditional social structure of Mesopotamia. In Neolithic times, social and economic differences within society had been minimal. Urban immigration increased the power, wealth, and status of two groups. In the first group were the religious authorities responsible for the temples. The second consisted of the emerging military and administrative elites, such as Gilgamesh, who were responsible for the construction and protection of the cities. These two groups probably encouraged much of the migration to the cities. The decision to enter the city was not always voluntary, but rather forced by these ruling classes who stood to gain the most from a concentration of population within the walls.

Whether they lived inside the city or on the farmland it controlled, Mesopotamians formed a highly stratified society that shared unequally in the benefits of civilization. Slaves, who did most of the unskilled labor within the city, were the primary victims of civilization. Most were prisoners of war but some were people forced by debt to sell themselves or their children. Most of the remaining rural people were peasants who were little better than slaves. Having lost their freedom to the religious or military elite, they were reduced to working the land of others and depended on markets and prices out of their control. Better off were soldiers, merchants, and workers and artisans who served the temple or palace. At the next level were landowning free persons. Above all of these were the priests responsible for temple services and the rulers. Rulers included the *ensi*, or city ruler, and the *lugal*, or king, the earthly representative of the gods. Kings were powerful and feared. The hero of the *Epic of Gilgamesh* is presented as a ruler so harsh that the gods created a wild man, Enkidu, to subdue him.

Urban life also redefined the role and status of women, who in the Neolithic period had enjoyed roughly the same roles and status as men. In cities, women tended to exercise private authority over children and servants within the household, while men controlled the household and dealt in the wider world. This change in roles resulted in part from the economic basis of the first civilization. Southern Mesopotamia has no sources of metal or stone. To acquire these precious commodities, trade networks were extended into Syria, the Arabian peninsula, and even India. The primary commodities that Mesopotamians produced for trade were textiles, and these were largely produced by women captured in wars with neighboring city-states. Their menfolk were normally killed or blinded and used for menial tasks such as milling. The enslaved women employed in urban textile production constituted a dependent female population. Some historians suggest that the disproportionate numbers of low-status women in Mesopotamian cities affected the status of women in general. Although women could own property and even appear as heads of households, by roughly 1500 B.C. the pattern of patriarchal households predominated. Throughout Western history, while individual women might at times exer-

Excavation of a mass grave at Ur yielded this ladies' headdress adorned with interwoven ribbons, leaves, disks, and flowers of gold. The heavy earrings are crafted of lapis lazuli, gold, and carnelian.

Long before the invention of writing by the Sumerians, farmers and business people in western Asia used clay tokens of various shapes and markings to keep accounts of amounts of grain, jars of oil, or units of land. Since some of the tokens are similar to Sumerian ideographs, it is thought that they may be the earliest precursor of writing.

cise great power, they did so largely in the private sphere. Public control of the house, the family, the city, and the state was largely in male hands.

Changes in society brought changes in technology. The need to feed, clothe, protect, and govern growing urban populations led to major technological and conceptual discoveries. Canals and systems of dikes partially harnessed water supplies. Farmers began to work their fields with improved plows and to haul their produce to town, first on sleds and ultimately on carts. These land-transport devices, along with sailing ships, made it possible not only to produce greater agricultural surplus but also to move this surplus to distant markets. Craft workers used a refined potter's wheel to produce ceramic vessels of great beauty. Government officials and private individuals began to use cylinder seals, small stone cylinders engraved with a pattern, to mark ownership. Metalworkers fashioned gold and silver into valuable items of adornment and prestige. They also began to cast bronze, an alloy of copper and tin, which came into use for tools and weapons about 3000 B.C.

Perhaps the greatest invention of early cities was writing. As early as 7000 B.C., small clay or stone tokens with distinctive shapes or markings were being used to keep track of animals, goods, and fruits in inventories and bartering. By 3500 B.C., government and temple administrators were using simplified drawings, today termed *pictograms*, which were derived from these tokens, to assist them in keeping records of their transactions. A scribe molded a small lump of clay into a square. Holding it between his thumb and forefinger, he divided the smooth surface into a series of squares by scratching it with a sharp reed. Within each square he then drew his pictograms. In the dry hot Mesopotamian air these lumps of clay dried quickly into firm tablets. If accidentally hardened by fire, they became virtually indestructible. Thousands have survived in the ruins of Mesopotamian cities.

The first tablets were written in Sumerian, a language related to no other known tongue. Each pictogram represented a single sound, which corresponded to a single object or idea. In time, these pictograms developed into a true system of writing. The drawings themselves became smaller and more abstract and were arranged in straight lines. Since the scribe first pressed the triangle-shaped writing instrument into the clay and then drew it across the square, this writing took on its characteristic wedge or "cuneiform" shape (from the Latin *cuneus*, wedge). Finally, scribes took a radical step. Rather than simply using pictograms to indicate single objects, they began to use cuneiform characters to represent concepts. For example, the pictogram for "foot" could also mean "to stand." Ultimately, pictograms came to represent sounds divorced from any particular meaning.

The implications of the development of cuneiform writing were revolutionary. Since symbols were liberated from meaning, they could be used to record any language. Over the next thousand years, scribes used these same symbols to write not only in Sumerian but also in the other languages of Mesopotamia, such as Akkadian, Babylonian, and Persian. The earliest extant clay tablets are little more than lists of receipts. Later, tablets were used to preserve contracts, maintain administrative records, and record significant events, prayers, myths, and proverbs. Writing soon allowed those who had mastered it to achieve greater centralization and control of government, to communicate over enormous distances, to preserve and transmit information, and to express religious and cultural beliefs. Writing reinforced memory, consolidating and expanding the achievements of the first civilization and transmitting them to the future. Writing was power, and for much of subsequent history a small minority of merchants and elites and the scribes in their employ wielded this power. In Mesopotamia, this power served to increase the strength of the king, the servant of the gods.

Gods and Mortals in Mesopotamia

Uruk had begun as a village like any other. Its rise to importance resulted from its significance as a religious site. A world of many cities, Mesopotamia was also a world of many gods, and Mesopotamian cities bore the imprint of the cult of their gods.

The gods were like the people who worshiped them. They lived in a replica of human society, and each god had a particular responsibility. Every object and element from the sky to the brick or the plow had its own active god. The gods had the physical appearance and personalities of humans as well as human virtues and vices, but always to an exaggerated extent. Like humans, they lived in a stratified society. The hundreds of ordinary divinities were overshadowed by greater gods like Nanna and Ufu, who were the protectors of Ur and Sippar. Others, such as Inanna or Ishtar, the goddess of love, fertility, and wars, and her husband Dumuzi, were worshiped throughout Mesopotamia. Finally, at the top of the pantheon were the gods of the sky, the air, and the rivers. The sky god was An, whose temple was in Uruk. Enki was god of earth and waters and Enlil the supreme ruler of the air.

The southwestern side of the ruins of the ziggurat of Ur. On top of a main platform fifty feet high, two successively smaller stages were built. The top stage was a temple containing a religious shrine. Ramplike stairways led up to the shrine from the ground.

Mesopotamians believed that the role of mortals was to serve the gods and to feed them through sacrifice. Towns had first developed around the gods' temples for this purpose. By around 2500 B.C., although military lords and kings had gained political power at the expense of the temple priests, the temples still controlled a major portion of economic resources. They owned vast estates where peasants cultivated wheat and barley as well as vegetable gardens, vineyards, flocks of sheep, and herds of cattle and pigs. The produce from temple lands and flocks supported the priests, scribes, craftsmen, laborers, farmers, teamsters, smiths, and weavers who operated these complex religious centers. At Lagash, for example, the temple of the goddess Bau owned over eleven thousand acres of land. The king held a quarter of this land for his own use. The priests divided the remainder into individual plots of about thirty-five acres, each to be cultivated for the support of the temple workers or rented out to free peasants. At a time when the total population was approximately forty thousand, the temple employed more than twelve hundred workers of various sorts, supervised by an administrator and an inspector appointed by the priests. The temple of Bau was one of only twenty temples in Lagash—and not the largest or most wealthy among them.

Temples dominated the city's skyline as they dominated the city's life. Square, rectangular, or oval, they consisted of the same essential elements. Worshipers entered through a vestibule that opened onto a spacious courtyard dominated by an altar. Here sacrifices were offered to the idol of the god. Spreading out from the courtyard was a maze of smaller chambers, which provided housing for the priests and storage facilities for the accumulated offerings brought to feed the god. By around 2000 B.C., a ziggurat, or tiered tower, dedicated to the god stood near many temples. The great Ziggurat of Ur, for example, measured nearly two thousand square feet at its base and originally stood more than 120 feet high. Ziggurats were constructed of mud bricks, covered with baked bricks set in bitumen, and were often ornamented with elaborate multicolored mosaics. Today their weathered remains are small hills rising unexpectedly from the Iraqi plain. It is easy to see why people of a later age

A Sumerian cylinder seal dating from 2500 B.C. made this impression of a hero fighting a bull and a creature that is half-man and half-bull fighting a lion. Incised cylinders were rolled on soft clay to seal documents and other objects.

thought that the people who had built the ziggurats wanted a tower that would reach to heaven—the origin of the biblical story of the Tower of Babel.

Although Mesopotamians looked to hundreds of personal divinities for assistance, they did not attempt to establish personal relationships with their great gods. They believed that these gods were little interested in humans and casual contact with them was dangerous. However, since they assumed that the gods lived in a structured world that operated rationally, they believed that mortals could deal with them and enlist their aid by following the right rituals. Rites centered on the worship of idols. The gods were thought to be present if their idols showed the appropriate features, clothing, ornaments, and equipment and if they were cared for in the proper manner. The most important care was feeding. At the temple of Uruk, the gods were offered two meals a day, each consisting of two courses served in regal quantity and style. The offerings were left before the idol so that it could consume their immaterial essence. Then the meals were served to the priests. The surplus of the vast amounts of food brought to the temple were distributed among the temple staff and servants.

Through the proper rituals, a person could buy the god's protection and favor. Still, mortal life was harsh and the gods offered little solace to the great issues of human existence. This attitude is powerfully presented in the *Epic of Gilgamesh* which, while not an accurate picture of Mesopotamian religion, still conveys much of the values of this civilization. In this popular legend Gilgamesh, king of Uruk, civilizes the wild man Enkidu, who had been sent by the gods to temper the king's harshness. Gilgamesh and Enkidu become friends and undertake a series of adventures. However, even their great feats cannot overcome death. Enkidu displeases the gods and dies. Gilgamesh then sets out to find the magic plant of eternal life with which to return his friend from the somber underworld. On his journey he meets Ut-napishtim, the Mesopotamian Noah, who recounts the story of the Great Flood and tells him where to find the plant. Gilgamesh follows Ut-napishtim's advice and is successful but loses the plant on his journey home. The message is that only the gods are immortal, and the human afterlife is at best a shadowy and mournful existence. In Mesopotamian society, this earthly life alone was considered worth living, and one had to accomplish all that one could in it.

Akkad Under Sargon

Sargon and Mesopotamian Expansion

The temple was one center of the city; the palace was the other. As representative of the city's god, the king was the ruler and highest judge. Like people at other strata of society, the king held privileges and responsibilities appropriate to his position. He was responsible for the construction and maintenance of religious buildings and the complex system of canals that maintained the precarious balance between swamp and arid steppe. Finally, he commanded the army, defending his community against its neighbors and leading his forces against rival cities.

The cultural and economic developments of early Mesopotamia occurred within the context of almost constant warfare. From around 3000 B.C. until 2300 B.C., the rulers of Ur, Lagash, Uruk, and Umma fought among themselves for control of Sumer, their name for the southern region of Mesopotamia. While their urban and political traditions were similar, the region had no political, linguistic, or ethnic unity. The population was a mixture of Sumerians and Semites, peoples speaking Semitic languages related to modern Arabic or Hebrew, all jealously protective of their cities and gods and eager to extend their domination over their weaker neighbors.

The extraordinary developments in this small corner of the Middle East might have remained isolated phenomena were it not for Sargon (ca. 2334–2279 B.C.), king of Akkad and the most important figure in Mesopotamian history. During his long reign of fifty-five years, Sargon built on the conquests and confederacies of the past to unite, transform, and expand Mesopotamian civilization. Born in obscurity, after his death he was worshiped as a god. Sargon was the son of a priestess and an unknown father. A legend similar to that of Moses says that Sargon's mother placed him in a reed basket and set him adrift on the Euphrates. In his youth he was the cupbearer to the king of Kish. Later, he overthrew his master and conquered Uruk, Ur, Lagash, and Umma. This made him lord of Sumer. Such glory had satisfied his predecessors, but not Sargon. Instead he extended his military operations east across the Tigris, west along the Euphrates, and north into modern Syria, thus creating the first great nation-state in the West.

This bronze head, dating from around 2300 B.C., was found at Nineveh. It is sometimes identified as Sargon, king of Akkad. Later invaders mutilated the nose and eyes, apparently making a political statement.

The Akkadian state, so named by contemporary historians for Sargon's capital at Akkad, consisted of a vast and heterogeneous collection of city-states and territories. Sargon attempted to rule it by transforming the traditions of royal government. First, he abandoned the traditional title of king of Kish in favor of "King of the Four Regions," a title emphasizing the universality of his rule. Second, rather than eradicating the traditions of conquered cities, he allowed them to maintain their own institutions, but replaced many of their autonomous ruling aristocracies with his own functionaries. He also reduced the economic power of local temples in favor of his supporters, to whom he apparently distributed temple property. At the same time, however, he tried to win the loyalty of the ancient cities of Sumer by naming his daughter high priestess of the moon-god Nanna at Ur. He was thus the first in a long tradition of Near Eastern rulers who sought to unite his disparate conquests into a true state.

Sargon did more than just conquer cities. Although a Semite, he spread the achievements of Sumerian civilization throughout his vast state. In the Akkadian pantheon, Sumerian and Semitic gods were venerated equally, and similar gods from various traditions were merged into the same divinities. Akkadian scribes used cuneiform to write the Semitic Akkadian language, thus continuing the tradition of literate administration begun by the Sumerians. So important did Sargon's successors deem his accomplishments that they ordered him worshiped as a god.

The Akkadian nation-state proved as ephemeral as Sargon's accomplishments were lasting. All Mesopotamian states tended to undergo a cycle of rapid rise under a gifted military commander, then begin to crumble under the internal stresses of dynastic disputes and regional assertions of autonomy. Thus weakened, they could then be conquered by other expanding states. First Ur, under its Sumerian king and first law-codifier, Shulgi (2094–2047 B.C.), and then Amoritic Babylonia, under its great ruler, Hammurabi (1792–1750 B.C.), assumed dominance in the land between the rivers. From about 2000 B.C. on, the political and economic centers of Mesopotamia were in Babylonia and in Assyria, the region to the north at the foot of the Zagros Mountains.

Hammurabi and the Old Babylonian Empire

In the tradition of Sargon, Hammurabi expanded his state through arms and diplomacy. He expanded his power south as far as Uruk and north to Assyria. In the tradition of Shulgi, he promulgated an important body of law, known as the Code of Hammurabi. In the words of its prologue, this code sought:

> To cause justice to prevail in the country
> To destroy the wicked and the evil,
> That the strong may not oppress the weak.

As the favored agent of the gods, the king held responsibility for regulating all aspects of Babylonian life, including dowries and contracts, agricultural prices and wages, commerce and money lending, and even professional standards for physicians and architects. Hammurabi's code thus offers a view of many aspects of Babylonian life, although always from the perspective of the royal law. This law lists offenses and prescribes penalties, which vary according to the social status of the victim and the perpetrator. The code creates a picture of a prosperous society composed of three legally defined social strata: a well-to-do elite, the mass of the population, and slaves. Each group had its own rights and obligations in proportion to its status. Even slaves enjoyed some legal rights and protection, could marry free persons, and might eventually obtain freedom.

Much of the code seeks to protect women and children from arbitrary and unfair treatment. Husbands ruled their households, but they did not have unlimited authority over their wives. Women could initiate their own court cases, practice various trades, and even hold public positions. Upon marriage, husbands gave their fathers-in-law a payment in silver or in furnishings. The father of the wife gave her a dowry over which she had full control. Some elite women personally controlled great wealth.

The law code held physicians, veterinarians, architects, and boat builders to standards of professional behavior. If a physician performed a successful eye operation on a member of the elite, the code specified that he receive ten shekels of silver. However, if he caused the loss of the eye, the physician lost his hand. Builders of houses had to repair any damages caused if their structures collapsed. If a free person died in the collapse, the builder had to pay with his life.

The Code of Hammurabi was less a royal attempt to restructure Babylonian society than an effort to reorganize, consolidate, and preserve previous laws in order to maintain the established social and economic order. What innovation it did show was in the extent of such punitive measures as death or mutilation. Penalties in earlier codes had been primarily compensation in silver or valuables. Hammurabi's extensive use of the law of retaliation was an assertion of royal authority in maintaining justice.

Law was not the only area in which the Old Babylonian kingdom began an important tradition. In order to handle the economics of business and government administration, Babylonians developed the most sophisticated mathematical system known prior to the fifteenth century A.D.

A seven-foot-high diorite stele dating from about 1750 B.C. is inscribed with the law code of Hammurabi. The relief at the top shows Hammurabi standing at left in the presence of the sun-god, perhaps explaining his code of laws.

Between the Two Rivers

ca. 3500 B.C.	Pictograms appear
ca. 3000–2316 B.C.	War for control of Sumer
ca. 2334–2279 B.C.	Sargon
ca. 2700 B.C.	Gilgamesh
1792–1750 B.C.	Hammurabi
ca. 1600 B.C.	Hittites destroy Old Babylonian state
ca. 1286 B.C.	Battle of Kadesh

Babylonian mathematics was based on a numerical system from one to sixty (we today still divide hours and minutes into sixty units). Babylonian mathematicians devised multiplication tables and tables of reciprocals that allowed quick calculations of all products from one to fifty-nine with each of the numbers from two to fifty-nine. They also devised tables of squares and square roots, cubes and cube roots, and other calculations needed for computing such important figures as compound interest. Babylonian mathematicians developed an algebraic system and solved linear and quadratic equations for such practical purposes as determining the shares of inheritance for several sons or the wages to be paid for a variety of workers employed for several days. Similar tables of coefficients made possible the calculation of areas of perimeters of various geometric figures as well as the amounts of standard building materials needed for buildings in these shapes. Although Babylonian mathematicians were not primarily interested in theoretical problems and were seldom given to abstraction, their technical proficiency indicates the advanced level of sophistication with which Hammurabi's contemporaries could tackle the problems of living in a complex society.

For all its successes, Hammurabi's state was no more successful than those of his predecessors at defending itself against internal conflicts or external enemies. Despite his efforts, the traditional organization inherited from his Sumerian and Akkadian predecessors could not ensure orderly administration of a far-flung collection of cities. Hammurabi's son lost over half of his father's kingdom to internal revolts. Weakened by internal dissension, the kingdom fell to a new and potent force in Western history, the Hittites.

From their capital of Hattushash (modern Bogazköy in Turkey), the Hittites established a centralized state based on agriculture and trade in the metals mined from the ore-rich mountains of Anatolia and exported to Mesopotamia. Perfecting the light, horse-drawn war chariot, the Hittites expanded into northern Mesopotamia and along the Syrian coast. They were able to destroy the Babylonian state around 1600 B.C. Unlike the Sumerians and the Semitic nomads, Akkadians, and Babylonians, the Hittites were an Indo-European people, speaking a language that was part of a linguistic family that includes most modern European languages as well as Persian, Greek, Latin, and Sanskrit. The Hittites' gradual expansion south along the coast was checked at the battle of Kadesh around 1300 B.C., when they encountered the army of an even greater and more ancient power—the Egypt of Ramses II.

The Gift of the Nile

Like that of the Tigris and Euphrates valleys, the rich soil of the Nile Valley can support a dense population. There, however, the similarities end. Unlike the Mesopotamian, the Nile floodplain requires little effort to make the land productive. Each year the river floods at exactly the right moment to irrigate crops and to deposit a layer of rich, fertile silt. South of the last cataracts, the fertile region called Upper Egypt is about eight miles wide and flanked by high desert plateaus. Near the Mediterranean in Lower Egypt, the Nile spreads across a lush, marshy delta more than a hundred miles wide. Egypt knew only two environments, the fertile Nile Valley and the vast wastes of the Sahara Desert surrounding it. This inhospitable and largely uninhabitable region limited Egypt's contact with outside influences. Thus while trade, communication, and violent conquest characterized Mesopotamian civilization, Egypt knew self-sufficiency, an inward focus in culture and society, and stability. In its art, political structure, society, and religion, the Egyptian universe was static. Nothing was ever to change.

The earliest sedentary communities in the Nile Valley appeared on the western margin of the Delta around 4000 B.C. In villages such as Merimda, which had a population of over ten thousand, huts constructed of poles and adobe bricks huddled together near *wadis*, fertile river beds that were dry except during the rainy season. Farther south, in Upper Egypt, similar communities developed somewhat later but achieved an earlier political unity and a higher level of culture. By around 3200 B.C., Upper Egypt was in contact with Mesopotamia and had apparently borrowed something of that region's artistic and architectural traditions. During the same period, Upper Egypt developed a pictographic script.

These cultural achievements coincided with the political centralization of Upper Egypt under a series of kings. Probably around 3150 B.C., King Narmer or one of his predecessors in Upper Egypt expanded control over the fragmented south, uniting Upper and Lower Egypt and establishing a capital at Memphis on the border between these two regions. For over twenty-five hundred years, the Nile Valley, from the first cataract to the Mediterranean, enjoyed the most stable civilization the Western world has ever known.

Tending the Cattle of God

Historians divide the vast sweep of Egyptian history into thirty-one dynasties, regrouped in turn into four periods of political centralization: pre- and early dynastic Egypt (ca. 3150–2770 B.C.), the Old Kingdom (ca. 2770–2200 B.C.), the Middle Kingdom (ca. 2050–1786 B.C.), and the New Kingdom (ca. 1560–1087 B.C.). The time gaps between kingdoms were periods of disruption and political confusion termed intermediate periods. While minor changes in social, political, and cultural life certainly occurred during these centuries, the changes were less significant than the astonishing stability and continuity of the civilization that developed along the banks of the Nile.

Divine kingship was the cornerstone of Egyptian life. Initially, the king was the incarnation of Horus, a sky and falcon god. Later, the king was identified with the sun god Ra (subsequently known as Amen-Re, the great god), as well as with Osiris, the god of the dead. As divine incarnation, the king was obliged above all to care for his people. It was he who assured the annual flooding of the Nile, which brought water to the parched land. His commands preserved *maat*, the ideal state of the universe and society, a condition of harmony and justice. In the poetry of the Old Kingdom, the king was the divine herdsman, while the people were the cattle of god:

Ancient Egypt

The pyramids at Giza, near modern Cairo. In the center rises the Great Pyramid, the royal tomb of the pharaoh Khufu.

Well tended are men, the cattle of god.
He made heaven and earth according to their
   desire
and repelled the demon of the waters . . .
He made for them rulers (even) in the egg,
   a supporter to support the back of the disabled.

Unlike the rulers in Mesopotamia, the kings of the Old Kingdom were not warriors but divine administrators. Protected by the Sahara Desert, Egypt had few external enemies and no standing army. A vast bureaucracy of literate court officials and provincial administrators assisted the god-king. They wielded wide authority as religious leaders, judicial officers, and, when necessary, military leaders. A host of subordinate overseers, scribes, metalworkers, stonemasons, artisans, and tax collectors rounded out the royal administration. At the local level, governors administered provinces called *nomes*, the basic units of Egyptian local government.

Women of ancient Egypt were more independent and involved in public life than were those of Mesopotamia. Egyptian women owned property, conducted their own business, entered legal contracts, and brought lawsuits. They also had an integral part in religious rites. They were not segregated from men in their daily activities and shared in the economic and professional life of the country at every level except one. Women were apparently excluded from formal education. The professional bureaucracy was open only to those who could read and write. As a result, the primary route to public power was closed to women, and the bureaucratic machinery remained firmly in the hands of men.

The role of this bureaucracy was to administer estates, collect taxes, and channel revenues and labor toward vast public works projects. These construction projects focused on the king. He lived in the royal city of Memphis in the splendor of a *Per-ao* or "great house," from which comes the word *pharaoh*, the Hebrew term for the Egyptian king. During the Old and Middle kingdoms, more imposing than the great house of the living king were the pyramid temple-tomb complexes of his ancestors. The vast size and superb engineering of these structures remain among the marvels of human creation.

The founder of the Old Kingdom, King Zoser, who was a rough contemporary of Gilgamesh, built the first of these pyramid temples, the Step Pyramid at Sakkara. The pyramid tombs were only part of elaborate religious complexes at whose center were temples housing royal statues. Within the temples priests and servants performed rituals to serve the dead kings just as they had served the kings when they were alive. Even death did not disrupt the continuity so vital to Egyptian civilization. The cults of dead kings reinforced the monarchy, since veneration of past rulers meant veneration of the kings' ancestors. The pyramids thus strengthened the image of the living king by honoring the physical remains of his predecessors.

Building and equipping the pyramids focused and transformed Egypt's material and human resources. Artists and craftsmen had to be trained, engineering and transportation problems solved, quarrying and stoneworking techniques perfected, and laborers recruited. In the Old Kingdom, whose population has been estimated at perhaps 1.5 million, more than seventy thousand workers at a time were employed in building these great temple-tombs. No smaller work force could have built such a massive structure as the Great Pyramid of Khufu (ca. 2600 B.C.), which stood 481 feet high and contained almost six million tons of stone. In comparison, the great Ziggurat of Ur rose only some 120 feet above the Mesopotamian plain. The pyramids were constructed by peasants working when the Nile was in flood and they could not till the soil. Although actual construction was seasonal, the work was unending. No sooner was one complex completed than the next was begun.

Feeding these masses of laborers absorbed most of the country's agricultural surplus. Equipping the temples and pyramids provided a constant demand for the highest-quality luxury goods, since royal tombs and temples were furnished as luxuriously as palaces. Thus the construction and maintenance of these vast complexes focused the organization and production of Egypt's economy and government.

Democratization of the Afterlife

In the Old Kingdom, future life was available only to the king or through the king. The graves of thousands of his attendants and servants surrounded his temple. All the resources of the kingdom went to maintaining existing cults and establishing new ones. All the wealth, labor, and expertise of the kingdom thus flowed into these temples, reinforcing the position of the king. Like the tip of a pyramid, the king was the summit, supported by all of society.

Gradually, however, the absolute power of the king declined. The increasing demands for consumption by the court and the cults forced agricultural expansion into areas where returns were poor, thus decreasing the flow of wealth. As bureaucrats increased their efforts to supply the voracious needs of living and dead kings and their attendants, they neglected the maintenance of the economic system that supplied these needs. The royal government was not protecting society, the "cattle of god" were not being well tended. Finally, tax-exempt religious foundations, established to ensure the perpetual cult of the dead, received donations of vast amounts of property and came to rival the power of the king. This removed an ever greater amount of the country's wealth from the control of the king and his agents. Thus the

In this illustration from the Ani Papyrus of 1250 B.C., the ba *hovers over the mummified body of an Egyptian in the tomb. The* ba, *or soul, is depicted as a bird whose head bears the likeness of the dead person.*

wealth and power of the kings declined at roughly the time that Sargon was expanding his Akkadian state in Mesopotamia. By around 2200 B.C., Egyptian royal authority collapsed entirely, leaving political and religious power in the hands of provincial governors.

After almost two hundred years of fragmentation, the governors of Thebes in Upper Egypt reestablished centralized royal traditions, but with a difference. Kings continued to build vast temples, but they did not resume the tremendous investments in pyramid complexes on the scale of the Old Kingdom. The bureaucracy was opened to all men, even sons of peasants, who could master the complex pictographic writing. Private temple-tombs proliferated and with them new pious foundations. These promised eternal care by which anyone with sufficient wealth could enjoy a comfortable afterlife.

The memory of the shortcomings of the Old Kingdom introduced a new ethical perspective expressed in the literature written by the elite. For the first time, the elite voiced the concern that justice might not always be served and that the innocent might suffer at the hands of royal agents. In the story of Sinuhe, a popular tale from around 1900 B.C., an official of Amenemhet I (d. 1962 B.C.) flees Egypt after the death of his king. He fears that through false reports of his actions he will incur the wrath of Amenemhet's son, Senusert I. Only in his old age, after years in Syria and Palestine, does Sinuhe dare to return to his beloved Egypt. There, through the intercession of the royal children, Senusert receives him honorably and grants him the ultimate favor, his own pyramid-tomb. In the "Tale of the Eloquent Peasant," a peasant is constantly mistreated by royal officials. Although he, like Sinuhe, ultimately receives justice, the moral is clear. The state system at times failed in its responsibility to safeguard *maat*. Still, these stories, in the end, reaffirm the existing system.

The greater access to power and privilege in the Middle Kingdom benefited foreigners as well as Egyptians. Assimilated Semites from Palestine rose to important administrative positions. By around 1600 B.C., when the Hittite armies were destroying the state of Hammurabi's successors, large bands of Palestinians had settled in the eastern Delta, setting the stage for the first foreign conquest of Egypt. A series of kings referred to by Egyptian sources as "rulers of foreign lands," or *Hyksos*, overran the country and ruled the Nile Valley as far south as Memphis. These foreigners adopted the traditions of Egyptian kingship and continued the tradition of divine rule, even using names compounded with that of the sun god, Ra.

The Hyksos kings introduced their military technology and organization into Egypt. In particular, they brought with them the light, horse-drawn war chariot. This mobile fighting platform, manned by warriors armed with bows, bronze swords of a type previously unknown in Egypt, and lances transformed Egyptian military tactics. These innovations remained even after the Hyksos were expelled by Ahmose I (1552–1527 B.C.), the Theban founder of the Eighteenth Dynasty, with whose reign the New Kingdom began.

The Egyptian Empire

The Egyptian Empire

Ahmose did not stop with the liberation of Egypt. He forged an empire. He and his successors used their new-found military might to extend the frontiers of Egypt south up the Nile

beyond the fourth cataract and well into Nubia. To the east they absorbed the caravan routes to the Red Sea from which they were able to send ships to Punt (probably modern Somalia), the source of the myrrh and frankincense needed for funeral and religious rituals. Most important was the Egyptian expansion into Canaanite Palestine and Syria. Here Egyptian chariots crushed their foes as kings pressed on as far as the Euphrates. Thutmose I (1506–1494 B.C.) proclaimed, "I have made the boundaries of Egypt as far as that which the sun encircles."

Thutmose's immediate successors were his children, Thutmose II (1494–1490 B.C.) and Hatshepsut (1490–1468 B.C.), who married her brother. Such brother-sister marriages, although not unknown in polygamous Egyptian society, were rare. After the death of Thutmose II, Hatshepsut ruled both as regent for her stepson Thutmose III (1490–1468 B.C.) and as co-ruler. She was by all accounts a capable ruler, preserving stability and even personally leading the army on several occasions to protect the empire. However, the traditions of male leadership were such that Hatshepsut could not present her public image as a female monarch. In royal inscriptions and in pictures, she had herself portrayed in the formal rigid pose and dress of a king, including a false beard.

In spite of the efforts of Hatshepsut and her successors, the Egyptian empire was never as grand as its kings proclaimed. Many of the northern expeditions were raids rather than conquests. Still, the expanded political frontiers meant increased trade and unprecedented interaction with the rest of the ancient world. The cargo excavated from the wreck of a ship that sank off the coast of modern Turkey around 1350 B.C. vividly portrays the breadth of international exchange in the New Kingdom. The nationality of the ship, its origins, and its destination are unknown, but it carried a cargo of priceless and exotic merchandise from around the Mediterranean world. From distant Cyprus came copper ingots. Tin ingots probably originated in the Hittite state of modern Afghanistan or Turkey. In the ship's hold lay numerous jars from Canaan and vases from Greece. When it sank, the ship was carrying Canaanite glass ingots, jewelry, and jars of ointment; ebony from Nubia; pottery from Cyprus; weapons from Egypt, Greece, and Syria;

This painted limestone head of Hatshepsut was originally from a statue. She is shown wearing the crown of Egypt and the stylized "beard" that symbolized royalty and was often seen on the statues and death masks of pharaohs.

cylinder seals from Mesopotamia or Syria; raw ivory; and a mass of damaged Egyptian gold jewelry probably intended for scrap.

The lost ship was probably not a merchant vessel in the modern sense; private merchants were virtually unknown in the Egyptian empire. Instead, most precious commodities circulated through royal ventures or as gifts and tribute. The ship may well have been carrying tribute to the king, for in the New Kingdom as in the Old, the ruler, as the incarnation of the great god, Amen-Re, was the pinnacle of the political and economic order.

Religion was both the heart of royal power and its only limiting force. Though the king was the embodiment of the religious tradition, he was also bound by that tradition, as it was interpreted by an ancient and powerful system of priesthoods, pious foundations, and cults. The intimate relationship between royal absolutism and religious cult culminated in the reign of Amenhotep IV (1364–1347 B.C.), the most controversial and enigmatic ruler of the New Kingdom, who challenged the very basis of royal religious control. In a calculated break with over a thousand years of Egyptian religious custom, Amenhotep attempted to abolish the cult of Amen-Re along with all of the other traditional gods, their priesthoods, and their festivals. In their place he promoted a new divinity, the sun-disk god Aten. Amenhotep moved his capital from Thebes to a new temple city, modern Tell al-'Amarna, and changed his own name to Akhenaten ("It pleases Aten").

Akhenaten has been called the first monotheist, a reformer who sought to revitalize a religion that had decayed into superstition and magic. Yet his monotheism was not complete. The god Aten shared divine status with Akhenaten himself. Akhenaten attacked other cults, especially that of Amen-Re, to consolidate royal power and to replace the old priesthoods with his own family members and supporters. In his artistic policies, he broke with the past, but again the break was limited. Official portraiture, which depicted Akhenaten with a long, thin face, a swollen stomach, and large thighs, was no more "realistic" than the earlier tradition. Instead, Akhenaten appeared as both man and woman, an image of his counterpart Aten, the godhead who was father and mother of all creation.

A relief from the temple of Aten at Tel el Amarna shows the pharaoh Akhenaten, Queen Nefertiti, and one of their daughters adoring the god Aten in the form of the sun's disk. The Aten sends down tiny hands to accept the libations of the royal pair.

Still, in attempting to reestablish royal divinity, Akhenaten did temporarily transform the aesthetics of Egyptian court life. Traditional archaic language gave way to the everyday speech of the fourteenth century B.C. Wall paintings and statues showed people in the clothing that they actually wore rather than in stylized parade dress. This new naturalism rendered the king at once more human and more divine. It differentiated him from the long line of preceding kings, emphasizing his uniqueness and his royal power.

The strength of royal power was so great that during his reign Akhenaten could command acceptance of his radical break with Egyptian

stability. However, his ambitious plan did not long survive his death. His innovations annoyed the Egyptian elite, while his abolition of traditional festivals alienated the masses. His son-in-law, Tutankhamen (1347–1337 B.C.), the son of Akhenaten's predecessor, was a child when he became king upon Akhenaten's death. Under the influence of his court advisors, probably inherited from his father's reign, he restored the ancient religious traditions and abandoned the new capital of Amarna for his father's palace at Thebes. Something of the relaxed artistic style introduced by Akhenaten survived in the art of Tutankhamen's reign. However, the religious themes and objects found in the young king's tomb, which was unearthed by the English archaeologist Howard Carter in 1922, show a complete return to the old ways within years of Akhenaten's death. (See Special Feature, "Discovering The Pharaohs," pp. 24–25).

Return to the old ways meant return to the old problems. Powerful pious foundations controlled fully 10 percent of the population. Dynastic continuity ended after Tutankhamen and a new military dynasty seized the throne. These internal problems provided an opportunity for the expanding Hittite state in Asia Minor to expand south at the expense of Egypt. Ramses II (1289–1224 B.C.) checked the Hittite expansion at the battle of Kadesh, but the battle was actually a draw. Eventually, Ramses and the Hittite King Hattusilis III signed a peace treaty whose terms included nonaggression and mutual defense. Archaeologists have found copies of the treaty, both in Hattushash and in Egypt. Written in Egyptian, Hittite, and the international diplomatic language of Akkadian, the agreement marked the failure of both states to unify the Fertile Crescent, the region stretching from the Persian Gulf northwest through Mesopotamia and down the Mediterranean coast to Egypt.

The mutual standoff at Kadesh did not long precede the disintegration of both Egypt and the Hittite state. Within a century, states large and small along the Mediterranean coast from Anatolia to the Delta and from the Aegean Sea in the west to the Zagros Mountains in the east collapsed or were destroyed in what seems to have been a general crisis of the civilized world. The various raiders, sometimes erroneously called the

Discovering the Pharaohs

The English archaeologist Howard Carter had been searching the Valley of the Kings, near Thebes, for the tomb of Tutankhamen for five fruitless years. Years later he described the events of 26, November 1922, the day that culminated his quest:

> With trembling hands I made a tiny breach in the upper left-hand corner [of the door]. Darkness and blank space, as far as an iron testing-rod could reach, showed that whatever lay beyond was empty, and not filled like the passage we had just cleared. Candle tests were applied as a precaution against possible foul gases, and then, widening the hole a little, I inserted the candle and peered in, Lord Carnarvon, Lady Evelyn [Herbert] and [A. R.] Callender standing anxiously beside me to hear the verdict. At first I could see nothing, the hot air escaping from the chamber causing the candle flame to flicker, but presently, as my eyes grew accustomed to the light, details of the room within emerged slowly from the mist, strange animals, statues, and gold—everywhere the glint of gold. For the moment—an eternity it must have seemed to the others standing by—I was struck dumb with amazement, and when Lord Carnarvon, unable to stand the suspense any longer, inquired anxiously, "Can you see anything?" it was all I could do to get out the words, "Yes, wonderful things."

"The wonderful things" Carter saw were over five thousand priceless objects, including translucent alabaster jars and cups, painted wooden caskets, life-size wooden statues of the king, four chariots, three large couches in the forms of animals, a golden throne, a shrine encased in thick sheet-gold, and a great number of smaller jars, boxes, baskets, and other burial offerings spread through four underground rooms. The burial chamber itself contained the shrine housing the remains of the king, its seals intact. Inside the shrine was another gilt shrine, and within it a third, and a fourth, each more exquisite and precious. Within the last lay the yellow quartzite sarcophagus that held the king's mummified remains in three coffins. The first was of gilded wood; the second, gilded wood with glass paste; the third, 450 pounds of solid gold. The tomb of Tutankhamen, the only royal tomb known to have escaped ancient grave robbers, remains the most spectacular archaeological discovery of all time.

As spectacular as it was, Carter's discovery was not the most important in the history of Egyptology. Actually, Carter's find would have been impossible without a more significant breakthrough that had occurred exactly 100 years earlier and which took place not on the banks of the Nile in Egypt but on those of the Seine in France. Carter was able to discover Tutankhamen's tomb only because an earlier scholar had discovered the secret of Egyptian hieroglyphics. Over the following century, archaeologists, historians, and philologists (scholars who study language) had pieced together the history of ancient Egypt and Tutankhamen's role in it.

The story begins in 1798 when Napoleon Bonaparte invaded Egypt with a view to adding this ancient land to the French Republic. He took with him not just soldiers but also a Commission of Science and Arts composed of over one hundred scientists, engineers, and mathematicians. During their three-year occupation of Egypt, they and their commander were captivated by the splendor of Egypt's ancient monuments. They mapped and sketched hundreds of temples, pyramids, and ruins and brought back to France thousands of objects, many covered with intriguing but unreadable hieroglyphics. Back in France, members of the commission worked for years studying, classifying, and publishing the first comprehensive and systematic survey of Egyptian antiquities. Still the hieroglyphics, and with them the rich history of ancient Egypt, remained a mystery.

The mystery was solved in 1822 by the young scholar, Jean François Champollion (1790–1832). Champollion had already mastered Latin, Greek, Hebrew, Syriac, Ethiopic, Arabic, Persian, Sanskrit, and Coptic when, at age eighteen, he began to devote himself to cracking the mystery of Egyptian writing. His key was a basalt fragment discovered at Rachid (in English, Rosetta) on the west branch of the Nile in 1799 by Napoleon's commission.

The stone contains three inscriptions. The uppermost is written in hieroglyphics; the second, in what is called demotic, the simplified common script of ancient Egypt; and the third in Greek. Champollion guessed that the three inscriptions might all contain the same text and spent the

next fourteen years working from the Greek to the demotic and finally to the hieroglyphics until he had deciphered the whole text and uncovered the basics of ancient Egyptian writing. In 1822 he reported his great discovery to the French Academy of Inscriptions. Champollion's discovery remains the most significant event in Egyptology, and he accomplished it without ever setting foot on Egyptian soil.

In the following century, scholars translated thousands of inscriptions and texts, identifying and dating monuments, tombs, and objects and gradually compiling a full and accurate picture of Egyptian history, including the reign of the rather obscure Tutankhamen. By the beginning of the twentieth century, archaeologists knew that he had been the successor of Akhenaten, that he had restored the cult of Amen-Re and the other traditional gods, that he had moved his court back to Thebes, and that he had probably been buried in the nearby Valley of the Kings. In 1906 a British archaeologist working in the valley came across a series of scattered finds that included objects containing hieroglyphic inscriptions pointing to Tutankhamen. An American Egyptologist at the Metropolitan Museum in New York recognized these as the remains of a ritual funeral banquet performed for Tutankhamen. Armed with all of this knowledge accumulated over decades, Carter began a systematic search for the lost tomb. On 26 November 1922, his search ended.

The Gift of the Nile

ca. 3150–2770 B.C.	Predynastic and early dynastic Egypt
ca. 2770–2200 B.C.	Old Kingdom
ca. 2600 B.C.	Pyramid of Khufu
ca. 2050–1786 B.C.	Middle Kingdom
ca. 1560–1087 B.C.	New Kingdom
1552–1527 B.C.	Ahmose I
1506–1494 B.C.	Thutmose I
1494–1490 B.C.	Thutmose II
1490–1468 B.C.	Hatshepsut
1364–1347 B.C.	Amenhotep IV (Akhenaten)
1347–1337 B.C.	Tutankhamen
1289–1224 B.C.	Ramses II

"Sea Peoples," who struck Egypt, Syria, the Hittite state, and elsewhere were not the primary cause of the crisis. It was rather internal political, economic, and social strains within both of these great states that provided the opportunity for various groups—including Anatolians, Greeks, Israelites, and others—to raid the ancient centers of civilization. In the ensuing confusion, the small Semitic kingdoms of Syria and Palestine developed a precarious independence in the shadow of the great powers.

Between Two Worlds

Civilization was an endangered species throughout antiquity. Just beyond the well tilled fields of Mesopotamia and the fertile delta of the Nile lay the world of anticivilization—that of the Semitic tribes of seminomadic shepherds and traders. Of course, not all Semites were uncivilized. Many had formed part of the heterogeneous population of the Sumerian world. Sargon's Semitic Akkadians and Hammurabi's Amorites created great Mesopotamian nation-states, adopting the ancient Sumerian cultural traditions. Along the coast of Palestine, other Semitic groups established towns modeled on those of Mesopotamia, which were involved in the trade between Egypt and the north. But the majority of Semitic peoples continued to live a life radically different than that of the floodplain civilizations. From these, one small group, the Hebrews, emerged to establish a religious and cultural tradition unique in antiquity.

A Wandering Aramaean Was My Father

Sometime after 2000 B.C., small Semitic bands under the leadership of patriarchal chieftains spread into what is today Syria and Palestine. These bands lived on the edge of civilization. They crisscrossed the Fertile Crescent, searching for pasture for their flocks. Occasionally they participated in the trade uniting Mesopotamia and the towns of the Mediterranean coast. For the most part, however, they pitched their tents on the outskirts of towns only briefly, moving on when their sheep and goats had exhausted the supply of pasturage. The biblical patriarch Abraham was typical of these chieftains. The story of his migration from Ur to Haron and then to Hebron, as described in the Book of Genesis, chapters 11–12, conforms to the general pattern of such wandering groups. Semitic Aramaeans and Chaldeans brought with them not only their flocks and families, but Mesopotamian culture as well.

Later Hebrew history records such Mesopotamian traditions as the story of the flood (Genesis, chapters 6–10), legal traditions strongly reminiscent of those of Hammurabi, and the worship of the gods on high places. Stories such as that of the Tower of Babel (Genesis, chapter 11) and the garden of Eden (Genesis, chapters 2–4) likewise have a Mesopotamian flavor, but with a difference. For these wandering shepherds, civilization was a curse. In the Hebrew Bible (the Christian Old Testament), the first city was built by Cain, the first murderer. The Tower of Babel, probably a ziggurat, was a symbol not of human achievement but of human pride.

At least some of these wandering Aramaeans, among them Abraham, as the Hebrews later described him, also rejected the gods of Meso-

The Kingdoms of Israel and Judah

potamia. Religion among these nomadic groups focused on the specific divinity of the clan. In the case of Abraham, this was the god El. Abraham and his successors were not monotheists. They did not deny the existence of other gods. They simply believed that they had a personal pact with their own god.

In its social organization and cultural traditions, Abraham's clan was no different from its neighbors. These independent clans were ruled by a senior male (hence the Greek term *patriarch*—rule by the father). Women, whether wives, concubines, or slaves, were treated as distinctly inferior, virtually as property. As a nonliterate society, these nomadic people had little access to the learned traditions of the Fertile Crescent. Indeed, nothing marked them for any greatness. They became significant only in retrospect, and not in the Palestine of the patriarchs but in the Egypt of the pharaohs.

Some of Abraham's descendants must have joined the steady migration from Palestine into Egypt that took place during the Middle Kingdom and the Hyksos period. Although initially well treated, after the expulsion of the Hyksos in the sixteenth century B.C., many of the Semitic settlers in Egypt were reduced to slavery. Around the thirteenth century B.C., a small band of Semitic slaves numbering less than one thousand left Egypt for Sinai and Palestine under the leadership of Moses. The memory of this departure, known as the Exodus, became the formative experience of the descendants of those who had taken part

and those who later joined them. Moses, a Semite who carried an Egyptian name and who, according to tradition, had been raised in the royal court, was the founder of the Israelite people.

During the years that they spent wandering in the desert and then slowly conquering Palestine, the Israelites forged a new identity and a new faith. From the Midianites of the Sinai Peninsula, they adopted the god Yahweh as their own. Although composed of various Semitic and even Egyptian groups, the Israelites adopted the oral traditions of the clan of Abraham as their common ancestor and identified his god, El, with Yahweh. They interpreted their extraordinary escape from Egypt as evidence of a covenant with this god, a treaty similar to those concluded between the Hittite kings and their dependents. Yahweh was to be the Israelites' exclusive god; they were to make no alliances with any others. They were to preserve peace among themselves, and they were obligated to serve Yahweh with arms. This covenant was embodied in the law of Moses, a series of terse, absolute commands quite unlike the conditional laws of Hammurabi. While Hammurabi's code listed a series of offenses and their penalties (if . . . , then . . .), the law of Yahweh was absolute: "Thou shall not . . . ."

Inspired by their new identity and their new religion, the Israelites swept into Palestine. Taking advantage of the vacuum of power left by the Hittite-Egyptian standoff following the battle of Kadesh, they destroyed or captured the cities of the region. In some cases the local populations welcomed the Israelites, abandoned or overthrew their local leaders, and accepted the religion of Yahweh. In other places, the indigenous peoples were slaughtered, down to the last man, woman, and child.

A King Like All the Nations

During its first centuries, Israel was a loosely organized confederation of tribes whose only focal point was the religious shrine at Shiloh. This shrine, in contrast with the temples of other ancient peoples, housed no idols, but only a chest, known as the Ark of the Covenant, which contained the law of Moses and mementos of the Exodus. At times of danger temporary leaders would lead united tribal armies. The power of these leaders, called judges in the Hebrew Bible, rested solely on their personal leadership qualities. This "charisma" indicated that the spirit of Yahweh was with the leader. Yahweh alone was the ruler of the people.

By the eleventh century B.C., this disorganized political tradition placed the Israelites at a disadvantage in fighting their neighbors. The Philistines, who dominated the Palestinian seacoast and had expanded inland, posed the greatest threat. By 1050 B.C., the Philistines had defeated the Israelites, captured the Ark of the Covenant, and occupied most of their territory. Many Israelites clamored for "a king like all the nations" to lead them to victory. To consolidate their forces, the Israelite religious leaders reluctantly established a kingdom. Its first king was Saul and its second was David.

David (ca. 1000–962 B.C.) and his son and successor, Solomon (ca. 961–922 B.C.) brought the kingdom of Israel to its peak of power, prestige, and territorial expansion. David defeated and expelled the Philistines, subdued Israel's other enemies, and created a united state that included all of Palestine from the desert to the sea. He established Jerusalem as the political and religious capital. No longer would the Ark of the Covenant rest in the tents of Israel's nomadic ancestors. Solomon went still further, building a magnificent temple complex to house the Ark and to serve as Israel's national shrine. Just as they transformed the worship of Yahweh from rural cult to urban religion, David and Solomon restructured Israel from a tribal to a monarchical society. The old tribal structure remained only as a religious tradition. Solomon centralized land divisions, raised taxes, and increased military service in order to strengthen the monarchy.

The cost of this transformation was high. The kingdom under David and especially under Solomon grew more tyrannical as it grew more powerful. Solomon behaved like any other king of his time. He contracted marriage alliances with neighboring princes and allowed his wives to practice their own cults. He demanded extraordinary taxes and services from his people to pay for his lavish building projects. When he was unable to pay his Phoenician creditors for supplies and craftsmen, he deported Israelites to work as slaves in Phoenician mines.

Not surprisingly, the united kingdom did not survive Solomon's death. The northern region broke off to become the Kingdom of Israel with its capital in Shechem. The south, the Kingdom of Judah, continued the tradition of David from his capital of Jerusalem. These small, weak kingdoms did not long maintain their independence. Beginning in the ninth century B.C., a new Mesopotamian power, the Assyrians, began a campaign of conquest and unprecedented brutality throughout the Near East. The Hebrew kingdoms were among their many victims. In 722 B.C., the Assyrians destroyed the Kingdom of Israel and deported thousands of its people to upper Mesopotamia. Judah escaped destruction for just over a century by submitting to Assyria and becoming a dependent client state. In 586 B.C., the Kingdom of Judah was conquered by Assyria's destroyers, the New Babylonian empire under King Nebuchadnezzar II (604–562 B.C.). The temple of Solomon was destroyed, Jerusalem was burned, and Judah's elite were deported to Babylon. This Babylonian captivity ended some fifty years later when the Persians, who had conquered Babylonia, allowed the people of Judah to return to their homeland.

In this gypsum bas-relief panel, Israelite refugees are seen sadly departing their home city of Lachish after its subjugation by the Assyrians in 701 B.C. The sculpture was commissioned by the tyrant Sennacherib to commemorate his victory.

Between Two Worlds

ca. 1050 B.C.	Philistines defeat the Israelites
ca. 1000–961 B.C.	David, king of Israel
ca. 961–922 B.C.	Solomon, king of Israel
722 B.C.	Assyrians destroy Kingdom of Israel
604–562 B.C.	Nebuchadnezzar II
586 B.C.	Nebuchadnezzar II conquers Kingdom of Judah

The Law and the Prophets

The religious significance of the people of Israel is as great as their political significance is small. The faith of the Israelites is the direct source of the three great Western religions: Judaism, Christianity, and Islam. Gradually, the relationship between Yahweh and the people of Israel was transformed from one of simple exclusivity to monotheism. Particularly after the Babylonian captivity, Yahweh was not simply one god among many but rather the one universal god, creator and ruler of the universe. Although Yahweh might be described in human terms, he was so beyond human understanding that he could not be depicted in any image.

Although beyond all earthly powers, Yahweh intervened in human history to accomplish his goals. He formed a covenant with Abraham and renewed it with Moses. The covenant promised that Israel would be Yahweh's special people, but in return for this favor he demanded not simply sacrifices but righteousness. Thus ethics were a central aspect of Israel's religion. Yahweh acted justly and he demanded that his people respond accordingly.

Religious leaders, termed *prophets*, constantly explained historical events in terms of the faithfulness of the Israelite or, later, Jewish people (the term *Jew* means a descendant of those who occupied the Kingdom of Judah) to their covenant with Yahweh. The prophets were inde-

pendent of royal control and spoke out constantly against any ruler whose immorality compromised the terms of the covenant. They called upon rulers and people to reform their lives and to return to Yahweh. The prophet Jeremiah (ca. 650–570 B.C.) boldly accused King Jehoiakim (ca. 609–598 B.C.) of Judah of reviving the cult of Ishtar and practicing child sacrifice and warned that Yahweh would send Babylon to destroy him. In Egypt or Mesopotamia, such dissenters would have been liquidated. Even in Israel and Judah, prophets often met with persecution. Jehoiakim burned Jeremiah's writings and he had to go into hiding for a time. Some prophets were killed. Still they persisted, establishing a tradition of religious opposition to royal absolutism, a tradition which, like monotheism itself, is an enduring legacy.

Nineveh and Babylon

The Assyrian state that destroyed Israel accomplished what no other power had ever achieved. It tied together the floodplain civilizations of Mesopotamia and Egypt. But the Assyrian state was not just larger than the nation-states that had preceded it; it differed in nature as well as in size. The nation-states of Akkadia, Babylonia, the Hittites, and even the Egyptian empire were essentially diverse collections of city-states. Each preserved its own institutions and cultural traditions while diverting its economic resources to the capital. The Assyrian empire was an integrated state in which conquered regions were reorganized and remade along the model of the central government. By the middle of the seventh century B.C., the Assyrian empire stretched from the headwaters of the Tigris and Euphrates rivers to the Persian Gulf, along the coast from Syria to beyond the Delta, and up the Nile to Thebes. Now the ancient gods of Sumer were worshiped in the sanctuaries of Memphis.

The Assyrian plain north of Babylonia had long been a small Mesopotamian state threatened by seminomads and great powers such as the Babylonians and later the Hittites. When King Assur-dan II mounted the throne in 934 B.C., his country was, as he himself later said, exhausted.

An Assyrian bas-relief shows the capture of a town. A siege engine at the right batters at the walls while soldiers shoot arrows at the town. Dead and wounded lie in the middle ground, and at left attackers scale the walls.

Gradually he and his successors began to strengthen the state against its enemies and to allow its population to rebuild its agricultural and commercial base. The Assyrian army, forged by constant warfare into a formidable military machine, began to extend the frontiers of the kingdom in the manner of so many earlier Mesopotamian empires, both toward the Mediterranean and down the twin rivers toward the Persian Gulf. However, like its predecessors, within a century this empire seemed destined for collapse.

Rapid growth and unprecedented wealth had created a new class of noble warriors who were resented and mistrusted by the petty nobility of the old heartland of the Assyrian kingdom. The old nobility demanded a greater share in the imperial wealth and a more direct role in the administration of the empire. When the emperors ignored their demands, they began a long and bitter revolt that lasted from 827 B.C. until 750 B.C. This internal crisis put Assyria at the mercy of its external enemies, who seemed on the verge of destroying the Assyrian state. Instead, the revolt paved the way for the ascension of Tiglath-pileser III (746–727 B.C.), the greatest empire builder of Mesopotamia since Sargon. Tiglath-pileser and his successors transformed the structure of the Assyrian state and expanded its empire. They created a model for empire that would later be copied by Persia, Macedonia, and Rome. In the sense that the Assyrians not only conquered but created an administrative system by which to rule, theirs was the first true empire.

From his palace at Nineveh, Tiglath-pileser combined all of the traditional elements of Mesopotamian statecraft with a new religious ideology and social system to create the framework for a lasting, multiethnic imperial system. This system rested on five bases: a transformed army, a new religious military ideology, a novel administrative system, a social policy involving large-scale population movements, and the calculated use of massive terror.

The heart of Tiglath-pileser's program was the most modern army the world had ever seen. In place of traditional armies of peasants and slaves supplied by great aristocrats, he raised professional armies from the conquered lands of the empire commanded by Assyrian generals. The Assyrian army was also the first to use iron weapons on a massive scale. The bronze swords and shields of their enemies were no match for the stronger iron weapons of the Assyrians. Assyrian armies were also well balanced, including not only infantry, cavalry, and chariots, but also engineering units for constructing the siege equipment needed to capture towns. Warfare had become a science.

In addition to the professional army, Tiglath-pileser created the most developed military-religious ideology of any ancient people. Kings had long been agents of the gods, but Ashur, the god of the Assyrians, had but one command: enlarge the empire! Thus warfare was the mission and duty of all, a sacred command paralleled through the centuries in the cries of "God wills it" of the Christian crusaders and the "God is great" of Muslims.

Tiglath-pileser restructured his empire, both at home in Assyria and abroad, so that revolts of the sort that had nearly destroyed it would be less possible. Within Assyria, he increased the number of administrative districts, thus decreasing the strength of each. This reduced the likelihood of successful rebellions launched by dissatisfied governors. Outside of Assyria proper, whenever possible the king liquidated traditional leaders and appointed Assyrian governors or at least assigned loyal overseers to protect his interests. Even then he did not allow governors and overseers unlimited authority or discretion; instead, he kept close contact with local administrators through a system of royal messengers.

In order to shatter regional identities, which could lead to separatist movements, Tiglath-pileser deported and resettled conquered peoples on a massive scale. He sent thirty thousand Syrians to the Zagros Mountains and moved eighteen thousand Aramaeans from the Tigris to Syria. Thousands must have died of exhaustion, hunger, and thirst during these forced marches of men, women, and children. The survivors, cut off from their homelands by hundreds of miles and surrounded by people speaking different languages and practicing different religions, posed no threat to the stability of the empire.

Finally, in the tradition of his Assyrian predecessors, Tiglath-pileser and his successors maintained control of conquered peoples through a policy of unprecedented cruelty and brutality. One, for example, boasted of once having flayed an enemy's chiefs and using their skins to cover a great pillar he erected at their city gate and on which he impaled his victims. The enemy officers were treated more kindly—he simply cut off their arms and legs.

Ironically, while the imperial military and administrative system created by the Assyrians became in time the blueprint for future empires, its very ferocity led to its downfall. The hatred inspired by such brutality led to the destruction of

Nineveh and Babylon

827–750 B.C.	Revolt of Assyrian petty nobility
746–727 B.C.	Tiglath-Pileser III
612 B.C.	Medes and Babylonians take Nineveh
539 B.C.	Cyrus II of Persia takes the city of Babylon

the Assyrian empire at the hands of a coalition of its subjects. In what is today Iran, Indo-European tribes coalesced around the Median dynasty. Egypt shook off its Assyrian lords under the leadership of the pharaoh Psamtik I (664–610 B.C.). In Babylon, which had always proven difficult for the Assyrians to control, a new Aramaean dynasty began to oppose Assyrian rule. In 612 B.C., the Medes and Babylonians joined forces to attack and destroy Nineveh. Once more, the pattern begun by Sargon, of imperial expansion, consolidation, decay, and destruction, was repeated.

However, the lessons that the Assyrians taught the world were not forgotten by the Babylonians, who modeled their imperial system on that of their predecessors, even while harkening back to traditions of the Old Babylonian kingdom of Hammurabi. Administration of the New Babylonian empire, which extended roughly over the length of the Tigris and extended west into Syria and Palestine, owed much to Assyrian tradition. The Code of Hammurabi once more formed the fundamental basis for justice. Babylonian kings restored and enriched temples to the Babylonian gods, and temple lands, administered by priests appointed by the king, played an important role in Babylonian economy and culture. Babylonian priests, using the mathematical methods developed during the Old Kingdom, made important advances in mathematical astronomy, laying the foundation for subsequent exact studies of heavenly bodies.

Under King Nebuchadnezzar II, the city of Babylon reached its zenith, covering some five hundred acres and containing a population of over a hundred thousand, over twice the population of Uruk at its height. The city walls, counted

The Assyrian and New Babylonian Empires

among the seven wonders of the world by the later Greeks, were so wide that two chariots could ride abreast on them. And yet this magnificent fortification was never tested. In 539 B.C., a Persian army under King Cyrus II (ca. 585–ca. 529 B.C.), who had ousted the Median dynasty in 550 B.C., slipped into the city through the Euphrates river bed at low water and took the city by surprise.

The legacy of the first three thousand years of civilization is more than a tradition of imperial conquest, exploitation, and cruelty. It goes beyond a mere catalogue of discoveries, inventions, and achievements, impressive as they are. The legacy includes the basic structure of Western civilization. The floodplain civilizations and their neighbors provided the first solutions to problems of social and political organization and complex government. They built what we now recognize to have been the first cities, city-states, nation-states, and finally multinational empires. They attacked the problems of uneven distribution of natural resources through irrigation, long-distance trade, and communication. Their religious traditions, from polytheism to monotheism, provided patterns for subsequent Western religious traditions. Mesopotamian astronomy and mathematics and Egyptian engineering and building were fundamental for future civilizations. The immediate successors of these civilizations, however, would be to the west of the great river valleys, in the mountainous peninsulas and scattered islands of southern Europe.

Suggestions for Further Reading

General Reading

Cambridge Ancient History, Vol. 1, Part 1 (Cambridge: Cambridge University Press, 1970). Contains essays on every aspect of ancient civilizations.

* A. Bernard Knapp, *The History and Culture of Ancient Western Asia and Egypt* (Chicago: Dorsey Press, 1987). A good general survey of the entire period.

* Gerda Lerner, *The Creation of Patriarchy* (New York: Oxford University Press, 1986). A study of gender and politics in antiquity by a leading feminist historian.

* Indicates paperback edition available.

* Barbara Lesko, "Women of Egypt and the Ancient Near East" in Renate Bridenthal, Claudia Koonz, and Susan Stuart, eds., *Becoming Visible*, 2nd ed. (Boston: Houghton Mifflin, 1987). A general survey of women in ancient civilizations.

Before Civilization

* Lewis R. Binford, *In Pursuit of the Past* (New York: Thames & Hudson, 1988). A general introduction to prehistorical archaeology, intended for a general audience by an expert.

Peter Ucko and G. W. Dimbleby, *The Domestication and Exploitation of Plants and Animals* (Chicago: Aldine, 1969). Technical essays on the origins of domestication.

Between the Two Rivers

Hans J. Nissen, *The Early History of the Ancient Near East, 9000–2000 B.C.* (Chicago: University of Chicago Press, 1988). An up-to-date survey of early Mesopotamia.

* A. L. Oppenheim, *Ancient Mesopotamia*, 2nd ed. (Chicago: University of Chicago Press, 1977). Another general introduction by an expert.

* Georges Roux, *Ancient Iraq* (New York: Penguin Books, 1980). A very readable general introduction intended for a broad audience.

Morris Silver, *Economic Structures of the Ancient Near East* (New York: B&N Imports, 1985). A controversial analysis of ancient Near Eastern economy.

* O. Neugebauer, *The Exact Sciences in Antiquity* (New York: Dover, 1970). A series of technical essays on ancient mathematics and astronomy.

The Gift of the Nile

H. Frankfort, *Ancient Egyptian Religion* (New York: Harper & Row, 1961). A classic study of Egyptian religion.

* B. B. G. Trigger et al., *Ancient Egypt: A Social History* (Cambridge: Cambridge University Press, 1983). A current survey of ancient Egyptian social history by a group of experts.

Between Two Worlds

John Bright, *A History of Israel*, 3rd ed. (Louisville, KY: Westminster John Knox Press, 1981). A standard history of the Israelites until the middle of the second century B.C.

A. T. Olmstead, *History of Assyria* (Chicago: University of Chicago Press, 1975). The fundamental survey of the Assyrian empire.

H. W. F. Saggs, *Everyday Life in Babylonia and Assyria* (New York: Putnam, 1965). A readable account of Babylonian and Assyrian society.

2

Early Greece

Hecuba and Achilles

The wrath of the great warrior Achilles is the subject of Homer's *Iliad*, the first and greatest epic poem of the West, written shortly after 750 B.C. Angered by a perceived slight to his honor, Achilles sulks in his tent while the other Achaeans, or Greeks, fight a desperate and losing battle against their enemies, the defenders of the city of Troy. Only after his friend Patroclus is slain by the Trojan Prince Hector does Achilles return to the battle to avenge his fallen comrade and propel the Achaeans to victory. Near the end of the epic, after he has slain Hector in hand-to-hand combat, Achilles ties his foe's body to the back of his chariot and drags it three times around Patroclus' tomb to appease his friend's spirit. The gods are horrified at this demeaning treatment of the body of one who had always been faithful in his sacrifices. Zeus, the chief god, sends his messenger Iris to Hector's mourning parents, his father, Priam, king of Troy, and his mother, Hecuba. Iris urges them to ransom their son's body from Achilles. Moved by the message, Priam goes to Achilles' tent to plead for Hector's body. Achilles, moved by pity and grief for his own father and for Patroclus, grants the old king his request, and Priam returns in sorrow to Troy bearing the body of his son for burial.

The first portions of this episode are brilliantly rendered on the side of the sixth-century B.C. *hydria*, or water pitcher, shown here. At the center, Achilles leaps into his chariot. The naked body of Hector stretches below him and the chariot rushes around the tumulus, or burial mound, of Achilles' friend, represented by the white hill to the right. Above it, the small winged spirit of Patroclus watches. In death he is a pale reflection, a shade of his former self, still attired in the clothing and arms of a warrior. But even as Achilles carries out his deed of vengeance, Iris, the winged messenger of Zeus, rushes to Hector's parents, who are shown under a columned portico, which represents Troy. Typically, the artist has taken some liberty with the story. It is not the grieving father the artist has chosen to feature but rather Hecuba, Hector's disconsolate mother. In a vivid manner, totally alien to previous artistic traditions, the Greek artist, like the Greek poet, has captured the essentials of human tragedy.

For all its violent action, the *Iliad* is concerned less with what people do than with how they face the great moments of their life, their time of suffering, their time of death. Hector had died well and in so doing won immortal fame from his enemies, the Greeks. Achilles eventually acted well, and in his encounter with Priam faced the universal elements of human destiny: life, love, suffering, endurance, death. Such sentiments, expressed by Homer, became an enduring heritage of Greek civilization and, through it, the civilization of the West. In the small, fragile, and violent communities of Greek speakers spread across the Mediterranean, citizen soldiers first struggled with these and other fundamental issues that have set the agenda for the West to the present day.

Greece in the Bronze Age

Early in the *Iliad* Homer pauses to list the captains and ships of the besieging forces. The roll call of heroes and their homelands is more than a literary device. It is the distant echo of a vanished world, the world of "the goodly citadel of Athens, wealthy Corinth, Knossos and Gortys of the great walls, and the established fortress of Mycenae." The poet lived in an age of illiterate warrior herdsmen, of impoverished, scattered, and sparsely populated villages. Still, in the depths of this "Dark Age," roughly from 1200 to 700 B.C., the distant memory of a time of rich palaces, teeming cities, and powerful kings lived on. Homer and his contemporaries could not know that these confused memories were of the last great Bronze Age (ca. 3500–1200 B.C.) civilization of the Mediterranean. Still less could they have imagined that at the very time when they were singing of the wrath of Achilles and the lost glory of his age, they were also preparing the foundations of a far greater and lasting civilization, that of classical Greece.

Unlike the rich floodplains of Mesopotamia and Egypt, Greece is a stark world of mountains and sea. The rugged terrain of Greece, only 10 percent of which is flat, and the scores of islands that dot the Aegean and Ionian seas favor the development of small, self-contained agricultural societies. The Greek climate is uncertain, constantly threatening Greek farmers with failure. While temperature remains fairly constant, rainfall varies enormously from year to year, island to island, valley to valley. Arid summers alternate with cool, wet winters. Greek farmers struggled to produce the Mediterranean triad of grains, olives, and wine, which first began to dominate agriculture around 3000 B.C. Wheat, barley, and beans were the staples of Greek life. Chickpeas, lentils, and bread, supplemented with olive oil, wine, and cheese filled the stomachs of Greek farmers and townspeople. Only on rare holidays did ordinary folk see fish or perhaps some mutton on their tables. When the rains came too soon or too late, even bread and beans might be missing. The constant fluctuations in climate and weather

Marble statue of a seated harp player from the Cyclades Islands, dating from the third millennium B.C. The statue is executed in great detail despite the primitive tools at the sculptor's disposal.

from region to region helped break down the geographical isolation by forcing isolated communities to build contacts with a wider world in order to survive.

Islands of Peace

To Homer, the Greeks were all Achaeans no matter whether they came from the Greek mainland, the islands in the Aegean Sea, or the coast of Asia Minor. Since the late nineteenth century, archaeologists have discerned three fairly distinct late Bronze Age cultures—the Cycladic, the

Minoan, and the Mycenaean—that flourished in the Mediterranean prior to the end of the twelfth century B.C.

The first culture appeared on the Cyclades, the rugged islands strewn across the bottom of the Aegean from the Greek mainland to the coast of Asia Minor. As early as 2500 B.C., craftsmen in small settlements on the islands of Naxos and Melos developed a high level of metallurgical and artistic skill. Veins of lead and silver run through the hills of the Cyclades. Local craft workers perfected techniques of working these metals, methods that later traveled both north to the mainland and south to Crete. The most impressive and enig-

matic remains of the Cycladic culture (ca. 3000–ca. 1550 B.C.) are marble figurines, both male and female, found in large numbers in graves on the mainland, the islands themselves, and in Asia Minor. These severe geometrical figures presumably had a religious significance, a significance now unknown.

Cycladic society was not concentrated into towns, nor apparently was it particularly warlike. Many of the largest Cycladic settlements were unfortified. Cycladic religion, to judge from fragments of large clay statues of female figures found in a temple on the island of Ceos, focused on female deities, perhaps fertility goddesses.

Greece in the Bronze Age

This early Bronze Age society faded slowly and imperceptibly but not before influencing its neighbors, especially Crete, the large Mediterranean island to the south. There, beginning around 2500 B.C., developed a remarkably sophisticated centralized civilization termed Minoan after the legendary King Minos of Crete.

Knowledge of Minoan civilization burst upon the modern world suddenly in 1899. In that year the English archaeologist Sir Arthur Evans made the first of a series of extraordinary archaeological discoveries at Knossos, the legendary palace of Minos. Since then, additional centers have been found on the southern and eastern coasts of the island as well as at Chania in the northwest. Crete's location between the civilizations of the Fertile Crescent and the barbarian worlds of the north and west made the island a natural point of exchange and amalgamation of cultures. Still, during the golden age of Crete, roughly between 2000 and 1550 B.C., the island developed its unique traditions. Great palace complexes were constructed at Knossos, Phaistos, Hagia Triada, and elsewhere on the island. They appear as a maze of storerooms, workrooms, and living quarters clustered around a central square. Larger public rooms may have existed at an upper level, but all traces of them have disappeared. The walls of these palaces still display frescoes, which present a vivid image of Cretan life in the late Bronze Age. Some frescoes depict crowds of prosperous Cretans watching as court ladies dance under olive trees or as male and female athletes practice the deadly sport of vaulting over the backs of ferocious bulls. Other wall paintings show aristocratic women, elaborately clothed in sumptuous dresses that leave their breasts exposed, engaged in conversation while the athletic spectacle unfurls before them.

Palace bureaucrats, using a unique form of syllabic writing known as Linear A, controlled agricultural production and distribution as well as the work of skilled artisans in their surrounding areas. A well-maintained road system connected the cities across the island, especially between Knossos, the capital, and Phaistos in the south, which may have been a winter palace. Towns with well-organized street plans, drainage systems, and clear hierarchies of elite and lesser homes dotted the landscape.

Like other ancient civilizations, Minoan Crete was a strongly stratified system in which the vast peasantry paid a heavy tribute in olive oil and other produce. Tribute or taxes flowed to local and regional palaces and ultimately to Knossos, which stood at the pinnacle of a four-tier network uniting the island. To some extent, the palace elites redistributed this wealth back down the system through their patterns of consumption. However, the abundance of luxury imports at Knossos, Phaistos, and elsewhere indicate that much of the wealth amassed by the elite was consumed by the great numbers of palace servants and craftsmen or went abroad to pay for the Egyptian and Syriac luxury goods, Italian metal, and Baltic amber found in abundance in the ruins.

Though the system may have been exploitative, it was not militaristic. None of the palaces or towns of Crete was fortified. The delicate and naturalistic frescoes and statues never depict warriors, weapons, or battles. Nor was the cult of the ruler particularly emphasized. The throne room at Knossos is modest and none of its decorations suggest the sort of royal aggrandizement typical in the Mesopotamian, Hittite, or Egyptian

A reconstructed portion of the Palace of Minos at Knossos, Crete. A fresco of frolicking dolphins adorns a wall. The mosaic-covered masonry walls and painted wooden columns are characteristic of Cretan architecture.

In "The Toreador Fresco" from the Cretan Palace of Minos, dating from about 1500 B.C., one daring, wasp-waisted athlete vaults over the back of a charging bull while another holds the bull by the horns. The bull played a major role in Minoan religious symbolism.

worlds. Monumental architecture and sculpture designed to exalt the ruler and to overwhelm the commoner is entirely absent from Crete. A key to this unique social tone may be Cretan religion and, with it, the unusually high status of women. Although male gods received veneration, Cretans particularly worshiped female deities, whose cults were centered in some twenty-five caves scattered across the island. Here and at the palaces, bulls and bull horns as well as the double-headed ax, or *labris*, played an important if today mysterious role in the worship of these gods. Chief among the female deities was the mother goddess, who was the source of good and evil. One must however be careful not to paint too idyllic an image of Cretan religion. Children's bones found in excavations of the palace of Knossos show traces of butchering and the removal of slices of flesh. Other hints at human sacrifice have been found at Archanes, immediately behind the Knossos palace.

Although evidence such as the frequent appearance of women participating in or watching public ceremonies and the widespread worship of female deities cannot lead to the conclusion that Minoan society was a form of matriarchy, it does suggest that Minoan civilization differed considerably from the floodplain

Faience statuette of a priestess, or perhaps a deity, from the Palace of Minos, holding two squirming snakes. The stiff, flounced skirt and bare breasts are typical of female figures found in Cretan frescoes and on gold signet rings.

civilizations of the Near East and the societies developing on the mainland. At least until the fourteenth century B.C., Cretan society was truly unique. Both men and women seem to have shared important roles in religious and public life and together built a structured society without the need for vast armies or warrior kings.

Around 1450 B.C., a wave of destruction engulfed all of the Cretan cities except Knossos, which finally met destruction around 1375 B.C. The causes of this catastrophe continue to inspire historical debate. Some argue that a natural disaster such as an earthquake or the eruption of a powerful volcano on Thera was responsible for the destruction. More likely, given the martial traditions of the continent and their total absence on Crete, the destruction was the work of mainland Greeks taking control of Knossos and other Minoan centers. An Egyptian tomb painting from the fifteenth century B.C. graphically illustrates the transition. An ambassador in Cretan dress was overpainted by one wearing a kilt characteristic of that worn by mainland Greeks. Around this same time, true warrior graves equipped with weapons and armor begin to appear on Crete and at Knossos for the first time. Following this violent conquest, only Knossos and Phaistos were rebuilt, presumably by Greek lords who had eliminated the other political centers on the island. A final destruction hit Knossos around 1200 B.C..

Mainland of War

The contrast between the islands and the Greek mainland was particularly marked. Around 1600 B.C., a new and powerful warrior civilization arose on the Peloponnesus at Mycenae. The only remains of the first phase of this civilization are thirty graves found at the bottom of deep shafts arranged in two circles, but they tell of a rich, powerful, and warlike elite. The delicate gold ornaments, bronze swords, spearheads, knives, axes, armor, and utensils that fill the graves emphasize the warrior lives of their occupants. By 1500 B.C., mainland Greeks were using huge *tholoi*, or beehive-shaped tombs, for royal burials. These structures were magnificent achievements of architecture and masonry, far beyond anything seen previously in Europe. The largest, found at Mycenae and erroneously called the "Treasury of Atreus" after a character of Greek myth, is forty-eight feet in diameter and forty-three feet from floor to its vaulted ceiling. This great vault, capped by a stone weighing over a hundred tons, was the largest vault in the world for over sixteen hundred years, surpassed only by Roman architects at the height of the Roman Empire. Over fifty such tombs have been found on the Greek mainland, as have the remains of over five hundred villages and great palaces at Mycenae, Tiryns, Athens, Thebes, Gla, and Pylos. This entire civilization, which encompassed not

A bronze dagger blade showing a lion hunt in inlaid gold and silver, dating from around 1500 B.C., was found at the Citadel of Mycenae.

only the mainland but also parts of the coast of Asia Minor, is called Mycenaean, although there is no evidence that the city of Mycenae actually ruled all of Greece.

The Mycenaeans quickly adopted artisanal and architectural techniques from neighboring cultures, especially from the Hittites and from Crete. However, the Mycenaeans incorporated these techniques into a distinctive tradition of their own. Unlike the open Cretan palaces and towns, Mycenaean palaces were strongly walled fortresses. From these palaces Mycenaean kings, aided by a small military elite, organized and controlled the collection of taxes and tribute from subordinate towns and rural districts. Through their palace administrators, they controlled the production of bronze, the weaving of woolen cloth, and the extensive maritime trade in agricultural produce with other regions.

Mycenaean administrators also adopted the Linear A script of Crete, transforming it to write their own language, a Greek dialect, in a writing known as Linear B. Linear B appears to have been used almost exclusively for record-keeping in palaces, indicating amounts of tribute, the organization of workers, and the quantities of weapons, sheep, and slaves engaged in various religious and palace duties.

Mycenaean domination did not last for long. Around 1200 B.C., many of the mainland and island fortresses and cities were sacked and totally destroyed. In some areas, such as Pylos, the population fell to roughly 10 percent of what it had been previously, while in others, such as Patras, population grew but remained dispersed. Centralized government, literacy, urban life, civilization itself disappeared from Greece for over four hundred years. Why and how this happened is one of the great mysteries of world history.

In later centuries the Greeks believed that following the Trojan War, new peoples, especially the Dorians, had migrated into Greece, destroying Mycenae and most of the other Achaean cities. More recently, some historians have argued that catastrophic climatic changes, volcanic eruptions, or some other natural disaster wrecked the cities and brought famine and tremendous social unrest in its wake. Neither theory is accurate. No single invasion or natural disaster caused the collapse of the civilizations of late Bronze Age Greece. Mycenaean Greece was destroyed neither

The Lion Gate at Mycenae. On a stone slab atop a huge lintel two lions face each other across a sacred column of the type found at Knossos on Crete. The heads, now lost, were made of separate pieces of metal or stone.

by barbarian invaders nor by acts of God. It self-destructed. Its disintegration was part of the widespread crisis affecting the eastern Mediterranean in the twelfth century B.C. (see chapter 1, pp. 23). The pyramid of Mycenaean lordship, built by small military elites commanding maritime commercial networks, was always threatened with collapse. Overpopulation, the fragility of the agrarian base, the risks of overspecialization in cash crops such as grain in Messenia and in sheep raising in Crete, and rivalry among states—all made Mycenaean culture vulnerable. The disintegration of the Hittite empire and the near-collapse of the Egyptian disrupted Mediterranean commerce, exacerbating hostilities among Greek states. As internal warfare raged, the delicate structures of elite lordship disappeared in the mutual sackings and destructions of the palace fortresses. The Dark Age poet Hesiod (ca. 800 B.C.), although writing about his own time, probably got it about right:

> Father will have no common bond with son
> Neither will guest with host, nor friend with friend
> The brother-love of past days will be gone ....
> Men will destroy the towns of other men.

The Dark Age

With the collapse of the administrative and political system on which Mycenaean civilization was built, the tiny elite that had ruled it vanished as well. Some of these rulers probably migrated to the islands, especially Cyprus, and the eastern Mediterranean. Others took to piracy, alternately raiding the coast from Anatolia to Egypt and serving as mercenaries in foreign armies. What later Greeks remembered as the Trojan War may have been a cloudy recollection of the last raids of free-booters along the edge of the collapsing Hittite empire. From roughly 1200 until 800 B.C., the Aegean world entered what is generally termed the Dark Age, a confused and little-known period during which Greece returned to a more primitive level of culture and society.

In the wake of the Mycenaean collapse, bands of northerners moved slowly into the Peloponnesus while other Greeks migrated out from the mainland to the islands and the coast of Asia Minor. As these tribal groups merged with the indigenous populations they gave certain regions distinctive dialectic and cultural characteristics. Thus the Dorians settled in much of the Peloponnesus, Crete, and southwest Asia Minor. Ionians made Attica, Euboea, and the Aegean islands their home, while a mixed group called Aeolians

Greece in the Bronze Age

ca. 2500 B.C.	Beginning of Minoan civilization in Crete
ca. 2000–1500 B.C.	Golden Age of Crete
ca. 1600 B.C.	Beginning of Mycenaean civilization in Greece
ca. 1450 B.C.	Cretan cities, except Knossos, destroyed
ca. 1375 B.C.	Knossos destroyed
ca. 1200–800 B.C.	Greek Dark Age
ca. 1200 B.C.	Mycenaean sites in Greece destroyed; Knossos destroyed again
ca. 1100–1000 B.C.	Writing disappears from Greece

An amphora from Mykonos is decorated with reliefs depicting the siege of Troy. On the neck of the jar, the Trojan Horse is being wheeled toward the walls of Troy by the unsuspecting defenders as Greek warriors lurk inside.

began to migrate to central and northwest Asia Minor. As a result, from the eleventh century B.C., both shores of the Aegean became part of a Greek-speaking world. Still later, Greeks established colonies in what is today southern Russia, Italy, North Africa, Spain, and France. Throughout its history, Greece was less a geographical than a cultural designation.

Everywhere in this world, between roughly 1100 and 1000 B.C., architecture, urban traditions, even writing disappeared along with the elites for whose exclusive benefit these achievements had served. The Greece of this Dark Age was much poorer, more rural, and more simply organized. It was also a society of ironworkers. Iron began to replace bronze as the most common metal for ornaments, tools, and weapons. At first this was a simple necessity. The collapse of long-distance trade deprived Greeks of access to tin and copper, the essential ingredients of bronze. Gradually, however, the quality of iron tools and weapons began to improve as smiths learned to work hot iron into a primitive steel.

What little is known of this period must be gleaned from archaeology and from two great epic poems written down around 750 B.C., near the end of the Dark Age. The archaeological record is bleak. Pictorial representation of humans and animals almost disappears. Luxury goods and most imports are gone from tombs. Gold ornaments and jewelry are so rare that they may have come from some Mycenaean hoard found by Dark Age Greeks rather than from contemporary artisans. Pottery made at the beginning of the Dark Age shows little innovation, crudely imitating forms of Mycenaean production.

Gradually, beginning in the eleventh century B.C., things began to change a bit. New geometric forms of decoration begin to appear on pottery. New types of iron pins, weapons, and decorations appeared, which owe little or nothing to the Mycenaean tradition. Cultural changes accompanied these material changes. Around the middle of the eleventh century B.C., Greeks in some locations stopped burying their dead and began to practice cremation. Whatever the meaning of these changes, they signaled something new on the shores of the Aegean.

The two epic poems, the *Iliad* and the *Odyssey*, hint at this something new. The *Iliad* is the older poem, dating probably to the second half of the eighth century B.C. The *Odyssey* dates from

This red-figured Greek vase from the fifth century B.C. depicts the hero Odysseus resisting the Sirens. He is tied to the mast of his ship to prevent him from being lured to destruction by the song of the bird-bodied temptresses.

perhaps fifty years later. Traditionally ascribed to Homer, these epics were actually the work of oral bards or performers who composed as they chanted, weaving the tale of traditional lines and expressions as they went along. The world in which the action of the Homeric epics takes place was already passing away when the poems were composed, but the world described is not really that of the late Bronze Age. Although the poems explicitly harken back to the Mycenaean age, much of the description of life, society, and culture actually reflects Dark Age conditions.

Thus Homer's heroes were petty kings, chieftains, and nobles, whose position rested on their wealth, measured in land and flocks, on personal prowess, on networks of kin and allies, and on military followings. The Homeric hero Odysseus is typical of these Dark Age chieftains. In the *Iliad* and the *Odyssey* he is king of Ithaca, a small island on the west coast of Greece. He had inherited his kingship from his father, but he derived his real authority from his skills as a speaker and warrior. To the Homeric poets he was "goodly Odysseus" as well as "the man of wiles" and "the waster of cities." He retained command of his men only as long as he could lead them to victory in the raids against their neighbors, which formed the most honorable source of wealth. Odysseus describes his departure for home after the fall of Troy with pride:

> "The wind that bore me from Ilios brought me . . . to Ismarus, whereupon I sacked their city and slew the people. And from the city we took their wives and much goods, and divided them among us, that none through me might go lacking his proper share."

Present, the king was judge, gift giver, lawgiver, and commander. Absent, no legal or governmental institutions preserved his authority. Instead the nobility, lesser warriors who were constantly at odds with the king, sought to take his place. In the *Odyssey* only their mutual rivalry saves Odysseus' wife, Penelope, from being forced to marry one of these haughty aristocrats eager to replace the king.

These nobles, warriors wealthy enough to possess horses and weapons, lived to prove their strength and honor in combat against their equals, the one true test of social value. The existence of chieftains such as Odysseus was a threat

PHOENICIAN	⟨ 𐤁 𐤂 𐤃 𐤄 Y 𐤆 B 𐤇 𐤈 𐤉 𐤊 𐤋 ○ 𐤍 Φ 𐤏 W † Y Y Y 𐤕 𐤒 I
EARLY GREEK	A 𐤁 𐤂 Δ ⊐ 𐤅 𐤆 B 𐤇 𐤈 𐤊 𐤋 𐤌 𐤍 O 𐤓 Φ 𐤖 𐤗 X Y Y Y 𐤕 I
ENGLISH	A B C D E F G H I J K L M N O P Q R S T U V W X Y Z

to their honor, and by the eighth century B.C., the aristocracy had eliminated kings in most places. Ranking beneath these proud warriors, as a shadowy mass, was the populace. Some of this group, like Odysseus' faithful servants who aided him in defeating his enemies upon his return home, were slaves. Most were shepherds or farmers too mired down in the laborious work of subsistence agriculture to participate in the heroic life-style of their social betters. Still, even the populace were not entirely excluded from public life. Odysseus' son Telemachus summoned the assembly of the people, the *dēmos*, to listen to his complaints against the noble suitors of his mother. This does not mean that the assembly was particularly effective. They listened to both sides and did nothing. Still, a time was coming when changes in society would give a new and hitherto unimagined power to the silent farmers and herdsmen of the Dark Age.

Archaic Greece

Between roughly 800 and 500 B.C., extraordinary changes took place in the Greek world. The descendants of the farmers and herdsmen of Homer's Dark Age brought about a revolution in political organization, artistic traditions, intellectual values, and social structures. In a burst of creativity forged in conflict and competition, they invented politics, invented abstract thought, invented the individual. Greeks of the Archaic Age (ca. 700–500 B.C.) set the agenda for the rest of Western history.

The first sign of radical change in Greece was a major increase in population in the eighth century B.C. In Attica for example, between 780 and 720 B.C., the population increased perhaps sevenfold. Similar rapid population growth occurred throughout the Greek world. The reasons for this extraordinary increase are obscure but may have resulted from a shift from herding to agriculture. In any case the consequences were enormous. First, population increase meant more villages and towns, greater communication among them, and thus the more rapid circulation of ideas and skills. Second, the rising population placed impossible demands on the agricultural system of much of Greece, overcrowding the land and forcing many farmers into poverty and many others into migration. Third, it led to greater division of labor and, with an increasingly diverse population, to fundamental changes in political systems. The old structure of loosely organized tribes and chieftains became inadequate to deal with the more complex nature of the new society.

The multiplicity of political and social forms developing in the Archaic Age set the framework in which developed the first flowering of Greek culture. Economic and political transformations laid the basis for intellectual advance by creating a broad class with the prosperity to enjoy sufficient leisure for thought and creative activity. At the same time, literacy and local pride allowed the new citizen populations of the Greek cities to participate in intellectual and cultural activities in an unprecedented manner. Finally, maritime relations brought people and ideas from around the Greek world together, cross-fertilizing artists and intellectuals in a way never before seen.

Ethnos and Polis

In general, two forms of political organization developed in response to the population explosion of the eighth century B.C. On the mainland and in much of the western Peloponnesus, people continued to live in large territorial units called *ethnē* (sing. *ethnos*). In each ethnos people lived in villages and small towns scattered across a wide region. Common customs and a common religion focusing on a central religious sanctuary united them. The ethnos was governed by an elite, or *oligarchy*, meaning rule by the few, made up of major landowners who met from time to time in one or another town within the region. This form of government, which had its roots in the Dark Age, continued to exist throughout the classical period.

A much more innovative form of political organization, which developed on the shores of the Aegean and on the islands, was the *polis* (pl. *poleis*), or city-state. Initially, *polis* meant simply "citadel." Villages clustered around these fortifications, which were both protective structures and cult centers for specific deities. These high, fortified sites—*acropolis* means "high citadel"—were sacred to specific gods: in Athens and Sparta, to Athena; in Argos and Samos, to Hera; at Corinth and Thermon, to Apollo. In addition to protection, the polis offered a marketplace, or *agora*, where farmers and artisans could trade and conduct business. The rapid population growth of the eighth century B.C. led to the fusion of these villages and the formation of real towns. Each town was independent, each was ruled by a monarch or oligarchy, and each controlled the surrounding region, the inhabitants of which were on an equal footing with the townspeople. At times of political or military crisis, the rulers might summon an assembly of the free males of the community to the agora to participate in or to witness the decision-making process. In the following centuries, these city-states became the center for that most dramatic Greek experiment in government, democracy.

The general model of the polis may have been borrowed from the eastern Mediterranean Phoenicians, the merchant society responsible for much of the contact Greeks of the eighth-century B.C. had with the outside world. On the other hand, by 800 B.C. the Greeks themselves had a permanent trading post at Al Mina on the Syrian coast and thus were in direct contact with the traditions of the Near East. The Phoenicians were certainly the source of a equally important innovation that appeared in Greece at the same time: the reintroduction of writing. The Linear B script, which the Mycenaeans had used exclusively for administrative and bureaucratic purposes, had entirely disappeared, along with the complex palace systems that it had served. Sometime in the eighth century B.C., Greeks adopted the Phoenician writing system. But this time the purpose was not primarily central administrative record keeping. From the start this writing system was intended for private, personal use and was available to virtually anyone. In a society fascinated with the oral traditions of the heroic past, it is no surprise that the Greeks radically transformed the Phoenician system, making its Semitic characters into arbitrary sounds (see the chart on page 44) and adding vowel notation in order to record poetry. Soon this writing system was being used to indicate ownership of objects, to record religious and secular vows, and even to entertain.

Within the polis, political power was not the monopoly of the aristocracy. The gradual expansion of the politically active population resulted largely from the demands of warfare. In the Dark Age, warfare had been dominated by heavily armed, mounted aristocrats who engaged their equals in single combat. In the Archaic Age, such individual combat between aristocratic warriors gave way to battles decided by the use of well-disciplined ranks of infantrymen called *phalanges* (sing. *phalanx*). Properly disciplined, the phalanx could withstand attacks of better-equipped aristocratic warriors. And while few Greeks could afford costly weapons, armor, and horses, between 25 and 40 percent of the landowners could provide the shields, lances, and bronze armor needed by the infantryman, or *hoplites*. These foot soldiers developed their own warrior pride, equal to but differing from that of the aristocrat. In the words of Tyrtaeus, a poet of the mid-seventh century B.C., the hoplite was to "stand near and take the enemy, strike with long spear or sword, set foot by foot, lean shield on shield, crest upon

A Greek hoplite

crest, helmet on helmet." The democratization of war led gradually to the democratization of political life. Those who brought victory in the phalanx were unwilling to accept total domination by the aristocracy in the agora. Growing demands of the common people, combined with demographic expansion and economic changes, created enormous social and political tensions throughout the Greek world. The rapid growth of the urban population, the increasing impoverishment of the rural peasantry, and the rise of a new class of wealthy merchant commoners were all challenges that traditional forms of government failed to meet. Everywhere traditional aristocratic rule was being undermined, and cities searched for ways to resolve this social conflict. No one solution emerged, and one of the outstanding achievements of archaic Greece was the almost limitless variety of political forms elaborated in its city-states.

Colonists and Tyrants

Colonization and tyranny were two intertwined results of the political and social turmoil of the seventh century B.C. Population growth, changes in economy, and opposition to aristocratic power led Greeks to seek change externally through emigration and internally through political restructuring.

Already late in the eleventh century B.C., Greeks began to migrate to new homes on the islands and along the coast of Asia Minor, in search of commercial advantages or a better life. Many of these communities, such as Rhodes, Miletus, Ephesus, and Erythrae, probably renewed older Greek traditions from the Mycenaean period. By the eighth century B.C., Greeks had pushed still farther east in search of sources for bronze. Euboeans established a permanent trading community at Al Mina in northern Syria and Greeks established themselves in other eastern towns such as Tarsus.

Beginning around 750 B.C., a new form of colonization began in the western Mediterranean. The impetus for this expansion was not primarily trade, but rather the need to reduce population pressure at home. The first noteworthy colony, Cumae near Naples, was founded by emigrants from Euboea. Soon other cities sent colonists to southern Italy and Sicily. Chalcis

founded Messina, Corinth founded Syracuse, and Achaea founded Sybaris, to name a few. Before long, these colonies themselves became mother cities, sending out parties to found still other colonies. Around 700 B.C., similar colonies appeared in the northeast in Thrace, on the shores of the Black Sea, and as far as the mouth of the Don River.

Colonists were not always volunteers. At Thera, for example, young men were chosen by lot to colonize Cyrene. The penalty for refusing to participate was death and confiscation of property. According to tradition, Sparta sent illegitimate sons to found Tarentum, and other cities forced political dissidents to emigrate. Usually colonists included only single males, the most volatile portion of the community. Colonies were thus a safety valve to release the pressures of population growth and political friction.

Although colonies remained attached culturally to their mother cities, they were politically independent. The men who settled them were warriors as well as farmers or traders and carved out their new cities at the expense of the local population. Intermarriage was the norm, but so was the conquest and enslavement of much of the original population, followed by a gradual absorption of natives into Greek civilization.

Colonization relieved some of the population pressure on Greek communities, but it did not solve the problem of political conflict. As opposition to entrenched aristocracies grew, first in Argos, then at Corinth, Sicyon, Elis, Mytilene, and elsewhere, individuals supported by those opposed to aristocratic rule seized power. These rulers were known as *tyrants*, a term which originally meant the same as king. In the course of the later sixth century B.C., *tyrant* came to designate those who had achieved supreme power without benefit of official position. Often, this rise to power came through popularity with hoplite armies. However, the term *tyrant* did not carry the negative connotation associated with it today. Early tyrants were generally welcomed by their fellow citizens and played a crucial role in the destruction of aristocratic government and the creation of civic traditions.

Generally, tyrants were motivated not so much by great civic spirit as they were by the desire to win and maintain power. Still, to this end they weakened the power of entrenched aristocratic groups, promoted the prosperity of their supporters by protecting farmers and encouraging trade, undertook public works projects, founded colonies, and entered marriage alliances with rulers of other cities, which provided some external peace. Although they stood outside of the traditional organs of government, tyrants were frequently content to govern through them, leaving magistracies and offices intact but ensuring that through elections these offices were filled with the tyrant's supporters. Thus at Corinth, Mytilene, Athens, and elsewhere, tyrants preserved and even strengthened constitutional structures as a hedge against the return to power of aristocratic factions.

The great weakness of tyrannies was that they depended for their success on the individual qualities of the ruler. Tyrants tended to pass their powers on to their sons and, as tyrannies became hereditary, cities came to resent incompetent or excessively harsh heirs' arbitrary control of government. This process seldom took more than three generations. As popular tyranny gave way to harsh and arbitrary rule, opposition brought on

Greek commerce expanded along with the colonies. In the painting on the interior of the Arkesilas Cup, dating from around 560 B.C., the king of Cyrene, a Greek colony in North Africa, is shown supervising the preparation of hemp or flax for export.

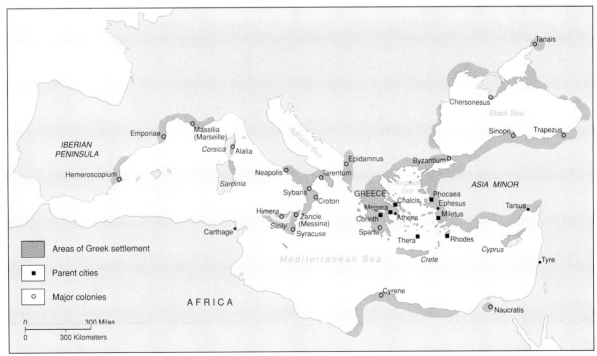

Greek Cities and Colonies of the Archaic Age

civil war and the deposition or abdication of the tyrant. Gradually tyranny acquired the meaning it bears today, and new forms of government emerged. Still, in spite of the bitter memory Greek tyranny left in people's minds, in many cities tyrants had for a time solved the crisis of political order and had cleared the way for broader participation in public life than had ever before been known.

Gender and Power

Military, political, and cultural life in the city-states became more democratic, but this democratization did not extend to women. Greek attitudes toward gender roles and sexuality were rigid. Except in a few cities, and in certain religious cults, women played no public role in the life of the community. They were isolated in the portions of the home reserved for them and remained firmly under male control throughout their lives, passing from the authority of their fathers to that of their husbands. Women were to be good mothers and obedient wives, not partners or close friends. For the most part friendship existed only between members of the same sex, and this friendship was often intensely sexual. Thus bisexuality was the norm in Greek society, although neither Greek homosexuality nor heterosexuality were the same as they are in modern society. Rather, both coexisted and formed a part of a sexuality of domination by those considered superior in age, rank, or sex over others. Mature men took young boys as their lovers, helped educate them, and inspired them by word and deed to grow into ideal warriors and citizens. We know less about such practices among women, but teachers such as Sappho of Lesbos (ca. 610–ca. 580 B.C.) formed similar bonds with their pupils, even while preparing them for marriage.

Those women who were in public life were mostly slaves, frequently prostitutes. These ranged from impoverished streetwalkers to *hetairai*, educated, sophisticated courtesans who entertained men at *symposia* (sing. *symposion*), or male banquets, which were the centers of cultural and social life. Many female slaves were acquired by collecting and raising infant daughters who had been abandoned by impoverished

A detail from a vase made in the fourth century B.C. in Sicily shows musical courtesans entertaining guests at a symposium, or drinking party.

families or those who simply did not want any more daughters. Greek society did not condemn or even question infanticide, prostitution, and sexual exploitation of women and slave boys. These practices formed part of the complex and varied social systems of the developing city-states.

Gods and Mortals

Greeks and their gods enjoyed an ambivalent, peculiar, almost irreverent relationship. On the one hand, Greeks made regular offerings to the gods, pleaded with them for help, and gave them thanks for assistance. On the other, the gods were thoroughly human, sharing in an exaggerated manner not only human strengths and virtues but also weaknesses and vices.

Greeks offered sacrifices to the gods on altars, which were raised everywhere—in homes, in fields, in sacred groves. Normally, the priests responsible for these rituals were lay people, often political and military leaders, but no group had the sort of monopoly on the cult of the gods enjoyed by Mesopotamian and Egyptian priests. Beginning in the Dark Age, cities dedicated open-air altars to the gods, often on the acropolis. In time, these altars were enclosed within temples. However, unlike the temples of other societies, Greek temples were houses of the gods, not centers of ritual. The earliest temples were constructed of wood or brick. Around 700 B.C., the first stone temples appeared and shortly afterward the Greek temple achieved its classic form. The so-called Doric temple consisted of an oblong or rectangular room covered by a pitched roof and circled by columns. These temples, which housed a statue of the god, were otherwise largely empty. Although dedicated to the gods, temples reflected the wealth and patriotism of the city. They stood as monuments to the human community rather than to the divine.

On special occasions, festivals celebrated at sanctuaries honored the gods of the city with processions, athletic contests, and feasts. Some of these celebrations were local, some involved the whole polis or ethnos, while others drew participants from all of the Greek world. The two greatest pan-Hellenic (meaning "all Greek," from *Hellas*, the Greek word for Greece) sanctuaries were Olympia and Delphi. Because both were remote from centers of political power, they were insulated from interstate rivalry and provided neutral ground on which hostile neighbors could meet in peace.

Olympia was the main sanctuary of Zeus and had been a cult site since the Bronze Age. Beginning in 776 B.C., every four years, wars and conflicts were temporarily suspended while athletes from the whole Greek world met at Olympia to participate in contests in honor of Zeus. Initially, the sports included only footraces and wrestling. In the sixth century B.C., horse races and other events were added and the games at Olympia grew in importance. (See Special Feature, "The Agony of Athletics," pp. 50–51.) The religious nature of the contests lowered neither their heated interstate rivalry nor the violence with which they were pursued. Wrestling in particular could be deadly, since matches continued until one participant signaled that he had had enough. Many wrestlers chose death rather than defeat. Victors were seen as the ideals of human society, the perfect triumph of body and soul, and Olympic victors were treated as national heroes. As Greek culture slowly spread through the Mediterranean world, so did participation in the Olympics, which continued for over one thousand years, ending only in A.D. 393.

Delphi, the site of the shrine of Apollo, god of music, archery, medicine, and prophecy, was the second pan-Hellenic cult center. Like Olympia, Delphi drew athletes from the whole Greek world to its athletic contests. However, Delphi's real fame lay in its oracle, or spokeswoman for the god Apollo. From the eighth century B.C., before undertaking any important decision such as establishing a colony, beginning a war, or even contracting a marriage, individuals and representatives of distant cities traveled to Delphi to ask Apollo's advice. In the turbulent seventh and sixth centuries B.C., Apollo was the acknowledged expert on justice. Through his oracle he guided petitioners seeking purification from the guilt attached to shedding others' blood and reconciliation with their fellow citizens. For a stiff fee, visitors were allowed to address questions to the god through a female medium. She entered a trance state and uttered a reply, which lay priests at the shrine then put into verse form and transmitted to the petitioner. The ambiguity of the

The Agony of Athletics

The Greeks did not play sports. Our word *play* is related to the Greek word *pais* (child), and there was nothing childish about Greek athletics. The Greek word was *agōnia*, and our modern derivation, *agony*, hits closer to the mark. From Homeric times, sports were a deadly serious affair. Poets, philosophers, and statesmen placed athletic victories above all other human achievements. "There is no greater glory for a man, no matter how long his life," proclaimed Homer, "than what he achieves with his hands and feet."

Athletic contests took place within a religious context, honoring the gods but glorifying the human victors. By 500 B.C., there were fifty sets of games across the Greek world held at regular intervals. Among the most prestigious contests were the so-called Crown Games at Delphi, Corinth, and Nemea; the most important were those held every four years as part of the cult of Zeus at Olympia. The most important event of the Olympic Games was the 192-meter race, or *stade*, from which comes the word *stadium*. So important was victory in this event that the name of the victor provided the basic system of Greek dating. Years were reckoned from the last Olympiad and were recorded as "three years after Epitelidas of Sparta won the stade" (577 B.C.), or "the year in which

Phanias of Pellene won the stade" (512 B.C.). In time, other events were added to the Olympics—other footraces (including one in which the contestants wore armor), throwing of the discus and javelin, the long jump, horse races, and chariot

races. The *pankration* combined wrestling and boxing in a no-holds-barred contest. The pentathlon included five events: discus, jumping, javelin, running, and wrestling.

The serious nature of sport was equaled by its danger. One

inscription from a statue erected at Olympia reads simply, "Here he died, boxing in the stadium, having prayed to Zeus for either the crown or death." The most celebrated pankration hero was Arrichion, who won but died in victory. Although his opponent was slowly strangling him, Arrichion managed to kick his adversary in such a way as to force the ball of his ankle free from its socket. The excruciating pain caused the opponent to signal defeat just as Arrichion died, victorious.

The ultimate disgrace was not injury or even death, but defeat. As one contemporary author put it, "In the Olympic Games you cannot just be beaten and then depart, but first of all, you will be disgraced not only before the people of Athens or Sparta or Nicopolis but before the whole world." Greeks did not honor good losers, only winners. As Pindar, the great lyric poet who celebrated victorious athletes, wrote, "As they [the losers] returned to their mothers no laughter sweet brought them pleasure, but they crept along the backroads, avoiding their enemies, bitten by misfortune."

If failure was bitter, victory was sweet indeed. Victors received enduring fame and enormous fortune. Poets composed odes in their honor, crowds hurried to meet them on their return home. Most games carried considerable cash prizes. At the four big games, winners received only crowns of olive or laurel leaves, but their home cities gave them more substantial gifts. Athens, for example, paid Olympic victors the equivalent of five hundred bushels of grain. This fabulous sum put the winner—for one year at least—in the ranks of the wealthiest Athenians. Most cities granted winners public honors and allowed them to eat at public expense for the rest of their lives. Thus the best athletes were essentially professionals, traveling from game to game. The Thasian boxer and pankratiast Theogenes claimed to have won over thirteen hundred victories during a professional career that spanned more than two decades. After his death he received the ultimate accolade: he was worshiped in Thasos as a god.

Competition among cities to field winning athletes was as sharp as the competition among the athletes themselves. Cities hired coaches, often themselves former Olympic champions, and actively recruited athletes from rival neighboring cities. The colony of Croton in Italy, for example, won the stade 44 percent of the time between 588 B.C. and 484 B.C. Then Croton's leading sprinter, Astylos, was lured to Syracuse and won three races, including the stade, for that city. Croton never again achieved an Olympic victory. Presumably its best athletes had been bought off.

In keeping with the rest of male-dominated Greece, only men were allowed to participate in or attend the Olympic games. Separate games dedicated to Zeus' wife, Hera, were held for unmarried women at Olympia. Women competed only in footraces over a short-ened track. While men competed naked, their bodies rubbed down with olive oil, in the Heraia women wore a short tunic. Victors in the Heraia did not receive the same honors as their male counterparts, but at least one woman found an indirect way to win a victory at the male Olympics. Cynisca, the daughter of a Spartan king, entered a team of horses in the race, encouraged, the story goes, by her brother, who wanted to show that victory in these events "required no excellence but was a victory of money and expense." Whatever her motivation, Cynisca was certainly proud of her achievement. Following the victory won for her by her male driver, she erected a statue of herself at Olympia with an inscription that read:

> Sparta's kings were fathers
>   and brothers of mine,
> But since with my chariot
>   and storming horses I,
>   Cynisca,
> Have won the prize, I place
>   my effigy here
> And proudly proclaim
> That of all Grecian women I
>   first bore the crown.

The Greeks' passion for games is unique in antiquity, and the progressive interest of Romans and "barbarians" in athletics was a sure sign of their absorption of Greek culture. Perhaps the best explanation of the place of athletics in the Greek world was that the single athlete, standing alone and naked and striving with all his being for excellence, was the purest expression of the individualism that animated Hellenic society.

Vase painting showing the Pythia, the priestess of Delphi, seated on her tripod. She holds a branch of the laurel plant, which is sacred to her patron, the god Apollo. The petitioner standing at right will most likely receive an enigmatic reply to his question.

Delphic replies was legendary. Petitioners had to interpret the answers they received as best they could.

Though gods were petitioned, placated, and pampered, they were not privileged or protected. Unlike the awe-inspiring gods of the Mesopotamians and Egyptians, the traditional Greek gods, inherited from the Dark Age, were represented in ways that showed them as all too human, vicious, and frequently ridiculous. Zeus was infamous for his frequent rapes of boys and girls. His lust was matched only by the fury of his jealous wife, Hera. According to one story, a visitor to Athens asked why its citizens so often used the exclamation "by Zeus." The answer came back, "Because so many of us are." Other gods received equally irreverent treatment. Poseidon, god of earthquakes, water, and the sea, was powerful and dangerous as well as brutal, arbitrary, and vindictive. Dionysus, a popular god of emotional religion and wine, was frequently drunk. The Greek gods were immortal, superhuman in strength, and able to interfere in human affairs. But in all things, they reflected the values and weaknesses of the Greek mortals, who could bargain with them, placate them, and even trick them.

Religious cults were not under the exclusive control of any priesthood or political group. Thus, there were no official versions of stories of gods and goddesses. This is evident both from Greek poetry, which often presents contradictory stories of the gods, and from pottery, which bears pictorial versions of myths that differ greatly from written ones. Although centers such as Delphi were universal religious sites, drawing visitors from the whole Greek world and even beyond, no one group or sacred site enjoyed a monopoly on access to the gods. Like literacy and government, the gods belonged to all.

Myth and Reason

The glue holding together the individual and frequently hostile Greek poleis and ethne scattered throughout the Mediterranean was their common stock of myths and a common fascination with the Homeric legends. Stories of gods and heroes, told and retold, were fashioned into *mythoi*, (myths, literally, "formulated speech"), which explained and described the world both as it was and as it should be. Myths were told about every city, shrine, river, mountain, and island. Myths explained the origins of cities, festivals, the world itself. Why are there seasons? Because Persephone, a daughter of Zeus, had been carried off by Hades, god of the dead, and for four months each year she had to dwell in his dark kingdom. What is the place of humans in the cosmos? They stand between beasts and gods because Prometheus tricked Zeus and gave men fire with which they cook their food and offer the bones and fat of sacrificial animals to the gods. Why is there evil and misfortune? Because, Greek men explained, in revenge for Prometheus' trickery, Zeus offered man Pandora (the name means "all gifts"), the first woman, whose beauty hid her evil nature. By accepting this gift, humans brought evil and misfortune on themselves.

Such stories were more than simply fanciful explanations of how things came to be. Myths sanctioned and supported the authority of social, political, and religious traditions. They presented how things had come to be in a manner that prescribed how they were to remain. The story of Prometheus and Pandora, for example, defined the ambivalent relationship between gods and humans, the evil nature of women, and the ritual role of fire and sacrifice to the gods.

As important as these myths were, they were not immutable. Archaic Greeks constantly reworked ancient myths, retelling them, adjusting their content and thus their meanings. Pandora began as evil. "Whoever is trusting a woman is trusting himself to a thief." But in another version of the myth, Pandora is curious rather than evil. She opens a jar given her by Zeus which contained all evils and thereby unintentionally releases them into the world. As colonists traveled to the far shores of the Mediterranean, their mythic heroes moved with them. New legends told of the travels of Heracles, Apollo, and other gods and heroes to Sicily, Italy, and beyond. In the process of revising and retelling, myths became a powerful and dynamic tool for reasoning about the world.

Archaic Greeks showed a similar combination of veneration and liberty in dealing with the Homeric legends. Young Greeks were urged to model themselves on the example of the ancients as described in the *Iliad* and the *Odyssey*. Increasingly, however, thoughtful Greeks approached the heroic ideals of these epics with a sense of detachment and criticism. Military values were still important, but the ancient aristocratic values were no longer universally accepted. Some mothers might tell their sons as they marched off to war, "Return with your shield or on it," that is, victorious or dead. Archilochus, a seventh-century B.C. lyric poet, could take a very different view of shields and honor:

> A perfect shield bedecks some Thracian now;
> I had no choice, I left it in a wood.
> Ah, well, I saved my skin, so let it go!
> A new one's just as good.

The new, open examination of traditional values extended into all areas of investigation. By the sixth century B.C., a number of Ionian Greeks began to investigate the origins and nature of the universe, not in terms of myth or religion, but by observation and rational thought. Living on the coast of Asia Minor, these Ionians were in contact

Greek pottery was often decorated with paintings of religious motifs. Here Hades, the ruler of the underworld, is shown with his wife, Persephone, a daughter of Zeus, who returned to earth every year, bringing the springtime.

with the ancient civilizations of Mesopotamia and learned much from the Babylonian traditions of astronomy, mathematics, and science. However, their primary interest went beyond observing and recording to speculating. They were the first philosophers, intellectuals who sought natural explanations for the world around them.

Thales of Miletus (ca. 625–ca. 547 B.C.) regarded water as the fundamental substance of the universe. For Anaximander (610–ca. 527 B.C.), the primary substance was matter—eternal and indestructible. It was Anaximenes of Miletus (fl. ca. 545 B.C.) who regarded air as the primary substance of the universe. Heraclitus of Ephesus (ca. 540–ca. 480 B.C.) saw the universe not as one unchanging substance but rather as change itself. For him, the universe is constantly in flux, changing like a flickering fire. One cannot step into the same river twice, Heraclitus taught, because no flowing stream is ever the same from one moment to another. Thus it is with the world. All is constantly in a state of becoming, not in a static state of being. And yet this constant change is not random. The cosmic tension between stability and flux is regulated by laws that human reason can determine. The universe is rational.

The significance of such speculative thought was not in the conclusions reached, but rather in the method employed. The Ionian philosophers no longer spoke in myth but rather in plain language. They reached their conclusions through observation and rational thought in which religion and the gods played no direct role. As significant as their original speculations was the manner in which these philosophers were received. Although as late as the fourth century B.C., intellectuals still occasionally fell prey to persecution, by the sixth century B.C., much of Greek society was ready to tolerate such nonreligious, rational teaching, which in other times and places would have been thought scandalous or atheistic.

This krater, called the François Vase, is a large vessel for mixing wine. It comes from the Greek colonies of Sicily and dates from around 570 B.C. The krater is decorated with bands on which are depicted martial and mythological scenes.

Art and the Individual

Archaic Greeks borrowed from everywhere and transformed all that they borrowed. Just as they adopted and adapted the Phoenician alphabet and Mesopotamian science, they took Near Eastern and Egyptian painting and sculpture and made them their own. During the Dark Age, the Mycenaean traditions of art had entirely disappeared. Pottery showed only geometric decorations; sculpture was unknown. Gradually, from the ninth century B.C., stylized human and animal figures began to appear within the tightly composed geometric patterns. As Greek traders increased their contacts with the Near East, lions, griffins, and other strange beasts, began to appear on vases, jugs, vials, and other pottery containers. But by the eighth century B.C., such exotic subjects had given way to the Greek passion for human images taken from their own myths and legends. The preferred technique was the so-called black figure style developed first at Corinth. Subjects were painted in black silhouette on red clay and then details were cut with a sharp point so that the background could show through. As the popularity of these mythic and heroic scenes increased, so too did the artists' technical competence. Unlike Egyptian and Syrian craftsmen, who were largely content within a static tradition of representation, Greek artists competed with one another to overcome technical problems of perspective and foreshortening. They also experimented with techniques of portraying long and complicated narratives on individual vases. Masters of the technique were proud of their skills and eager to proclaim their accomplishments. From the sixth century B.C., many of the finest examples were signed, sometimes, as in the case of the François vase shown here. By both potter or the owner of the pottery shop and the painter. Such masterpieces celebrated not only the heroes of the past but also the artist as individual and as the interpreter of culture no less original than the poet.

Greek sculpture underwent a similar dramatic development. The earliest and most common subject of Archaic sculpture was the standing male nude or *kouros* figure, which was in wide demand as grave monument, dedication to a god, or even cult statue of male deity. In Egypt, seventh-century B.C. Greeks had seen colossal statues

Female korē *and male* kouros *figures from the Greek Archaic period, seventh century* B.C. *Egyptian influence can be seen in the stiff, formal poses, the broad, square shoulders, and the rigid symmetry of the design.*

creations of the individual sculptor. To this end, they experimented with increasingly natural molding of limbs and body and began signing their works. Thus, as in vase painting, Greek sculpture reflected the importance of the individual, not in its subject matter, but in its creator. The widely popular kouros figures left little room for experimentation with more complex problems of composition and action. Their female counterparts, *korai*, followed similarly rigid traditions to which sculptors added female attributes. In the korai figures it was the clothing rather than the anatomy that allowed some scope to the artist's talents.

The real challenges in sculpture came, as in poetry and vase painting, in the portrayal of narrative in decorations on monuments, primarily temples. Unlike kouroi, which were usually private commissions intended to adorn the tombs of aristocrats, these public buildings were constructed as expressions of civic pride and were accessible to everyone. Here the creativity and dynamism of Greek cities could be paralleled in stone. Figures such as the calf-bearer (ca. 590) and the Rampin horseman (ca. 560) from the

The Calf-Bearer

and had learned to work stone. They brought these techniques home, improved on them by using iron tools (the Egyptians knew only bronze ones), and began to create their own human images. The kouros was a relatively easy figure to carve. Essentially, the sculptor began with a prism-shaped block of stone about 6 feet by 1 foot by 1 ½ feet. Applying a system of widely accepted ratios, the artist then carved it into a recognizable three-dimensional human form. The rigidly formulaic position of the kouros—standing, arms by the sides, looking straight ahead, left foot extended—followed Egyptian tradition and left little room for originality. Thus sculptors sought to give their statues originality and individuality, not as representations of individuals, but as the

Athenian acropolis are daring in the complexity of composition and the delicacy of execution. These are statues that tell stories. In the former, a

master farmer carries a calf to be sacrificed to Athena. The two gentle heads, the cross formed by the farmer's hands and the calf's legs are individual traits without precedent in ancient art. In the latter, the earliest-known Greek equestrian statue, the rider's head is turned naturally, possibly peeking out from behind the head of his mount. The horseman wears a wreath of parsley, probably an indication that

The Rampin horseman   he had won the prize in a race held in connection with a religious feast. Both statues surpass the monotony and anonymity of tradition. Although formally intended for religious purposes, these figures serve not only the gods and the aristocratic elite, but rather the whole community.

Archaic Greece

ca. 780–720 B.C.	Population increase in Greece
776 B.C.	First Olympic Games held
ca. 750–700 B.C.	Greeks develop writing system based on Phoenician model; Greeks begin colonizing western Mediterranean
ca. 700–500 B.C.	Archaic Age of Greece
ca. 700 B.C.	First stone temples appear in Greece
ca. 650 B.C.	Cypselus breaks rule of Bacchaids in Corinth; rules city as tyrant
594 B.C.	Solon elected chief archon of Athens; institutes social and political reforms
586 B.C.	Death of Periander ends tyrants' rule in Corinth
499 B.C.	Ionian cities revolt

A Tale of Three Cities

The political, social, and cultural transformations that occurred in the Archaic Age took different forms across the Greek world. No community or city-state was typical of Greece. The best way to understand the diversity of Archaic Greece is to examine three very different cities which, by the end of the sixth century B.C., had become leading centers of Greek civilization. Corinth, Sparta, and Athens present something of the spectrum of political, cultural, and social models of the Hellenic world. Corinth, like many cities, developed into a commercial center in which the assembly of citizens was dominated by an oligarchy. Sparta developed into a state in which citizenship was radically egalitarian but restricted to a small military elite. In Athens, the Archaic Age saw the foundations of an equally radical democracy.

Wealthy Corinth

Corinth owed its prosperity to its privileged site, dominating both a rich coastal plain and the narrow isthmus connecting the Peloponnesus to the mainland. In the eighth century B.C., as Greeks turned their attention to the west, Corinthians led the way. Corinthian pottery appeared throughout western Greece and southern Italy. Corinthian trade led to colonization, and settlers from Corinth founded Syracuse and other cities in Sicily and Italy. These colonies reduced the population pressure on the city and provided markets for its grain and manufactured goods, primarily pottery and textiles. Even more important to Corinthian prosperity was its role in the transport of other cities' products from east to west. By carrying goods across the isthmus and loading them onto other ships, merchants could avoid the long and dangerous passage around the Peloponnesus. Duties imposed on other cities using this unique passage added to Corinthian wealth from agriculture and its own commerce.

The precise details of early Corinthian government are uncertain. Still, it appears that in Corinth as in many other cities, a tyranny replaced a ruling clan and in time this tyranny ended with an oligarchic government. Until the middle of the seventh century B.C., Corinth and its wealth were ruled in typical Dark Age fashion by an aristocratic clan known as the Bacchiads. There were approximately two hundred members of this clan, all of whom claimed descent from the mythical hero Heracles. Corinth began its rise under this aristocratic rule and individual Bacchiads led colonizing expeditions to Italy and Sicily. However, the increasing pressures of population growth, rapidly expanding wealth, and dramatic changes in the economy produced social tensions that the traditional aristocratic rulers were unable to handle. As in cities throughout the Greek world, these tensions led to the creation of a new order.

The early history of Corinth is obscure, but apparently around 650 B.C. a revolution led by a dissident Bacchiad named Cypselus (ca. 657–627 B.C.) and supported by non-Bacchiad aristocrats and other Corinthians broke the Bacchiads' grip on the city. The revolution led to the establishment of Cypselus as tyrant. Cypselus and his son Periander (ca. 627–586 B.C.) seem to have been generally popular with most Corinthians. As Periander himself said, "The safety of the tyrant is better guarded by the goodwill of the citizens than by the spears of a bodyguard."

In Corinth, as in many other cities, the tyrants restructured taxes, relying primarily on customs duties, which were less of a burden on the peasantry. Around 600 B.C., Periander began construction of a causeway across the isthmus on which ships could be hauled from the Aegean to the western Mediterranean. In this way merchant vessels (and warships) could enter the Gulf of Corinth without having to unload. This causeway eventually became a major source of Corinth's wealth. Periander also attacked conspicuous consumption on the part of the aristocracy. He forbade women to wear expensive clothes and jewelry. He introduced laws against idleness and put thousands of Corinthians to work in extensive building programs. He erected temples and sent colonists to Italy. Under his leadership the Corinthian fleet developed into the most powerful naval force in the Adriatic and Aegean seas. Under its tyrants, Corinth led the Greek world in the production of black figure pottery, which spread throughout the Mediterranean. A great seaport, Corinth also became known as the center of prostitution, and a popular saying ran "not every man has the luck to sail to Corinth," implying both

that not everyone would be fortunate enough to enjoy its pleasures and that not everyone had the luck to survive such a trip without considerable expense.

The tyrants also lay the foundation for broader political participation. Cypselus divided the population into eight tribes, based not on traditional ethnic divisions, but on arbitrary groupings by region. All of Corinth was divided into three large regions. The population of each region was distributed among each of the eight tribes. This assignment prevented the emergence of political factions based on regional disputes. Ten representatives from each tribe formed a council of eighty men. Under the tyrants, this council was largely advisory and provided a connection between the autocratic rulers and the citizens.

In Corinth as elsewhere, the strength or weakness of tyranny rested on the abilities and personality of individual tyrants. The benefits they brought their cities could not entirely overcome the negative impression made by the arbitrary nature of their rule. Thus their popularity declined rapidly. Cypselus had been a beloved liberator. His son Periander, in spite of his accomplishments, was remembered for his cruelty and violence. To later Greeks, Periander was the originator of the brutal, arbitrary rule later considered typical of repressive tyranny. Shortly after Periander's death in 586 B.C., a revolt killed his successor and tyranny in Corinth ended.

The new government continued the tribal and council system established by Cypselus. From the sixth century B.C. until its conquest by Macedonia in 338 B.C., Corinth was ruled by an oligarchy. Although an assembly of the *dēmos*, or adult males, met occasionally, actual government was in the hands of eight deliberators, or *probouloi*, and nine other men from each tribe who together formed the council of eighty. How council members and probouloi were selected is unknown. Presumably they were elected for very long periods if not for life and the council tended to be self-perpetuating. Still, the oligarchs who made up the council avoided the kind of exclusive and arbitrary tendencies that had destroyed both the Bacchiads and the tyrants. They were remarkably successful in maintaining popular support among the citizens and provided a reliable and effective government.

Thus Corinth flourished, a city more open to commerce and wealth than most, moderate in its political institutions and eager for stability. As one fourth-century B.C. poet wrote:

(There) lawfulness dwells, and her sister,
Safe foundation of cities,
Justice, and Peace, who was bred with her;
They dispense wealth to men.

Martial Sparta

At the beginning of the eighth century B.C., the Peloponnesus around Sparta and Laconia faced circumstances similar to those of Corinth and other Greek communities. Population growth, increasing disparity between rich and poor, and an expanding economy created powerful tensions. However, while Corinthian society developed into a complex mix of aristocrats, merchants, artisans, and peasants, ruled by an oligarchy, the Spartan solution presented a rigid, two-tiered social structure. By the end of the Archaic Age, a small, homogeneous class of warriors called *homoioi*, or equals, ruled a vast population of state serfs, or *helots*. The two classes lived in mutual fear and mistrust. Spartans controlled the helots through terror and ritual murder. The helots in turn were "an enemy constantly waiting for the disasters of the Spartans." And yet, throughout antiquity the Spartans were the Greeks most praised for their courage, simplicity of life, and service to the state.

War was the center of Spartan life, and war lay at the origin of the Spartans' extraordinary social and political organization. In the eighth century B.C., the Spartans conquered the fertile region of Messenia and compelled the vanquished Messenians to turn over one-half of their harvests. The spoils were not divided equally, but went to increase the wealth of the aristocracy, thus creating resentment among the less privileged. Early in the seventh century B.C., the Spartans attempted a similar campaign to take the plain of Thyreatis from the city of Argos. This time they were not so fortunate; they were defeated and resentment of the ordinary warriors toward their aristocratic leaders flared into open conflict. The Messenians seized upon this time as a moment to revolt, and for a time Sparta was forced to fight at home and abroad for its very existence. In many cities, such crises gave rise to tyrants. In Sparta, the crisis led to radical political and social reforms that transformed the polis into a unique military system.

The Spartans attributed these reforms to the legendary lawgiver Lycurgus (seventh century B.C.). Whether or not Lycurgus ever existed and was responsible for all of the reforms, they saved the city and ended its internal tensions at the expense of abandoning the mainstream of Greek development. Traditionally, Greeks had placed personal honor above communal concerns. During the crisis of the second Messenian war, Spartans of all social ranks were urged to look not to individual interest but to *eunomia*, good order and obedience to the laws, which alone could unite Spartans and bring victory. Faced with certain defeat as the only alternative, Spartans answered the call and became the first Greeks to elevate duty and patriotism above individual interest. United, the Spartans crushed the Messenians. In return for obedience, poor citizens received equality before the law and benefited from a land distribution that relieved their poverty. Conquered land, especially that in Messenia, was divided and distributed to Spartan warriors. However, the Spartan warriors were not expected to work the land themselves. Instead, the state reduced the defeated Messenians to the status of helots and assigned them to individual Spartans. While this system did not erase all economic inequalities among the Spartans (aristocrats continued to hold more land than others), it did decrease some of the disparity. It also provided a minimum source of wealth for all Spartan citizens and allowed them to devote themselves to full-time military service.

This land reform was coupled with a political reform that incorporated elements of monarchy, oligarchy, and democracy. The state was governed by two hereditary kings and a council of elders, the *gerousia*. The two royal families probably represented the combination of differing groups that had formed the Spartan polis at some earlier date. Their authority in peacetime was limited to familial and religious affairs. In war, they commanded the army and held the power of life and death.

In theory at least, the central institution of Spartan government was the gerousia, which was composed of thirty men at least sixty years of age and included the two kings. The gerousia directed all political activity, especially foreign affairs, and served as high court. Members were elected for life by the assembly, or *apella*, which was composed of all equals over the age of thirty and which approved decisions of the gerousia.

Bronze statue of a Greek warrior from the sixth century B.C. The figure is slightly less than six inches high and stands on a base of red marble. The warrior is draped in a cloak and wears a helmet of the Corinthian type, covering the head and face.

However, this approval, made by acclamation, could easily be manipulated, as could the course of debate within the gerousia itself. Wealth, cunning, and patronage were more important in the direction of the Spartan state than were its formal structures.

Actual administration was in the hands of five magistrates termed *ephors*. Ephors were not members of the gerousia and often came from fairly obscure backgrounds. However, their powers were extremely broad. They presided over joint sessions of the gerousia and *apella*. They held supreme authority over the kings during wartime and acted as judges for noncitizens. Finally, the ephors controlled the *krypteia*, or secret police, a band of youths who practiced state terrorism as part of their rite of passage to the status of equal. On the orders of the ephors, the krypteia assassinated, intrigued, arrested powerful people, and terrorized helots. Service in this corps was considered a necessary part of a youth's education.

The key to the success of Sparta's political reform was an even more radical social reform that placed everyone under the direct supervision and service of the state from birth until death. Although admiring aristocratic visitors often exaggerated their accounts of Spartan life, the main outlines are clear enough. *Eunomia* was the sole guiding principle, and service to the state came before family, social class, and every other duty or occupation.

Spartan equals were made, not born. True, only a man born of free Spartan parents could hope to become an equal, but birth alone was no guarantee of admission to this select body, or even of the right to live. Elsewhere in Greece, parents were free to decide whether children should be raised or abandoned. In Sparta, public officials examined infants and decided whether they were sufficiently strong to be allowed to live or should be exposed on a hillside to die. From birth until age seven, a boy lived with his mother, but then he entered the state education system or *agōgē*, living in barracks with his contemporaries and enduring thirteen years of rigorous military training. Harsh discipline and physical deprivation were essential parts of this training, which was intended to teach men to endure pain and to conquer in battle.

At age twelve, training with swords and

spears became more intense, as did the rigors of the life-style. Boys were given only a single cloak to wear and slept on thin rush mats. They were encouraged to supplement their meager diet by stealing food, although if caught they were severely whipped, not for the theft but for the failure. All of this they were expected to endure in silence.

Much of the actual education of the youths was entrusted to older accomplished warriors who selected boys as their homosexual lovers. Such relationships between youths and adults were the norm throughout Greece, although in Sparta they were more important than elsewhere. Not only did the lover serve as tutor and role model, but in time the two became a fighting team, each inspiring the other to show the utmost valor. Ultimately, the older warrior would even help his young lover select a wife.

At age twenty, Spartan youths were enrolled in the krypteia. Each was sent out into the countryside with nothing but a cloak and a knife and forbidden to return until he had killed a helot. This finishing school for killers kept helots in a constant state of terror and gave ephors an deadly efficient mechanism for enforcing their will.

If a youth survived the rigors of his training until age thirty, he could at last be incorporated into the rank of equals, provided he could pass the last obstacle. He had to be able to furnish a sufficient amount of food from his own lands for the communal dining group to which he would be assigned. This food might come from inherited property or, if he had proved himself an outstanding warrior, from the state. Those who passed this final qualification became full members of the assembly, but they continued to live with the other warriors. Now they could marry, but family life in the usual sense was nonexistent. To symbolize the furtive nature of marriage, the prospective groom acted out a ritual abduction of his bride. Thereafter he would slip out occasionally at night to sleep with her.

Although their training was not as rigorous as the education of males, Spartan women were given an upbringing and allowed a sphere of activity unknown elsewhere in Greece. Girls, like boys, were trained in athletic competition and, again like them, competed naked in wrestling, footraces, and spear throwing. This training was based not on a belief in the equality of the sexes but simply on the desire to improve the physical stamina and childbearing abilities of Spartan women. Women were able to own land and to participate widely in business and agricultural affairs, the reason being that since men were entirely involved in military pursuits, women were expected to look after economic and household affairs. When a foreign woman commented that Spartan women were the only women who could rule men, a Spartan wife replied, "With good reason, for we are the only women who bring forth men."

Few Lacedaemonians (as Spartans were also called) ever became equals. Not only were there far more helots than Spartans, but many inhabitants of the region, termed *perioikoi*, or peripherals, although they were free citizens of their local communities, were not allowed into the agoge. Others were washed out, unable to endure the harsh life, and still others lacked the property qualifications to supply their share of the communal meals. Thus for all the trappings of egalitarianism, equality in Sparta was the privilege of a tiny minority.

The total dedication to military life was reinforced by a deliberate rejection of other activities. Prior to the eighth century B.C., Sparta had participated in the general cultural and economic transformations of the Greek world. Legend even made Sparta the birthplace of music. However, from the time of the second Messenian war, Sparta withdrew from the mainstream of Greek civilization. Equals could not engage in crafts, trade, or any other forms of economic activity. Because Sparta banned silver and gold coinage, it could not participate in the growing commercial network of the Greek world. Although a group of free citizens of subject towns could engage in such activities, the role of Sparta in the economic, architectural, and cultural life of Greece was negligible after the seventh century B.C. Militarily, Sparta cast a long shadow across the Peloponnesus and beyond, but the number of equals was always too small to allow Sparta both to create a vast empire and to maintain control over the helots at home. Instead, Sparta created a network of alliances and nonaggression pacts with oligarchic neighbors. In time this network came to be known as the Peloponnesian League.

Democratic Athens

Athens enjoyed neither the advantages of a strategic site such as that of Corinth nor that of the rich plains of Sparta. However, the "goodly citadel of Athens" was one of the few Mycenaean cities to have escaped destruction at the start of the Dark Age. Gradually Athens united the whole surrounding region of Attica into a single polis, by far the largest in the Greek world. Well into the seventh century B.C., Athens followed the general pattern of the polis seen in Corinth and Sparta. Like other Dark Age communities, Athens was ruled by aristocratic clans, particularly the Alcmaeonids. Only the members of these clans could participate in the *areopagus*, or council, which they entered after serving a year as one of the nine *archons*, or magistrates elected yearly. Until the seventh century B.C., Athens escaped the social pressures brought on by population growth and economic prosperity that led to civil strife, colonialism, and tyranny elsewhere. This was due largely to its relative abundance of arable land and its commercial prosperity based on the export of grain.

By the late seventh century B.C., however, Athens began to suffer from the same class conflict that had shaken other cities. Newly rich merchants and craftsmen of the middle classes resented the aristocratic monopoly on political power. Poor farmers were angry because, far from participating in the growing prosperity, they were being forced into debt to the wealthy. When they were unable to pay their debts, they or their children were sold as slaves by their creditors. Sometime around 630 B.C., an aristocrat named Cylon attempted to seize power as tyrant. His attempt failed, but when he was murdered by one of the Alcmaeonids, popular revulsion drove the Alcmaeonids from the city. A decade of strife ensued as aristocratic clans, wealthy merchants, and farmers fought for control of the city. Violence between groups and families threatened to tear the community apart. In 621 B.C., the Athenians granted a judge, Draco, extraordinary powers to revise and systematize traditional laws concerning vengeance and homicide. His restructuring of procedures for limiting vengeance and preventing bloodshed were harsh enough to add the term *Draconian* to Western legal vocabulary.

When asked why death was the most common penalty he imposed, Draco explained that minor offenses merited death and he knew of no more severe penalty for major ones. Still, these measures did nothing to solve the central problems of political control. Finally in 594 B.C., Solon (ca. 630–ca. 560 B.C.), an aristocratic merchant, was elected chief archon and charged with restructuring the city's government. Solon based his reform on the ideal of eunomia as had the Spartans, but he followed a very different path to secure good order.

In Sparta, Lycurgus had begun with a radical redistribution of land. In Athens, Solon began with the less extreme measure of eliminating debt bondage. Athenians who had been forced into slavery or into sharecropping because of their debts were restored to freedom. A law forbade mortgaging free men and women as security for debts. Athenians might be poor, but they would be free. This free peasantry formed the basis of Athenian society throughout its history.

Solon also reorganized the rest of the social hierarchy and broke the aristocracy's exclusive control of the areopagus by dividing the society into four classes based on wealth rather than birth and opening the archonship to the top two classes. He further weakened the areopagus by establishing a council of four hundred members drawn from all four classes to which citizens could appeal decisions of the magistrates.

Although Solon's reforms established the framework for a resolution of Athens' social tensions, they did not entirely succeed. Solon himself did not consider his new constitution perfect, only practical. Asked if he had given the Athenians the best laws that he could give them, he answered, "The best that they could receive." Resistance from the still-powerful aristocracy prompted some Athenians to urge Solon to assume the powers of a tyrant in order to force through his reforms. He refused, but after his death, Peisistratus (d. 527 B.C.), an aristocrat strongly supported by the peasants against his own class, hired a mercenary force to seize control of the city. After two abortive attempts, Peisistratus ruled as tyrant from 545 B.C. until his death.

With his bodyguard firmly established on the acropolis, Peisistratus might have governed the city, for a while at least, as an absolute tyrant.

Instead, he and later his son Hippias (d. 490 B.C.), who succeeded him until 510 B.C., continued to rule through Solon's constitution but simply ensured that the archons elected each year were their agents. Thus the Athenian tyrants strengthened Solon's constitution even while they further destroyed the powers of the aristocracy.

Peisistratus and Hippias drew their support from the demos, or people at large, rather than from an aristocratic faction. They claimed divine justification for their rule and made a great show of devotion to the Athenian gods. At one point, Peisistratus even dressed a very tall, beautiful girl to look like the goddess Athena, patron of the city, and had her driven into town in a chariot while heralds went before her announcing that Athena herself was supporting him. He also promoted annual festivals, and in so doing began the great tradition of Athenian literature. At the festival of Athena, professional reciters of *rhapsōidiai* (epic poetry) recited large portions of the *Iliad* and the *Odyssey.* During a festival in honor of Dionysus, actors performed the first tragedies and comedies. The tyrants also directed a series of popular, nationalistic public works programs that beautified the city, increased national pride, and provided work for the poor. They rebuilt the temple of Athena on the acropolis, for which both the statues of the Rampin horseman and the calf-bearer were commissioned. The tyrants also constructed a system of terra-cotta pipes by which clear mountain water was brought into the agora and they built public halls and meeting places. These internal measures were accompanied by support for commerce and export, particularly of grain. The tyrants introduced the silver "owl" coin, which became the first international Greek currency. Soon, Athens was challenging Corinth as the leading commercial power and trading in grain as far away as the Black Sea.

Athenian silver coin called a tetradrachm, dating from the fifth century B.C. The owl is the symbol of the goddess Athena.

Peisistratus was firm. His son Hippias was harsh. Still, even Hippias enjoyed the support of the majority of the citizens of both popular and aristocratic factions. Only after the assassination of his younger brother did Hippias become sufficiently oppressive to drive his opponents into exile. Some of these exiles obtained the assistance of Sparta and returned to overthrow Hippias in 510 B.C. Hippias' defeat ended the tyrants' rule in Athens and won for Sparta an undeserved reputation as the opponent of all tyranny.

Following the expulsion of Hippias, some aristocrats attempted to return to the "good old days" of aristocratic rule. However, for more than eighty years, Athenians had been accustomed to Solon's constitution and were unwilling to give it up. Moreover, the tyrants had created a fierce sense of nationalistic pride among all ranks of Athenians, and few were willing to turn over government to the hands of only a few. Thus, when the aristocrats made their bid to recover power, their primary opponent, Cleisthenes (ca. 570–ca. 507 B.C.), "made the demos his faction" and pushed through a final constitutional reform that became the basis for Athenian democracy.

The essence of Cleisthenes' reform lay in his reorganization of the major political units by which members of the council were selected. Previously, each citizen had belonged to one of four tribes, further broken down into twelve brotherhoods, or *phratries*, which were administrative and religious units. In a manner similar to that of Cypselus in Corinth, Cleisthenes reshuffled these phratries into thirty territorial units, or *demes*, comprising urban, inland, or coastal regions. These thirty units in turn were grouped into ten tribes, each consisting of one unit from each of the urban, inland, and coastal regions. The tribes elected the members of the council, military commanders, jurors, and magistrates. As in Corinth, this reorganization destroyed the traditional kin-based social and political pattern and integrated people of differing social, economic, and regional backgrounds. Aristocrats, merchants, and poor farmers had to work together to find common ground for political action, both regionally and nationally. With this new, integrated democracy and its strong sense of nationalism, Athens emerged from the Archaic Age as the leading city of the Hellenic world.

The Fragility of the Archaic Creation

By the end of the sixth century B.C., the products of Greek experimentation were evident throughout the Mediterranean. Greek city-states had resolved the crises of class conflict. Greek merchants and artisans had found ways to flourish despite poor soil and uncertain climate. Greek philosophers, poets, and artists had begun to celebrate the human form and the human spirit. Still, these achievements were the product of small, independent, and relatively weak communities on the fringe of the civilized world. The Greeks' insignificance and isolation had kept them out of the sphere of interest of the great floodplain empires to the east.

In the second half of the sixth century B.C., all this changed. The Persian empire, under its dynamic king Cyrus II, began a process of conquest and expansion west into Asia Minor, absorbing the kingdom of Lydia and conquering Ionia on the coast of Asia Minor. The Persians put tyrants loyal to Cyrus to rule over these Greek communities and for a few decades these centers of Greek culture and thought accepted foreign control. In 499 B.C., the passion for democracy, which had swept much of mainland Greece, reached Ionia. Cities such as Miletus, Ephesus, Chios, and Samos revolted, expelled their Persian-appointed tyrants, established democracies, and sent ambassadors to the mainland to seek assistance. Eretria and Athens, two mainland cities with Ionian roots, responded, sending ships and men to aid the Ionian rebels. Athenian interests were more than simple solidarity with their Ionian cousins. Athens depended on grain from the Black Sea region and felt its direct interests to lie with the area. The success of the revolt was short-lived. The puny Greek cities were dealing with the largest empire the West had yet known. By 500 B.C., the Persian empire included Asia Minor, Mesopotamia, Palestine, and Egypt, uniting all the peoples from the Caucasus to the Sudan.

The giant Persian empire responded slowly, but with force, to the Greek revolt. King Darius I (522–486 B.C.) gathered a vast, international force from throughout his empire and set about to recapture the rebellious cities. The war lasted five years and ended in a Persian victory. By 494 B.C., the Persians had retaken the cities of the coast and nearby islands. In the cities deemed most responsible for the revolt, the population was herded together, the boys were castrated and made into royal eunuchs, the girls sent to Darius' court, the remainder of the population sold into slavery, and the towns burnt to the ground. Once the rebels had been disposed of, Darius set out to punish their supporters on the mainland, Eretria and Athens. With the same meticulous planning and deliberate pace, the Persian king turned his vast armies toward the Greek mainland.

Civilization developed much later in the Mediterranean world than it had in the floodplains of the Near East. The earliest Bronze Age societies of Greece and the neighboring islands, while influenced by contact with the great civilizations of Mesopotamia and Egypt, developed distinctive societies and cultures tied closely to the sea around them. Still, they too were caught up in the general cataclysm of the twelfth century B.C. Out of the ruins emerged a society much less centralized, wealthy, or powerful, but possessing an extraordinary dynamism.

The Archaic Age was an age of experimentation. Greeks, propelled by demographic and political pressures and inspired by the legends of vanished heroes, began in the eighth century B.C. to recast traditions and techniques acquired from their ancient neighbors into new forms. The multiplicity of independent communities, their rela-

The Persian Empire, ca. 500 B.C.

tive isolation, and their differing traditions created a wide spectrum of political forms, social structures, and cultural values. And yet from Sicily to Asia Minor, Greeks felt themselves united by a common language, a common cultural heritage, and a common commitment to individual freedom within the community, whether that freedom was protected within a monarchy, a tyranny, an oligarchy, or a democracy. That commitment to freedom, fostered in the hoplite ranks, protected in the assembly, and increasingly expressed in poetry and sculpture, hung in the balance as Darius and the Persians marched west.

Suggestions for Further Reading

General Reading

John Boardman, Jasper Griffin, and Oswyn Murray, *Greece and the Hellenistic World* (Oxford: Oxford University Press, 1988). An excellent collection of essays on Greek civilization by British scholars.

Cambridge Ancient History, vol. 4. Contains more detailed essays on all aspects of early Greek history.

Greece in the Bronze Age

* M. I. Finley, *Early Greece: The Bronze and Archaic Ages*, 2d ed. (New York: W. W. Norton, 1982). A very readable overview by a leading Greek historian.

* N. K. Sandars, *The Sea Peoples* (New York: Thames & Hudson, 1985). A recent survey of the controversy over the crisis of the twelfth century B.C.

* Emily Vermeule, *Greece in the Bronze Age* (Chicago: University of Chicago Press, 1964). A standard though somewhat dated study, particularly for the early material.

O. Krzyszkowska and L. Nixon, eds., *Minoan Society* (Bristol: Bristol Classical Press, 1983). Excellent collection of essays on early Crete.

J. T. Hooker, *Mycenaean Greece* (New York: Routledge, Chapman & Hall, 1976). The best introduction to Mycenaean history.

* M. I. Finley, *The World of Odysseus*, 2d. rev. ed. (New York: Penguin Books, 1979). A brilliant analysis of the Dark Age through the Homeric epics.

Archaic Greece

Anthony Snodgrass, *Archaic Greece: The Age of Experiment* (Totowa, NJ: Biblio Distribution Center, 1980). Excellent survey of the creative achievements of the Archaic period.

* Indicates paperback edition available.

* John Boardman, *The Greeks Overseas* (New York: Thames & Hudson, 1982). Description of varieties of Greek involvement abroad and their effects on Greece by a distinguished archaeologist.

* A. J. Graham, *Colony and Mother City in Ancient Greece* (Chicago: Ares, 1983). A synthetic look at Greek colonies.

G. E. R. Lloyd, *Magic, Reason and Experience* (New York: Cambridge University Press, 1979). Enlightening analysis of early Greek thought and culture.

E. Hussey, *The Presocratics* (New York: Scribners, 1972). Standard study of early Greek philosophers.

* Walter Burkert, *Structure and History in Greek Mythology and Ritual* (Berkeley: University of California Press, 1980). Relates myth and religion to society and history.

W. G. Forrest, *The Emergence of Greek Democracy* (New York: McGraw-Hill, 1966). Covers the politics of the Archaic period.

A. Andrewes, *The Greek Tyrants* (Atlantic Highlands, NJ: Humanities Press International, 1956). Standard survey of Greek tyranny.

Eva. C. Keuls, *The Reign of the Phallus: Sexual Politics in Ancient Athens* (New York: Harper & Row, 1985). Controversial study of sexual politics.

* S. B. Pomeroy, *Goddesses, Whores, Wives, and Slaves: Women in Classical Antiquity* (New York: Schocken Books, 1975). Pioneering study of gender in antiquity.

T. B. L. Webster, *Everyday Life in Classical Athens* (New York: Putnam, 1969). A general look at ordinary life but concentrating on the classic period.

W. B. Dinsmoor, *The Architecture of Ancient Greece* (New York: W. W. Norton, 1952). An old but still valuable survey.

* J. Boardman, *Preclassical Style and Civilization* (Harmondsworth: Penguin Books, 1967). A study of early Greek art by a leading archaeologist.

J. Boardman, *Greek Sculpture: Archaic Period* (New York: Thames & Hudson, 1985). A well-illustrated survey of early Greek sculpture.

R. M. Cook, *Greek Painted Pottery*, 2d. ed. (New York: Routledge, Chapman & Hall, 1972). The basic handbook of Greek vase painting.

A Tale of Three Cities

David Whitehead, *The Demes of Attica (ca. 508–250 B.C.)* (Princeton, NJ: Princeton University Press, 1986). An excellent, recent study of Athenian politics and society.

Paul Cartledge, *Sparta and Lakonia: A Regional History 1300–362 B.C.* (New York: Routledge, Chapman & Hall, 1978). The best survey of Spartan history.

J. B. Salmon, *Wealthy Corinth: A History of the City to 338 B.C.* (New York: Oxford University Press, 1984). A comprehensive history of early Corinth.

Classical Greece

Alexander at Issus

War with Persia opened and closed the centuries of Greek glory. The invasion of the Greek mainland by Darius I in 490 B.C. pitted the greatest empire the West had ever known against a few small, mutually suspicious states. His failure created among the Greeks a new belief in the superiority of the Greek world over the barbarian and of free men over Eastern despots. Darius III (336–330 B.C.) suffered a far more devastating defeat than his ancestor at the hands of Alexander the Great (336–323 B.C.) and a combined Greek army 157 years later. Darius I had lost his pride. Darius III lost his empire and, shortly afterward, his life.

Alexander had announced his expedition as a campaign to punish the Persians for their invasion of Greece over a century and a half earlier. Greeks rightly viewed Alexander's victory at Issus in 333 B.C. as the beginning of the end for the Persians, and it was long celebrated by Greek poets and artists. The most famous of these was Philoxenus of Eretria, whose paintings marked the high point of Greek pictorial art. His masterpiece, like all other Greek paintings executed on wood, is long vanished. However sometime in the first century B.C., a wealthy Roman commissioned a mosaic copy of the painting for his villa at Pompeii in southern Italy. The mosaic, measuring some six-

teen feet by eight feet and containing a million and a half stones, each the size of a grain of rice, is itself a masterpiece. It is also a faithful copy of Philoxenus' painting, which a Roman critic had characterized as "surpassed by none."

Alexander, with reckless disregard for his own safety, had led his right wing across a small stream at a gallop and routed the Persians' left flank. At the same time the Persian center, which consisted of Greek mercenaries, managed to push Alexander's center back into the stream. Finally, Alexander and his right wing swung left, cutting Darius' Greeks to pieces, scattering his Persian guard, and forcing Darius to flee for his life.

In muted tones of red, brown, black, and yellow, Philoxenus brings all the skills developed through two centuries of Greek art to capture this most dramatic moment of the battle. The action takes place on a dusty and barren plain. The only landscape features are a lone dead tree and a forest of spears. Bold foreshortening, first used in the previous century, renders the rear of the horse in the center almost three dimensional as it runs in blind fury toward Darius' chariot. Although the entire scene is wildly chaotic, each man and each mount is portrayed as an individual, with his own expression of emotion and his own part to play in the violent action.

The young Alexander, his hair blowing free and his eye fixed not on Darius but on his greater destiny, exudes the reckless courage and violence for which he was so famous. And yet he is not the center of the composition. That place of honor goes to Darius, whose kindly, tortured face looks back as his horses pull his chariot to safety. His hand stretches out in helpless sympathy toward the young Persian who has thrown himself between his king and Alexander, taking through his chest the spear that the Greek king had intended for the Persian ruler.

The effect of the painting is at once heroic and disconcerting. Who is the hero of the battle? Is it the wild-eyed Alexander in his moment of victory, or is it the aged Persian monarch, whose infinite sadness at his moment of defeat is not for himself but for his young aide, who has given his life so that Darius might live? The picture here is no simple juxtaposition of civilization against barbarity. Greeks fought on both sides at Issus, just as they had in the Persian wars of the fifth century B.C. Nor did Alexander's warriors despise their Persian enemies. Alexander told Darius' mother, captured after the battle, that he felt no personal bitterness toward her son. By the fourth century

B.C., Greeks had learned that right and wrong, good and evil, civilized and barbarian were not simple issues. In the past century and a half, they had seen many wars, many leaders, and many defeats. Greek intellectuals had explored the complexity of human existence, agreeing with the philosopher Socrates, that the unexplored life was not worth living. Greek dramatists had taught that suffering brought wisdom. Philoxenus' depictions of Darius and Alexander reflect the same complexity. Who is the hero here? Who is the man of wisdom?

Learning to ask these questions was a painful education for Greeks of the fifth and fourth centuries. The victories over the Persian forces of Darius and his successors brought an unprecedented period of political and cultural freedom and creativity, but also deadly rivalry between Athens and Sparta, the leaders of the victorious Greeks. Democratic Athens transformed its wartime alliance into an empire, and only a generation after Athenian and Spartan troops had faced the Persians, they fought each other in a long and futile war, which left the Greek world exhausted and easy prey for the ambitious Macedonian dynasty.

War and Politics in the Fifth Century

The vast Persian army moving west in 490 B.C. threatened the fruits of three centuries of Greek political, social, and cultural experimentation. The shared ideal of freedom within community and the common bond of language and culture seemed no basis on which to build an effective resistance to the great Persian Empire. Moreover, Darius I was not marching against the Greeks as such. Few Greek states other than Athens had supported the Ionians against their Persian conquerors. Many Greeks saw the Persians as potential allies or even rulers preferable to their more powerful Greek neighbors and rivals within their own states. Separated by political traditions, intercity rivalries, and cultural differences, the Greeks did not feel any sense of national or ethnic unity. Particular interest, rather than patriotism or love of freedom, determined which cities opposed the Persian march. In the end, only Eretria, a badly divided Athens, and the small town of Plataea were prepared to refuse the Persian king's demand for gifts of earth and water, the traditional symbols of submission.

The Persian Wars

Initially, the Persian campaign followed the pattern established in Ionia. In the autumn of 490 B.C., Darius quickly destroyed the city of Eretria and carried off its population in captivity. The victorious Persian forces, numbering perhaps twenty thousand infantrymen and mounted archers, then landed at the Bay of Marathon, one of the few locations in Attica where horses could pasture that late in the year. Even with around six hundred Plataeans, the total Athenian force was no more than half that of its enemies, but the Greeks were better armed and commanded the hills facing the Marathon plain on which the Persian troops had massed. The Athenians also benefited from the leadership of Miltiades (ca. 544–489 B.C.), an experienced soldier who had served Darius and who knew the Persian's strengths and weaknesses. For over a week the two armies faced each other in a battle of nerves. Growing dissension in the Athenian ranks finally led the Greek generals to make a desperate and unexpected move. Abandoning the high ground, the Athenian hoplites rushed in disciplined phalanxes over almost a mile of open fields and then attacked the amazed Persian forces at a run. Although the Persians broke through the center of the Greek lines, the Athenians routed the Persian flanks and then turned in, enveloping the invaders in a deadly trap. In a few hours it was all over. Six thousand Persians lay dead, while fewer than two hundred Athenians were buried in the heroes' grave that still marks the Marathon plain. The Persians retreated to their ships and sailed for the Bay of Phalerum near Athens, hoping to attack the city itself before its victorious troops could return. However, the Athenians, though exhausted from the battle, rushed the twenty-three miles home in under eight hours, beating

The plain of Marathon. The Greek hoplites formed up in the foothills at the left for the decisive battle against the Persian invaders in 490 B.C.

the Persian fleet. When the Persians learned that they had lost the race, they turned their ships for Asia.

The almost miraculous victory at Marathon had three enormous consequences for Athens and for Greece in general. First, it established the superiority of the hoplite phalanx as the finest infantry formation in the Mediterranean world. Not only Athenians but all Greeks were thereafter convinced of the superiority of their soldiers. Second, Greeks expanded this belief in military superiority to a faith in the general superiority of Greeks over the "barbarians" (those who spoke other languages). Finally, by proving the value of the citizen army, the victory of the Athenians solidified and enhanced the democratic reforms of Cleisthenes.

Common citizens were determined that the victory won by the hoplite phalanx at Marathon should not be lost to an aristocratic faction at home. To guard against this danger, the Athenian assembly began to practice *ostracism*, ten-year exile without loss of property, imposed on those who threatened to undermine the constitution of Cleisthenes. Each year every Athenian citizen had the opportunity to write on a potsherd (in Greek, *ostrakon*) the name of the man he most wished to leave Attica. If at least six thousand citizens voted, the state sent the individual receiving the most votes into temporary exile. No charges or accusations had to be made, much less proven. Anyone who had offended the Athenians or who, by his prominence, seemed a threat to democracy, could be ostracized. Aristides (ca. 530–ca. 486 B.C.), known as "The Just" and a hero of the Battle of Marathon, was ostracized in 482 B.C. During the vote, an illiterate farmer, taking him for an ordinary citizen, approached Aristides and asked him to write the name *Aristides* on a potsherd for him. When asked if Aristides had done him any wrong, the farmer replied, "None at all, nor do I know him. I am just tired of hearing everyone call him The Just." Aristides complied and, gaining the most votes, sadly left Attica.

At the same time, Athenians also began to select their chief officers not simply by direct election but by lot. This practice prevented any individual from rising to power by creating a

This ostrakon was found in the Athenian agora. It was used to cast a vote to choose a person who would be ostracized — banished from Athens for a period of ten years. The name on the first line is Themistocles.

powerful faction. Themistocles (ca. 528–462 B.C.), the son of a noble father and a non-Greek mother, took the lead in using the tools of ostracism and selection by lot to hold the aristocratic factions at bay. He also used his influence to convince Athens to fortify its harbor at Piraeus and to invest in a powerful fleet as protection against the inevitable return of the Persians.

Occupied by problems elsewhere in their vast empire and the unexpected death of Darius I in 486 B.C., Persia paid little attention to Greece for six years. After Darius' death, his son Xerxes (486–465 B.C.), probably more interested in securing the western frontier of his empire than avenging his father's loss at Marathon, began to amass foodstuffs, weapons, and armies for a land assault on his Greek enemies. In response to these preparations, Greek cities began to attempt to close ranks against the invaders. Still, however, many Greek communities saw their neighbors as greater threats than the Persians. Some states, including Thebes, Argos, and Thessaly, more or less willingly allied with the Persians against Athens or Sparta. More distant cities such as Syracuse refused assistance except on their own terms, and north of the Peloponnesus only Athens, Plataea, and a few other small states were willing to fight. Sparta was prepared to defend itself and its league but was not interested in campaigns far from home. Finally, in 481 B.C., when the Persian invasion was imminent, representatives of what a contemporary called "the

Greeks who had the best thoughts for Greece" met in Sparta to plan resistance. The allies agreed that the Spartans would take command of the combined land and sea forces, which probably totaled roughly 35,000 helots, 5,000 hoplites, and 378 ships.

Although larger than those mustered by Athens against Darius, the Greek forces were puny compared with Xerxes' estimated two hundred thousand infantry and one thousand light and highly maneuverable Ionian and Phoenician ships. The Spartan commanders sought a strategic point at which the numerical superiority of the Persian forces would be neutralized. The choice fell on the narrow pass of Thermopylae and the adjacent Euboean strait. While a select force of hoplites held the pass, the Greek fleet, following a strategy devised by Themistocles, harried the larger Persian one. Neither action produced a Greek victory, but none could have been expected.

At Thermopylae, the Greeks held firm for days against wave after wave of assaulting troops ordered forward by an amazed and outraged Xerxes. Finally, Greek allies of the Persians showed them a narrow mountain track by which they were able to attack the Greek position from the rear. Seeing that all was lost, the Spartan king Leonidas (490–480 B.C.) sent most of his allies home. Then he and his three hundred Spartan equals faced certain death with a casual disdain characterized by the comment made by one Spartan equal. Told that when the Persians shot their arrows, they were so numerous that they hid the sun, the Spartan replied, "Good. If the Persians hide the sun, we shall have our battle in the shade." The epitaph raised later by the Spartan state to Leonidas and his men read simply, "Go tell the Spartans, you who read: we took their orders, and are dead." Dead they were, but they had bought precious time for the Greek allies.

While the Persian troops were blocked at Thermopylae, their fleet was being battered by fierce storms in the Euboean straits and harassed by the heavier Greek ships. Here the Greeks learned that in close quarters, they could stand up to Xerxes' Phoenician navy. This lesson proved vital a short time later. While the Persian army burned Athens and occupied Attica, Themisto-

The Persian Wars

cles lured the fleet into the narrow strait between Salamis and the mainland. There the slower Greek vessels bottled up the larger and vastly more numerous enemy ships and cut them to pieces.

After Salamis, Xerxes lost his appetite for fighting Greeks. Without his fleet, he could not supply a vast army far from home in hostile territory. Leaving a force to do what damage it could, he led the bulk of his forces back to Persia. At Athenian urging, the Greek allies under Leonidas' kinsman Pausanias (d. ca. 470 B.C.) met the Persians at Plataea in 479 B.C. Once more hoplite discipline and Greek determination meant more than numerical superiority. That night the Spartan king dined in the splendor of the captured tent of the defeated Persian commander. Athenian sea power and Spartan infantry had proven invincible. Soon the Athenians were taking the offensive, liberating the Ionian cities of Asia Minor and, in the process, laying the foundations of an Athenian empire every bit as threatening to their neighbors as that of Xerxes.

The Athenian Empire

Sparta, not Athens, should have emerged as the leader of the Greek world after 479 B.C. The Spartans, after all, had provided the crucial military force and leadership. Sparta and the Peloponnesus, unlike Attica, had emerged unscathed from the Persian wars. Finally, Sparta already had its own league, which might have formed the nucleus of an empire. However, the constant threat of a helot revolt and the league members' desire to go their separate ways left Sparta too preoccupied with internal problems to fill the power vacuum left by the Persian defeat. Nor did Spartan values encourage international ambitions. Sparta's militarism at home did not translate into military expansion abroad.

Athens, on the other hand, was only too ready to take the lead in bringing the war home to the Persians. From the start, Athenian motives were a combination of altruism, self-interest, and greed, in ascending proportions. With Sparta out of the picture, the Athenian fleet was the best hope of liberating the Aegean from Persians and pirates. Athenian propaganda emphasized the Persian menace and Ionian solidarity. Athens accepted control in 478 B.C. of what historians have come to call the Delian League, after the island of Delos, a religious center that housed the league's treasury. Athens and some of the states with navies provided ships; others contributed annual payments to the league. Initially, the league pursued the war against the Persians, not only driving them back along the Aegean and the Black seas, but also supporting rebels in the Persian Empire as far away as Egypt. At the same time, Athens hurriedly rebuilt its defensive fortifications, a move correctly interpreted by Sparta and other states as directed more against them than against the Persians.

Athens' domination of the Delian League assured its prosperity. Athenian citizens came to rely on the wages they earned each summer pulling at the oars of the league's ships. This annual source of cash was an essential cushion against the unreliability of agriculture. Attica, with its fragile agriculture, depended on Black Sea wheat and the league kept these regions under Athenian control. Since Athens received not only cash "contributions" from league members but also one-half of the spoils taken in battle, the state's public coffers were filled. The new riches made possible the reconstruction of the city that was burned by the Persians into the most magnificent city of Greece.

The league was too vital to Athenian prosperity to stand and fall with the Persian threat. The drive against the Persian empire began to falter after a league expedition to Egypt in 454 B.C. ended in total defeat. Discouraged by this and other setbacks, the Athenian Callias, acting for the league, apparently concluded a treaty of peace with Persia in 449 B.C., making the alliance no longer necessary. For a brief moment it appeared that the Delian League might disband. But it was too late. The league had become an empire and Athens' allies were its subjects.

The Athenian empire was an economic, judicial, religious, and political union held together by military might. Athens controlled the flow of grain through the Hellespont to the Aegean, ensuring its own supply and heavily taxing cargoes to other cities. Athens controlled the law courts of member cities and used them to repress anti-Athenian groups. Major cases were brought to Athens itself, where large politicized, democratic juries ensured that the Athenian *dēmos*, or people, would emerge as winners. Everywhere the goddess Athena received official worship as the patroness of Ionia. The goddess, through her temples, owned great amounts of land leased out to Athenians. Rich and poor citizens alike acquired territory throughout the empire. The rich took over vast estates confiscated from local opponents of Athenian dominance, while the poor replaced hostile populations in the colonies. Control over this empire depended on the Athenian fleet to enforce cooperation. Athenian garrisons were established in each city and "democratic" puppet governments ruled according to the wishes of the garrison commanders. Revolt, resignation from the league, or refusal to pay the annual tribute resulted in brutal suppression. The whole population of one rebellious city in Euboea was expelled and replaced with Athenian colonists. Athens sold the population of another into slavery. Persian tyranny had hardly been worse than Athenian imperialism.

Private and Public Life in Athens

During the second half of the fifth century B.C., Athens, enriched by tribute from its over 150 subject states, was a vital, crowded capital drawing merchants, artisans, and laborers from throughout the Greek world. At its height, the total population of Athens and surrounding Attica numbered perhaps 350,000, although probably fewer than 60,000 were citizens, that is, adult males qualified to own land and participate in Athenian politics. Over one-quarter of the total population were slaves. Historians have often described Athens as a slave-based society, and certainly slavery was a fundamental institution throughout its history. Ever since the reforms of Solon had prohibited debt bondage, great land-owners, unable to force ordinary free men to work their estates, had turned to slave labor. Slaves were also vital in mining and other forms of craft and industrial work. In addition, most citizen households, even modest ones, boasted at least one or two domestics.

Greek slaves were not distinguished by race, ethnicity, or physical appearance. Anyone could become a slave. Prisoners of war, foreigners who failed to pay taxes, victims of pirate raids, could all end up on the auction blocks of the ancient world. Pirates even captured the great philosopher Plato while he was traveling from Sicily to Athens and sold him into slavery in Egypt. Only a payment by his family saved him from an obscure life in the household of some wealthy Egyptian.

Slaves were as much the property of their owners as their land, houses, cattle, and sheep. Many masters treated their slaves well. After all, the cost of a slave was higher than the annual wage of a skilled free man. However, masters were under no obligation to treat their slaves kindly. Beatings, tattooing, starvation, and shackling were all common means of enforcing obedience. The bodies of male and female slaves were always at the disposition of their masters, who could use them as they wished or hand them over to others.

Still, the variety of slave experience was enormous. Rural slaves generally fared worse than urban ones, and those who worked the mines led the most appalling lives, literally worked to death. Others worked side by side with their masters in craft shops or even set up their own businesses, from which they were allowed to keep some of their profit to ultimately purchase their freedom. One slave left an estate worth over 33,000 drachmas (the equivalent of 165 years' salary for an ordinary free man), which included slaves of his own!

Roughly half of Athens' free population were foreigners—*metoikoi*, or metics. These were primarily Greek citizens of the tributary states of the empire, but they might also be Lydians, Phrygians, Syrians, Egyptians, Phoenicians, or Carians. The number of metics increased after the middle of the fifth century B.C. both because of the flood of foreigners into the empire's capital and because Athenian citizenship was restricted to persons with two parents who were of citizen families. Under these rules, neither Cleisthenes, the great reformer of the sixth century B.C., nor Themistocles, the architect of the victory against Persia, both of whose mothers had been foreigners, could have been Athenian citizens.

A small clay plaque discovered in Corinth shows workmen laboring in a pit quarrying clay for the pottery industry, which brought prosperity to the city. Refreshments are being lowered to the workers in the jar at the center.

Metics could not own land in Attica nor could they participate directly in politics. They were required to have a citizen protector and to pay a small annual tax. Otherwise, they were free to engage in every form of activity. The highest concentration of metics was found in the port of Piraeus, where they participated in commerce, manufacturing, banking, and skilled crafts. Educated metics also contributed to the intellectual and cultural life of the city. One of the wealthiest and most influential residents of Athens in the late fifth century B.C. was Cephalas of Syracuse. The great historian of the Persian wars, Herodotus, was a foreigner from Halicarnassus.

More than half of those born into citizen families were entirely excluded from public life. These were the women, who controlled and directed the vital sphere of the Athenian home, but who were considered citizens only for purposes of marriage, transfer of property, and procreation. During the Archaic period, aristocratic women had enjoyed some independence. However, the triumph of democracy reduced the public role of all women to that of breeder and property conduit. From birth to death, every female citizen lived under the protection of a male guardian, either a close relative such as father or brother, or a husband or son. Women spent almost their entire lives in the inner recesses of the home, emerging only for funerals and a very few religious festivals. Fathers arranged marriages, the purposes of which are abundantly clear from the ritualized exchange of words sealing the betrothal:

> I give this woman for the procreation of legitimate children.
> I accept.
> And (I give a certain amount as) dowry.
> I am content.

A wife had no control over her dowry, which passed to her son. In the event of divorce or the death of her husband, the woman and her dowry returned to her father. Should a woman's father die without a will or an heir, his closest male relative could demand her as his wife and thus claim the inheritance, even if the woman were already married to someone else.

An honorable Athenian woman stayed at home and managed her husband's household. Wealthy women directed the work of servants and slaves. In modest homes women were expected to participate along with the slaves in domestic chores such as spinning and in rearing children. Only the poorest citizens sent their wives and daughters to work in the marketplace or the fields. Even the most casual contact with other men without permission was strictly forbidden, although men were expected to engage in various sorts of extramarital affairs. In the words of one Athenian male, "Hetairai we have for our pleasure, mistresses for the refreshment of our bodies, but wives to bear us legitimate children and to look after the house faithfully."

Within the home, Athenian women were vital, if subordinate, partners. The household, as Athenians never tired of repeating, was the foundation of all society. Thus the role of women was indeed important. The public sphere was entirely closed to them, although even some men realized the potential for resentment. A woman in one of Euripides' tragedies describes her status:

> We women are the most unfortunate creatures.
> Firstly with an excess of wealth it is required
> For us to buy a husband and take for our bodies
> A master; for not to take one is even worse. . . .
> What they say of us is that we have a peaceful time
> Living at home, while they do the fighting in war.
> How wrong they are! I would very much rather stand
> Three times in the front of battle than bear one child.

Male control over women may have resulted in part from fear. Women were identified with the forces of nature, which included both positive forces such as fertility and life and negative forces such as chaotic irrationality, which threatened civilization. These two poles were epitomized by the cult of Dionysus. He was the god of wine, life blood, and fertility, but he was also the deity whose female devotees, the *maenads*, were portrayed as worshiping him in a state of frenzied savagery that could include tearing children and animals limb from limb.

Attic black figure hydra, or water jar, from the sixth century B.C. The scene depicted on the jar is related to its function. Women at a fountain are dancing and talking as they fill similar hydrae from the water spouts.

The male citizens of fifth-century B.C. Athens were free to an extent previously unknown in the world. But Athenian freedom was freedom in community, not freedom from community. The essence of their freedom lay in their participation in public life, especially self-government, which was their passion. This participation was always within a complex network of familial, social, and religious connections and obligations. Each person belonged to a number of groups: a deme, a tribe, a family, various religious associations, and occupational groups. Each of these communities placed different and even contradictory demands on its members. The impossibility of satisfying all of these demands, of responding to the special interests of each, forced citizens to make hard choices, to set priorities, and to balance conflict-

ing obligations. This process of selection was the essence of Athenian freedom, a freedom which, unlike that of the modern world, was based not on individualism but on a multitude of collectivities. The sum of these overlapping groupings was Athenian society, in which friends and opponents alike were united.

Unity did not imply equality. Even in fifth-century B.C. Athens, not all Athenians were socially or economically equal. Most were farmers who looked to military service as a means of increasing their meager income. Others engaged in trade or industry, although metics, with their commercial contacts in their cities of origin, dominated much of these activities in Athens. However, the aristocracy was still strong, and most of the popular leaders of the century came from the ranks of old wealth and influence. They used their wealth to attract supporters from the poorer ranks of the citizenry. Still, sovereignty lay not with these aristocrats but with the demos, the people.

In theory the adult male citizens of Athens were Athens' sovereigns. Since the time of Solon, they had formed the *ekklēsia*, or assembly. On particularly solemn occasions, as many as six thousand citizens might convene in the *pnyx*, the meeting place of the assembly. They also made up the large juries, always composed of several hundred citizens, who decided legal cases less on law than on the political merits of the case and the quality of the orators who pleaded for each side. Such large bodies were too unwieldy to deal with the daily tasks of government. Thus, control of these tasks fell to the council, or *boulē*, composed of five hundred members selected by lot by the tribes; the magistrates, who were also chosen by lot; and ten military commanders or generals, the only major officeholders elected rather than chosen at random.

Paradoxically, the resolute determination of Athenian democrats to prevent individuals from acquiring too much power helped to create a series of extraconstitutional power brokers. Since most offices were filled by lot and turned over frequently, real political leadership came not from officeholders but from generals and from popular leaders. These so-called demagogues, while at times holding high office, exercised their power through their speaking skills, informal networks, and knowledge of how to get things done. They acquired this knowledge through their willingness to serve for long periods in various capacities on committees, as unpaid government workers, and in minor elected offices. Demagogues tended to be wealthy aristocrats who could afford to put in the time demanded by these largely voluntary services. Governing an empire demanded skill, energy, and experience, but Athenian democracy was formally run by amateurs. Small wonder that the city's public life was dominated by these popular leaders.

Although many demagogues competed for power and attracted the support of the people, the Athenian demos was not kind to its heroes. Ten years after the Greek victory at Salamis in 480 B.C., Athens ostracized Themistocles, whose leadership there had saved Athens. Mistrusted by many of his co-citizens, he ended his days ironically in the service of the Persian king. Cimon (ca. 510–451 B.C.), the son of the Marathon hero Miltiades, helped destroy Themistocles and succeeded him as the most influential leader of the city. As long as he lavished his wealth on the populace and led Athenian armies to victory against the Persians, Cimon remained popular. He also fought to hold the Athenian empire together when the island of Thasos attempted to secede in 465 B.C. However, his luck ran out three years later. In 462 B.C., Cimon led an army to assist Sparta in suppressing a revolt of its helots. The Spartans, fearing that he was actually planning to plot with the helots against them, sent him and his army home in disgrace. This disgrace was fatal, and Athens ostracized Cimon upon his return.

For the next thirty years, one individual dominated Athenian public life, the general Pericles (ca. 495–429 B.C.). Although not an original thinker, he was a great orator and a successful military commander, who proved to be the man most able to win the confidence of Athens and to lead it during the decades of its greatest glory. The Athenian political system of radical democracy reached its zenith under the leadership of Pericles, even while its imperial program drew it into a long and fatal war against Sparta, the only state powerful enough to resist it.

Pericles and Athens

Pericles was descended from the greatest aristocratic families of Athens. Nevertheless, as one ancient author put it, he "took his side, not with the rich and the few, but with the many and the poor." Pericles acquired intimate knowledge of government through long service on various public works projects, projects that provided lucrative income to poorer citizens who had supplemented their incomes as oarsmen before being idled by the peace of Callias of 449 B.C. Pericles was also president of the commission responsible for constructing the great ivory and gold statue of Athena that stood in the Parthenon, the main temple in Athens. He served on the commission that built the Lyceum, or city exercise center, and the Parthenon itself. These enormous projects won him a great popular following while giving him an intimate knowledge of public finance and the details of Athenian government. He enhanced his position further through his great powers of persuasion. His speaking ability was described by an opponent, Thucydides, son of Melesias (d. ca. 410 B.C.). When asked by the king of Sparta whether he or Pericles was the better wrestler, Thucydides was said to have replied that while he could throw Pericles, the latter was so eloquent that he could easily convince those who had seen him thrown that he had not fallen but rather had won the match.

Pericles had been a young supporter of Themistocles and had commissioned the dramatist Aeschylus to write a play glorifying him at the time of his ostracism. Pericles never ruled Athens. As a general he could only carry out the orders of the ekklesia and the boule, and as a citizen he could only attempt to persuade his fellows. Still he was largely responsible for the extension of Athenian democracy to all free citizens. Under his influence Athens abolished the last property requirements for officeholding. He convinced the state to pay those who served on juries, thus making it possible for even the poorest citizens to participate in this important part of Athenian government. But he was also responsible for a restriction of citizenship to those whose mothers and fathers had been Athenians. Such a law would have denied citizenship to many of the most illustrious Athenians of the sixth century B.C., including his own ancestors. By adopting such a measure, Athens was closing the door to persons of talent and energy who might have been of great service to the city in the future. The law also prevented citizens of Athens' subject states from developing a real stake in the fate of the empire.

Perikles had been an opponent of the aristocratically oriented Kimon at home and disputed Kimon's foreign policy, which saw Athens and Sparta as "yoke mates" against Persia. Perikles had little fear of Persia, but shared Kimon's view that the Athenian empire had to be preserved at all costs. This policy ultimately drew Athens into deadly conflict with Sparta. The first clash between the two great powers came around 460 B.C. Megara, which lay between the Peloponnesus and Attica, withdrew from the Spartan alliance and sought Athens' assistance against nearby Corinth in a border dispute. The Athenians, eager to add Megara to their empire, went to their assistance. Soon Sparta and Aegina entered the fray, but Athens emerged victorious, checking Sparta and absorbing Megara, Aegina, and Boeotia. However, in 446 B.C., after the Athenian defeat in Egypt, Megara and Boeotia rebelled and Sparta invaded the disputed region. Unable to face this new threat at home after its disastrous loss abroad, in 445 B.C. the Athenians, under the leadership of Perikles, concluded a peace treaty with Sparta whereby Athens abandoned all of its continental possessions. The treaty was meant to last for thirty years. It held for fourteen.

The two great powers were eager to preserve the peace, but the whole Greek world was a tinderbox ready to burst into flame. The spark came from an unexpected direction. In 435 B.C., Corinth and its colony Corcyra on the Adriatic Sea came to blows and Corcyra sought the assistance of Athens. Athens had never had much interest or involvement in the west, but it did not want the Corinthian fleet, vital to the Spartan alliance, augmented by absorbing the ships of Corcyra. Therefore the Athenians agreed to a defensive alliance with Corcyra and assisted it in defeating its enemy. This assistance infuriated Corinth, an ally of Sparta, and in 432 B.C., the Corinthians con-vinced the Spartans that Athenian imperial ambitions were insatiable. In the words of the great historian of the war, Thucydides (d. ca. 401 B.C.), "What made war inevitable was the growth of Athenian power and the fear which this caused in Sparta." The next year, Sparta invaded Attica. The Peloponnesian War, which would destroy both great powers, had begun.

The Peloponnesian War

The Peloponnesian War was actually a series of wars and rebellions. Athens and Sparta waged two devastating ten-year wars, from 431 B.C. to 421 B.C. and then again from 414 B.C. to 404 B.C. At the same time, cities in each alliance took advantage of the wars to revolt against the great powers, eliciting terrible vengeance from both Athens and Sparta. Within many of the Greek city-states, oligarchs and democrats waged bloody civil wars for control of their governments. Moreover, between 415 and 413 B.C., Athens attempted to expand its empire in Sicily, an attempt that ended in disaster. Before it was over, the Peloponnesian War had become an international war, with Persia entering the fray on the side of Sparta. In the end, there were no real victors, only victims.

Initially, Sparta and Athens both hoped for quick victory. Sparta's strength was its army and its strategy was to invade Attica, devastate the countryside, and force the Athenians into an open battle. Given the Spartan infantry's strength, numbers, and skill, such a battle could only end in an Athenian defeat. Perikles urged Athens to a strategy of conserving its hoplite forces while exploiting its naval strength. Athens was a naval power and, with its empire and control of Black Sea grain, could hold out for years behind its fortifications, the great wall linking Athens to its port of Piraeus. At the same time, the Athenian fleet could launch raids along the coast of the Peloponnesus, thus bringing the war home to the Spartans. Perikles hoped in this way to outlast the Spartans. In describing the war, Thucydides uses the same word for "survive" and "win."

The first phase of the war, called the Archidamian War after the Spartan king Archidamos

(431–427 B.C.), was indecisive. Sparta pillaged Attica but could not breach the great wall nor starve Athens. In 430 B.C., the Spartans received unexpected help in the form of plague, which ravaged Athens for five years. By the time it ended in 426 B.C., as much as a third of the Athenian population had died, including Pericles. Still Athens held out, establishing bases encircling the Peloponnesus and urging Spartan helots and allies to revolt. At Pylos in 425 B.C., the Athenian generals Cleon and Demosthenes captured a major force of Spartan equals. The Spartans offset this defeat by capturing the city of Amphipolis on the northern Aegean. The defeated Athenian commander, Thucydides, was exiled for his failure and retired to Spartan territory to write his great history of the war. Exhausted by a decade of death and destruction, the two sides contracted peace in 421 B.C. Although Athens was victorious in that its empire was intact, the peace changed nothing and tensions festered for five years.

The Delian League and the Peloponnesian War

After the peace of 421 B.C., Pericles' kinsman Alcibiades (ca. 450–404 B.C.) came to dominate the demos. Well-spoken, handsome, and brave, but also vain, dissolute, and ambitious, Alcibiades led the city into disaster. Although a demagogue who courted popular support, he despised the people and schemed to overturn the democracy. His personal life, perhaps typical of privileged young Athenian aristocrats, had little room for the traditional religious or patriotic values of the city. In 415 B.C., he urged Athens to expand its empire west by attacking Syracuse, the most prosperous Greek city of Sicily, which had largely escaped the devastation of the Archidamian War. The expedition went poorly and Alcibiades, accused at home of having profaned one of the most important Athenian religious cults, was ordered home. Instead, he fled to Sparta, where he began to assist the Spartans against Athens. The Sicilian expedition ended in disaster. Athens lost over two hundred ships and fifty thousand men. At the same time, Sparta resumed the war, this time with naval support provided by Persia.

Suddenly Athens was fighting for its life. Alcibiades soon abandoned Sparta for Persia and convinced the Athenians that if they would abandon their democracy for an oligarchy, Persia would withdraw its support of Sparta. In 411 B.C., the desperate Athenian assembly established a brutal oligarchy controlled by a small faction of antidemocratic conspirators. Alcibiades' promise proved hollow and the war continued. Athens reestablished its democracy, but the brief oligarchy left the city bitterly divided. The Persian king renewed his support for Sparta, sending his son Cyrus (ca. 424–401 B.C.) to coordinate the war against Athens. Under the Spartan general Lysander (d. 395 B.C.), Sparta and its allies finally closed in on Athens. Lysander captured the Athenian fleet in the Hellespont, destroyed it, killed three thousand Athenian prisoners, and severed Athens' vital grain supply. Within months Athens was entirely cut off from the outside world and starving. In 404 B.C., Sparta accepted Athens' unconditional surrender. Athens' fortifications came down, its empire vanished, and its fleet, except for a mere twelve ships, dissolved.

Athenian Culture

Throughout the fifth century B.C., the turbulent issues of democracy and oligarchy, war and peace, hard choices and conflicting obligations found expression in Athenian culture even as the glory of the Athenian empire was manifested in art and architecture. During this century, Athens transformed Greek and indeed Western civilization. Most of what we today call Greek is actually Athenian: the great dramatists Aeschylus, Sophocles, and Euripides were Athenian, as were the sculptor Phidias, the Parthenon architects Ictinus and Callicrates, the philosophers Socrates and Plato. To Athens came writers, thinkers, and artists from throughout the Greek world.

The Examined Life

A primary characteristic of Athenian culture was its critical and rational nature. In heated discussions in the assembly and the agora, the courtroom and the private symposium, Athenians and foreigners drawn to the city no longer looked to the myths and religion of the past for guidance. Secure in their identity and protected by the openness of their radical democracy, they began to examine past and present and to question the foundations of traditional values. From this climate of inquiry emerged the traditions of moral philosophy and its cousin, history.

The Ionian interest in natural philosophy, the explanation of the universe in rational terms, continued throughout the fifth century B.C. But philosophers began also to turn their attention to the human world, in particular to the powers and limitations of the individual's mind and the individual's relationship with society. By the end of his life, the philosopher Heraclitus (see ch. 2, p. 53) had become intrigued with the examination of the rational faculties themselves rather than what one could know with them. In part, this meant a search for personal, inner understanding that would lead to proper action within society, in other words, to the search for ethics based in reason. In part, too, such an inquiry led to a study of how to formulate arguments and persuade others through logic.

In the political world of fifth-century B.C. Athens, rhetoric, the art of persuasion, was particularly important, because it was the key to political influence. Ambitious would-be successors to Pericles and Alcibiades were prepared to pay well to learn the art of persuasion. Teachers, called *sophists* ("wise people"), traveled throughout Greece offering to provide an advanced education for a fee. Although the sophistic tradition later gained a negative reputation, teachers such as Gorgias (ca. 485–ca. 380 B.C.) and Protagoras (ca. 490–421 B.C.) trained young men not only in the art of rhetoric but also in logic. By exercising their students' minds with logical puzzles and paradoxical statements, the sophists taught a generation of wealthy Greeks the powers and complexities of human reason.

Socrates (ca. 470–399 B.C.) was considered by many of his contemporaries as but one more sophist, but he himself reacted against what he saw as the amoral and superficial nature of sophistic education. Although as a young man he had been interested in natural philosophy, he abandoned this tradition in favor of the search for moral self-enlightenment urged by Heraclitus. "Know thyself" was Socrates' plea. An unexamined life, he argued, was not worth living. Socrates refused any pay for his teaching, arguing that he had nothing to teach. He knew nothing, he said, and was superior to the sophists only because he recognized his ignorance while they professed wisdom.

Socrates' method infuriated his contemporaries. He would approach persons with reputations for wisdom or skill and then, through a series of disarmingly simple questions, force them to defend their beliefs. The inevitable result was that in their own words the outstanding sophists, politicians, and poets of the day demonstrated the inadequacy of the foundations of their beliefs. While his opponents were left in confusion and outrage, Socrates' young followers, who included many of the sons of the aristocracy, delighted in seeing their elders so humiliated and embarrassed.

Since Socrates refused to commit any of his teaching to writing, we have no direct knowledge

This statuette is a realistic portrait of the philosopher Socrates, who was celebrated for his mind rather than his physical endowments. Our verbal portraits of Socrates and his ideas come to us from Plato and Xenophon.

of the content of his instruction. We know of him only from the conflicting reports of his former students and opponents. One thing is certain, however. While demanding that every aspect of life be investigated, Socrates never doubted the moral legitimacy of the Athenian state. Condemned to death in 399 B.C. on the trumped-up charges of corrupting the morals of the Athenian youth and introducing strange gods, he rejected the opportunity to escape into exile. For seventy years, he argued, he had accepted the laws of Athens. Now, he must accept their sentence, for by rejecting the laws of the city, he would in fact be guilty of the charges against him. Rather than reject Athens and its laws, he drank the fatal potion of hemlock given him by the executioner.

The philosophical interest in human choices and social constraints found echo in the historical writing of the age. Herodotus (ca. 484–ca. 420 B.C.), the first historian, was one of the many foreigners who found in Athens the intellectual climate and audience he needed to write an account of the Persian Wars of the preceding generation. His book of inquiries, or *historia*, into the origins and events of the conflict between Greeks and Persians is the first true history. Herodotus had traveled widely in the eastern Mediterranean, collecting local stories and visiting famous temples, palaces, and cities. In his study he presents a great panorama of the civilized world at the end of the sixth century B.C. His descriptions range from the peoples of the Persian empire to the construction of the great pyramids (he reports that sixteen hundred talents of silver were paid for supplies of radishes, onions, and leeks for the workers who built the pyramid of Cheops). The story builds gradually to the heroic clash between the ancient civilizations of the East and the Greeks. Herodotus does not hesitate to report myths, legends, and outrageous tales. His faith in the gods is strong and he believes that the gods intervene in human affairs. Still, he is more than just a good storyteller or a chronicler of legends. Often, after reporting conflicting accounts he will conclude, "Both stories are told and the reader may take his choice between them." In other cases, after recounting a particularly far-fetched account heard from local informants, he comments, "Personally, I think this story is nonsense."

As he explains in his introduction, Herodotus' purpose in writing was twofold. First, he sought to preserve the memory of the past by recording the achievements of both Greeks and Orientals. Second, he set out to show how the two came into conflict. It was this concern to explain, to go beyond mere storytelling, that earned Herodotus the designation of the "father of history." Still, his understanding of cause and effect was fairly simple. He believed that wars arise from grievances and retribution. Thus the Persian Wars appear rather like large-scale feuds, the origins of which are lost in myth. At the same time, Herodotus is less interested in the mythic dimensions of the conflict than in the human, and his primary concern is the action of individuals under the press of circumstances. Ultimately, the Persian Wars become for Herodotus the conflict between freedom and despotism, and he describes with passion how different Greek states chose between the two. The choice, as he phrased it, was "to live in a rugged land and rule or to cultivate rich plains and be slaves."

The story of the Peloponnesian War was recorded by a different sort of historian, one who focused more narrowly on the Greek world and on political power. Through oral interviews and reading, Herodotus painstakingly recovered information about the events he described. Thucydides had been an Athenian general and a major actor in the first part of the Peloponnesian War. He began his account at the very outbreak of the conflict, thus writing a contemporary record of the war rather than a history of it. As Herodotus is called the father of history, Thucydides might be called the first social scientist.

Not myth, nor religion, nor morality takes center stage in Thucydides' account of what he saw from the outset to be "a great war and more worth writing about than any of those which had taken place in the past." For him, the central subject is human society in action. His passion is the open, self-conscious political life characteristic of the Greek polis, and his view of the give-and-take of politics shows a strong debt to the sophistic tradition. Thucydides views the Greek states acting out of rational self-interest. His favorite device for showing the development of such policies is the political set speech in which two opposing leaders attempt to persuade their fellow citizens on the proper course of action. Thucydides was seldom actually present at the events he describes. Even when he was, he could not have transcribed the speakers' exact words. Rather he attempted to put into the mouths of the speakers "whatever seemed most appropriate to me for each speaker to say in the particular circumstances." Although fictitious by modern standards, these speeches penetrate to the heart of the tough political choices facing the opposing forces. This hard-nosed approach to political decisions continues to serve as a model to historians and practitioners of power politics.

Still, morality is always just below the surface of Thucydides' narrative. Even as he unflinchingly chronicles the collapse of morality and social order in the face of political expediency, he recognizes that this process will destroy his beloved

The interior of a black-figured kylix, or drinking cup, dating from about 540 B.C., is decorated with a scene of the god of wine, Dionysus, reclining in a boat. He is surrounded by dolphins and bunches of grapes.

Athens. In his account of the second phase of the war, Athens acts with the full arrogance of a tyrant. Its overwhelming pride leads it to attack and destroy its weaker neighbors and, ultimately, to invade Sicily, with all the disastrous consequences of that campaign. The consequences of political self-interest, devoid of other considerations, follow their own natural course to disaster and ruin. In the later, unfinished chapters (Thucydides died shortly after Athens' final defeat), the Peloponnesian War takes on the characteristics of a tragedy. Here Thucydides, the ultimate political historian, shows the deep influence of the dominant literary tradition of his day, Greek drama.

Athenian Drama

Since the time of its introduction by Peisistratus in the middle of the sixth century B.C., drama had become popular, not only in Athens, but throughout the Greek world. Plays formed part of the annual feast of Dionysus and dealt with mythic subject matter largely taken from the *Iliad* and the *Odyssey*. As the dramatist Aeschylus said, "We are all eating crumbs from the great table of Homer." Three types of plays honored the Dionysian festival. Tragedies dealt with great men who failed because of flaws in their natures. Their purpose was, in the words of the philosopher Aristotle, to effect "through pity and terror the correction and refinement of passions." Comedies were more directly topical and political. They parodied real Athenians, often by name, and amused even while making serious points in defense of democracy. Somewhere between tragedies and comedies, satyr plays remained closest to the Dionysian cult. In them lecherous drunken satyrs, mythical half-man, half-goat creatures, interact with gods and men as they roam the world in search of Dionysus.

Athenian drama became more secular and less mythic as dramatists began to deal with human topics explosive in their immediacy and timeless in their portrayal of the human condition. Only a handful of the hundreds of Greek plays written in the fifth century B.C. survive. The first of the great Athenian tragedians whose plays we know is Aeschylus (525–456 B.C.), a veteran of

Fragment of a vase from Tarentum showing an actor holding a mask. Greek dramas were presented in outdoor theaters. Men played women's roles and the actors wore masks to indicate the nature of the characters they played.

Marathon and an eyewitness of the battle of Salamis. His one surviving trilogy, the *Oresteia*, traces the fate of the family of Agamemnon, the Greek commander at Troy. The three plays of the trilogy explore the conflicting obligations of filial respect and vengeance, which ultimately must be settled by rational yet divinely sanctioned law. Upon his return from Troy, the victorious Agamemnon is murdered by his unfaithful wife Clytemnestra. Orestes, his son, avenges his father's murder by murdering Clytemnestra, but in so doing incurs the wrath of the Furies, avenging spirits who pursue him for killing his mother. The conflict of duties and loyalties cannot be resolved by human means. Finally, Orestes arrives at the shrine of Apollo at Delphi, where the god purifies him from the pollution of the killing. Then at Athens, Athena rescues Orestes, creating the Athenian law court and transforming the Furies into the Eumenides, the kindly guardian spirits of Athens.

The mature plays of Aeschylus' younger contemporary, Sophocles (496–406 B.C.), are tragedies in which religion plays a less important role. Instead, Sophocles sought to express human character. Although the Athenian audience knew the stories on which he based his plays, his plots move in a natural pace. He shows how humans make decisions and carry them out, constrained by their pasts, their weaknesses, and their vices, but free nonetheless. Sophocles' message is endurance, acceptance of human responsibility and, at the same time, of the ways of the gods, who overrule people's plans. The heroine of *Antigone* is the sister of Polynices, exiled son of King Oedipus of Thebes. Polynices has died fighting his city and Creon, its new ruler, commands under penalty of death that Polynices' body be left unburied. This would mean that his soul would never find rest, the ultimate punishment for a Greek. Antigone, with a determination and courage equal to her love for her brother, buries Polynices and is entombed alive for her crime. Here the conflict between the state, which claims the total obedience of its people, and the claims of familial love and religious piety meet in tragic conflict. Creon, warned by a prophet that he is offending heaven, orders Antigone's release, but it is too late. Rather than wait for death, she has already hanged herself.

Sophocles was the most successful of the fifth-century B.C. tragedians and in the next century his plays came to be considered the most "classic" of the tragedies. His younger contemporary, Euripides (485–406 B.C.), was far more original and daring in his subject matter and treatment of human emotions. Unlike the stately dramas of Aeschylus and the deliberate progressions of Sophocles, Euripides' plays abound in plot twists and unexpected, violent outbursts of passion. His characters are less reconciled to their fates and less ready to accept the traditional gods:

> Does someone say that there are gods in heaven?
> There are not, there are not—unless one choose
> to follow old tradition like a fool.

Euripides' women were often wronged and seldom accepted their lot. Medea, the central figure of his most famous tragedy, made it possible for the adventurer Jason to complete his quest for the mythical Golden Fleece. Abandoning her land in the east, she returns with the hero, bears his children, and settles with him at Corinth. Jason hopes to marry the daughter of the king, his only child, but must send Medea away. He tries to reason with her and she pretends to agree.

Instead, she murders the Corinthian princess and her own children by Jason before escaping in a magical chariot drawn by dragons. Passion, not reason, rules Euripides' world.

Neither passion nor reason, but politics rules the world of Greek comedy. Rather than the timelessness of the human condition, Athenian comic playwrights focused their biting satire on the political and social issues of the moment. Particularly the comic genius Aristophanes (ca. 450–ca. 388 B.C.) used wit, imagination, vulgarity, and great poetic sensitivity to attack everything that offended him in his city. In his plays he mocks and ridicules statesmen, philosophers, rival playwrights, and even the gods. His comedies are full of outrageous twists of plot, talking animals, obscene jokes and puns, and mocking asides. And yet Aristophanes was a deeply patriotic Athenian, dedicated to the democratic system and equally dedicated to the cause of peace. In his now-lost *Babylonians*, written around 426 B.C., as Athenians struggled to recover from the plague and Cleon continued to pursue the bloody war against Sparta, he mocks Cleon and the Athenian demagogues while portraying the cities of the Delian League as slaves forced to grind grain at a mill. In *Lysistrata*, written in 411 B.C., after Athens had once more renewed the war, the women of Greece force their men to make peace by conspiring to refuse them sex as long as war continues. Through the sharp satire and absurd plots of his plays, Aristophanes communicates his sympathy for ordinary people, who must match wits with the charlatans and pompous frauds who attempt to dominate Athens' public life.

The Human Image

The humanity in Greek drama found its parallel in art. In the late sixth century B.C., a reversal of the traditional black figure technique had revolutionized vase painting. Artists had begun to outline scenes on unfired clay and then fill in the background with black or brown glaze. The interior details of the figures were also added in black. The result was a much more lifelike art, a lighter, more natural coloring, and the possibility of more perspective, depth, and molding. The drinking cup shown here, signed by Douris, one of the finest fifth-century B.C. vase painters, ex-

Man and Youth, a
fifth-century B.C.
drinking cup in terra
cotta from Attica in
Greece. The cup is
signed by Douris. Over
two hundred extant
vases are ascribed to
him.

emplifies this fluidity and naturalness. The subject matter is erotic: a mature man is offering a handsome youth money for sex. The execution is masterful. The two figures interact and yet balance each other, exactly filling the circular space of the cup's interior. Douris has captured the animation of the two figures' faces and their naturally expressive gestures as they bargain, as well as the fine detail of their musculature and clothing.

Sculpture reflected the same development toward balance and realism contained within an ideal of human form. The finest bronzes and marbles of the fifth century B.C. show freestanding figures whose natural vigor and force, even when engaged in strenuous exertion, are balanced by the placidity of their faces and their lack of emotion. The tradition established by the Athenian sculptor Phidias (ca. 500–ca. 430 B.C.) sought a naturalism in the portrayal of the human figure, which remained ideal rather than individual.

Even those statues explicitly commemorative, dedicated for victories in games or battle, showed people as they participated in the larger context of humanity.

The greatest sculptural program of the fifth century B.C. was that produced for the Athenian acropolis. The reconstruction of the acropolis, which had been destroyed by the Persians, was the culmination of Athenian art. Originally, the Athenians had not planned to rebuild its temples. However, Pericles decided to use the tribute collected from the Delian League to launch an enormous building project, which transformed the Athenian acropolis into the greatest complex of buildings in the ancient world. A first-century A.D. author, who had visited all the great cities of the Mediterranean, remarked, "they seem to have within them some everlasting breath of life and an ageless spirit intermingled with their composition."

The Acropolis

The Erechtheum

The Propylaea

The Parthenon

The acropolis complex was so designed that a visitor was guided to see it in the proper order and perspective. One entered through the monumental *Propylaea*, or gateway, a T-shaped structure approached by a flight of steps. From the top of the steps, one could glimpse both Phidias' great bronze statue of Athena Promachos in the center of the acropolis and, to the right, the Parthenon. As visitors entered the acropolis itself, they passed on the right the small temple of Athena as Victory. This small temple, built slightly later than the Parthenon, looks out toward Salamis. It was constructed in the Ionic style, or order, an architectural tradition distinguished chiefly by the simple but fluid patterns of flowers and scrolls on its capitals, patterns borrowed from Oriental architecture. Continuing on the Sacred Way, one saw on the left the delicate Ionic Erechtheum, which housed the oldest Athenian cults. On the right, visitors were overawed by the Parthenon, a monument as much to Athens as to Athena.

Even today, the ruined temple seems a rectangular embodiment of order, proportion, and balance, an effect achieved through irregularity, illusion, and variation. The Parthenon is the most perfect example of Doric order, an austerely beautiful building tradition reminiscent of earlier wooden structures. Every surface, from the floor to the columns to the horizontal beams, curves slightly. The spacing of the columns varies and each leans slightly inward. Those at the rear are larger than those at the front to compensate for the effect of viewing them from a greater distance. Just as the idealization of Athenian statues leaves the viewer with the impression of seeing a perfect individual, the illusion of flatness, regularity, and repetition in the Parthenon is the intended effect of an optical illusion.

An illusion, too, was the sense of overwhelming Athenian superiority and grandeur the acropolis was intended to convey. By the time the Erechtheum was completed in 406 B.C., the Athenian empire was all but destroyed, the city's population devastated, and its democracy imperiled. Two years later Athens surrendered unconditionally to Sparta.

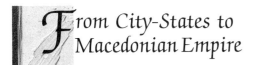

From City-States to Macedonian Empire

The Peloponnesian War touched every aspect of Greek life. The war brought changes to the social and political structures of Greece by creating an enduring bitterness between elites and populace and a distrust of both democracy and traditional oligarchy. The mutual exhaustion of Athens and Sparta left a vacuum of power in the Aegean. Finally, the war raised fundamental questions about the nature of politics and society throughout the Greek world.

Politics after the Peloponnesian War

Over the decades-long struggle, the conduct of war and the nature of politics had changed, bringing new problems for victor and vanquished alike. Lightly armed professional mercenaries willing to fight for anyone able to pay gradually replaced hoplite citizen soldiers as the backbone of the fighting forces. Just as the rise of hoplite phalanxes in the sixth century B.C. had weakened oligarchies, the rise of these poorer warriors weakened the political importance of hoplites in favor of those who could pay and outfit rootless mercenaries. The rise of mercenary armies meant trouble for democracies such as Athens as well as for Sparta with its class of equals.

As war became professional and protracted, it became more brutal. When the Spartans and their band of allies captured Plataea in 427 B.C., they slaughtered all the men, enslaved the women, and razed the city. Despite Cleon's urgings, Athens refused to treat Mytilene in the same way when it captured that city in the same year. But by 416 B.C., when Athens captured Melos, it did not hesitate to treat its citizens as Sparta had dealt with those of Plataea. Lysander's slaughter of Athenian prisoners of war in 405 B.C. was business as usual. The moment of Greek unity experienced during the second Persian war was forgotten in the horrors of the Peloponnesian conflict.

Victory left Sparta no more capable of assuming leadership in 404 B.C. than it had been in 478 B.C. Years of war had reduced the population of equals to less than three thousand. The city could no longer maintain its traditional isolation from the outside world. Sparta could not control the Greek world without a powerful fleet, but ships and crews were costly and could only be maintained by taxing its empire or by accepting subsidies from Persia. Greedy and ambitious Spartans began to accumulate much of the wealth that poured in as booty and tribute from throughout the Aegean while other equals lost the land they needed to maintain their place in society.

The Spartans also proved extremely unpopular imperialists. As reward for Persian assistance, Sparta returned the Ionian cities to Persian control. Elsewhere it established hated oligarchies to rule in a way favorable to Sparta's interests. In Athens, a brutal tyranny of thirty men took control in 404 B.C. With Spartan support, they executed fifteen hundred democratic leaders and forced five thousand more into exile. The Thirty Tyrants evoked enormous hatred and opposition. Within a year the exiles recaptured the city, restored democracy, and killed or expelled the tyrants.

Similar opposition to Spartan rule emerged throughout the Greek world, shattering the fragile peace created by Athens' defeat. For over seventy years the Greek world boiled in constant warfare. Mutual distrust, fear of any city that seemed about to establish a position of clear superiority, and the machinations of the Persian empire to keep Greeks fighting each other produced a constantly shifting series of alliances.

Persia turned against its former ally when Sparta supported an unsuccessful attempt by Cyrus to unseat his brother Artaxerxes II. Soon the unlikely and unstable alliance of Athens, Corinth, Argos, Thebes, and Euboea, financed by Persia, entered a series of vicious wars against Sparta. Rapidly shifting alliances and mutual hostility ensured that there was no real victor. The first round ended in Spartan victory, due to the shifting role of Persia, whose primary interest was the continued disunity of the Greeks. By 377 B.C., however, Athens had reorganized its league and with Thebes as ally was able to break Spartan sea power. The decline of Sparta left a power vacuum soon filled by Thebes. Athens, concerned by this new threat, shifted alliances, making peace with its old enemy. However, Spartan military fortunes had so declined that when Sparta attacked Thebes in 371 B.C., its armies were destroyed and Spartan power broken. The next year Thebes invaded the Peloponnesus and freed Messenia, the foundation of Sparta's economic prosperity. Sparta never recovered. Deprived of its economic base, its body of equals reduced to a mere eight hundred, and its fleet gone, Sparta never regained its historic importance.

Theban hegemony was short-lived. Before long the same process of greed, envy, and distrust that had devastated the other Greek powers destroyed Thebes. In 355 B.C., when Thebes attempted to conquer the small state of Phocis, its enemies seized Delphi and used the vast treasure that had accumulated there over the years as gifts to Apollo to hire mercenaries. These professionals gradually wore down the Theban forces over the course of ten years. During the same time, Athens' reconstituted league disintegrated as members opposed Athenian attempts once more to convert a free association of states into an empire. By the 330s, all of the Greek states had proven themselves incapable of creating stable political units larger than their immediate polis.

Philosophy and the Polis

The failure of Greek political forms, oligarchy and democracy alike, profoundly affected Athenian philosophers. Plato (ca. 428–347 B.C.), an aristocratic student of Socrates, grew up during the Peloponnesian War and had witnessed the collapse of the empire, the brutality of the Thirty Tyrants, the execution of Socrates, and the revival of the democracy and its imperialistic ambitions. From these experiences he developed a hatred for Athenian democracy and a profound distrust of ordinary people's ability to tell right from wrong. Disgusted with public life, Plato left Attica for a time and traveled in Sicily and Italy, where he encountered different forms of government and different philosophical schools. Around 387 B.C., he returned to Athens and opened the Academy, a school to provide Athenian youth with what he considered to be knowledge of what was true and good for the individual and the state.

Plato chose a most unlikely literary form for transmitting his teachings. He used the dialogue, in the form of discussions between his teacher, Socrates, and a variety of students and opponents, to develop his ideas. While Plato shared with his mentor the conviction that human actions had to be grounded in self-knowledge, Plato's philosophy extended much further. His arguments about the inadequacy of all existing forms of government and the need to create a new form of government through the proper education of elite philosopher rulers were part of a complex understanding of the universe and the individual's place in it. (See Special Feature, "The First Utopia, pp. 88–89.)

Plato argued that true knowledge is impossible as long as it focuses on the constantly changing, imperfect world of everyday experience. Real knowledge can only be of that which is eternal, perfect, and beyond the experience of the senses, the realm of what Plato calls the Forms. When we judge that individuals or actions are true or good or beautiful, we do so not because these particular persons or events are truly virtuous, but because we recognize that they participate in some way in the Idea or Form of truth or goodness or beauty. Consistent with Socrates' insistence on looking within oneself, Plato argues that we rec-

Roman copy of a Greek statue of Aristotle. Many ancient Greek sculptures are known to us only through Roman copies.

only to the extent to which it participates in the Forms.

The evils of the world and in particular the vices and failures of government and society result from ignorance of the truth. Most people live as though chained in a cave in which all they can see are the shadows cast by a fire on the walls. In their ignorance, they mistake these flickering, imperfect images for reality. Their proper ruler must be a philosopher, one who is not deceived by the shadows. The philosopher's task is to break their chains and turn them toward the source of the light so that they can see the world as it really is. Ultimately, the philosopher will lead them from the cave to see the ultimate source of light, the sun outside. Truth will make them free.

Plato's idealist view (in the sense of the Ideas or Forms) of knowledge dominated much of ancient philosophy. His greatest student, Aristotle (384–322 B.C.), however, rejected this view in favor of a philosophy rooted in the natural world. Aristotle came from a medical family of northern Greece and, although a student in Plato's Academy for almost twenty years, he never abandoned observation for speculation. Systematic investigation and explanation characterize Aristotle's vast work, and his interests ranged from biology to statecraft to the most abstract philosophy. In each field, he employed essentially the same method. He observed as many individual examples of the topic as possible and from these specific observations extracted general theories. His theories, whether on the nature of matter, the species of animals, the working of the human mind, ethics, or the proper form of the state, are distinguished by clarity of logical thinking, precision in the use of terminology, and respect for the world of experience. While ready to acknowledge his debt to Plato and other thinkers whose books he collected and read with great interest, he remained steadfastly opposed to Plato's Forms. For Aristotle, understanding of this world remains basic, and no valid theory can make it unintelligible.

Aristotle brought this approach to the question of life in society. He defined humans as "political animals," that is, animals particularly characterized by life in the polis. He analyzed over 150 city constitutions in order to find what con-

ognize these Forms, not in the object itself, but within our memories, memories of a previous existence when our spirits or souls had direct contact with the universe of the Forms. Thus all knowledge is recollection, and everything exists

The First Utopia

If the Greeks were fixated on good government, it might be because they had seen so many examples of bad. The bewildering variety of political forms that replaced the tyrants of the sixth century B.C. had proved no better than the evil they had sought to correct. By the end of the fourth century B.C., Lysander's brutal rule disillusioned many about the advantages of the Spartan mixture of monarchy, oligarchy, and democracy. The oligarchy of Corinth and the federalism of Thebes proved no better. And the radical democracy of Athens had brought disaster not only to the city but to all of Greece.

Aristotle and Plato each tackled the problem according to his own philosophical inclinations. Aristotle, ever the empiricist, collected over 150 city constitutions, which he hoped to analyze in order to discover the best form of government. His teacher Plato would have thought such an exercise a waste of time. To Plato, all existing constitutions were bad. No place had the perfect form of government. He thus set about in his *Republic* to describe the constitution of "no place" (in Greek, *utopia*, a term coined over eighteen hundred years later), the ideal government.

In his description, Plato tackles the ultimate problem of politics: how should the state be ordered? His answer is a disturbing and fascinating image of a just society, created by a philosopher king and ruled by a hand-picked body of Guardians.

Plato's ideal state resembles the Greek polis in size. A relatively small, territorially limited state is all that he can imagine. It is populated by four groups of people: slaves, craftsmen, auxiliaries, and Guardians. The first group is implied but never discussed. Plato, like any other Greek, could not have imagined a society existing without slave labor. The bulk of the citizens are farmers, craft workers, and tradesmen, each specializing in that form of economic activity for which he or she is most suited. They are the only property owners in the republic, form the basis of its prosperity, and lead lives much like those of the ordinary citizens of a Greek polis, except that they have no role in defense or government.

The third group, in part self-perpetuating, in part recruited from the most promising children of the first, are the auxiliaries, who devote themselves exclusively to protecting the state from internal and external dangers. Auxiliaries are made, not born, and the program of education outlined by Plato is the critical ingredient in his ideal state. Boys and girls destined to be auxiliaries (equality of the sexes is fundamental in the republic) must be trained to know what is true and good and must be protected from lies and deception. Thus Plato bans poets and dramatists from his educational program. After all, Homer, Hesiod, Aeschylus, and Sophocles clothe fictions about the immorality of the gods and men in language of great beauty. Instead, the auxiliaries will be taught music and lyric poetry to instill in them a love of the harmony and order of the world. They also undertake physical training appropriate for soldiers, which not only prepares them for battle but, like music, develops the proper harmony of body and soul.

The auxiliaries must be free of private interests or ambitions, which would distract them from the needs of the state. Thus, they must live without private property or private family. Their needs are to be provided for by the craftsman class, making it unnecessary and impossible for the auxiliaries to amass anything of their own. Because family concerns might distract them from their duty, they must live in a garrisonlike arrangement. Rulers would select appropriate male and female auxiliaries to mate and produce the best offspring. The children of such unions would be brought up together, regarding themselves and the adult auxiliaries as one large family identical with state.

The best of these children, distinguished by their intellectual and moral ability, are to be selected as rulers or Guardians. They undergo further education in the exact sciences and logic to train them to recognize the fundamental principles on which all truth depends. Finally, at the age of thirty-five, after years of study, a Guardian undertakes the hard task of governing, which Plato sees as a process of sharing with those less fortunate the enlightenment that education has given them.

Plato did not consider his republic an exercise in imagination. He firmly believed that it was practical and possible. The best means by which to establish it was by a philosopher-king, a ruler in whom "political power and philosophy meet together."

Plato's contemporaries as well as subsequent generations have been at once fascinated and horrified by this ideal state. For many, the idea of total equality of the sexes was too absurd to consider. For others, the abolition of the family or the banning of poetry went beyond the realm of reason. Aristotle thought that the effects of such a system would be the opposite of that Plato intended, creating dissension and rebellion rather than reducing them. Modern readers praise or condemn Plato's republic because it smacks of communism, thought control, and totalitarianism. The modern social philosopher Karl Popper, for example, has termed Plato's political demands "purely totalitarian and anti-humanitarian," and considers Plato the most determined enemy of freedom ever known. Goaded by Plato's challenge, political theorists ever since have taken up the task of devising their own image of the perfect society, seeking their own answer to Plato's challenge, "where shall we find justice?"

tributed to their successes and failures. Unlike Plato, he did not regard any particular form of government as ideal. Rather, he concluded that the type of government ultimately mattered less than the balance between narrow oligarchy and radical democracy. Consistent with his belief that "virtue lies in a mean," he advocated governments composed of citizens who were neither extremely wealthy nor extremely poor. Moderation was the key to stability and justice.

Aristotle's teaching had little effect on his most famous student, Alexander, the son of King Philip of Macedon. Nor apparently did Aristotle's firsthand observation of this traditional hereditary monarchy in northern Greece influence the philosopher's understanding of the realities of Greek politics. And yet, during the very years that Aristotle was teaching, the vacuum created by the failure of the Greek city-states was being filled by the dynamic growth of the Macedonian monarchy that finally ended a century of Greek warfare and with it, the independence of the Greek city-states.

The Rise of Macedon

The polis had never been the only form of the Greek state. Alongside the city-states of Athens, Corinth, Syracuse, and Sparta were more decentralized ethne ruled by traditional hereditary chieftains and monarchs. Macedonia, in the northeast of the mainland, was one such ethnos. Its kings, chosen by the army from within a royal family, ruled in cooperation with nobles and clan leaders. Kings enhanced their position by marrying a number of wives from among the families of powerful supporters and allies. The Macedonian people spoke a Greek dialect and Macedonian kings and elite identified with Greek culture and tradition. However, constant rivalry for the throne, relative impoverishment, and loose organization prevented the Macedonians from playing much of a role in the events and achievements of the fifth and sixth centuries B.C. Macedonia had, however, long served as a buffer between the barbarians to the north and the Greek mainland, and its tough farmers and pastoralists were geared to constant warfare. As Athens, Sparta, and Thebes fought each other to

mutual exhaustion, Macedonia under King Philip II (359–336 B.C.) moved into the resulting power vacuum.

Philip was called by a contemporary "the greatest man Europe had ever produced." If political acumen and military skill are the only criteria, he deserves the title. These Philip had in abundance, but his ambition exceeded them both. During his twenties he murdered his way to the throne (the usual Macedonian procedure) and set about consolidating his position at home and strengthening his influence abroad through military and diplomatic means. Philip showed a particular genius for rapidly organizing and leading armies and for conducting complex, multiple campaigns each year. He secured his borders against northern barbarians and captured the northern coast of the Aegean, including the gold and silver mines of Mount Pangaeus, which gave him a ready source of money for his campaigns. Then he turned his attention to the south.

In 346 B.C., Philip intervened in the war between Thebes and Phocis, ending that conflict but forcing himself into the center of Greek affairs. From then on he was relentless in his efforts to swallow up one Greek state after another. In spite of the powerful oratory of the Athenian statesman Demosthenes (384–322 B.C.), who recognized Philip's threat, the Greek states resisted uniting against Philip, and one by one they fell. In 338 B.C., Philip achieved a final victory at Chaeronea and established a new league, the League of Corinth. However, unlike all those that had preceded it, this league was no confederation of sovereign states. It was an empire ruled by a king and supported by wealthy citizens whose cooperation Philip rewarded well. This new model of government, a monarchy drawing its support from a wealthy elite, became a fixture of the Mediterranean world for over two thousand years.

Philip's success was based on his powerful military machine, which combined both Macedonian military tradition and the new mercenary forces that had emerged over the past century in Greece. The heart of his army was the infantry trained in the use of pikes some fourteen feet long, four feet longer than those of the Greek hoplites. Tribesmen from the Macedonian hills formed the core of this fighting force. Allies and Greek mercenaries, paid for with Mount Pangaeus gold, could swell their ranks to armies of over forty thousand. Macedonian phalanxes moved forward in disciplined ranks, pushing back their foes, whose shorter lances could not reach the Macedonians. When the enemy were contained, the Macedonian cavalry charged from the flank and cut them to pieces. The cavalry, composed of nobles and tribal chieftains, lived in close proximity to the king and felt tremendous personal loyalty to Philip. Known as the Royal Companions, they were the elite of Macedon and the greatest beneficiaries of Philip's conquests.

No sooner had Philip subdued Greece than he announced a campaign against Persia. He intended to lead a combined Greek force in a war of revenge and conquest to punish the great empire for its invasion of Greece 150 years earlier and its subsequent involvement in the Greek world. Before he could begin, however, he met the fate of his predecessors. At the age of forty-six he was cut down by an assassin's knife, leaving his twenty-year-old son, Alexander (336–323 B.C.), to lead the expedition. Within thirteen years Alexander conquered the world.

The Empire of Alexander the Great

Alexander was less affected by his teacher, the philosopher Aristotle, than he was by the poet Homer. Envisioning himself a new Achilles, Alexander sought to imitate and surpass that legendary warrior and hero of the *Iliad.* Shortly after moving his troops across the Hellespont from Europe to Asia, Alexander visited Troy, where he lay a wreath on the supposed tomb of his hero and took from a temple weapons said to have belonged to Achilles. These he had carried before him in all of his battles.

Alexander's military genius, dedication to his troops, reckless disregard for his own safety, and ability to move both men and supplies across vast distances at great speed inspired the war machine developed by Philip and led it on an odyssey of conquest that stretched from Asia Minor to India. In 334 B.C., the first year of his campaign, Alexander captured the Greek cities of Asia Minor. Then he continued east. At Gordium, according to legend, he confronted an ancient puzzle, a complex knot tied to the chariot of the ancient king of that city. Whoever could loosen the

The Empire of Alexander the Great

knot, the legend said, would become master of Asia. Alexander solved that puzzle, as he did all of his others, with his sword. Two months later he defeated the Persian king Darius III at Issus and then headed south toward the Mediterranean coast and Egypt. After his victories there, he turned again to the north and entered Mesopotamia. At Gaugamela in 331 B.C., he defeated Darius a second, decisive time. Shortly after, Darius was murdered by the remnants of his followers. Alexander captured the Persian capital of Persepolis with its vast treasure and became the undisputed ruler of the vast empire.

A partially guilded silver rhyton, or drinking vessel, is an example of Persian art. A horned griffin forms the base and lotus buds encircle the rim. Treasures such as this were looted from the Persians by Alexander's conquering army.

The conquest of Persia was not enough. Alexander pushed on, intending to conquer the whole world. His armies marched east, subduing the rebellious Asian provinces of Bactria and Sogdiana. He negotiated the Khyber Pass from modern Afghanistan into the Punjab, crossed the Indus River, and defeated the local Indian king. Everywhere he went he reorganized or founded cities, entrusting them to loyal Macedonians and other Greeks, settling there veterans of his campaigns, and then pushed on toward the unknown. At Bucephala on the Hydaspes River in modern Pakistan, his Macedonian warriors finally halted. Worn out by years of bloody conquest and exhausting travel, they refused to go further, even if Alexander himself were to lead them. "If there is one thing above all others a successful man should know," their spokesman told him, "it is when to stop." Furious but impotent, Alexander turned south, following the Indus River to its mouth in the hope that it might turn out to be an extension of the Nile encircling the earth. Upon reaching the Indian Ocean he at last turned west, leading his army across the barren Gedrosia desert and finally back to Persepolis in 324 B.C. No mortal had ever before accomplished such a feat. Even in his own lifetime, Alexander was venerated as a god.

Alexander is remembered as a greater conqueror than ruler, but his plans for his reign, had he lived to complete them, might have won him equal fame. Unlike his Macedonian followers who were interested mainly in booty and power, he recognized that only by merging local and Greek peoples and traditions could he forge a lasting empire. Thus, even while founding cities on the Greek model throughout his empire, he carefully respected the local social and cultural traditions of the conquered peoples. In fact, after his return from India, he executed many Macedonian governors found guilty of misrule or corruption. Alexander enlisted elite units of Persian youths to be trained in Macedonian-style warfare and traditions. At the same time he encouraged marriages between his companions and the daughters of local elites. In one mass ceremony at Susa thousands of his warriors married Persian women. Alexander himself led the way, marrying Darius' daughter Stateira just as he had previously married Roxane, daughter of the king of Bactria.

Classical Greece

525–456	B.C.	Aeschylus
ca. 500–ca. 430	B.C.	Phidias
496–406	B.C.	Sophocles
490	B.C.	Battle of Marathon
485–406	B.C.	Euripides
ca. 484–ca. 420	B.C.	Herodotus
480	B.C.	Battles of Thermopylae and Salamis
478	B.C.	Athens assumes control of Delian League
ca. 470–399	B.C.	Socrates
ca. 460–430	B.C.	Perikles dominates Athens
ca. 450–ca. 388	B.C.	Aristophanes
431–421; 414–404	B.C.	Peloponnesian War
ca. 428–347	B.C.	Plato
384–322	B.C.	Aristotle
384–322	B.C.	Demosthenes
338	B.C.	Philip of Macedon defeats Athens
336–323	B.C.	Reign of Alexander the Great

Whether his program of cultural and social amalgamation could have succeeded is a moot point. In 323 B.C., two years after his return from India, he died at Babylon at the age of thirty-two.

The empire did not outlive the emperor. Vicious fighting soon broke out among his generals and his kin. Alexander's wife Roxane and son Alexander IV (323–317 B.C.) were killed, as were all other members of the royal family. The various units of the empire broke apart into separate kingdoms and autonomous cities in which each ruler attempted to continue the political and cultural tradition of Alexander in a smaller sphere. Alexander's empire became a shifting kaleidoscope of states, kingdoms, and cities, dominated by priest-kings, native princelings, and territorial rulers, all vying to enhance their positions while preserving a relative balance of power. By 275 B.C., three large kingdoms dominated Alexander's former domain. The most stable was Egypt, which Ptolemy I (323–285 B.C.), one of Alexander's closest followers, acquired upon Alexander's death and which he and his descendants ruled until Cleopatra VII (51–30 B.C.) was defeated by the Roman Octavian in 31 B.C. In the east, the Macedonian general Seleucus (246–226 B.C.) captured Babylon in 312 B.C., and he and his descendants ruled a vast kingdom reaching from what is today western Turkey to Afghanistan. Whittled away in the east by both the Greek kingdom of Bactria and the non-Greek Parthians and in the west by the Greek Attalids in Pergamum, the Seleucid kingdom gradually shrank to a small region of northern Syria before it fell to Rome in 64 B.C. After fifty years of conflict, Antigonus Gonatas (276–239 B.C.), the grandson of another of Alexander's commanders, secured Macedon and Greece. His Antigonid successors ruled the kingdom until it fell to the Romans in 168 B.C.

The Hellenistic World

Although vastly different in geography, language, and custom, the Hellenistic kingdoms (so called to distinguish them from the Hellenic civilization of the fifth and early fourth centuries B.C.) shared two common traditions. First, great portions of the Hellenistic world, from Asia Minor to Bactria and south to Egypt, had been united at various times by the Assyrian and Persian empires. During these periods they had absorbed much of Mesopotamian civilization and in particular the administrative traditions begun by the Assyrian Tiglath-pileser. Thus the Hellenistic kings ruled kingdoms already accustomed to centralized government and could rely on the already existing machinery of tax collection and administration to control the countryside. For the most part, however, these kings had little interest in the native populations of their kingdoms beyond the amount of wealth that they could extract from them. Hellenistic monarchs remained Greek and lavished their attentions on the newly created Greek cities which absorbed vast amounts of the kingdom's wealth.

These cities and their particular form of Greek culture were the second unifying factor in the Hellenistic world. In the tradition of Alexander himself, the Ptolemys, Seleucids, and Antigonids cultivated Greek urban culture and recruited Greeks for their most important positions of responsibility. Alexander had founded over thirty-five cities during his conquests. The Seleucids established almost twice as many throughout their vast domain, even replacing the ancient city of Babylon with their capital, Seleucia, on the Tigris. In Egypt the Ptolemys replaced the ancient capital of Memphis with the new city of Alexandria. These cities became the centers of political control, economic consumption, and cultural diffusion throughout the Hellenistic world.

Urban Life and Culture

The Hellenistic kingdoms lived in a perpetual state of warfare with one another. Kings needed Greek soldiers, merchants, and administrators and competed with their rivals in offering Greeks all the comforts of home. Hellenistic cities were Greek in physical organization, constitution, and language. Each had an agora, or marketplace, that would not have been out of place in Attica. They boasted temples to the Greek gods and goddesses, theaters, baths, and most importantly, a *gymnasion*, or combination sports center and school. In the gymnasion young men competed in Greek sports and absorbed Greek poetry and philosophy just as did their cousins on the Peloponnesus. Sophocles' tragedies played to enthusiastic audiences in an enormous Greek theater in what is today Ai Khanoum on the Oxus River in Afghanistan, and the rites of Dionysus were celebrated in third-century B.C. Egypt with processions of satyrs, maenads, free wine for all, and a golden phallus 180 feet long. Since these Greeks were drawn from throughout the Greek-speaking world, in time a universal Greek dialect, *koinē*, became the common language of culture and business, similar to the Latin of the medieval West, the German of the Habsburg empire, or basic English in much of the world today.

For all their Greek culture, Hellenistic cities differed fundamentally from Greek cities and colonies of the past. Not only were they far larger than any earlier Greek cities, but their government and culture were different from other cities or colonies. Colonies had been largely independent poleis. The Hellenistic cities were never politically sovereign. The regional kings maintained firm control over the cities, even while working to attract Greeks from the mainland and the islands to them. On the one hand, this policy weakened the political significance of Greek life and culture. Politics was no longer the passion that it had been in the fifth and early fourth centuries B.C. In each city a council elected from among the Greek inhabitants was largely self-governing in domestic matters. However, while these cities were in theory democracies, kings firmly controlled city government, and participation in the city councils and magistracies became the affair of the wealthy.

On the other hand, the Hellenistic cities were much less closed than were the traditional poleis of the Hellenic world. There, citizenship had been largely restricted by birth and social identity had been determined by deme, tribe, and family. In the new cities of the east, Greeks from all over were welcomed as soldiers and administrators regardless of their city of origin. By the second century B.C., Greeks no longer identified themselves by their city of origin but as "Hellenes," that is, Greeks. Moreover, to a limited extent, native elites could, through the adoption of Greek language, culture, and traditions, become Greek themselves, an achievement that had been impossible for the metics of Athens, Corinth, or Sparta.

The great social and geographical mobility possible in the new cities extended to women as well as men. No longer important simply as transmitters of citizenship, women began to assume a greater role in the family, in the economy, and in public life. Marriage contracts, particularly in Ptolemaic Egypt, emphasized the theoretical equality of husband and wife. In one such contract, the wife was granted "mastery in common with (her husband) over all their possessions." The husband and wife were further enjoined to take no concubines or male or female

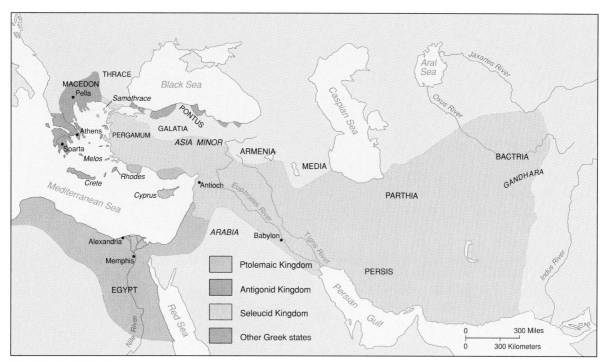

The Hellenistic Kingdoms

lovers. The penalty for the husband was loss of the wife's dowry; for the wife, the punishment was divorce.

Since women could control their own property, many engaged in business and some became wealthy. Wealth translated into civic influence and power. Phyle, a woman of the first century B.C. from Priene in Asia Minor, spent vast sums on a reservoir and aqueducts to bring water to her city. She was rewarded with high political office, as was a female archon in Histria on the Black Sea in the second century B.C.

The most powerful women in Hellenistic society were queens, especially in Egypt, where the Ptolemys adopted the Egyptian tradition of royal marriages between brothers and sisters. Four of the first eight Ptolemys married sisters in order to eliminate foreign dynastic influences in court. Arsinoë II (ca. 316–270 B.C.) ruled as an equal with her brother-husband Ptolemy II (286–246 B.C.) She inaugurated a tradition of powerful female monarchs that ended only with Cleopatra VII, the last independent ruler of Egypt, who

successfully manipulated the Roman generals Julius Caesar (100–44 B.C.) and Mark Antony (81–30 B.C.) to maintain Egyptian autonomy.

Just as monarchs competed with one another in creating Greek cities, they vied in making their cities centers of Greek culture. Socially ambitious and newly wealthy citizens supported poets, philosophers, and artists as a means of demonstrating their status. Queens, in particular, patronized poets and dramatists, and cities and wealthy individuals endowed gymnasia and libraries. The largest library was in Alexandria in Egypt, where the Ptolemys established the *Mouseion*, or Museum, as the house of the muses, the goddesses of the arts and literature. In time the library at Alexandria housed half a million book-rolls, including all of the great classics of Greek literature. In order to acquire still more, ships arriving in Alexandria were boarded and searched for books to copy. Generations of poet-scholars edited and commented on the classics, in the process inventing literary criticism and preserving much of what is known about classical authors.

Hellenistic writers were not simply book collectors or critics. They developed new forms of literature, including the romance, which often recounted imaginary adventures of Alexander the Great, and the pastoral poem, which the Sicilian Theocritus (ca. 310–250 B.C.) developed out of popular shepherd songs. Callimachus (ca. 305–ca. 240 B.C.), the cataloger of the library in Alexandria and royal tutor, was the acknowledged (and envied) master of the short, witty epigram. With equal skill he could poke fun at himself as a frustrated lover of boys and parties or move the reader with touching poems on his deceased friends.

Political rivalry also encouraged architectural and artistic rivalry, as kings competed for the most magnificent Hellenistic cities. Temples, porticoes, and public buildings grew in size and ornamentation. Architects experimented with multitiered buildings, combining traditional Doric and Ionian orders. In the Seleucid kingdom, the more flamboyant Corinthian order with its luxuriantly foliated capitals was especially popular. The Seleucid king Antiochus IV (176–165 B.C.) completed in the Corinthian order the great temple of Olympian Zeus in Athens, until Roman times the largest building in Europe.

Hellenistic architects not only developed more elaborate and monumental buildings, they also combined these buildings in harmonious urban ensembles. New cities presented unprecedented opportunities for urban planners and Hellenistic rulers provided the funds to undertake major urban renewal projects in older cities. In cities such as Rhodes and Pergamum, planners incorporated their constructions into the terrain, using natural hills and slopes to create elegant terraced vistas.

Freestanding statues and magnificent murals and mosaics adorned the public squares, temples, and private homes of Hellenistic cities. While artists continued the traditions of the Hellenic age, they displayed more freedom in portraying tension and restlessness as well as individuality in the human form. Little remains of Hellenistic painting, although Roman mosaics such as that of Alexander at Issus suggest the virtuosity with which mural painters managed multifigure compositions, perspective, and realistic portrayal of landscapes. Sculptors also demonstrated their skill in the portrayal of drapery tightly folded or falling naturally across the human form. The Nike (Victory) from Samothrace (ca. 200 B.C.) and the Aphrodite from Melos, known more commonly as the Venus de Milo (ca. 120 B.C.), are supreme examples of Hellenistic sculptural achievement.

The Nike, or Winged Victory, was found in fragments on the island of Samothrace in the Aegean Sea in 1863. The head and arms were never discovered. The statue is now in the Louvre Museum in Paris.

Hellenistic Philosophy

Philosophy, too, flourished in the Hellenistic world, but in directions different from those initiated by Plato and Aristotle, who were both deeply committed to political involvement in the free polis. Instead, Cynics, Epicureans, and Stoics turned inward, advocating types of morality less directly tied to the state and society. These philosophies appealed to the rootless Greeks of the Hellenistic east no longer tied by bonds of religion or patriotism to any community. Each philosophy was as much a way of life as a way of thought and offered different answers to the question of how the individual, cut loose from the security of traditional social and political networks, should deal with the whims of fate.

The Cynic tradition, established by Antisthenes (ca. 450–ca. 350 B.C.), a pupil of Socrates, and Diogenes of Sinope (d. ca. 320 B.C.), taught that excessive attachment to the things of this world was the source of evil and unhappiness. Individual freedom comes through renunciation of material things, society, and pleasures. The more one has, the more one is vulnerable to the whims of fortune. The Cynics' goal was to reduce their possessions, connections, and pleasures to the absolute minimum. "I would rather go mad than enjoy myself," Antisthenes said. The story was told that once, while Diogenes was sunning himself, Alexander the Great came to see the philosopher and, standing before him, offered to do for him anything that he desired. "Stand out of my sun," was Diogenes' reply.

Like the Cynics, the Epicureans sought freedom, but from pain rather than from the conventions of ordinary life. Epicurus (341–270 B.C.) and his disciples have often been attacked for their emphasis on pleasure ("You need only possess perception and be made of flesh, and you will see that pleasure is good," Epicurus wrote), but this search for pleasure was not a call to sensual indulgence. Pleasure must be pursued rationally. Today's pleasure can mean tomorrow's suffering. The real goal is to reduce desires to that which is simple and attainable. Thus Epicureans urged retirement from politics, retreat from public competition, and concentration instead on friendship and private enjoyment. Epicurus'

Hellenistic bronze statue of a veiled dancer from the third century B.C. The figure is a remarkable example of the effect created by the treatment of flowing draperies, which was a hallmark of the art of the Hellenistic period.

garden became a tranquil retreat for himself and his disciples. For Epicurus, reason properly applied illuminates how best to pursue pleasure. The universe is entirely material, consisting of atoms, and the gods have no interest or role in this world. Alone, humans must search for their pleasure through reason, which will make them free. The traditional image of the Epicurean as an indulgent sensualist is a gross caricature. As Epicurus advised one follower, an Epicurean "revels in the pleasure of the body—on a diet of bread and water."

The Stoics also followed nature, but rather than leading them to retire from public life, it led them to greater participation in it. Just as the universe is a system in which stars and planets move according to fixed laws, so too is human society ordered and unified. As the founder of Stoicism, Zeno (ca. 335–ca. 263 B.C.), expressed it, "All men should regard themselves as members of one city and people, having one life and order." Every person has a role in the divinely ordered universe, and all roles are of equal value. True happiness consists in freely accepting one's role, whatever it may be, while unhappiness and evil result from attempting to reject one's place in the divine plan. Stoic virtue consists in applying reason to one's life in such a way that one knowingly lives in conformity to nature. Worldly pleasures, like worldly pain, have no particular value. Both are to be accepted and endured.

All three philosophical traditions emphasized the importance of reason and the proper understanding of nature. Hellenistic understanding of nature was one area in which Greek thinkers were influenced by the ancient Oriental traditions brought to them through the conquests of Alexander. Particularly for mathematics, astronomy, and engineering, the Hellenistic period was a golden age.

Mathematics and Science

Ptolemaic Egypt became the center of mathematical studies. Euclid (ca. 300 B.C.), whose *Elements* was the fundamental textbook of geometry until the twentieth century, worked there, as did his student Apollonius of Perga (ca. 262–ca. 190 B.C.), whose work on conic sections is one of the greatest monuments of geometry. Both Apollonius and his teacher were as influential for their method as for their conclusions. Their treatises follow rigorous logical proofs of mathematical theorems, which established the form of mathematical reasoning to the present day. Archimedes of Syracuse (ca. 287–212 B.C.) corresponded with the Egyptian mathematicians and made additional contributions to geometry, such as the calculation of the approximate value of pi, as well as to mechanics, arithmetic, and engineering. Archimedes was famous for his practical application of engineering, particularly to warfare, and legends quickly grew up about his marvelous machines with which he helped Syracuse

defend itself against Rome. Although it was not true, as reported, that the rumor of him on the city's walls was sufficient to cause the Roman fleet to flee in terror, such traditions indicate the esteem in which applied science was held in the Hellenistic world.

Many mathematicians, such as Archimedes and Apollonius, were also mathematical astronomers, and the application of their mathematical skills to the exact data collected by earlier Babylonian and Egyptian empirical astronomers greatly increased the understanding of the heavens and earth. Archimedes devised a means of measuring the diameter of the sun, and Eratosthenes of Cyrene (ca. 276–194 B.C.) calculated the circumference of the earth to within two hundred miles. Aristarchus of Samos (ca. 270 B.C.) theorized that the sun and fixed stars were motionless and that the earth moves around the sun. His theory, unsupported by mathematical evidence and not taking into account the elliptical nature of planetary orbits or their nonuniform speeds, was rejected by contemporaries. Hipparchus of Nicea (ca. 146–127 B.C.) offered an alternative theory, placing the earth at the center of the universe. Backed by more mathematically acceptable arguments, his system remained, with slight adjustments made three hundred years later by Ptolemy of Alexandria, the dominant theory until the sixteenth century.

Like astronomy, Hellenistic medicine combined theory and observation. In Alexandria, Herophilus of Chalcedon (ca. 270 B.C.) and Erasistratus of Ceos (ca. 260 B.C.) conducted important studies in human anatomy. The Ptolemaic kings provided them with condemned prisoners whom they dissected alive and thus were able to observe the functioning of the organs of the body. The terrible agonies inflicted on their experimental subjects were considered to be justified by the argument that there was no cruelty in causing pain to guilty men to seek remedies for the innocent.

For all of the vitality of the Hellenistic civilization, these cities remained parasites on the local societies. No real efforts were made to merge the two and to develop a new civilization. Some ambitious members of the indigenous elites tried to adopt the customs of the Greeks, while others plotted insurrection. The clearest example of these conflicting tensions was that of the Jewish community. Early in the second century B.C., a powerful Jewish faction, which included the High Priest of Yahweh, supported hellenization. With the assistance of the Seleucid king, this faction set up a gymnasion in Jerusalem where Jewish youths and even priests began to study Greek and participate in Greek culture. Some even underwent painful surgery to reverse the effects of circumcision so that they could pass for Greeks in naked athletic contests. This rejection of tradition infuriated a large portion of the Jewish population. When the Seleucids finally attempted to introduce pagan cults into the temple in 167 B.C., open rebellion broke out and continued intermittently until the Jews gained independence in 141 B.C.

This violent opposition was repeated elsewhere from time to time, especially in Egypt and Persia, where, as in Judea, old traditions of religion and monarchy provided rallying points against the transplanted Greeks. In time the Hellenistic kingdoms' inability to bridge the gap between Greek and indigenous populations proved fatal. In the East, the non-Greek kingdom of Parthia replaced the Seleucids in much of the old Persian empire. In the West, continuing hostility between kingdoms and within kingdoms prepared the way for their progressive absorption by the new power to the west: Rome.

In the fifth century B.C., the rugged slopes, fertile plains, and arid islands of the Greek world developed characteristic forms of social, political, and cultural organization that have reappeared in varying forms wherever Western civilization has taken root. In Athens, which emerged from the ruins of the Persian invasion as the most powerful and dynamic state in the Hellenic world, the give-and-take of a direct democracy challenged men to raise fundamental questions about the relationship between individual and society, freedom and absolutism, gods and mortals. At the same time, this society of free males excluded the majority of its inhabitants— women, foreigners, and slaves—from participation in government and fought a long and ultimately futile war to hold together an exploitative empire.

The interminable wars among Greek states ultimately left the Greek world open to conquest by a powerful, semi-Greek monarchy that went on to spread Athenian culture throughout the known world. Freed from the particularism of individual city-states, Hellenistic culture became a universal tradition emphasizing the individual rather than the community of family, tribe, or religious association. And yet, this universal Hellenistic cultural tradition remained a thin veneer, hardly assimilated into the masses of the ancient world. Its proponents, except for Alexander the Great, never sought a real synthesis of Greek and barbarian tradition. Such a synthesis would only begin with the coming of Rome.

Suggestions for Further Reading

General Reading

John Boardman, Jasper Griffin, and Oswyn Murray, *Greece and the Hellenistic World* (New York: Oxford University Press, 1988). An excellent, up-to-date survey of Greek history by a series of experts.

* Michel M. Austin and Pierre Vidal-Naquet, *Economic and Social History of Ancient Greece* (Berkeley, CA: University of California Press, 1977). An excellent survey of Greek society.

Cambridge Ancient History, 2d ed., Vols. 5 (1989) and 7 (1984). Contains essays on most aspects of Greek history.

* Simon Hornblower, *The Greek World, 479–323 B.C.* (New York: Routledge, Chapman & Hall, 1983). An up-to-date survey concentrating on political history.

War and Politics in the Fifth Century

John Manuel Cook, *The Persian Empire* (New York: Schocken Books, 1983). The standard history of Persia from the perspective of history and archaeology.

R. Meiggs, *The Athenian Empire* (New York: Oxford University Press, 1979). The standard account.

P. J. Rhodes, *The Athenian Empire* (1985). A short summary.

* A. H. M. Jones, *Athenian Democracy* (Baltimore, MD: Johns Hopkins University Press, 1957). A collection of essays by a major traditional historian.

* M. I. Finley, *Democracy Ancient and Modern*, 2d ed. (New Brunswick, NJ: Rutgers University Press, 1985). A valuable essay on Athenian democracy by a leading historian of antiquity.

W. R. O'Connor, *The New Politicians of Fifth-Century Athens* (Princeton, NJ: Princeton University Press, 1971).

* Indicates paperback edition available.

Reappraises the demagogues within the context of Athenian political life.

A. W. Gomme, *Historical Commentary on Thucydides*, 5 volumes (New York: Oxford University Press, 1945–80). The fundamental study of the sources.

G. E. M. de St. Croix, *The Origins of the Peloponnesian War* (Ithaca, NY: Cornell University Press, 1972). An interpretation of the Peloponnesian War broader than the title indicates.

* David M. Schaps, *Economic Rights of Women in Ancient Greece* (New York: Columbia University Press, 1979). An examination of the roles of women in Greek society, focusing on property rights.

* W. K. Lacey, *The Family in Classical Greece* (Ithaca, NY: Cornell University Press, 1984). Ordinary life in the Greek world.

Renate Bridenthal and Claudia Koonz, eds., *Becoming Visible: Women in European History*, 2d ed. (Boston: Houghton Mifflin, 1988). Includes essays on women in classical Greece.

Eva C. Keuls, *The Reign of the Phallus: Sexual Politics in Ancient Athens* (New York: Harper & Row, 1985). A controversial history of sexual relations in Athens.

* Yvon Garlan, *Slavery in Ancient Greece* (Ithaca, NY: Cornell University Press, 1988). A recent study of Greek slavery.

Athenian Culture

* W. K. C. Guthrie, *History of Greek Philosophy*, Vol. 3 (New York: Cambridge University Press, 1971). Covers the Sophists.

I. Crombie, *An Examination of Plato's Doctrines*, 2 vols. (Atlantic Highlands, NJ: Humanities Press International, 1963). A safe guide into works on Plato.

* G. E. R. Lloyd, *Aristotle: The Growth and Structure of His Thought* (New York: Cambridge University Press, 1968). A developmental approach to Aristotle.

W. Burkert, *Greek Religion* (Cambridge, MA: Harvard University Press, 1985). General survey of the topic.

* J. Boardman, *Greek Art*, 3d ed. (New York: Thames & Hudson, 1985). A handbook introduction by period.

* Simon Goldhill, *Reading Greek Tragedy* (New York: Cambridge University Press, 1986). A general introduction to Athenian tragedy.

From City-States to Macedonian Empire

G. Cawkwell, *Philip of Macedon* (Boston: Faber & Faber, 1978). A political biography of the Macedonian king.

* A. B. Bosworth, *Conquest and Empire* (New York: Cambridge University Press, 1988). A scholarly but readable account of Alexander the Great.

R. L. Fox, *Alexander the Great* (New York: Dial, 1973). Lively recent biography.

The Hellenistic World

* R. W. Walbank, *The Hellenistic World* (Cambridge, MA: Harvard University Press, 1981). General overview.

P. M. Fraser, *Ptolemaic Alexandria* (New York: Oxford University Press, 1972). Especially good on Hellenistic literature in Egypt.

A. A. Long, *Hellenistic Philosophy* (Wolfeboro, NH: Longman Publishing Group, 1974). On Hellenistic thought.

* J. J. Pollitt, *Art in the Hellenistic Age* (New York: Cambridge University Press, 1986). A recent survey.

J. Barnes et al., *Science and Speculation* (New York: Cambridge University Press, 1982). A collection of papers on Hellenistic science.

Early Rome

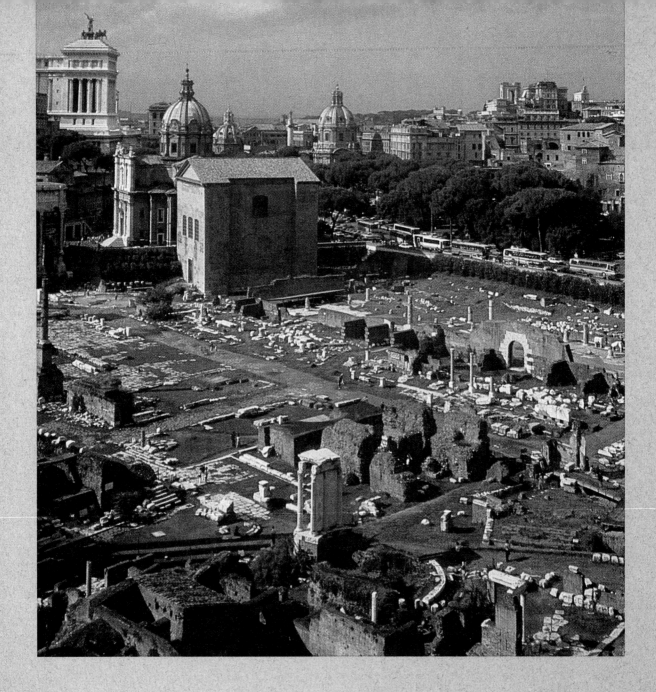

Eternal Rome

Five miles from its mouth, the Tiber River snakes in a lazy S around the first highlands that rise from the marshes of central Italy. These weathered cliffs, separated by tributary streams, look down on the river valley that broadens to over a mile and a half wide, the first and only natural ford for many miles. Only three promontories, the Capitol, Palatine, and Aventine, are separate hills. The others, the Quirinal, Viminal, Caelian,

Oppian, and Esquiline, are actually spurs of the distant Apennines. Gradually the pastoral villages founded on these hills spread down to the valleys between them, united, and grew to a city whose name for over two thousand years was synonymous with empire.

Rome wasn't built in a day. The earliest Roman villages were found on the Palatine, from whose heights the picture was taken and which remained throughout Rome's history the favored residential area. Here first Latin shepherds erected their crude huts and then republican senators built their homes. Later, emperors built on its slopes their increasingly splendid residences until the term *palace* became synonymous with the seat of royalty. The Capitol with its steep cliffs, which begin at the extreme left of the photograph, served as an acropolis, the religious center of the community. Here were found not only temples but also the state archives and the city mint beside the temple of Juno the Admonisher, *Juno Moneta*, hence our word for money. The Capitol, so the Romans thought, was indestructible and became a symbol of the eternal city. As Romans established colonies across Italy and throughout the Mediterranean, the colonies too had their hill temples, their so-called capitols.

The area shown in the center of the photograph between the Palatine and Capitol was originally a low, marshy burial ground. In the seventh century B.C., Etruscan kings drained the marshes, making it possible to pave the area between and turn it into a public meeting place, or forum. The Forum became the heart of the city. Through it ran the Sacred Way, the road that cuts diagonally from left to right in the photograph. At the south end, to the right of the photograph, was the marketplace, which bustled with shops and businesses. To the north, where the domed church of Saints Luca and Magartina now stand, was the *Comitium*, the meeting place of the citizens' assembly. Here the king and, in republican times, the popular assembly conducted political business. Just below it still stands the *Curia*, the meeting place of the Roman Senate, which survived because it was converted into a Christian church in the seventh century A.D.

Here too temples and monuments rose to meet religious and public needs. Perhaps the most ancient structure was the circular temple of Vesta, the hearth goddess, the surviving columns of which can be seen in the lower center of the photograph. In this temple consecrated virgins, the most honored women of Rome, tended the sacred fire, the symbol of the life of Rome. The ruins of the virgins' magnificent residence fill the lower right of the photograph. Just above it stood the royal residence, the *Regia*, which during the Republic came to be the quarters of one of Rome's chief priests, the *pontifex maximus*. To the lower right stood the temple to the twin gods Castor and Pollux, who were credited with bringing victory in the early days of the Republic against Rome's Latin neighbors. In, time, still other temples joined these, for honoring the gods and honoring Rome were one.

As Rome grew from a simple city to an empire, the Forum reflected these changes. Simple Etruscan architecture gave way to the Greek style of building. Marble replaced brick and stucco. Near the Curia, the golden milestone marked the point from which all distances were measured and to which all roads of the empire led. The turmoil of the last years of the Republic also left its mark. In the center of the picture the semicircular brown stone ruin is all that remains of the temple of the Divine Julius, erected on the spot where Julius Caesar's remains were cremated after his murder on the Ides of March. After his death, Caesar received divine honors, the first Roman to be so treated by his city. Next to the temple stands all that remains of the monumental arch of Caesar's adopted son, Octavian, known to history as Augustus, the first and greatest of the Roman emperors.

By the time of Caesar and Augustus, Rome had replaced its Forum, just as it had replaced its republican constitution. Caesar had begun and Augustus completed new forums, known collectively as the Forum of the Caesars, which lay beyond the trees at the top of the picture. Their successor Trajan (A.D. 98–117) would build a still greater one just beyond it. Still, for centuries of Romans and for the Western societies that succeeded them, the narrow space encompassing the Capitoline, Palatine, and the Forum was the epicenter of the city and the world.

The Western Mediterranean

Civilization came late to the western Mediterranean, carried in the ships of Greeks and Phoenicians. While the great floodplain civilizations of Mesopotamia and Egypt and the Greek communities of the eastern Mediterranean were developing sophisticated systems of urban life and political organization, western Europe and Africa knew only the scattered villages of simple farmers and pastoralists. These populations, such as the Ligurians of northern Italy, were the descendants of Neolithic peoples only remotely touched by the developments in the East. The West was, however, rich in metals, and an indigenous Bronze Age culture developed slowly between 1500 and 1000 B.C., spreading widely north of the Alps and south into Italy and Spain. By the twelfth century B.C., workshops in northern Italy were producing bronze spearheads, swords, and axes both for local use and for export to Crete, Naxos, Corfu, and Mycenae. At the same time, southern Italians were importing bronze knives and ornaments from Greece. In addition to finished weapons and other objects, the eastern cities sought in Italy and Spain unworked bronze, silver bullion, tin, and iron.

Hut-shaped impasto funerary urn from Vulci in Italy, dating from the ninth century B.C. Such urns were used by the Villanovans to hold the ashes of the dead.

The western shores of the Mediterranean did not escape the widespread crisis of the twelfth century B.C., which transformed so profoundly the established civilizations of Mycenae and the Near East, but its exact effects on the West are unknown. Sometime around the year 1000 B.C., a new, distinctive iron-using civilization first appeared in northern Italy. These Villanovans, so called for a major archaeological discovery of this civilization at Villanova near Bologna, differed from earlier Italian peoples in their use of iron, in the practice of cremating their dead and burying their ashes in large urns, and in the greater size and complexity of their settlements.

No one knows whether the Villanovans were new arrivals in Italy or simply the descendants of previous inhabitants. However, around this same time small groups of warrior peoples did begin to infiltrate Italy from the east and the north, occupying the mountainous terrain of the Apennines and pushing the indigenous society west. These new arrivals shared no common organization or identity, but all spoke related Indo-European languages we call Italic, including Latin. These newcomers were warriors, and their steady progress is marked by the appearance of their distinctive form of burial, in which their dead were cremated and buried with weapons. This practice contrasted with the urn burials of the earlier inhabitants. Like the Dark Age Greeks, these peoples soon developed the art of making iron weapons, which gave them a decided advantage over the older inhabitants of the peninsula. By 800 B.C., they were in firm control of the mountainous region of central Italy and threatened the coastal societies of the West and South.

Merchants of Baal

Also around 800 B.C., Phoenicians arrived in the West, first as traders and then as colonists. Phoenicians were known as the best seafarers of antiquity and the most ruthless. Setting out in warships from the regions of Tyre, Sidon, and Byblos, they ventured beyond the Straits of Gibraltar in search of supplies of silver and tin. They established a trading post at Cadiz (Gadir, "walled place" in Phoenician) at which they could trade with the local inhabitants for silver from

The Western Mediterranean

the Sierra Morena and tin, which the Spanish (Iberians) obtained from distant Britain and Ireland. Because sailing vessels hugged the coastline whenever possible rather than braving the open sea, the Phoenicians established a series of bases along the route to and from Spain on the coast and on the islands of Corsica and Sicily. There Phoenician ships on their way to and from Cadiz could find safe harbor, food, and supplies. Phoenicians established bases on the islands of Ibiza and Motya in the Mediterranean, at Panormus on Sicily, and at Utica and Carthage on the coast of North Africa. Carthage was initially no more than a small anchorage for ships. Gradually, its population grew as overcrowding forced emigration from Tyre. When, in the sixth century B.C., Tyre was conquered by Nebuchadnezzar and incorporated into the Babylonian empire, Carthage became an independent city and soon established itself as the center of an expanding Phoenician presence in the western Mediterranean.

The city was perfectly situated to profit both from the land and the sea. Its excellent double harbor, which had attracted the Phoenicians ini-

tially, made it an ideal port. Here ships could lie at rest, protected from storms as well as from enemies by a narrow, seventy-foot entrance to the sea which could be closed with iron chains. In good weather, captains could anchor their ships outside of the harbor proper along a pier some three hundred yards long. The city was equally protected on land, situated on a narrow isthmus and surrounded by massive walls over forty feet high and thirty feet thick. As long as Carthage controlled the sea, its commercial center was secure from any enemies.

The wealth of Punic (from *Puni* or *Poeni*, the Roman name for the Carthaginians) commerce was supplemented by the agricultural riches of the surrounding region. The fertile coastal plain produced grain and fruits for export in abundance, while inland the subject native population engaged in cattle raising and sheep herding for their masters.

By the middle of the sixth century B.C., Carthage was the center of a real empire. But in contrast with the Athenian empire of the following century, that of Carthage was much more successful at integrating other cities and peoples into its military and thus sharing the burden of warfare. Carthaginian mercenary armies consisted of Libyan light infantry, Numidian cavalry, Spanish hill people, Balearic sling throwers, Gallic infantry, Italians, and often Greeks. Only the fleet was composed primarily of Carthaginians. This multiethnic empire proved far more stable than any of those created by the Greeks, succeeding in victory and withstanding defeat to endure for over three centuries.

Carthage was governed by a mixed constitution that combined elements of monarchical, aristocratic, and popular rule. The assembly of citizens annually elected the heads of state. In spite of the role of the free citizenry in their selection, however, these officials consistently came from among the wealthy and powerful merchant aristocracy. They presided over the popular assembly and the smaller, aristocratic senate, and dispensed justice. In their governmental tasks these officials were assisted by "judges," actually a select body of magistrates chosen from the senate who had broad judicial and administrative responsibility.

As a society of merchants, Carthaginians mistrusted military leaders and carefully separated military authority from civil. Generals were elected and served open-ended terms. Because almost all of Carthage's wars were conducted far from home, using mercenaries or citizens of subject cities, selection of commanders was often based more on the aristocracy's concern to avoid giving too much power to ambitious, capable leaders than to select the best soldiers. Unlike commanders in Greek states, successful generals found themselves more distrusted than honored by their fellow citizens.

Although superficially similar to many Greek cities, the Punic state differed profoundly in the relationship between citizen and state. Compared with that of the Greek states, Punic popular politics has been termed essentially apolitical. In spite of the formal role of the assembly, ordinary citizens had little involvement and, apparently, little interest in government. Unlike the Greeks, they normally did not serve in the military and thus did not develop a sense of solidarity and involvement in the state. According to Aristotle,

The influence of Carthaginian culture throughout the western Mediterranean area is seen in this terra-cotta female figurine, found in Spain and dating from about the fourth century B.C.

the aristocracy treated the rest of the population generously, sharing with it profits in the exploitation of its commercial and imperial wealth. Thus the kinds of class pressures that created the Greek tyrants never emerged in Carthage.

This traditional, conservative perspective of Carthaginian government was also evident in

Carthaginian religion. The gods of Carthage were local variations of the Phoenician gods, especially Baal Hammon, the supreme god El of the Semitic world, and the goddess Tanit, a version of the Near Eastern goddess Asherat. Baal Hammon was an awesome figure. The Greeks equated him not with Zeus but with the more ancient supreme god, Kronos, a cruel tyrant who devoured his children. Tanit, goddess of fertility, assumed an importance equal to that of Baal Hammon, probably under the influence of the indigenous Libyan society. Submission of humans to the will of the gods and the appeasing of the deities through human sacrifice characterized Carthaginian religion.

According to hostile Greek and Roman sources, all Carthaginian citizens were obligated to sacrifice their firstborn sons and the sacrifice of children constituted the most important and, to their Greek and barbarian neighbors, the most repulsive aspect of Punic culture. The basic reliability of these reports was dramatically confirmed in 1922, when archaeologists excavated the sanctuary of Tanit at Salammbo, site of the earliest Punic settlement. It was found to contain urns filled with the remains of hundreds of children. Other similar sacred sites have since been found. While some scholars have suggested that these are simply infant burial sites, the gradual appearance of animal bones mixed in with those of children in levels from the fourth century B.C. and then, in the level from the following century, the appearance of only animal remains, indicates that child sacrifice did indeed take place, only gradually disappearing toward the end of Carthaginian history.

Stable, prosperous, and devout, Carthage was the master of the western Mediterranean. But its dominion was not undisputed. From the sixth century B.C., the Punic empire felt the pressure of ambitious and expansive Greek cities eager to gain a share of the West's riches.

The Western Greeks

The Greek arrival in the West was the result of a much more complex process than the trading policy of the Phoenicians. As we saw in chapter 2, toward the end of the Dark Age, commerce, over-population, and civic tension sent Greek colonists out in all directions. In the eighth century B.C., Crete, Rhodes, Corinth, Argos, Chalcis, Eretria, and Naxos all established colonies in Sicily and southern Italy. One of the earliest of these colonies, Cumae on the Bay of Naples, began like Cadiz as a trading post. There Corinthians could trade for copper ore from Etruria and Campania. Other colonies such as Catane, Leontini, Tarentum, Sybaris, and Messina were primarily agricultural.

In the seventh century B.C., Syracuse became the greatest city of Sicily and one of the most prosperous cities of the Greek world. Greek colonies spread slowly up the boot of Italy, known as Greater Greece, in pursuit of trade and arable land. Initially, this expansion posed no problem for the Phoenicians and Carthaginians, who concentrated primarily on the Spanish and African coasts. But by the last quarter of the seventh century B.C., the autonomous Greek colonies began to encroach on the Carthaginian empire's sphere of influence. Around 631 B.C., Greeks from Thera founded a colony at Cyrene in North Africa. The Greek city of Phocaea in Asia Minor established a colony at Marseilles around 600 B.C. and began to trade down the coast of Spain.

Etruscan gold jewelry from the seventh century B.C., found in a tomb in Cerveteri. Eastern influence is evident in the motif of the Mistress of the Animals and other elements of the design.

Both commercial rivalry and open warfare characterized the relationship between Greeks and Phoenicians in the western Mediterranean. In the course of the sixth century B.C., Greeks in Sicily attempted to expel the Phoenicians from the island. In the fifth century B.C., Syracuse, under its tyrant Gelon (ca. 540–478 B.C.), threatened both Punic and Greek cities on the island. In an attempt to defend its colonies, in 480 B.C. Carthage launched an enormous force to support Gelon's Greek enemies. The attack took place, probably not coincidentally, at the same moment that Xerxes invaded Greece. At the battle of Himera, fought, we are told, on the same day as the battle of Salamis, the Syracusans soundly defeated the Carthaginians. The Carthaginian commander, in a fruitless attempt to summon Baal to his aid, is said to have thrown himself into a sacrificial fire and perished.

Gelon's victory at Himera ushered in a period of prosperity and cultural achievement in Sicily only slightly less extraordinary than that which followed the battles of Marathon and Salamis in Greece. The tyrants of Syracuse, enriched with the spoils of victory, created a court whose magnificence, wealth, and generosity won the admiration of poets and admirers from throughout the Greek world. This prosperity continued after the elimination of the tyranny in mid-century, and in 415 B.C., Syracuse was able to withstand Athens' attempt at conquest (see chapter 3, p. 77).

A far more serious threat appeared in 410 B.C., when a new Carthaginian army arrived in Sicily seeking revenge. The Carthaginians rapidly captured and destroyed Himera, sacrificing three thousand prisoners on the site where the earlier commander had offered himself up, and extending the boundaries of Punic Sicily. This invasion initiated a century of inconclusive conflict between Syracuse and Carthage.

Early on in their struggle with the Sicilian Greeks, the Carthaginians found allies in the third major civilization of the West. These were the Etruscans, who in the seventh century B.C. dominated the western part of central Italy known as Etruria. The region today is Tuscany; its name derives from *Tusci*, the Roman name for this early people.

Italy's First Civilization

Etruscan civilization was the first great civilization to emerge in Italy. The Etruscans have long been regarded as a people whose origins, language, and customs are shrouded in mystery. Actually, the mystery is more apparent than real. The Greek historian Herodotus thought that the Etruscans had emigrated from Lydia in Asia Minor, and many historians, noting similarities between Etruscan and Eastern traditions, have subsequently accepted the thesis of Eastern origins. A second ancient tradition, reported by the Greek scholar Dionysius of Halicarnassus, is that the Etruscans did not emigrate from anywhere but rather had always been in western Italy. In recent years, archaeologists have demonstrated that this latter thesis is probably correct. The earliest materials from Etruscan sites indicate no break with the civilization of pre-Italic Villanovan Italy but rather a gradual development from it. Probably, just as in the Aegean, an indigenous cultural tradition was overwhelmed by the chaos of the twelfth-century B.C. crisis and the migration of Indo-Europeans from the north. This tradition shares much with Eastern civilizations, such as the importance of underworld gods, fertility cults, and the high status of women. Some scholars even speak of a common Mediterranean civilization submerged for a time but reemerging transformed centuries later.

Etruscan language is commonly seen as the second great mystery. Unlike the early Minoan writing, which was found to be early Greek written in an unknown script, Etruscan is written in an alphabet derived from that of Greece. Still, despite the derivation of the alphabet, the Etruscan language appears unrelated to any other language and even today some of the extant Etruscan texts remain incompletely deciphered. Bilingual inscriptions and careful analysis, however, have made it possible to read many of the extant Etruscan texts, and in the process the mysteries of the Etruscans have become much less mysterious.

Etruscan civilization coalesced slowly in Etruria over the course of the seventh century B.C. from diverse regional and political groups sharing a similar cultural and linguistic tradition. In the mid-sixth century B.C., in the face of Greek pressure from the south, twelve of these groups united in a religious and military confederation. Over the next hundred years, the confederation expanded north into the Po Valley and south to Campania, creating a loose Etruscan alliance that included almost all of the peninsula. Cities, each initially ruled by a king, were the centers of Etruscan civilization, and everywhere the Etruscans spread they either improved upon

On the Etruscan sarcophagus of Larthia Scianti a matron reclines as at a banquet. Much of our knowledge of this first Italian civilization comes from the elaborate paintings and statuary found in Etruscan cemeteries.

existing towns or founded new ones. Towns in the north included Bologna, Parma, Modena, Ravenna, Milan, and Mantua; in the south, there were Nola, Nuceria, Pompeii, Sorrento, and Salerno. The Etruscan confederation remained a loose one and, unlike that of the Carthaginians, never developed into a centralized empire. Etruscan kings assumed power in conquered towns, but between the sixth and fifth centuries B.C., Etruscan kingship gave way to oligarchic governments, much as Greek monarchies did a bit earlier. In the place of kings, aristocratic assemblies selected magistrates, often paired together or combined into "colleges" to prevent individuals from seizing power. These republican institutions provided the foundation for later Roman republican government.

The remnants of an ancient civilization, the Etruscans retained throughout their history social and cultural traditions long since vanished elsewhere in the Mediterranean. Society divided sharply into two classes, lords and servants. The lords' wealth was based on the rich agricultural regions of Etruria where grain grew in abundance and on the equally rich deposits of copper and iron. The vast majority of the population were actual slaves, working the lands and mines of the aristocracy.

The aristocrats were aggressive and imaginative landowners. They developed hydraulic systems for draining marshes, established a wine production famous throughout the Mediterranean, and put their slaves to work in mines and in smelting. Still, they were largely absentee landlords, spending much of their time in the towns that characterized Etruscan civilization. These cities, with their massive walls, enclosed populations of as many as twenty thousand. Etruscans built largely in wood, so little remains of their houses, temples, and public buildings. However, their extensive cemeteries have preserved a vivid image of Etruscan life. In the tombs of Caere and other Etruscan settlements, the dead were buried in family chamber tombs which recall the homes of the living. These were furnished with the wares of everyday life, including benches, beds, ornaments, utensils, and vessels and platters of Etruscan and Corinthian manufacture. The walls of the more sumptuous tombs are decorated with lively, brilliantly colored scenes of feasting, processions, and activities of daily life.

The most striking aspect of Etruscan life to Greek contemporaries and to later Romans was the elevated status of Etruscan women. The decorations and furnishings of tombs, inscriptions, and reports by contemporaries indicate that, as in the much earlier Minoan civilization, women played an active, public role in society. Unlike honorable Greek women, Etruscan women took part in banquets, reclining beside their male companions on couches from which they ate. They attended and even occasionally presided over dances, concerts, and sporting events. Women, as wives and mothers, were also active in political life. When a king died, his successor had to be designated and consecrated by the Etruscan queen to establish his legitimacy. Greeks such as Aristotle regarded the public behavior of Etruscan women as lewd. The great philosopher accused them of lying under the same cloak with men at banquets. To later Romans, the political role of women such as Tullia, wife of King Lucius Tarquin (Tarquin the Proud), the Etruscan king of Rome, was equally shocking. The Roman historian Livy (59 B.C.–A.D. 17) pretends that when Tullia first recognized her husband as king, he was so shocked that he sent her home. In truth, he was surely grateful.

While the Etruscans were consolidating their hegemony in western Italy, they were at the same time establishing their maritime power. From the seventh to the fifth centuries B.C., Etruscans controlled the Italian coast of the Tyrrhenian Sea as well as Sardinia, from which their ships could reach the coast of what is today France and Spain. Attempts to extend farther south into Greek southern Italy and toward the Greek colonies on the modern French coast brought the Etruscans and the Greeks into inevitable conflict. Etruscan cities fought sporadic sea battles against Greek cities in the waters of Sicily as well as off the coasts of Corsica and Etruria. Common hostility toward the Greeks as well as complementary economic interests soon brought the Etruscans into alliances with Carthage. Toward the end of the sixth century B.C., Etruscan cities including Rome signed a series of pacts with Carthage which created military alliances against the Phocaeans

and Syracuse. Etruscan fleets were victorious over the Phocaeans, driving them from Corsica, but they were no match for Syracuse. In 474 B.C., shortly after the battle of Himera, the Syracusan fleet destroyed that of the Etruscans off Cumae. Cumae marked the beginning of Etruscan decline. Through the fifth century B.C., Etruscan cities lost control of the sea to the Greeks. Around the same time, Celts from north of the Alps invaded and conquered the Po Valley. And to the south, Etruscans saw their inland territories progressively slipping into the hands of their former subjects, the Romans.

From City to Empire

What manner of people were these who, from obscure origins, came to rule an empire? Their own answer would have been simple: They were farmers and soldiers, simple people accustomed to simple, straightforward actions. Throughout their long history, Romans liked to refer to the clear-cut models provided by their semilegendary predecessors: Cincinnatus, the farmer, called away to the supreme office of dictator in time of danger, then returning to his plow; Horatius Cocles, the valiant warrior who held back an Etruscan army on the Tiber bridge until it could be demolished and then, despite his wounds, swam across the river to safety; Lucretia, the wife who chose death after dishonor. These were myths, but they were important myths to Romans, who preferred concrete models to abstract principles.

Later Romans liked to imagine the history of their city as one predestined by the gods for greatness. Some liked to trace the origins of Rome to Romulus and Remus, twin sons of the war god Mars and a Latin princess. According to legend, the children, after having been thrown into the Tiber River, were raised by a she-wolf. Other Romans, having absorbed the Homeric traditions of Greece, taught that the founder of Rome was Aeneas, son of the goddess of love Aphrodite and the Trojan Anchises, who had wandered west after the fall of Troy. All agreed that Rome had been ruled by kings, who underwent a steady decline in ability and morals until the last, Tar-

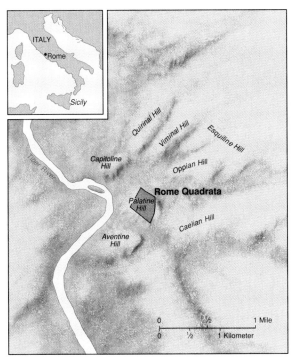

Ancient Rome

was one of several hills overlooking a natural ford on the Tiber; it constituted the first high ground some fourteen miles from the sea. The strategic importance of the site, as well as its relatively healthy climate above the disease-ridden marshes, made it a natural location for a settlement. This Alban village, called Roma Quadrata, was soon joined by other Latin and Sabine settlements on nearby hills. By the end of the eighth century B.C., seven Latin villages that clustered along the route from the Tiber to Alba had formed a league for mutual defense and shared religious cults.

Early Roman society was composed of households; clans, or *gentes;* and village councils, or *curiae* (sing. *curia*). The male head of each household, the *paterfamilias,* had power of life and death over its members and was responsible for the proper worship of the spirits of the family's ancestors, on whom continued prosperity depended. Within some villages, these families were grouped into gentes, which claimed descent from a semimythical ancestor.

Male members of village families formed councils, which were essentially religious organizations but also provided a forum for public discussion. These curiae tended to be dominated by gentes, but all males could participate, including those who belonged to the *plebs,* that is, families not organized into gentes. Initially the distinction between *plebeian* families and those families grouped into gentes was one of custom rather than economic, social, or political importance. Only later did the leaders of the gentes call themselves *patricians* ("descendants of fathers") and claim superiority to the plebs.

Important plebeian and patrician families increased their power through a system of *clientage,* which remained a fundamental aspect of social and political organization throughout Roman history. Clients were free men who depended on the protection of a more powerful individual or family and who owed various services, including political support, in return for this protection.

Villages themselves grouped together for military and voting purposes into ethnic *tribus,* or tribes, each composed of a number of curiae. Each individual curia supplied a contingent of infantry and each tribe cooperated to supply a unit of horsemen to the Roman army.

quin the Proud, was expelled by outraged Latins. These legends tell much about the attitudes and values of later Romans. They tell nothing about the origins of the city, its place in the Latin and Etruscan worlds, and its rise to greatness.

Latin Rome

Civilization in Italy meant Etruria to the north and Greater Greece to the south. In between lay Latium, a marshy region punctured by hills on which a sparse population could find protection from disease and enemies. This population was an amalgam of aboriginal Ligurians and the more recently arrived Latins and Sabines who lived a pastoral life in small scattered villages.

The Alban hills south of the Tiber were a center of Latin population. Sometime in the eighth century B.C., roughly forty Latin villages formed a loose confederation, the Alban League, for military and religious purposes. Not long after, in the face of an expanding Etruscan confederation from the north and Sabine penetration from the east, the Albans established a village on the steep Palatine hill to the north. The Palatine

Assemblies of all members of the curiae expressed approval of major decisions, especially declaration of war and the selection of new kings, and thus played a real if limited political role. More powerful although less formal was the role of the *senate* (assembly of elders), which was composed of heads of families. The senate's power derived from the individual importance of its members and from its role in selecting a candidate for king, who was then presented to the assembly of the curiae for approval.

Kings served as religious leaders, the primary means of communication between gods and men. In time, kings attained some political and judicial authority, but through the early Latin period royal power remained fundamentally religious and limited by the senate, curiae, gentes, and families.

The seven villages that made up primitive Rome developed independently of their Etruscan and Greek neighbors. Initially, Romans lived in thatched huts, tended their flocks on the hillsides, and maintained their separate village identities. By the seventh century B.C., they had begun fortifications and other structures indicating the beginnings of a dynamic civic life. This independent course of development changed in the middle of the seventh century B.C., when the Etruscans overwhelmed Latium and absorbed it into their civilization. Under its Etruscan kings, Rome first entered civilization.

Etruscan Rome

The Etruscans introduced in Latium and especially in Rome their political, religious, and economic traditions. Etruscan city organization partially replaced Latin tribal structures. Etruscan kings and magistrates ruled Latin towns, increasing the power of traditional Latin kingship. The kings were not only religious leaders, directing the cults of their humanlike gods, but also led the army, served as judges, and held supreme political power. In Rome a series of Etruscan kings, notably Tarquin the Elder and Servius Tullius, used the city's location on the Tiber ford as a strategic position from which to control Latium to the south. As Latium became an integral part of the Etruscan world, the Tiber became an important commercial route, carry-

ing the agricultural produce of Latium throughout Etruria and bringing to Rome the products of Etruscan and Greek workshops. For the first time, Rome began to enter the wider orbit of Mediterranean civilization. The town's population swelled with the arrival of merchants and craftsmen.

As Rome's importance grew, so did its size. Surrounding villages were added to the original seven, as were the Sabine colonies on the Quirinal and Capitoline hills. Etruscan engineers drained the marshes into a great canal flowing to the Tiber, thus opening the lowlands between the hills to settlement. This in turn allowed them to create and pave the Forum. The Etruscans were also builders, constructing a series of vast fortifications encircling the town. Under Etruscan influence, the fortified Capitoline hill, which served much like a Greek acropolis, became the cult center with the erection of the temple to Jupiter, the supreme god; Juno, his consort; and Minerva, an Etruscan goddess of craftwork similar to Athena. In its architecture, religion, commerce, and culture, Latin Rome was deeply indebted to its Etruscan conquerors.

As important as the physical and cultural changes brought by the Etruscans was their reorganization of the society. As in Greece, this restructuring was tied to changes in the military. The Etruscans had learned from the Greeks the importance of hoplite tactics, and King Servius Tullius (578–534 B.C.) introduced this system of warfare into Rome. This led to the abolition of the earlier curia-based military and political system in favor of one based only on property holding. Weakening the traditional Latin social units, the king divided Roman society into two groups. Those landowners wealthy enough to provide armed military service were organized into five *classis* (from which the word *class* is derived), ranked according to the quality of their arms and hence their wealth. Each class was further divided into military units called centuries. This military reorganization had fundamental political importance as well. Members of these centuries constituted the centuriate assembly, which replaced the older curial assemblies for such vital decisions as the election of magistrates and the declaration of war.

The constitution and operation of this centuriate assembly ensured control by the most conservative forces within the society. Small centuries of wealthy, well-armed cavalrymen and fully armed warriors outnumbered the more modestly equipped but numerically greater centuries. Likewise, men over the age of forty-seven, although in a minority, controlled over half of the centuries in each class. Since votes were counted not by individuals but by centuries, this ensured within the assembly the domination of the rich over the poor, the elder over the younger. The remainder of the society was the *infra classem*, those literally "under class" who owned no property and were thus excluded from military and political activity.

With this military and political reorganization came a reconstruction of the tribal system. Servius Tullius abolished the old tribal organization in favor of geographically organized tribes into which newcomers could easily be incorporated. Henceforth, while the family remained powerful, involvement in public life was based on property and geography. Latins, Sabines, Ligurians, and Etruscans could all be active citizens of the growing city.

While the old tribal units and curiae declined, divisions between the patricians and the plebeians grew more distinct. During the monarchy the patricians came to compose an upper stratum of wealthy nobles. They forbade marriage outside their own circle, forming a closed, self-perpetuating group that monopolized the senate, religious rites, and magisterial offices. Although partially protected by the kings, the plebeians, whether rich or poor, were pressed into a second-class status and denied access to political power.

When the Etruscans came to Rome, they found it a small collection of wood and reed villages only beginning to develop into an urban center. In less than two centuries, they transformed it into a prosperous, unified urban center that played an important role in the economic and political life of central Italy. They laid the foundations of a free citizenry, incorporating Greek models of military and social organization. The transformations brought about by the Etruscan kings became an enduring part of Rome. The Etruscans themselves did not. Just as the hoplite revolution in Greece saw the end of most Hellenic monarchies, around the tradi-

tionally reported date of 509 B.C. the Roman patricians expelled the last king, Tarquin the Proud, and established a republic. Then a republic (from the Latin *res publica*, public property, as opposed to *res privata*, private property of the king) was established.

Rome and Italy

Always the moralizers, later Roman historians made the expulsion of King Tarquin the dramatic result of his son's lust. According to legend, Sextus, the son of Tarquin, raped Lucretia, a virtuous Roman matron. She told her husband of the crime and then took her own life. Outraged, the Roman patricians were said to have driven the king and his family from the city. Actually, monarchy was giving way to oligarchic republics across Etruria in the sixth century B.C. Rome was hardly exceptional. However, the establishment of the Roman republic coincided roughly with the beginning of the Etruscan decline, allowing the city of Rome to assert itself and to develop its Latin and Etruscan traditions in unique ways. This development took place within an atmosphere of internal dissension and external conquest.

The patrician oligarchy had engineered the end of the monarchy and patricians dominated the offices and institutions of the new republic at the expense of the plebs who, in losing the king, lost their only defender. Governmental institutions of the early republic developed within this context of patrician supremacy.

Characteristic of republican institutions was that at every level, power was shared by two or more equals elected for fixed terms. This practice of shared power was intended to ensure that magistrates would consult with each other before making decisions and that no individual could achieve supreme power at any level. Replacing the king were the two *consuls*, each elected by the assembly for a one-year term. Initially only the consuls held the *imperium*, the supreme power to command, to execute the law, and to impose the death penalty. Only in moments of grave crisis might a consul, with the approval of the senate, name a single *dictator* with extraordinary absolute power for a very brief period, never more than six months. In time other magistracies developed to perform specialized functions. *Praetors*, who in time also exercised the imperium, administered justice, and defended the city in the absence of the consuls. *Quaestors* controlled finances. *Censors* assigned individuals their places in society, determined the amount of their taxes, filled vacancies in the senate, and negotiated contracts for public construction projects. A variety of military commanders directed wars against neighboring cities and peoples under the imperium of the consuls. In all their actions these officeholders consulted with each other and with the senate, which was composed of roughly three hundred powerful former magistrates. The centuriate assembly functioned as the legislative organ of the state, but it continued to be dominated by the eldest and wealthiest members of society.

During the early republic, wealthy patricians, aided by their clients, monopolized the senate and the magistracies. Successful magistrates rose through a series of increasingly important offices, which came to be known as the *cursus honorum*, to the position of consul. Censors selected from among former magistrates in appointing new senators, thus ensuring that the senate would be dominated by the patrician elite. Patricians also controlled the system of priesthoods, which they held for life. With political and religious power came economic power. The poorer plebs in particular found themselves sinking into debt to wealthy patricians, losing their property, and with it the basis for military service and political participation. In the courtroom, in the temple, in the assembly, and in the marketplace, plebeians found themselves subjected to the whims of an elite from which they were excluded.

The plebs began to organize in response to patrician control. On several occasions in the first half of the fifth century B.C., the whole plebeian order withdrew a short distance from the city, refusing to return or to serve in the military until conflicts with the patricians were resolved. In time the plebs created their own assembly, the Council of the Plebs, which enacted laws binding on all plebeians. This council founded its own temples and elected magistrates called *tribunes*, whose persons were declared sacred to the gods. The tribunes protected the plebs from arbitrary

By the middle of the second century B.C., the Roman republic had evolved to the point where private citizens could cast private ballots. This Roman coin of 137 B.C. features a Roman voter dropping a stone tablet into a voting urn.

patrician power. Anyone harming the tribunes, whether patrician or plebeian, could be killed by the plebs without trial. With their own assembly, magistracies, and religious cults, the plebeians were well on the way to creating a separate republic. This conflict between the plebeians and the patricians, known as the Struggle of Orders, threatened to tear the Roman society apart, just as pressure from hostile neighbors placed Rome on the defensive. Roman preeminence in Latium had ended with the expulsion of the last king. The Etruscan town of Veii just north of the Tiber began launching periodic attacks against Rome. To the south, the Volscians had begun to expand north into the Litis and Trerus valleys.

This military pressure, and the inability of the patricians to meet it alone, ultimately forced them to a compromise with the plebeians. One of the first victories won by the plebs around 450 B.C. was the codification of basic Roman law, the Law of the Twelve Tables, which recognized the basic rights of all free citizens. As important as the specific provisions of the law, which covered private, criminal, sacred, and public matters, was the fact that it was written and posted publicly. Thus anyone, not only patrician magistrates, could have access to it. Around the same time, the state began to absorb the plebeian political and religious organizations intact. Gradually, priesthoods, magistracies, and thus the senate were opened to plebeians. The consulship was the last prize finally won by the plebs in 367 B.C. In 287 B.C., as the result of a final secession of the plebs, the decisions of the plebeian assembly became binding on all citizens, patrician and plebeian alike.

Bitter differences at home did not prevent patricians and plebs from presenting a united front against their enemies abroad. External conquest deflected internal hostility and profited both orders. By the beginning of the fourth century B.C., the united patrician-plebeian state was expanding its rule both north and south. Roman legions, commanded by patricians but formed of the whole spectrum of property-owning Romans, reestablished Roman preeminence in Latium and then began a series of wars that brought most of Italy under Roman control. In 396 B.C., Roman forces captured and destroyed Veii and shortly after conquered the rest of southern Etruria. In the south, Roman and Latin forces turned back the Volscians. In 390 B.C., Rome suffered a temporary setback at the hands of the Gauls, or Celts, of northern Italy, who raided south and sacked much of the city before being bought off with a large tribute payment. Even this event had a silver lining. The damage to Rome was short-lived, but the Gauls had dealt a deathblow to the Etruscan cities of the north, clearing the way for later Roman conquest. A last-ditch effort by the Latins to preserve their autonomy was crushed in 338 B.C., and by 295 B.C., Rome had secured its rule as far north as the Po Valley. In the south, Roman infantry and persistence proved the equal of professional Greek armies. Rome won a war of attrition against a series of Hellenistic commanders, the last of whom was the Greek king Pyrrhus of Epirus (319–272 B.C.). Pyrrhus, regarded as the greatest tactician of his day, won a series of victories that proved more costly to him than to his Roman opponents. In 275 B.C., after losing two-thirds of his troops in these "Pyrrhic victories," he withdrew to Sicily. By 265 B.C., Rome had absorbed the Hellenistic cities of the south.

The Roman conquest benefited patrician and plebeian alike. While the patricians acquired

Relief of a Roman war galley. The deck is crowded with infantrymen. Galleys were usually rowed by slaves while the soldiers remained fresh for the task of subduing enemy ships.

wealth and power, the plebeians received a prize of equal value: land. After the capture of Veii, for example, the poor of Rome received shares of the conquered land. Since landowning was a prerequisite for military service, this distribution created still more peasant soldiers for further expeditions. Some citizens received land in organized colonies similar to those of Greece while others received individual plots spread about the conquered territories. Still, while the constant supply of new land did much to diffuse the tensions between orders, it did not actually resolve them. Into the late third century B.C., debt and landlessness remained major problems creating tensions in Roman society. Probably not more than one-half of the citizen population owned land by 200 B.C.

The Roman manner of treating conquered populations, radically different from anything seen before, also contributed to Rome's success. In war, no one could match the Roman legions for ruthless, thorough destruction. Yet no conquerors had ever shown themselves so generous in victory. After crushing the Latin revolt of 338 B.C., virtually all of the Latins were incorporated into the Roman citizenry. Later colonies founded outside of Latium were given the same status as Latin cities. Other more-distant conquered peoples were considered allies and required to provide troops but no tribute to Rome. In time, they too might become citizens. In its wars against the Hellenistic cities of the south, Rome took pains to portray itself as defending Greek civilization against the barbarism of marauding mercenary armies.

The implications of these measures were revolutionary. By extending citizenship to conquered neighbors and by offering the future possibility to allies, Rome tied their fate to its own. Rather than potentially subversive subjects, conquered populations became strong supporters. Thus, in contrast to the Hellenistic cities of the east where Greeks jealously guarded their status from the indigenous population, Rome's colonies acted as magnets, drawing local populations into the Roman cultural and political orbit. In time a fortunate few who cooperated with Rome might, with luck, talent, and money, share the benefits of Roman citizenship. Greeks were scandalized by the Roman tradition of giving citizenship even to

freed slaves. By the end of the fourth century B.C., some of the sons of these freedmen were finding a place in the senate. Finally, in all of its wars of conquest, Rome claimed a moral mandate. Romans went to great lengths to demonstrate that theirs were just wars, basing their claims on alleged acts of aggression by their enemies, on the appeal to Rome by its allies, and, increasingly, by presenting themselves as the preservers and defenders of Greek traditions of freedom. Both these political and propagandistic measures proved successful. Between 265 B.C. and 91 B.C., few serious revolts shook the peace and security of Italy south of the Po.

Benevolent treatment of the conquered spurred further conquest. Since subject cities and peoples did not pay tribute, the only way for Rome to benefit from its conquests or to exercise its authority was to demand and use troops. These troops aided still further conquests, which brought the spoils of war to them as well as to Rome. By 264 B.C., all of Italy was united under Roman hegemony. Roman expansion finally brought Rome into conflict with the great Mediterranean power of the west, Carthage.

Rome and the Mediterranean

Since its earliest days, Rome had allied itself with Carthage against the Greek cities of Italy. The zones of interest of the two cities had been quite separate. Carthage was a sea empire, while Rome was a land-based power without a navy. The Greeks, aspiring to power on land and sea, posed a common threat to both Rome and Carthage. However, once Rome had conquered the Greek cities to the south, it became enmeshed in the affairs of neighboring Sicily, a region with well-established Carthaginian interests. There, in 265 B.C., a group of Italian mercenary pirates in Messina, threatened by Syracuse, requested Roman assistance. The senate refused but the plebeian assembly, eager for booty, exercised its newly won right to legislate for the republic and accepted. Shortly afterward the Romans invaded Sicily, and Syracuse turned to its old enemy, Carthage, for assistance. The First Punic War had begun.

The First Punic War, which lasted from 265 to

Roman territory (people given Roman citizenship)

Allied areas (people not given citizenship)

0   100 Miles

0   100 Kilometers

Rome in 264 B.C.

ranean storms took their toll of opposing fleets. Finally, in 241 B.C., Rome forced the Carthaginian commander, Hamilcar Barca (ca. 270–229 B.C.), to surrender simply because the Romans could afford to build one more fleet than he. Carthage paid a huge indemnity and abandoned Sicily. Syracuse and Messina became allies of Rome. In a break with tradition, Rome obligated the rest of Sicily to pay a true tribute in the form of a tithe (one-tenth) of their crops. Shortly after that, Rome helped itself to Sardinia as well, from which it again demanded tribute, not simply troops. Rome had established an empire.

During the next two decades Roman legions kept busy in the north, defeating the Ligurians on the northwest coast, the Celtic Gauls south of the Alps, and the Illyrians along the Adriatic coast. At the same time, Carthage fought a bitter battle against its own mercenary armies, which it had been unable to pay off after its defeat. Carthage then began the systematic creation of an empire in Spain. Trade between Carthage and Rome reached the highest level in history, but trade did not create friendship. The two former enemies maintained a wary peace. On both sides, powerful leaders saw the treaty of 241 B.C. as just a pause in a fight to the death. Hamilcar Barca had his nine-year-old son Hannibal swear to be Rome's eternal enemy. Fearful and greedy Romans insisted that Carthage had to be destroyed for the security of Rome. They were particularly disturbed by the growth of Carthage's Spanish empire, even though Hamilcar Barca assured the senate that he was simply trying to raise funds to pay off its indemnity.

Carthaginian successes in Spain, led after Hamilcar's death by his son-in-law Hasdrubal (d. 221 B.C.) and his son Hannibal (247–183 B.C.), finally provoked Rome to war in 218 B.C. As soon as this Second Punic War had begun, Hannibal began an epic march north out of Spain, along the Mediterranean coast, and across the Alps. In spite of great hardships, he was able to transport over 23,000 troops and approximately eighteen war elephants into the plains of northern Italy. (See Special Feature, "Hannibal's Elephants," pp. 118–19.) Hannibal's brilliant generalship brought victory after victory to the Carthaginian forces. In the first engagement on the Trebia River in the Po Valley the Romans lost twenty thousand men,

241 B.C., was a costly, brutal, and drawn-out affair which Rome won by dint of persistence and methodical calculation rather than strategic brilliance. Rome invaded and concluded an alliance with Syracuse in 263 B.C. The war rapidly became a sea war. Rome had little previous naval experience but quickly learned the rules of the game then rewrote them to its own advantage. Taking a wrecked Carthaginian ship as a model, Roman builders constructed twenty fast ships propelled by roughly two hundred oarsmen to ram and sink opposing ships. Rome also built one hundred larger ships with crews of three hundred, manned by Roman allies. Unaccustomed to fighting at sea, Roman engineers turned sea battles into land by placing on their ships heavy gangplanks that could be dropped onto enemy ships. The gangplanks were equipped with a heavy iron spike to secure them to the enemy's deck. This allowed a contingent of legionnaires to march onto the enemy ship and fight as though on dry land.

With these innovations, the Romans won impressive initial victories but still could not deliver a knockout blow either in Sicily or North Africa for over twenty years. Warfare and Mediter-

Hannibal's Elephants

"What do you get when you cross an Alp with an elephant?" Hannibal hoped that the answer was "Rome." Elephants were the most spectacular, extravagant, and unpredictable element in ancient warfare. Since the time of Alexander the Great, Hellenistic kings and commanders tried to use the great strength, size, and relative invulnerability of these animals to throw opposing infantry into confusion and flight. Elephants' unusual smell and loud trumpeting also panicked horses not accustomed to these strange beasts, wreaking havoc with cavalry units. *Mahouts,* or drivers, who were usually Indians, controlled and directed the animal from a seat on the elephant's neck. Normally each elephant carried a small, towerlike structure from which archers could shoot down on the massed infantry. However, like modern tanks, the primary importance of the beasts was the enormous shock effect created by a charge of massed war elephants. Still, they often created more problems than they solved.

Indian princes had used elephants in warfare for centuries. When Alexander the Great crossed the Indus in 326 B.C., the Indian king Porus came within an ace of defeating the Greek conqueror, thanks largely to his more than two hundred elephants. In 302 B.C., Seleucus I received five hundred war elephants from an Indian king as part of a peace treaty. The next

year these animals contributed greatly to Seleucus' victory over Antigonus at Ipsus, which made possible the creation of his separatist kingdom in Syria. Thereafter Seleucid kings used elephants as an integral part of their military and even attempted, without much success, to breed elephants in Syria.

The Ptolemys, too, used elephants in Egypt, but lacking access to Indian animals, they had to be content with the smaller African forest elephant. The great African bush elephant, the largest land animal and a far greater beast than either the forest or the Indian elephants, remained unknown to the Western world until the nineteenth century. The Ptolemys sent large-scale hunting parties into Ethiopia to capture forest elephants. Captured animals were trained and driven by Indians. In battles between Seleucids and Ptolemys, however, the larger Indian elephants usually brought victory.

The Romans first experienced the terror of elephant charges in their war against Pyrrhus in the south of Italy. They next encountered them in the Punic wars. The Carthaginians had learned to use elephants around the middle of the third century B.C., capturing them in the Atlas Mountains of North Africa and putting them to good use in Spain. When Hannibal decided to invade Italy via the Alps, he naturally wanted to take along these formidable beasts.

This was easier said than done. In 217 B.C., Hannibal set out from Cartagena and some weeks later arrived at the Rhone River with an army that

included roughly 38,000 infantry, 8,000 cavalry, and thirty-seven elephants. Ferrying the pachyderms across the river was a major undertaking, since the frightened animals refused to walk onto rafts. Finally, the Carthaginians lashed together a series of rafts, the first two on dry land, the others forming a pontoon into the river. The sides were piled with earth so that the elephants could not see that they were not walking on dry land. Their Indian mahouts led them a few at a time to the end rafts which were then cut free and towed across the river by boats. Most of the animals, seeing water on all sides, remained terrified but still. Others panicked, upsetting the rafts, falling into the river, and drowning their mahouts. Once in the water, however, most of the elephants were able to swim to the far shore.

As difficult as the river crossing was, it paled in comparison with the problems of crossing the Alps. As Hannibal moved slowly up the valley of the Arc, his troops were under constant harassment from local Celtic tribes eager to ambush them at every occasion. From high up in the passes, the Celts showered down rocks, throwing the pack animals into confusion and causing them to hurl themselves off the narrow paths. Landslides carried away portions of the track and, as Hannibal advanced, the path became too narrow for elephants and, eventually, even for horses and mules. Engineers had to rebuild paths, taking up valuable time. Great boulders had to be cleared away by heating them and then pouring vinegar into won without the assistance of the pachyderm shock force. In 207 B.C., Hannibal's brother Hasdrubal (d. 207 B.C.) entered Italy with ten elephants, but at the battle of Metaurus they panicked, stampeded, and did more harm to the Carthaginians than to the Romans.

The next time Hannibal faced a Roman army with his full contingent of war elephants was at Zama. There his eighty animals proved a bitter disappointment. Ordered to charge, many of the elephants panicked at the sound of trumpets and horns, wheeled about, and went raging into the massed African cavalry arrayed on the Punic side. Some elephants did charge, but with limited effect. The Romans had learned to take aim at the mahouts, killing them and leaving the animals without direction. The Romans also allowed the elephants to charge past, then attacked their flanks with javelins and their legs with swords. Finally, the Roman commander had taken the precaution of leaving wide paths between his formations. Many of the animals simply charged down these paths and disappeared into the open fields beyond the Roman lines.

The Romans themselves made little use of elephants in warfare. These exotic beasts better suited the inflated egos of Eastern kings than the practical minds of Roman generals. The Romans preferred the disciplined advance of a well-trained cohort of Roman legionnaires to the charge of a war elephant. It was with these steadfast and resolute infantrymen rather than with raging elephants that they won an empire.

crevices to cause them to explode. At the top of the pass, new snow forced a three-day halt while a new road wide enough for the elephants to descend was constructed down the more precipitous Italian side of the mountain. During this time the elephants were without fodder and suffered enormously. Finally, after fifteen days Hannibal's depleted troops reached the fertile plains of the Po Valley. He had lost almost half of his infantry and cavalry since reaching the Rhone and more than half of his elephants.

Was it worth it? In his first major encounter with the Romans at the Trebia River, Hannibal split his elephants into two groups to protect the wings of his infantry. The beasts were a major factor in the devastating defeat inflicted on the Romans. However, shortly after, the cold and snow killed all but one of the animals. This lone survivor became Hannibal's personal command post. The great Punic victories at Lake Trasimene and Cannae were two-thirds of their army. Carthaginian success encouraged the Gauls to join the fight against the Romans. Initially, Italian, Etruscan, and Greek allies remained loyal, but after Rome's catastrophic defeats at Lake Trasimene in Etruria in 217 B.C. and especially at Cannae in 216 B.C., a number of Italian colonies and allies and especially the cities of Capua and Syracuse went over to the enemy. In the east, Philip V of Macedon (238–179 B.C.) made a treaty with Carthage in the hope of taking Illyria (today the coast of Yugoslavia) from a defeated Rome.

As commanders chosen by the patrician-dominated senate failed to stop the enemy, the Roman plebs became increasingly dissatisfied with the way the oligarchy was conducting the war. However, popular pressure to appoint new commanders did little to alleviate the situation. In 217 B.C., following the battle of Lake Trasimene, the senate named the capable general Quintus Fabius Maximus (d. ca. 203 B.C.) dictator. He used delaying tactics successfully to slow the Carthaginians, thus earning the title *Cunctator*, or Delayer. The popular assembly, impatient for a decisive victory, elected a second dictator, thus effectively canceling the position of Quintus Fabius Maximus. The next year popular pressure forced the election of Gaius Terentius Varro as consul. Varro quickly led the army to the greatest defeat in Roman history at Cannae. There Hannibal surrounded and annihilated Varro's numerically superior army.

Three things saved the Roman state. First, while some important allies and colonies defected, the majority held firm. Rome's traditions of sharing the fruits of victory with its allies, extending the rights of Roman citizenship, and protecting central and southern Italy against its enemies proved stronger than the appeals of Hannibal. Although victorious time and again, without local support Hannibal could not hold the terrain and cities he won. New allies such as Syracuse, which fell in 212 B.C., were forcibly returned to the Roman camp. Fabius resumed his delaying tactics and gradually Hannibal's victories slipped from his hands.

The second reason for Rome's survival was the tremendous social solidarity all classes and factions of its population showed during these desperate years. In spite of the internal tensions between patricians and plebeians, their ultimate dedication to Rome never faltered. Much of this loyalty was due to the Roman system of strong family and patronage ties. Kinsmen and clients answered the call of their patriarchs and patrons to bounce back repeatedly from defeat. Roman farmer-soldiers stood firm.

The final reason for Rome's ultimate success was Publius Cornelius Scipio (236–184 B.C.), also known as Scipio the Elder, a commander able to force Hannibal from Italy. Scipio, who earned the title Africanus for his victory, accomplished this not by attacking Hannibal directly, but by taking the war home to the enemy, first in Spain and then in Africa. In 210 B.C. Scipio arrived in Spain and rapidly captured the city of Cartagena (New Carthage). Within four years he destroyed Punic power in Spain. Riding the crest of popular enthusiasm at home, he raised a new army and in 204 B.C. sailed for Africa. His victories there drew Hannibal home, where at Zama in 202 B.C. the Roman commander destroyed the Carthaginian army. Zama put an end to both the Second Punic War and Carthaginian political power. Saddled with a huge indemnity and forced to abandon all

The Punic Wars

of its territories and colonies to Rome, reduced to a small portion of the North African coast, Carthage had become in effect a Roman subject.

But still this humiliating defeat was not enough for Rome. While some Roman senators favored allowing Carthage to survive as a means of keeping the Roman plebs under senatorial control, others demanded destruction. Chief among them was the censor Marcus Porcius Cato, known as Cato the Elder (234–149 B.C.), who ended every speech with *Delenda est Carthago,* "Carthage must be destroyed." Ultimately trumped-up reasons were found to renew the war in 149 B.C. In contrast to the desperate, hard-fought campaigns of the Second Punic War, the Third was an unevenly matched slaughter. In 146 B.C., Scipio Aemilianus (184–129 B.C.), or Scipio the Younger, the adopted grandson of Scipio the Elder, overwhelmed Carthage and sold its few survivors into slavery. As a symbolic act of final destruction, he then had the site razed, plowed, and cursed. Carthage's fertile hinterland became the property of wealthy Roman senators.

In the same year that Carthage was destroyed, Roman armies destroyed Corinth, a second great center of Mediterranean commerce. This victory marked the culmination of Roman imperialist expansion east into the Greek and Hellenistic world, which had begun with the conquest of Illyria. This expansion was not simply the result of Roman imperialist ambitions. The Hellenistic states, in their constant warring and bickering, drew Rome into their conflicts against their neighbors. Greek states asked the Roman senate to arbitrate their disputes. Pergamum requested military assistance against Macedonia. Appealing to Rome's claims as "liberator," cities pressed the senate to preserve their freedom in the face of aggressive expansion by their more powerful neighbors. In a series of intermittent, uncoordinated, and sporadic engagements, Rome did intervene, although its real focus was on its life-and-death struggle with Carthage. Roman intentions may not have been conquest, but Roman intervention upset the balance of power in the Hellenistic world. Although Rome became a major player in the eastern Mediterranean more by chance than by design, it rapidly became the winner. The price of Roman arbitration, intervention, and protection was loss of independence.

Gradually the Roman shadow fell over the eastern Mediterranean.

The treaty Philip V of Macedon concluded with Carthage during the Second Punic War provided an initial excuse for war, one seized upon more eagerly by the plebeian assembly than by the senate. Shortly after its victory at Zama, Rome provoked Philip to war and then easily defeated him in 197 B.C., proclaiming the freedom of the Greek cities and withdrawing from Greece. In 189 B.C., the Seleucid Antiochus III (223–187 B.C.) of Syria suffered the same fate, and Rome declared the Greek cities in Asia Minor he had controlled free. The Greeks venerated the Roman commander, Titus Quinctius Flamininus (228–174 B.C.), as a god—the first Roman to be accorded this Eastern honor. In reality, the control of the cities lay in the hands of local oligarchs favorable to Rome. In 179 B.C., Philip's son Perseus (179–168 B.C.) attempted to stir up democratic opposition to Rome within the cities. This time Rome responded more forcefully. The Macedonian kingdom was divided into four republics governed by their own senates and magistrates selected from among the local aristocrats. In Epirus, seventy cities were destroyed and 150,000 people sold into slavery. This harsh punishment prompted other Greek cities to react with panic even to the mere threat of Roman retribution. When the citizens of Rhodes heard that the senate was contemplating declaring war on them, they quickly executed all of their anti-Roman fellows.

The final episode of Rome's expansionist drama unfolded during the Third Punic War. When Rome resumed its war with Carthage in 149 B.C., several Greek cities attempted once more to assert their autonomy from the hated oligarchies established by Rome. Retribution was swift. The Roman legions crushed the rebel forces and, as an example to all, Corinth was razed as thoroughly as was Carthage. Vast booty from wealthy Corinth poured into Rome while the survivors found themselves enslaved in the homes and estates of Roman victors.

In the west, in northern Italy, Spain, and Africa, Roman conquest had been direct and complete. Tribal structures had been replaced with Roman provinces governed by former magistrates or proconsuls. In the east, Rome preferred to work through the existing political hierarchies.

Still, Rome cultivated its image as protector of Greek liberties against the Macedonian and Seleucid monarchies and preferred indirect control to annexation. Its power was no less real for being indirect.

By 146 B.C., the Roman republic controlled the whole rim of the Mediterranean from Rhodes in the east across Greece, Dalmatia, Italy, southern Gaul, Spain, and North Africa. Even Syria and Egypt, although nominally independent, had to bow before Roman will. This subjugation had been graphically demonstrated in 168 B.C., when the Seleucid Antiochus IV (175–164 B.C.) invaded the kingdom of the Egyptian ruler Ptolemy VI (180–145 B.C.) and besieged Alexandria. The Ptolemys had long before made a treaty with Rome, and the senate sent an envoy to Antiochus with written instructions to withdraw immediately from Egypt. The king replied that he would like to consult before making a decision. The Roman envoy immediately drew a circle around Antiochus, ordering him to give an answer before he stepped out of the ring. Such directness was unknown in the world of Hellenistic diplomacy. After a moment's hesitation, the deeply shocked Antiochus replied that he would do whatever the Romans demanded. Roman perseverance and determination had brought it from obscurity

The Roman Republic

509 B.C.	Expulsion of last Etruscan king; beginning of Roman republic
ca. 450 B.C.	Law of the Twelve Tables
396 B.C.	Rome conquers southern Etruria
295 B.C.	Rome extends rule north to Po Valley
265–241 B.C.	First Punic War
264 B.C.	All of Italy under Roman control
218–202 B.C.	Second Punic War
149–146 B.C.	Third Punic War; Carthage is destroyed

to the greatest power the West had ever known. The republic had endured great adversity. It would not survive prosperity.

Republican Civilization

Territorial conquest, the influx of unprecedented riches, and exposure to sophisticated Hellenistic civilization ultimately overwhelmed earlier Roman civilization. This civilization had been created by stubborn farmers and soldiers who valued above all else authority, simplicity, and piety. This unique culture was the source of strength that led Rome to greatness, but its limitations prevented the republic from resolving its internal social tensions and the external problems caused by the burden of empire.

Farmers and Soldiers

The ideal Roman farmer was not the great estate owner of the Greek world, but the smallholder, the dirt farmer of central Italy. A typical farm might be as little as ten acres worked by the owner and his family. Such farms produced grain and beans and raised hogs for family consumption. In addition, Roman farmers cultivated vineyards and olive groves for cash crops. But the most important crop of Roman farms was citizens. "From farmers come the bravest men and the sturdiest soldiers," wrote Cato the Elder.

Nor was the ideal Roman soldier the gallant cavalryman but rather the solid foot soldier. Cavalry, composed of wealthy citizens who made up the elite equestrian order (from the Latin *equus*, horse), and especially allies, provided reconnaissance and protected Roman flanks. However, the main fighting force was the infantry. Sometime in the early Republic the Greek phalanx was transformed into the Roman legion, a flexible unit composed of thirty companies of 120 men each. Legions maneuvered in three rows of squares of men each containing 120 soldiers. The first row engaged the enemy, first with javelins, and then with short swords. As men in the first row tired, members of the second and eventually the third could step in to relieve them. Likewise,

Roman mosaics illustrating tasks appropriate to the months of the year. At left, two laborers are using an olive press with a horizontal screw for the December olive-pressing. At right, workers use a ladder to reach the fruit during September apple-picking time.

the whole square could move back in formation, its place taken by a fresh unit that could keep up the pressure on the enemy. Such tactics demanded less virtuoso military ability than solid discipline.

Constant training, careful preparation, and painstaking execution characterized every aspect of Roman military expeditions. Wars were won as much by engineering feats as by feats of arms. Engineers constructed bridges, siege machines, and catapults. By the time of the late republic, Roman armies on the march could construct identical camps each night, quickly building a strong square fort 2,150 feet on a side. Within the camp, every unit had exactly the same location for its quarters, as did the commander and paymaster. The chain of command was rigidly maintained from the commander, a Roman consul, through military tribunes and centurions, two of whom commanded each company of 120 men. Even the slaughter and pillage that followed the capture of an enemy city were carried out with firm Roman discipline. When Scipio the

Elder took Cartagena in 210 B.C., he ordered his troops to exterminate every form of life they encountered, sparing none, and not to start pillaging until ordered to do so. After the citadel had fallen, the order went out to stop killing and start pillaging. Half of the army collected the spoils and brought them to a central location while the other half stood guard. The military tribunes then distributed the booty among their legions.

These solid, methodical troops, the backbone of the republican armies that conquered the Mediterranean, were among the victims of that conquest. The pressures of constant international warfare were destroying the farmer-soldiers whom the traditionalists loved to praise. When the Roman sphere of interest had been confined to central Italy, farmers could do their planting in spring, serve in the army during the summer months, and return home to care for their farms in time for harvest. When Rome's wars became international expeditions lasting for years, many soldiers, unable to work their lands while doing military service, had to mortgage their farms in order to support their families. When they returned they often found that during their prolonged absences they had lost their farms to wealthy aristocratic moneylenders. While aristocrats amassed vast landed estates worked by imported slaves, ordinary Romans and Italians lacked even a family farm capable of supporting themselves and their families. Without land, they and their sons were excluded from further military service and sank into the growing mass of desperately poor, disenfranchised citizens.

In many ways typical of such soldiers was Spurius Ligustinus, an ordinary soldier who by 177 B.C. had served twenty-two years in foreign campaigns. Born on a minuscule Sabine farm, he had entered the army and served two years in Macedonia against Philip V, then immediately reenlisted to serve in Spain. During a third enlistment he fought in Aetolia and was promoted to centurion. Later he served in three additional Spanish campaigns. Ligustinus held the rank of chief centurion four times and was thirty-four times rewarded for bravery. When he was well past fifty years of age, his sole means of support besides the military was the half-acre farm inherited from his father, from which he was expected to support six sons and two daughters. For such men and their families, the benefits of conquest must have seemed illusory indeed.

The Roman Family

In Roman tradition, the *paterfamilias* was the master of the family, which in theory included his wife, children, and slaves, over whom he exercised the power of life and death. This authority lasted as long as he lived. Only at his death did his sons, even if long grown and married, achieve legal and financial independence. The family was the basic unit of society, of the state. The authority of the paterfamilias was the foundation of this essentially patriarchal society and the key to its success.

Although not kept in seclusion as in Greece, Roman women theoretically never exercised independent power in this male-dominated world. Before marriage, a Roman girl was subject to the authority of her father. When she married, her father traditionally transferred legal guardianship to her husband, thus severing her bonds to her paternal family. A husband could divorce his wife at will, returning her and her dowry to her father. Wives did exercise real though informal authority within the family. Part of this authority came from their role in the moral education of their children and the direction of the household. Part also came from their control over their dowries. Widows might exercise even greater authority in the raising of their children.

M·CORNELIO·M·F·PALE·STATIO·B·   FECER·

The progress of a Roman son. At left the baby nurses while the proud father looks on. The toddler in his father's arms soon gives way to the young boy playing with a donkey and cart. The maturing youth is seen at right reciting his lessons.

The atrium of the House of the Silver Wedding in Pompeii. The pool in the floor caught the rainwater that entered through the opening in the high roof.

Paternal authority over children was absolute. Not all children born into a marriage became members of the family. The Law of the Twelve Tables allowed defective children to be killed for the good of the family. Newborn infants were laid on the ground before the father, who decided whether the child should be raised. By picking up a son, he accepted the child into the family. Ordering that a daughter be nursed similarly signified acceptance. If there were too many mouths to feed or the child were simply unwanted, the father could command that the infant be killed or abandoned. Abandoned children might be adopted by childless couples. Frequently, if they survived at all, it was as slaves or prostitutes.

Nor were all sons born into Roman families. Romans made use of adoption for many purposes. Families without heirs could adopt children. Powerful political and military figures might adopt promising young men as their political heirs. These adopted sons held the same legal rights as the natural offspring of the father and thus were integral members of his family. Some adoptions even took place posthumously. An important Roman might name a younger man as his adopted son in his will.

Slaves, too, were members of the family. On the one hand, slaves were property without personal rights. On the other, they might live and work alongside the free members of the family, worship the family gods, and enjoy the protection and endure the authority of the paterfamilias. In fact, the authority of the paterfamilias was roughly the same over slave and free members of the family. If he desired, he could sell the free members of the family into slavery. Even freed slaves remained obligated to their former owner throughout life. They owed him special respect and could never oppose him in lawsuits or other conflicts under penalty of returning to servitude.

The center of everyday life for the Roman family was the *domus,* the family house whose architectural style had developed from Etruscan traditions. Early Roman houses, even of the wealthy and powerful, were simple, low buildings well suited to the Mediterranean climate, constructed around an open courtyard, or *atrium.* Cato the Elder described the home of the great general Manius Curius, who had driven Pyrrhus from Italy, as a small, plain dwelling, and this simplicity predominated through the second century B.C. The house looked inward, presenting nothing but blank walls to the outside world. Visitors entered through the front door into the atrium, a central courtyard containing a collecting pool into which rainwater for household use flowed from the roof through terra-cotta drains. Originally, the atrium not only provided sunlight but allowed smoke from the hearth to escape. In niches or on shelves stood wax or terra-cotta busts of ancestors and statues of the household gods. The walls, constructed of blocks of stone, were often painted in bands of different colors in imitation of polychrome marble. Around the atrium, openings gave on to workrooms, storerooms, bedrooms, offices, and small dining rooms.

In the wake of imperial conquests, the Roman family and its environment began to change in ways disturbing to many of the oligarchy. Some women, perhaps in imitation of their more liberated Hellenistic sisters, began to take a more active role in public life. One example is Cornelia, a daughter of Scipio Africanus, who bore her husband twelve children, only three of whom survived to maturity. After her husband's death in 154 B.C., she refused to remarry, devoting herself instead to raising her children, administering their inheritance, and directing their political careers.

Some married women, too, escaped the authority of their husbands. Fewer and fewer fathers transferred authority over their daughters to their husbands. Instead, daughters remained under their father's authority as long as he lived. This meant that upon the father's death, they became independent persons, able to manage their own affairs without the consent of or interference by their husbands. Although some historians believe that sentimental bonds of affection may have increased between many husbands and wives and parents and children as legal bonds loosened, it also meant that the wife's relationship to her children was weakened. Roman mothers had never been legally related to their children. Wives and mothers were not fully part of their husband's families. Thus their brothers' families, not their own children, were their natural heirs. Just as adoption created political bonds, marriage to daughters sealed alliances between men. However, when these alliances fell apart or more advantageous ones presented themselves, fathers could force their daughters to divorce their husbands and to marry someone else. Divorce became increasingly common in the second century B.C. More and more, wives were temporary visitors in their husband's homes.

Homes grew in size, wealth, and complexity for those who participated in the wealth of empire. With increasing prosperity, the atrium became more elegant, intended to impress visitors with the wealth of the family and its traditions. The water basin became a reflecting pool, often endowed with a fountain and surrounded by towering columns. In many cases a second open area, or *peristyle*, appeared behind the first. The wealthy surrounded the atrium and peristyle with glass-enclosed porticoes and decorated their walls with frescoes, mosaics, and paintings looted from Hellenistic cities of the East. Furniture of fine inlaid woods, bronze, and marble and Eastern carpets and wall hangings increased the exotic luxury of the patrician *domus*.

Not every Roman family could afford its own *domus* and in the aftermath of the imperial expansion, housing problems for the poor became acute. In Rome and other towns of Italy, shopkeepers lived in small houses attached to their shops or in rooms behind their workplaces. Peasants forced off their land and crowded into cities found shelter in multistory apartment buildings, an increasingly common sight in the cities of the empire. In these cramped structures, families crowded into small, low rooms about ten feet square. All the families shared a common enclosed courtyard. These apartment buildings and shops were not hidden away from the homes of the wealthy. In Roman towns throughout Italy, simple dwellings, luxurious mansions, shops, and apartment buildings existed side by side. The rich and the poor rubbed shoulders every day, producing a friction that threatened to burst into flame.

Roman Religion

Romans worshiped many gods, the more the better. Every aspect of daily life and work was the responsibility of individual powers, or *numina*. Every man had his *genius* or personal *numen*, just as every woman had her *juno*. Each family had its household powers, the *lares familiares*, whose proper worship was the responsibility of the paterfamilias. The *Vesta* was the spirit of the hearth-fire. The *lares* were the deities of farmland, the *domus*, and the guardians of roads and travelers. The *penates* guarded the family larder or storage cupboard. These family spirits exercised a binding power, a *religio*, upon the Romans, and the pious Roman householder recognized these claims and undertook the *officia*, or duties, to which the spirits were entitled.

Bronze statuette of a Lar, a Roman household god representing an ancestral spirit. In some houses, such statuettes were placed in miniature shrines fashioned after Roman temples. At mealtimes bits of food were burned as offerings to the ancestors.

These basic attitudes of religion, piety, and office lay at the heart of Roman reverence for order and authority. They extended to other traditional Roman and Latin gods such as Jupiter, the supreme god; Juno, his wife; Mars, the god of war; and the two-faced Janus, spirit of gates and new beginnings. This piety extended also to the anthropomorphic Etruscan gods for whom temples were erected on the Capitoline hill, and to the Greek deities whom the Romans absorbed along with the Hellenic world.

Outside the household, worship of the gods and the reading of the future in the entrails of sacrificed animals, the flight of birds, or changes in weather were the responsibilities of colleges of priests. Roman priests did not, as did those in the Near East, form a special caste but rather were important members of the elite who held priesthoods in addition to other public offices. Religion was less a matter of personal relationship with the gods than a public, civic activity binding society together. State-supported cults with their colleges of priests, Etruscan- and Greek-style temples, and elaborate ceremonies were integral parts of the Roman state and society. The world of the gods reflected that of mortals.

As the Roman mortal world expanded, so did the divine. Romans were quick to identify foreign gods with their own. Thus Zeus became Jupiter, Hera became Juno, and Aphrodite became Venus. Whenever possible, Romans interpreted foreign cults in familiar Roman terms. This *interpretatio romana* allowed for the incorporation of conquered peoples into the Roman religious world, which was one with the state. It also made possible the introduction of Roman gods into newly conquered regions, where shrines and temples to indigenous gods could be rededicated to the gods of Rome under their local names.

Still, the elasticity of Roman religion could stretch just so far. With the empire came not only the cults of Zeus, Apollo, and Aphrodite to Rome but that of Dionysus as well. Unlike the formal, public cults of the other Greek deities, which were firmly in the control of authorities, that of Dionysus was largely outside of state control. Women, in the tradition of the maenads, controlled much of the ecstatic and overtly sexual rituals associated with the god. Moreover, these rituals took place in secret, open only to the initiates of the god. Following the Second Punic War, the cult of Dionysus, known in Latin as Bacchus, spread rapidly in Italy, drawing thousands of devotees from all social orders. To the members of the oligarchy everything about the cult seemed to threaten traditional Roman values: it was Greek; it was dominated by women; most significantly, its rituals were secret. At these rites, or *Bacchanalia*, men and women were rumored to engage in every kind of sexual act. The Roman senate was ready to believe anything about this

Detail from a wall painting in the Villa Item (Villa of the Mysteries) near Pompeii. A female satyr suckles a young goat while another plays the panpipes. At right, a young woman recoils before the apparition of Dionysus and Ariadne and the symbols of the mysteries, which are seen on the adjacent wall.

rapidly spreading cult. As Titus Livius or Livy (59 B.C.–A.D. 17), a later Roman moralist and historian, put it:

> The corruption was not confined to one kind of evil, the promiscuous violation of free men and of women; the cult was also a source of false witnesses, forged documents and wills, and perjured evidence, dealing also in poisons and in wholesale murders among the devotees, and sometimes ensuring that not even the bodies were found for burial.

In 186 B.C., the senate decreed the cult of Bacchus a conspiracy and ordered an inquiry. The consul Spurius Postumius Albinus, acting on the spurious testimony of a former prostitute, began a brutal persecution. Rituals were banned, priests and adherents arrested, and rewards offered to informants who provided lurid and fanciful accounts of what had taken place at the Bac-

chanalia. Panic spread throughout Italy as thousands of devotees fled in fear of their lives. Others took their own lives in despair. Hundreds of people were imprisoned and greater numbers were executed. The senate ordered all shrines to Bacchus destroyed and Bacchanalia banned throughout Italy. Perhaps more than any other episode, the suppression of the Bacchic cult showed the fear that the oligarchy felt about the changes sweeping Roman civilization.

Republican Letters

As Rome absorbed foreign gods, it also absorbed foreign letters. From the Etruscans the Romans adopted and adapted the alphabet, the one in which most Western languages are written to this day. Early Latin inscriptions are largely funeral monuments and some public notices such as the Law of the Twelve Tables. The Roman high priest responsible for maintaining the calendar of annual feasts also prepared and updated *annals*, short accounts of important religious and secular events of each year, which he put on public display outside his home. Important treaties, records of booty, and decrees of the senate found their way onto inscriptions as well. However, prior to the third century B.C., apart from extravagant funerary eulogies carefully preserved within families, Romans had no apparent interest in writing or literature as such. The birth of Latin letters began with Rome's exposure to Greek civilization.

Early in the third century B.C., Greek authors had begun to pay attention to expanding Rome. The first serious Greek historian to focus on this new western power was Timaeus (ca. 356–ca. 260 B.C.), who spent most of his productive life in Athens. There he wrote a history of Rome up to the Pyrrhic war, interviewing Roman and Greek witnesses in order to gain an understanding of this Italian city that had defeated a Hellenistic army. Polybius (ca. 200–ca. 118 B.C.), the greatest of the Greek historians to record Rome's rise to power, gathered his information firsthand. As one of a thousand eminent Greeks deported to Rome for political investigation, he became a close friend of Scipio Aemilianus and accompanied him on his Spanish and African campaigns. Polybius became a strong supporter of Roman expansion. His history of the Punic and eastern wars, in the tradition of Thucydides, searches for truth in eyewitness testimony, in the writings of earlier authors, and in the personal experience of the author. Polybius' history is both the culmination of the traditions of Greek historiography and its transformation, since it centers on the rise of a non-Greek power to rule "almost the whole inhabited world."

At the same time that Greeks began to take Rome seriously, Romans themselves became interested in Greece and in particular in the international Hellenistic culture of the eastern Mediterranean. The earliest Latin literary works were clearly adaptations if not translations of Hellenistic genres and texts. Still, they indicated an independence typically Roman. Although Polybius dated the Roman interest in things Greek from the fall of Syracuse in 212 B.C., already in 240 B.C., plays in the Greek tradition were said to have been performed in Rome. The earliest extant literary works, ironically for the sober image of the Roman farmer-soldier, are the plays of Plautus (ca. 254–184 B.C.) and Terence (186–159 B.C.), lightly adapted translations of Hellenistic comedies.

Scheming servants, mistaken identities, bedroom farces, young lovers, and lecherous elders make up the plots of the Roman plays. What is most remarkable about these comedies, however, is the extent to which their authors experimented with and transformed Greek literature. Plautus in particular, while maintaining superficially the Greek settings of his plays, actually creates a world more Roman than Greek. References to Roman laws, magistrates, clients, and social situations abound, as do humorous, derogatory comments on Greek mores. Terence, although remaining closer to Greek models, romanized his material through the creation of an elegant, natural style. Although criticized by many at the time, his plays rapidly became classics of Latin writing, influencing subsequent generations of Latin authors who worked to create a literary language separate from but equal to Greek.

Relief of Roman comic actors at work. The action of many Roman comedies took place on a street. The back wall of the stage represented house fronts with doorways for entrances and exits.

The Burden of Empire

The effects of Rome's rise to world power within less than a century profoundly affected every aspect of Republican life. Magistrates operating far from senatorial control in conquered provinces exercised power and found opportunities for enrichment never before seen. Successful commanders, honored and even deified by eastern cities, felt the temptation to ignore the strict requirements of senatorial accountability. There were fortunes to be made in the empire, and these fortunes distanced the oligarchy ever further from ordinary Roman citizens. A cynical saying circulating in the later Republic summed up the situation well. During the time of a provincial command, it was said, one had to make three fortunes: the first to pay off the bribes it took to get the office, the second to pay off the jury that would investigate corruption after the command had expired, and a third to live on for the rest of one's life. Thus provincial commanders enriched themselves through extortion, collusion with dishonest government contractors and tax collectors, and wholesale bribe taking. Ordinary citizens, aware of such abuses, felt increasingly threatened by the wealthy and powerful. The old traditions of the farmer-soldier, the paterfamilias, the pious venerator of the gods, and the plain-speaking Latin dissolved before the vast new horizons, previously unimagined wealth, alien culture, and unprecedented opportunities of empire.

In the second century B.C., Romans found themselves in a dilemma as the old and the new exerted equal pressures. These tensions led to almost a century of bitter civil strife and ultimately to the disintegration of the Republic. The complex interaction of these tensions can best be seen in the life of one man, Marcus Porcius Cato.

Cato the Elder is often presented as the preserver of the old traditions, in contrast to Scipio Aemilianus, destroyer of Carthage and proponent of Hellenism in the Roman world. True, as censor fighting against conspicuous consumption and as self-conscious defender of the past, Cato cast himself in the mold of the traditional Roman. And Scipio, with his love of Hellenism and his political career defined more by personal achievement than traditional magistracies, represented a new type of Roman. But if the division between old and new, between Cato and Scipio, had been so clear cut, the dilemma of republican Rome would not have been so great. As it was, Cato reflected in himself this contradictory clash of values. Like the two-faced god Janus whom he invoked in all his undertakings, Cato was the stern censor, the guardian and proponent of traditional Roman virtue, as well as the new Roman of shrewd business acumen, influence, and power unimaginable to the simple farmers he professed to admire.

Cato was born in the Latin town of Tusculum in 234 B.C. and grew to maturity on a family estate in Sabine territory. Although he boasted that he had spent his entire youth in frugality, rigor, and industry, his was a moderately wealthy family of Roman citizens. He came of age just at the start of the Second Punic War and distinguished himself in campaigns against Hannibal in Italy and Syracuse in Sicily. In between campaigns he became even more famous for his eloquence in pleading legal cases. His talents, matched by his drive and energy, brought him to the attention of a number of powerful members of the senatorial aristocracy, under whose patronage he came to Rome. There he began to rise through the offices of military tribune, quaestor, and ultimately consul and censor.

This first-generation senator became the spokesman for the traditional values of Rome, for severity and simplicity, for honesty and frugality in private and public life. Never known for his personal charm or tact, Cato was constantly embroiled in controversy. He saved his particular venom for those who enriched themselves with the spoils of conquest, who adopted Greek traditions of culture, and who displayed their new wealth and culture in fine furniture, expensive clothes, and gangs of Greek slaves. He made a great show of his own frugality, glorifying his simple farm life and the care he took in the management of his estates and of his extended *familia*, and working his fields side by side with his slaves. He despised senators who were profiting from the expansion of the empire to become involved in trade and supported legislation to keep senators out of commerce. In public office

Cato was equally frugal, drinking the same cheap wine as his men when on military campaign and boasting of how little public money he spent. He ridiculed Greek philosophy and education, warning his son that the Romans would be destroyed once they were infected with Greek learning. Cato presented himself as the epitome of the old Roman farmer-soldier, a man of simplicity and traditional values.

Actually, Cato, as much as anyone else, was deeply involved in the rapid changes brought about by the empire. He may have worked along with his slaves and shared their table, but as soon as they grew old he sold them to the state to avoid having to support them, something no conscientious paterfamilias would ever have done. Although he led the battle to prevent senators from participating in commerce, he was perhaps the first of that body to diversify his holdings and investments. He bought up land, hot baths, and mineral deposits. He invested his surpluses in maritime commerce, being careful to use middlemen to circumvent his own laws. He also grew rich through moneylending, not only to merchants but also to slaves. Although he avoided conspicuous consumption himself, as consul and censor he was responsible for many of the sumptuous building projects in Rome through which ordinary Romans first experienced the luxuries of the Hellenistic world. While scorning Greek culture, his extant writings and speeches show how deeply indebted he was to Greek literature. Even in his own day he was called the Roman Demosthenes, and he worked bits of Greek authors even into his attacks on Greek civilization.

Cato was neither duplicitous nor hypocritical. He was simply typical. Many senators agreed with him that the old values were slipping away and with them the foundation of the republic. Many feared that personal ambition was undermining the power of the oligarchy. And yet these same people could not resist exploiting the changed circumstances for their own benefit.

Rome had come a long way since its origin as an outpost of the Alban League. At first overshadowed by its more civilized neighbors to the north and south, it had slowly and tenaciously achieved independence from and then domination over its more ancient neighbors. It is difficult to point to particular Roman ideas, institutions, or techniques that made this possible. Virtually all of these were absorbed or adapted from the Etruscans, Greeks, and others with whom Rome came into contact. Rome's great success was largely due to Roman authoritarianism as well as to its genius for creative adaptation, flexibility, and thoroughness, and its willingness to give those it conquered a stake in Roman victory. Until the middle of the second century B.C., this formula had served the republic well. After the final destruction of Carthage, however, an isolated and fearful oligarchy appeared unwilling or unable to broaden the base of those participating in the Roman achievement. The result was a century of conflict and civil war that destroyed the Republican empire.

Suggestions for Further Reading

Primary Sources

Much of the works of Polybius, Livy, Cato, and other Roman authors are available in English translation from Penquin Books. The first volume by Naphtali Lewis and Meyer Reinhold, *Roman Civilization Selected Readings Vol. I: The Republic* (1951) contains a wide selection of documents with useful introductions.

The Western Mediterranean

B. H. Warmington, *Carthage*, rev. ed. (New York: F. A. Praeger, 1969). A basic introduction.

Massimo Pallottino, *The Etruscans* (Bloomington, IN: Indiana University Press, 1975). A general introduction to Etruscan history, language, and civilization.

From City to Empire

Leon Homo, *Primitive Italy and the Beginnings of Roman Imperialism* (Philadelphia: Century Bookbindery, 1968). Classic introduction to early Italian history.

Michael Crawford, *The Roman Republic* (Cambridge, MA: Harvard University Press, 1978). A modern survey of the Republican period, emphasizing political history.

John Boardman, Jasper Griffin, and Oswyn Murray, *The Roman World* (New York: Oxford University Press, 1988). A balanced collection of essays on all aspects of Roman history and civilization.

* P. A. Brunt, *Social Conflicts in the Roman Republic* (New York: Norton, 1971). Analyzes the continuing struggle between patricians and plebeians until the end of the republic.

Keith Hopkins, *Conquerors and Slaves* (New York: Cambridge University Press, 1978). A sociological study of the effects of slavery on imperial society and government.

* Mary Beard and Michael Crawford, *Rome in the Late Republic* (Ithaca, NY: Cornell University Press, 1985). A short interpretative essay on the crisis of the late republic.

Republican Civilization

Suzanne Dixon, *The Roman Mother* (Norman, OK: University of Oklahoma Press, 1988). A balanced view of Roman mothers in law and in society.

* Erich S. Gruen, *The Hellenistic World and the Coming of Rome*, 2 vols. (Berkeley, CA: University of California Press, 1984). A detailed history of the Hellenistic world, presenting Rome's gradual and unintended rise to dominance in it.

Géza Alföldy, *The Social History of Rome* (Berlin: Walter de Gruyter, 1988). A survey of Rome that emphasizes the relationship between social structure and politics.

The Burden of Empire

Alan E. Astin, *Cato the Censor* (New York: Oxford University Press, 1978). An excellent biography of Cato that also analyzes his writings.

* Indicates paperback edition available.

5

Imperial Rome

A Day in the Pax Romana

The street scene in the picture above records a moment arrested in time: 24 August A.D. 79. That morning Vesuvius, the great volcano whose summit towers only five miles from the small seaside resort town of Herculaneum, exploded in a tremendous eruption of fire, ash, pumice, and hot gases that rose in a mushroomlike cloud some twelve miles into the atmosphere. Prevailing winds brought the residue down mostly to the east, filling the region of Oplontis and the town of Pompeii with hot ash. But that evening, "a fearful black cloud ripped by sudden bursts of fire" rolled down the mountainside toward Herculaneum. This hot, black cloud—reaching a temperature of more than 750° F—was a wave of ash and pumice mixed with limestone, mud, and rock. Six successive waves swept through the town, burying it more than sixty-five feet deep. As it cooled into solid rock, it trapped not only stone structures but often even metal, wood, and cloth, preserving them to the present day. As archaeologists patiently chip away the stone, the city reemerges exactly as it was on its final day during the height of the Roman Empire.

Here as nowhere else we can sense what living in the Roman world meant to rich and poor alike. Preserved under the mass of pumice is the Villa of the Papyri, a vast suburban mansion that sprawls eight hundred feet along the Bay of Naples. Its magnificent peristyle, its fine Greek bronzes and marble busts, its complex aqueduct and hydraulic system, and its marble-floored library containing over seventeen hundred papyrus scrolls, all reflect the extraordinary opulence of the great families, those who benefited most from the *pax Romana*, or Roman peace. Standing in marked contrast is the cheaply constructed Trellis House. In the twenty-two-foot frontage, tiny inner courtyard, and two dark floors of this house, which sheltered two families, we get a sense of the life of more ordinary urban Italians of the first century A.D. This flimsy wood frame building with its small, low rooms averaging ten square feet still contains the simple wood beds, clothes cabinet, and cupboard complete with utensils, glassware, and cups used by the inhabitants. The rope by which the families, too poor to tie into the town's aqueduct, drew water

from a well in the courtyard lies coiled around its windlass.

A visitor to Herculaneum can wander the streets and visit the shops exactly as they were on that August day. Wine jugs and a variety of cheeses, nuts, cakes, and fruits line the shelves and countertops of the town's numerous snack bars or wine shops. In the bakeries, ovens almost identical to those used today in nearby Naples produced bread and pastries. Other shops sold vegetables, fruits, grain, and cloth. In small workshops craftsmen cut gems, made and repaired metal objects, and painted decorative panels for their wealthier neighbors. In all, the tools and merchandise lie as they were left that day by their terrified owners.

Both rich and poor could rub shoulders in either of the town's two bathhouses, one centrally located near the forum, the other near the marina beyond the town walls. There men could exercise or play ball in an open courtyard, then choose a warm or hot bath to be followed by a cold plunge in the *frigidarium*. Similar but smaller facilities were available in the women's portion of the bath. Throughout the building, an elaborate hydraulic system of boilers, pipes, and drains supplied the baths with water at the proper temperature.

Everywhere the spirit of the departed inhabitants lingers in the graffiti written on Herculaneum's walls: "To live is vain" on the wall of a wine shop; professions of undying love or scurrilous attacks on rivals; obscenities in the brothel

attached to the suburban bath. Even more eloquent are the silent remains of over a hundred victims of the disaster, most found near the marina where they fled in a desperate attempt to escape by sea. Even in death, the contrast between rich and poor is striking. Near the marina lay the remains of a wealthy woman about forty-five years old, still wearing two gold rings, bracelets, and earrings. Analysis showed her to be tall, well nourished, and in perfect health. Not too far distant were found the remains of a fourteen-year-old slave girl, still cradling the skeleton of a seven-month-old infant who was her charge. The slave had endured a hard life. As an infant she had suffered severe malnutrition, possibly the result of abandonment. Her skeleton also showed the stresses of excessive work for a girl her age. Her owners were certainly getting their money's worth from her.

The streets, buildings, and remains of the inhabitants of Herculaneum strike us with an immediacy often missing in ancient history. Here we observe the ordinary activities of Romans living in a privileged corner of the empire. Their ancestors had survived the turmoil of the republic's collapse. Most lived far removed from the great events of empire and conquest. And yet in their daily lives, their homes, their shops, their luxuries, and their amusements, they show the vitality of Roman civilization, a civilization that ruled the world by the force of its armies but also by the attraction of its culture.

The Price of Empire

Roman victory defeated the republic. Roman conquest of the Mediterranean world and the establishment of the Roman Empire spelled the end of the republican system. Roman society could not withstand the tensions caused by the enrichment of the few, the impoverishment of the many, and the demands of the excluded populations of the empire to share in its benefits. Traditional Roman culture could not survive the attraction of Hellenistic civilization with its wealth, luxuries, and individualistic values. Finally, Roman government could not restrain the ambitions of its oligarchs or protect the interests of its ordinary citizens. The creation of a Mediterranean empire brought in its wake a century of revolutionary change before new, stable social, cultural, and political forms emerged in the Roman world.

Winners and Losers

Rome had emerged victorious in the Punic and Macedonian wars against Carthage and Macedon, but the real winners were the members of the oligarchy, the *optimates* or the "best," as they called themselves, whose wealth and power had grown beyond all imagining. These optimates included roughly three hundred senators and magistrates, most of whom had inherited wealth, political connections, and long-established clientages. Since military command and government of the empire were entrusted to magistrates who were answerable only to the senate of which they were members, the empire was essentially their private domain. Their combination of landed wealth, political experience, and social ties placed them at the pinnacle of Roman society.

But new circumstances created new opportunities for many others. Italian merchants, slave traders, entrepreneurs, and bankers, many of lowly origin, poured into the cities of the east in the wake of the Roman legions. These newly enriched Romans constituted a second elite and formed themselves into a separate order, that of the *equites*, or equestrians, distinguished by their wealth and honorific military service on horseback, but connected with the old military elite. Since the senate did not create a government bureaucracy to administer the empire, equestrian tax farmers became essential to provincial government. Companies of these publicans, or tax collectors, purchased the right to collect rents on public land, tribute, and customs duties from provincials. Whatever they collected beyond the amount contracted for by Roman officials was theirs to keep. Publicans regularly bribed governors and commanders to allow them to gouge the local populations with impunity and on occasion even obtained Roman troops to help them make their collections. Gradually, some of these "new men," their money "laundered" through investments in land, managed to achieve lower magistracies and even move into the senatorial order. Still, the upper reaches of office were closed to all but a tiny minority. By the end of the Punic wars, only some twenty-five families could hope to produce consuls.

The losers in the wars included the vanquished who were sold into slavery by the tens of thousands, the provincials who bore the Roman yoke, the Italian allies who had done so much for the Romans, and even the citizen farmers, small shopkeepers, and free craftsmen of the republic. All four groups suffered from the effects of empire, and over the next century all resorted to violence against the optimates.

The slaves revolted first. Thousands of them, captured in battle or taken after victory, flooded

Roman slaves sifting grain. Roman victories in the Punic and Macedonian wars brought in a huge influx of slaves from the conquered lands. Slaves were pressed into service on the estates and plantations of wealthy landowners.

This relief shows mounted Roman equites, led by musicians, proceeding to a temple for sacrificial rites. As Roman power expanded, Roman religion was increasingly influenced by Greek ideas and by eastern mystery cults such as those of Mithras, Isis, and Serapis.

the Italian and Sicilian estates of the wealthy. Estimates vary, but in the first century B.C., the slave population of Italy was probably around two million, fully one-third of the total population. This vastly expanded slave world overwhelmed the traditional role of slaves within the Roman *familia.* Rural slaves on absentee estates enjoyed none of the protections afforded traditional Roman servants. Cato sold off his slaves who reached old age; others simply worked them to death. Many slaves, born free citizens of Hellenistic states, found such treatment unbearable. In 135 B.C., a small group of particularly badly mistreated slaves in Sicily took up arms against their masters. Soon other slaves joined, swelling the ranks of the rebels ultimately to over two hundred thousand. It took the Roman state three years to crush the revolt.

A generation later slaves revolted in southern Italy and, between 104 and 101 B.C., again in Sicily. This time the cause was more specific. The senate had passed a decree freeing enslaved citizens of Roman allies, but Sicilian slave owners blocked implementation of the order in Sicily. The rebel ranks quickly swelled to over thirty thousand, and only a full-scale military campaign was able to defeat them.

The most serious slave revolt occurred in Italy between 74 and 71 B.C. Gladiators, professional slave fighters trained for Roman amusement, revolted in Capua. Under the competent leadership of the Thracian gladiator Spartacus, over a hundred thousand slaves took up arms against Rome. Ultimately eight legions, more troops than had met Hannibal at Zama, were needed to put down the revolt.

All slave revolts were doomed to failure. The revolutionaries lacked a unified goal, organization, discipline, or strategy. Some wanted freedom to return home. Others sought to establish themselves as autonomous kings with slaves of their own. Still others wished simply to avenge themselves against their masters. Their desperate struggles proved unequal to the numerical and military superiority of the disciplined legions, and retribution was always terrible. After the defeat of Spartacus, crucified rebels lined the road from Rome to Naples.

Revolts profoundly disturbed the Roman state, all the more because it was not just slaves who revolted. In many cases poor free peasants and disgruntled provincials rose up against Rome. The most significant provincial revolt was that of Aristonicus, the illegitimate half brother of Attalus III (ca. 138–133 B.C.) of Pergamum, a Roman client state. Attalus had left his kingdom to Rome at his death. In an attempt to assert his right to the kingdom, Aristonicus armed slaves and peasants and attacked the Roman garrisons. The Hellenized cities of Asia Minor remained loyal to Rome, but this provincial uprising, the first of many over the centuries, lasted more than three years, from 133 to 130 B.C. In 88 B.C., Mithridates VI (120–63 B.C.), the king of Pontus, led an uprising against Roman soldiers, merchants, businessmen, and publicans in Asia Minor. The revolt spread to Greece and tens of thousands of Romans died at the hands of poor freemen.

Revolts by slaves and provincials were disturbing enough. Revolts by Rome's Italian allies were much more serious. After the Second Punic War, these allies, on whose loyalty Rome had depended for survival, found themselves badly treated and exploited. Government officials used state power to undermine the position of the Italian elites. At the same time Roman aristocrats used their economic power to drive the Italic peasants from their land, replacing them with slaves. Some reform-minded Romans attempted to diffuse tensions by extending citizenship to the allies, but failure of this effort led to a revolt at Fregellae south of Rome in 125 B.C. A broader and more serious revolt took place between 91 and 89 B.C. after the senate blocked an attempt to extend citizenship to the allies. During this so-called Social War (from *socii*, the Latin word for *allies*), almost all the Italian allies rose against Rome. These revolts differed from those in the provinces in that the Italian elites as well as the masses aligned themselves against the Roman oligarchy. Even some ordinary Roman citizens joined the rebel forces against the powerful elite.

Optimates and Populares

The despair that could lead ordinary Roman citizens to armed rebellion grew from the social and economic consequences of conquests. While aristocrats amassed vast landed estates worked by cheap slaves, ordinary Romans often lacked

The Roman Empire, ca. 133 B.C.

The walls of this Pompeian dining room are decorated with scenes of mythical animals and gods. The diners reclined on couches around the central sunken fountain while musicians played at the far end of the room.

even a family farm capable of supporting themselves and their families. Many found their way to Rome, where they swelled the ranks of the unemployed, huddled into shoddily constructed tenements and living off the public subsidies.

While many senators bemoaned the demise of the Roman farmer-soldier, few were willing to compromise their own privileged position to help. In the face of the oligarchy's unwillingness to deal with the problem, the tribune Tiberius Gracchus (ca. 163–133 B.C.) in 133 B.C. attempted to introduce a land-reform program that would return citizens to agriculture. Gracchus was the first of the *populares*, political leaders appealing to the masses. His motives were probably a mixture of compassion for the poor, concern over the falling numbers of citizens who had the minimum land to qualify for military service, and personal ambition. Over the previous century, great amounts of public land had illegally come into private hands. With the support of reform-minded aristocrats and commoners, Gracchus proposed a law that would limit the amount of public land an individual could hold to about 312 acres. He also pro-

posed a commission to distribute to landless peasants the land recovered by the state as a result of the law. Because many senators who illegally held vast amounts of public land strongly opposed the measure, it faced certain failure in the senate. Gracchus therefore took it to the plebeian assembly. Since 287 B.C., assembly measures had been binding on all society and only the ten elected tribunes could veto its decisions. Here Gracchus' proposal was assured of support by the rural poor who flocked to Rome to vote for it. When optimates, aristocratic opponents hoping to preserve their position, influenced one of the other nine tribunes to oppose the law, Gracchus had him deposed by the assembly, a move that shocked many senators. Senators, bound by custom and tradition, found Gracchus' maneuver to avoid the senate and his unprecedented deposition of a tribune novel and deeply disturbing. The law passed and a three-person commission to distribute land was established. However, Gracchus' maneuvering lost him many of his aristocratic supporters, who feared that a popular democracy led by a demagogue was replacing the senatorial oligarchy.

Also in 133 B.C., Gracchus introduced another bill that provided that the royal treasury of the kingdom of Pergamum bequeathed to Rome by Attalus III be used to help citizens receiving land purchase livestock and equipment. These laws, which challenged the senate's traditional control over finance and foreign affairs, deeply disturbed the conservative elite, but as long as Gracchus held office, he was protected from any sort of attack by the traditional immunity accorded tribunes. It was no secret, however, that the senate planned to prosecute him as soon as his one-year term expired. To escape this fate, he appealed to the assembly to reelect him for an unprecedented second consecutive term. To his opponents, this appeal smacked of an attempt to make himself sole ruler, a democratic tyrant on the Greek model. A group of senators and their clients, led by one of Gracchus' own cousins, broke into the assembly meeting at which the election was to take place and murdered the tribune and three hundred of his supporters.

The optimates in the senate could eliminate Tiberius Gracchus, but they could not so easily eliminate the movement he had led. In 123 B.C., his younger brother, Gaius Sempronius Gracchus

(153–121 B.C.), became tribune and during his two one-year terms initiated an even broader and more radical reform program. Tiberius had been concerned only about poor citizens. Gaius attempted to broaden the citizenry and to shift the balance of power away from the senate. Alarmed by the revolt at Fregellae, he attempted to extend citizenship to all Latins and improve the status of Italian allies by extending to them the right to vote in the assembly. In order to check the power of senatorial magistrates in the provinces, he transferred to the equestrians the right to investigate provincial corruption. This move brought the wealthy equestrian order into politics as a counterbalance to the senate. Gaius also improved the supply and distribution of grain in Rome and other Italian cities to benefit the urban poor. He reestablished his brother's land-distribution project, extended participation to Latins and Italians, and encouraged colonization as a means to provide citizens with land. Finally, in order to protect himself and his party from the anticipated reaction of the senate and to prepare to avenge his brother's death, he pushed through a law stipulating that only the people could condemn a citizen to death.

Gaius' program was extraordinary for several reasons. In the first place, it was exactly that, a program, the first comprehensive attempt to deal with the problems facing Roman society. Secondly, it proposed a basic shift of power, drawing the equestrian order for the first time into the political arena opposite the senate and making the assembly rather than the senate the initiator of legislation. Finally, it offered a solution to the problem of the allies which, although rejected at the time, was finally adopted some twenty years later. In the short run, however, Gaius' program was a failure. In 121 B.C., he failed to be reelected for a third term and thus lost the immunity of the tribunate. Recalling the fate of his brother, he armed his supporters. Once more the senate acted, ordering the consul to take whatever measures he deemed necessary. Gaius and some three thousand of his supporters died.

The deaths of Tiberius and Gaius Gracchus marked a new beginning in Roman politics. Not since the end of the monarchy had a political conflict been decided with personal violence. The whole episode provided a model for future attempts at reform. Reformers would look not to the senate or the aristocracy but to the people, from whom they would draw their political power. The experience of the Gracchi also provided a model for repression of other reform programs: violence.

The End of the Republic

With the Gracchi dead and the core of their reforms dismantled, the senate appeared victorious against all challengers. At home, the masses of ordinary Roman citizens and their political leadership were in disarray. The conquered lands of North Africa and the Near East filled the public coffers as well as the private accounts of Roman senators and publicans.

In reality, Rome had solved neither the problem of internal conflict between rich and poor nor that of how to govern its enormous empire. The apparent calm ended when revolts in Africa and Italy exposed the fragility of the senate's control and ushered in an ever increasing spiral of violence and civil war.

The Crisis of Government

In 112 B.C., the senate declared war against Jugurtha (ca. 160–104 B.C.), the king of a North African client state who, in his war against a rival, had killed some Roman merchants in the Numidian city of Cirta. The war dragged on for five years amid accusations of corruption, incompetence, and treason. Finally in 107 B.C., the people elected as consul Gaius Marius (157–86 B.C.), a "new man" who had risen through the tribunate, and entrusted him with the conduct of the war. In order to raise an army, Marius ignored property qualifications and enlisted many impoverished Romans and armed them at public expense. Although recruiting of landless citizens had probably taken place before, no one had done it in such an overt and massive manner. Senators looked on Marius' measure with great suspicion, but the poor citizen recruits, who had despaired of benefiting from the land reforms proposed by the Gracchi, looked forward to receiving a grant of land at the end of their military service.

Marius quickly defeated Jugurtha in 106 B.C. In the next year Celtic and Germanic barbarians crossed the Alps into Italy and, although technically disqualified from further terms, Marius was elected consul five times between 104 and 100 B.C. to meet the threat. During this period he continued to recruit soldiers from among the poor and on his own authority extended citizenship to allies. To his impoverished soldiers, Marius promised land but, after his victory in 101 B.C., the senate refused to provide veterans with farms. As a result, Marius' armies naturally shifted their allegiance away from the Roman state and to their popular commander. Soon this pattern of loyalty became the norm. Politicians forged close bonds with the soldiers of their armies. Individual commanders, not the state or the senate, ensured that their recruits received their pay, shared in the spoils of victory, and obtained land upon their retirement. In turn, the soldiers became fanatically devoted to their commanders. Republican armies had become personal armies, potent tools in the hands of ambitious politicians.

The outbreak of the Social War in 91 B.C. marked the first use of these armies in civil war. Both Marius and the consul Lucius Cornelius Sulla (138–78 B.C.) raised armies to fight the Italians, who were only pacified after Roman citizenship was extended to all Italians in 89 B.C. The next year Mithridates VI, the king of Pontus, took advantage of the Roman preoccupation in Italy to invade the province of Asia. As soon as the Italian threat receded, Sulla, as the representative of the optimates, raised an army to fight Mithridates. Marius, as leader of the populares who favored reform, attempted to have Sulla relieved of command. Sulla marched on Rome, initiating a bloody civil war. In the course of this war Rome was occupied three times, once by Marius, twice by Sulla. Each commander ordered mass executions of his opponents and confiscated their property, which he then distributed to his supporters.

Ultimately Sulla emerged victorious and ruled as dictator from 82 to 79 B.C., using this time to shore up senatorial power. He doubled the size of the senate to six hundred, filling the new positions with men drawn from the *equites*. He reduced the authority of tribunes and returned jury courts from the equites to the senators. In order to weaken the military power of magistrates, he abolished the practice of assigning military commands to praetors and consuls. Rather, they were to be held by proconsuls, or former magistrates, who would serve for one year as provincial governors.

In 79 B.C., his reforms in place, Sulla stepped down to allow a return to oligarchic republican rule. Although his changes bought a decade of peace, they did not solve the fundamental problems dividing optimates and populares. If anything, his rule had proven that the only real political option was a dictatorship by a powerful individual with his own army. During the last generation of the republic, idealists continued their hopeless struggle to prop up the dying republican system while more forward-thinking generals fought among themselves for absolute power.

The Civil Wars

Marcus Tullius Cicero (106–43 B.C.) reflected the strengths and weaknesses of the republican tradition in the first century B.C. Although cultivated, humane, and dedicated to the republican constitution, he was also ambitious, blind to the failings of the optimates, a poor judge of character, and out of touch with the political realities of his time. Like Cato in an earlier age, he was a "new man," the son of a wealthy equestrian who provided his children with the best possible education both in Rome and in Athens and Rhodes. In Greece, Cicero developed a lifelong attachment to Stoic philosophy and developed the oratory skills necessary for a young Roman destined for public life. After returning to Rome he quickly earned a reputation for his skills as a courtroom orator. At the same time he began his climb up the political ladder by championing popular causes while protecting the interests of the wealthy and soliciting the assistance of young optimates. Cicero identified firmly with the elite, hoping that the republic could be saved through

The Career of Julius Caesar

the harmonious cooperation of the equestrian and senatorial orders. Neither group was interested in following his program, but most considered him a safer figure than military strongmen like Sulla, who sought high office. In 63 B.C. Cicero was elected consul, the first "new man" to hold the office in over thirty years. The real threat to the existence of the republic was posed by the ambitions of powerful military commanders—Pompey (106–48 B.C.), Crassus (ca. 115–53 B.C.), and Julius Caesar (100–44 B.C.).

Pompey and Crassus, both protégés of Sulla, rose rapidly and unconstitutionally through a series of special proconsular commands by judicious use of fraud, violence, and corruption. Pompey first won public acclaim by commanding a victorious army in Africa and Spain. Upon his return to Rome in 70 B.C., he united with Crassus, who had won popularity for suppressing the Spartacus rebellion. Together they worked to dismantle the Sullan constitution to the benefit of the populares. In return, Pompey received an extraordinary command over all of the coasts of the Mediterranean, in theory to suppress piracy

but actually to give him control over all of the provinces of the empire. When in 66 B.C., King Mithridates of Pontus again attacked Greece, Pompey assumed command of the provinces of Asia. His army not only destroyed Mithridates but continued on, conquering Armenia, Syria, and Palestine, acquiring an impressive retinue of client kings and increasing the income from the provinces by some 70 percent.

While Pompey was extending the frontiers of the empire to the Euphrates, Crassus, whose wealth was legendary—"no one should be called rich," he once observed, "who is not able to maintain an army on his income"—was consolidating his power. He allied himself with Julius Caesar, a young, well-connected orator from one of Rome's most ancient patrician families, who nevertheless promoted the cause of the populares. The senate feared the ambitious and ruthless Crassus, and it was to block the election of Crassus' candidate Catiline (Lucius Sergius Catilina, ca. 108–62 B.C.) to the consulate in 63 B.C. that the senate elected Cicero instead. Catiline soon joined a conspiracy of Sullan veterans and populares, but Cicero quickly uncovered and suppressed the conspiracy and ordered Catiline's execution.

When Pompey returned from Asia in triumph in 62 B.C., he expected to find Italy convulsed with the Catiline revolt and in need of a military savior in the tradition of Sulla. Instead, thanks to Cicero's quick action, all was in order. Although he never forgave Cicero for stealing his glory, Pompey disbanded his army and returned to private life, asking only that the senate approve his organization of the territories he had conquered and grant land to his veterans. The senate refused. In response Pompey formed an uneasy alliance with Crassus and Caesar. This alliance was known as the first triumvirate, from the Latin for *three men*. Caesar was elected consul in 59 B.C. and the following year received command of the province of Cisalpine Gaul in northern Italy.

Pompey and Crassus may have thought that this command would remove the ambitious young man from the political spotlight. Instead, Caesar, who has been called with only some exaggeration "the sole creative genius ever produced by Rome," used his province as a staging ground for the conquest of a vast area of western Europe to the mouth of the Rhine. His brilliant military skills beyond the Alps and his dedication to his troops made him immensely popular with his legions. His ability for self-promotion ensured that this popularity was matched at home, where the populares eagerly received news of his Gallic wars. In 53 B.C. Crassus died leading an army in Syria, leaving Pompey and the popular young Caesar to dispute supreme power. As word of Caesar's military successes increased his popularity at Rome, they also increased Pompey's suspicion of his younger associate. Finally, in 49 B.C., Pompey's supporters in the senate relieved Caesar of his command and ordered him to return to Italy.

Return he did, but not as commanded. Rather than leave his army on the far side of the Rubicon River, which marked the boundary between his province of Cisalpine Gaul and Italy as ordered, he marched on Rome at the head of his legions. This meant civil war, a vicious bloodletting that convulsed the whole Mediterranean world. In 48 B.C., Caesar defeated Pompey in northern Greece, and

Pompey was assassinated shortly after in Egypt. Still the wars went on between Pompey's supporters and Caesar until 45 B.C., when with all his enemies defeated, Caesar returned to Rome. There, unlike Sulla, he showed his opponents clemency as he sought to heal the wounds of war and to undertake an unprecedented series of reforms. He enlarged the senate to nine hundred and widened its representation, appointing soldiers, freedmen, provincials, and above all wealthy men from the Italian towns. He increased the number of magistracies to broaden participation in government, founded colonies at Carthage and Corinth, and settled veterans in colonies elsewhere in Italy, Greece, Asia, Africa, Spain, and Gaul. Still, he made no pretense of returning Rome to republican government. In early 44 B.C., although serving that year as consul together with his general Antony (ca. 81–30 B.C.), Caesar had himself declared perpetual dictator. This move was finally too much for some sixty diehard republican senators. On March 15, a group led by two enemies whom Caesar had pardoned, Cassius Longinus and Marcus Junius Brutus, assassinated him as he entered the senate chamber.

This silver coin was struck to commemorate the assassination of Julius Caesar. Two daggers flank a cap symbolizing liberty. The legend reads "the Ides of March." On the other side is a profile of Brutus.

Cicero rejoiced when he heard of the assassination, clear evidence of his political naivete. The republic was dead long before Caesar died, and the assassination simply returned Rome to civil war, a civil war that destroyed Cicero himself. Mark Antony, Marcus Lepidus (d. 12 B.C.), another of Caesar's generals, and Caesar's grand-nephew and adopted son Octavian (63 B.C.–A.D. 14), who took the name of his great uncle, soon formed a second triumvirate to destroy Caesar's enemies. After a bloody purge of senatorial and equestrian opponents including Cicero, Antony and Octavian set out after Cassius and Brutus, who had fled into Macedonia. At Philippi in 42 B.C. Octavian and Antony defeated the armies of the two assassins (or, as they called themselves, liberators), who preferred suicide to capture.

After the defeat of the last republicans at Philippi, the members of the second triumvirate began to look suspiciously at one another. Antony took command of the east, protecting the provinces of Asia Minor and the Levant from the Parthians and bleeding them dry in the process. Lepidus received Africa, and Octavian was left to deal with the problems of Italy and the west.

Initially Octavian had cut a weak and unimposing figure. He was only eighteen when he was named adopted son and heir in Caesar's will. He had no military or political experience and was frequently in poor health. Still, he had the magic of Caesar's name with which to inspire the army, he had a visceral instinct for politics and publicity, and he combined these with an absolute determination to succeed at all costs. Aided by more competent and experienced commanders, notably Marcus Agrippa (ca. 63–12 B.C.), and Maecenas (ca. 70–8 B.C.), he began to consolidate his power at the expense of his two colleagues. Lepidus attempted to gain a greater share in the empire but found that his troops would not fight against Octavian. He was forced out of his position and allowed to retire in obscurity, retaining only the honorific title of *pontifex maximus.*

Antony, to meet his ever growing demand for cash, became dependent on the Ptolemaic ruler of Egypt, the clever and competent Cleopatra. For her part, Cleopatra manipulated Antony in order to maintain the integrity and independence of her kingdom. Octavian seized the opportunity to portray Antony as a traitor to Rome, a weakling controlled by an Oriental woman who planned to move the capital of the empire to Alexandria. Antony's supporters replied with propaganda of their own, pointing to Octavian's humble parentage and his lack of military ability. The final break came in 32 B.C. Antony, for all his military might, could not attack Italy as long as the despised Cleopatra was with him. Nor could he abandon her without losing her essential financial support. Instead, he tried to lure Octavian to a showdown in Greece. His plan misfired. Agrippa forced him

The End of the Republic

135–81 B.C.	Revolts against the Republic
133–121 B.C.	Gracchi reform programs
107 B.C.	Gaius Marius elected consul
91–82 B.C.	Social War and civil war (Marius vs. Sulla)
82–79 B.C.	Sulla rules as dictator
79–27 B.C.	Era of civil wars
63 B.C.	Cicero elected consul First Triumvirate (Pompey, Crassus, Caesar)
59 B.C.	Caesar elected consul
45 B.C.	Caesar defeats Pompey's forces
44 B.C.	Caesar assassinated Second Triumvirate (Mark Antony, Lepidus, Octavian)
42 B.C.	Octavian and Mark Antony defeat Cassius and Brutus at Philippi
31 B.C.	Octavian defeats Mark Antony and Cleopatra at Actium
27 B.C.	Octavian is declared Augustus

into a naval battle off Actium in 31 B.C. in which Antony was soundly defeated. He and his Egyptian queen committed suicide and Octavian ruled supreme in the Roman empire.

The Good Life

Mere survival was a difficult and elusive goal through the last decades of the republic. Still, some members of the elite sought more. They tried to make sense of the turmoil around them and formulate a philosophy of life to provide themselves with a model of personal conduct. By now Rome's elite were in full command of Greek literature and philosophy, and they naturally turned to the Greek tradition to find their answers. However, they created from it a distinctive Latin cultural tradition. The most prominent figure in the late republic is Cicero, who combined his active life as lawyer and politician with an abiding devotion to Stoic philosophy. In stoicism's belief in divine providence, morality, and duty to one's allotted role in the universe, he found a rational basis for his deeply committed public life. In a series of written dialogues, Cicero presented Stoic values in a form that created a Latin philosophical language freed from slavish imitation to Greek. He also wrote a number of works of political philosophy, particularly *The Republic* and *The Laws*, in conscious imitation of Plato's concern for the proper order of society. For Cicero, humans and gods are bound together in a world governed not simply by might but by justice. The universe, while perhaps not fully intelligible, is nonetheless rational, and reason must be the basis for society and its laws.

These same concerns for virtue are evident in the writings of the great historians of the late republic, Sallust (86–ca. 34 B.C.) and Livy (59 B.C.– A.D. 17). Sallust was a supporter of Julius Caesar, who had written his own stylistically powerful histories of the Gallic and Civil wars. For him as well as for his younger contemporary Livy, the chaos of civil war was the direct result of moral corruption and decline that followed the successes of the empire. For Sallust, the moral failing was largely that of the senate and its members, who trampled the plebs in their quest for power and personal glory. Livy, who was much more conservative, condemned plebeian demagogues as well as power-hungry senators. Only those aristocratic conservatives who, like Cato, had stood for the ancient Roman traditions merited praise. In the second century B.C. the Greek historian Polybius had been fascinated with the rise of the Roman Republic to world supremacy. A century later the Roman historians were even more fascinated with its decline.

A different kind of morality dominated the work of Lucretius (ca. 100–55 B.C.), the greatest poet of the late republic. Just as Cicero had molded stoicism into a Roman civic philosophy, Lucretius presented Epicurean materialist philosophy as a Roman alternative to the hunger for power, wealth, and glory. In his great poem, *On the Nature of Things*, Lucretius presents the Epicurean's thoroughly physical understanding of the universe. He describes its atomic composition, the evolution of man from brutish beginnings to civilization, and the evil effects not only of greed and ambition but also of religion. All that exists is material reality. Religion, whether the state-supported cults of ancient Rome or the exotic cults introduced from the East, plays on mortals' fear of death, a fear that is irrational and groundless. "Death is nothing to us," Lucretius writes. "It is only the natural fulfillment of life. A rational, proportional enjoyment of life is all that matters. Sorrow and anxiety come from but an ignorant emotionalism."

Emotion was precisely the goal of another poetic tradition of the late republic, that of the "neoteric" or new-style poets, especially Catullus (ca. 84–ca. 54 B.C.). Avoiding politics or moralistic philosophy, these poets created short, striking lyric poems which, although inspired by Hellenistic poetry, combine polished craftsmanship with a direct realism that is without precedent. Roughly two dozen of Catullus' poems are addressed to his lover, whom he calls Lesbia. Mostly poems of rejection and disillusion, they are both artful and direct, a cry from the heart, but from a very sophisticated heart:

> My lady says that she wants to marry no one
> so much as me,
> Not even should Jupiter himself ask her.
> So says she. But what a woman says to her
> eager lover
> Should be written in the wind and rushing
> water.

One of the most striking differences between this Latin poetry and its Greek antecedents is the reality and individuality of the persons and relationships expressed. Catullus' poems follow the complex twists and turns of his real affair with Lesbia, who was in reality the cultured, emancipated, and wealthy Clodia, wife of the consul Metellus Celer. Lesbia and the other individuals in Catullus' poems are both very real persons and universal representatives of humanity. Such poetry could exist only because the late republic produced women sufficiently educated and independent to appreciate it.

The same interest in the individual affected the way artists of the late republic borrowed from Greek art. Since Etruscan times, Romans had

Statue of a patrician exhibiting busts of his ancestors in a funeral procession. Roman portrait sculpture developed on Hellenistic Greek models, but the Romans never achieved the realism of the Greek sculptors.

commemorated their ancestors in wax or wooden busts displayed in the atria of their homes. Hellenistic artists concentrated on the ideal, but Romans cherished the individual. The result was a portraiture that caught the personality of the individual's face, even while portraying him or her as one of a type. Statues of the ideal nude, the armored warrior, or the citizen in his simple toga followed the proportions and conventions of Hellenistic sculpture. The heads however, created in hard, dry style, are as unique and personal as the characters who live in Catullus' lyric poems. We see in them the strengths and weaknesses, the stresses and the privileges, that marked the last generation of the Roman republic.

The Augustan Age

It took Octavian two years following his victory at Actium in 31 B.C. to eliminate remaining pockets of resistance and to work out a system to reconcile his rule with Roman constitu-tional traditions and yet not surrender any of his power. That power rested on three factors: his immense wealth, which he used to secure sup-port; his vast following among the surviving elites as well as among the populares; and his total command of the army. It also rested on the exhaustion of the Roman people, who were eager, after decades of civil strife, to return to peace and stability. Remembering the fate of Julius Caesar, however, Octavian had no intention of rekindling opposition by establishing an overt monarchy. Instead, in 27 B.C., as he himself put it in the autobiographical inscription he had erected out-side his mausoleum years later, he returned the republic from his own charge to the senate and the people of Rome. In turn the senate decreed him the title of *Augustus*, meaning "exalted."

What this meant was that Augustus, as he was now called, continued to rule no less strongly than before, but he did so not through any auto-cratic office or title—he preferred to be called simply the "first citizen," or *princeps*—but by preserving the form of the traditional Roman magistracies. For four years he rested his authority on consecutive terms as consul, and after 23 B.C., held a life position as tribune. The senate granted him proconsular command of the provinces of Gaul, Spain, Syria, and Egypt, the major sources of imperial wealth and the loca-tions of more than three-quarters of the Roman army. Later the senate declared his command *imperium* of these "imperial" provinces superior to that of any governors of other provinces. Thus Augustus, through the power of the plebeian office of tribune, stood as the permanent protec-tor of the Roman people. As simultaneously either consul or proconsul, he held the imperium, the command of the army, the basis of the ancient patrician authority. He was the first and greatest emperor.

These formalities deceived no one. Augustus' power was absolute. However, by choosing not to exercise it in an absolutist manner, he forged a new constitutional system that worked well for himself and his successors. By the end of his ex-traordinarily long reign of forty-one years, few living could remember the days of the republic and fewer still mourned its passing. Under Augustus and his successors the empire enjoyed two centuries of stability and peace, the *pax Romana.*

The Empire Renewed

Cicero had sought in vain a concord of the orders, a settlement of the social and political frictions of the empire through the voluntary efforts of a public-minded oligarchy. What could not happen voluntarily, Augustus imposed from above, reforming the Roman state, society, and culture.

Key to Augustus' program of renewal was the senate, which he made, if not a partner, then a useful subordinate in his reform. He gradually reduced the number of senators, which had grown to over a thousand, back down to six hundred. In the process he eliminated the unfit and incompetent as well as the impoverished and

This idealized marble portrait statue of the emperor Augustus addressing his army was found in the Villa of Livia, wife of Augustus, at Prima Porta in Rome. The carvings on his breastplate recall a diplomatic incident during his reign.

those who failed to show the appropriate *pietas* toward the *princeps*. At the same time he made membership hereditary, although he continued to appoint individuals of personal integrity, ability, and wealth to the body. Under Augustus and his successors, access to the senate became easier and more rapid than ever before and the body was constantly renewed by the admission of wealthy sons of provincials and even of freed slaves. Most conspicuous among the "new men" to enter the senate under Augustus were the wealthy leaders of Italian cities and colonies. These small-town notables formed the core of Augustus' supporters and worked most closely with him to renew the Roman elite.

Augustus also shared with the senate the governance of the empire, although again not on an equal footing. The senate named governors to the peaceful provinces, while Augustus named commanders to those frontier "imperial" provinces where were stationed the bulk of the legions. Senators themselves served as provincial governors and military commanders. The senate also functioned as a court of law in important cases. Still in all, the senate remained a creature of the emperor, seldom asserting itself even when asked to do so by Augustus or his successors and competing within its own ranks to see who could be first to do the emperor's bidding. "Men fit for slaves!" was how Augustus' successor Tiberius disgustedly described senators.

Augustus undertook an even more fundamental reform of the equites, those wealthy businessmen, bankers, and tax collectors who had vied with the senatorial aristocracy since the reforms of Tiberius Gracchus. After Actium many equites found themselves proscribed—sentenced to death or banishment—and had their property confiscated. Augustus began to rebuild their ranks by enrolling a new generation of successful merchants and speculators, who became the foundation of his administration. Equestrians formed the backbone of the officer corps of the army, of the treasury, and of the greatly expanded imperial administration. The equestrian order was open at both ends. Freedmen and soldiers who acquired sufficient wealth moved into the order, and the most successful and accomplished equestrians were promoted into the senate. Still, the price for a renewed equestrian order was its removal from the political arena. No longer was provincial tax collection farmed out to companies of equestrian publicans nor were they allowed a role in executive or judicial deliberations. For most, these changes were a small price to pay for security, standing, and avenues to lucrative employment. Small wonder that emperors often had difficulty persuading the most successful equites to give up their positions for the more public but less certain life of a senator.

The land crisis had provoked much of the unrest in the late republic, and after Actium, Augustus had to satisfy the needs of the loyal soldiers of his sixty legions. Drawing on his immense wealth, acquired largely from the estates of his proscripted enemies, he pensioned off thirty-two legions, sending them to colonies he purchased for them throughout the empire. The remaining twenty-eight legions became a permanent professional army stationed in imperial provinces. In time the normal period of enlistment became fixed at twenty years, after which time Augustus provided the legionnaires with land and enough cash to settle in among the notables of their colonies. After A.D. 5 the state assumed the payment of this retirement bonus. Augustus also enrolled over a hundred thousand noncitizens into auxiliary units stationed in the imperial provinces. Auxiliaries served for twenty-five years and upon retirement were rewarded with colonies and Roman citizenship. Finally, Augustus established a small, elite unit, the praetorian guard, in and around Rome as his personal military force. Initially, the praetorians protected the emperors. In later reigns, they would make them.

These measures created a permanent solution to the problem of the citizen-soldier of the late republic. Veteran colonies, all built as model Roman towns with their central forum, baths, temples, arenas, and theaters as well as their outlying villas and farms, helped Romanize the far provinces of the empire. These colonies, unlike the independent colonies of Greece in an earlier age, remained an integral part of the Roman state. Thus Romanization and political integration went hand in hand, uniting through peaceful means an empire first acquired by arms. Likewise, ambitious provincials, through service as auxiliaries and later as citizens, acquired a stake in the destiny of Rome.

Not every citizen, of course, could find prosperity in military service and a comfortable retirement. The problem of urban poverty in Rome continued to grow. By the time of Augustus, the capital city had reached a population of perhaps 600,000 people. A tiny minority relaxed in the comfortable homes built on the Palatine. Tens of thousands more crammed into wooden and brick tenements and jostled each other in the crowded, noisy streets. (See Special Feature, "Living in Rome" pp. 152–153.) Employment was hard to find since free labor had difficulty competing against slaves. The emperors, their power as tribunes making them protectors of the poor, provided over 150,000 resident citizens with a basic dole of wheat brought from Egypt. They also built aqueducts to provide water to the city. In addition, they constructed vast public recreation centers. These included both the sumptuous baths, which were combination bathing facilities, health clubs, and brothels; and arenas such as the Colosseum, where fifty thousand spectators could watch gladiatorial displays, and the Circus Maximus, where a quarter of the city's population could gather at once to watch chariot races. Such mass gatherings replaced the plebeian assemblies of the republic as the occasions on which the populace could express its will. Few emperors were foolish enough to ignore the wishes of the crowd roared out in the Circus.

Divine Augustus

Augustus' renewal of Rome rested on a religious reform. In 17 B.C. he celebrated three days of sacrifices, processions, sacred games, and theater performances known as the secular games. Although celebrations marking the beginning of each one-hundred-year generation, or *saeculum*, had been a part of ancient Roman tradition, Augustus revived the games and expanded them to mark the beginning of a new age. After the death of Lepidus in 12 B.C., he assumed the office of *pontifex maximus* and used it to direct a reinvigoration of Roman religion. He restored numerous temples and revived ancient Roman cults that had fallen into neglect during the chaos of the civil wars. He established a series of public religious festivals, reformed priesthoods, and encouraged citizens to participate in the traditional cults of Rome. His goals in all these religious reforms were twofold. After decades of public

This fourth-century mosaic depicts gladiatorial combatants, some of whom are identified by name. Roman gladiators were lionized by society much like the sports stars of today. Some, who began as slaves, became men of wealth and substance.

authority controlled by violence and naked aggression, he was determined to restore the traditions of Roman piety, morality, sacred order, and faith in relationship between the gods and Roman destiny. An equally important goal was Augustus' promotion of his own cult. His adoptive father, Julius Caesar, had been deified after his death, and Augustus benefited from this association with a divine ancestor. His own *genius*, or guiding spirit, received special devotion in temples throughout the West dedicated to "Rome and Augustus." In the East, citizens and noncitizens alike worshiped him as a living god. In this manner the emperor became identical with the state and the state religion closely akin to emperor worship. After his death Augustus and virtually all of the emperors after him were worshiped as official deities in Rome itself.

Closely related to his fostering of traditional cults was Augustus' attempt to restore traditional Roman virtues, especially within the family. Like the reformers of the late republic, he believed that the declining power of the paterfamilias was at the root of much that was wrong with Rome. To reverse the trend and to restore the declining population of free Italians, Augustus attempted to encourage marriage, procreation, and the firm control of husbands over wives. He imposed penalties for those who chose not to marry and

bestowed rewards on those who produced large families. He enacted laws to prevent women from having extramarital affairs and even exiled his own daughter and granddaughter for promiscuity.

Augustus' call for a return to ancient virtue echoed that of leading figures of the late republic, in particular Cicero. The story is told that Augustus himself, although he had been partially responsible for Cicero's proscription and death, recognized the merit of his philosophy. He once came upon one of his grandchildren reading Cicero. The child, knowing that Cicero had been his grandfather's enemy, attempted to hide the book. Augustus took it, looked through it, and returned it, saying, "My child, this was a learned man and a lover of his country."

Augustus actively patronized those writers who shared his conservative religious and ethical values and who might be expected to glorify the *princeps* and used his power to censor and silence writers he considered immoral. Chief among the favored were the poets Virgil (70 B.C.–19 B.C.) and Horace (65 B.C.–8 B.C.). Both came from provincial and fairly modest origins, although both received excellent educations. Each lost his property in the proscriptions and confiscations during the civil wars, but their poetry eventually won them the favor of Augustus. In time Horace received a comfortable estate at Licenza east of Rome and Virgil's family estates were returned to him and he received a villa at Nola and houses in Rome and Naples. In return, through their poetry in praise of the emperor, Horace and Virgil conferred immortality on Augustus.

Horace celebrated Augustus' victory at Actium, his reform of the empire, and reestablishment of the ancient cults that had brought Rome divine favor. In Horace's poems, Augustus is almost a god. His deeds are compared to those of the great heroes of Roman legend and judged superior. Interspersed with the poems praising Augustus are poems of great beauty praising the love of both boys and girls and the enjoyment of wine and music. To Horace, the glories of the new age inaugurated by Augustus with the secular games of 17 B.C. included not only the splendor of empire but also the enjoyment of privileged leisure.

Virgil began his poetic career with pastoral poems celebrating the joys of rural life and the bitterness of the loss of lands in the civil wars. By 40 B.C. he was turning to greater themes. In his fourth *Eclogue*, he announced the birth of a child, a child who would usher in a new golden age. This prophetic poem may have anticipated the birth of a son to Octavian's sister and Mark Antony; it may simply have been an expression of hope for renewal. Later, under the patronage of Maecenas and Augustus, Virgil turned directly to glorify Augustus and the new age. The ultimate expression of this effort was the *Aeneid*, an epic consciously intended to serve for the Roman world the role of the Homeric poems in the Greek.

As he reworked the legend of Aeneas, a Trojan hero who escaped the destruction of the city, wandered throughout the Mediterranean, and ultimately came to Latium, Virgil presented a panoramic history of Rome and its destiny. Unlike the Homeric heroes, Achilles and Odysseus, who were driven by their own search for glory, Aeneas is driven by his piety, that is, his duty toward the gods and his devotion to his father. Aeneas must follow his destiny, which is the destiny of Rome, to rule the world in harmony and justice. In the midst of his wanderings, Aeneas (like Odysseus before him) enters the underworld to speak with his dead father. Here he sees a vision of Rome's greatness to come. He sees the great heroes of Rome, including Augustus, "son of a god," and he is told of the particular mission of Rome:

Let others fashion in bronze more lifelike,
    breathing images
Let others (as I believe they will) draw living
    faces from marble
Others shall plead cases better and others will
    better
Track the course of the heavens and announce
    the rising stars.
Remember, Romans, your task is to rule the
    peoples
This will be your art: to teach the habit of
    peace
To spare the defeated and to subdue the
    haughty.

The finest of the poets who felt the heavy hand of Augustus' disfavor was Ovid (43 B.C.–A.D. 17), the great Latin poet of erotic love. In *Art of Love* and *Amores*, he cheerfully preaches the art of seduction and adultery. He delights in poking irreverent fun at everything from the sanctity of Roman marriage to the serious business of warfare. In his great *Metamorphoses*, a series of artfully told myths, he parodies the heroic epic, mocking with grotesque humor the very material Virgil used to create the *Aeneid*. By A.D. 8 Augustus had had enough. He exiled the witty poet to Tomis, a miserable frontier post on the Black Sea. There Ovid spent the last nine years of his life, suffering from the harsh climate, the constant danger of nomadic attacks and, most of all, the pain of exile from the center of the civilization he loved. Exactly what offense he had committed is not clear. Perhaps for Augustus what was most intolerable was that, in spite of the emperor's efforts to foster an immortal poetic tradition glorifying the Roman virtues, Ovid was clearly appreciated by his contemporaries as the greatest poet of the age.

Augustus' Successors

Horace and Virgil may have made Augustus' fame immortal. His flesh was not. The problem of succession occupied him throughout much of his long reign and was never satisfactorily solved. Since the princeps was not a specific office, but a combination of offices and honors held together by military might and religious aura, formal dynastic succession was impossible. Instead Augustus attempted to select a blood relative as successor, include him in his reign, and have him voted the various offices and dignities that constituted his own position.

Unfortunately, Augustus outlived all of his first choices. His nephew and adopted son Marcellus, to whom he married his only child Julia, died in 23 B.C. He then married Julia to his old associate Agrippa and began to groom him for the position, but Agrippa died in 12 B.C. Lucius and Gaius, the sons of Julia and Agrippa, also died young. Augustus' final choice, his stepson Tiberius (A.D. 14–37) proved to be a gloomy and unpopular successor but nevertheless a competent ruler under whom the machinery of the empire functioned smoothly. The continued smooth functioning of the empire even under the subsequent members of Augustus' family—the mad Gaius, also known as Caligula (37–41), the bookish but competent Claudius (41–54), and initially under

Nero (54–68)—is a tribute to the soundness of Augustus' constitutional changes and the vested interest that the descendants of Augustus' military and aristocratic supporters had in them.

Nero was, however, more than even they could bear. Profligate, vicious, and paranoid, Nero divided his time between murdering his relatives and associates, including his mother, his aunt, his wife, his tutors, and eventually his most capable generals, and squandering his vast wealth on mad attempts to gain recognition as a great poet, actor, singer, and athlete. (When he competed in games, other contestants wisely lost.) Finally in A.D. 68, the exasperated commanders in Gaul, Spain, and Africa revolted. Once more war swept the empire. Nero slit his own throat (one of his last sentences was "Dead, and so great an artist!"), and in the next year, the "Year of the Four

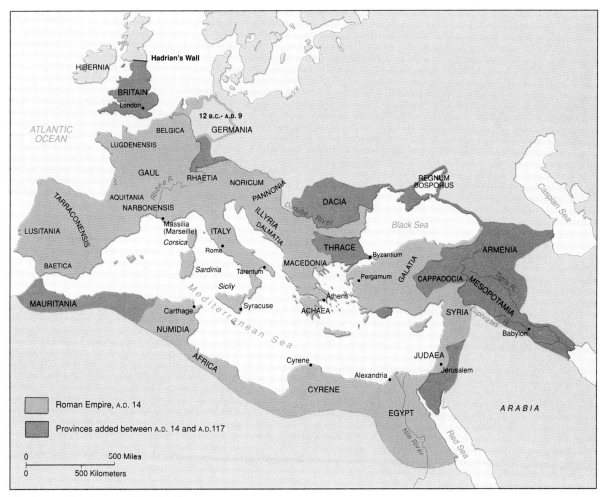

The Roman Empire, A.D. *14 and 117*

Living in Rome

In spite of its magnificent temples, palaces, and forums, the Rome of the empire had more in common with the teeming cities of the third world—Nairobi or Calcutta—than with the modern capitals of Washington, Paris, or London. The narrow, twisted streets; the din of hawkers, animals, and shoppers; the stench of garbage and sewage; and above all, the teeming masses of the desperately poor made Rome a nightmare for those not rich enough to isolate themselves in the luxury of a Palatine mansion.

At its height in the second century, the population of Rome and Ostia, its port, numbered well over a million. Feeding, housing, employing, and maintaining even a minimum of sanitation for so many people were almost beyond the ability of the Roman state. The poor crowded together in dark, dank apartment buildings thrown up with little care and in constant danger of collapse. In his biting satire on life in Rome, the poet Juvenal (ca. 55–after 127 A.D.) complained of the constant fear that Roman tenements would come crashing down on their inhabitants. Even if the buildings did not collapse, they were likely to catch fire from one of the many poorly protected fireplaces tended by each family. Fires were frequent, and the fire brigade organized under Augustus could do little to stop fire from racing through the crowded buildings. In 64 A.D., a

disastrous fire (rumored to have been started by the Emperor Nero) swept from the area of the Circus Maximus near the Palatine hill through the city. Tacitus described the fire: "there were no residences fenced with masonry or temples surrounded by walls, or anything else to act as an obstacle. The blaze in its fury ran through the level portions of the city, rose to the hills, then again devastated the lower places . . . ." When it was over, of the fourteen districts of the city, only four remained undamaged. Three had been leveled; in seven

there remained only a few shattered, half-burned relics of houses.

While catastrophes on so grand a scale were infrequent, daily life held sufficient terrors for most inhabitants. The city was filthy. Although the streets were mostly paved, they were thick with mud in rainy weather and dust in dry. To this were added garbage, animal excrement, and human sewage illegally dumped from tenement windows. The *cloaca maxima*, or great sewer, could accommodate only a small portion of the city's wastes and in any case

152

flowed into the Tiber, polluted with garbage, offal of slaughtered animals, and every sort of waste. By law, sewage was to be carried outside the city limits and dumped into foul-smelling pits that ringed Rome, pushed back year to year as the suburban slums expanded with the city's growth.

During their short lives (urban men could hope to live to an average age of perhaps twenty-six, women to twenty-three), Rome's masses were constantly engaged in a desperate search for food. The famous "bread and circuses" provided by the emperors were too little and reached only a fraction of the urban poor. Only about one-third of Roman families received the monthly ration of thirty-three kilograms of wheat, hardly enough to sustain them.

Even these had to find some sort of income with which to supplement their diet with oil, beans, cheese, fruits, and meat, as well as to pay for rent and clothing.

Since Rome had virtually no industry, the majority of the middle classes supported themselves by working to transport the vast quantities of foodstuffs and other necessities the city consumed each day. The poor, if they found work at all, did so in menial service positions, often in public enterprises such as baths.

Competition for even the most humble positions was keen and, in order to protect their jobs, Roman workers of all levels organized into colleges or guilds, trade associations with social and religious functions. These guilds protected mem-

bers from unauthorized competition, set salaries, and at the same time provided the city government with a means of policing its vast population. Guilds ranged from teachers, physicians, scribes, and shippers, to sewer cleaners, muleteers, and over twenty specialized guilds in the public baths such as bath attendants, masseuses, and even armpit-hair pluckers.

Their meager incomes protected by their guilds, their precarious diets supplemented by the public dole, Rome's masses lived their short lives in a condition exceeded in wretchedness only by that of the worst slaves. When they died, not even a pauper's grave awaited them. Their remains were simply dumped into the sewage pits beyond the city's walls.

Emperors," four men in quick succession won the office only to lose their lives just as quickly. Finally, in 70 Vespasian (A.D. 69–79), the son of a "new man" who had risen through the ranks to the command in Egypt, secured the principate and restored order.

The first emperors had rounded off the frontiers of the empire, transforming the client states of Cappadocia, Thrace, Commagene, and Judaea in the east and Mauritania in North Africa into provinces. Claudius (A.D. 41–54) presided over the conquest of Britain in A.D. 43. These emperors introduced efficient means of governing and protecting the empire, and tied together its inhabitants, roughly fifty million in the time of Augustus, in networks of mutual dependence and common interest. Augustus established peaceful relations with the Parthian empire, which permitted unhampered trade between China, India, and Rome. In the west, after a disastrous attempt to expand the empire to the Elbe ended in the loss of three legions in A.D. 9, the frontier was fixed at the Rhine. The northern border stopped at the Danube. The deserts of Africa, Nubia, and Southern Arabia formed the southern borders of what in the first century A.D. many saw as the "natural" boundaries of the empire.

When Vespasian's troops fought their way into Rome in vicious hand-to-hand street fighting, the populace watched with idle fascination. The violence of A.D. 69, unlike that of the previous century, involved mostly professional legions and their commanders. The rest of the empire sat back to watch. In a few restive regions of the empire some Gauls, the Batavians along the Rhine, and die-hard Jewish rebels tried to use the momentary confusion to revolt, but by and large the empire remained stable. This stability was the greatest achievement of Augustus and his immediate successors.

The emperors of the Flavian dynasty, Vespasian and his sons and successors Titus (79–81) and Domitian (81–96), were stern and unpretentious provincials who restored the authority and dignity of their office, although they also did away with much of the trappings of republican legitimacy that Augustus and his immediate successors had used. They solidified the administrative system, returned the legions to their fairly permanent posts, and opened the highest reaches of

power as never before to provincial elites. After the Flavian emperors, the Antonines (96–193), especially Trajan (98–117), Hadrian (117–138), and Antoninus Pius (138–161), ruled for what has been termed "the period in the history of the world, during which the human race was most happy and prosperous."

The Pax Romana

Not all was peaceful during this period. Trajan initiated a new and final expansion of the imperial frontiers. Between 101 and 106 he conquered Dacia (modern Romania). He resumed war with the Parthians, conquering the provinces of Armenia and Mesopotamia by 116. During the second century, the Palestinian Jews revolted in 115–117 and again in 132–135. The emperor Hadrian put down this second revolt and expelled the surviving Jews from Judaea. Along both the eastern and western frontiers legions had to contend with sporadic border incidents. However, within these borders a system of Roman military camps, towns, and rural estates constituted a remarkably heterogeneous and prosperous civilization.

Administering the Empire

The imperial government of this vast empire was as oppressive as it was primitive. Taxes, rents, forced labor service, military levies and requisitions, and outright extortion weighed heavily on its subjects. Still, fewer than one thousand officials ever held direct official imperium or command within the empire at any time. These were largely the governors and officials of the senatorial provinces, but even they had little direct control over the daily lives of the governed. The daily exercise of government fell to local elites, the army, and members of the imperial household.

To a considerable extent, the inhabitants of the empire continued to be governed by the indigenous elites whose cooperation Rome won by giving them broad autonomy. Thus Hellenistic cities continued to manage their own affairs under the supervision of essentially amateur Roman governors. Local town councils in Gaul, Germany, and Spain supervised the collection of taxes, maintained public works projects, and kept the peace. In return for their participation in Roman rule, these elites received Roman citizenship, a prize that carried prestige, legal protection, and the promise of further advancement in the Roman world.

In those imperial provinces controlled directly by the emperor, the army was much more in evidence, and the professional legions were the ultimate argument of imperial tax collectors and imperial representatives, or *procurators*. Moreover, as the turmoil of the Year of the Four Emperors amply demonstrated, the military was the ultimate foundation of imperial rule itself. Still, soldiers were as much farmers as fighters. Legions usually remained in the same location for years, and around military camps veterans' colonies sprang up. These settlements created a strong Roman presence and blurred the distinction between army post and town.

Finally, much of the governing of the empire was done by the vast households of the Roman elite, particularly that of the princeps. Freedmen and slaves from the emperor's household often governed vast regions, oversaw imperial estates, and managed imperial factories and mines. These slaves and former slaves were loyal, competent, and easily controlled. The vast, powerful, and efficient imperial household was also a means of social and economic advancement. Proximity to the emperor brought power and status, regardless of birth. The descendants of the old Roman nobility might look down their noses at imperial freedmen, but they obeyed their orders.

The empire worked because it rewarded those who worked with it and left alone those who paid their taxes and kept quiet. Local elites, auxiliary soldiers, and freedmen could aspire to rise to the highest ranks of the power elite. Seldom has a ruling elite made access to its ranks so open to those who cooperated with it. As provincials were drawn into the Roman system, they were also drawn into the world of Roman culture. Proper education in Latin and Greek, the ability to hold one's own in philosophical discussion, the absorption of Roman styles of dress, recreation,

religious cults, and life itself, all were essential for ambitious provincials. Thus, in the course of the first century A.D., the disparate portions of the empire competed, not to free themselves from the Roman yoke but to become Roman themselves.

Eastern Religions

The same openness that permitted the spread of Latin letters and Roman baths to distant Gaul and the shores of the Black Sea provided paths of dissemination for other distinctly un-Roman religious traditions. For many in the empire, the traditional rituals offered to the household gods and the state cults of Jupiter, Mars, and the other official deities were insufficient foci of religious devotion. Many educated members of the elite were actually vague monotheists, believing in a supreme deity even while

A painting from Herculaneum depicts priests of the cult of Isis, an Egyptian goddess of procreation and birth. By the time of the Empire, many Romans had turned from the spiritually unrewarding state religion to eastern mystery cults.

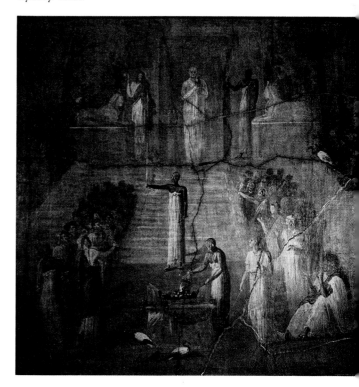

convinced that the ancient traditional cults were essential aspects of patriotism, the cornerstone of the piety necessary to preserve public order. Many others in the empire sought personal, emotional bonds with the divine world.

As discussed in chapter 4, already in the second century B.C. the Roman world had been caught up in the emotional cult of Dionysus, an ecstatic, personal, and liberating religion entirely unlike the official Roman cults. Again in the first century A.D., so-called mystery cults, that is, religions promising immediate, personal contact with a deity that would bring immortality, spread throughout the empire. Some were officially introduced into Rome as part of its open polytheism. These included the Anatolian Cybele or great mother-goddess cult, which was present in Rome from the late third century B.C. Devotees underwent a ritual in which they were bathed in the blood of a bull or a ram, thereby obtaining immortality. The cult of the Egyptian goddess Isis spread throughout the Hellenistic world and to Rome in the republican period. In her temples, staffed by Egyptian priests, water from the Nile

was used in elaborate rites to purify initiates. From Persia came the cult of Mithras, the ancient Indo-Iranian god of light and truth who, as bringer of victory, found special favor with Roman soldiers and merchants eager for success in this life and immortality beyond the grave. Generally Rome tolerated these alien cults as long as they could be assimilated or at least reconciled in some way into the cult of the Roman gods and the genius of the emperor.

With one religious group this assimilation was impossible. The Jews of Palestine had long refused any accommodation with the polytheistic cults of the Hellenistic kingdoms or with Rome. Roman conquerors and emperors, aware of the problems of their Hellenistic predecessors, went to considerable lengths to avoid antagonizing this small and unusual group of people. When Pompey seized Jerusalem in 63 B.C., he was careful not to interfere in Jewish religion and even left Judaea under the control of the Jewish high priest. Later, Judaea was made into a client kingdom under the puppet Herod. Jews were allowed to maintain their monotheistic cult and were

Spoils From the Temple in Jerusalem, *a marble relief from the Arch of Titus. The arch was begun by Titus' father, the emperor Vespasian, to commemorate Titus' victory over the Jews in* A.D. *78.*

excused from making sacrifices to the Roman gods.

Still, the Jewish community remained deeply divided about its relationship with the wider world and with Rome. At one end of the spectrum were the Sadducees, a party composed largely of members of priestly families who enjoyed considerable influence with their foreign rulers. They were staunch defenders of the ancient Jewish law, or Torah, but not to the exclusion of other later religious and legal traditions. In particular the Sadducees rejected the idea of resurrection and predictions of a coming liberator and the end of the world. They were willing to work with Rome and even adopt some elements of Hellenism, as long as the services in the temple could continue.

At the other end of the spectrum were the Hasidim, those who rejected all compromise with Hellenistic culture and collaboration with foreign powers. Many expected the arrival of a messiah, a liberator who would destroy the Romans and reestablish the kingdom of David. One party within the Hasidim were the Pharisees, who practiced strict dietary rules and rituals to maintain the separation of Jews and Gentiles (literally, "the peoples," that is, all non-Jews). The Pharisees accepted the writings of the Hebrew prophets along with the Torah and abided by a still larger body of orally transmitted law, the "tradition of the elders." The most prominent figure in this movement was Hillel (ca. 30 B.C.–A.D. 10), a Jewish scholar from Babylon who came to Jerusalem as a teacher of the law. He began a tradition of legal and scriptural interpretation which, in an expanded version centuries later, became the Talmud. Hillel was also a moral teacher who taught peace and love, not revolt. "Whatever is hateful to you, do not to your fellow man: this is the whole Law; the rest is mere commentary," he taught. He also looked beyond the Jewish people and was concerned with the rest of humanity. "Be of the disciples of Aaron; loving peace and pursuing peace; loving mankind and bringing them near to the Torah."

For all their insistence on purity and separation from other peoples, the Pharisees did not advocate violent revolt against Rome. They preferred to await divine intervention. Another group of Hasidim, the Zealots, were less willing to wait. After A.D. 6, when Judaea, Samaria, and Idumaea were annexed and combined into the province of Judaea administered by imperial procurators, the Zealots began to organize sporadic armed resistance to Roman rule. As ever, armed resistance was met with violent suppression. Through the first century A.D., clashes between Roman troops and Zealot revolutionaries grew more frequent and more widespread.

The already complex landscape of the Jewish religious world became further complicated by the brief career of Joshua ben Joseph (ca. 6 B.C.–A.D. 30), known to history as Jesus of Nazareth and to his followers as Jesus the Messiah or the Christ. Jesus came from Galilee, an area known as a Zealot stronghold. However, while Jesus preached the imminent coming of the kingdom, he did so in an entirely nonpolitical manner. He was, like many popular religious leaders, a miracle worker. When people flocked around him to see his wonders, he preached a message of peace and love of God and neighbor. His teachings were entirely within the Jewish tradition and closely resembled those of Hillel—with one major exception. While many contemporary religious leaders announced the imminent coming of the messiah, Jesus informed his closest followers, the apostles and disciples, that he himself was the messiah.

For roughly three years Jesus preached in Judaea and Galilee, drawing large, excited crowds. Many of his followers pressed him to lead a revolt against Roman authority and reestablish the kingdom of David, even though he insisted that the kingdom he would establish was not of this world. Other Jews saw his claims as blasphemy and his assertion that he was the king of the Jews, even if a heavenly one, as a threat to the status quo. Jesus became more and more a figure of controversy, a catalyst for violence. Ultimately the Roman procurator, Pontius Pilate, decided that he posed a threat to law and order. Pilate, like other Roman magistrates, had no interest in the internal religious affairs of the Jews. However, he was troubled by anyone who had the potential for causing political disturbances, no matter how unintentionally. Pilate ordered Jesus scourged and put to death by crucifixion, a common Roman form of execution for slaves, pirates, thieves, and noncitizen troublemakers.

The cruel death of this gentle man ended the popular agitation he had stirred up, but it did not deter his closest followers. They soon announced that three days after his death he had risen and

The Roman Empire

Julio-Claudian Period	Augustus (27 B.C.–A.D. 14)
	Tiberius (A.D. 14–37)
	Caligula (37–41)
	Claudius (41–54)
	Nero (54–68)
Year of the Four Emperors A.D. 69	
Flavian Period A.D. 69–96	Vespasian (69–79)
	Titus (79–81)
	Domitian (81–96)
Antonine Period 96–193	Trajan (98–117)
	Hadrian (117–138)
	Marcus Aurelius (161–180)
	Commodus (180–192)

had appeared to them numerous times over the next weeks. They took this resurrection as proof of his claims to be the messiah and confirmation of his promise of eternal life to those who believed in him. Soon a small group of his followers, led by Peter (d. ca. A.D. 64), formed another Jewish sect, preaching and praying daily in the temple. New members were initiated into this sect, soon known as Christianity, through baptism, a purification rite in which the initiate was submerged briefly in flowing water. They also shared a ritual meal in which bread and wine were distributed to members. Otherwise, they remained entirely within the Jewish religious and cultural tradition and Hellenized Jews and pagans who wished to join the sect had to observe strict Jewish law and custom.

Christianity spread beyond its origin as a Jewish sect because of the work of one man, Paul of Tarsus (ca. A.D. 5–ca. 67), a follower of the Hillel school and an early convert to Christianity. Although Paul was an observant Jew, he was part of the wider cosmopolitan world of the empire and from birth enjoyed the privileges of Roman citizenship. He saw Christianity as a separate tradition, completing and perfecting Judaism but intended for the whole world. Non-Jewish converts, he convinced Peter and most of the other leaders, did not have to become Jews. The Christian message of salvation was to be preached to all nations and people of all estates, for "there is neither Jew nor Greek, slave nor free, male or female, for all are one in Christ Jesus."

Paul set out to spread his message, crisscrossing Asia Minor, Greece, and even traveling to Rome. Wherever he went, Paul won converts and established churches, called *ecclesiae*, or assemblies. Everywhere Paul and the other disciples went they worked wonders, cast out demons, cured illnesses, and preached. In his preaching and his letters to the various churches he had established, Paul elaborated the first coherent system of beliefs or theology of the Christian sect. His teachings, while firmly rooted in the Jewish historical tradition, were radically new. God had created the human race, he taught, in the image of God and destined it for eternal life. However, by deliberate sin of the first humans, Adam and Eve, humans had lost eternal life and introduced evil and death into the world. Even then God did not abandon his people but began, through the Jews, to prepare for their eventual redemption. That salvation was accomplished by Jesus, the son of God, through his faith, a free and unmerited gift of God to his elect. Through faith, the Christian ritual of baptism, and participation in the church, men and women can share in the salvation offered by God.

How many conversions resulted from Paul's theological message and how many resulted from the miracles he and the other disciples worked will never be known. People of the ancient world believed firmly in the power of demons, the supernatural spirits of various types who influenced humans for good or ill. Christian preachers were recognized as having power over spirits, and people who could cast out demons were considered worth listening to. A third factor certainly played a part in the success of conversions. That was the courage Christians showed in the face of persecution.

Even the tolerance and elasticity of Rome for new religions could be stretched only to a point. The Christians' belief in the divinity of their founder was no problem. Their offer of salvation to those who participated in their mysteries was only normal. But their stubborn refusal to acknowledge the existence of the other gods and to participate in the cult of the genius of the emperor was intolerable. Judaism, which accepted these same tenets, was generally tolerated because it was not actively seeking to convert others. Christianity was an aggressive and successful cult, attracting followers throughout the empire. This was not religion, it was subversion. Beginning during Nero's reign, Roman officials sporadically rounded up Christians, destroyed their sacred scriptures, and executed those who refused to sacrifice to the imperial genius. But instead of decreasing the cult's appeal, persecution only aided it. For those who believed that death was birth into a new and better life, martyrdom was a reward, not a penalty. Christian men, women, and children suffered willingly, enduring unto death the most gruesome tortures Roman cruelty could devise. The strength of their convictions convinced others of the truth of their religion. Still, Christianity remained in the first

centuries a minor irritation characterized by one cultured senator as "nothing but a degenerate sort of cult carried to extravagant lengths."

A Tour of the Empire

Each town in the sprawling empire, from York in the north of Britain to Dura Europus on the Euphrates, was a center of *Romanitas* in provinces still closely tied to local provincial traditions. Each boasted a forum where locals conducted business and government affairs. Each had an arena for gladiatorial games, baths, a racetrack, and a theater where Greek and Latin plays entertained the populace. Temples to the Capitoline Jupiter and to the deified emperors adorned the cities. Aqueducts brought fresh

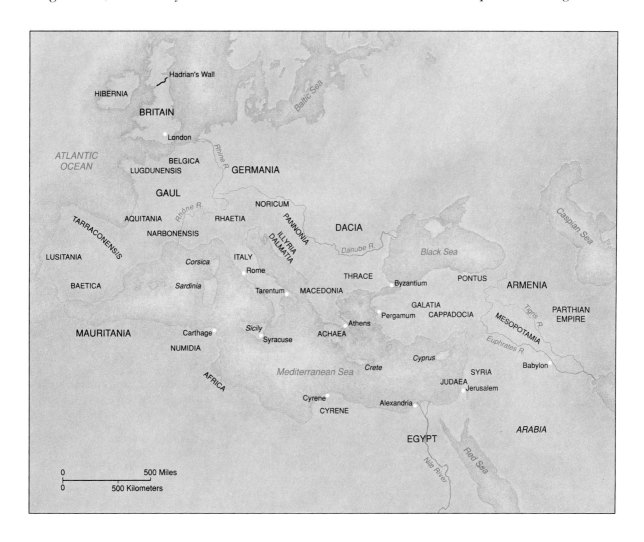

water from distant springs into the heart of the cities. Local property owners made up the senate or curia of each town in imitation of that of Rome. These included both wealthy provincials who had tied their future to Rome and retired veterans whose pensions made them immediately part of the local gentry. Local aristocrats competed with each other in their displays of civic duty, often constructing public buildings at their own expense, dedicating statues or temples to the emperor or influential patrons, and endowing games and celebrations for the amusement of their communities.

Connecting these towns was a network of well-maintained roads frequented by imperial administrators, merchants, the idle rich, and soldiers. Beginning in 120 the roads of the empire saw a most unusual traveler: the emperor Hadrian, who traveled them to conduct an extraordinary inspection of the length and breadth of his empire.

Hadrian, the adopted son and heir of Trajan, had received an excellent Greek education and was an accomplished writer, poet, connoisseur, and critic. Still, he had spent most of his early career as a successful field commander and administrator in Dacia and the lower Danube. This region, newly conquered by Trajan, presented particular security problems. The great Pannonian plain was a natural invasion route into southern and western Europe. The Danube, while broad, was easily crossed by barbarian raiders and made for a long and poorly defensible frontier. Years of military experience in the region had made Hadrian very aware of the potential weaknesses of the vast Roman borders and his primary interest was to inspect those military commands most critical for imperial stability.

Thus he set out west, traveling first through the provinces of Gaul, prosperous and pacific

regions long integrated into the Roman world. Gaul was known for its good food, its pottery manufacture, and its comfortable if culturally slightly backward local elites. Much of Gaul's prosperity came from supplying the legions guarding the Rhine-Danube frontier, and it was across the Rhine toward Germany, where the legions faced the barbarians of "Free Germany," that Hadrian was headed. Legions stationed at Xanten, Cologne, and Trier were far removed from the Mediterranean world that formed the heart of the Empire. The dark forests, cold winters, and crude life made Germany a hardship post. Hadrian threw himself into the harsh camp life of Germany in order to bolster discipline and combat readiness. He shared rough field rations, long marches, and simple conditions with his troops, improving their equipment even while demolishing creature comforts such as dining rooms, covered walks, and ornamental gardens erected by their commanders.

From Germany, Hadrian traveled down the Rhine through what is today Holland and then crossed over to Britain. Here too defense was utmost on his mind. Celts from the northern, unconquered portion of the island had been harassing the Romanized society to the south. The emperor ordered the erection of a great wall over fifty miles long across Britain from coast to coast. The most critical eastern half of this wall, much of which still stands, was built of stone ten feet thick and fifteen feet high, while the western half was constructed of turf. Battlements, turrets, and gates as well as garrison forts extended the length of the wall. South of the wall, Roman Britain was studded with hundreds of Roman villas, ranging from simple country farmhouses to vast mansions with over sixty rooms. Over a hundred towns and villages were large enough to boast walls, ranging from London with a population of roughly thirty thousand to numerous settlements of between two thousand and ten thousand.

No sooner had he put things straight in Britain than Hadrian returned to Gaul, paused in Nîmes in the south, and then headed south toward his native Spain. By the second century A.D., Spain was even more thoroughly Romanized than most of Gaul, having been an integral part of the empire since the Second Punic War. It was also far richer. Spanish mines yielded gold, iron, and tin, and Spanish estates produced grain and cattle. Since the reign of Vespasian, the residents of Spanish communities had been given some of the

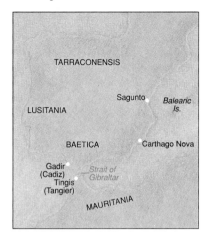

rights of Roman citizens, thus making them eligible for military service, a value even greater to the empire than Spain's mineral wealth. Problems with military service brought Hadrian to Spain. The populace was becoming increasingly resistant to conscription, a universal phenomenon, and Hadrian's presence strengthened the efforts of recruiters.

From Spain, the emperor may have crossed the Straits of Gibraltar to deal personally with a minor revolt of Moorish tribes in Mauritania, a constant low-level problem with these semi-nomadic peoples living on the edge of the desert. In any event, he soon set sail for the provinces of Asia. Here he was in the heart of the Hellenistic world so central to the empire's prosperity. Its great cities were centers of manufacture and its ports the vital links in Mediterranean trade. As in Hellenistic times, these cities were the organizing principle of the region, with local senates largely self-governing and rivalries among cities prevent-

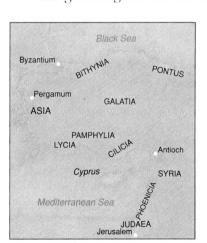

ing the creation of any sort of provincial identities. Thus in Asia Hadrian worked with individual communities, showering honors and privileges on the most cooperative, checking no doubt on the financial affairs of others, and founding new communities in the Anat-

olian hinterland. The last activity was particularly important because, for all of the civilized glory of urban Asia, the rural areas remained strongly tied to traditions that neither Greeks nor Romans had managed to weaken. The empire remained two worlds: one urban, Hellenized, mercantile, and collaborationist; the other rural, traditional, exploited, and potentially separatist.

In 125, Hadrian left Asia for Greece, where he participated in traditional religious cults. Greek culture continued to be vital for Rome, and by participating in the rituals of Achaia and Athens the emperor placed himself in the traditions of the legendary Herakles and Philip of Macedon. He no doubt also seized the opportunity to audit the accounts of provincial governors and procurators, whose reputation for misuse of their powers was infamous. Finally, in 127 Hadrian returned to Rome via Sicily, a prosperous amalgam of Greek and Latin cultures dominated by vast senatorial estates, or *latifundia*, stopping to climb Mount Etna, it was said, to see the colorful sunrise.

This restless emperor spent less than twelve months in Rome before setting out again, this time for Africa. There, as in Germany, his concern was the discipline and preparedness of the troops guarding the rich agricultural areas and thriving commercial centers of

the coast from the marauding nomads on the edges of the desert. Shortly after that, he was again in Athens to dedicate public works projects he had undertaken as well as an altar to himself—like all emperors in the East, Hadrian was venerated as a living god. From Greece he headed east, again crossing Asia and this time moving into Cappadocia and Syria. His concerns here were again defense, but against a powerful civilized Parthian empire, not barbarian tribes. Hadrian renewed promises of peace and friendship with the Parthian king, even returning the latter's daughter, whom Trajan had captured in the last Parthian war.

Moving south, Hadrian stopped in Jerusalem, where he dedicated a shrine to Jupiter Capitolinus on the site of the destroyed Jewish temple before heading to Egypt for an inspection trip up the

Nile. Egypt remained the wealthiest Roman province and the most exploited. Since Augustus, Egypt had been governed directly by the imperial household, its agricultural wealth from the Nile Delta going to feed the Roman masses. At the same time Alexandria continued to be one of the greatest cultural centers of the Roman world. This culture, however, was a fusion of Greek and Egyptian traditions, constantly threatening to form the basis for a nationalist opposition to Roman administrators and tax collectors. Hadrian sought to defuse this powder keg by disciplining administrators and by founding a new city, Antinopolis, which he hoped would create a center of loyalty to Rome.

Hadrian finally returned to the imperial residence on the Palatine in 131. He had spent over ten years on the road and had no doubt done much to strengthen and preserve the *pax Romana*, or Roman peace. Still, to the careful observer the weaknesses of the empire were as evident as its strengths. The frontiers were vast and constantly tested by a profusion of hostile tribes and peoples. Roman citizens from Italy, Gaul, and Spain were increasingly unwilling to serve in such far-flung regions. As a result, the legions were manned by progressively less Romanized soldiers, and their battle readiness and discipline, poorly enforced by homesick officers, declined dangerously. In the more civilized eastern provinces, corrupt local elites, imperial governors, and officials siphoned off imperial revenues destined for the army to build their personal fortunes. Also, in spite of centuries of Hellenization and Roman admin-

istration, city and countryside remained culturally and politically separated. Early in the second century, such problems were no more than small clouds on the horizon, but in the following century they would grow into a storm that would threaten the very existence of the empire.

The Culture of Antonine Rome

Annius Florus, a poet friend of Hadrian, commenting on the emperor's exhausting journeys, wrote:

> I do not want to be Caesar,
> To walk about among the Britons,
> To endure the Scythian hoar-frosts.

To which Hadrian replied:

> I do not want to be Florus,
> To walk about among taverns,
> To lurk about among cook-shops.

Like the other members of his dynasty, Hadrian enjoyed an easy familiarity with men of letters, and like other men of letters of the period, Florus was a provincial, an African drawn from the provincial world to the great capital. Another provincial, Rome's greatest historian, Cornelius Tacitus (ca. 56–ca. 120), recorded the history of the first century of the empire. Tacitus wrote to instruct and to edify his generation and did so in a style characterized by irony and a sharp sense of the differences between public propaganda and the realities of power politics. He was also unique in his ability to portray noble opposition to Roman rule. His picture of Germanic and British societies served as a warning to Rome against excessive self-confidence and laxity.

Tacitus' contemporaries, Plutarch (ca. 46–after A.D. 119) and Suetonius (ca. 69–after A.D. 122), were biographers rather than historians. Plutarch, who wrote in Greek, composed *Parallel Lives*, a series of character studies in which he compared an eminent Greek with an eminent Roman. His purpose was to portray public virtue, to show how philosophical principles could be integrated into lives of civic action. Suetonius also wrote biographies, using anecdotes to portray character. Suetonius' biographies of the emperors fall short of the literary and philosophical qualities of Plutarch's character studies and far short of Tacitus' histories. Suetonius delighted in the rumors of private scandals that surrounded the emperors and used personal vice to explain public failings. Still, the portraits Suetonius created remained widely popular through the centuries, while Tacitus' histories fell out of fashion.

In the later second century, Romans in general preferred the study and writing of philosophy, particularly stoicism, over history. The most influential Stoic philosopher of the century was Epictetus (ca. A.D. 55–135), a former slave who taught that man could be free by the control of his will and the cultivation of inner peace. Like the early Stoics, Epictetus taught the universal brotherhood of humankind and the identity of nature and divine providence. He urged his pupils to recognize that dependence on external things was the cause of unhappiness and therefore they should free themselves from reliance on material possessions, public esteem, and all other things prized by the worldly. Each individual would find happiness by adapting himself to his own particular expression of nature and by accepting with indifference the advantages and disadvantages that this role entailed.

The slave's philosophy found its most eager pupil in an emperor. Marcus Aurelius (A.D. 161–180) reigned during a period when the stresses glimpsed by Hadrian were beginning to show in a much more alarming manner. Once more the Parthians attacked the eastern frontier, while in Britain and Germany barbarians struck across the borders. In 166 a confederation of barbarians known as the Marcomanni crossed the Danube and raided as far south as northern Italy. A plague, brought west by troops returning from the Parthian front, ravaged the whole empire. Like his predecessor Hadrian, Aurelius felt bound to endure the Scythian hoar-frosts rather than luxuriate in the taverns of Rome. He spent virtually the whole of his reign on the Danubian frontier, repelling the barbarians and shoring up the empire's defenses.

Throughout his reign Aurelius found consolation in the Stoic philosophy of Epictetus. In his soldier's tent at night he composed his *Medita-*

The emperor Marcus Aurelius performing a sacrifice in front of the temple of Jupiter, Juno, and Minerva. The relief captures Marcus Aurelius in the role of Stoic disciple rather than in his position as Roman emperor.

tions, a volume of philosophical musings. Like the slave, the emperor sought freedom from the burden of his office in his will and in the proper understanding of his role in the divine order. He called himself to introspection, to a constant awareness, under the glories and honors heaped upon him by his entourage, of his true human nature: "A poor soul burdened with a corpse."

Aurelius played his role well, dying in what is today Vienna, far from the pleasures of the capital. His Stoic philosophy did not, however, serve the empire well. For all his emphasis on understanding, Aurelius badly misjudged his son Commodus (A.D. 180–192), who succeeded him. Commodus, whose chief interest was in being a gladiator, saw himself the incarnation of Herakles and appeared in public clad as a gladiator and as consul. As Commodus sank into insanity, Rome was once more convulsed with purges and proscriptions. Commodus' assassination in 192 did not end the violence. The pax Romana was over.

The haphazard conquest of the Mediterranean world threw Roman republican government, traditional culture, and antagonistic social groups into chaos. The result was a century and a half of intermittent violence and civil war before a new political and social order headed by an absolute monarch established a new equilibrium. During the following two centuries, a deeply Hellenized Roman civilization tied together the vast empire by incorporating the wealthy and powerful of the Western world into its fluid power structure while brutally crushing those who would not or could not conform. The binding force of the Roman Empire was great and would survive the political crises of the third century as great as those that had brought down the republic three hundred years before.

Suggestions for Further Reading

Primary Sources

Major selections of the works of Caesar, Cicero, Tacitus, Plutarch, Suetonius, and Marcus Aurelius are available in English translation from Penguin Books. The second volume, * Naphtali Lewis and Meyer Reinhold, *Roman Civilization Selected Readings Vol. II: The Empire* (1951), contains a wide selection of documents with useful introductions.

The Price of Empire

* Mary Beard and Michael Crawford, *Rome in the Late Republic* (Ithaca, NY: Cornell University Press, 1985). An analysis of the political processes of the last republic as part of the development of Roman society, not simply the decay of the republic.

* E. Badian, *Roman Imperialism in the Late Republic* (Ithaca, NY: Cornell University Press, 1968). A study of the contradictory forces leading to the development of the empire.

The End of the Republic

Ronald Syme, *The Roman Revolution*, 2d ed. (New York: Oxford University Press, 1960). A classic study of the social groups who made up the party of Augustus.

E. S. Gruen, *The Last Generation of the Roman Republic* (Berkeley: University of California Press, 1973). A recent and controversial analysis of the politics of the late republic.

D. Stockton, *Cicero: A Political Biography* (London: Oxford University Press, 1971). A biography of the great orator in the context of the end of the republic.

* Indicates paperback edition available.

The Augustan Age

G. W. Bowersock, *Augustus and the Greek World* (New York: Oxford University Press, 1965). A cultural history of the Augustan Age.

D. A. West and A. J. Woodman, *Poetry and Politics in the Age of Augustus* (New York: Cambridge University Press, 1984). The cultural program of Augustus.

J. B. Campbell, *The Emperor and the Roman Army* (New York: Oxford University Press, 1984). Essential for understanding the military's role in the Roman Empire.

Richard Duncan-Jones, *The Economy of the Roman Empire*, 2d ed. (New York: Cambridge University Press, 1982). A series of technical studies on Roman wealth and its economic context and social applications.

The Pax Romana

Fergus Millar, *The Roman Empire and Its Neighbors*, 2d ed. (New York: Holmes & Meier, 1981). A collection of essays surveying the diversity of the empire.

Peter Garnsey and Richard Saller, *The Roman Empire: Economy, Society, and Culture* (Berkeley: University of California Press, 1987). A topical study of imperial administration, economy, religion, and society, arguing the coercive and exploitative nature of Roman civilization on the agricultural societies of the Mediterranean world.

Fergus Millar, *The Emperor in the Roman World* (Ithaca, NY: Cornell University Press, 1977). A study of emperors, stressing their essential passivity, responding to initiatives from below.

Philippe Ariès and Georges Duby, eds., *History of Private Life. Vol. 1. From Pagan Rome to Byzantium* (Cambridge, MA: Harvard University Press, 1986). Essays on the interior, private life of Romans and Greeks by leading French and British historians.

* Judith P. Hallett, *Fathers and Daughters in Roman Society & the Elite Family* (Princeton, NJ: Princeton University Press, 1984). A study of indirect power exercised by elite women in the Roman world as daughters, mothers, and sisters.

* Ramsay MacMullen, *Paganism in the Roman Empire* (New Haven, CT: Yale University Press, 1981). A description of the varieties and levels of pagan religion in the Roman world.

Jane F. Gardner, *Women in Roman Law and Society* (Bloomington, IN: Indiana University Press, 1986). A study of the extent of freedom and power over property enjoyed by Roman women.

Edward Champlin, *Fronto and Antonine Rome* (Cambridge, MA: Harvard University Press, 1980). A cultural history of Antonine court life through the letters of the second century's greatest rhetorician.

* Joseph Jay Deiss, *Herculaneum: Italy's Buried Treasure* (New York: Harper and Row, 1985). A vividly written and well-illustrated introduction to Herculaneum for a general audience.

6

The
Transformation
of the
Classical World

Coin of the Realm

The magnificent medallion shown here depicts on one side likenesses of the imperial brothers Valentinian I and Valens, who jointly ruled the Roman Empire from 364 to 375. On the obverse is pictured a mounted emperor, surrounded by a nimbus, the symbol of divinity, and the gods Tellus (earth) and Fortuna (good fortune). The inscription reads, "The glory of the Romans," and the AN indicates that the medallion was struck at the imperial mint at Antioch. Beneath these facts about the medallion, however, lies a much broader story. It is the story of the transformation of the Roman Empire in late antiquity.

The medallion fairly bristles with apparent contradictions and incongruities. Now two emperors instead of one rule the empire. The emperors are Christian, yet they are surrounded with pagan symbols and appear to be equated with the gods. Finally, the inscription on the face, "King of the Romans," reveals the medallion for what it is: a counterfeit. The Romans never called their emperors kings, but that was the term the barbarian Goths, who did not have kings themselves, used for the Roman emperors. Although the medallion is counterfeit, it is not worthless. Its gold is of higher purity than many genuine Roman coins of the period.

By the last quarter of the fourth century, the barbarian and Roman worlds were inextricably connected, like the two sides of the coin itself. The Goths had struck the coin to show their esteem for the Roman Empire and its rulers. Yet, only a few years after this coin had been struck, the Emperor Valens and his army were destroyed by the very Goths who had produced it in his honor. This counterfeit medallion demonstrates the considerable extent to which the Goths had absorbed and imitated Roman cultural and political traditions. At the same time it reflects the radical transformations of Roman and barbarian culture, society, and institutions that took place in the two centuries following the death of Marcus Aurelius in 180.

By the end of the second century, most of the Mediterranean world had been part of the Roman Empire for more than two centuries—a longer period than the fifty states have been part of the United States. It was, however, the empire's success in expanding its frontiers and in incorporating greatly diverse peoples that was the cause of its radical change during late antiquity. Even while the provinces were becoming Romanized, the meaning of "Roman" was being altered. Accelerating this process of change and transformation was the combination of events collectively referred to as the crisis of the third century.

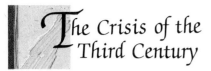 The Crisis of the Third Century

From the reign of Septimius Severus (193–211) to the time of Diocletian (284–305), both internal and external challenges shook the Roman Empire. The empire survived, but its social, political, and economic structures were radically transformed.

Sheer size was a fundamental problem for the empire. Haphazard expansion in many regions—to the north and west for instance—overextended the frontiers. The manpower and resources needed to maintain this vast territory strained the economic system of the empire. Like a thread stretched to the breaking point, the thin line of border garrisons and forts was ready to snap.

The economic system itself was part of the reason for this strain on resources. For all of its commercial networks, the economy of the empire remained tied to agriculture. To the aristocrats of the ancient world, agriculture was the only honorable source of wealth. Thus the prosperous Roman citizen bought slaves and land, not machinery. The goal of the successful merchant was to liquidate his commercial assets, buy estates, and rise into the leisured land-holding elite. As a result, liquid capital either for investment or taxation was always scarce.

The lack of sophistication in commercial and industrial business practice characterized the financial system of the empire as well. Government had always been conducted on the cheap. The tax system of the empire had never been very efficient at tapping into the real wealth of the aristocracy. Each individual city made its own collective assessments. Individuals eager to win the gratitude of their local communities were expected to provide essential services from their own pockets. Even with the vast wealth of the empire at its disposal, the government never developed a system of public debt—that is, a policy of borrowing against future revenues. As a result, the only way to solve short-term cash-flow problems was to debase the coinage by using more copper and less silver. This practice became epidemic in the third century, when the price of a bushel of wheat rose over 200 percent.

The failure of the empire to develop a stable political base complicated its economic problems. In times of emergency, imperial control relied on the personal presence and command of the emperor. As the empire grew, it became impossible for this presence to be felt everywhere. Moreover, the empire never developed either a regular system of imperial succession or an adequate power base. Control of the army, which was the ultimate source of imperial power, was possible only as long as the emperor was able to lead his armies to victory.

Enrich the Army and Scorn the Rest

Through much of the late second and third centuries, emperors failed dismally to lead their armies to victory. The pressure on the borders temporarily halted by Marcus Aurelius resumed under his successors. The barely Romanized provincials in the military bore the brunt of these attacks. When the emperors selected by the distant Roman Senate failed to win victory, front-line armies unhesitatingly raised their own commanders to the imperial office. These commanders, such as the Pannonian general Septimius Severus, set about restructuring the empire in favor of the army. They opened important administrative posts to soldiers, expanded the army's size, raised military pay, initiated expensive building programs in frontier settlements, and in general introduced authoritarian military discipline throughout society. To finance these costly measures, the new military government confiscated senatorial wealth, introduced new forms of taxation, and increasingly debased the coinage.

The old senatorial elite and the people living in the more civilized regions of the empire thought these measures disastrous. Soldiers in the provinces welcomed the changes. With their first rise in real income soldiers could improve their standard of living while in service and buy their way into provincial elites upon retirement. At long last they were allowed to marry even while on active service. Free-spending soldiers and imperial extravagance helped the bleak settlements on the edges of military camps grow into prosperous cities with all the comforts of the older parts of the empire.

For the first time capable soldiers could hope to rise to the highest levels of public power regardless of their birth. One extraordinarily successful soldier was Publius Helvius Pertinax. Born the son of a freed slave in the north of Italy (Liguria) in 126, he abandoned a career as a schoolteacher to enter the military. His rise to the top of the military and bureaucratic ladder began in Syria. From Syria he was promoted to a post in Britain. He then returned to the continent and served in the Danubian region during the Marcomannian wars in both civil and military capacities for approximately ten years. By the time he was fifty, his success as a military commander won for him the office of consul. He then held a series of military, civil, and proconsular positions in Syria, Britain, Italy, and Africa before returning to Rome. When the Emperor Commodus was murdered in 192, the palace guard proclaimed Pertinax emperor—the first emperor who had not come from the privileged senatorial class.

Career of Publius Helvius Pertinax

Soon, however, the military control of the empire turned into a nightmare even for the provinces and their armies. Exercising their newly discovered power, armies raised and then destroyed pretender after pretender, offering support to whichever imperial candidate promised them the greatest riches. Pertinax, the first of these soldier-emperors, set the precedent. Less than three months after becoming emperor he was murdered by his soldiers. The army's incessant demands for higher pay led emperors to lower the amount of silver in the coins with which the soldiers were paid. But the less the coins were worth, the more of them were necessary to purchase goods. And the more goods cost, the less valuable was the salary of the soldiers. Wages doubled but the price of grain tripled in the third century. Thus soldiers were worse off at the end of the period than at the beginning. Such drastic inflation wrecked the economic stability of the empire and spurred the army on to greater and more impossible demands for raises. Emperors who could not meet the demands were killed by their troops. In fact, the army was much more effective at killing emperors than enemies. Between 235 and 284 seventeen of the twenty more or less legitimate emperors were assassinated or killed in civil war.

The crisis of the third century did not result only from economic and political instability within the empire. Rome's internal imperial crises coincided with an increase of attacks from outside the empire. In Africa, Berber tribes harassed the frontiers. The Sassanid dynasty in Persia threatened Rome's eastern frontier. When the Emperor Valerian (253–260) attempted to prevent the Persian king of kings Shapur I from seizing Roman Mesopotamia and Armenia, he was captured and held prisoner for the rest of his life. Valerian became such a curiosity that after his death his skin was reportedly stuffed and kept on display for centuries in a Persian temple.

The greatest danger to Rome came not from the south or east, but rather from the west. There, along the Rhine, various Germanic tribes known collectively as the Franks and the Alemanni began raiding expeditions into the empire. Along the lower Danube and in southern Russia, the Gothic confederation raided the Balkans and harassed Roman shipping on the Black Sea.

This cameo was made to the order of Shapur I after the capture of Valerian during the great battle near Antioch in A.D. 260. The symbolic scene has Shapur seizing Valerian simply by grasping his hand.

An Empire on the Defensive

The central administration of the empire simply could not deal effectively with the numerous barbarian attacks. Left on their own, regional provincial commanders at times even headed separatist movements. Provincial aristocrats who despaired of receiving any help from distant Rome often supported these pretenders. One such commander was Postumus, whom the armies of Spain, Britain, and Gaul proclaimed emperor. His nine-year separatist reign (ca. 258–268) was the longest and most stable of that of any emperor, legitimate or otherwise, throughout this whole troubled period.

Political and military instability had devastating effects on the lives of ordinary people. Citizenship had been extended to virtually all free inhabitants of the empire in 212, but that right was a formality given simply to enlarge the tax base, since only citizens paid inheritance taxes. In reality the legal and economic status of all but the richest declined. Society became sharply divided into the privileged *honestiores*—senators, municipal gentry, and the military—and the increasingly burdened *humiliores*—everyone else. The *humiliores* suffered the most from the tax increases because unlike the *honestiores* they could neither bribe their way out of them nor intimidate tax collectors with private armies. They were also frequent targets of extortion by the military and of violence perpetrated by bandits.

It was the impossible burden of taxation that drove many individuals into banditry. Such crime had long been endemic to the Roman Empire, and slave and peasant bandits, rustlers, and even pirates played an ambivalent role in society. Often they terrorized the countryside, descending from the hills to attack villages or travelers. However, at times they also protected peasants from greedy tax collectors and military commanders. In Gaul and Spain, peasants and local leaders organized armed resistance movements to withstand the exorbitant demands of tax collectors. Although these resistance movements, termed *Bacaudae*, were always ruthlessly crushed, they continued to reappear—a sure sign of the desperation of ordinary people. In the first centuries of the empire bandits operated primarily in peripheral areas recently and poorly subjugated to Roman rule. In the late second and third centuries they became an increasing problem in Italy itself.

The most famous of the bandits was Bulla the Lucky, who headed a band of over 600 men and plundered Italy during the reign of Septimius Severus. No simple thief, Bulla was more like a Roman Robin Hood. He often robbed his prisoners of only a portion of their goods, which he distributed to the needy. He detained skilled artisans and made use of their skills, then let them go with a parting gift. On one occasion he captured the centurion charged with hunting him down and, dressed in the official robes of a Roman magistrate, summoned the centurion in his own "court." The centurion, his head shaved like a slave, was brought before Bulla and told: "Carry

This relief shows landowners collecting rents from peasants. The peasantry, displaced by slaves, congregated in the capital and formed a poverty-stricken urban underclass.

this message back to your masters: let them feed their slaves so that they might not be compelled to turn to a life of banditry."

Bulla lived and died outside the law, but as the third century progressed, such lawlessness increasingly became the law. The life of Maximinus the Thracian, known as Little Big Man (173–238), typifies this change. He began life as a shepherd, then drifted into rustling; but he also protected the local community. Later he entered the Roman army, where his extraordinary physical size and skills caught the attention of Septimius Severus, who promoted him to centurion. Maximinus rose quickly through the ranks and in 235 was proclaimed emperor at Mainz by a mutinous army, which had overthrown the grandson of Septimius Severus. Although he reigned only a bit more than two years, Maximinus' career showed how fluid the boundaries between legitimate violence and banditry had become during the third century.

The Barbarian World

Compounding the internal violence that threatened to destroy the Roman Empire were the external attacks of the Germanic barbarians. These attacks reflected changes within the Germanic world as profound as those within the empire. Between the second and fifth centuries the Germanic world was transformed from a mosaic of small, decentralized, agricultural tribes into a number of powerful military tribal confederations capable of challenging Rome itself. We cannot understand the impact of the barbarians on the empire without understanding the social and political organization and the transformation of these people living beyond the frontier.

The Germanic peoples typically inhabited small villages organized into patriarchal households, integrated into clans, which in turn composed tribes. The boundaries between each of these groups were fluid, and central government was extremely weak. For the most part, clans governed themselves, and except in war tribal leaders had little authority over their followers. In the second century many tribes had kings, but they were religious rather than political leaders.

Germanic communities lived by farming, but cattle raising and especially warfare carried the highest social prestige. Men measured their status by the number of cattle they owned and by their martial ability. Women took care of agricultural chores and household duties. Like the number of cattle, the number of wives showed a man's social position. Polygyny was common among chiefs.

Warfare defined social groupings and warriors dominated public life. Only within the clan was fighting inappropriate. But rival clans within the same tribe dealt with one another brutally. Conflict took the form of the feud, and each act of aggression was repaid in kind. If an individual within a clan had a grievance with an individual within another clan, all his kinsmen were obliged to assist him. Thus a single incident could result in a continuous escalation of acts of revenge. Murder piled upon murder as sons and brothers retaliated for each act of vengeance.

Clans in other tribes were fair game for raiding and conquering. The wars that resulted formed the normal mechanisms by which wealth circulated among tribes, either as booty or as gifts exchanged to conclude peace. Individuals, clans, and tribes built their reputations on warfare. The more successful a tribe was in warfare, the more clans it attracted and the greater its position became in the barbarian world.

The practice of feuding, especially within the tribe, had enormous costs. Families were decimated and strong warriors who were needed to defend the tribe from outside attack faced constant danger from members of their own tribe. Thus tribal leaders attempted to reduce hostilities by establishing payments called *wergeld* in place of the blood vengeance demanded in reparation for crimes. Such *wergeld*, normally paid in cattle or slaves, was voluntary, since the right of vengeance was generally recognized, and the unity of the tribe remained precarious.

Tribes also attempted to reinforce unity through religious cults involving shared myths of common ancestry and rituals intended to underline group cohesion. Drinking was the most important of these rituals. When not fighting, Germanic warriors spent much of their time drinking beer together at the table of their war leader. Because it provided the most ready means of preserving grain, beer was a staple of Germanic diet. Communal beer drinking was also a way of uniting potentially hostile neighbors. Not surprisingly, it could also lead to drunken brawls that reopened the very feuds drinking bouts were intended to end. These feuds could in turn lead to the hiving off of irreconcilable factions, which might in time form their own tribes.

In contrast to the familial structure of barbarian society stood another warrior group that cut across kindred and even tribal units. This was the warrior band, called in Latin the *comitatus*. Some young warriors formed personal bonds with particularly able leaders and pledged them absolute loyalty. In return the leaders were obligated to lead their warriors to victory and to share with them the spoils of war. These warrior societies, far from being the basic units of a larger tribal military force, were organized for their own plunder and fighting. While they might be a valuable aid in intertribal warfare, they could also shatter the fragile peace by conducting raids on neighbors, thus bringing whole tribes into internal conflict. Although nontribal, successful *comitatus* could form the nuclei of new tribes. Successful warrior leaders might draw sufficient numbers of followers and conquer so many other groups that in time the band would become a new tribe.

This intratribal and intertribal violence produced a rough equilibrium of power and wealth as long as small Germanic tribes lived in isolation. The presence of the Roman Empire, felt both directly and indirectly in the barbarian world, upset this equilibrium. Unintentionally, Rome itself helped transform the Germanic tribes into the major threat to the imperial system.

The direct presence of Roman merchants extended only about 100 miles beyond the frontiers into "free Germany." However, the attraction of Roman luxury goods and the Romans' efforts to establish friendly Germanic buffer zones along the borders drew even distant tribes into the Roman imperial system. Across the barbarian world, tribal leaders and *comitatus* leaders sought the prestige that Roman goods brought them. Roman provincial commanders encouraged these leaders to enter into commercial arrangements with the Romans. In exchange for their cattle, which the Romans needed for their troops, the Germanic leaders received gold and grain. This outside source of wealth greatly increased

An ivory plaque portraying Stilicho, a Vandal by birth, who rose to be Master of Soldiers and Consul of Rome. He is shown here in the patrician robes of a consul and carrying the weapons of a soldier, suggesting his dual role.

economic disparity within Germanic society. In addition, some leaders made treaties with Rome, thus receiving the advantage of Roman support, which other tribal leaders lacked. In return for payments of gold and foodstuffs, chieftains of these "federated" tribes agreed to oppose tribes hostile to Rome and to prevent young hotheads of their own tribes from raiding across the frontier. Some chiefs supplied warriors for the Roman army. Others even led their *comitatus* into Roman service. By the late third century the Roman army included Franks, Goths, and Saxons serving as far away from their homes as Egypt. Such "imperial Germans" moved back and forth between the Roman and barbarian worlds, using each as a foundation for increased power in the other and obscuring the cultural and political differences between the two.

The inherent attraction of Roman material civilization and the Romans' policy of supporting "their" barbarians tended to upset Germanic society and to accentuate political, social, and economic differences within tribal units. This in turn led to the formation of pro- and anti-Roman factions, which further splintered barbarian tribes. New and powerful groups appeared, older tribal units vanished, and new forms of military organization came to predominate.

The effects of contact between barbarians and Romans reached far and wide throughout the empire and beyond the frontier. Along the Rhine and Danube, the result was the so-called West Germanic Revolution. In order to survive in a time of constant warfare, tribes had to become armies. The armies needed a united and effective leadership. Among most of the western Germanic peoples, the tradition of the older tribal king was abandoned. A new kind of nonroyal chieftain emerged as the war leader of the people and as the representative of the war god Woden. In the later second and third centuries the turmoil resulted in the formation of new tribes and tribal confederations—the Marcomanni, the Alemanni, and the Franks. By the end of the second century this internal barbarian transformation spilled over into the empire in the form of the Marcomannian wars and the Saxon, Frankish, and Alemannic incursions into the western provinces.

Around the same time, along the Oder and Vistula rivers to the north, a group later known as the Goths began their slow consolidation around a royal family. The Goths were unique in that their kings exercised more military authority than was usual for a Germanic tribe. These kings formed the nucleus of a constantly changing barbarian group. A Goth was not necessarily a biological descendant of the small second-century tribe living along the shore of the Baltic. Anyone who fought alongside the Gothic king was a Goth.

Between the second and fourth centuries, the bearers of this Gothic royal tradition began to filter to the south and east, ultimately transferring their model of barbarian organization to the area of present-day Kiev in southern Russia. This move was not so much a physical migration of thousands of people across Europe as the gradual confederation under Gothic leadership of various Germanic, Slavic, and Scythian peoples living around the Black Sea. By the early third century this Gothic confederation was strong enough to challenge Roman supremacy in the region. These first Gothic wars in the east were even more devastating than were the later wars in the west.

The Empire Restored

By the last decades of the third century, the empire seemed in danger of crumbling under combined internal and external pressure. That it did not was largely due to the efforts of the soldier-emperor Aurelian (270–275), who was able to repulse the barbarians, restore the unity of the empire, and then set about stabilizing the internal imperial structure. Although Aurelian was assassinated, his successors were able to build on his efforts. Restoration came to fruition under Diocletian (284–305), who summed up and solidified the transformations made under his predecessors. However, the restored empire bore under Diocletian little resemblance to the Roman Empire of the first and second centuries.

Diocletian the God-Emperor

Diocletian, a Dalmatian soldier who had risen through the ranks to become emperor, completed the process of stabilization and reorganization of the imperial system begun by Aurelian. The result was a regime that in some ways increased imperial power and in other ways simply did away with the pretenses that had previously masked the emperor's true position.

No longer was the emperor *princeps*, or "first citizen." Now he was *dominus*, or "lord," the term of respect used by slaves in addressing their masters. He also assumed the title of *Iovius*, or Jupiter, thus claiming divine status, and demanded adoration as a living god. Diocletian emphasized the imperial cult and the autocratic power of the emperor, but he did not grasp this power exclusively for himself. He recognized that the empire was too large and complex for one man to rule. To solve the problem, he divided the empire into eastern and western parts, each part to be ruled by both an augustus and a junior emperor, or caesar. Diocletian was augustus in the east, supported by his caesar, Galerian. In the west the rulers were the augustus Maximian and his caesar, Constantius.

In theory this tetrarchy, or rule by four, provided for regular succession. The caesars, who were married to daughters of the augusti, were to succeed them. The new system also made revolts and assassinations less likely to be successful, since a person would have to kill all four rulers in order to seize power. Although from time to time subsequent emperors would rule alone, Diocletian's innovation proved successful and enduring. The empire was divided administratively into eastern and western parts until the death of Julius Nepos, the last legitimate emperor in the west, in 480.

In addition to this constitutional reform, Diocletian enacted or consolidated a series of measures to improve the functioning of the imperial administration. He reorganized and expanded the army, approximately doubled the number of provinces, separated their military and civil administration, and greatly increased the number of bureaucrats to administer them. He attempted to stem runaway inflation by increasing the amount of silver in coins and fixing maximum prices and wages throughout the empire. He restructured the imperial tax system, basing it on payments in goods and produce in order to distribute the burden more equitably on all citizens and to avoid problems of currency debasement.

The pillar of Diocletian's success was his victorious military machine. He was effective because, like the barbarian chieftains who had turned their tribes into armies, he militarized society and led this military society to victory. Like Diocletian himself, his soldiers were drawn from provincial, marginal regions. They showed tremendous devotion to their god-emperor. By the time of Diocletian's reign, a career such as that of Pertinax (p. 169) had become the rule for emperors rather than the exception.

The career of Aurelius Gaius, an obscure provincial officer, is typical of that of soldiers of Diocletian's army. Gaius was born in a Galatian village in what is today Turkey. Like many other young men from his village, he sought his fortune by entering military service in a Danubian legion that traditionally drew recruits from Galatia. He served in infantry and cavalry units in Pannonia and then in Gaul near Strasbourg, advancing through the ranks from simple recruit to cavalryman, adjutant, and finally centurion in Diocletian's personal guard. He traveled the length and breadth of the empire with Diocletian. Six times he fought outside the empire in campaigns that penetrated the Gothic kingdom, Per-

The tetrarchy was an attempt to regulate the succession. Here, the emperors Diocletian and Maximian are depicted with their caesars, Constantius of the West and Galerius of the East, who were their respective sons-in-law.

sia, North Africa, and Numidia.

Compared with that of Pertinax, Gaius' career reflects the differences between successful careers at the end of the second century and those at the end of the third. Unlike Pertinax, Gaius served his entire career within the military. Diocletian had largely ended the tradition of mixing civil and military offices, a measure that perhaps prevented undue military meddling in civil government but that also cut off most bureaucrats from the army, the real source of power. Second, Gaius' military service took him to an even wider range of provinces than did that of Pertinax. However, as remarkable as the regions in which he served are the places he apparently never visited. Except for a short time in Strassbourg, Gaius spent no time in Gaul and never visited Britain. The extreme west of the empire was increasingly irrelevant to the interests of central government. Neither did Gaius visit Italy and Greece, the centers of the old classical world. For him, as for Diocletian, the periphery of the empire had become its center; the center was increasingly marginal to the program of the empire.

Some aspects of Diocletian's program, such as the improvement of the civil administration and the military, were successful. Others, such as the reform of silver currency and wage and price controls were dismal failures. One effect of the fiscal reforms was to bind *colons*, or hereditary tenant farmers, to their lands, since they were forbidden to leave the villages where they were registered to pay their taxes. In this practice lay the origins of European serfdom. Another effect was the gradual destruction of the local city councils since their members, the *decurions*, were held personally responsible for the payment of local assessments whether or not they could be collected from the other inhabitants. In time this led to the dissolution of local civil government.

All of these measures were designed to marshal the entire population in the monumental task of preserving *Romanitas*. Central to this task was the proper reverential attitude toward the divine emperors who directed it. (See Special Feature, "Portraits of the Soul," pp. 186–187.) One group seemed stubbornly opposed to this heroic effort: the Christians. In 298 an incident occurred that seemed to confirm their subversive attitude. At a sacrifice in the presence of Diocletian, the Roman priests were unable to obtain the desired

favorable omens, and they attributed their failure to the presence of Christians, who were crossing themselves to ward off demons. Such blasphemous conduct—it might be compared, for instance, to desecrating the flag at a public assembly—led to the beginning of the Great Persecution, which formally began in 303 and lasted sporadically until 313. Although unevenly pursued across the empire, it resulted in the destruction of churches, the burning of copies of Christian scriptures, the exclusion of Christians from access to imperial courts, and the torture, maiming, and death of hundreds of Christians who refused to sacrifice to the pagan gods.

Constantine the Emperor of God

In 305, in the midst of the Great Persecution, Diocletian and his co-augustus Maximian took the extraordinary step of abdicating in favor of their caesars, Galerius and Constantius. This abdication was intended to provide for an orderly succession. Instead, the sons of Constantius and Maximian, Constantine (306–337) and Maxentius (306–312), drawing on the prejudice of the increasingly barbarian armies toward hereditary succession, set about wrecking the tetrarchy. In so doing they plunged the empire once more into civil war as they fought over the western half of the empire.

Victory in the west came to Constantine in 312, when he defeated and killed Maxentius in a battle at the Mulvian Bridge outside Rome. Constantine attributed his victory to a vision telling him to paint a ☥ on the shields of his soldiers. For pagans this symbol indicated the solar emblem of the cult of the Unconquered Sun. For Christians it was the Chi-Rho, ☧ , formed from the first two letters of the Greek word for Christ. The next year in Milan Constantine rescinded the persecution of Christians and granted Christian clergy the same privileges enjoyed by pagan priests. Constantine himself was not baptized until near death, a common practice in antiquity. However, during his reign Christianity grew from a persecuted minority to the most favored cult in the empire.

Almost as important as Constantine's conversion to Christianity was his decision to establish his capital not in Rome, with its strong association with the cult of the traditional gods, nor in

The Empire Under Diocletian, A.D. 284–305

Painting of Christ from a catacomb ceiling. The cata-combs were underground passages near Rome used by the early Christians as cemeteries, for funeral and memorial services, and as places of refuge during times of persecution.

Milan or Trier, the military capitals of the west, but in Byzantium, a city founded by Greek colonists on the narrow neck of water connecting the Black Sea to the Mediterranean. He transformed and enriched this small town, calling it the New Rome. Later it was known as Constantinople, the city of Constantine. For the next eleven centuries Constantinople served as the heart of the Roman and then the Byzantine world. Even to barbarians, it was known simply as "the City," a title once held by Rome. From his new city, Constantine began to transform the empire into a Christian state and Christianity into a Roman state religion.

We will never know just what Constantine's conversion meant to him in personal terms. Its effects on the empire and on Christianity were obvious and enormous. Constantine himself continued to maintain cordial relations with representatives of all cults and to use ambiguous language that would offend no one when talking about "the deity." His successors were less broad-minded. They quickly reversed the positions of Christianity and paganism. In 341 pagan sacrifice was banned, and by 355 the temples had been closed and the death penalty for sacrificing to the gods had been decreed, although not enforced. In 357 the altar of Victory, on which senators had offered incense since the time of Augustus, was removed from the senate.

While paganism was being disestablished, Christianity was rapidly becoming the established religion. Conversion in no way meant a break with the theocratic consolidation initiated by Diocletian. On the contrary, Constantine was one of the most ruthless and ambitious emperors Rome had ever known. He sought in the Christian cult exactly the kind of support Diocletian had looked for in a return to Jupiter and the traditional gods. Constantine made enormous financial contributions to Christian communities to repay them for their losses during persecutions. He erected rich churches on the model of Roman basilicas, or administrative buildings, and converted temples into Christian places of worship. He gave bishops the authority to act as magistrates within the Christian community. Once the particular objects of persecution, bishops became favored courtiers. Constantine attempted to make himself the de facto head of the Church. He even presided at the Council of Nicaea in 325, at which the assembled bishops condemned the Arian teaching that Jesus as Son of God was not equal to God the Father. Constantine and his successors, with the exception of his nephew Julian (361–363), who attempted unsuccessfully both to reestablish paganism and to promote traditional Hellenism, sought to use the cult of the one God to strengthen their control over the empire.

Although imperial support was essential to the spread of Christianity in the fourth century, other factors encouraged conversion as well. Christian miracles, particularly that of exorcism, or casting out of demons, won many converts. The ancient world was filled with *daimons*, supernatural creatures whose power for good or ill no one doubted. Every village had its possessed persons—madmen and women, troubled youths, and hate-filled citizens. Much of traditional pagan ritual was aimed at dealing with the spirits bedeviling such people. Wandering Christian preachers seemed more competent than others to deal with these tormentors, proving that their God was more powerful than the spirits and that their message was worthy of a hearing.

Over the course of the fourth century, the number of Christians rose from five to thirty million. Imperial support, miracles, and preaching could not, by themselves, account for this phenomenal growth. Physical coercion played a large part. The story was told, for example, of the conversion of the town of Gaza under its first bishop, Porphyry, around 400. Although the account is largely fictional, it describes what must have been a fairly typical progression in the process of conversion. Porphyry arrived to find a pagan city. He began to make converts almost at once through the force of his miracles. His prayers to God ended a drought, aided a woman in childbirth, and expelled demons. The eloquence of his preaching struck his opponents dumb. Enormous imperial gifts enriched the local church. Then finally, upon imperial command, all of the local temples were destroyed and "a great number" of leading pagans who refused conversion were tortured to death. The remaining pagan population converted. Whether or not the story is true, it illustrates the essential role that naked force often played in the process of conversion. This suited Church leaders such as Porphyry who, when questioned about the value of conversions resulting from terror, is said to have quoted St. Paul: "Whether falsely or truly, Christ is preached, and I rejoice in that." Conversion—by whatever method—also suited the emperors, who saw a unified cult as an essential means of bolstering their position.

A Parting of the Ways

The emperor and the empire needed bolstering in 376 when the Huns, a nomadic horse people from central Asia, swept into the Black Sea region and threw the entire barbarian world once more into chaos. The Huns quickly destroyed the Gothic confederation and absorbed many of the peoples who had constituted the Goths. Others sought protection in the empire. The Visigoths, as they came to be known, were the largest of these groups, and their fate illustrated how precarious existence could be for all the occupants of the imperial frontier. Driven from their lands and thus from their food supply, the Visigoths turned to the empire for assistance. But the Roman authorities treated them as brutally as had the Huns, forcing some to sell their children into slavery in return for morsels of dog flesh. In despair the Visigoths rose up against the Romans, and against all odds their desperate rebellion succeeded. They annihilated an imperial army at Adrianople in 378, and the emperor Valens himself was killed. His successor, Theodosius, was forced to allow the Visigoths to settle along the Danube and to be governed by their own leaders despite the fact that they lived within the boundaries of the empire.

Theodosius' treaty with the Visigoths set an ominous precedent. Never before had a barbarian people been allowed to settle as a political unit within the empire. Within a few years, the Visigoths were again on the move, traveling across the Balkans into Italy under the command of their chieftain Alaric (ca. 370–410). In 410 they captured Rome and sacked it for three days, an event that sent shock waves throughout the entire empire. Rome had been sacked before, but ever since the Celtic sack of Rome in 390 B.C., the sacking had always been done by Romans. The symbolic effect of the Visigoths' victory far exceeded the amount of real damage, which was relatively light. Only after Alaric's death did the Visigoths leave Italy, ultimately settling in Spain and southern Gaul with the approval of the emperor.

Missorium of Theodosius made in A.D. 388. Theodosius is presented as a godlike figure detached from the struggles of ordinary people. Beside him are his sons Valentinianus II and Arcadius.

The Barbarization of the West

Rome did not fall. It was transformed. Romans participated in and even encouraged this transformation. Roman accommodation with the Visigoths set the pattern for subsequent settlement of barbarians in the western half of the empire. By this time, barbarians made up the bulk of the imperial army, and commanders were frequently themselves barbarians. However, these barbarian troops had been integrated into existing Roman military structures. Indeed, these so-called imperial Germans had often proven even more loyal to Rome than the Roman provincial populations they were to protect. In the late fourth and fifth centuries, emperors accepted whole barbarian peoples as integral parts of the Roman army and settled them within the empire. Usually the emperors diverted a percentage of tax revenues from the region's estates in order to support these "guests."

The Visigothic kingdom in southern Gaul and Spain was typical in this respect. Alaric's successor, Ataulf, was extremely eager to win the approval of the emperor. He married Galla Placidia, the daughter of the Emperor Theodosius and the sister of Emperor Honorius, in a Roman ceremony in Narbonne in 414. Soon afterward he established a government at Bordeaux directed by Gallo-Roman aristocrats. Although his opponents soon assassinated him, his successors concluded a treaty with Constantinople in which the Visigoths were recognized as a legitimate, established political presence within the empire. This so-called Kingdom of Toulouse endured for almost a century. South of the Pyrenees the Gothic kingdom of Toledo continued for almost three hundred years.

The Visigoths were not the only powerful barbarian people to challenge the empire. The Vandals, who had entered the empire in 406, crossed over into Africa, the richest region of the western empire, and quickly conquered it. Avowed enemies of the empire, the Vandals used their base in North Africa to raid the European coastline and attack Roman shipping. In 455 they sacked Rome much more thoroughly than had the Goths forty-five years earlier.

Another threat appeared in the 430s, when the Huns, formerly Roman allies, invaded the empire under their charismatic leader Attila (ca.

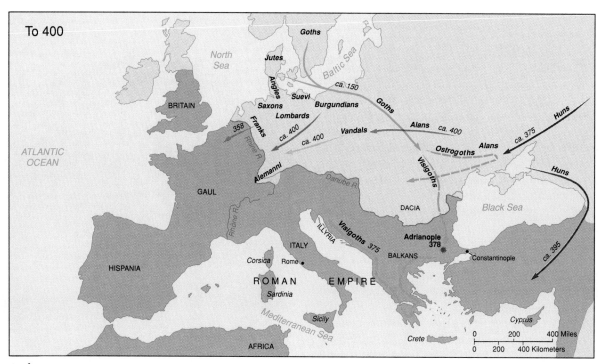

Barbarian Migrations and Invasions

406–453). Although defeated in Gaul by a combined army of barbarians under the command of the Roman general Flavius Aëtius in 451, they turned toward Italy and penetrated as far as Rome. There they were stopped not by the rapidly disintegrating imperial forces but by the bishop of Rome, Pope Leo I, who met Attila before the city's gates. What transpired between the two is not known, but Attila's subsequent withdrawal from Italy vastly increased the prestige of the papacy. Now not only were popes successors of Saint Peter and bishops of the principal city of the west, but they were replacing the emperor as protector of the city. The foundations of the political power of the papacy were established.

The confederation of the Huns collapsed after the death of Attila in 453, but imperial power did not revive in Italy. A series of incompetent emperors were pushed aside by barbarian generals who assumed power in the peninsula and sought recognition from Zeno, the emperor in the east. However, after the death of the last legitimate western emperor, Julius Nepos, in 480, Zeno conferred the title of patrician on the Ostrogothic king Theodoric. In 489 Theodoric invaded Italy with imperial blessing and established himself as ruler of Italy.

In Theodoric's kingdom, the Roman and Ostrogothic institutions remained separate, united only at the top in the person of Theodoric. To his barbarians Theodoric was king; to the Romans he was patrician and military commander in the west. In reality, imperial presence had ceased to exist in Italy.

In Gaul, between the Seine and the Loire, the Roman general Flavius Aëtius and, after his death, the general Syagrius continued to represent some imperial presence. But the armies that Aëtius and Syagrius commanded consisted entirely of barbarians, particularly of Visigoths and Franks, and they represented the interests of local aristocratic factions rather than those of Constantinople. So thoroughly barbarized had these last Roman commanders become in their military command and political control that the barbarians referred to Syagrius as "king of the Romans." Ultimately in 486 Syagrius was defeated and replaced by the Frank Clovis, son of his military commander Childeric, probably with the blessing of the emperor.

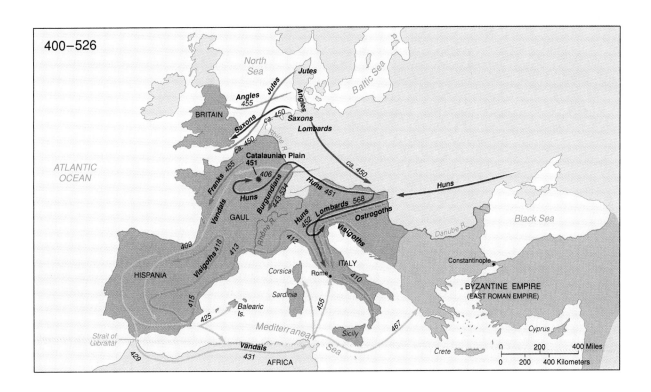

Britain met a similar fate. Abandoned by Roman legions around 407, the Romano-Celtic population in this province concluded a treaty with bands of Saxons and Angles to protect Britain from other barbarian raiders. As had happened elsewhere in the empire, the barbarians came as federated troops and stayed as rulers. Gradually, during the fifth century, Germanic warrior groups conquered much of the island. The Anglo-Saxons pushed the native inhabitants to the west and the north. There, as the Cornish and the Welsh (in Anglo-Saxon *Welsh* means simply "enemy"), they preserved the Christian religion but largely lost their other Roman traditions.

The establishment of barbarian kingdoms within the Roman world meant the end of the western empire as a political entity. However, the emperors east and west continued to pretend that all these barbarian peoples, with the exception of the Vandals, were Roman troops commanded by loyal Roman officers who happened to be of barbarian origin. Following the precedent established with the Visigoths, the emperors gave their kings or war leaders official status within the empire as Roman generals or patricians. They generally rewarded their leaders by redirecting to them imperial taxes from areas where they were settled. Occasionally emperors granted them portions of abandoned lands or existing estates. Local Roman elites considered these leaders rude and uncultured barbarians who nevertheless could be made to serve these elites' own interests more easily than better educated imperial bureaucrats.

As a result, the aristocracy of the west, the *maiores*, viewed the decay of the civil government without dismay. This decay was due largely to the poverty of the imperial treasury. In the fifth century the entire public revenues of the west amounted to little more than the annual incomes of a few wealthy private aristocrats. Managing to escape both taxation and the jurisdiction of public officials, these individuals carved out for themselves vast estates, which they and their families controlled with private armies and which they governed as virtually autonomous lordships. Ordinary freemen, pressed by the remnants of imperial taxation and by barbarians, were forced into accepting the protection and hence control offered by these aristocrats, who thereby came to control whole villages and districts.

The primary source of friction between barbarians and provincial elites was religion. Many Goths had converted to Christianity around the time that the Huns had destroyed the Gothic confederation. However, they had chosen the Arian form of Christianity in order to appease the Arian emperors Constantius and Valens. But the Goths and most other barbarian peoples held to the Arian form of faith long after it had been abandoned in the Empire. Thus, wherever the barbarians settled, they were met with distrust and hostility from the orthodox clergy. In southern Gaul and Italy this hostility created serious difficulties because during the fifth century bishops had assumed many of the traditional duties and powers held by provincial Roman administrators.

Although during the fifth century the western aristocracy had largely given up on the civil administration, these wealthy landowners increasingly identified with the episcopacy. In Gaul, bishops were regularly selected from members of the greatest Gallo-Roman senatorial families, establishing veritable episcopal dynasties. In Italy and Spain too, bishops were drawn from the landed aristocracy. These bishops, most of whom were elected after long years of outstanding secular leadership, served as the primary protectors and administrators of their communities, filling the vacuum left by the erosion of other civil offices. They, more than either local civil officials or the Bacaudae, were successful in representing the community before imperial tax collectors or barbarian chieftains.

Barbarian military leaders needed local ties by which to govern the large indigenous populations over whom they ruled. They found cooperation with these aristocrats both necessary and advantageous. Thus while individual landowners might have suffered in the transition from Roman to barbarian rule, for the most part this transition took place with less disturbance of the local social or political scene than was once thought. During the fifth century the imperial presence simply faded away as barbarian kings came to rule in the name of the emperor. After 480, the emperor resided exclusively in the east. The last western emperors disappeared without serious opposition either from western aristocrats or from their eastern colleagues.

The Hellenization of the East

The eastern half of the empire, in contrast to the west, managed to survive and even to prosper in the fifth and sixth centuries. In the east, beginning in 400, the trends toward militarization and barbarization of the administration were reversed, the strength of the imperial government was reaffirmed, and the vitality and integrity of the empire were restored.

Several reasons account for the contrast between east and west. First, the east had always been more urbanized and civilized than the west. It had an old tradition of civil control that antedated the Roman Empire itself. When the decay of Roman traditions allowed regionalism and tribalism to arise in the west, the same decay brought in the east a return to Hellenistic traditions. Second, the east had never developed the tradition of public poverty and private wealth characteristic of the west. In the east tax revenues continued to support an administrative apparatus, which remained in the hands of civilians rather than barbarian military commanders. Moreover, the local aristocracies in the eastern provinces never achieved the wealth and independence of their western counterparts. Finally, Christian bishops, frequently divided over doctrinal issues, never managed to monopolize either sacred power, which was shared by itinerant holy men and monks, or secular power, which was wielded by imperial agents. Thus under the firm direction of its emperors, especially Theodosius and later Zeno, the eastern empire not only survived but prepared for a new expansionist phase under the emperor Justinian.

Everywhere, the patina of Latin culture began to wear thin as provincials began to rise to positions of prominence and power. In the east, this meant the reemergence of regional cultures and especially of Hellenistic traditions. It also meant that Christian and pagan thinkers would use these traditions to interpret the crises of their world.

The Crisis of Elite Culture

The transformation of the classical world from a pagan empire, secure in its mastery over the civilized world, to a fragmented Christian one was as profoundly felt in the cultural sphere as it was in the political and social spheres. Crisis forces choice, and in the third through fifth centuries the choices faced by intellectuals were as profound as those faced by emperors. Where should one look for peace—within or without? Ought Christians to reject the intellectual tradition of the Greco-Roman world or recast it in Christian form? Finally, was the Roman political system in which Christianity had become so deeply embedded essential to its survival?

Three very different figures—Plotinus, Origen, and Augustine—exemplify this transformation and set the stage for future European cultural developments. During the crisis of the third century, Hellenistic culture reached its zenith in the life and work of the pagan Egyptian philosopher Plotinus (205–270), who recast Platonism into the form that was the foundation of Christian, Islamic, and Jewish thought through the Middle Ages. His contemporary and compatriot Origen (185–254) began to intellectualize the meaning of the Christian Scriptures and transformed pagan philosophy into a Christian

The Vandals crossed into North Africa from Spain and founded a state centered on Carthage. This mosaic of the late fifth or early sixth century shows a prosperous Vandal lord leaving his villa. His costume is typical of barbarians.

intellectual tradition. As a result of his work Christian intellectuals could no longer be dismissed as "wool seekers, cobblers, laundry workers, and the most illiterate and rustic yokels." In the following century Augustine of Hippo (354–430) faced a new, internal challenge. Victory over paganism was quickly followed by serious disagreements over the proper relationship between the Christian community and the Christian empire. In the early period of Christianity the question was whether to be a Christian meant to be a Jew. Now Augustine had to decide whether to be a Christian meant to be a Roman.

Living in Harmony with the Universe

Plotinus exemplified the vital Hellenistic high culture of late antiquity. He was born in a small provincial town in Upper Egypt, but his restless intellect led him first to dabble in Gnosticism and then to travel to Mesopotamia in the hope of studying Persian and Indian philosophy. The crucial event in his life was his introduction to Platonic philosophy as a student in Alexandria in his late twenties. The new or Neoplatonic tradition, which he studied and of which he became the principal spokesperson, was by the third century much more than a philosophy. It was a virtual religion, combining Platonic and Stoic thought and demanding withdrawal from the world and full-time dedication to the pursuit of wisdom. The serenity and tranquillity demanded of the philosopher was available only to a tiny elite. To cultured people everywhere, this was the most worthy life-style, and Plotinus was its embodiment. His reputation as a serene and gentle teacher continued to spread, especially after he settled in Rome, where he spent the last and most productive decades of his life.

Plotinus and his fellow Neoplatonists believed that through rational contemplation it was possible to see beyond material existence and to recognize the intimate connection between the invisible God and the visible world. This intimate connection was made through an unbroken chain of intermediate beings linking God, who was beyond all knowing, to creatures and especially to man. The most important link in this chain was the World Soul, and this link between the universe and God was reflected in the relationship

Relief from the tomb of a Roman man of letters, thought to be Plotinus (late third to fourth century). As he studies a scroll, he is surrounded by sages and disciples. A bundle of books reposes at his feet.

between the body and the soul. Classical Platonism had considered the body as the prison of the soul, and the extremists of Christian and Gnostic asceticism saw the body as evil. For Plotinus, however, the body was the instrument through which the soul sought expression. Material and spiritual reality were thus intimately and properly associated. Man was at home in the universe, just as he was at home in his body. The harmony of matter and spirit could be recognized in philosophical contemplation just as it could be seen in the balanced, perfect lives of the philosophers themselves.

Plotinus thus molded the major philosophical traditions of antiquity into a way of life and an understanding of the universe in which man and God were intimately interconnected. The serenity and acceptance of life that this tradition promised to those able to dedicate themselves to it stood in sharp contrast to the violent and disordered world in which Plotinus and his students lived. For those too ignorant or superstitious to see the beauty of this harmony, especially Christians, Plotinus and his followers had nothing but scorn. And yet the same Alexandrian teacher who instructed Plotinus had another, even more influential student. He also taught Origen, who would reconcile Christianity and classical philosophy.

Inventing the Christian Intellectual

Origen was born into a Christian family in Alexandria, then the most cultivated city of the Hellenistic world, and grew up with an acute sense of the challenge of being a Christian. When Origen was seventeen his father was executed for his faith and his property was confiscated. Origen so wanted to share in his father's martyrdom that his mother had to hide his clothes to keep him at home. To support his mother and six younger brothers, he began to teach rhetoric, that is, traditional pagan learning. Later he headed the Christian education program of Alexandria. Although he was a layman, his reputation spread throughout the empire. Important Christians and pagans, even including the mother of the pagan emperor Alexander Severus, sought his advice. However, his brilliant career and his bold teachings infuriated his jealous bishop in Alexandria, who attacked him for personal and heretical improprieties. The pope ultimately confirmed these charges, but this judgment was never recognized in much of the east. Moving to Palestine, Origen continued to teach and write until a new outbreak of persecution in the 250s. Arrested and tortured, he finally followed in his father's footsteps and died a martyr in 254.

Origen invented a new sort of Christian, the Christian intellectual. Intellectuals like Plotinus had condemned Christians as superstitious ignoramuses because they sought truth in Scripture rather than in philosophical reason. Origen moved Christian teaching from a literal to a symbolic understanding of Scripture and gave it a sound philosophical foundation by synthesizing the Neoplatonic tradition, represented by Plotinus, with Christianity.

Initially Origen had accepted the literal sense of Scripture, going so far as to castrate himself after reading the biblical injunction: "There are eunuchs who make themselves eunuchs for the kingdom of heaven's sake." Eventually he rejected such a literal and destructive meaning of Scripture as he came to realize the importance of symbolism. He applied to Scripture the same sort of symbolic analysis pagan scholars had used to understand the classics of the Greek and Roman traditions. For Origen the Scriptures became a symbol of God's eternal teaching—incomprehensible to those who sought a literal meaning but

apparent to those who looked for the hidden spiritual message. This allegorical tradition would dominate Christian biblical studies for over a thousand years.

Against the charge of anti-intellectualism leveled at Christianity, Origen replied that since God endowed man with reason, he must have intended that humans reach true wisdom through reason. Only because people failed at the task did God give them revelation. "It is far better to accept doctrines with reason and wisdom," he wrote, "than with mere faith." Thus he insisted that his Christian students first study the best of the pagan intellectual tradition, particularly Neoplatonism, not with the intention of refuting its "errors" but rather of finding in it that which was true. Only after his students had thoroughly mastered human wisdom was he prepared to teach them divine wisdom. So completely did Origen combine the Neoplatonic tradition with Christianity that he was often accused of being more devoted to the former than the latter. Nevertheless his insistence that there was no contradiction between faith and reason established an intellectual basis for Christianity that continued through Western history.

Finding the City of God

Origen was the father of Christian philosophy. Augustine was the father of Christian political science. Born into a well-off North African family in the town of Tagaste, he was quickly drawn into the good life and upward mobility open to bright young provincials in the fourth century. In his *Confessions*, the first psychological autobiography, Augustine describes how his skills in rhetoric took him to the provincial capital of Carthage and then on to Rome and finally Milan, the western imperial residence, where he gained fame as one of the foremost rhetoricians of the empire.

Connections as well as talent contributed to his rise to fame. Although his mother was a Christian, he was not baptized at birth, and while in Carthage he joined the Manichees, a materialist, dualist sect which taught that good and evil were caused by two different ultimate principles and which rejected the notion of spiritual reality. As protégé of the Manichees, Augustine gained introductions to the leading pagan aristocrats of his day.

While in Milan, Augustine came into contact with kinds of people he had never encountered in Africa, particularly with Neoplatonists and Christians. The most important of these was Ambrose, bishop of Milan. The encounter with a spiritual philosophy and a Christianity compatible with it profoundly changed the young professor. After a period of agonized searching, Augustine converted to the new religion. With characteristic enthusiasm, he embraced Christianity as wholeheartedly as he had previously embraced his career. Abandoning his Italian life, he returned to the North African town of Hippo to found a monastery where he could devote himself to reading the Scriptures. However, his neighbors were determined to harness the intellectual talents of their brilliant native son. When their bishop died, they forcibly seized Augustine and made him their bishop.

Augustine spent the remainder of his life as bishop of this small provincial town, but his reputation as spokesperson for the Christian tradition spread throughout the empire. As a professor of rhetoric he had become an expert in debate, and much of his episcopal career was spent in debates with enemies within and without the Church. Chief among the former were the Donatists, a North African sect, and the Pelagians, who taught that humans were responsible for their own salvation. Enemies outside the Church were the defenders of the pagan Roman tradition, who blamed Christians for the sacking of Rome in 410.

All three of these groups represented sincere responses to the challenges of the new Christian empire. The Donatists had developed in North Africa as a response to the political conversions of the early fourth century. During the last persecutions many Christians and even bishops had collaborated with Roman authorities, handing over sacred Scriptures to be burned. Disturbed by the ease with which these traitors (our word *traitor* comes from the Latin verb *tradere* "to hand over") had returned to positions of power in the Church under Constantine and by the growth of political conversions, the Donatists insisted that the Church had to be pure and that its ministers had to be blameless. Thus they argued that baptisms and ordinations performed by these traitors were invalid. The visible Church on earth had to be as perfect as the invisible one, and only the Donatists had preserved this purity.

The Pelagians also held themselves to a higher standard than that of ordinary Christians, who accepted sin as an inevitable part of human life. Pelagians believed rather that human nature had been so created that people could achieve perfection in this life. God's will, like the will of the emperor, was absolute. Moreover, humans had both the duty and the ability to obey it. Like the Donatists, Pelagians believed that members of the true Church were those who perfected themselves by the force of their own wills, thus making a radical break with the compromising world in which they lived.

These appeals to heroic virtue were paralleled in the attacks launched against Christianity by the remaining adherents to the cult of the old Roman gods. The disasters of recent history and in particular the sack of Rome had occurred, they argued, because the west had abandoned the gods and the traditions of Roman virtue and justice that had made Rome great.

In responding to these attacks, Augustine elaborated a new Christian understanding of human society and the individual's relationship to God, which dominated Western thought for the next fifteen centuries. He rejected the elitist attempt of the Donatists and Pelagians to identify the true Church with any earthly community. Likewise he rejected the claim of pagans that the Roman tradition was the embodiment of true virtue. Instead he argued that the true members of God's elect necessarily coexisted in the world with sinners. No earthly community, not even the empire or the Church, was the true "city of God." Earthly society participated in the true "city of God" through the sacraments and did so quite apart from the individual worthiness of the recipients or even of the ministers of these rites. Belief that the presence of sinners within the Church blocked the plan of salvation or that responsibility for salvation lay with the individual was to deny the omnipotence of God.

Thus neither the Donatist sect nor the Pelagian community nor even the imperial Church was essential for salvation. Salvation came through the Church, but the saved were not identified solely with any particular group of Christians. In this way, Augustine argued for a distinction between the visible Christian empire and the Christian community. Earlier Paul, the pharisaic Jew, had determined that Christianity would survive Judaism even as the latter was being destroyed by Rome. Now Augustine, the Roman rhetorician, determined that Christianity would survive the disappearance of the Roman empire just as it was disintegrating into barbarian kingdoms. Even as Augustine lay dying in Hippo, the city was under siege by the Vandals.

The Transformation of Popular Culture

The responses of Plotinus, Origen, and Augustine to the choices of late antiquity were fundamental for the subsequent intellectual development of Western civilization. On a more popular level a different sort of Christian had an equally profound influence on the future. This was the hermit, monk, or recluse, who taught less by his or her words than by his or her life, a life often so unusual that even the most ignorant and worldly citizen of the late empire could recognize in it the power of God. Beneath the apparent eccentricity, however, lay a fundamental principle: the radical rejection of society's values in favor of absolute dedication to God's.

While Plotinus was teaching in the serenity of his Roman villa, and shortly after Origen had died fighting for the integrity of the Christian intellectual tradition, another Egyptian was undertaking a different path to enduring fame. Anthony (ca. 250–355), a well-to-do peasant, heard the same text that later converted Augustine, "Go, sell all you have and give to the poor and follow me." Anthony was uneducated; it was said that he had been too shy as a boy to attend school. This straightforward peasant did exactly what the text commanded. He disposed of all his goods and left his village for the Egyptian desert. There, for the next seventy years, he sought to follow Christ in a life of constant self-mortification and prayer.

This dropout from civilization deeply touched his fellow Christians, many of whom were disturbed by the abrupt transformation of their religion from persecuted minority to privileged majority. By the time of his death this

monk—the word comes from the Greek *monos*, alone—found himself the head of a large, loosely knit community of like-minded persons who looked to him as spiritual father, or abbot. Over the next centuries thousands rejected the worldliness of civilization and the easy life of the average Christian to lead a monastic life in the wildernesses of the empire.

Monastic Communities

Monasticism took two forms, communal organization or solitary life. Pachomius (ca. 290–346) and Basil the Great (ca. 329–379) in the east and Benedict of Nursia (ca. 480–547) in the west perfected the communal life. Faced with the impossibility of surviving in a harsh environment without cooperation, Egyptian monks banded together into small monastic towns. In these monasteries lived as many as two thousand monks. They placed themselves under the control of the abbot, who served as spiritual guide and administrator of the community. These men and women sought spiritual perfection through physical self-mortification and through the subordination of their own wills to that of the abbot. Monks drank no wine, ate no meat, used no oil. They spent their days in prayer, either communal or individual. These monastic communities survived by maintaining a symbiotic relationship with the civilized world the monks had sought to escape. Abbots organized their monks into houses according to their various crafts, and the surplus of their gardening, baking, basket making, and the like was sold in the villages and towns of Egypt.

The fame of these religious communities spread throughout the Roman world, carried initially by the local peasants, then by inhabitants of nearby cities who came to see the desert dwellers and ask their advice. Pilgrims from across the empire visited the Egyptian monasteries on their way to and from Jerusalem. Some of these pilgrims returned home with the desire to imitate the Egyptian monks in their native provinces. During the fourth century this monastic tradition spread east to Bethlehem, Jerusalem, Caesarea, and Constantinople and west to Rome, Milan, Trier, Marseille, and Tours. In the following centuries it reached beyond the borders of the empire

Portraits of the Soul

The art of late antiquity confronts us with the powerful complexities of Mediterranean civilization in the fourth through the sixth centuries. Pagans, Christians, and Jews all jostled together in the turbulent and exciting cities of the empire, as much connected by a common culture as they were separated by religion. Integral to this common culture were portraiture and representational art. The official images of the emperor in every town; the busts of ancestors preserved in every home; miniatures given to friends as mementoes; encaustic representations of beloved dead on wooden sarcophagi; statues of philosophers, gods, heroes, and poets—everywhere one confronted the faces, the persons, and the souls of present and past generations.

Portraits, while individualized, nevertheless differed greatly from the traditions of Roman portraiture, which had striven for precise representation of physical likenesses. Beginning in the third century, artists transformed the actual appearance of their subjects in order to capture their inner reality. In busts of the tetrarchs, for example, artists often used a "hard" military style. In the example here, Diocletian is captured in compact, geometric forms in Egyptian basalt. The sculptor suggested the emperor's close-cropped hair and beard by incising the stone rather than by traditional molding. The savior of the empire looks out on the world from enlarged, staring eyes, his harsh features and tight lips suggesting the tension and controlled cruelty with which he transformed the civilized world.

In contrast, the colossal head shows Constantine in the tradition of early emperors. His long, clean-shaven face, his molded hair, and serene expression all hark back to the first century. His great eyes peer off into the heavens; they are the windows from which he views the ultimate truths that lie beyond this world and through which one can glimpse his inner spirit. What matters is much less the appearance of the man Constantine than the impact of the image. Its huge size (the whole seated figure was over thirty feet high) and inner-worldly expression emphasize the emperor's position. If not a god, he was, in Constantine's own words, "a fitting instrument of His will."

The representation of private individuals followed the same pattern as that of emperors. In a gold glass portrait from fourth-century Alexandria, members of a family gaze serenely at the viewer, their faces emotionless, only their eyes penetrating and alive. This is the magic of the encaustic (colored wax painted on wood)

mortuary images found in Egyptian burials from the fourth and fifth centuries. The apparent verisimilitude of this woman's portrait (showing the person much younger than she was at the time of death) is less significant than the power of the eyes, which reach out and draw the viewer into her soul. This, rather than faithful representation, was the goal of the artist and accorded with the dominant Neoplatonic philosophy of Christians and pagans alike. Plotinus had refused to sit for a portrait, objecting that it would only show the mundane and not his true spiritual and intellectual reality. By returning to Hellinistic traditions and by moving to stylized, nonrepresentational forms, the artists of late antiquity sought to capture invisible truth in visible form.

When Christians and Jews

wished to represent the heroes of their cults, they turned to the same traditions and even the same artists as did their pagan neighbors. Just as the inner spirit of emperors of the fourth and fifth centuries could be captured by the evocation of subtly altered classical portraiture, so too could Christ, his mother Mary, and the Christian saints be best captured within established classical traditions.

Jewish representations of David followed a similar tradition. In 508–509 an artist decorating a synagogue in Gaza represented David as Orpheus, the pagan philosopher-musician who conveyed his doctrines in song. Christians too adopted the image of Orpheus, both as David and, since David was a prefiguration of Christ, as Christ himself, "the New Musician, who sings a new song," in the words of one Christian theologian. Since Orpheus was often depicted carrying a sheep on his shoulders, this image was adapted to Christ, the Good Shepherd.

Mary, venerated as the "Mother of God" in the east, inherited the traditional imagery of the Egyptian goddess Isis suckling Horus. Mary nursing the Christ child became a common representation in fifth-century Egypt and from there it eventually spread across the Christian world.

Such explicit mixing and borrowing from pagan iconographic tradition parallels the adoption by Origen and Augustine of the pagan philosophical tradition. Uneducated monks in the wilderness might greet such adaptations with alarm and violence. For cultured persons of all religious traditions, however, these representations led the viewer from the visible world into a higher, invisible one. The artists portrayed emperors, family, gods, or saints not as they appeared, but rather they used appearance to reach into the very souls of their subjects.

when Egyptian-style monasticism was introduced into Ireland.

Intellectuals as well as peasants heard the call of monastic life. Chief among the intellectuals was Jerome (ca. 347–420), the greatest linguist of antiquity, who was so impressed by a visit to the monastic communities of the east that he became a priest and founded a monastery in Bethlehem. There he translated the Bible into Latin. This Latin translation, known as the Vulgate, became the standard version of Christian Scripture in the west until the Reformation and, in Roman Catholic countries, until the twentieth century.

In the Greek-speaking world, the definitive form of the monastic community was provided by Basil the Great. Basil had visited the monasteries of Egypt, Palestine, and Syria before founding his own monastery at Pontus near his family estate at Annesi in present-day Turkey. Although he did not write a specific rule for the governance of his monastery, his collection of commentaries and spiritual advice to his followers outlined a form of monastic life in which a day of agriculture, craft work, and care for the sick and the poor was organized within an ordered progression of liturgical prayer. His emphasis on communal life rather than on heroic acts of individual asceticism provided the model for eastern monasticism from his day to the present.

Unlike Anthony of Egypt, Basil was a brilliant and well-educated intellectual who frequently left his monastery to throw himself into the ecclesiastical politics of the empire. By the end of his life Basil had become bishop of Caesarea. Eastern monastic communities continued this active involvement in political and secular affairs. Monasteries provided the early religious training for most religious leaders. Monks and abbots often involved themselves wholeheartedly in the politics of the empire. Monks rioting in the streets of Constantinople over political issues was a familiar sight for over a thousand years.

In the west, Benedict of Nursia was as influential in structuring communal religious life as was Basil in the east. Like Anthony before him, Benedict had fled the city for the countryside. In time Benedict became abbot of a small community of monks at Monte Cassino, between Rome and Naples. The rule that he drafted for the governance of his community, while drawn largely

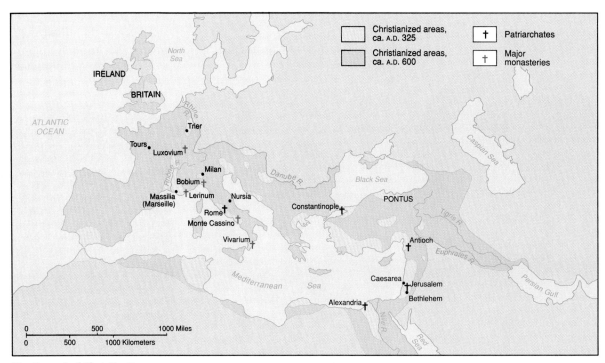

The Spread of Christianity

from earlier monastic rules circulating in Italy, became the definitive statement of western monasticism. Benedict's rule encouraged moderation and flexibility while emphasizing a life of poverty, chastity, and obedience to an elected abbot. Monks were required to perform some physical labor, and the monastery was intended to be a self-sufficient community. However, the real task of the monk was the continuous praise of God. This consisted of gathering at regular intervals through the day and night for communal prayer. Although Benedict lived and died in obscurity, within two and one half centuries his rule became the universal rule for western monasticism.

Western monasteries, too, provided their share of bishops, but unlike those in the east, western monks remained more isolated from population centers and from direct involvement in public affairs. Western monasteries were not, however, peripheral to western society and religion. Rather, these rustic communities were centers of religious and economic activity as well as education and learning in the largely rural west. They remained under the authority of the local bishops who were usually drawn from the lay aristocracy of the empire in the west. Also, western monasteries depended upon the political and economic support that they received from lay patrons.

Solitaries and Hermits

Although Anthony had begun as a hermit, he and most Egyptian monks eventually settled into communal lives. Elsewhere, particularly in the desert of Syria, the model of the monk remained the individual hermit. The Syrian desert, unlike that of Egypt, was particularly suitable for such an ascetic life. Here the desert was milder, an individual could find food in wild roots and water in rain-pools, and villages were never too far off. Moreover, the life of the wandering hermit was closely connected to traditional seminomadic life-styles in the Fertile Crescent. But the Christian hermits who appeared across Syria in late antiquity were unlikely to be mistaken for Bedouin. The Christian hermits were wild men and women who came down from the mountainsides and galvanized the attention of their contemporaries by their life-styles. Their lives were characterized by the most extreme forms of self-mortification

Gold plaque from a sixth-century Syrian reliquary. The subject is Simeon Stylites on his pillar. The snake represents the vanquished devil. Clients could consult the holy man by climbing up the ladder on the left.

and radical rejection of civilization. The most famous of the hermits, Simeon Stylites (ca. 390–459), spent thirty-six years perched at the top of a pillar fifty feet high. Two women, Marana and Cyra, lived forty-two years chained in a small open-roofed enclosure.

Such people of God, rejecting civilized life in the most overt and radical ways, nevertheless met very real social and cultural needs of the population. Their lack of ties to human society made them the perfect arbitrators in the constant disputes that threatened to disrupt village life. They were "individuals of power," whose proven ability to cast out demons and work miracles made them ideal community patrons at a time when traditional power brokers of the village were being lured away to imperial service or provincial cities. The greatest of these holy people, like Simeon Stylites, received as visitors not only local peasants but also emperors and empresses, who eagerly sought their advice. In an age of individualism, the Syrian hermits were, along with the emperors, the most prominent examples of individuals who had risen above humanity and who stood (literally in the case of the pillar dwellers) somewhere between the divine and the human.

Unlike the eastern monks, the Syrian hermits of the fourth and fifth centuries had few parallels in the west. Hermits did inhabit the caves and forests of Italy and Gaul, and pious women found solitude as recluses even in the center of Rome. But these westerners did not establish themselves either as independent sources of religious power or as political power brokers. Their monasticism remained a personal religious commitment. When one Roman woman was asked why she remained shut up in her cell, she replied, "I am on a journey." When asked where she was going, she answered simply, "to God."

In the west, in spite of the creation of the barbarian kingdoms, cultural and political leadership remained firmly in the hands of the aristocracy. Aristocratic bishops, rather than hermits, monopolized the role of mediators of divine power just as their lay brothers, in cooperation with barbarian rulers, monopolized the role of mediators of secular power.

The divergence in religious power between east and west was characteristic of the growing differences between the two halves of the Roman Empire at the close of late antiquity. The east remained more firmly attached not only to Roman traditions of government but also to the much more ancient traditions of social complexity, urban life, and religious culture that stretched back to the dawn of civilization. The emperors continued to rule from Constantinople for another thousand years, but the extent of their authority gradually shrank to little more than the city itself. Furthermore, their empire was so profoundly Hellenized in nature that it is properly called Byzantine (from the original name of Constantinople) rather than Roman.

The west experienced a transformation even more profound than that of the east. The triple heritage of late Roman political and military forms, barbarian society, and Christian culture coalesced into a new civilization that was perhaps less the direct heir of antiquity than that of the east, but the more dynamic for its distinctiveness. In culture, politics, and patterns of urban and rural life, the west and the east had gone separate ways, and their paths diverged ever more in the centuries ahead.

Suggestions for Further Reading

The Crisis of the Third Century

* A. H. M. Jones, *The Later Roman Empire, 284–602: A Social, Economic and Administrative Survey*, 2 vols. (Baltimore: The Johns Hopkins University Press, 1986). The standard, detailed survey of late antiquity by an administrative historian.

* Peter Brown, *The World of Late Antiquity*, A.D. 150–750 (New York: Harcourt Brace Jovanovich, 1971). A brilliant essay on the cultural transformation of the ancient world.

E. A. Thompson, *The Early Germans* (Oxford: Oxford University Press, 1965). An important social and economic view of Germanic society.

The Empire Restored

* Ramsay MacMullen, *Paganism in the Roman Empire* (New Haven, CT: Yale University Press, 1981). A sensible introduction to the varieties of Roman religion in the imperial period.

T. D. Barnes, *The New Empire of Diocletian and Constantine* (Cambridge, MA: Harvard University Press, 1982). A current examination of the transformations brought about under these two great emperors.

A Parting of the Ways

* Patrick J. Geary, *Before France and Germany* (New York: Oxford University Press, 1988). On the origins of the barbarian West.

Herwig Wolfram, *History of the Goths* (Berkeley, CA: University of California Press, 1988). An ethnologically sensitive history of the formation of the Gothic peoples.

The Crisis of Elite Culture

* Ramsay MacMullen, *Christianizing the Roman Empire (100–400)* (New Haven, CT: Yale University Press, 1984). A view of Christianity's spread from the perspective of Roman history.

* Judith Herrin, *The Formation of Christendom* (Princeton, NJ: Princeton University Press, 1987). A history of early Christianity from the perspective of a noted Byzantinist.

* Karl F. Morrison, Ed., *The Church in the Roman Empire* (Chicago: University of Chicago Press, 1986). Major documents of early Christianity.

The Transformation of Popular Culture

Peter Brown, *Society and the Holy in Late Antiquity* (Berkeley, CA: University of California Press, 1982). Imaginative essays on religion and society, emphasizing the role of saints.

* David Knowles, *Christian Monasticism* (New York: McGraw-Hill, 1969). A very readable introduction by a great historian of monastic history.

* Indicates paperback edition available

7

The Classical Legacy in the East: Byzantium and Islam

From Temple to Mosque

First a temple dedicated to the Syriac god Hadad and then to the Roman Jupiter, later the Christian church of St. John, and finally a mosque, the Great Mosque of Damascus in Syria bears testimony to the great civilizations that have followed one another in the Near East. Like the successive houses of worship, each civilization rose upon the ruins of its predecessor, incorporating and transforming the rich legacy of the past into a new culture. Little of the pagan and Christian structures is visible, although the mosque owes much to both, as does the civilization it represents.

Nothing remains of the pre-Roman structure. In the first century the Romans rebuilt the temple to include an outer enclosure 1,233 by 1,000 feet with four monumental gateways. In the interior was a porticoed court marked by four corner towers. Monumental portals, or gateways, in the east and west with triple doorways provided access to this inner court, in the center of which stood a structure housing the statue of Jupiter.

Around the time of Constantine, the temple was converted into a Christian church dedicated to Saint John the Baptist. Apparently a portion of the interior porticoed court, which measured roughly 517 by 318 feet, was enclosed to provide a space for worshipers. Two of the four towers were raised to serve as bell towers. For a time after Damascus fell to the Arabs in 635, Christians and Muslims shared the church. Initially, there were only a few Muslims, who required no more than a small place in the exterior courtyard.

However, the Muslim population of the city grew rapidly, and by 705 Damascus was the capital of a vast, expanding Muslim empire, which would soon stretch from the Pyrenees to the Indus River. The caliph al-Walid (705–15) wanted a place of prayer befitting his capital's glory. He invited the Christian community to choose a site for another church. When they refused, he expelled them and hired Greek architects to adapt the structure to Muslim worship. They demolished the interior walls of the church, leaving only the ancient walls of the porticoed court and the tower at each of the four corners. These four Christian towers became the first minarets, towers from which Muslim religious leaders call the faithful to prayer five times each day. Within the ancient walls, the courtyard was surrounded by porticoes on three sides and by the facade of the sanctuary on the fourth.

Al-Walid wanted his mosque to be the most magnificent in his empire, and he determined to employ the finest artists in the world to cover its walls with mosaics. The supreme center of mosaic art was Constantinople, capital of the Byzantine, or eastern Roman, Empire. Although the caliphate and the Byzantine Empire were bitter enemies, the Christian emperor loaned the caliph Byzantine artists for the task. Even today, the surviving Barada mosaics show Damascus as it appeared to al-Walid's Byzantine artists: a rich, verdant valley of palaces and houses.

The Christian antecedents of the mosque did not entirely disappear. During the preliminary work, an underground chapel was said to have been found, containing a chest with a human head. On the chest was written, "This is the head of John, son of Zacharias." Al-Walid had the sacred relic placed under one of the pillars and a monument erected over it. To this day the shrine survives in the mosque, a symbol of the continuity among Judaism, Christianity, and Islam.

This moment of artistic and religious cooperation was brief. Only a few years later, in 717, al-Walid's successor subjected Constantinople to the most fearful siege it would endure for five hundred years. Still, the continuity of religious worship and the common taste for classical art show how deeply both the caliphate and the empire were bound together in the common heritage of late antiquity, of which both were the true heirs.

The Byzantines

At the end of the fifth century, the eastern empire of Theodosius and Zeno had escaped the fate that its western counterpart had suffered at the hands of the Germanic peoples. Wealthier and more urbanized than the west, its population had also been accustomed to centralized government for more than a thousand years. Still, the long-term survival of the eastern empire seemed far from certain. Little unified the empire of Constantinople. The population of the capital split into rival political factions, whose violent conflicts often threatened the stability of the government. These rival groups, organized militarily and politically, controlled the Circus, or Hippodrome, where the games and chariot races that were the obsession of the city's population took place. These factions took their names, the Greens and the Blues, from their circus colors. When these two factions joined forces with the army, they were powerful enough to create or destroy emperors. Beyond Constantinople, the empire's population consisted of the more or less Hellenized peoples of Asia Minor, Armenians, Slavs, Arabs, Syrians, Egyptian Copts, and others. Unlike western Europe, the east was still a world of cities, which were centers of commerce, industry, and Hellenistic culture. But the importance of these urban centers began to decline in favor of the rural, peasant world, which not only fed the

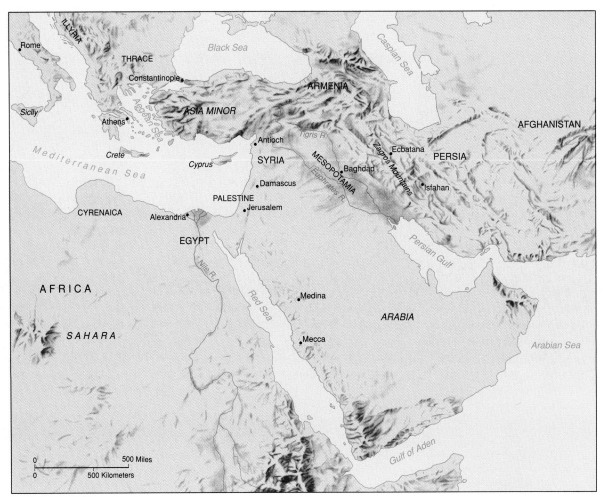

The Eastern Mediterranean

empire and was the source of its great wealth but also provided the generations of tough soldiers necessary to protect it from its enemies.

Finally, the eastern empire was more divided than unified by its Christianity. Rivalry among the great cities of Antioch, Alexandria, Jerusalem, Rome, and Constantinople was expressed in the competition among their bishops, or patriarchs. The official "right teaching" or orthodox, faith of Constantinople and its patriarch was bitterly opposed by "deviant," or heterodox bishops of other religious traditions, around which developed separatist ethnic political movements. In Syria and Egypt in particular, theological disagreements on the nature of God had become rallying points of political opposition. By the time of Justinian (527–65), emperors were obsessed with maintaining absolute authority and imposing uniformity on their empire.

Justinian and the Creation of the Byzantine State

Strong-willed, restless, and ambitious, Justinian is remembered as "the emperor who never slept." Although his goals were essentially conservative, he transformed the very foundations of the imperial state, its institutions, and its culture. He hoped to restore the territory, power, and prestige of the ancient Roman Empire, but his attempts to return to the past created a new world. With the assistance of his dynamic wife Theodora, his great generals Belisarius and Narses, his brilliant jurist Tribonian, his scientists Anthemius of Tralles and Isidorus of Miletus, and his brutally efficient administrator and tax collector John of Cappadocia, he remade the empire.

Spurred on by the ambitious Theodora, in 532 Justinian checked the power of the circus factions by brutally suppressing a riot that left thirty thousand dead in the capital city. Belisarius and Narses recaptured North Africa from the Vandals, Italy from the Ostrogoths, and part of Spain from the Visigoths, restoring for one last moment some of the geographical unity of the empire of Augustus and Constantine. Tribonian revised and organized the existing codes of Roman law into the *Justinian Code*, a great monument of Western

jurisprudence that remains today the foundation of most of Europe's legal systems. Anthemius and Isidorus combined their knowledge of mathematics, geometry, kinetics, and physics to build the Church of the Holy Wisdom (Hagia Sophia) in Constantinople, one of the largest and most innovative churches ever constructed. This structure was as radical as it was simple. In essence it is a huge rectangle, 230 by 250 feet, above which a vast dome 100 feet in diameter rises to a height of 180 feet and seems to float, suspended in air. As spectacular but not as well appreciated were the achievements of John of Cappadocia, who was able to squeeze the empire's population for the taxes to pay for these conquests, reforms, and building projects. Justinian may have been referring to more than just his new church when, upon entering it for the first time, he compared himself to the biblical builder of the first temple in Jerusalem, declaring "Solomon, I have vanquished thee!"

This gold medallion of Justinian may have been issued to commemorate the emperor's triumph over the Vandals in 534. The angel on the right is seen leading the Christian ruler to victory over the barbarians.

Ultimately, Justinian's spectacular achievements came at too high a price. He left his successors an empire virtually bankrupt by the costs of his wars and his building projects, bitterly divided by his attempts to settle religious controversies, and poorly protected on its eastern border, where the Sassanid Empire was a constant threat. Most of Italy and Spain soon returned to barbarian control. In 602 the Sassanid emperor Chosroes II (d. 628) invaded the empire, capturing Egypt, Palestine, and Syria, and threatening Constantinople itself. In a series of desperate campaigns, the emperor Heraclius (610–41) turned back the tide and crushed the Sassanids, but it was too late. A new power, Islam, had emerged in the deserts of Arabia. This new power was to challenge and ultimately absorb both the Sassanids and much of the eastern Roman Empire. As a result, the east became increasingly less Roman and more Greek or, specifically, more Byzantine, a term derived from the original name of Constantinople, Byzantium.

For over seven hundred years the Byzantine Empire played a major role in Western history. From the seventh through tenth centuries, when most of Europe was too weak and disorganized to defend itself against the expansion of Islam, the Byzantines stood as the bulwark of Christianity. When organized government had virtually disappeared in the west, the Byzantine Empire provided a model of a centralized, bureaucratic state ruled according to principles of Roman law. When, beginning in the fourteenth century, western Europeans began once more to appreciate the heritage of Greek and Roman art and literature, they turned to Constantinople. There the manuscripts of Greek writers such as Plato and Homer had been preserved and studied and were available to contribute to a rebirth of classical culture in the west. When the Slavic north, caught between the Latin Christians and the Muslims, sought its cultural and religious orientation, it looked to the liturgical culture of Byzantine orthodoxy. Perhaps most importantly, when urban civilization had all but disappeared from the rest of Europe, Greeks and Latins could still look to "The City," *eis tēn polin*, or as the Turks pronounced it, *Istanbul.*

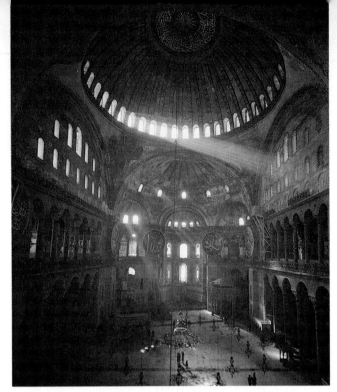

The interior of Hagia Sophia. The building was converted into a mosque after the Ottoman conquest of 1453. The magnificent mosaics were painted over to conform to Islamic religious dictates against representing human figures.

Emperors and Individuals

The classic age of Byzantine society, roughly from the eighth through the tenth centuries, has been described as "individualism without freedom." The Byzantine world was intensely individualistic—unlike the Roman, which emphasized public and private associations; unlike the western barbarian kingdoms, in which hierarchical gradations connected everyone from peasant to kings; and unlike the communal society of Islam. But Byzantine individualism did not lead to a great amount of individual initiative or creativity. Still less did it imply individual freedom of action within the political sphere, a concept that hardly existed for the vast majority of the empire's population. Instead Byzantine individualism meant that individuals and small family groups stood as isolated units in a society characterized, until the mid-eleventh century, by the direct relationship between an all-powerful emperor and citizens of all ranks.

In part this individualism resulted from the Byzantine form of government. The Byzantine state was in theory and often in fact an autocracy. Since the time of Diocletian, all members of society were subjects of the emperor, who alone was the source of law. How a person became emperor remained, as it had been in the Roman Empire, more a question of military power than constitutional succession. Although in theory the emperor was elected by the senate, army, and people of Constantinople, generally emperors selected their own successors and had them crowned in their own lifetime.

As long as the empire remained a civilian autocracy, it was even possible for a woman to rule, either as regent for a minor son or as sovereign. Thus Irene (780–802), widow of Leo IV (725–780), ruled as regent for her son Constantine VI (780–797). However, when he reached his majority, she had him blinded and deposed and ruled alone from 797 to 802, not merely as the *basilissa*, or wife of the *basileus*, but as the *basileus*, or emperor, herself. In the eleventh century the empire was ruled for a time by two sisters, Zoe (1028–34), daughter of one emperor and widow of another, and Theodora (1042–56), who was dragged out of a church by an enthusiastic mob and proclaimed empress.

Male or female, emperors were above and beyond their subjects, often quite literally. In the tenth century, a mechanical throne was installed in the main audience room. The throne would suddenly lift the emperor high above the heads of astonished visitors. Like God the Father, with whom he was closely identified in imperial propaganda, the emperor was separated from the people by an unbridgeable gulf. For great lords and peasants alike, the only proper attitude toward such a ruler was adoration and abject humility.

Thus the traditional corporate bodies of the Roman Empire wasted away or became window dressing for the imperial cult. The senate, which had received the rights and privileges of the Roman Senate in 359, gradually ceased to play any autonomous role. Long before its powers were officially abolished in the ninth century, the senate had become simply a passive and amorphous body of prominent people called upon from time to time to participate in public ceremonies. Senators were present when important foreign ambassadors were received. Senatorial acclamation of new emperors was always a part of the imperial coronation ceremony. But such roles were simply part of an elaborate ritual emphasizing the dignity and power of the emperor.

The circus factions, which in the sixth century had the power to make or break emperors, met the same fate. From autonomous political groups, they too gradually became no more than participants in imperial ceremonies. By the tenth century, the Greens and the Blues were simply officially constituted groups whose role was to praise the emperor by mouthing traditional formulas on solemn occasions. The Hippodrome games themselves became aristocratic pastimes. Chariot races, increasingly amateurish, ended in the early thirteenth century. By the end of that century the great Hippodrome was nearly deserted except for occasional games of polo played by young aristocrats.

The Empress Irene, widow of Leo IV, was the only woman to rule the Byzantine Empire in her own right. As regent during the minority of her son, she reestablished the worship of icons. In 802 Irene was dethroned and exiled to Lesbos.

This ivory panel, one half of a diptych, celebrates the Lampadius family. The bottom scene depicts chariot races in the Hippodrome at Constantinople. The stone pillar in the middle is a hieroglyphic-covered obelisk brought from Egypt.

While the emperor was the source of all authority, the actual administration of the empire was carried out by a vast bureaucracy composed of military and civilian officers. The empire was divided into roughly twenty-five provinces, or themes. The soldiers in each theme were also farmers, rather than full-time warriors. Each soldier received a small farm by which to support himself and his family. Soldiers held their farms as long as they served in the army. When a soldier retired or died, his farm and his military obligation passed to his eldest son. These farmer-soldiers were the backbone of both the imperial military and the economic system. They not only formed a regular, native, locally based army, but they also kept much of Byzantine agriculture in the hands of small free peasants rather than great aristocrats. The themes were governed by military commanders, or *stratēgoi*, who presided over both civilian and military bureaucrats. Although virtually all-powerful in their provinces, strategoi could be appointed, removed from office, or transferred at the whim of the emperor.

In contrast to the military command of the themes, the central administration, which focused on the emperor and the imperial family, was wholly civil. The most important positions at court were occupied by eunuchs, castrated men who offered a number of advantages to imperial administration. Eunuchs often directed imperial finance, served as prime ministers, directed the vast bureaucracy, and even undertook military commands. Because they could not have descendants, there was no danger that they would attempt to turn their offices into hereditary positions or that they would plot and scheme on behalf of their children. Moreover, since the sacred nature of the emperor required physical perfection, eunuchs could not aspire to replace their masters on the throne. Finally, although at times their influence with the emperor made them immensely powerful, eunuchs were at once feared and despised by the general population. Thus they had little likelihood of building autonomous power bases outside of imperial favor. One Byzantine historian described the powerful eunuch John the Orphanotrophos (mid-eleventh century) by saying that "nothing at all escaped his notice nor did anyone even try to do so, for everyone feared him and all dreaded his vigilance." The

A tenth-century Greek manuscript of the gospels from Constantinople is decorated with a drawing of laborers in a vineyard. Such illustrated texts often recorded the daily activities of the ordinary people, including plowing, fishing, farming, and sheep shearing.

extensive use of eunuchs was one of the keys to the survival of absolutist authority in the empire. While many eunuchs promoted the interests of their brothers and nephews, they were less dangerous than ambitious aristocrats. They preserved imperial authority at a time when both Islamic and Latin states were experiencing a progressive erosion of central power to the benefit of ambitious aristocratic families.

A godlike emperor and a centralized bureaucracy left little room for the development of the hierarchies of private patronage, lordship, and group action, which were characteristic of western Europe. In the Byzantine Empire, aristocrat and peasant were equal in their political powerlessness. Against the emperor and the bureaucracy, no extended kin group or local political unit offered security or comfort. Thus Byzantine society tended to be organized at the lowest level, that of the nuclear family. This structure was imprinted even on the physical landscape of Byzantine cities. Single-family dwellings replaced the public spaces and buildings of antiquity. Public assemblies and communal celebrations either disappeared or were absorbed into the ritual of imperial dignity. Daily life focused on the protective enclosure of the private home, which served

as both shelter and workplace. Professional and craft associations continued to exist as they had in antiquity. However, like everything else in Byzantium, these were not autonomous professional groups intended to protect the interests of their members. Instead, they were fostered and controlled by imperial officials to regulate and tax urban industry.

The countryside, which was the backbone of Byzantine prosperity into the eleventh century, was also a world with limited horizontal and vertical social bonds. Villages were the basic elements in the imperial system. The village court handled local affairs and tax assessments, but it in turn dealt directly with the imperial bureaucracy. Occasionally, villages might unite against imperial tax collectors, but normally villagers dealt with each other and with outside powers as wary individuals. This attitude was an outgrowth of agricultural techniques practiced in Greece and Asia Minor, where a peasant's prosperity depended not on teamwork but rather on individual effort. Most peasants, whether they were landowners, peasant soldiers, or renters on great estates, survived on the labor of their own family and perhaps one or two slaves. In the eleventh century, tax records indicated only three types of peasants, distinguished according to their equipment: those with two yoke of cattle, those with one, and those with none. Large cooperative undertakings as in Islamic lands or the use of communal equipment as became the rule in the west was unknown. Individual families worked their own fields, which were usually enclosed with protective stone or brick walls. Byzantine peasants would have agreed with the New England poet Robert Frost saying that "good fences make good neighbors."

Like the villages, Byzantine towns were isolated in location and activities. The mountainous terrain of Greece and Asia Minor contributed to this isolation, cutting off ready overland communication among communities and forcing them to turn to the sea. In this respect Constantinople was ideally situated to develop into the greatest commercial center of the West, at its height boasting a population of over one million. Because of Constantinople's strategic location on the Bosporus, that slim ribbon of water uniting the Black and Mediterranean seas, all of the products of the empire and those of the Slavic, Latin, and Islamic worlds, as well as Oriental goods arriving overland from central Asia, had to pass through the city. Silks, spices, and precious metals were loaded onto ships at Trebizond and then transported south to Constantinople. Baltic

amber, slaves, and furs from the Slavic world were carried down the Dnepr River to the Black Sea and then to the capital. There, all goods passing north or south had to be unloaded, assessed, and subjected to a flat import-export tariff of 10 percent.

The empire's cities were centers for the manufacture of luxury goods in demand throughout the Islamic and Christian worlds. The secret of silk manufacture had been smuggled out of China by a Christian monk who had hidden silkworms in his pilgrim's staff during his journey home. Imperial workshops in Constantinople and closely regulated workshops in Corinth and Thebes produced fine silks, brocades, carpets, and other luxury products marketed throughout the Mediterranean, again subject to the state's customary 10 percent tax.

As vital as maritime commerce was to the empire, most Byzantines despised the sea. They feared it as a source of constant danger from Muslim and Christian pirates. They dreaded its sudden storms and hidden dangers. When they did travel by ship, they prayed to their sacred icons and tried to sail, as one Byzantine put it, "touching the shore with an oar." Moreover, particularly among the elite, commerce was considered demeaning. The story is told that when one ninth-century emperor learned that his wife owned a ship, he ordered it and its cargo burned.

The Byzantine Empire Under Justinian and in 814

Never great mariners, Byzantines were largely content to allow others—first Syrians and Slavs and later Italians—to monopolize the empire's commerce.

A Foretaste of Heaven

The cultural cement that bound emperor and subjects together was Orthodox Christianity. The Islamic capture of Alexandria, Jerusalem, and Antioch had removed the centers of regional religious particularism from the empire. The barbarian domination of Italy had isolated Rome and reduced its influence. These two processes left Constantinople as the only remaining patriarchate in the empire and thus the undisputed center of Orthodox Christianity. However, like virtually every other aspect of Byzantine society and culture, the patriarch and the Orthodox faith he led were subordinated to the emperor. Although in theory patriarchs were elected, in reality emperors appointed them. Patriarchs in turn controlled the various levels of the Church hierarchy, which included metropolitans, bishops, and the local clergy. This ecclesiastical structure reflected the organization of the state bureaucracy, which it reinforced. Local priests were drawn from the peasant society of which they were a part. They were expected to be married and to live much like their neighbors. Bishops, metropolitans, and patriarchs were recruited from monasteries and remained celibate. They were, so to speak, spiritual eunuchs who represented the emperor. In rare instances, a patriarch might threaten to excommunicate an emperor, as the patriarch Polyeuct did Emperor John Tzimisces (969–76) when he proposed to marry his predecessor's wife Theophano, but such threats could seldom be carried out with impunity. Generally the Church supported the emperor and the imperial cult.

The essence of Orthodox religion was the liturgy, or ceremonies, of the Church, which provided, it was said, a foretaste of heaven. Adoration of God and veneration of the emperor went hand in hand as the cornerstone of imperial propaganda. Ecclesiastical and court processions assured that everything and everyone was in the proper place, that order and stability reigned in this world as a reflection of the eternal order of the next. This confirmation, in churches and in court, of stability and permanence in the face of possible crisis and disruption calmed and reassured the liturgically oriented society. The effects of Byzantine ceremonial reached far beyond the Byzantines themselves. According to Russian sources, when the prince of Kiev sent observers to

St. Catherine's at the foot of Mount Sinai. Justinian built a church here, and the hermits who had been scattered in separate cells among the rocks came to live in this early monastery.

report on the manners of worship in Islamic, Latin, and Greek societies, the effect of the Byzantine liturgy was overpowering: "We knew not whether we were in heaven or on earth, for on earth there is no such splendor or such beauty." So strong was the impression made by the rituals of the Church that the prince decided to invite Byzantine clergy to instruct his people.

The one aspect of religious life not entirely under imperial control was monasticism. Since the time of the desert fathers, monastic communities had been an essential part of Christianity. From the sixth century, numerous monastic communities were founded throughout the empire, and by the eleventh century there were at least three hundred monasteries within the walls of Constantinople alone. Following the Muslim invasions of the eleventh century, Anatolia became the major center of monastic life outside the city. Monasteries were often wealthy and powerful. Moreover, their religious appeal, often based on the possession of miracle-working religious images, or icons, posed an independent source of religious authority at odds with the imperial centralization of all aspects of Byzantine life. To the faithful, icons were not simply representations or reminders of Jesus and the saints. They had a real if intermediary relationship with the person represented, and as such themselves merited veneration and, some argued, adoration.

Beginning with Emperor Leo III, the Isaurian (717–41), the military emperors who had driven back Islam sought to curtail the independence of monastic culture and particularly the cult of icons that was an integral part of it. These emperors and their supporters, termed *iconoclasts* (literally, "breakers of images"), objected to the mediating role of sacred images in worship. While the iconoclasts may have been influenced by Jewish and Islamic prohibitions of images, they were also fighting the sort of decentralization in religion that the imperial bureaucracy prevented in government. Monasteries, with their miracle-working icons, became the particular object of imperial persecution. Monasteries were closed and their estates confiscated. Monks, termed by one emperor "idolaters and lovers of darkness," were forced to marry. Everywhere imperial agents destroyed icons, statues, and illustrated manuscripts, and painted over frescoes in churches. The defenders of icons, *iconodules*, or image venerators, were imprisoned, tortured, and even executed. Most bishops, the army, and much of the non-European population of the empire supported the iconoclast emperors, but monks, the lesser clergy, and the majority of the populace, particularly women, violently resisted the destruction of their beloved images. For over a century, the iconoclast dispute threatened to tear the empire apart. The first phase, which began in

726, ended in 787, when a council summoned by the Empress Irene confirmed the adoration of images. After her deposition in 802, a milder iconoclastic persecution revived until the Empress Theodora (842–58), who ruled during the minority of her son, ended the persecution and restored image veneration in 843. Monasteries reopened and regained much of their former wealth and prestige. Images were brought out of hiding or new ones created, and they resumed their role in the eastern Christian church. The longest-lasting effect of the iconoclastic struggle was in Byzantium's relations with the west. Christians in western Europe and particularly the popes of Rome never accepted the iconoclast position. The popes considered the iconoclast emperors heretics and looked increasingly to the Frankish Carolingian family for support against them and the Lombards of Italy. In this manner the Franks first entered Italian politics and began, with papal support, to establish themselves as a rival imperial power in the west, which culminated in the coronation of Charlemagne in 800.

The Rise of Islam

Recite: in the name of your Lord,
The Creator Who created man from clots of blood!
Recite: Your Lord is the Most Bounteous One,
Who taught by the pen,
Taught mankind things they did not know.

This command to recite, to reveal God's will, communicated directly by God, launched an obscure merchant in the Arabian city of Mecca on a career that would transform the world. Through faith, Abu al-Qasim Muhammad ibn 'Abd Allah ibn 'Abd al-Muttalib ibn Hashim (ca. 570–632), or more simply Muhammad, united the tribes of the Arabian peninsula and propelled them on an unprecedented mission of conquest. Within a century of Muhammad's death, the world of Islam—a word that means "submission to the will of God"—included all of the ancient Near East and extended from the Syr Darya River in Asia, south into the Indian subcontinent, west across the African coast to the Atlantic, north through Spain, and along the Mediterranean coast to the Rhone River. Just as their faith combined elements of traditional Arab worship with Christianity and Judaism, the Arabian conquerors and their subject populations created a vital civilization from a mix of Arabian, Roman, Hellenistic, and Sassanid traditions.

Arabia Before the Prophet

Although Arabs did not appear in written sources as such before the ninth century B.C., their ancestors had played an important if supporting role in Near Eastern history for thousands of years. Already in the Egyptian Old Kingdom, the incense trees of southern Arabia had drawn Egyptians to the region, then known as the land of Punt. Trade routes between the Fertile Crescent and Egypt had crossed northern Arabia for just as long, drawing its inhabitants into contact with civilization. By the sixth century A.D., Arabic-speaking peoples from the Arabian peninsula had spread through the Syrian Desert as far north as the Euphrates.

Those who lived on the fringes of the Byzantine and Sassanid empires had been largely absorbed into the cultural and political spheres of these two great powers. The northern borders of Arabia along the Red Sea formed Roman provinces that even produced an emperor, Philip the Arab (244–49). Hira, to the south of the Euphrates, became a Sassanid puppet principality that, although largely Christian, often provided the Persians with auxiliaries. At times the Sassanid Empire also controlled Bahrain on the Persian Gulf, as well as Yamama and the Yemen, both vital in the spice trade. Within both empires, the distinction between Arab and non-Arab populations was blurred. Except for a common language and a hazy idea of common kinship, nothing differentiated Arabs from their neighbors.

Southern Arabia, with a relatively abundant rainfall and fertile soils, was an agricultural region long governed by monarchs. Here was the kingdom of Saba, the Sheba of the Bible, which had existed since the tenth century B.C. During the fifth century A.D. the kings of the Yemen had extended their influence north over the Bedouin tribes of central Arabia in order to control and protect the caravan trade between north and south. However, in the late sixth century Ethiopian and then Persian conquerors destroyed the Arabian kingdom of the Yemen and absorbed it into their empires. The result was a power vacuum that left central Arabia and its trade routes across the deserts in confusion.

The interior of the Arabian peninsula was much less directly affected by the great empires to the north or the Arabian kingdoms to the south. Waterless steppes and seas of shifting sand dunes had long defeated Roman and Persian or Sassanid efforts to control the Arabic Bedouin. These nomads roamed the peninsula in search of pasturage for their flocks. Theirs was a life of independence, simplicity, and danger.

Although they acknowledged membership in various tribes, the Bedouin's real allegiance was to much more narrow circles of lineages and tenting groups. As in the Germanic tribes of Europe, kin relationships rather than formal governmental systems protected individuals through the obligation for vengeance and blood feud. In the words of a pre-Islamic poet, "Blood for blood—wiped out were the wounds, and those who had gained a start in the race profited not by their advantage." Tribal chieftains, called sheikhs, chosen from ruling families, had no coercive power, either to right wrongs or to limit feuds. They served only as arbitrators and executors of tribal consensus. The patriarch of each family held final say over his kin. He could ignore the sheikh and go his own way with his flocks and herds, wives and slaves.

The individual was unimportant in Bedouin society. Private land ownership was unknown and flocks and herds were often held in common by kindreds. The pastoral economy of the Bedouin provided meat, cheese, and wool. Weapons, ornaments, women, and livestock could be acquired through exchange at the market towns that developed around desert oases. More commonly, these goods were taken in raids against other tribes, caravans, and settlements or by exacting payments from weaker neighbors in return for protection. Raids, however, yielded much more than mere booty. Often launched in defense of family honor, they were the means of increasing prestige and glory in this warrior society. Prizes won in battle were lightly given away as signs of generosity and marks of social importance.

Some of the Arabs of the more settled south, as well as inhabitants of towns along caravan routes, were Christian or Jewish. As farmers or merchants, these groups were looked down upon by the nomadic Bedouin, most of whom remained pagan. Although they recognized some important gods and even a high god usually called Allah, Bedouin worshiped local, tribal deities often thought of as inhabiting a sacred stone or spring. Worship involved gifts and offerings and played only a small part in nomadic life. Far more important was commitment to the tribe, expressed through loyalty to the tribal cult and through unity of action against rival tribes.

Rivalry and feuding among tribes could be set aside at a mutually accepted neutral site, which might grow up around a religious sanctuary. A sanctuary, or haram, which was often on the border between tribal areas, was founded by a holy man not unlike the Christian holy men of the Syrian Desert. The holy man declared the site and surrounding area neutral ground on which no violence could take place. Here enemies could meet under truce to settle differences under the direction of the holy man or his descendants. Merchant communities sprang up within the safety of these sites, since the sanctuary gave them and their goods protection from their neighbors.

Mecca was just such a sanctuary, around whose sacred black rock, or *Ka'bah*, a holy man named Qusayy established himself and his tribe, the Quraysh, as its guardians sometime early in the sixth century. In the next century Mecca grew into an important center under the patronage of the Quraysh, who made it the center of a commercial network. Through religious, diplomatic, and military means, they organized camel caravans, which could safely cross the desert from the Yemen in the south to Iran and Syria in the north. During the early seventh century, when increased hostilities between the Byzantine and Sassanid empires severed the direct trading links between the empires, the Quraysh network became the leading commercial organization in northern Arabia. Still, its effectiveness remained tied to the religious importance of Mecca and the Ka'bah. When Muhammad, a descendant of Qusayy, began to recite the monotheistic message of Allah, his preaching was seen as a threat to the survival of his tribe and his city.

Muhammad, Prophet of God

More is known about Muhammad's life than about that of Moses, Jesus, Buddha, or any of the other great religious reformers of history. Still, Muhammad's early years were quickly wrapped in a protective cloak of pious stories by his followers, making it difficult to discern truth from legend. A member of a lesser branch of the Quraysh, Muhammad was an orphan raised by relatives. At about age twenty he became the business manager for Khadijah, a wealthy widow whom he later married. This marriage gave him financial security among the middle ranks of Meccan merchants. During this time he may have traveled to Syria on business and heard the preaching of Christian monks. He certainly became familiar with Judaism through contact with Jewish traders. In his thirties, he began to devote an increasing amount of time to meditation, retiring to the barren, arid mountains outside the city. There, in the month of Ramadan in the year 610, he reported a vision of a man, his feet astride the horizon. The figure commanded: "O Muhammad! Thou art the Messenger of God. Recite!"

Khadijah, to whom he confided his revelation in fear and confusion, became his first convert. Within a year he began preaching openly. His early teachings stressed the absolute unity of God, the evils of idolatry, and the threat of divine judgment. Further revelations to Muhammad were copied word for word in what came to be the *Qur'an*, or Koran. These messages offered Arabs a faith founded on a book. In their eyes, this faith was both within the tradition of and superior to the Christianity and Judaism of their neighbors. The *Qur'an* was the final revelation and Muhammad the last and greatest prophet. To Muslims—the term means "true believers"—Muhammad is simply the Prophet.

Allah's revelation emphasized above all his power and transcendence. The duty of humans is worship. The prayers of Islam, in contrast with those of Christianity and Judaism, are essentially prayers of praise, seldom prayers of petition. This reverential attitude places little premium on scriptural interpretation or theological speculation. Muslims regard the whole *Qur'an* as the exact and complete revelation of God, literally true, and forming a unified whole, though revelations contained in it came at various times

Arabic manuscripts were decorated with intricate geometric designs. This page from an eighth- or ninth-century copy of the Koran illustrates the elegance and formality of the Kufic form of Arabic calligraphy. Vowel marks appear as dots of various colors.

throughout the Prophet's life. It is the complete guide for secular and religious life, the fundamental law of conduct for Islamic society. The Prophet emphasized constantly that he was simply God's messenger and that he merited no special veneration or worship. For this reason Muslims have always rejected the label *Muhammadan*, which nonbelievers often apply to them. Muslims are not followers of Muhammad but of the God of Abraham and Jesus, who chose to make the final and complete revelation of his power and his judgment through the Prophet.

Initially, such revelations of divine power and judgment neither greatly bothered nor influenced Mecca's merchant elite. Muhammad's earliest followers, such as his cousin 'Ali ibn Abi (ca. 600–661), came from his own clan and from among the moderately successful members of the Mec-

Illustration from the Maqamat *of al-Hariri, painted by Yahya ibn Mahmud al-Wasiti, from Baghdad, Iraq, 1237. Mounted musicians carry banners in a parade at the Great Festival, which marked the final days of the annual pilgrimage to Mecca.*

can community, the "nearly haves" rather than the "have nots" as one scholar put it. Elite clans such as the Umayya, who controlled the larger Quraysh tribe, saw little to attract them to the upstart. But soon Muhammad began to insist that those who did not accept Allah as the only God were damned, as were those who continued to venerate the sorts of idols on which Mecca's prosperity was founded. With this proclamation, toleration gave way to hostility. Muhammad and his followers were ostracized and even persecuted.

Around 620, some residents of Medina, a smaller trading community populated by rival pagan, Jewish, and Islamic clans and racked by internal political dissension, approached the Prophet and invited him to govern the community in order to end the factional squabbles. Rejected at home, he answered their call. On 24 September 622, Muhammad and one supporter secretly made their way from Mecca to Medina. This short journey of less than three hundred miles, known as the *Hijra*, was destined to change the world.

The Hijra marks the beginning of the Islamic dating system in the way that the birth of Jesus begins the Christian. The Hijra was the Prophet's first step—or steps—in the shift from preaching to action. He organized his followers from Mecca and Medina into the *Umma*, a community that transcended the old bonds of tribe and clan. He set about turning Medina into a haram like Mecca, with himself as founding holy man and the Umma as his new family. But this was not to be a haram nor indeed a family like any other. Muhammad was not merely a sheikh whose authority rested on consensus. He was God's messenger, and his authority was absolute. His goal was to extend this authority far beyond his adopted town of Medina to Mecca and ultimately to the whole Arab world.

First, he gained firm control of Medina at the expense of its Jewish clans. He had expected these monotheists to embrace his teachings. Instead, they rejected the unlettered Arab's attempt to transform Judaic and Christian traditions into an Arab faith. Rejection was their undoing. The Prophet expelled them in the name of political and religious unity. Those not expelled were executed.

Muhammad then used this unified community to attack the Quraysh where they were most vulnerable—in their protection of camel caravans. Inability to destroy the upstarts or protect its trading network cost the Quraysh tribe much of its prestige. More and more members of Meccan families and local tribes converted to Islam. In 629, Muhammad and 10,000 warriors marched on Mecca and captured the city in a swift and largely bloodless campaign.

During the three years between Muhammad's triumphant return to Mecca and his death, Islam moved steadily toward becoming the major force in the Arabian peninsula. The divine revelations increasingly took on legal and practical dimensions as Muhammad was forced to serve, not just as Prophet, but as political leader of a major political and economic power. The Umma had become a sort of supertribe, open to all individuals who would accept Allah and his Prophet. The invitation extended to women as well as to men.

Islam brought a transformation of the rights of women in Arabian society. This did not mean that they achieved equality with men any more than they did in any premodern civilization east or west. Men continued to dominate Islamic society in which military prowess and male honor were so valued. Women remained firmly subordinate to men, who could have up to four wives, could divorce them at will, and often kept women segregated from other men. When in public, Islamic women in many regions adopted the Syriac Christian practice of wearing a veil that covers all of the face but the eyes. Islam did, however, forbid female infanticide, a common practice in pre-Islamic society. Brides, and not their fathers or other male relatives, received the dowry from their husbands, thus making marriage more a partnership than a sale. All wives had to be treated equally. If a man was unable to do so, he had to limit himself to a single wife. Islamic women acquired inheritance and property rights, and protection against mistreatment in marriage. Although they remained second-class in status, at least women had a status, recognized and protected within the Umma. (See Special Feature, "Harems and Gynaiconites", pp. 210–211.)

The rapid spread of Islam within the Arab world can be explained by a number of religious

The seven-tiered heaven of Islam. The Bedouin, in their harsh, dry land under the implacable sun, conceived of paradise as a cool, shaded garden full of lush, fruiting plants and washed by the waters of murmuring fountains.

and material factors. Perhaps most attractive, though actually least important, was the sensuous vision of the afterlife promised to believers. Paradise is presented as a world of refreshing streams and leafy bowers, where redeemed men lie upon divans, eat exotic foods served by handsome youths, and are entertained by beautiful virgins called *Houris*, created especially for them by Allah. Probably more compelling than the description of heaven was the promise of the torments awaiting nonbelievers on the day of judgment. "For the wrong-doers we have prepared a fire which will encompass them like the walls of a pavilion. When they cry out for a drink they shall be showered with water as hot as melted brass, which will scald their faces. Evil shall be their drink, dismal their resting-place." But as central as these otherworldly considerations were, the concrete attractions of Islam in this world were equally important. These included both economic prosperity and the opportunity to continue a life-style of raiding and warfare in the name of Allah.

Muhammad won over the leaders of the Quraysh by making Mecca the sacred city of Islam and by retaining the Ka'bah, cleansed of idols, as the center of Islamic pilgrimage. Not unlike the Roman courtiers of Constantine's day who rapidly adopted Christianity, the once disdainful elite now rushed to convert and reestablish their preeminent position within the community. The rapid rehabilitation of old families such as the Umayyads greatly disturbed many of Muhammad's earliest followers, especially those from Medina whose timely invitation had been essential in launching the Prophet's career.

Muhammad's message spread to other tribes through diplomatic and, occasionally, military means. The divisive nature of Bedouin society contributed to his success. Frequently factions within other tribes turned to Muhammad for mediation and support against their rivals. In return for his assistance, petitioners accepted his religious message. Since the *Qur'an* commanded Muslims to destroy idol worship, conversion provided the occasion for holy wars (*jihads*) of conquest and profitable raids against their still-pagan neighbors. Converts showed their piety by sending part of their spoils as alms to Medina. The *Qur'an* permitted Christians and Jews living under the authority of Islamic communities to continue to practice their faith, but they were forced to pay a head tax shared among members of the Umma.

The Spread of Islam

Muhammad died in the summer of 632 after a short illness, leaving no successor and no directions concerning the leadership of the Umma. Immediately his closest and most influential followers selected Abu Bakr (632–34), the fourth convert to Islam, to be caliph, or successor of the Prophet. Abu Bakr and, after his death two years later, the caliph 'Umar (634–44) faced formidable obstacles. Within the Umma, tensions

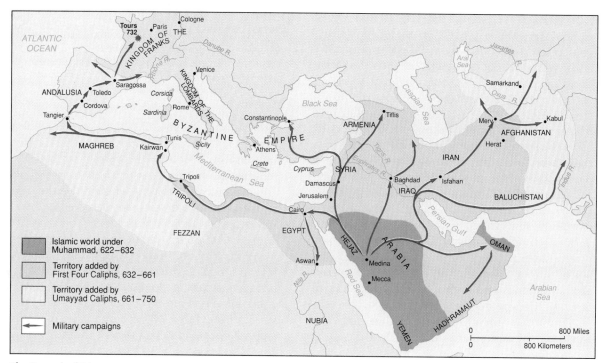

The Spread of Islam

between the early Medina followers of the Prophet and the Meccan elite were beginning to surface. A more critical problem was that the tribes that had accepted the Prophet's leadership believed that his death freed them from their treaty obligations. Now they attempted to go their own ways. Some sent emissaries to announce that while they would remain Muslims, they would no longer pay alms. Others attempted to abandon Islam altogether.

To prevent the collapse of the Umma, Abu Bakr launched a war of reconversion. Purely by chance, this war developed into wars of conquest that reached far beyond the Arab world. Commanded by Khalid ibn al-Walid (d. 642), the greatest early Islamic general, Muslim forces defeated tribe after tribe and brought them back into the Umma. But long-term survival demanded expansion. Since Muslims were forbidden to raid fellow believers, and raids were an integral part of Bedouin life, the only way to keep recently converted Bedouin in line was to lead them on military expeditions against non-Muslims. Khalid and his armies were people of the desert and they used this sea of sand as the British Empire would later use the oceans in the nineteenth century. Arab armies could move men and supplies quickly across the arid wastes, crush their enemies, and then retreat back into the desert, beyond the reach of Byzantine and Sassanid forces. Under Abu Bakr, Muslim expansion covered all of Arabia. Under 'Umar, Islam conquered Iran, Iraq, Syria, and Egypt.

The swift and total collapse of the Sassanid Empire and the major portion of the Byzantine Empire astounded contemporaries, not least the Muslims themselves. Their success seemed to be irrefutable proof that Muhammad's message was from God. By 650 Islam stretched from Egypt to Asia Minor, from the Mediterranean to the Indus River.

The Islamic Conquest

Of course, there were other factors that contributed to the Muslims' phenomenal success. Protracted wars between the Byzantine and Sassanid empires as well as internal divisions within the Byzantine world helped. For over a decade Egypt, Palestine, and Syria had been under Persian control. Although eventually reconquered by the Byzantine emperor Heraclius, these provinces had not yet recovered from the decades of warfare, and within them a whole generation had grown up with no experience of Byzantine government.

In addition, the reimposed Byzantine yoke was widely resented because of profound cultural differences between Greeks and the inhabitants of Syria, Iraq, and Egypt. Many looked on the Byzantines not as the liberators but as the enemy. Syria and Egypt had always been different from the rest of the Roman world. Although their great cities of Antioch and Alexandria had long been centers of Hellenistic learning and culture, the hinterlands of each enjoyed ancient cultural traditions totally alien to those of their urban neighbors. In Syria, this rural society was Aramaic and Arabic speaking. In Egypt, it was Coptic. With the steady decay of urban life and the rising demands on the rural economy, these local traditions rose to greater prominence. Eventually these traditions coalesced around religious traditions sustained by liturgies in the vernacular and sharply at odds with the Orthodox Christianity of Constantinople.

These profound cultural, ethnic, and social antagonisms were largely fought out in the sphere of doctrine, particularly over the nature of Jesus Christ. The form of Christianity that the emperors sought to impose, defined at the Council of Chalcedon in 451, insisted that Jesus was only one person but had two complete natures, one fully human, the other entirely divine. Such a distinction rested less on the language of the New Testament than on the Greek philosophical tradition. To the Syrian and Egyptian communities, this position was heresy. "Anathema to the unclean Synod of Chalcedon!" wrote one Egyptian monk. Closer to the Jewish tradition of the transcendence of God, the Syriac and Egyptian Monophysite (meaning "one nature") Christians insisted that Christ had but a single nature and it was divine.

The two groups vented their intense hatred of each other in riots, murders, and vicious persecutions directed by zealous emperors. As a result, for many Christians of the Near East, the arrival of the Muslims, whose beliefs about the unity and transcendence of God were close to their own and who promised religious toleration and an end to persecution, was seen initially as a divine blessing.

Harems and Gynaiconites

"Lay injunctions on women kindly," Muhammad is reputed to have said in his farewell address to his followers, "You have taken them only as a trust from God." Islamic teachers did not share with many Christian monks and clerics the notion of woman as the source of evil and sin, the weak temptress and daughter of Eve. Nevertheless, Islamic society was unambiguously male-oriented. Women were firmly excluded from public view and, in normal circumstances, from public roles. As in pre-Islamic times, Muslims practiced resource polygyny, much like the Germanic tribes in Europe. That is, although most men could afford only one wife, the rich and powerful might have several wives (the Qur'an limited the number to four) and numerous concubines and slave women. Muslim conquerors adopted the tradition of veiling women. To safeguard them better, they often kept them in a harem, that is, a secure and secluded section of the home or palace, watched over by trustworthy eunuchs.

If Byzantines did not much remark on the treatment of women in Islam, it is probably because their own traditions were not very different. Although polygyny was not officially permitted, the practice of veiling women was first popular among the Christians of Syria and was adopted by the Muslims after the conquest. As for the harem, the institution, if not the name, existed in Byzantium as well. The imperial court had its *gynaiconites*, or women's section. Most women seldom left their homes. A Byzantine jurist, describing an earthquake in 1068, remarked with surprise that after the quake women who normally stayed secluded in the interior rooms of their houses "forgot their innate shame" and ran out into the street.

Every rule has its exceptions. In Islam individual women, particularly the mothers of powerful commanders, could exercise considerable indirect power. Al-Khayzuran was a servant in the caliph's household when she bore his son al-Mahdi two boys. After al-Mahdi became caliph in 755, he freed and married her. She soon became the most important figure in his administration.

Byzantine women could also wield enormous power either in their own right as empress or through their sons and husbands. Anna Dalassena, mother of the emperor Alexius I Comnenus, managed the bureaucracy for her son. Her granddaughter, Anna Comnena, wrote that her father Alexius "took upon himself the wars against the barbarians and whatever battles and combats pertained to them, while he entrusted to his mother the complete management of civil affairs." These were, however, exceptions to normal practice. Women normally had no access to public power and for every Al-Khayzuran or Anna Dalassena, there were thousands of women cut off from the public sphere.

Muslim women, when they did act in public, did so at a decided disadvantage. In matters of inheritance and in witnessing and giving testimony, women, even if free, were valued at one half of a man. Byzantines were also reluctant to allow women to participate in public affairs. In the ninth century Emperor Leo VI (886–912) forbade women to act as witnesses in contracts because "the power to act as witness in the numerous assemblies of men with which they mingle, as well as taking part in public affairs, gives them the habit of speaking more freely than they ought, and, depriving them of the morality and reserve of their sex, encourages them in the exercise of boldness and wickedness, which, to some extent, is even insulting to men."

Subordination, seclusion, and control over women were for both societies a primary means of showing masculine honor and prestige. Byzantines and especially Muslims were shocked that Latin Christian women appeared in public, talked to men, and at times exercised "masculine" power. Crusaders and their wives and mistresses were a particular scandal to Muslims. One reported with horror that "the Franks have no trace of jealousy or feeling for the point of honor. One of them may be walking along with his wife, and he meets another man, and this man takes his wife aside and chats with her privately, while the husband stands apart for her to finish her conversation; and if she takes too long he leaves her alone with the companion and goes away." A later Muslim visitor to France concluded that "in France women are of higher station than men, so that they do what they wish and go where they please; and the greatest lord shows respect and courtesy beyond all limits to the humblest of women." To be delivered from such scandal, one Muslim visitor to Europe "prayed to God to save us from the wretched state of these infidels who are devoid of manly jealousy and are sunk in unbelief."

Many Christians and Jews in Syria, Palestine, Egypt, and North Africa shared this view of the Muslim conquest as liberation rather than enslavement. Jews and Christians may have been second-class citizens in the Islamic world, but at least they had a defined place. Conquered populations were allowed to practice their religion in peace. Their only obligation was to pay a head tax to their conquerors, a burden considerably less onerous than the exactions of the Byzantine tax collectors.

The Byzantines' defeat of the Sassanids indirectly facilitated the Muslims' conquest of Iraq. When the Bedouin realized that the Persians were too weakened to protect their empire against raiders, they intensified their attacks. Soon, recent converts to Islam, too late to profit from the conquests of Syria and Egypt, were spearheading the conquest. By 650 the great Sassanid Empire had disappeared and the Byzantine Empire had lost Egypt, Syria, Mesopotamia, Palestine, portions of Asia Minor, and much of North Africa. During the reigns of Constantine IV (668–85) and Leo III (717–41), Constantinople itself fought for its own survival against besieging Muslim fleets. Each time it survived only through the use of a secret weapon, so-called Greek fire, an explosive liquid that burst into flame when sprayed by siphons onto enemy ships. Although the city itself survived, the Muslim conquests left the once-vast empire a small state reduced to little more than Greece, western Asia Minor, southern Italy, and the Balkans.

Authority and Government in Islam

Conquering the world for Islam proved easier than governing it. What had begun as a religious movement within Arabian society had created a vast, multinational empire in which Arabs were a tiny minority. Nothing in the *Qur'an*, nothing in Arabian experience, provided a blueprint for empire. Thus, the Muslims' ability to consolidate their conquests is even more remarkable than the conquests themselves. Within the first decades following the death of the Prophet, two models of governance emerged, models that continue to dominate Islamic politics to the present.

The first model was that of pre-Islamic tribal authority. The Umma could be considered a supertribe, governed by leaders whose authority came from their secular power as leaders of the superior military and economic elements within the community. This model appealed particularly to Quraysh and local tribal leaders who had exercised authority before Muhammad. The second model was that of the authority exercised by the Prophet. In this model, the Umma was more than a supertribe, and its unity and purity had to be preserved by a religiously sanctioned rule exercised by a member of the Prophet's own family. This model was preferred by many of the more recent converts to Islam, especially the poor. Governance under each of the two models was attempted successively in the seventh and eighth centuries.

Regardless of their disagreements on the basis of political authority, both groups adopted the administrative systems of their conquered lands. Byzantine and Sassanid bureaucracy and government, only slightly adjusted, became the models for government in the Islamic world until the twentieth century. In Syria and Egypt, Byzantine officials and even churchmen were incorporated into the government, much as had been the case in Europe following the Germanic conquests. John of Damascus (ca. 676–ca. 754), a Christian theologian venerated as a saint, for example, served as the caliph's chief councillor. His faithfulness to the Islamic government and opposition to Byzantine imperial iconoclasm earned him the title of "cursed favorer of Saracens (Muslims)" from the Byzantine emperor.

Likewise, the Muslims left intact the social structures and economic systems of the empires they conquered. Lands remained in the hands of their previous owners. Only state property or, in the Sassanid Empire, that of the Zoroastrian priesthood, became common property of the Muslim community. The monastery of Saint Catherine on Mount Sinai, founded by the emperor Justinian around 540, for example, survived without serious harm and still shelters Orthodox monks today.

The division of the spoils of conquest badly divided the Umma and precipitated the first crises in the caliphate. Under 'Umar, two groups received most of the spoils of the conquests. First were the earliest followers of the Prophet, who received a disproportionate share of revenues.

The terrifying weapon known as Greek fire is turned on an enemy during a naval battle.
This early example of chemical warfare was a mixture of unknown ingredients that
ignited and burned furiously when it came into contact with water. The sailors in the
illustration are using it like a flamethrower.

Second were the conquerors themselves, who were often recent converts from tribes on the fringes of Arabia. After 'Umar's death, his successor 'Uthman (d. 656), a member of the powerful Umayya clan of Mecca, attempted to consolidate control over Islam by Quraysh elite. He began to reduce the privileges of early converts in favor of the old Meccan elite. At the same time, he demanded that revenue from the provinces be sent to Medina. The result was rebellion, both within Arabia and in Egypt. 'Uthman's only firm support lay in distant Syria, ruled by members of his own clan. Abandoned at home and abroad, he was finally murdered as he sat reading the *Qur'an* in his home.

In spite of 'Uthman's unpopularity, his murder sent shockwaves throughout the Umma. The fate of his successor, Muhammad's beloved son-in-law and nephew 'Ali (656–61), had an even more serious effect on the future of Islam. Although chosen as fourth caliph, 'Ali was immediately charged with complicity in 'Uthman's murder and strongly opposed by the Umayyad

commander of Syria. To protect himself, 'Ali moved the caliphate from Arabia to Iraq. There he sought the support of underprivileged, recent converts by stressing the equality of all believers and the religious role of the caliph, who was to be less governor and tax collector than spiritual guide of Islam.

'Ali's spiritual appeal could not make up for his political weakness. At home and abroad his support gradually crumbled as the Quraysh and their Syrian supporters gained the upper hand. In 661 'Ali was murdered by supporters of his Umayyad rivals. Still, the memory of the "last orthodox caliph" remained alive in the Islamic world, especially in Iraq and Iran. Centuries later, a tradition developed in Baghdad that legitimate leadership of Islam could come only from the house of 'Ali. Adherents of this belief developed into a political and religious sect known as Shi'ism. Although frequently persecuted as heretical by the majority of Muslims, Shi'ism remains a potent minority movement within the Islamic world today.

The immediate effect of 'Ali's death, however, was the triumph of the old Quraysh and in particular the Umayyads, who established at Damascus in Syria a caliphate that lasted a century. The Umayyads made no attempt to base their rule on spiritual authority. Instead, they ruled as secular leaders, attempting to unite the Islamic empire through an appeal to Arab unity. Profits from this state went entirely to the Quraysh and members of Arabian tribes who formed the backbone of the early Umayyad army, monopolized high administration, and acquired rich estates throughout the empire.

The Umayyads extended the Islamic empire to its farthest reaches. In the north, armies from Syria marched into Anatolia and were only stopped in 677 by the Byzantine fleet before Constantinople itself. In the east, Umayyad armies pressed as far as the Syr Darya River on the edge of the Chinese T'ang empire. In the south and southwest, Umayyad progress was even more successful. After the conquest of the Mediterranean coast of Africa, the general Tariq ibn Ziyad (d. ca. 720) in 711 crossed the strait separating Morocco from Spain near the Rock of Gibraltar (the name comes from the Arabic *jabal Tariq*, "Tariq's mountain") and quickly conquered virtually the entire peninsula. Soon raiding parties had ventured as far north as the Loire Valley of what is today France. There they were halted by the Frankish commander Charles Martel in 732. Much of Spain, however, remained part of the *Dar al-Harab* (the House of Islam) until 1492.

The Umayyad caliphate's external success in conquering failed to extend to its dealings with the internal tensions of the Umma. The Umayyads could not build a stable empire on the twin foundations of a tiny Arabian elite and a purely secular government taken over from their Byzantine predecessors. Arabs as well as Jews, Zoroastrians, and Christians converted in great numbers. Not all Muslim commanders looked favorably on such conversions. Far from practicing "conversion by the sword," as was often the case in Christian missionary activity, Muslim leaders at times even discouraged the spread of Islam among the non-Arabs they had conquered. The reason was simple. Christians and Jews had to pay the head tax imposed upon them. If they converted, they no longer paid the tax. In time, this growing population of non-Arab Muslims

began to demand a share in the empire's wealth.

Not only were the numbers of Muslims increasing, so also was their fervor. Growing numbers of devout Muslims—Arabs and non-Arabs alike—were convinced that leadership had to be primarily spiritual, and that this spiritual mandate was the exclusive right of the family of the Prophet. Ultimately, a coalition of dissatisfied Persian Muslims and Arabian religious reformers united under the black banners of the descendants of Muhammad's paternal uncle, 'Abbas (566–ca. 653). In 750 this group overthrew the Umayyads everywhere but in Spain and established a new caliphate in favor of the 'Abbasids.

With the fall of the Umayyad caliphate, Arabs lost control of Islam forever. The 'Abbasids attempted to govern the empire according to religious principles. These were found in the *Qur'an* and in the *sunnah* or practices established by the Prophet and preserved first orally and then in the *hadith*, or traditions, which were somewhat comparable to the Christian Gospels. This new empire was to be a universal Muslim commonwealth in which Arabs had no privileged position. "Whoever speaks Arabic is an Arab," ran a popular saying. The 'Abbasids had risen to power as "the group of the saved," and they hoped to make the moral community of Islam the cornerstone of their government, with obedience to 'Abbasid authority an integral part of Islamic belief.

The institutional foundations of the new caliphate, however, like those of the Umayyads, remained firmly in the ancient empires they had conquered. The great caliph Mansur (754–75) moved the capital from Damascus to Baghdad, an acknowledgment of the crucial role of Iraqi and Iranian military and economic strength. The city, a few miles from the ruins of Ctesiphon on the Tigris, was largely constructed from building stones hauled by slaves from the old city to the new. In the same manner, the 'Abbasids constructed an autocratic imperial system on the model of their Persian predecessors. With their claims to divine sanction as members of the "holy family" and their firm control of the military, increasingly composed of slave armies known as *Mamluks*, the 'Abbasids governed the Islamic empire at its zenith.

Ultimately, however, the 'Abbasids were no more successful than the Umayyads in maintaining authority over the whole Muslim world. By the tenth century, local military commanders, termed *emirs*, took control of provincial governments in many areas while preserving the fiction that they were appointed by the 'Abbasid caliphs. The caliphs maintained the symbolic unity of Islam while the emirs went their separate ways. The majority of Muslims accepted this situation as a necessary compromise. In contrast to the Shi'ites, who continued to look for a leader from the family of 'Ali, the Sunnis, as they came to be known, remain to the present the majority group of Muslims. The Sunnis had no fixed theory of government or succession to the caliphate. Instead, they accepted the events of history in a practical manner, secure in the truth of the hadith, "My umma will never agree upon an error."

In the west the 'Abbasids could not maintain even a facade of unity. Supporters of 'Ali's family had never accepted the 'Abbasid claims to be the legitimate spiritual leaders of the Islamic community. These Shi'ites launched sporadic revolts and separatist movements. The most successful was that of 'Ubayd Allah the Fatimid (d. 934), who claimed to be the descendant of 'Ali and rightful leader of Islam. In 909, with the support of North African seminomadic Berbers, he declared himself caliph in defiance of the 'Abbasids at Baghdad. In 969 'Ubayd's Fatimid successors conquered Egypt and established a new city, Cairo, as the capital of their rival caliphate. By the middle of the eleventh century, the Fatimid caliphate controlled all of North Africa, Sicily, Syria, and western Arabia.

In Umayyad Spain, although the Muslim population remained firmly Sunni, the powerful emir 'Abd ar-Rahman III (891–961) took a similar step. In 929 he exchanged his title for that of caliph, thus making his position religious as well as secular. Everywhere the political and religious unity of Islam was being torn apart.

The arrival in all three caliphates of Muslim peoples not yet integrated into the civilization of the Mediterranean world accelerated this disintegration. From the east, Seljuq Turks, long used as slave troops, entered Iraq and in 1055 conquered Baghdad. Within a decade they had conquered Iran, Syria, and Palestine as well. Around the same time Moroccan Berbers conquered much of North Africa and Spain, while Bedouin

raided freely in Libya and Tunisia. These invasions by Muslims from the fringes of the Islamic commonwealth had catastrophic effects on the Islamic world. The Turks, unaccustomed to commerce and to the administrative traditions of the caliphate, divided their empire among their war leaders, displacing traditional landowners and disrupting commerce. The North African Berbers and Bedouins destroyed the agricultural and commercial systems that had survived successive Vandal, Byzantine, and Arabian invasions.

Islamic Civilization

The Islamic conquest of the seventh century brought peace to Iraq and Iran after generations of struggle and set the stage for a major agricultural recovery. In the tradition of their Persian predecessors, the caliphs organized vast irrigation systems, which made Mesopotamia the richest agricultural region west of China. Peasants and slaves raised dates and olives in addition to wheat, barley, and rice. Sophisticated hydraulics and scientific agriculture brought great regions of Mesopotamia and the Mediterranean coast into cultivation for the first time in centuries.

By uniting the Mediterranean world with Arabia and India, the 'Abbasid empire created the greatest trade network ever seen. Muslim merchants met in busy, bustling ports on the Persian Gulf and the Red Sea. There they traded silks, paper, spices, and horses from China for silver and cotton from India. Gold from the Sudan was exchanged for iron from Persia. Carpets from Armenia and Tabaristan, what is today Iran, were traded; from western Europe came slaves. Much of these luxury goods found their way to Baghdad, known as the marketplace for the world.

The marketplace for ideas was as active as that for merchandise. Within a few generations, descendants of Bedouin established themselves in the great cities of the ancient Near East and absorbed the traditions of Persian, Roman, and Hellenistic civilization. However, unlike the Germanic peoples of western Europe, who quickly adopted the Latin language and Roman Christianity, the Muslims recast Persian and Hellenistic culture in an Arabic form. Even in Iran, where Farsi, or Persian, survived as the majority lan-

Sufi mysticism existed side by side with orthodox Islam. The members of an Islamic religious order known as the dancing dervishes whirl round and round in a ritual meant to help the dancers achieve psychic illumination.

guage, Arabic vocabulary and structure transformed the traditional language. While 'Abassid political unity was falling apart, this new civilization was reaching its first great synthesis.

As desert conquerors, the Arabs might have been expected to destroy or ignore the heritage of Persian and Hellenistic culture. Instead, they became its protectors and preservers. As early as the eighth century, caliphs collected Persian, Greek, and Syriac scientific and philosophical

works and had them translated into Arabic. Legal scholars concerned with the authenticity of hadith used Greek rationalist methods to distinguish genuine from spurious traditions. Religious mystics called *Sufis* blended Neoplatonic and Muslim traditions to create new forms of religious devotion. The medical writings of Hippocrates and Galen circulated widely in the Islamic world, and Muslim physicians were by far the most competent and respected in the West through the fifteenth century. Mathematics and astronomy were both practical and theoretical fields. Muslim intellectuals introduced the so-called Arabic numerals from India and by the tenth century had perfected the use of decimal fractions and algebra. Although theoretical astronomy was limited to reforming rather than recasting Ptolemaic theory, Muslim astronomers absorbed and continued the highly accurate traditions of Mesopotamian planetary observation. The tables they compiled were more accurate than those known in the Byzantine and Latin worlds.

Although most Islamic scientists were professional physicians, astronomers, or lawyers, they were also deeply concerned with abstract philosophical questions, particularly those raised by the works of Plato and Aristotle, which had been translated into Arabic. Many sought to reconcile Islam with this philosophical heritage in the same manner that Origen and Augustine had done for Christianity. Ya'qub al-Kindi (d. 873), the first Arab philosopher, noted that "The truth . . . must be taken wherever it is to be found, whether it be in the past or among strange peoples." The Persian physician Ibn Sina (980–1037), known in the west as Avicenna, wrote over a hundred works on all aspects of science and philosophy. He compiled a vast encyclopedia of knowledge in which he attempted to synthesize Aristotelian thought into a Neoplatonic view of the universe. In the next century the Cordoban philosopher Ibn Rushd (1126–98), called Averroës in the west, went still further, teaching an authentic Aristotelian philosophy stripped of Neoplatonic mystical trappings. His commentaries on Aristotle were enormously influential even outside the Islamic world. For Christian philosophers of the thirteenth century, Averroës was known simply as "the Commentator."

At the same time that Muslim thought and culture was at its most creative, Islam faced invasion from a new and unaccustomed quarter: Constantinople. In the tenth and early eleventh centuries, the Byzantines pressed the local rulers of northern Syria and Iraq in a series of raids, which reached as far as the border of Palestine. At the end of the eleventh century western Europeans, encouraged and supported by the Byzantines, captured Jerusalem and established a western-style kingdom in Palestine that survived for over a century. Once more, Constantinople was a power in the Mediterranean world.

This engraved brass astrolabe was made by the Yemeni sultan al-Ashraf in 1291. Astrolabes such as this were used by seafarers from ancient times to measure the angles of celestial bodies above the horizon.

The Byzantine Apogee

During the tenth and eleventh centuries, Byzantium dominated the Mediterranean world for the last time. Imperial armies under the Macedonian dynasty (867–1059) began to recover some lands lost to Islam during the previous two centuries. Antioch was retaken in 969, and for over a century Byzantine armies operated in Syria and pushed to the border of Palestine. By the middle of the eleventh century Armenia and Georgia, which had formed independent principalities, had been reintegrated into the empire. To the west Sicily remained in Muslim hands, but southern Italy, which had been subject to Muslim raids and western barbarian occupation, was secured once more. Byzantine fleets recaptured Crete, cleared the Aegean of Muslim pirates, and reopened the vital commercial sea routes. To the north, missionaries spread not only the Christian religion but also Byzantine culture among the Slavic peoples beyond the frontiers of the empire. The most important missionaries were the brothers Cyril (ca. 827–69) and Methodius (ca. 827–85), who preached to the Khazars and the Moravians. They also invented the Cyrillic alphabet, which they used to translate the Bible and other Christian writings into Slavic. Their missionary activities laid the foundation for the conversion of Serbia, Bulgaria, and Russia. In 1018 Basil II (976–1025) destroyed the Bulgarian kingdom and brought peace to the Balkan peninsula.

The conquests of the Macedonian dynasty laid the foundation for a short-lived economic prosperity and cultural renaissance. Conquered lands, particularly Anatolia, brought new agricultural wealth. Security of the sea fostered a resurgence of commerce, and customs duties enriched the imperial treasury. New wealth financed the flourishing of Byzantine art and literature. However, just as in the spheres of Byzantine liturgy and court ceremonial, the goal of Byzantine art was not to reflect the transient "reality" of this world but rather the permanent, classical values inherited from the past. Thus rarely in Byzantine art, literature, or religion was innovation appreciated or cultivated. The language, style, and themes of classical Greek literature, philosophy, and history completely dominated Byzantine culture. Only in rare works such as the popular epic *Digenis Akrites* does something of the flavor of popular Byzantine life appear. The title of the work means roughly "the border defender born of two peoples," for the hero, Basil, was the son of a Muslim father and a Christian Greek mother. The epic consists of two parts, one describing the exploits of the father, a Muslim emir or general, and the other those of Digenis Akrites himself, fighting against both Muslims and bandits. The descriptions of his battles, his encounters with wild beasts and dragons, and his heroic death, as well as those of his intelligence, learning, and magnificent palace, are at once part of the western epic tradition and a reflection of life on the edge of the empire. *Digenis Akrites* is unique for its close relation to popular oral traditions of Byzantine society.

Another picture of Byzantine life was created by cultivated authors who were able to master completely their ancient models and to fashion within these inherited forms of literature compelling works of enduring value. One such author was the historian and imperial courtier Michael Psellus (1018–ca. 1078). His first-hand descriptions of rampaging mobs in Constantinople, hounding their enemies "like wild beasts," his acute analyses of imperial politics, and his descriptions of the inner workings of court intrigues bring to life Byzantine society at its height.

The Disintegration of the Empire

In all domains, however, the successes of the Macedonian emperors set the stage for serious problems. Rapid military expansion and economic growth allowed new elites to establish themselves as autonomous powers and to position themselves between the imperial administration and the people. The constant demand for troops always exceeded the supply of traditional salaried soldiers. In the eleventh century, emperors began to grant imperial estates to great magnates in return for military service. These grants, termed *pronoia*, often included immunity from imperial taxation and the right to certain administrative activities traditionally carried out by the central government. The practice created in effect a largely independent, landed military aristocracy that stood between the peasantry and the imperial government. This policy weakened the centralized state and reduced its income from taxes.

As generals became dissatisfied with the civilian central administration, they began to turn their armies against the emperors, launching over thirty revolts in as many years. To defend itself against both the Muslims without and the generals within, the central government, composed of intellectuals, eunuchs, and urban aristocrats, had to spend vast sums on mercenary armies. These armies, composed largely of Armenians, Germans, and Normans, soon began to plunder the empire they were hired to protect. Further danger came from other, independent Normans who, under their commander Robert Guiscard (ca. 1015–85), conquered Byzantine Bari and southern Italy and then Muslim Sicily. Soon Guiscard was threatening the empire itself. The hostility between military aristocracy and imperial administration largely destroyed the tradition of civilian government. "Do not wish to be a bureaucrat," one general advised his son. "It is not possible to be both a general and a comedian."

Under increasing pressure from local magnates on the one hand and desperate imperial tax collectors on the other, villages began to make deals with powerful patrons who would represent them in return for the surrender of their independence. Through the eleventh and twelfth centuries, the Byzantine peasantry passed from the condition of individualism without freedom to collectivism without freedom. Through the same process landlords and patrons acquired the means to exercise a political role, which ended the state's monopoly on public power.

At the same time that civil war and external pressure were destroying the provincial administration, Byzantine disdain for commerce was weakening the empire's ability to control its income from customs duties. Initially the willingness to turn over commerce to Italians and others posed few problems. Those engaged in actual commerce were for the most part citizens of the empire and were in any case subject to the 10 percent tariffs. However, in the tenth and eleventh centuries, merchants of Amalfi, Bari, and then Venice came to dominate Byzantine commerce. Venetian merchant fleets could double as a powerful navy in times of need, and by the eleventh century the Venetians were the permanent military and commercial power in the Mediterranean. When Robert Guiscard and his Normans threatened the empire, the emperors had to turn to the Venetians for protection and were forced to cede them major economic privileges. The Venetians acquired the right to maintain important self-governing communities in major ports throughout the empire and were allowed to pay lower tariffs than the Byzantines themselves.

In 1071, the year that Robert Guiscard captured the last Byzantine city in Italy, the empire suffered an even more disastrous defeat in the east. At Manzikert in Anatolia the emperor Romanus IV (1067–71) and his unreliable mercenary army fell to the Seljuq Turks, who captured Romanus himself. Manzikert sealed the fate of the empire. Anatolia was lost and the gradual erosion of the empire both west and east had begun.

The Conquests of Constantinople and Baghdad

At the end of the eleventh century the Comnenian dynasty (1081–1185) briefly halted the political and economic chaos of the empire. Rather than fighting the tendency of the centralized state to devolve into a decentralized aristocratic one, Alexius I Comnenus (1081–1118) tied the aristocracy to his family, thus making it an instrument of imperial government. In the short run the process was successful. He expanded the use of pronoia to strengthen loyal aristocrats and he granted them offices in the central administration that had been traditionally reserved for eunuchs. He stabilized Byzantine currency, which was the international exchange medium in the Islamic and Christian worlds and which had been dangerously devalued by his predecessors. Still, by the late twelfth century, the empire was a vulnerable second-rate power caught between Latin Europe and Islam.

Initially, the Christian west was a more deadly threat than the Islamic east. In the eleventh century, after more than five hundred years

of economic and political weakness, western Europe was beginning to reach parity with Byzantium. Robert Guiscard and his Normans, who had conquered Sicily and southern Italy, were typical examples of the powerful, militaristic aristocracy developing in the remains of the old western empire. This military threat from the west was paralleled by a religious one. In the centuries that Rome had been largely cut off from Constantinople, western Christianity had developed a number of rituals and beliefs differing from Orthodox practice. This parting of the ways had already appeared during the iconoclastic controversies of the eighth and ninth centuries. In the eleventh, it was directed by an independent and self-assertive papacy in Rome, which claimed supreme authority throughout Christendom. Disagreements between the patriarchs of Constantinople and the popes of Rome prevented cooperation between the two Christian worlds and led to further deterioration of relationships between Greeks and Latins. These disagreements came to a head in 1054, when the papal representative, or legate, Cardinal Humbert (ca. 1000–61) met with the patriarch of Constantinople, Michael Cerularius (ca. 1000–59), to negotiate ecclesiastical control over southern Italy and Sicily. Humbert was arrogant and demanding, Michael Cerularius haughty and uncompromising. Acting beyond his authority, Humbert excommunicated the patriarch and all his followers. The patriarch responded in kind, excommunicating Humbert and all connected with him. This formal excommunication was lifted in the 1960s, but the schism, or split, between the churches of Rome and Constantinople continues to the present.

Excommunication was probably the least of the dangers the Byzantines faced from the west. The full fury of this ignorant, greedy, and violent western society reached the empire when, after the defeat at Manzikert, the emperor Alexius called on western Christians for support against the Muslims. To his horror, adventurers of every sort eager to conquer land and wealth in the name of the cross of Jesus flooded the empire. In the penetrating and often cynical biography of her father, Alexius' daughter Anna (ca. 1083–1148) describes how, as quickly as possible, Alexius hurried these crusaders (from the Latin *cruciata*, "marked with a cross") on to Palestine before they could turn their violence against his empire. Even while recognizing that the crusaders were uncouth and barbarous, the Byzantines had to admit that the Latins were effective. Despite enormous hardships, the First Crusade was able to take advantage of division in the Muslim world to conquer Palestine and establish a Latin kingdom in Jerusalem in 1099.

The crusaders' initial victories and the growth of Latin wealth and power created in Constantinople a temporary enthusiasm for western European styles and customs. The Byzantines soon realized, however, that the Latin kingdom posed a threat not only to Islam but to them as well. While crusaders threatened Byzantine territories, Venetian merchants imposed a stranglehold on Byzantine trade. When emperors granted other Italian towns concessions equal to those of the Venetians, they found that they had simply amplified their problems. Anti-Latin sentiment reached the boiling point in 1183. In the riots that broke out in that year Italians and other westerners in Constantinople were murdered and their goods seized. Just twenty-one years later, in 1204, a wayward crusade, egged on by Venice, turned aside from its planned expedition to Palestine to capture a bigger prize: Constantinople. After pillaging the city for three days—the Byzantine survivors commented that even the Saracens would have been less cruel—the westerners established one of their own as emperor and installed a Venetian as patriarch.

The Byzantines did manage to hold on to a portion of their empire centering on Nicaea, and before long the Latins fell to bickering among themselves. In 1261 the ruler of Nicaea, Michael Palaeologus (ca. 1224–82), recaptured Constantinople with the assistance of the Genoese and had himself crowned emperor in the Hagia Sophia. Still, the empire was fatally shattered, its disintegration into autonomous lordships complete. The restored empire consisted of little more than the district around Constantinople, Thessalonica, and the Peloponneseus. Bulgarians and Serbs had expanded far into the Greek mainland. Most of the rich Anatolian regions had been lost

The Crusades

The Byzantine Empire and the Rise of Islam

caliph, ending a five-hundred-year tradition. The Mongol armies then moved west, shattering the Seljuq principalities in Iraq, Anatolia, and Syria and turning back only before the fierce resistance of the Egyptian Mamluks.

From the ruins of the Seljuq kingdom arose a variety of small Turkish principalities, or emirates. After the collapse of the Mongol empire, one of these, the Ottoman, began to expand at the expense of both the weakened Byzantine and the Mongol-Seljuq empires. In the next centuries the Ottomans expanded east, south, and west. Around 1350, they crossed into the Balkans as Byzantine allies but soon took over the region for themselves. By 1450 the Ottoman stranglehold on Constantinople was complete. The final scene of the conquest, long delayed but inevitable, occurred three years later.

For Greeks and for Italian intellectuals of the Renaissance, the conquest of Constantinople by the Ottomans was the end of an imperial tradition that reached back to Augustus. But Mehmed the Conqueror (1452–1481) could as easily be seen as its restorer. True, the city was plundered by the victorious

The Ottoman Empire, ca. 1450

army. But this was simply the way of war in the fifteenth century. The city, its palaces, and its religious edifices fared better under the Turks than they had under its previous, Christian conquerors. The Latins had placed a prostitute on the patriarch's throne in the Hagia Sophia. Mehmed, after purging the church of its Christian trappings, rededicated it to the worship of the one God. Once more Constantinople, for centuries a capital without a country, was the center of a great Mediterranean empire. In the following centuries, Ottoman rule stretched from the gates of Vienna to the Caspian Sea and from the Persian Gulf to the Strait of Gibraltar. The legacy of absolutism, of imperial government, and of cultural pluralism, inherited from Sassanid Persia and imperial Rome, survived until the beginning of the twentieth century.

to the Turks, and commercial revenues were in the hands of the Genoese allies. The restored empire's survival for almost two hundred years was due less to its own prerogative than to the internal problems of the Islamic world.

The caliphs of Baghdad, like the emperors of Constantinople, succumbed to invaders from the barbarous fringes of their empire. In 1221 the Mongol prince Temujin (ca. 1162–1227), better known to history as Genghis Khan (Universal Ruler), led his conquering army into Persia from central Asia. From there, a portion of the Mongols went north, invading Russia in 1237 and dividing it into small principalities ruled by Slavic princes under Mongol control. In 1258 a Mongol army captured Baghdad and executed the last 'Abbasid

Although often deadly enemies, the Byzantine and Islamic worlds were both genuine heirs of the great eastern empires of antiquity. The traditions of the Assyrian, Alexandrian, Persian, and Roman empires lived on in their cities, their bureaucracies, their agricultural and commercial systems. Both also shared the monotheistic religious tradition that had emerged from Judaism. In their schools and libraries, they preserved and transmitted the literary and scientific heritage of antiquity. Through Islam, the legacy of the West reached the Far East. Through Byzantium, the peoples of the Slavic world became heirs of the caesars. The inhabitants of western Europe long viewed these two great civilizations with hostility, incomprehension, and fear. Still, in the areas of culture, government, religion, and commerce, the west learned much from its eastern neighbors.

Suggestions for Further Reading

The Byzantines

George Ostrogorsky, *History of the Byzantine State* (Rutgers, NJ: Rutgers University Press, 1969). The standard one-volume history of Byzantium.

Cyril Mango, *Byzantium: The Empire of New Rome* (New York: Scribner's, 1980). An imaginative and provocative reevaluation of the Byzantine world.

Joan M. Hussey, *The Orthodox Church in the Byzantine Empire* (New York: Oxford University Press, 1986). An introduction to Orthodox Christianity.

* Dimitri Obolensky, *The Byzantine Commonwealth: Eastern Europe 500–1453* (Crestwood, NY: St. Vladimir's Seminary Press, 1983). Relates Byzantium to the Slavic world.

* J. W. Barker, *Justinian and the Later Roman Empire* (Madison, WI: University of Wisconsin Press, 1975). A survey of Justinian's reign intended for a general public.

Speros Vryonis, Jr., *Byzantium and Europe* (New York: Harcourt Brace Jovanovich, 1967). A survey of the relationship between Byzantium and the West.

A. A. Vasiliev, *History of the Byzantine Empire* (Madison, WI: University of Wisconsin Press, 1952). A classic survey of Byzantine history by a great Russian scholar.

Alexander Kazhdan and Giles Constable, *People and Power in Byzantium* (Washington, DC: Dumbarton Oaks, 1982). An imaginative and controversial analysis of Byzantine culture by a Russian Byzantinist and a western medievalist.

The Rise of Islam

* Bernard Lewis, *The Arabs in History* (New York: Harper & Row, 1966). A well-written general introduction by an authority.

* Hugh Kennedy, *The Prophet and the Age of the Caliphates* (White Plains, NY: Longman, 1986). A valuable summary of the early political history of Islam.

* John L. Esposito, *Women in Muslim Family Law* (Syracuse, NY: Syracuse University Press, 1982). A general introduction to the topic, with historical material in the first two chapters.

G. E. Von Grunebaum, *Classical Islam: A History 600–1258* (Chicago: Aldine, 1970). A general introduction to early Islamic history.

Aziz Al-Azmeh, *Arabic Thought and Islamic Societies* (London: Routledge, Chapman & Hall, 1986). A demanding but valuable introduction to Islamic intellectual history.

Roy P. Mottahedeh, *Loyalty and Leadership in an Early Islamic Society* (Princeton, NJ: Princeton University Press, 1980). An important introduction to the social values and structures of western Iran and southern Iraq in the tenth and eleventh centuries.

Bernard Lewis, ed., *Islam and the Arab World* (New York: Knopf, 1976). An illustrated collection of essays on Islamic history and culture.

* Bernard Lewis, *The Muslim Discovery of Europe* (New York: W. W. Norton, 1985). Views of the West by Muslim travelers.

The Byzantine Apogee

* Michael Agold, *The Byzantine Empire 1025–1204.* (White Plains, NY: Longman, 1985). A solid recent survey of the Byzantine Empire prior to the capture of Constantinople by the Latins.

* P. M. Holt, *The Age of the Crusades: The Near East from the Eleventh Century to 1517.* (White Plains, NY: Longman, 1986). An excellent up-to-date survey of the political history of the Near East in the later Middle Ages.

* Indicates paperback edition available

8

The West
in the Early
Middle Ages

The Chapel at the Waters

The Palatine Chapel in Aachen, now a small German city near the Belgian border, brings together a fascination with the traditions of the Roman past with the creativity of a new epoch. These two strands describe Europe during the early Middle Ages, generally the period between 500 and 1000. Aachen was a favorite residence of the Frankish king Charles the Great, or Charlemagne (768–814), who often came there to enjoy its natural hot springs. In time it came to be his primary residence, the capital of his vast kingdom, which stretched from central Italy to the mouth of the Rhine River. Around 792 Charlemagne, a descendant of barbarian warriors, commissioned an architect to design a palace complex as his residence, one that would rival the great Roman and Byzantine buildings of Italy and Constantinople.

Royal agents scoured Europe for Roman ruins from which columns, precious marble, and ornaments could be salvaged and reused. From these ancient stones masons raised a complex of audience rooms, royal apartments, baths, and quarters for court officials. The whole ensemble was intentionally reminiscent of the Lateran Palace in Rome, which had been the residence of the emperors before being given to the popes.

The central building of Charlemagne's palace complex was the chapel, a symmetrical octagon three hundred feet on its principal axes, modeled on San Vitale in Ravenna. The choice of model was significant. Ravenna had been the former capital of Roman Italy and of Theodoric the Great, the Ostrogothic king whom Charlemagne greatly admired. But although modeled on Roman buildings, the Palatine Chapel was admirably suited to the glorification of Charlemagne.

The building was divided into three tiers. The first tier on the ground floor held the sanctuary, where priest and people met for worship. The topmost tier, supported by ancient Roman pillars shipped to Aachen from Rome and Ravenna, represented the heavens. Between the two was a gallery connected by a passage to the royal residence. On this gallery sat the king's throne. From his seat, Charlemagne could look down upon the religious services being conducted below. Looking up to where he sat, worshipers were constantly reminded of the king's intermediary position between ordinary mortals and God.

This architectural design boldly asserted that Charlemagne was more than a barbarian king. By 805 when the chapel was dedicated, he had made good this assertion. As a contemporary chronicler wrote, while in Rome in the year 800

> On the most holy day of Christmas, when the king rose from prayer in front of the shrine of the blessed apostle Peter to take part in the Mass, Pope Leo placed a crown on his head, and he was hailed by the whole Roman people . . . He was now called Emperor and Augustus.

Thus, to Charlemagne and to his supporters, this coronation ceremony revived the Roman Empire in the west. Charlemagne, with his vast empire and his imperial palace, was a true successor of the ancient Roman emperors. Like his chapel in Aachen (long after known as Aix-la-Chapelle, the chapel at the waters), this empire was built on the remains of Roman traditions grafted onto a vigorous tradition of Germanic kinship and society. According to the Byzantines, who looked on Charlemagne and his imperial coronation with alarm, the western empire could not be revived because it had never really ended. According to them, the death of the last western emperor Julius Nepos in 480 had ended the division of the empire. Since then, the Byzantine emperors had pretended that they ruled both east and west. Charlemagne's claims, made through the ceremony in Rome and more subtly in the imperial architecture of his palace, represented to them not a revival of the empire but a threat to its existence.

The Making of the Barbarian Kingdoms

The existence of a united empire had long been but a dream. In the year 500, Emperor Anastasius I (491–518) could delude himself that he ruled the whole empire of Augustus, Diocletian, and Constantine, both east and west. Never mind that in the east war against the Persians dragged on. Never mind that along the northern border of the empire the Bulgarians, a new multiethnic barbarian confederation, had begun to raid into the Balkans. Neither of these conflicts, Anastasius contended, threatened the stability of the empire. In the west, the governor who ruled Italy had sworn that he "rejoiced to live under Roman law, which we are prepared to defend by arms." The king of the once troublesome Vandals had concluded a marriage alliance with the Italian governor and seemed ready to accept Roman statecraft. Beyond the Alps a Roman officer called a patrician ruled the regions of the upper Rhone, and a consul controlled Gaul. In Aquitaine and Spain, legitimate, recognized officers of the empire ruled both Romans and barbarians. What need was there to speak of the end of the empire in the west?

This imperial unity was more apparent than real. The Italian governor was the Ostrogothic king Theodoric the Great (493–526), whose Roman title meant less than his Ostrogothic army. The patrician was the Burgundian king Gondebaud (480–516). The Roman officer in Aquitaine and Spain was the Visigothic king Alaric II (485–507), and the Gallic consul was the Frankish king Clovis (482–511). Each of these rulers courted imperial titles and recognition, but not one of them regarded Anastasius as his sovereign. In Britain, the chieftains of the Anglo-Saxons did not even bother with the charade of imperial recognition. Within each barbarian kingdom in the west, the process of merging barbarians and Romans into new political and social entities had begun. No longer were east and west a united empire. The west had gone its own way.

The Goths: From Success to Extinction

In the early sixth century all of the Germanic peoples settled within the old Roman Empire acknowledged the Goths as the most successful of the "blond-haired peoples," as the Romans called the barbarians. The Ostrogoths had created an Italian kingdom in which Romans and barbarians lived side by side. The Visigoths ruled Spain and southern Gaul by combining traditions of Roman law and barbarian military might. Yet neither Gothic kingdom endured more than two centuries.

Theodoric the Ostrogoth was the most cultivated, capable, and sophisticated barbarian ruler. He was also the most powerful. Burgundians, Visigoths, and Alemanni looked to him for leadership and protection. Even Clovis, the ambitious Frankish king, usually bowed to his wishes.

Theodoric's success was the result of his deep understanding of Roman and barbarian traditions. He had spent his teenage years as a pampered hostage in Constantinople. There he had learned to understand and admire Roman ways. Later, after he had conquered Italy at the head of

A gold solidus coin bears a portrait of Theodoric. His left hand holds a globe on which stands a victory. The inscription reads "King Theodoric," but the absence of a robe and diadem shows that he was not considered the equal of the emperor.

The Barbarian Kingdoms, ca. 526

his Gothic army, he put his knowledge of Roman law and governance to good use. He established a dual government, which respected both the remains of Roman civil administration and Gothic military organization. Using the authority granted him as patrician, or theoretical representative of the Byzantine emperor, Theodoric governed the Roman population through the traditional Roman bureaucracy. As hereditary king he led his Ostrogoths, a small but powerful military minority.

Religion as well as government divided Italy's population. The Ostrogoths were Arians, while the majority of the Romans were orthodox Christians. Initially, Theodoric made no effort to interfere with the religion of his subjects, stating that "We cannot command the religion of our subjects,

since no one can be forced to believe against his will." This religious toleration attracted into his government outstanding Roman intellectuals and statesmen. Boethius (480–524), while serving in Theodoric's government, was also trying to synthesize the philosophical traditions of Plato and Aristotle. Cassiodorus (ca. 490–ca. 585), a cultivated Roman senator, served as Theodoric's secretary and held important positions in his government before retiring to found monasteries, where he and his monks worked to preserve the literary and philosophical traditions of Rome.

What might have been the fate of Italy and the West had Theodoric's kingdom survived the sixth century is a matter of speculation. Tensions grew between Ostrogoths and Romans. Some Ostrogothic warriors feared that their children were abandoning Gothic traditions for those of their Roman neighbors. The early atmosphere of toleration soured into suspicion. Boethius himself was accused of treason and executed. Following Theodoric's death in 526, internal conflict over the succession paved the way for a protracted and devastating invasion, which destroyed not only the Ostrogothic kingdom but also much of what remained of Roman Italy. These new, destructive invaders were not another barbarian tribe but the civilized Byzantines.

Italy was simply too close to Constantinople and too important for the ambitious Emperor Justinian I (527–65) to ignore. Encouraged by his easy victory over the Vandals, he sent an army into Italy, where he anticipated an easy reconquest of the peninsula (see p. 196). He got instead almost twenty years of vicious warfare. Not only were the Goths more formidable foes than he had expected, but when Roman tax collectors arrived with the Roman armies Justinian found that the Italian people did not greet their "liberators" with open arms. In addition, in the midst of the reconquest a new and terrible disease appeared throughout the Mediterranean world. The plague cut down as much as one-third of Europe's population in the next two centuries.

The destruction of Italy by war and disease paved the way for its conquest by the Lombards. As allies in Justinian's army, some members of this Germanic tribe from along the Danube had learned of the riches of Italy first-hand. In 568 the whole Lombard people left the Carpathian basin to their neighbors, the Avars, and invaded the exhausted and war-torn Italian peninsula. By the end of the sixth century the Ostrogoths had disappeared and the Byzantines retained only the boot of Italy and a narrow strip stretching from Ravenna to Rome. The Byzantine presence in Rome was weak and by default the popes, especially Gregory the Great (590–604), became the defenders and governors of the city. Gregory organized the resistance to the Lombards, fed the population during famines, and comforted them through the dark years of plague and warfare. A vigorous political as well as spiritual leader, he laid the foundations of the medieval papacy.

The Lombards were more brutal and less sophisticated than their Ostrogothic predecessors. They had little use for Roman administrative

tradition and instead divided Italy into military districts under the control of dukes whose authority replaced that of Roman bureaucrats. But it is an ill wind indeed that blows no good. The Lombards largely eliminated the Roman tax system under which Italians had long suffered. Moreover, they were less concerned with preserving their own cultural traditions than were the Ostrogoths, even in the sphere of religion. Initially the Lombards were Arians, but in the early seventh century the Lombard kings and their followers accepted orthodox Christianity. This conversion paved the way for the unification of the society. Italy may have been less civilized under the Lombards than under the Goths or Romans, but life for the vast majority of the population was probably better than it had been for centuries.

Rather than accepting a divided society as did the Ostrogoths or merging into an orthodox Roman culture as did the Lombards, the Visigoths of Gaul and Spain sought to unify the indigenous population of their kingdom through law and religion. Roman law deeply influenced Visigothic law codes and formed an enduring legal heritage to the West. Religious unity was a more difficult goal. The kings' repeated attempts to force conversion to Arianism failed and created tension and mistrust. This mistrust proved fatal. In 507 Gallo-Roman aristocrats supported the Frankish king Clovis in his successful conquest of the Visigothic kingdom of Toulouse. Defeat drove the Visigoths deeper into Spain, where they gradually forged a unified kingdom based on Roman administrative tradition and Visigothic kingship.

Spain was a rich country, and its Visigothic kings profited accordingly. Cordovan leather, olive oil, and grain cultivated on vast estates still owned by the Romans were exported throughout the known world. Greek, Jewish, and Syrian merchants crowded into the ports of the kingdom and carried its products as far as Ireland to the northwest and Palestine in the east. This prosperity benefited Spain's rulers, since some of the Roman tax system survived, filling royal coffers with gold. Both the Franks to the north and the Muslims to the south eyed the riches greedily.

The long-sought-after religious unity was finally achieved when King Recared (586–601) and, along with him, the Gothic aristocracy embraced orthodox Christianity. This conversion further blurred the differences between Visigoths and Roman provincials in the kingdom. It also initiated an unprecedented use of the Church and its ideology to strengthen the monarchy. Visigothic kings modeled themselves after the Byzantine emperors, proclaimed themselves new Constantines, and used Church councils, held regularly at Toledo, as governing assemblies.

Still, Visigothic distrust directed toward anyone who was different continued. It focused especially on the considerable Jewish population, which had lived in Spain since the diaspora, or dispersion, in the first century of the Roman Empire. Almost immediately after Recared's conversion, he and his successors began to enact a series of anti-Jewish measures, culminating in 613 with the command that all Jews accept baptism or leave the kingdom. Although this mandate was never fully carried out, the virulence of the persecution of the Jews grew through the seventh century. At the same time rivalry within the aristocracy weakened the kingdom and left it vulnerable to attack from without. In 711 Muslims from North Africa invaded and quickly conquered the Visigothic kingdom. While some remnants of the Visigoths held on in small kingdoms in the northwest, most of the population quickly came to terms with their new masters. Jews rejoiced in the religious toleration brought by Islam, and many members of the Christian elite converted to Islam and retained their positions of authority under the new regime. (See Special Feature, "The Jews in the Early Middle Ages," pp. 230–31.)

The Anglo-Saxons: From Pagan Conquerors to Christian Missionaries

The motley collection of Saxons, Angles, Jutes, Frisians, Suebians, and others who came to Britain as federated troops and stayed on as rulers did not coalesce into a united kingdom until almost the eleventh century. Instead, these Germanic warriors carved out small kingdoms for themselves, enslaving the Romanized Britons or driving them into Wales. Although independent, these little kingdoms (their number varied from five to as many as eleven at different times) maintained some sort of identity as a group. The king of the dominant kingdom was accorded the honorific title of Bretwalda or "wide ruler." Other kings looked to him as first among equals and sought his advice and influence in their dealings with one another. Unlike the Goths, none of these peoples had previously been integrated into the Roman world. Thus rather than fusing Roman and Germanic traditions, they eradicated the former.

This gilded copper plate, one of the Lombard treasures, was part of a helmet decoration. The Lombard king Agilulf (590-615) is shown receiving tribute from his conquered subjects. On either side of the king are winged victories carrying signs saying victoria.

The Jews in the Early Middle Ages

The intolerance and persecution of Jews by the Visigoths was the exception rather than the rule in early medieval Europe. Since the diaspora, Jews had settled throughout the West, primarily in towns. In Italy, Rome, Ravenna, and Pavia had important communities. In the Frankish kingdom Jews were particularly numerous in the southern cities of Lyon, Vienne, Arles, Marseille, and Narbonne, although Jewish communities could be found in more northern towns such as Orléans, Soissons, Nantes, Aachen, and Frankfurt. In contrast with later practice, Jews appeared no different from their Christian neighbors. They spoke the same language, wore no distinctive clothing, and occupied no designated section of town, or ghetto. Although they worshiped in their synagogues and studied in their yeshivas, they otherwise were very much integrated into the fabric of society.

Some Jews owned rural estates, where they cultivated vineyards and farms alongside their Christian neighbors. Jewish farmers and landowners were particularly common in the areas of Vienne, Mâcon, and Arles, where they appear in records of land transactions, buying, selling, and exchanging property with individuals and Christian churches. However, most Jews were merchants or practiced other urban professions such as goldsmithing or medicine. Some acted as tax collectors and emissaries for lay and ecclesiastical lords. The reasons for these specializations were obvious. First, Jewish communities in the West maintained ties with other Jews in the Byzantine and Muslim worlds, exchanging letters on religious and legal affairs and traveling back and forth. Second, while not frequent, sporadic attacks on Jews did occur. In the sixth century, for example, the Frankish king Chilperic (561–84) attempted to force Jews in his kingdom to be baptized. Thus Jews concentrated in occupations that allowed them to move easily and quickly in time of danger. Finally, the lack of interest on the part of their Christian neighbors in trade and the disappearance of Syriac and Greek merchants in the seventh century left long-distance commerce almost entirely in the hands of Jews. Royal documents speak frequently of "Jews and other merchants," implying that Gentile merchants were an unimportant minority.

Jewish merchants traveled widely, from Scandinavia to Iran, India, and even as far as China, exporting western slaves, furs, and weapons and returning with such exotic luxuries as spices and silks. This trade was important to western monarchs not only for supplies of luxuries but also for the tariff income it provided. In the ninth century Jewish merchants were so vital to the empire of Louis the Pious that he granted them special privileges and took them under his royal protection. A palace official, the master of the Jews, was responsible for protecting them throughout the empire and appeals against them to the king usually were settled in the Jews' favor.

Not everyone was equally pleased with the tolerance shown this non-Christian minority. Bishop Agobard of Lyon (799–840) complained bitterly to Louis about his policy of tolerance. The bishop was particularly disturbed by the fact that, while few Jews could be persuaded to convert, in the area of Lyon many Christians found the sermons of rabbis preferable to those of their priests and that conversions to Judaism were becoming frequent.

The most celebrated conversion was that of Bodo, a young Frankish aristocrat raised in Louis' palace and educated in his school. In 838, while on what he had pretended to be a pilgrimage to Rome, he converted to Judaism, sold his entourage into slavery, married a young Jewish woman, and fled to Saragossa in Muslim Spain. From there he wrote scathing attacks on the immorality and doctrinal ignorance of the Christian clergy he had known

הסוחר ריענו אשר תכתוב על הכיס אותותי את שמי ואת שם אבותי
כי הרואים רבים יסלועם וסרבם: ויאמר הנע כתב כפי חפצך שוך

in Aachen. Fourteen clerics there, he claimed, had held fourteen different opinions on their faith. Disgusted by what he considered to be the ignorance and idolatry of Christianity, he saw his conversion as a return to the worship of the one true God.

Christian churchmen were scandalized by Bodo and embarrassed by their inability to convert Jews through peaceful persuasion, but they were powerless to do anything about the situation. Traditional Christian doctrine asserted that the conversion of the Jews would be one of the signs of the end of the world. Until then, they had the right to toleration. Moreover, the early medieval world was one of many peoples, laws, and traditions. In a society in which different people in the same towns and even households might live according to Roman, Frankish, Gothic, or Burgundian law, Jews were but one more group with a distinct identity. Kings refused to limit the civil and religious rights of their Jewish subjects, forbade Christians to baptize Jewish slaves, and in general protected them as valued members of society.

Although the ruined walls of Roman cities such as London, Gloucester, and Carlisle continued to offer some protection to a handful of people, urban life disappeared and with it the Roman traditions of administration, taxation, and culture.

In their place developed a world whose central values were honor and glory, whose primary occupation was fighting, and whose economic system was based on plunder and the open-handed distribution of riches. In many ways this Anglo-Saxon world resembled the heroic age of ancient Greece. This was a society dominated by petty kings and their aristocratic war leaders. These invaders were not, like the Goths, just a military elite. They also included free farmers who replaced the Romanized British peasantry, introducing their language, agricultural techniques, social organization, and folkloric traditions to the southeastern part of the island. These ordinary settlers, much more than the kings and aristocrats, were responsible for the gradual transformation of Britain into England, the land of the Angles.

The Anglo-Saxons were pagans, and although Christianity survived, the relationship between conquered and conquerors did not provide a climate conducive to conversion. Christianity came instead from without. The conversion of England resulted from a two-part effort. The first originated in Ireland, the most western society of Europe and the one in which Celtic traditions had survived little changed for over a thousand years. Ireland had never formed part of the Roman Empire and thus had never adapted the forms of urban life and centralized, hierarchal government or religion characteristic of Britain and the continent. In the fifth century merchants and missionaries introduced an eastern, monastic form of Christianity to Ireland, which adapted easily to the rural, tribal organization of Irish society. Although Irish Christianity was entirely orthodox in its beliefs, the isolation of Ireland led to the development of numerous practices at odds with those common to Constantinople and Rome. Thus, although Ireland had important bishops, the most influential churchmen were powerful abbots of strict, ascetic monasteries, closely connected with tribal chieftains, who directed the religious life of their regions. Around 565 the Irish

monk Columba (521–97) established a monastery on the island of Iona off the coast of Scotland. From there wandering Irish monks began to convert northern Britain.

The second effort at Christianizing Britain began with Pope Gregory the Great. In 596 he sent the missionary Augustine (known as Augustine of Canterbury to distinguish him from the bishop of Hippo) to attempt to convert the English. Augustine arrived in the southeast kingdom of Kent, where the pagan King Ethelbert, encouraged by his wife Bertha, a Christian Frankish princess, gave him permission to preach.

The Anglo-Saxon burial site at Sutton Hoo, dating from the seventh century, yielded this solid-gold buckle. The front of the buckle is decorated with intricate interlaced animal patterns much like those found in Celtic art.

Augustine laid the foundations for a hierarchal, bishop-centered church based on the Roman model. In time Ethelbert and much of his kingdom accepted Christianity, and Augustine was named archbishop of Canterbury by the pope. Augustine had similar success in nearby Essex and established a second bishopric at London shortly before his death in 604.

As Irish missionaries spread south from Iona and Roman missionaries moved north from Canterbury, their efforts created in England two opposing forms of orthodox Christianity. One was Roman, episcopal, and hierarchical. The other was Celtic, monastic, and decentralized. The Roman and Celtic churches agreed on basic doctrines. However, each had its own calendar of religious feasts and its own rituals. These differences posed serious problems since they existed not only in the same society but sometimes even within the same family. Thus a wife who followed Roman custom might be fasting and abstaining from meat during the season of penance that preceded Easter, while her husband, who followed the Celtic calendar according to which Easter came earlier, was already feasting and celebrating. It was precisely this situation that led King Oswy of Northumbria (d. 670), the Bretwalda, to call in 664 an episcopal meeting, or *synod*, at Whitby to settle the issue. After hearing arguments from both sides, Oswy accepted the customs of the Roman Church, thus allying himself and ultimately all of Anglo-Saxon England with the centralized, hierarchical form of Christianity, which could be used to strengthen his monarchy.

During the century and a half following the Synod of Whitby, Anglo-Saxon Christian civilization blossomed. Contact with the Continent and especially with Rome increased. The monasteries of Monkwearmouth and Jarrow became centers of learning, culminating in the writings of Bede (673–735), the greatest scholar of his century. He probably never set foot outside the monasteries of Monkwearmouth, to which he had been given as a child of seven, and Jarrow, which he entered in 681. Still, his knowledge of natural science, rhetoric, chronology, scripture, and especially history spread his fame throughout the West. His history of the English church and people is the finest historical work of the early Middle Ages. His influ-

A portrait of Bede, known as The Venerable. This illustration is from a manuscript of his Vita Sancti Cuthberti. Bede's Ecclesiastical History of the English Nation *earned him the title Father of English History.*

ence lives on today, for he was the scholar responsible for the popularization of dating history from before or after the birth of Jesus.

By the eighth century, England was no longer a mission land but had itself begun to send out Christian missionaries. From around 700, descendants of the Anglo-Saxon conquerors started traveling to "Old Saxony," the region of the Continent from which their ancestors had originally come, as well as to other parts of the Germanic world to convert their still pagan cousins. Until the late eighth and ninth centuries, when new waves of Germanic invaders known as the Vikings began to destroy Anglo-Saxon civilization, England furnished the Continent with many of its leading thinkers and scholars.

The Franks: An Enduring Legacy

The name *Frank* means "fierce" or "free"; actually in their early history most Franks were virtual slaves of the Romans. In the fourth century various small Germanic tribes along the Rhine coalesced into a loose confederation known as the Franks. A significant group of them, the Salians, made the mistake of attacking Roman garrisons and were totally defeated. The Romans resettled the Salians in a largely abandoned region of what is now Belgium and Holland. There they formed a buffer to protect Roman colonists from other Germanic tribes and provided a ready supply of recruits for the Roman army. During the fourth and fifth centuries, these Salian Franks and their neighbors assumed an increasingly important role in the military defense of Gaul and began to spread out of their "reservation" into more settled parts of the province. Although many high-ranking Roman officers of the fourth century were Franks, most were neither conquerors nor members of the military elite. They were rather soldier-farmers who settled beside the local Roman peoples they protected.

In 486 Clovis, leader of the Salian Franks and commander of the barbarized Roman army, staged a successful coup (possibly with the approval of the Byzantine emperor), defeating and killing Syagrius, the last Roman commander in the west. Although Clovis ruled the Franks as king, he worked closely with the existing Gallo-Roman aristocracy as he consolidated his control over various Frankish factions and over portions of Gaul and Germany held by other barbarian kingdoms.

Clovis' early conversion to orthodox Christianity helped ensure the effectiveness of this Gallo-Roman cooperation. Like other barbarian kings allied with Theodoric the Ostrogoth, Clovis may have been at least nominally an Arian. However, urged on by his wife Clotilda, he embraced orthodox Christianity. His religious conversion was very much in the tradition of Constantine. Clovis converted to orthodox Christianity hoping that God would give him victory over his enemies and that his new faith would win the support of the Roman aristocracy in Gaul. The

The Horseman's Stone of Hornhausen, a seventh-century relief from a Frankish tomb. The horseman with lance and shield rides above a two-headed serpent. Such pictorial stones are found mainly in Sweden.

king's baptism convinced many of his subjects to convert as well and paved the way for assimilation of Franks and Romans into a new society. This Frankish society became the model for European social and political organization for over a thousand years.

The mix of Frankish warriors and Roman aristocrats spread rapidly across western Europe. Clovis and his successors absorbed the Visigothic kingdom of Toulouse, the Thuringians, and the kingdom of the Burgundians, and expanded Frankish hegemony through modern Bavaria and south of the Alps into northern Italy. Unlike other barbarian kingdoms such as those of the Huns or Ostrogoths, which evaporated almost as soon as their great founders died, the Frankish synthesis was enduring. Although the dynasty established by Clovis, called the Merovingian after a legendary ancestor, lasted only until the mid-eighth century, the Frankish kingdom was the direct ancestor of both France and Germany.

After Clovis' death in 511, his kingdom was divided among his four sons. This decision to fragment his lands probably resulted from a compromise agreement among his sons, his Germanic warriors, and his Roman advisors. For the next two hundred years the heart of the Frankish kingdom, the region between the Rhine and Loire rivers, was often divided into the kingdoms of Neustria, Burgundy, and Austrasia, each ruled by a Merovingian king. The outlying regions of Aquitaine and Provence to the south and Alemania, Thuringia, and Bavaria to the east were governed by Frankish dukes appointed by the kings. Still, the Frankish world was never as divided as Anglo-Saxon England. In the early eighth century a unified Frankish kingdom reemerged as the dominant force in Europe.

Living in the New Europe

The substitution of Germanic kings for imperial officials made few obvious differences in the lives of most inhabitants of Italy, Gaul, and Spain. The vast majority of Europeans were poor farmers whose lives centered on their villages and fields. For them the seasons in the agricultural year, the burdens of rent and taxation, and the frequent poor harvests, food shortages, famines, and epidemics were more important than empires and kingdoms. Nevertheless, fundamental if imperceptible changes were transforming ordinary life.

These changes took place at every level of society. The slaves and semifree peasants of Rome gradually began to form new kinds of social groups and to practice new forms of agriculture as they merged with the Germanic warrior-peasants. Elite Gallo-Roman landowners came to terms with their Frankish conquerors, and these two groups began to coalesce into a single, unified aristocracy. In the same way that Germanic and Roman society began to merge, Germanic and Roman traditions of governance united between the sixth and eighth centuries to create a powerful new kind of medieval kingdom.

Creating the European Peasantry

Three fundamental changes transformed rural society during the early Middle Ages. First, Roman slavery virtually disappeared. Next, the household emerged as the primary unit of social and economic organization. Finally, Christianity spread throughout the rural world.

Economics, not ethics, destroyed Roman slavery. In the kind of slavery typical of the Roman world, large gangs of slaves were housed in dormitories and directed in large-scale operations by overseers. This form of slavery demanded a highly organized form of estate management and could be quite costly since slaves had to be fed and housed year-round. Since slaves did not always reproduce at a rate sufficient to replace themselves, the supply had to be replenished from without. However, as the empire ceased to expand, the supply of fresh captives dwindled. As cities shrank, many markets for agricultural produce disappeared, making market-oriented, large-scale agriculture less profitable. Enterprising landlords in the west sold off some of their slaves to the east, particularly to the Muslims. Furthermore, the Germanic societies that settled in the west had no tradition of gang slavery.

As a result, from the sixth through the ninth centuries, owners abandoned the practice of keeping gang slaves in favor of the less complicated practice of establishing slave families on individual plots of land. The slaves and their descendants cultivated these plots, made annual payments to their owners, and also cultivated the undivided portions of the estate, the fruits of which went directly to the owner. Thus slaves became something akin to sharecroppers. Gradually they began to intermarry with colons and others who, though nominally free, found themselves in an economic situation much like that of slaves. By the ninth century, the distinction between slaves who had acquired traditional rights to their farms, or manses, and free peasants who held and worked manses belonging to others was blurred. By the tenth and eleventh centuries, peasant farmers throughout much of Europe were subject to the private justice of their landlords, no matter whether their ancestors had been slave or free. Although not slaves in the classical sense, the peasantry had fused into a homogeneous unfree population.

The division of estates into separate peasant holdings contributed to the second fundamental transformation of European peasant society: the formation of the household. Neither the Roman tradition of slave agriculture nor the Germanic tradition of clan organization had encouraged the household as the basic unit of society. Now individual slaves and their spouses were placed on manses, which they and their children were expected to cultivate. The household had become the basic unit of Western economy.

The household was, however, more than an economic unit. It was also the first level of government. The head of the household, whether slave or free, male or female—women, particularly widows, were often heads of households—exercised authority over its other members. This authority made the householder a link in the chain of the social order, which stretched from the peasant hovel to the royal court.

Households became the basic form of peasant life, but not all peasants could expect to establish their own household. The number of manses was limited, a factor that condemned many men and women to life within the household of a more fortunate relative or neighbor. On one ninth-century estate, for example, 43 percent of the peasant households contained more than one adult male. Some of these unmarried men lived with relatives or wealthier peasants until they could be established in their own household. Many others spent their whole lives as servants in the house of another.

Peasant life centered on the house, the village, and the field. In the Mediterranean world, peasants constructed their houses of fieldstone; in the north, they built primarily in wood. Often these structures consisted simply of two or three rooms in which dwelt both the human and animal members of the household. Archaeologists can often distinguish the areas of human and animal habitation in such houses only by the relatively higher frequency of animal dung in one section than in the other. The hovel was heated by the body warmth of the cattle and sheep and by a hearth fire. Smoke escaped, not through a chimney, but through a hole in the roof.

The rhythm of peasant life was tied to the agricultural cycle, which had changed little since antiquity. January and February were the dead season. During these dormant months, the family huddled together from the cold and tried to survive on the previous harvest. They lived on coarse bread made from the previous year's grain, onions and leeks for vitamins, and nuts gathered from the forest. They drank wine or, in the north, a thick beer, which was a major source of protein. On special occasions they might enjoy a bit of pork. In March, they trimmed the vines for the growing season. Cattle were put out to pasture in April. In May peasants cut the fodder needed by the lord's horses. June meant plowing, July haying, August harvesting. In September and October grapes were harvested and winter grain (an innovation of perhaps the eighth century) was planted. In November the new wine was stored in barrels, the grain was milled, and the pigs (the primary source of meat for peasants) were allowed into the forest to gorge themselves on nuts and grubs. December was slaughter month, and then the family faced another winter.

Although women and men worked together on the harvest, normally peasants divided labor into male and female tasks. Husbands and sons tended to the work in the fields. Wives and daughters cared for chickens, prepared the dark bread that was the staple of the peasant diet, spun, and wove.

Occasionally peasants used new tools or technical innovations in their labor. Some lords had established water mills for grinding grain on their estates. Here and there peasants used heavy plows capable of cutting and turning the heavy clay soil of northern Europe. Some far-sighted lords had their peasants fertilize the fields with lime to restore the soil, but ninth-century peasants resented the extra labor that this recent innovation required. Technological progress was sporadic and uneven, and agricultural returns were correspondingly low.

In fact, returns were much lower than they had been in antiquity. Careful Roman landlords, using better tools and coordinating the work of their slaves more efficiently, were accustomed to harvesting eight times as much grain as they had sown. Frankish estates were doing well if they recorded harvests of three or four to one. In some

"The labors of the months" was a popular motif in medieval art. This illustration from the Astronomical Notices *was found in Salzburg. The annual round of agricultural tasks, such as sowing and reaping and grape-picking, is depicted along with scenes of hunting and hawking.*

years, no more grain was harvested than the seed necessary to plant the following June. Peasants had to choose between starving through the winter or eating the seed and starving the following year. Actually, the choice was not theirs, but rather that of their aristocratic lords, whose noble life-style they were forced to support.

Peasant culture, like peasant society, experienced a fundamental transformation during the early Middle Ages. During this period the peasantry became Christian. In antiquity Christianity had been an urban phenomenon. The term for the rural population had long been synonymous with "unbelievers." They were called pagans, that is, the inhabitants of the countryside,

or *pagus*. The spread of Christianity throughout the rural world began in earnest in the sixth century, when bishops and monks began to replace the peasants' traditional agrarian cults with Christian feasts, rituals, and beliefs. In sixth-century Gaul, for example, peasants regularly held a three-day celebration beside a mountain lake into which they threw food and valuable objects as an offering to the local god. The local bishop was unable to convince them to abandon the practice. Instead, he built a church on the spot in honor of Saint Hilary of Poitiers and placed there relics of the saint. Peasants continued to travel to the lake to celebrate the feast, but now the feast was in honor of Hilary.

Christianity penetrated more deeply into rural society with the systematic establishment of parishes, or rural churches. By the ninth century this parish system began to cover Europe. Bishops founded parish churches in the villages of large estates, and owners were obligated to set aside one-tenth of the produce of their estates for the maintenance of the parish church. The priests who staffed these churches came from the local peasantry and received a basic education in Latin and in Christian ritual from their predecessors and from their bishops. The continuing presence of priests in each village had a profound effect on the daily lives of Europe's peasants. Christian ritual came to be a regular part of peasant life.

Creating the European Aristocracy

At the same time that a homogeneous peasantry was emerging from the blend of slaves and free farmers, a homogeneous aristocracy was evolving out of the mix of Germanic and Roman traditions. In Germanic society, the elite had owed its position to a combination of inherited status and wealth, perpetuated through military command. Families who produced great military commanders were thought to have a special war-luck granted by the gods. The war-luck bestowed on men and women of these families a near-sacred legitimacy.

This legitimacy made the aristocrats largely independent of their kings. In times of war kings might command, but otherwise the extent to which they could be said to govern aristocrats was minimal. The earliest Frankish laws, which prescribe payments, or wergeld, for offenses in place of unlimited blood feuds do not mention aristocrats. The reason is probably that the kings had no recognized authority to command aristocrats to forego their right to settle disputes among themselves. The freedom of the aristocracy meant freedom from royal governance.

The Roman aristocracy was also based on inheritance, but of land rather than leadership. During the third and fourth centuries Roman aristocrats' control of land extended over the persons who worked that land. At the same time, great landowners were able to free themselves from provincial government.

Like their Germanic counterparts, Roman aristocrats acquired a sacred legitimacy, but within the Christian tradition. They monopolized the office of bishop and became identified with the sacred and political traditions associated with the Church. The family of the Gallo-Roman bishop and historian, Gregory of

The Episcopal Kin of Gregory of Tours

Tours (539–94) exemplifies this aristocratic tradition. By the time he took office in 573, thirteen of the previous eighteen bishops of Tours had come from his family. In addition he was related to generations of bishops from Langres, Lyon, Clermont-Ferrand, and elsewhere.

In Spain and Italy, the religious differences separating Arians and orthodox Christians impeded the fusion of the Germanic and Roman aristocracies. In Gaul, the conversion of Clovis and his people facilitated the rapid blending of the two worlds. North of the Loire River, where the bulk of the Franks had settled, Roman aristocrats soon became Franks. By the mid-sixth century the descendants of Bishop Remigius of Reims, who had baptized Clovis, had Frankish names and considered themselves Franks. Still, the Roman aristocratic tradition of great landholders became an integral part of the identity of the Frankish elite.

In the late sixth century, this northern Frankish aristocracy found its own religious identity and legitimacy in the Irish monasticism introduced by Saint Columbanus (543–615) and other wandering monks. At home in Ireland, these monks had been accustomed to working not with kings but with leaders of clans. In Gaul they worked closely with the Frankish aristocrats, who encouraged them to build monasteries on their estates. Eventually these monasteries amassed huge landholdings and became major economic and political centers headed by aristocrats who abandoned secular life for the cloister. The abbots and abbesses who headed the monasteries were venerated after their deaths as saints and wonder-workers. Their descendants drew on the inherited prestige of being members of the "family of saints" in the same way that earlier aristocrats had claimed legitimacy as carriers of war-luck.

South of the Loire, conditions were decidedly different. Here Irish monasticism was less important than episcopal office. The few Frankish and Gothic families who had settled in the south were rapidly absorbed into the Gallo-Roman aristocracy, which drew its prestige from control of local religious and secular power. Latin speech and Roman culture distinguished these "Romans," regardless of their ancestry.

Aristocratic life was similar whether north or south of the Loire, in Anglo-Saxon England, Visigothic Spain, or Lombard Italy. Aristocratic family structures were loosely knit clans that traced descent from important ancestors through either the male or the female line. Clans jealously guarded their autonomy against rival clans and from royal authority.

The aristocratic life-style focused on feasting, on hospitality, and on the male activities of hunting and warfare. In southern Europe, great nobles lived in spacious villas, often surrounded by solid stone fortifications, an inheritance of Roman traditions. In the north, Frankish and Anglo-Saxon nobles lived in great wooden halls, richly decorated but lacking fortifications. In winter, both kinds of lordly residences were the centers of banqueting and drinking bouts. Here important aristocrats gathered their supporters, entertained them at extravagant banquets, fed them vast stores of food, wine, and beer, and lavished on them gifts of jewelry, weapons, and fine horses. Here too they received their rivals, planned their alliances, and settled their disputes.

Also during the fall and winter, aristocratic men spent much of their time hunting deer and wild boar in their forests. Hunting was not merely sport. Essentially it was preparation for war, the activity of the summer months. In March, as soon as the snows of winter had begun to melt and roads had become passable, aristocrats gathered their retainers, who had enjoyed their winter hospitality, and marched to war. The enemy varied. It might be rival families with whom feuds were nursed for generations. It might be raiding parties from a neighboring region. Or the warriors might join a royal expedition led by the king and directed against a rival kingdom. Whoever the enemy, warfare brought the promise of booty and, as important, glory.

Within this aristocratic society women played a wider and more active role than had been the case in either Roman or barbarian antiquity. In part women's new role was due to the influence of Christianity, which recognized the distinct—though always inferior—rights of women, fought

This scene is from the lid of the Franks Casket, a whalebone box that was made in the north of England at the beginning of the eighth century. The carving depicts Egil the Archer defending his home. The other sides of the box are carved with a mixture of Christian and pagan scenes.

against the barbarian tradition of allowing chieftains numerous wives, and recognized women's right to lead a cloistered religious life. In addition, the combination of Germanic and Roman familial traditions permitted women to participate in court proceedings, to inherit and dispose of property, and, if widowed, to serve as tutors and guardians for their minor children. Finally, the long absence of men at the hunt, at the royal court, or on military expeditions left wives in charge of the domestic scene for months or years at a time.

The religious life in particular opened to aristocratic women possibilities of autonomy and authority previously unknown in the West. Women administered large and wealthy institutions and even exercised this authority over mixed monasteries, in which men and women lived in separate quarters but recognized the rule of the abbess. Saint Hilda of Whitby (614–80), an Anglo-Saxon princess, for example, established and ruled a religious community that included both women and men. This community was one of the most important in England. Five monks of Whitby later became bishops, and kings and aristocrats regularly traveled to the monastery to ask Hilda's advice. It was in Hilda's community that the Synod of Whitby took place, and Hilda played an active role advising the king and assembled bishops.

Governing Europe

The combination in the early Middle Ages of the extremes of centralized Roman power and fragmented barbarian organization produced a wide variety of governmental systems. At one end of the spectrum were the politically fragmented Celtic and Slavic societies. At the other end were the Frankish kingdoms, in which descendants of Clovis, drawing on the twin heritages of Roman institutions and Frankish tradition, attempted not simply to reign but to rule.

Rulers and aristocrats both needed and feared each other. Kings had emerged out of the Germanic aristocracy and could rule only in cooperation with aristocrats. Aristocrats were primarily concerned with maintaining and expanding their own spheres of control and independence. They perceived royal authority over them or their dependents as a threat. Still, they needed kings. Strong kings brought victory against external foes and thus maintained the flow of booty to the aristocracy. Aristocrats in turn redistributed the spoils of war among their followers to preserve the bonds of warrior society. Thus under capable kings aristocrats were ready to cooperate, not as subjects but as partners.

Gregory of Tours provides an account that illustrates the nature of the relationship between king and aristocrat. After his victory at Soissons, Clovis was dividing up the booty when the bishop of the city approached him and asked him to return a large pitcher. Clovis wished to do so and asked his warriors to grant him the pitcher over and above Clovis' normal share of the spoils. All agreed except for one Frank, who struck the pitcher with his battle-ax, declaring, "You shall have none of this booty except your fair share." Clovis did nothing to this warrior until the annual military muster the following March. When he came to the man who had struck the pitcher, he berated him for the poor condition of his weapons and threw his ax to the ground. As the man bent over to pick it up, Clovis used his own ax to split open the man's head. "That," he said, "is for what you did to my pitcher in Soissons."

This story illustrates both the strength and the weakness of early medieval monarchs. Clovis was the most powerful Frankish king before the eighth century, yet even he was unable to redress a blatant affront to his authority except under very specific circumstances. As the successors of Germanic war leaders and late Roman generals, kings were primarily military commanders. During campaigns and at the annual "March-field," when the free warriors assembled, the king was all-powerful. At those times he could cut down his enemies with impunity. At other times, the king's role was strictly limited. His direct authority extended only over the members of his household and his personal warrior band.

The king's role in administering justice was similarly ambivalent. He was not the source of law, which was held to be simply the customs of the past, nor was he responsible for enforcing this customary law. Enforcement was the duty of individuals and families. Only if they wished did they bring their grievances to the king or his agents for arbitration or judgment. However, even though they could not formally legislate, kings effectively molded law and legal procedure by collecting, selecting, clarifying, and publishing customary laws. Again Clovis presents a model for such legislative activity in the compilation of Salic law made during his reign. Anglo-Saxon and Visigothic kings of the seventh through tenth centuries did the same.

As heirs of Roman governmental tradition, kings sought to incorporate these traditions into their roles. By absorbing the remains of local administration and taxation, kings acquired nascent governmental systems. Through the use of written documents, Roman scribes expanded royal authority beyond the king's household and personal following. Tax collectors continued to fill royal coffers with duties collected in markets and ports.

Finally, by assuming the role of protector of the Church, kings acquired the support of educated and experienced ecclesiastical advisors and the right to intervene in disputes involving clergy and laity. Further, as defenders of the Church, kings could claim a responsibility for the preservation of peace and the administration of justice—two fundamental Christian (but also Roman) tasks.

Early medieval kings had no fixed capitals from which they governed. Instead they were constantly on the move, supervising their kingdoms and consuming the produce of their estates. The arrival of the king and his entourage was a major event long remembered in a region. A chronicler writing years later recalled the arrival in Burgundy (eastern France) of the Frankish king Dagobert I (623–38):

> "The profound alarm that his coming caused among the Burgundian bishops, magnates and others of consequence was a source of general wonder; but his justice brought great joy to the poor."

Since kings could not be everywhere at once, they were represented locally by aristocrats who enjoyed royal favor. In the Frankish world these favorites were called *counts* and their districts *counties*. In England royal representatives were termed *ealdormen* and their regions were known as *shires*. Whether counts or ealdormen, these representatives were military commanders and judicial officers drawn from aristocratic families close to the king. Under competent and effective kings, partnership with these aristocratic families worked well. Under less competent rulers and during the reigns of minors, these families often managed to turn their districts into hereditary, almost autonomous regions. The same thing happened when rival members of the royal house sought supporters against their cousins and brothers. The sphere of royal authority shrank or expanded in large measure in response to the individual qualities of the king. The personality of the king mattered far more than the institution of kingship itself.

The Carolingian Achievement

The Merovingian dynasty initiated by Clovis presided over the synthesis of Roman and Germanic society. It was left to the Carolingians who followed to forge a new Europe. In the seventh century, members of the new aristocracy were able to take advantage of royal minorities and dynastic rivalries to make themselves into virtual rulers of their small territories. By the end of the century the kings had become little more than symbolic figures in the Frankish kingdoms. The real power was held by regional strongmen called dukes. The most successful of these aristocratic factions was that led by Charles Martel (ca. 688–741) and his heirs, known as the Carolingians.

This family had risen to prominence in the seventh century by controlling the office of mayor of the palace in Austrasia, the highest court official who advised the king as spokesman for the aristocracy. The Carolingians increased their influence by marrying their sons to daughters of other aristocratic families. In the late seventh century they extended their control to include Neustria and Burgundy as well as Austrasia. By the second quarter of the eighth century Charles Martel, while not king, was the acknowledged ruler of the Frankish kingdom.

Charles Martel was ruthless, ambitious, and successful. He crushed rivals in his own family, subdued competing dukes, and united the

Frankish realm. He was successful in part because he molded the Frankish cavalry into the most effective military force of the time. His mounted, heavily armored warriors, using the newly introduced stirrup to keep them steady on their mounts, were extremely effective but extremely costly. He financed them with property confiscated from his enemies and from the Church. In return for oaths of absolute fidelity he gave his followers, or vassals, estates, which they held as long as they served him faithfully. With this new army he practiced a scorched-earth policy against his opponents that left vast areas of Provence and Aquitaine desolate for decades.

Charles Martel looked beyond military power to the control of religious and cultural institutions. He supported Anglo-Saxon missionaries such as Boniface (ca. 680–755), who were trying to introduce on the Continent the Roman form of Christianity they knew in England. This hierarchal style of Christianity served Carolingian interests in centralization, especially since Charles appointed his loyal supporters as bishops and abbots. Missionaries and Frankish armies worked hand in hand to consolidate Carolingian rule.

The ecclesiastical policy that proved most crucial to later Carolingians was Charles' support of the Roman papacy. Charles caught the attention of Pope Gregory III (731–41) in 732, when he defeated a Muslim force near Tours, which had attempted to continue the northward expansion of Islam. A few years later, when the pope needed protection from the Lombards to maintain his central Italian territories, he sought and obtained help from the Frankish leader.

The alliance with the papacy solidified during the lifetime of Charles' son Pippin (ca. 714–68). Pippin inherited his father's power. However, since he was not of the royal Merovingian family, he had no more right to supreme authority than any other powerful aristocrat. Pippin needed more than the power of a king: he needed the title. No Frankish tradition provided a precedent by which a rival family might displace the Merovingians. Pippin turned instead to the pope. Building on his increasingly close relationship with the papacy and the Frankish church dominated by his supporters, Pippin sought legitimacy in religious authority. In a carefully orchestrated exchange between Pippin and Pope Zacharias (741–52), the latter declared that the individual who exercised the power of king ought also to have the title. Following this declaration the last Merovingian was deposed and in 751 a representative of the pope anointed Pippin king of the Franks.

The alliance between the new dynasty and the papacy marked the first union of royal legitimacy and ecclesiastical sanction in European history. Frankish, Gothic, and Anglo-Saxon kings had been selected on secular criteria. Kings combined royal descent with military power. Now the office of king required the active participation of the Church. The new Frankish kingship led Europe into the first political, social, and cultural restructuring of the West since the end of the Roman Empire.

Charlemagne and the Renewal of the West

Pippin's son Charlemagne was the heir of the political, religious, and social revolutions begun by his grandfather and father. He was a large man, over six feet tall, with piercing eyes, a robust physique, and a restless spirit. To his intimates he was a generous lord constantly surrounded by friends, whether at table consuming vast quantities of wine and roast, in the baths in Aachen, where he often swam with more than a hundred courtiers, or on the march with his Frankish army. To his enemies he was the man of iron—the grim and invincible warrior clad head to foot in steel, sweeping all before him. He was a conqueror, but he was also a religious reformer, a state builder, and a patron of the arts. As the leader of a powerful, united Frankish kingdom for over forty years, Charlemagne changed the West more profoundly than anyone since Augustus.

Almost every spring Charlemagne assembled his Frankish armies and led them against internal or external enemies. He subdued the Aquitainians and Bavarians, conquered the kingdom of the Lombards and assumed the title of King of the Lombards, crushed the Saxons, annexed the Spanish region of Catalonia, and destroyed the vast Pannonian kingdom of the Avars. In wars of aggression, his armies were invincible. The heavy cavalry first employed by Charles Martel simply mowed down the more lightly armored and equipped enemy. Moreover, Charlemagne's logistical support was unmatched in the early Middle Ages. His ability to ship men and supplies down the Danube enabled him to capture the enormous hoard of gold the Avars had amassed from raids and annual payments by the Byzantines. As Einhard, Charlemagne's councillor and advisor, boasted, "These Franks, who until then had seemed almost paupers, now discovered so much gold and silver in the palace and captured so much previous booty in their battles, that it could rightly be maintained that they had in all justice taken from the Huns (Avars) what these last had unjustly stolen from other nations."

War booty fueled Charlemagne's renewal of European culture. As a Christian king he considered it his duty to reform the spiritual life of his kingdom and to bring it into line with his concept of the divinely willed order. To achieve this goal, he needed a dedicated and educated clergy. In the previous three centuries, secular schools had disappeared and Frankish monasteries had ceased to be centers of learning. Most of the native clergy were poorly educated and indifferent in their observance of the rules of religious life. Creating a reformed, educated clergy was an effort every bit as complex and demanding as organizing the army.

Charlemagne recruited leading intellectuals from England, Spain, Ireland, and Italy to the royal court to lead a thorough educational program. The architect of his cultural reform, Alcuin of York (ca. 732–804), directed a school for young lay and ecclesiastical aristocrats in the king's palace and encouraged the king to finance a wide variety of educational programs. Charlemagne supported schools in great monasteries such as Fulda and St. Gall for the training of young clerics and laymen. Schools needed books. Charlemagne's educational reformers scoured Italy for fading copies of works by Virgil, Horace, and Tacitus with the same determination that his builders hunted antique marbles and columns for is chapel. Alcuin and others corrected and copied classical texts corrupted by generations of haphazard transmission. The earliest extant manuscripts of virtually all the classics of Roman antiquity date from the late eighth or early ninth century. Caroline minuscule, the new style of

This bronze equestrian statue of a king dates from the ninth century. The rider wears the typical Frankish attire of hose, tunic, and long riding cloak. The subject is often identified as Charlemagne.

handwriting developed to preserve these texts, was so clear and easily readable that during the Renaissance, humanists (mistakenly thinking that these manuscripts dated from Roman times) adopted it as their standard script. It remains essentially the form of printing common today this book is printed in a version of Caroline minuscule.

Charlemagne's Empire, 814

The first decades of educational reform produced little that was new, but the reformers of this era laid the necessary foundation for what has been called the Carolingian renaissance. Their successors in the ninth century built on this foundation to make creative contributions in theology, philosophy, and historiography, and to some extent in literature. For the first time since Augustine, the West produced a really first-class theologian and philosopher, John Scotus Erigena (ca. 810–ca. 877), who mastered Greek and created a unique and influential synthesis of Neoplatonic philosophy.

The pursuit of learning was not a purely clerical affair. In the later ninth century, great aristocrats were highly literate and collected their own personal libraries. Count Everard of Friuli, who died in 866, left an estate that included over fifty books, among them works by Augustine, histories, saints' lives, and seven law books. Elite women participated fully in the Carolingian renaissance. One example is the noblewoman Dhuoda, who composed a manual of instruction for her son. Her writings show her as a woman of deep piety and learning familiar with the Bible,

the works of Augustine, Gregory the Great, and other theologians, and some classical authors as well.

Educational reform went hand in hand with reform of ecclesiastical institutions. Charlemagne and his son Louis the Pious (814–40) worked to establish the Benedictine rule as the norm for monastic life. They also tried to ensure that parish clergy were competent and committed to serving the needs of the people. The goal was the formation of a purified and organized clergy performing its essential role of celebrating Christian ritual and praying for the Frankish king. At the same time, the monasteries were to provide competent clerics to serve the royal administration at every level.

These reforms were expensive. The fiscal reorganization of ecclesiastical institutions was as far-reaching as their cultural reform. For the first time, Frankish synods or councils made tithing mandatory, specifying that one-tenth of all agricultural harvests were to go to the maintenance of church buildings, the support of the clergy, and the care of the poor. Monasteries grew rich with donations of land and slaves captured in battle. Monastic estates were reorganized, records of dues and revenues revised for greater efficiency, and dependent workers shifted around to maximize productivity.

Carolingian Government

Charlemagne recognized that conquest alone could not unify his enormous kingdom with its vast differences in languages, laws, customs, and peoples. The glue that held it together was loyalty to him and to the Roman Church.

In the tradition of his father and grandfather, he appointed as counts throughout Europe members of the great Frankish families who had been loyal to his family for generations. Thus he created what might be termed an "imperial aristocracy" truly international in scope. In addition to supervising the royal estates in their counties, each spring these counts led the local military contingent, which included all the free men of the county. Counts also presided over local courts, which exercised jurisdiction over the free persons of the county. The king maintained his control over the counts by sending teams of emissaries, or *missi dominici*, composed of bishops and counts to examine the state of each county.

Charlemagne recognized that while his representatives might be drawn from Frankish families, he could not impose Frankish legal and cultural traditions on all his subjects. The only universal system that might unify the kingdom was Roman Christianity. Unity of religious practices, directed by the reformed and educated clergy, would provide spiritual unity. Furthermore, since the clergy could also participate in the administration of the kingdom, they could guarantee administrative unity as well. Carolingian monarchs did not intend the enriched and reformed Church to be independent of royal authority; it was rather to be an integral part of the Carolingian system of government. However, at least some of the educated clerics and lay aristocrats who participated in the system formed a clear political ideology based on Augustinian concepts of Christian government. They attempted to educate Charlemagne and his successors to the duties of a king: maintaining peace and providing justice.

The mobile palace was the center of Carolingian government. It included the royal household and ecclesiastical and secular aristocrats who directed the various activities of the central administration. Within this palace the king held his own court. There too clerics maintained written records, produced official records of royal grants or decisions called *diplomas*, and prepared *capitularies*, which were written instructions for the implementation of royal directives at the local level.

Carolingian government was no modern bureaucracy or state system. The laymen and clerics who served the king were tied to him by personal oaths of loyalty rather than by any sense of dedication to a state or nation. Still, the attempts at governmental organization were far more sophisticated than anything that the West had

In this illustration from the Coronation Sacramentary of Charles the Bald, Emperor Charlemagne is shown flanked by Pope Gelasius and Pope Gregory the Great.

seen for four centuries or would see again for another four. The system of counts and missi provided the most effective system of government prior to the thirteenth century and served as the model for subsequent medieval rulers.

The size of Charlemagne's empire approached that of the old Roman Empire in the west. Only Britain, southern Italy, and parts of Spain remained outside Frankish control. With the reunification of most of the West and the creative adaptation of Roman traditions of culture and government, it is not surprising that Charlemagne's advisors began to compare his empire to that of Constantine. This comparison was accentuated by Charlemagne's conquest of

A page from the Book of Kells, which was made around 800. It was the work of scribes in Columba's monastery at Kells, Ireland. The intricate interlaced decorations of the letters are derived from traditional Celtic and Anglo-Saxon designs.

Lombard Italy and his protection of Pope Leo III—a role traditionally played by the Byzantine emperors. By the end of the eighth century the throne in Constantinople was held by a woman. Irene (752–802) was powerful and capable, but western male leaders considered her unfit by reason of her sex for such an office. All these factors finally converged in one of the most momentous events in Western political history: Charlemagne's imperial coronation on Christmas Day in the year 800.

Historians debate the precise meaning of this event, particularly since Charlemagne was said to have remarked afterward that he would never have entered St. Peter's Basilica in Rome had he known what was going to happen. Presumably he meant that he wished to be proclaimed emperor by his Frankish people rather than by the pope, since this is how he had his son Louis the Pious acclaimed emperor in 813. Moreover, Charlemagne apparently saw his title of emperor more as a reflection of his accomplishments than as a political title indicating the foundation of his authority.

Nevertheless, the imperial coronation of 800 subsequently took on great significance. Louis attempted to make his imperial title the sole basis for his rule, and for the next thousand years Germanic kings traveled to Rome to receive the imperial diadem and title from the pope. In so doing they inadvertently strengthened papal claims to enthrone—and at times to dethrone—emperors.

Carolingian Art

The same creative adaptation of the classical heritage that gave birth to a new Western empire produced a new Western art. The artistic traditions of the barbarian world consisted almost entirely of the decoration of small, portable objects such as weapons, jewelry, and, after conversion, manuscripts. Although some Mediterranean motifs penetrated northward, barbarian art was essentially nonrepresentational and consisted primarily of elaborate, interlaced geometric forms of great sophistication and craftsmanship. When animal and human forms did appear, as in the Lindisfarne Gospels, produced around 700, or the magnificent Book of Kells,

The Twenty-fourth Psalm (Twenty-third in the Vulgate), from the Utrecht Psalter, Reims, made in about 820. The imagery of the drawings in red-brown ink and the arrangement of the script on the page recall models from late antiquity.

created by Irish monks around a century later, they were transformed into intricate patterns of decoration.

For Charlemagne and his reformers, such abstract art was doubly inappropriate. Not only was it too distant from the Roman heritage that they were trying to emulate, but neither could it be used for instruction or propaganda. Thus Charlemagne invited Italian and Byzantine artists and artisans to his kingdom to teach a form of representational art that would decorate as well as educate. However, these southern traditions were no more slavishly followed by northern artists than were Roman political traditions wholly taken over by Charlemagne's government. Instead the artistic styles from the East were transformed. The synthesis of Mediterranean and northern artistic traditions produced a dynamic,

plastic style of representation in which figures seem intensely alive and active. These figures, which appear in manuscript illuminations, frescoes, ivories, and bas reliefs, are often arranged in narrative cycles that engage the mind as well as the eye. The Utrecht Psalter is the consummate masterpiece of this tradition. Each psalm is accompanied by a crowded, complex visual interpretation of the text in which verbal and visual metaphors move from scene to scene. In its arrangement and use of classical allusions, the whole work is clearly intended to echo classical antiquity. And yet the execution breathes with a dramatic vision and reality beyond any of its numerous classical models and is fully equal to the religious themes it represents. In art as in every other sphere, the Carolingian rebirth was actually a new birth.

A Tour of Europe in the Ninth Century

The Carolingian empire stretched from the Baltic Sea to the Adriatic and linked, through a network of commerce and exchange, the Germanic and Slavic worlds of the north, the Islamic world of Spain and the Near East, and the Mediterranean world of Byzantium. Carolingian kings rebuilt roads, bridges, and ports to facilitate trade. Charlemagne also reformed Western currency, abandoning gold coinage in favor of the more easily obtainable and liquid silver.

Silver was the medium of exchange at the northern ports of Durstede near the mouth of the Rhine and Quentovic near modern Étaples, where Frankish merchants haggled with Anglo-Saxon and Danish traders over cloth, furs, and amber from the Baltic. Merchants along the Slavic frontier and down the Danube dealt primarily in human commodities. Great slave trains passed from these regions into the Rhine region. In Verdun young boys were castrated at "eunuch factories" before being sent down the Rhone River to the cities of lower Provence, where they were sold to Muslim agents from Spain and North Africa. Jewish and Greek merchants supplied the Frankish church and aristocracy with luxury goods from Constantinople and the East. The travels of such a merchant in the early ninth century might begin with a short trip from Quentovic to the English coast and then continue clockwise around the Frankish world.

England

A continental visitor in England would be well treated. In 796 Charlemagne had written to King Offa of Mercia (757–96), offering English merchants protection in his kingdom and agreeing that "Our men, if they suffer any injustice in your dominion, are to appeal to the judgment of your equity, lest any disturbance should arise." Offa, the only king Charlemagne referred to as "brother," ruled a prosperous southeast England and was acknowledged as Bretwalda by other Anglo-Saxon rulers. His success was based partly on military actions against the Welsh. He had led raids deep into Wales and had constructed a great dike 25 feet high and 150 miles long along the whole length of the Welsh frontier. Charlemagne's letter indicates, though, that Mercia's prosperity was also based on extensive trading with the Continent, a trade in which Anglo-Saxon woolens and silver were exchanged for wine, oil, and other products of the Continent.

Mercian supremacy did not long survive Offa. In the constant warfare among Anglo-Saxon kingdoms during the first half of the ninth century Mercia fell to Wessex. The cycle of rise and fall of little kingdoms might have continued had the Vikings not come onto the scene. These Scandinavian raiders had been harassing the coast since 786. They did not pose a serious threat to England, however, until 865, when a great Viking army interested not in raiding but in conquest landed north of the Humber River. All but one of the Anglo-Saxon kingdoms were destroyed. Three kings were killed and a fourth was forced to abdicate.

The surviving king, Alfred of Wessex (870–99), reorganized his army, established a network of fortifications, created a navy, and thus temporarily halted the Viking conquest. Still, he realized that his military achievement could be consolidated only by the transformation of his political base. Few of Alfred's contemporaries saw him as the savior of England. He had first to win the loyalty of people in his own kingdom and then attract that of Anglo-Saxons outside it.

He won support by reforming the legal and cultural foundations of his kingdom. Alfred's legal reforms aimed to reassure subjects of the various Anglo-Saxon kingdoms of equal treatment. At the same time they emphasized the importance of oaths of loyalty and the gravity of treason. Alfred further reassured Anglo-Saxon nobles by arranging marriage alliances with influential noble families. Finally, Alfred inaugurated a religious and cultural program to extend literacy and learning so that his people might better understand and follow God's word. Because by this time Latin was almost entirely unknown in England, Alfred and his reformers used the vernacular Anglo-Saxon. Alfred encouraged the translation of the greatest books of the Christian tradition into Anglo-Saxon, even translating some of them himself.

By the time Alfred died in 899, southern England was united under Wessex leadership. The north, from the Thames to Chester, was occupied and colonized by Danes. In this region, known as the Danelaw, the Vikings settled down as farmers and slowly merged with the local population.

Scandinavia

Scandinavians in England were merchants as well as raiders. They sold furs, amber, and fish for English silver and cloth. A merchant interested in the northern trade might depart England from York and travel down the Ouse and the Humber to the North Sea. To make this passage, he might sail with a Scandinavian merchant-Viking in his longboat, that supreme expression of Viking culture. These magnificent ships, over seventy feet long, were fast, flexible, and easily maneuverable. They allowed Scandinavians to cross the ocean to America or to navigate the shallow rivers of Europe. A merchant's journey would begin with passage across the Channel, followed by a two-day sail north along the coast of Jutland to the mouth of the Eider. From here travelers could take advantage of the newly established trade route that crossed the peninsula to Hedeby at the head of the Slie Fjord on the Baltic, thus avoiding the long and dangerous sea voyage around The Skaw. After a few days a serious trader would press on, passing the Swedish archipelago, out past Öland and Gotland, through the narrow straits where Stockholm now stands, to Birka, the greatest port of Scandinavia. Here Danes, Swedes, Franks, Frisians, Anglo-Saxons, Balts, Greeks, and Arabs met to trade furs, ivory, and amber for weapons, fine English cloth, silver, and gold.

Like England, Scandinavia had long been an area of Frankish commercial and political interest. The Saxons had previously formed a buffer between the Scandinavians and the Frankish world, but Charlemagne's conquests had brought the two societies into direct contact.

Scandinavian society resembled Germanic society of the first century. It was composed of three social classes. At the top were wealthy chiefs or *jarlar* (earls) who had numerous servants, slaves, and free retainers. At the bottom were thralls, or bondsmen. In between were peasant freeholders, who formed the bulk of the population. Scandinavians lived for personal glory and war booty. Military ability and political cunning were equally prized, in women as well as men. In this society women enjoyed considerable freedom and authority that shocked more "civilized" observers. An Arab merchant who visited Hedeby in 950 reported that women could claim the right to divorce whenever they wished. But in the ninth century internal developments began to threaten the traditional independence of men and women alike, contributing to the Scandinavian expansion into the rest of Europe.

Scandinavian kings were traditionally selected by groups of earls and exercised a position more as first among equals than as ruler. However, around the end of the eighth century, possibly in imitation of Frankish and Anglo-Saxon royalty, Scandinavian kings began to consolidate power at home and to look to the wealthy Anglo-Saxon and Frankish worlds as sources of booty and glory. Earls and royal pretenders, threatened or displaced by the kings, also began to go "viking," that is, raiding, in order to replace abroad what they had lost at home.

The directions in which Northmen went viking depended on the region of Scandinavia from which they came. Swedes looked east, trading with the Slavic world and Byzantium. Norwegians looked to Ireland and Scotland and later to Greenland, Iceland, and North America. The Danes tended to focus on England and the Frankish empire.

Swedish merchant-Vikings, known as the *Rus'*, traveled down the Volga, Dvina, and Dnepr rivers as far as the Black and Caspian seas in search of furs and slaves. There they met the trading routes of the Byzantine Empire and the caliphate of Baghdad. Rus' fortified trading settlements at Novgorod, Smolensk, and Kiev became the nuclei of a Slavic-Scandinavian political unit to which they eventually gave their name: Russia.

Norwegians began their viking in the western islands in the late eighth century. Ireland, until then undisturbed either by Roman or Germanic invaders, was the first victim. Other Norwegians raided south along the coast of the Frankish kingdom, Spain, and even into the Mediterranean where they raided Provence, North Africa, and Italy. There a wily Norwegian plundered the city of Luna (which he mistook for Rome—he had probably never before seen a city of any size) by a ruse so bold that it captured the imagination of even the Franks. Unable to take the town by storm, the commander had his men inform the Italians that the Norwegian leader had died. Since he had been a Christian, they wished him to receive Christian burial. When the chieftain's body was brought into the city by his "mourning" followers, he suddenly rose from the dead, killed the bishop, and then he and his men sacked the town.

The political consolidation in Norway under Harold Finehair (860–933), which culminated in 872, led more Norwegians to go viking, as earls who objected to Harold's consolidation went abroad to maintain their freedom. Some settled in the Faroe Islands, while others colonized Iceland.

The southernmost Scandinavians, the Danes, were most intimately familiar with the Frankish and Anglo-Saxon realms. During the reigns of Charlemagne's successors Danish viking progressed from scattered raids against wealthy monasteries or trading towns like Durstede to organized expeditions and finally to massive conquests. Some of these Vikings, led by Danish kings, colonized whole areas such as Northumbria and the region of the mouth of the Seine. It was this region that later became known as Normandy— land of the Northmen.

The Slavic World

A merchant in Scandinavia might join an expedition of Swedish Rus' to cross the Baltic Sea and enter the Slavic world in search of ermine and slaves. Here too the Carolingians' effects were felt, both in merchant activity and in the presence of imperialist armies and missionaries. The Slavic world of the ninth century was a rapidly changing amalgam of Germanic and Slavic peoples whose ultimate orientation—north to Scandinavia, east to Constantinople, or west to Aachen—was an open question.

In antiquity and the early Middle Ages distinctions between Slavic and Germanic peoples were hazy, and the development of Slavic society and culture was quite similar to that of the Germans. In the sixth century, Slavic tribes had begun to filter west. In the seventh century, a Frank named Samo (d. ca. 660) organized a brief but powerful confederation of Slavs in the area between the Sudeten Mountains and the eastern Alps. For a time this confederation resisted both the Avars and the Merovingians.

In the following century the Great Moravian empire developed out of Slavic tribes along the March River. Both the Byzantine and Carolingian empires sought to bring Moravia into their spheres of influence. In the middle of the ninth century Frankish, Italian, and Greek missionaries began to compete to organize a Christian church in this Slavic empire. In 852 a Slavic prince, particularly suspicious of the Franks, turned to the Greeks. He encouraged the missionary efforts of Cyril and Methodius, who enjoyed the encouragement of both the Byzantines and the papacy. Through their translation of liturgical texts into Slavonic, for which they probably invented the Cyrillic script used today in Russia, they not only laid the basis for a Slavic church but they also began a tradition of Slavic literacy.

The promising beginning made by the two brothers was short-lived, as the Franks feared an independent Slavic church. In 864 the Carolingian king Louis the German (843–76) conquered Moravia. Methodius, who had been appointed archbishop of Moravia and Pannonia by the pope, was imprisoned in a German monastery for the rest of his life. The Frankish hegemony lasted only a few decades. In 895 a new steppe people, the Magyars, or Hungarians, swept into Pannonia as had the Huns and Avars before them. These new invaders destroyed the Franks' puppet Moravian empire and split the Slavic world in two. The south Slavs in the present-day Balkans were cut off from the northern Slavs in what is now Poland, Russia, and the Ukraine.

The Magyar kingdom proved a greater threat to the Franks than the Slavs or Avars. The Magyars not only conquered Pannonia as far as the Enns River, but they raided deep into the Carolingian empire. For fifty years swift bands of Magyar horsemen crossed the Alps and pillaged the Po Valley, terrorizing the eastern portions of the empire, and even striking as far west as modern Burgundy.

Muslim Spain

The Slavic world was not only in contact with the Christian societies of Byzantium and the West. Muslim merchants used Arab gold to buy furs and slaves from Rus' traders at settlements along the Dnepr. A Spanish merchant might depart from Kiev and, to avoid the Magyars, travel down the Dnepr to the Black Sea, past Constantinople, and then across the length of the Mediterranean to Al-Andalus, as the Muslims called Spain.

After the disintegration of the Umayyad caliphate (see pp. 214–215), the last Umayyad, 'Abd ar-Rahman I (731–88), made his way to Spain, where in 756 he established an independent emirate. Under the centralized control of the Umayyad emirs, the economic and cultural life of urban Spain, which had stagnated under the Visigoths, experienced a renaissance as vital as that taking place across the Pyrenees in the Frankish empire.

To secure the emirate, 'Abd ar-Rahman and his successors had to overcome internal division and external aggression. The Spanish population included an elite minority of Arabs, recently arrived Syrians, North African Berbers, converted Spaniards, Christian Spaniards, and Jews. In addition, Frankish aggression and Scandinavian Vikings continually harassed Al-Andalus.

In the short run, 'Abd ar-Rahman secured control by brute force. Relying on a professional army composed mainly of slaves, the emirs crushed revolts mounted by various Muslim factions. They strengthened a series of semi-autonomous districts, or marches, commanded by military governors as buffers against the Frankish kingdom to the north. Finally, they established a line of guard posts along the coast to protect themselves against the Northmen.

In the long run, the emirs sought stability in religion and law. They presented themselves as the champions and protectors of Islam, assuming in 926 the titles of "caliph," "commander of the believers," and "defender of the religion of God," thus building a religious foundation for their rule. Likewise, they cultivated the study and application of Islamic law as a source of justice and social order.

The economic prosperity of Al-Andalus was based on an enlightened system of agriculture, which included the introduction of oranges, rice, sugarcane, and cotton from the eastern Mediterranean. Complementing agriculture was a renewed urban life bolstered by vigorous trade to the north, east, and south. From the later ninth century, this trade was supplemented by raiding expeditions into Italy and southern Gaul. In the ninth and tenth centuries, Spain was the most prosperous region of Europe and one of the wealthiest areas of the Muslim world.

In this climate of security and prosperity developed the most sophisticated and refined culture in the West. Arabic poetry and art developed in a manner exactly the opposite of that in the Carolingian world. Poetry, visual art, and architecture deemphasized physical forms and encouraged abstraction and meditation. Meditation drew the individual away from the reality of objects and images toward the unseen divinity. Such abstract, contemplative art did not develop in western Christendom for centuries.

Alien, dynamic, and potentially threatening neighbors surrounded the Carolingian kingdom. To the west was Anglo-Saxon England, to the east were the Slavic and Byzantine worlds. Scandinavia lay to the north, and Al-Andalus threatened to the south. In the later ninth and tenth centuries, the Frankish kingdom collapsed, due in part to the actions of these neighbors, but primarily to its own internal weaknesses.

After the Carolingians: From Empire to Lordships

Charlemagne, despite his imperial title, had remained dependent on his traditional power base, the Frankish aristocracy. For them, learned concepts of imperial renovation meant little. They wanted wealth and power. Under Charlemagne, the empire's prosperity and relative internal peace had resulted largely from continued, successful expansion at the expense of neighbors. Its economy had been based on plunder and the redistribution of booty among the aristocracy and wealthy churches. As wars of conquest under Charlemagne gave place to defensive actions against Magyars, Vikings, and Saracens, the supply of wealth dried up. Aristocratic supporters had to be rewarded with estates within the empire. Aristocrats thus became enormously wealthy and powerful. Count Everard, whose library was mentioned earlier (p. 224), left to his sons estates scattered from Friuli in northern Italy to modern-day Belgium.

Competition among Charlemagne's descendants as well as grants to the aristocracy weakened central authority. By fate rather than by design, Charlemagne had bequeathed a united empire to his son Louis the Pious (814–40). Charlemagne had intended to follow Frankish custom and divide his estate among all his sons but only Louis survived him. Louis' three sons, in contrast, fought one another over their inheritance, and in 843 they divided the empire among them. The eldest son, Lothair (840–55), who inherited his father's imperial title, received an unwieldy middle portion that stretched from the Rhine south through Italy. Louis the German (840–876) received the eastern portions of the empire. The youngest son, Charles the Bald (840–77), was allotted the western portions. In time the western kingdom became France, and the eastern kingdom became the core of Germany. The middle kingdom, which included modern Holland, Belgium, Luxembourg, Lorraine (or Lotharingia, from Lothair), Switzerland, and northern Italy, remained a disputed region into the twentieth century.

The disintegration of the empire meant much more than its division among Charlemagne's heirs. In no region were his successors able to provide the degree of peace and public control that he had established. The Frankish armies, designed for wars of aggression, were too clumsy and slow to deal with the lightning raids of Northmen, Magyars, and Saracens. The constant need to please aristocratic supporters made it impossible for kings to prevent aristocrats from absorbing free peasants and churches into their economic and political spheres. Increasingly, these magnates were able to transform the offices of count and bishop into inherited familial positions. They also determined who would reign in their kingdoms and sought kings who posed no threat to themselves.

Most aristocrats saw this greater autonomy as their just due. Only dukes, counts, and other local lords could organize resistance to internal and external foes at the local level. They needed both economic means and political authority to provide protection and maintain peace. These

The Division of Charlemagne's Empire

resources could be acquired only at the expense of royal power. Thus during the late ninth and tenth centuries, much of Europe found its equilibrium at the local level as public powers, judicial courts, and military authority became the private possession of wealthy families. Charlemagne's empire had become a patchwork of local lordships.

Ultimately, new royal families emerged from among these local leaders. The family of the counts of Paris, for example, gained enormous prestige from the fact that they had led the successful defense of the city against the Vikings in 885–886. For a time they alternated with Carolingians as kings of the West Franks. After the

THE CAROLINGIANS

Charles Martel ca. 688–741

Pippin
King of the Franks 751–768

CHARLEMAGNE
King of the Franks 768–814
Emperor 800–814

LOUIS the PIOUS
Emperor 814–840

LOTHAIR I
Emperor 840–855

LOUIS the GERMAN
King of the East Franks 843–876

CHARLES THE BALD
King of the West Franks
843–877
Emperor 875–877

CARLOMAN
King of
Bavaria
876–880

LOUIS
King of
Saxony
876–882

CHARLES the FAT
King of the
Franks 884–887
Emperor 884–887

LOUIS II
King of the West Franks
877–879

ARNULF
King of the East Franks
887–899
Emperor 896–899

LOUIS III
King of the
West Franks
879–882

CARLOMAN
King of the
West Franks
879–884

CHARLES the SIMPLE
King of the
West Franks
893–923

LOUIS the CHILD
King of the East Franks
899–911

LOUIS IV
King of the West Franks
936–954

LOUIS
Emperor
855–875

CHARLES
King of
Provence
855–863

LOTHAIR II
King of
Lorraine
855–869

LOTHAIR
King of the West Franks
954–986

CHARLES
Duke of
Lorraine

LOUIS V
King of the West Franks
986–987

ascension of Hugh Capet in 987, they entirely replaced the Carolingians.

In a similar manner, the eastern German kingdom, which was divided into five great duchies, began to elect non-Carolingians as kings. In 919 the dukes of this region elected as their king Duke Henry of Saxony (919–36), who had proven his abilities fighting the Danes and Magyars. Henry's son, Otto the Great (936–73), proved to be a strong ruler who subdued the other dukes and definitively crushed the Magyars. In 962 Otto was crowned emperor by Pope John XII (955–64), thus reviving the empire of Charlemagne, although only in its eastern half. However, the dukes of this eastern kingdom chafed constantly at the strong control the Ottonians attempted to exercise at their expense. Although the empire Otto reestablished endured until 1806, he and his successors never matched the political or cultural achievements of the Carolingians.

By the tenth century, the early medieval kingdoms, based on inherited Roman notions of universal states and barbarian traditions of charismatic military leadership, had all ended in failure. After the demise of the Carolingian empire, the West began to find stability at a more local but also more permanent level. The local nature of western society did not mean, however, that the Roman and Carolingian traditions were forgotten. Carolingian religious reform, classical learning, and political ideology were preserved in the following centuries.

Church reform took on new life in 909 with the foundation of the monastery of Cluny in eastern France. Cluniac monks, drawn from the lesser aristocracy, were God's shock troops, fighting evil with their prayers with the same vigor that their secular cousins fought the enemy with their swords. Inspired by the monastic program of Louis the Pious and granted immunity from secular interference, Cluny became the center of an extraordinary expansion of Benedictine monasticism throughout the West.

The revival of classical learning begun in Carolingian schools, although hampered by the new wave of invasions that began in the later ninth century, continued in centers such as St. Gall, Auxerre, and Corvey. During the late ninth and tenth centuries western Christian civilization spread north and east. By the year 1000 Scandinavia, Poland, Bohemia, and even Hungary had become Christian kingdoms with national churches whose bishops were approved by the pope.

Among the aristocracy, just as all restraints on this warrior elite seemed to have been thrown off, a gradual process of transformation of their material and mental world began. Encouraged by Cluniac monasticism and by episcopal exhortations, nobles began to consider limiting their violence against one another and of placing it instead in the service of Christendom.

According to a ninth-century legend, Charlemagne once dreamed that he was visited by a sword-carrying spirit from the other world. The sword, a gift to the emperor from God, bore on its blade four Germanic words: *Rhat, Radoleiba, Nasg,* and *Enti.* The next day Charlemagne explained to his courtiers that the dream was a prophecy of the future. *Rhat* was the assistance God had given Charlemagne in conquering his enemies. *Radoleiba* indicated how, under Charlemagne's son, all of this would quickly dissipate. *Nasg* foretold the greed of his grandsons, who would allow their followers to plunder the Church and spread poverty through the land. *Enti* indicated the end, either of his royal family or of the world.

The anonymous author of this legend recognized that, although the Magyar, Viking, and Saracen raids contributed to the disintegration of the Carolingian empire, their role was secondary. The internal dynamics of the Frankish world and its unresolved social and political tensions were the essential causes for the collapse of the Carolingian synthesis.

In the long run, however, the Carolingian synthesis left a powerful and enduring legacy. At the start of the Middle Ages in the West, a variety of Germanic kingdoms experimented with a whole spectrum of ways to reconcile the twin elements of barbarian and Roman tradition. The Ostrogoths attempted to preserve the two as separate entities and soon vanished. The Visigoths sought unification through coercion and found themselves isolated and weakened. In England, Germanic invaders sought to replace Roman traditions entirely. Only the Franks found a lasting means of amalgamating Roman and Germanic societies.

The key elements of this synthesis were orthodox Christianity, Roman administration, and Frankish military kingship. Between 500 and 800, these three elements coalesced into a vital new civilization. Although the political structure created by Charlemagne did not survive his grandsons, the Frankish model proved enduring in every other respect. The cultural renaissance laid the foundation of all subsequent European intellectual activities. The alliance between Church and monarchy provided the formula for European kings for almost a thousand years. The administrative system with its central and local components, its counts and its missi, its diplomas and capitularies, provided the model for later medieval government in England and on the Continent. Finally, the idea of the Carolingian empire, the symbol of European unity, has never entirely disappeared from the West.

Suggestions for Further Reading

The Making of the Barbarian Kingdoms

Lucien Musset, *The Barbarian Invasions* (University Park, PA: Penn State University Press, 1975). A survey of the barbarian peoples in late antiquity and the early Middle Ages.

* Herwig Wolfram, *History of the Goths* (Berkeley, CA: University of California Press, 1987). An outstanding study of the formation of the Goths in late antiquity.

Thomas Burns, *The Ostrogoths* (Bloomington, IN: Indiana University Press, 1984). A recent study of Italy under the Goths.

Edward James, *The Origins of France From Clovis to the Capetians 500–1000* (London: Macmillan, 1982). A brief survey of the Franks with special attention to the archaeological sources.

* Patrick J. Geary, *Before France and Germany: The Origins and Transformation of the Merovingian World* (New York: Oxford University Press, 1988). A study of the Merovingians from the perspective of late Roman traditions.

James Campbell, ed., *The Anglo-Saxons* (Oxford: Phaidon, 1982). A collection of essays on Anglo-Saxon England by an outstanding group of archaeologists and historians.

* Indicates paperback edition available.

Living in the New Europe

Suzanne Fonay Wemple, *Women in Frankish Society: Marriage and the Cloister 500–900* (Philadelphia: University of Pennsylvania Press, 1981). A pioneering study of women in the early Middle Ages.

* David Herlihy, *Medieval Households* (Cambridge, MA: Harvard University Press, 1985). An important survey of medieval peasant society.

The Carolingian Achievement

* Rosamond McKitterick, *The Frankish Kingdoms Under the Carolingians, 751–987* (New York: Longmans, 1983). A very detailed study of Carolingian history with an emphasis on intellectual developments.

* Heinrich Fichtenau, *The Carolingian Empire: The Age of Charlemagne* (Toronto: University of Toronto Press, 1957). A classic reevaluation of the weaknesses of the Carolingian empire.

Pierre Riché, *Daily Life in the World of Charlemagne* (Philadelphia: University of Pennsylvania Press, 1978). A look at the lives of men and women in the ninth century by a leading French scholar.

A Tour of Europe in the Ninth Century

* Peter Sawyer, *The Age of the Vikings* (New York: St. Martins Press, 1971). A good introduction to Scandinavian history.

* Geoffrey Barraclough, ed., *Eastern and Western Europe in the Middle Ages* (New York: Harcourt Brace Jovanovich, 1970). Essays by specialists on Eastern Europe and its relationship to the West.

W. Montgomery Watt, *A History of Islamic Spain* (Edinburgh: Edinburgh University Press, 1965). An intelligent introduction to Spain under Islam for the non-specialist.

After the Carolingians: From Empire to Lordships

Heinrich Fichtenau, *Living in the Tenth Century: Studies in Mentalities and Social Orders* (Chicago: University of Chicago Press 1990). A brilliant evocation of the quest for order on the Continent following the dissolution of the Carolingian empire.

Georges Duby, *The Early Growth of the European Economy: Warriors and Peasants From the Seventh to the Twelfth Century* (Ithaca: Cornell University Press, 1974). An imaginative survey of the economic and social forces forming Europe in the early Middle Ages.

9

The High Middle Ages

HAROLD·SACRAMENTVM·FECIT:~ HIC HAROLD·DV
VVILLELMO DVCI:~

Harold, King of the English

A few decades after William the Conqueror's victory at Hastings in 1066, his half brother, Bishop Odo of Bayeux (ca. 1036–97), commissioned a great tapestry recording the Norman version of the conquest. An unknown Anglo-Saxon artist sketched the cartoon, drawing on models taken from Anglo-Saxon and Carolingian manuscript illumination. Anglo-Saxon women then embroidered the tapestry, a strip of linen 230 feet long and 20 inches high, a masterful piece of art.

Using such techniques familiar to modern moviemakers as jump cuts, flashbacks, close-ups, panoramas, and decomposing movement into freeze-frames, the artist and embroiderers vividly present life in eleventh-century warrior society. It is almost exclusively masculine. Of the 623 people represented, only six are women. We see peasants working the fields, craftsmen felling trees and building ships for William's Channel crossing. We see cities, palaces, and churches. We see cooking and banqueting, hunting, traveling, and of course we see fighting and dying. The artists accurately render clothing, armor, and even hairstyles. But the tapestry is not simply a naive piece of artistry, it is a masterpiece of propaganda.

When King Edward the Confessor (1042–66) died, two major claimants disputed the succession. Anglo-Saxon sources insist that Edward and his nobles chose Earl Harold Godwinson (ca. 1022–66). William insisted that Edward had designated him and that years before, when Harold had been shipwrecked on the Norman coast and befriended by the duke, he had sworn an oath to assist William in gaining the crown. This is the scene presented in the panel on the opposite page. Harold's death, portrayed in the panel below right, suggests divine vengeance for his perjury. The message seems clear. William was the rightful heir and Harold, by his perfidy, merited his tragic fate.

And yet the Anglo-Saxon artists who executed the tapestry for their Norman lord may have subtly introduced a different reading into the story of Harold. Nothing in the tapestry itself specifically labels him a perjurer or usurper. In the critical scene following his coronation, shown above, the legend declares him unambiguously the legitimate king: "Here sits Harold, King of the English." Moreover, in this scene he is acknowledged by representatives of the whole of society, that is, the workers, represented by the unarmed man at far left; the fighters, represented by the man holding the sword; and the prayers, present in the person of Stigand, the Archbishop of

Canterbury.

In its vividness, its political subtlety, and its essential ambiguity, the Bayeux tapestry is a fitting introduction to the world of the High Middle Ages, that is, the period from about 1000 to 1300. It was a world of workers, fighters, and prayers, but also one of cities, merchants, and scholars. Its culture and religion combined, like the tapestry, the extremes of brutal warfare and subtle artistry.

The Countryside

From the tenth through the thirteenth centuries enormous transformations re-created the rural landscape. The most significant of these changes concerned the peasantry, but they are difficult to chronicle since until the nineteenth century the majority of the common people left no record of their lives. What we know of them was written by a tiny literate elite whose interest in the masses was primarily either economic or judicial. The peasants and their lives, work, and aspirations were worth recording only to the extent that so doing could improve the collection of rents, tithes, and taxes or that it could better control this potential threat to the established order. With few exceptions, the only medieval peasants whose voices we hear are those who were forced to testify before the court of a secular lord or an ecclesiastical inquisitor.

By the tenth century the population of Europe was growing, and with this population growth came new forms of social organization and economic activity. Between the years 1000 and 1300 Europe's population almost doubled, from approximately 38 million to 74 million. Various reasons have been proposed for this growth. Perhaps the end of the Viking, Magyar, and Saracen raids left rural society in relative peace to live and reproduce. The decline of slavery meant that individual peasant families could grow and reproduce themselves without constraints imposed by masters. Gradually improving agricultural techniques and equipment lessened somewhat the constant danger of famine. Possibly, too, a slowly improving climate increased agricultural yields. None of these explanations are entirely satisfactory. Whatever the cause of the population growth, it changed the face of Europe.

During the tenth century the great forests that had covered most of Europe began to be cut back as population spread out from the islands of cultivation, which had characterized the ninth century, into the "desert," that is, the wilderness. In the north of Germany and in what is today Holland, from around 1100 enterprising peasants began to drain marshes, a slow process of creating new land that would continue into the present century. This progress was not everywhere linear.

In this medieval farmstead newly cut from the forest, men beat acorns out of the trees for the pigs to eat while horses wearing collars pull the plow. Note the fenced-in vegetable garden at the right.

In England, for example, forests actually gained on plowland after the Norman Conquest of 1066. However, by the mid-twelfth century the acrid smoke from slash-and-burn clearing of the forest could be smelled all across Europe.

The Peasantry: Serfs and Freemen

The peasants who engaged in the opening of this internal frontier were the descendants of the slaves, unfree farmers, and petty free persons of the early Middle Ages. In the east along the frontier of the Germanic empire, in the Slavic world, in Scandinavia, in southern Gaul, in northern Italy, and in the reconquered portions of Christian Spain, they were free persons who owned land, entered into contracts with magnates, and remained responsible for their own fates. Across much of northwestern Europe and in particular in France in the course of the eleventh century the various gradations in status disappeared, and the peasantry formed a homogeneous social category loosely described as serfs. While they were not slaves in a legal sense, their degraded status, their limited or nonexistent access to public courts of law, and their enormous dependency on their lords left them in a situation similar to that of those Carolingian slaves settled on individual farmsteads in the ninth century. Each year, peasants had to hand over to their lords certain fixed portions of their meager harvests. In addition, they were obligated to work a certain number of days the *demesne*, or reserve of the lord, the produce of which went directly to him for his use or sale. Finally, they were required to make ritual payments symbolizing their subordination.

Inadequately housed, clothed, and fed, subject to the constant scrutiny of their lords, and defenseless against natural or man-made disasters, most peasants led lives of constant insecurity. Their homes offered little protection from the elements. Most were small shacks constructed of mud and wood, with one or two rooms inhabited by the entire family and their most precious domestic animals. Roofs were so low that village gossips would often lift up a corner of the roof to listen in on their neighbors—the origin of the term *eavesdrop*. These huts must have been extremely dark and sooty. They usually had no windows and until the sixteenth century no chimneys. Instead smoke from the open hearth was allowed to escape through a hole in the roof. It is small wonder that tuberculosis and other lung diseases were endemic.

Across Europe, peasant houses were clustered in villages on manors or large estates. In part this was due to the peasants' need for security and companionship against the dangers and terrors of a hostile world. However, in some parts of Europe it was the result of their lord's desire to keep a close eye on his labor supply. Beginning in the tenth century in central Italy and elsewhere, lords forced peasants to abandon isolated farmsteads and traditional villages and to move into small fortified settlements. In these new villages peas-

ants were obligated to settle disputes in the lord's court, to grind their grain in the lord's mill, and to bake their bread in the lord's oven—all primary sources of revenue for the lord. At the center of the village was the church. Often it was the only stone or brick building in the village. Even the lord's castle was until the thirteenth century often simply a wooden structure similar to an Old West frontier fort. The same sort of monopoly enforced on the lords' mills and ovens applied to the church. Villagers had to contribute a tenth of their revenues to the church and to make donations in order to receive the sacraments. In some villages these payments may have actually gone to the church; usually they too went to the lord.

Each morning men went out to their fields, which surrounded the village. In some villages each peasant householder held thin strips of widely scattered land, while pasturage and woodland were exploited in common. While this arrangement was perhaps inefficient from the perspective of time lost traveling to work different plots of land, such an open-field system allotted all peasant households a portion of all of the different sorts of land. In addition, the physical separation of plots provided families insurance against total loss of crops due to sudden storms or other localized disasters. In other villages, each household tended a unified parcel of land. Such closed fields generally corresponded with greater divergences in wealth within the village and encouraged more independence.

While the men plowed and worked the fields, women took charge of the domestic tasks. These included wool carding, spinning, weaving, caring for the family's vegetable garden, bearing and raising children, and brewing the thick souplike beer that was a primary source of carbohydrates in the peasant diet. During harvest women worked in the fields alongside the men.

Beer, black bread, beans, cabbage, onions, and cheese made up the typical peasant fare. Meat was a rarity. Cattle and sheep were too precious to slaughter, and what little meat peasants ate came from the herds of pigs left free to forage in nearby forests for acorns and grubs. Only in northern Europe, where inadequate winter fodder necessitated culling herds each winter, did peasants occasionally enjoy beef. Inadequate agricultural methods and inefficient storage systems left the peasantry in constant threat of famine. A bad year could send mobs of desperate peasants roaming the land in search of food. In the mid-eleventh century the archbishop of Trier was on his way to church with his mounted retinue when he was stopped by a crowd of starving beggars. He offered them money but they refused, forcing him and his entourage to dismount and watch in disbelief while the crowd ripped the horses apart and devoured them on the spot.

The expansion of arable land offered new hope and opportunities to peasants. As rapid as it was, between the tenth and twelfth centuries population growth did not keep up with the demand for laborers in newly settled areas of Europe. Thus labor was increasingly in demand and lords were often willing to make special arrangements with groups of peasants to encourage them to bring new land under cultivation. From the beginning of the twelfth century peasant villages acquired from their lord the privilege to deal with him and his representatives collectively rather than individually. Villages purchased the right to control petty courts and to limit fines imposed by the lord's representative; peasants acquired protection from arbitrary demands for labor and extraordinary taxes.

These good times did not last forever. Gradually during the late twelfth and thirteenth centuries, the labor market stagnated. Europe's population, particularly in France, England, Italy, and western Germany, began to reach a saturation point. As a result, lay and ecclesiastical lords found that they could profit more by hiring cheap laborers than by demanding customary services and payments from their serfs. They also found that their serfs were willing to pay for increasing privileges.

Peasants could purchase the right to marry without the lord's consent, to move to neighboring manors or to nearby towns, and to inherit. They acquired personal freedom from their lord's jurisdiction, transformed their servile payments into payments of rent for their manses, purchased their own land, and commuted their labor services into annual or even one-time payments. In other words, they began to purchase their freedom. This free peasantry benefited the emerging states of western Europe, since kings and towns could extend their legal and fiscal jurisdictions

over these persons and their lands at the expense of the nobility. Governments thus encouraged the extension of freedom and protected peasants from their former masters. By the fourteenth century, serfs were a rarity in many parts of western Europe.

This is not to say that these freed serfs and their descendants necessarily gained prosperity. Freedom often meant freedom from the protection that lords had provided. It meant the freedom to fail and even to starve. While some peasants acquired their own lands and prospered and others moved to towns to make their fortune, still others sank into the ranks of landless beggars. Nevertheless, free peasants were increasingly able to involve themselves in the emerging world of cash-crop farming and to tie into a growing trend toward agricultural specialization. Northern Germany and Sicily focused on grain production, the river valleys of France and Germany on vineyards. Areas around emerging towns concentrated on truck gardening to supply produce for these growing urban centers. Clever and successful peasants acquired land, employed their own workers, and established a level of wealth equivalent at times to that of the lesser nobility. On the other hand, by the fourteenth century bands of unsuccessful landless and starving peasants, expelled from rented property by lords seeking to cut labor costs, began to roam the countryside, occasionally becoming the source of political and social turmoil.

Even as western serfs were acquiring a precious though fragile freedom, the free peasantry in much of eastern Europe and Spain were losing it. In much of the Slavic world, through the eleventh century, peasants lived in large, roughly territorial communes of free families. Gradually, however, princes, churches, and aristocrats began to build great landed estates. By the thirteenth century, under the influences of western and Byzantine models and of the Mongols, who dominated much of the Slavic world from 1240, lords began to acquire political and economic control over the peasantry. The process was gradual, however, and was not completed until the sixteenth century. In Hungary during the twelfth century free peasants and unfree servants merged to form a stratum of serfs tied to the emerging landed aristocracy and the lesser nobility composed of free warriors. A similar process took

"September" from the Duc de Berry's Très Riches Heures, *an illuminated French manuscript of the 1400s by the Limbourg brothers. The peasants are harvesting grapes in the shadow of the splendid castle of their lord.*

place in parts of Spain. In all of these regions, the decline of the free peasantry accompanied the decline of public authority to the benefit of independent nobles. The aristocracy rose on the backs of the peasantry.

The Aristocracy: Fighters and Breeders

Beginning in the late tenth century, writers of legal documents began to employ an old term in a novel manner to designate certain powerful free persons who belonged neither to the old aristocracy nor to the peasantry. The term was *miles*. In classical Latin *miles* meant "soldier." As used in the Middle Ages, we would translate it as "knight." Initially, a knight was simply a mounted

warrior—the term said nothing about his social status. Some knights were serfs, and in Germany knights remained a distinctly lower social group well into the thirteenth century. However, in France, northern Italy, England, and much of Spain, beginning in the eleventh century, the term *knight* (in French, *chevalier*; in Spanish, *caballero*) worked its way up the social ladder. By the end of the twelfth century even kings such as Richard the Lion-hearted of England (1189–99) identified themselves as part of a knightly, or chivalric, world. A term that originally described a function had come to designate a life-style.

The center of this life-style was northern France. From there, the ideals of knighthood, or chivalry, spread out across Europe, influencing aristocrats as far east as Byzantium. The essence of the knightly life-style was fighting. Through warfare this aristocracy had maintained or acquired its freedom and through warfare it justified its privileges. The origins of this small elite (probably nowhere more than 2 percent of the population) were diverse. Many were descended from the old aristocracy of the Carolingian age. In the region of Burgundy in eastern France, for example, by the twelfth century approximately forty-one families were considered "noble." These families, or "houses," had sprung from six great clans of the Carolingian period. They traced descent through the male line, inheritance was usually limited to the eldest sons, and daughters were given a dowry but did not share in inheritance. Younger sons had to find service with some great lord or live in the household of their older brothers. Even the eldest sons who became heads of these households could not freely dispose of family property without consulting their kinsmen.

Such noble families, proud of their independence and ancestry, maintained their position through complex kin networks, mutual defense pacts with other nobles, and control of castles, from which they could dominate the surrounding countryside. Safe behind the castle walls, they were by the twelfth century often independent even of the local counts, dukes, and kings. This lesser nobility absorbed control of such traditionally public powers as justice, peace, and taxation.

For the sons of such nobles preparation for a life of warfare began early, often in the entourage of a maternal uncle or a powerful lord. There boys learned to ride, to handle a heavy sword and shield, to manage a lance on horseback, to swing an axe with deadly accuracy. They also learned more-subtle but equally important lessons about honor, pride, and family tradition. The feats of ancestors or heroes, sung by traveling minstrels at the banqueting table on long winter nights, provided models of knightly action. In the *Song of Roland*, a legend loosely based on the exploits of an eighth-century count in Charlemagne's army who was killed in an ambush as the Franks crossed the Pyrenees from Spain, they learned the importance of loyalty and fierce dedication to duty but also the dangers of pride and reckless faith in one's own sword. In the legends of King Arthur, they learned the disasters that weak leadership could bring to a band of warriors or to a whole country. The culmination of this education for English and French nobles came in a ceremony of knighting. An adolescent of age sixteen to eighteen received a sword from an older, experienced warrior. No longer a "boy," he now became a "youth," ready to enter the world of fighting for which he had trained.

This miniature illustrates the adventures of the French epic hero Roland. He is seen fighting (at center) and laid out in death (bottom) after he was ambushed in the Pyrenees by Muslims.

A "youth" was a noble who had been knighted but who had not married or acquired land either through inheritance or as a reward from a lord for service, and thus had not yet established his own "house." The length of time one remained a youth varied enormously. It could easily extend into one's thirties or beyond. During this time the knight led the life of a warrior, joining in promising military expeditions and amusing himself with tournaments—mock battles that often proved as deadly as the real thing—in which one could win an opponent's horses and armor as well as renown. Drinking, gambling, and lechery were other common activities. This was an extraordinarily dangerous life-style, and many youths did not survive to the next stage in a knight's life, that of acquiring land, wife, honor, and his own following of youths. The basic plot outline of most medieval romances is in essence the dream of every young knight: kill an older opponent, marry his wife, acquire his lands, and found a house.

The period between childhood and maturity was no less dangerous for noblewomen than for men. Marriages were the primary forms of alliances between noble houses, and the production of children was essential to the continued prosperity of the family. Thus daughters were raised as breeders, married at around age sixteen, and then expected to produce as many children as possible. Given the primitive knowledge of obstetrics, bearing children was even more dangerous than bearing a lance. Many noblewomen died in childbirth, often literally exhausted by frequent successive births. Although occasionally practiced, contraception was condemned both by the Church and by husbands eager for offspring, and even the natural contraceptive effects of nursing were not available to noblewomen, who normally gave their infants to wet nurses to suckle.

In this martial society, the political and economic status of women declined considerably. Because they were considered unable to participate in warfare, in northern Europe women were also frequently excluded from inheritance, estate management, courts, and public deliberations. Although a growing tradition of "courtliness" glorified the status of aristocratic women in literature, women were actually losing ground in the real world. Some noblewomen did control property and manage estates, but usually such roles were possible only for widows who had borne sons and who could play a major part in raising them. Such women were not uncommon. If a noblewoman was able to bear children successfully, she stood an excellent chance of surviving her husband, who was probably at least fifteen years her senior and whose military pursuits placed him in constant danger. Such a role was not likely to endear her to her male contemporaries. For all their martial valor, medieval men feared women and female sexuality. They mistrusted this representative of another lineage who was essential to the continuance of their own. Both secular tradition and Christian teaching portrayed women as devious, sexually demanding temptresses often responsible for the corruption and downfall of men. Many men felt threatened by this aggressive sexual stereotype. They resented the power wielded by wealthy widows and abbesses.

The noble life-style for men and women demanded specific virtues. A knight and his lady were to be "gentle," a term that meant simply "of good birth"; men were to be "preu," that is, powerful fighters; both men and women were praised for graciousness—open-handed generosity to their followers or retainers. To maintain a life-style of conspicuous consumption required wealth, and wealth meant land. The nobility was essentially a society of heirs who had inherited not only land but also the serfs who worked their manors. Lesser nobles acquired additional property from great nobles and from ecclesiastical institutions in return for binding contracts of mutual assistance. This tradition was at least as old as the Carolingians, who granted their followers land in return for military service. In later centuries, counts and lesser lords continued this tradition, exchanging land for support. Individual knights became *vassals* of lay or ecclesiastical magnates, swearing fealty or loyalty to the lord and promising to defend and aid him. Normally this oath included serving a certain number of days in the lord's military expeditions, guarding his castles, escorting him, and providing other military services. In some regions the knight also underwent a ritual of homage whereby he placed his hands in the hands of the lord and acknowledged himself the man (in French, *homme*) of the

A knight and lady in a fifteenth-century garden. The ideals of chivalry and courtly love glorified women in literature and song, but in real life the subordinate status of women reflected the values of a martial society.

lord, ready to serve him as far as his freedom permitted. In return the lord swore to protect his vassal and granted him a means of support by which the vassal could maintain himself while serving his lord. Usually this grant, termed a fief, was a parcel of productive land and the serfs and privileges attached to it. The vassal and his heirs had the right to hold the fief as long as they were able to provide the service demanded for it. Should they ever be unable to continue or should their lineage die out, the fief returned to the lord.

Individual lords often had considerable numbers of vassals, who might also be the vassals of other lay and secular lords. The networks thus established formed vital social and political structures. In some unusual situations, such as in England immediately after the Norman Conquest and in the Latin Kingdom of Jerusalem founded following the First Crusade in 1099, these structures of lords and vassals constituted systems of hierarchical government. Elsewhere, individuals often held fiefs from and owed service to more than one lord, and not all of the individuals in a given county or duchy owed their primary obligation to the count or duke. Likewise, often most of a noble's land was owned outright rather than held in fief, thus making the feudal bond less central to his status. As a result these bonds, anachronistically called *feudalism* by French lawyers of the sixteenth and seventeenth centuries, constituted just one more element of a social system tied together by kinship, regional alliances, personal bonds of fealty, and the surviving elements of Carolingian administration inherited by counts and dukes. Outside Germany, Hungary, and a few regions such as Normandy and Anjou, the society of the eleventh and twelfth centuries was one of intensely local autonomous powers in which public order and political authority were spread as widely as ever in European history.

The Church: Saints and Monks

The religious needs of the peasantry remained those that their pre-Christian ancestors had known: fertility of land, animals, and women; protection from the ravages of climate and the warrior elite; supernatural cures for the ailments and disabilities of their harsh life. The cultural values of the nobility retained the essentials of the Germanic warrior ethos, including family honor, battle, and display of status. The rural Church of the High Middle Ages met the needs of both, although it subtly changed them in the process.

Most medieval people, whether peasants or lords, lived in a world of face-to-face encounters, a world in which abstract creeds counted for little and in which interior state and external appearance were rarely distinguished. In this world, religion meant primarily action, and the essential religious actions were the liturgical celebrations performed by the clergy. Many of the parish priests who celebrated the eucharist, performed baptisms, solemnized marriages, and conducted funerals were themselves peasants who had received only rudimentary instruction from their predecessors and whose knowledge of Latin and theology was minimal. But these intellectual factors would become significant only centuries later. The essential qualification was that priests could perform the rites of the Church.

What contemporaries complained about was not the clergy's ignorance but its greed and immorality. Ordinary lay people wanted priests who would not extort them by selling the sacraments and would not seduce their wives and daughters. They wanted priests who would not leave the village for months or years at a time to seek clerical advancement elsewhere rather than remaining in the village performing the rituals necessary to keep the supernatural powers well disposed toward men and women in the community.

The most important of these supernatural powers was not some distant divinity but the saints—local, personal, even idiosyncratic persons. During their lives saintly men and women had shown that they enjoyed special favor with God. After their deaths, they continued to be the link between the divine and the earthly spheres. Through their bodies, preserved as relics in the monasteries of Europe, they continued to live among mortals even while participating in the heavenly court. Thus they could be approached just like local earthly lords and like them be won over through offerings, bribes, oaths, and rituals of supplication and submission. Just as peasants who surrendered their liberty to a lord by entering his special *familia* could expect the lord's protection, so too could petitioners enter the *familia* of a saint, become the saint's serf, and thus expect the saint's supernatural assistance.

Saints were approached directly. Praying and fasting, petitioners pilgrimaged to a saint's tomb and kept vigil there, beseeching the saint's protection. These tombs were normally found in monasteries, the "cities of God" that dotted the landscape. As houses of the saints, monasteries orchestrated and controlled the places and times by which the laity could have access to these patrons. As the recipients of gifts to the saints, made in expectation of or in gratitude for supernatural assistance, monastic communities became wealthy and powerful institutions. Every community had its own local saints, either early martyrs of the region or saints whose remains had been transported there. In addition there were regional or national pilgrimages to saints such as Saint Fides and Saint Denis in France, Saint Stephen in Hungary, and Saint Theodosij in Kiev. Finally, there were the great international pil-

This gold-plated statue contains the skull of Saint Foy, a young girl who was martyred during the last Roman persecution of the Christians in 303. The image illustrates the medieval veneration of the physical relics of the saints.

grimages to Saint James of Compostela in Spain, to the tombs of the martyrs in Rome, and finally the greatest, the pilgrimage to the empty sepulcher of Jesus in Jerusalem.

Monasteries did more than orchestrate the cult of the special category of the dead who were the saints. They were also responsible for the cult of the ordinary dead, for praying for the souls of ordinary mortals. In particular, monastic communities commemorated and prayed for those members of noble families who, through dona-

tions of land, had become especially associated with the monastic community. It was widely believed in the eleventh century that the devil himself had complained that the monastery of Cluny was capable of snatching the souls of dead sinners from him through the power of its prayers. Association with such monasteries through gifts and exchanges of property, and particularly through burial in the monastic cemetery, provided the surest means of continuing noble families' honor and prestige into the next world. Across Europe noble families founded monasteries on their own lands or invited famous abbots to reorganize existing monasteries. These monasteries formed integral parts of the institutional existence of families. They continued the ritual remembrance of the family, providing it with a history and forming an important part of its material as well as spiritual prestige.

Supported by both peasants and nobles, Benedictine monasteries reached their height in the eleventh and twelfth centuries. Within their walls developed a religious culture that was one of the greatest achievements of the Middle Ages. Entry into a monastery was usually reserved for young nobles, whose families entrusted them to the monastery at the age of seven. There they were to remain until the end of their lives, first as novices in the religious culture of the monastery and later as mature monks and nuns, the professionals in the dance of medieval religion. The essence of the monastic life was the passionate pursuit of God. The goal was not simply salvation but perfection, and this required discipline of the body through a life of voluntary chastity and poverty and discipline of the spirit through obedience and learning. The Benedictine's life moved to the rhythm of the divine office, the ancient series of eight hours each day when the monks put aside work, study, or rest and assembled in the monastic church for the communal chanting of prayers, psalms, and hymns. Some of the prayers were fixed. Others varied according to the liturgical calendar and corresponded to the events in the history of salvation and the life of Christ. From matins, recited after midnight, until compline, the last evening prayer, the monks praised God and asked his aid and that of his saints on behalf of themselves, their secular patrons, their families, and all of society.

Proper participation in this communal liturgy required an education closely in tune with the needs of monastic prayer. Its essence was the *lectio divina*, the process of reading and studying the Old and New Testaments, for which the study of pagan classics and the writings of the Church Fathers was essential. Reading and studying were active, physical pursuits. Monks and nuns read out loud, the murmur of their voices filling the monastery even when they read in their own rooms or cells. Study did not mean primarily logical analysis. Rather it was a system that combined the tools of grammar, memorization, and word association. It emphasized imaginative description, concordance of scriptural passages related only by similar words, and the application of such "scientific" methods as the allegorical meanings of stones, parts of the body, animals, and so on, culled from ancient and medieval scientific texts. This study was combined with the allegorical analysis developed by Origen and the early Church Fathers to produce a distinctive, nonrational but extremely powerful form of intellectual and emotional spirituality. Far from denying the physical and erotic side of human nature, the monastic tradition saw in erotic love a metaphor of divine love. The most popular scriptural text in monastic study was the *Song of Songs*, that remarkable love poem in the Old Testament that never once mentions God.

Monasteries were communities of professional prayers and therein found their social justification. They were also enormously rich and powerful social and political institutions. The monastery of Cluny, in saving souls through prayer, became the first international organization of monastic centers, with abbeys and dependent communities, called priories, throughout Europe. The abbots of Cluny were among the most powerful and influential people of the eleventh and twelfth centuries, dealing as equals with kings, popes, and emperors. In order to remain in form for the strenuous liturgical commemoration of living and dead patrons, Cluniac monks largely abandoned the tradition of manual work, leaving such mundane activities rather to their thousands of serfs and lay agents.

The Cluniac monks' comparative luxury and concentration on liturgy to the neglect of other spiritual activities led some monastic reformers to call for a return to simplicity, separation from

Cluniac and Cistercian Monasteries

the rest of society, and a deeper internal spirituality. Chief among these groups were the Cistercians, who under the dynamic leadership of Bernard of Clairvaux (1090–1153), spread a rigorous, ascetic form of monasticism from England to the Vienna woods. The Cistercians built monasteries in the wilderness and discouraged the kinds of close ties with secular society established by the Cluniacs. They wished to avoid the crowds of pilgrims and the intense involvement with local affairs that characterized other types of monasticism. Paradoxically, by establishing themselves in remote areas, organizing their estates in an efficient manner, and gaining a great reputation for asceticism, the Cistercians became enormously wealthy and successful leaders in the economic changes taking place in the twelfth and thirteenth centuries.

The rural Church not only served the lay population but worked to transform it. Although monks and bishops were spiritual warriors, most abhorred bloodshed among Christians and sought to limit the violence of aristocratic life. This attitude combined altruistic and selfish motives, since Church property was often the focus of aristocratic greed. The decline of public power and the rise of aristocratic autonomy and violence were particularly marked in southern France. There, beginning in the tenth century, churchmen organized the Peace of God and the Truce of God, movements that attempted to protect peasants, merchants, and clerics from aristocratic violence and to limit the times when warfare was allowed. During the eleventh century, the goals of warfare were shifted from attacks against other Christians to the defense of Christian society. This redirection produced the Crusades, those religious wars of conquest directed against Europe's non-Christian neighbors.

In order to direct noble violence away from Christendom, Pope Urban II (1088–99) in 1095 urged Western knights to use their arms to free the Holy Land from Muslim occupation. In return he promised to absolve them from all of the punishment due for their sins in this life or the next. The First Crusade was remarkably successful. The crusaders took Jerusalem in 1099 and established a Latin kingdom in Palestine. For over two centuries bands of Western warriors went on armed pilgrimage to defend this precarious kingdom and, after the reconquest of Jerusalem by the Muslim commander Saladin in 1187, to attempt to recapture it. Crusades appealed particularly to younger sons and knights who hoped to acquire in the East the status that constricting lineages denied them in the West. Other such holy wars were directed against the Muslims in Spain, the Slavs in eastern Europe, and even against heretics and political opponents in France and Italy.

The Crusades, glorified in the nineteenth century by European imperialists who saw them as the model for Europe's expansion into the east, were brutal and vicious, and the crusaders were often motivated as much by greed as by piety. Some began with the wholesale slaughter of Jews in Europe and ended with equally bloody massacres in Palestine. When Jerusalem was taken in 1099, eyewitnesses reported that blood ran ankle deep in the old city. Scalping and head-hunting were practiced by both sides, as was the indiscriminate killing of captives. By the end of the thirteenth century the military failure of the Crusades, the immorality of many of the participants, and doubts about the spiritual significance of such wars contributed to their decline. So too did the rise of centralized monarchies, whose rulers, with few exceptions, viewed Crusades as wasteful and futile distractions. Although later preachers from time to time urged kings and nobles to take up the cross against the infidel, the age of the Crusades passed with the age of the independent warrior aristocracy.

In the first third of the eleventh century, a French bishop, Adalbero of Laon (d. 1030), described the ideal structure of society as composed of three groups: those who worked, those who fought, and those who prayed. Adalbero identified the workers as the peasants, the fighters as the king, and the prayers as the bishops. Not long after, monastic writers adopted but adjusted his schema. The workers remained the peasants, but the fighters were the nobles and the prayers the monks. While there were always people who did not fit neatly into either of these systems, in the eleventh and twelfth centuries most Europeans did fall roughly into one of these three categories. Peasants, lords, and monks made up the great majority of Europe's population and lived together in mutual dependence, sharing involvement with the rhythm of the agrarian life. From the later part of the twelfth century, however, this rural world became increasingly aware of a different society, that of the growing cities and towns of Europe, whose citizens had no place in the simplistic tripartite scheme of Adalbero and who moved to a different rhythm, that of commerce and manufacture.

Medieval Towns

Monastic preachers liked to remind their listeners that according to the Bible, Cain had founded the first town after killing his brother Abel. For monks, nobles, and peasants, the town was an anomaly—a center of commerce and manufacture populated by persons who did not fit well into the traditional social structure that was promoted by representatives of the rural aristocratic order. Towns seemed somehow immoral and perverse but at the same time fascinating. Monks saw the city as the epitome of evil from which they had fled, and yet in the twelfth century new monasteries were being established in or near towns, while older monasteries established on the outskirts of towns found themselves being incorporated into growing urban areas. Nobles disdained urban society for its lack of respect for aristocracy and its disinterest in their cult of violence. Still, as rude warriors were transformed into courtly nobles, these nobles were drawn to the luxuries provided by urban merchants and became indebted to urban moneylenders in order to maintain their "gracious" lifestyles. For many peasants, towns were refuges from the hopelessness of their normal lives. "Town air makes one free," they believed, and many serfs fled the land to try their fortunes in the nearby towns. Clearly, something was very different about the urban communities that emerged, first in Italy, then in the Low Countries and across Europe in the later eleventh and twelfth centuries.

Italian Communes

Urban life had never ceased to be an essential ingredient in Italy, which had maintained its urban traditions and ties with the Mediterranean world since antiquity. Although their populations had shrunk in late antiquity and they were dominated by their bishops, who exercised secular and ecclesiastical lordship, the towns of the peninsula had continued to play commercial and political roles and to attract not only runaway serfs but even nobles, who maintained fortified towers within the town walls.

The coastal cities of Amalfi, Bari, Genoa, and especially Venice had continued to play important roles in commerce both with the Byzantines and with the new Muslim societies. For Venice, this role was facilitated by its official status as a part of the Byzantine Empire, which gave it access to Byzantine markets. The geographical isolation of most of these cities from prosperous hinterlands gave them an additional advantage as commercial centers. With nothing of their own to trade but perhaps salt and, in Venice, glass, they were forced to look to trade, serving as go-betweens for the transport of eastern spices, silks, and ivories, which they exchanged for western iron, slaves, timber, grain, and oil. In order to protect their merchant ships, Italian coastal cities developed their own fleets, and by the eleventh century they were major military forces in the Mediterranean. Venice's fleet became the primary protector of the Byzantine Empire and was thereby able to win more favorable commercial rights than those enjoyed by Greek merchants.

As the merchants of the Italian towns penetrated the markets at the western end of the great overland spice routes connecting China, India, and central Asia with the Mediterranean, they established permanent merchant colonies in the East. When expedient, they did not hesitate to use military force to win concessions. In 1088, for example, the Venetians sacked the capital of Tunis in North Africa in order to force concessions to their merchants.

The Crusades, armed pilgrimages for pious northern nobles, were primarily economic opportunities for the Italians, who had no scruples about trading with Muslims. Furthermore, only the Italians had the ships and the expertise to transport the crusaders by sea, the only option that offered hope of success, since every Crusade but the first that had followed an overland route had ended in failure. Moreover, the ships of the Italian cities were the only means of supplying the crusading armies once they were in Palestine. Crusaders paid the Italian merchants handsomely for their assistance and also granted them economic and political rights in the Palestinian port cities such as Tyre and Acre, where both the Venetians and the Genoese had their own quarters governed by their own laws. The culmination of this relationship between northern crusaders and Italians was the Fourth Crusade. In 1204 a renegade Crusade short on funds was sidetracked

Italian Towns and Cities, ca. 1000

An illustration from a fourteenth-century manuscript. Marco Polo, with his father and uncle, is seen departing from Venice for points east in 1271. Marco did not return home to Venice until twenty-four years later.

by the Venetians into capturing and sacking Constantinople. As discussed in chapter 7 (see p. 220), the Byzantine Empire never recovered from this disaster, and Venice emerged as the undisputed Mediterranean power.

By the thirteenth century, Italian merchants had spread far beyond the Mediterranean. The great merchant banking houses of Venice, Florence, and Genoa had established offices around the Mediterranean and Black seas; south along the Atlantic coast of Morocco; east into Armenia and Persia; west to London, Bruges, and Ghent; and north to Scandinavia. Some individual merchants, the Venetian Marco Polo (1254–1324) for example, traded as far east as China.

These international commercial operations required more sophisticated systems of commercial law and credit than the West had ever known. Italian merchants developed the practices of double-entry bookkeeping, limited-liability partnership, commercial insurance, and international letters of exchange. Complex commercial affairs also required the development of a system of credit and interest-bearing loans, an idea abhor-

rent to traditional rural societies. Since usury, that is, borrowing and lending at credit, was regarded as making money by manipulating time, which belonged only to God, churchmen condemned the practice as a form of simony, the buying and selling of spiritual goods. In spite of ecclesiastical prohibitions, bankers found ways of hiding interest payments in contracts, thus allowing lender and seller to participate in the growing world of credit-based transactions. Long before the emergence of the Protestant work ethic, Italian capitalists had developed the tools of modern business.

Just as significant as the international trade networks established by these traders were the cultural and institutional infrastructures that made these far-flung operations possible. The most basic of these was a mentality that considered commerce an honorable occupation. Since antiquity, aristocratic culture had considered only warfare and agriculture as worthy pursuits. Even the great commercial operations of the Roman world tended to be in the hands of equestrians and freedmen. The strength of the Italian towns was that they were able to throw off such a rural, aristocratic value system. Already in the ninth century, even the doge, or duke, of Venice had invested much of his wealth in commercial operations. By the later tenth and eleventh centuries this passion for commerce had spread from the seacoasts to the towns throughout Italy and from there to cities such as Marseilles, Barcelona, and others in southern Europe. Urban dwellers generally found nothing ignoble in commerce and banking. By the twelfth century wealthy citizens, whether descended from successful merchants or from landed aristocrats, were indifferently termed "magnates." The rest of the town's population was called "populars." The difference between the two was essentially economic. Since commercial activity offered a means of social mobility, the two could act in close accord, particularly when dealing with urban lords or outside powers. In the eleventh and early twelfth centuries, many Italian towns bought off or expelled their traditional lords such as counts and bishops, thus allowing the magnates and populars of these cities to create their own governing institutions or communes.

During the twelfth and thirteenth centuries Italy played host to a bewildering variety of experiments in self-government as urban populations banded together in communes of citizens who sought to govern themselves. These relatively small communities of citizens (the largest was approximately one hundred thousand adults) developed a keen sense of patriotism, local pride, and fierce independence reminiscent of the ancient Greek city-states. They manifested this pride in artistic and architectural competition as individual cities and their citizens sought to surpass each other in the construction of beautiful plazas, town halls, and sumptuous urban palaces. The communes also sought to control every aspect of civic life: prices, markets, weights and measures, sanitation, and medical care. Who might wear what forms of dress and jewelry? How many inches of lace might the wife of a merchant wear on her dress? Could an ordinary citizen wear a cloak trimmed with sable? Might Christian women wear earrings or were these reserved for Jews? Such questions were considered appropriate topics of public legislation.

The unity and patriotism the Italian cities showed the rest of the world was matched in intensity by the violence of their internal disputes. Every adult male was expected to participate in government, usually in his free time and at the expense of his private business activities. This involvement was intensely partisan as magnates disputed among themselves and with the ordinary populace for control of the town. These conflicts frequently turned violent as citizens took sides on wider issues of Italian and European politics.

Within many towns, the magnates formed their own corporation, the society of knights, to protect their privileged position. Families of nobles and magnates, whose cultural values were similar to those of the rural aristocracy, competed with each other for honor and power. Often they erected lofty towers on their urban palaces, both for prestige and for defense against their neighbors. Feuds fought out between noble families and their vassals in city streets were frequent events in Italian towns.

Opposing the magnates were popular corporations, the society of the people, which sought to rein in the violent and independent-minded nobles. These popular organizations could include anyone who was not a member of the society of knights, although in reality they were dominated by the prominent leaders of craft and trade associations, or guilds. In many towns, the society of the people was organized both by residential district and by guild and sought to prevent the formation of special interest groups or conspiracies within the commune. To enforce its measures, the society had its own elected officers and its own military, headed by a "captain of the people," who might command as many as one thousand troops against the magnates.

In order to tip the scales in their favor, differing parties frequently invited outside powers into local affairs. The greatest outside contenders for power in the Italian cities were the Germanic empire and the papacy. Most towns had an imperial faction (named Ghibelline after Waiblingen castle, which belonged to the family of Frederick II), bitterly opposed by a papal faction (in time called Guelph after the Welf family, which opposed Frederick's family). In time, the issues separating Guelphs and Ghibellines changed, and the Guelphs became the party of the wealthy eager to preserve the status quo, while those out of power rallied to the Ghibelline cause.

In order to maintain civic life in spite of these conflicts, cities established complex systems of government in which officers were selected by series of elections and lotteries designed to prevent any one faction from seizing control. Sovereignty lay with the *arengo*, or assembly, which comprised all adult male citizens. Except in very small communes this body was too large to function efficiently, so most communes selected a series of working councils. The great council might be as large as 400; an inner council had perhaps 24 to 40 members. Generally, executive authority was vested in consuls, whose numbers varied widely and who were chosen from various factions and classes. When these consuls proved unable to overcome the partisan politics of the factions, many towns turned to hiring *podestàs*, nonpolitical, professional city managers from outside the community. These were normally magnates from other communes who had received legal educations and who served for relatively short periods. In Modena, for example, they served six months. They were required to bring with them four judges, twenty-four cavalrymen, and sergeants and grooms to help maintain order.

They could not have any relatives in Modena, could not leave town without permission of the great council, and could not eat or drink with local citizens lest they be drawn into factional conflicts. Their salaries were paid every two months, the last third not being handed over until after a final audit of their term. Only by such stringent means could the commune hope to keep partisan politics from corrupting their podestà!

Northern "Towns"

The Mediterranean, or "mid-earth," Sea was so named because, to the Greeks and Romans, it seemed to be in the middle of the world. In this sense, there was another "mediterranean" sea to the north. The Baltic and North seas and the English Channel tied together the peoples of Scandinavia, Lithuania, northern Germany, Flanders, and England. Scandinavian fish and timber, Baltic grain, English wool, and Flemish cloth circulated around the edges of these lands, linking them in a common economic network. Here, as in the south, there developed urban merchant and manufacturing communities linked by sea routes, distinguished from the surrounding countryside by the formation of a distinctly urban, commercial mentality.

The earliest of these interrelated communities were the cloth towns of Flanders, Brabant, and northern France. Chief among them were Ghent, Bruges, and Ypres, and the wool-exporting towns of England, particularly London. Both areas had been known for their cloth production since Roman times, but in the eleventh century Flanders, lacking the land for large-scale sheep grazing and facing a growing population, began to specialize in the production of high-quality cloth made from English wool. At the same time England, which experienced an economic and population decline following the Norman Conquest, began to export the greater part of its wool to Flanders to be worked. The production of wool cloth began to develop from a cottage occupation into Europe's first major industry.

Woolen manufacture was a natural for such a transformation. The looms required to manufacture heavy wool cloth were large and expensive and the skills needed to produce the cloth were

Medieval Trade Networks

complex. No less than thirteen separate steps were required to turn raw wool into finished cloth, and each step demanded special expertise, chemicals such as dyes and color fixers, and equipment. The need for water both to power looms and to wash the cloth during production tended to concentrate cloth manufacture along waterways. Finally, as competition increased, only centralization and regulation of manufacture could ensure quality control and thus enhance marketability. Moreover, wool cloth was a necessity of life across Europe, and the growing population provided the first large-scale market for manufactured goods since the disintegration of the Roman Empire.

For all of these reasons, by the late eleventh century, the traditional image of medieval cloth production had been transformed. No longer did individual women sit in farmhouses spinning and weaving. Now manufacture was concentrated in towns and men replaced women at the looms. Furthermore, production was closely regulated and controlled by a small group of extremely wealthy merchant-drapiers (cloth makers).

Concentration of capital, specialization of labor, and increase of urban population created vibrant, exciting cities essentially composed of three social orders. At the top were wealthy patricians, the merchant-drapiers. Their agents traveled to England and purchased raw wool, which they then distributed to weavers and other master craftsmen. These craftsmen, often using equipment rented from the patricians, carded, dyed, spun, and wove the wool into cloth. Finally, the finished cloth was returned to the patricians, whose agents then marketed it throughout Europe. Through their control of raw materials, equipment, capital, and distribution, the merchant-drapiers controlled the cloth trade and thus the economic and political life of the Flemish wool towns. Through their closed associations, or guilds, they controlled production and set standards, prices, and wages. They also controlled communal government by monopolizing urban councils. In wealth and power, the merchant-drapiers were almost indistinguishable from the great nobles with whom they often intermarried.

At the bottom of urban society were the unskilled and semiskilled artisans, called "blue nails," because constant work with dye left their

As towns grew, the numbers and types of jobs grew as well. In this fifteenth-century Flemish manuscript illumination, a guild master of the dyer's guild supervises as men of the guild dye cloth.

fingers permanently stained. These workers led an existence more precarious than that of most peasants. Employed from week to week, paid barely living wages, and entirely dependent on the woolen industry for their livelihood, they often hovered on the edge of subsistence. In the early fourteenth century, the temporary interruption of grain shipments from northern Germany to Ypres left thousands dead of starvation. Small wonder that from the thirteenth century on, "blue nails" were increasingly hostile to patricians. Sporadic rebellions and strikes spread across Flanders, Brabant, and northern France. Everywhere they were ruthlessly suppressed. The penalty for organizing a strike was death.

Between the patricians and the workers stood the masters—the skilled craftsmen who controlled the day-to-day production of cloth and lesser crafts. Masters organized into guilds with which they both regulated every aspect of their trades and protected them from competition. The masters often leased their looms or other equipment from the merchant-drapiers and from them received raw materials and wages to be distributed to their workers. If the hope of the common artisan was someday to move up into the rank of master, masters hoped to amass sufficient capital to purchase their own looms and perhaps someday move up into the rank of patrician.

Tying together the northern and southern commercial worlds were the great fairs of Champagne. Six times during the year the towns of Champagne, particularly Troyes and Provins, swelled with exotic crowds of merchants from Flanders, England, Scandinavia, Germany, Brabant, Spain, and Italy. Rich and poor from the surrounding countryside also poured into the towns, as merchants from north and south met to bargain and trade under the protection of the local counts.

Representing Flanders were agents of the merchant-drapiers of each town, whose carefully inspected and regulated products carried the prestige and financial prosperity of their communities. Cloth was known by the name of the town in which it was made and thus quality control was a corporate rather than an individual issue. From Italy came merchants of the great Italian trading companies to purchase northern cloth for resale throughout the Mediterranean. Often these Italians were young merchants whose trip was financed by wealthy capitalists, who had entered into a limited-liability contract with the young adventurers for the duration of the journey.

Southern merchants brought silks, sugar, salt, alum (a chemical essential in cloth manufacture), and, most importantly, spices to trade at the fairs. Medieval cooks gloried in the use of spices, of which they knew over two hundred. The liberal use of exotic spices may have served as a preservative, and spices probably hid the taste of half-rotten food. But primarily the use of spices was a part of the conspicuous consumption by which the rich displayed their wealth and status.

In addition to the trade in cloth and spices, leather from Spain, iron from Germany, copper and tin from Bohemia, salted or smoked fish and furs from Scandinavia, and local wines, cheeses, and foodstuffs also changed hands under the watchful eyes of fair officials, who supervised weights, measures, and currency exchanges. The fair staff also provided courts to settle disagreements among merchants. These great international exchanges connected the financial and marketing centers of the south with the manufacturing and trading communities of the north, tying the northern world to the south more effectively than had any system since the political institutions of the Roman Empire.

Urban Culture

The urban world of the twelfth and thirteenth centuries created forms of religious and cultural expression particularly suited to it. During the eleventh century, cathedrals had become centers of learning as young clerics sought training in schools established by bishops. Initially these urban schools in Germany, Italy, France, and England were similar to centers of monastic education. However, unlike monks, young men who attended the cathedral schools received an education aimed more at participation in the affairs of the world than in the worship of God. They learned the skills of writing and computation and received the legal training that allowed them to rise to positions of prominence in an increasingly literate and complex urban world. Basic education consisted of the study of the *trivium*, that is, grammar, rhetoric, and logic, the first three of the seven liberal arts, which had formed the basis of Roman liberal education. In some cathedral schools students went on to study the *quadrivium*, the mathematical disciplines of geometry, theory of numbers, astronomy, and musical harmonies. In Italy students traveled to Ravenna and Bologna to study Roman law.

In the late eleventh and early twelfth centuries, the pace of urban intellectual life quickened. The combination of population growth, improved agricultural productivity, political stability, and educational interest culminated in what has been called the "renaissance of the twelfth century." Bologna and Paris became the undisputed centers of the new educational movements. Bologna specialized in the study of law. There from the eleventh century a number of important teachers began to make detailed, authoritative commentaries on the *Corpus iuris civilis*, the sixth-century compilation of law prepared on the order of the Roman emperor Justinian. In the next century the same systematic study was applied to Church law, culminating in the *Decretum Gratiani*, or "Concord of Discordant Canons," prepared around 1140 in Bologna by the monk Gratian. The growing importance of legal knowledge in politics, international trade, and Church administration drew students from across Europe to Bologna, where they organized a *universitas*, or guild of students, the first true university. In Bologna law students, many of them adults from wealthy merchant or aristocratic backgrounds, controlled every aspect of the university from the selection of administrators to the exact length of professors' lectures. Professors and administrators were firmly subject to the guild's control and were fined if they broke any of the regulations.

North of the Alps, Paris became the center for study of the liberal arts and of theology during the twelfth century. The city's emergence as the leading educational center of Europe resulted from a convergence of factors. Paris was the center of an important cathedral school as well as of a monastic school, that of the Victorines on the left bank of the Seine. In the twelfth century it became the capital of the French kings, who needed educated clerics, or clerks, for their administration. Finally, in the early twelfth century, students from across Europe flocked to Paris to study with the greatest and most original intellect of the century, Peter Abelard (1079–1142).

Brilliant, supremely self-assured, and passionate, Abelard arrived in Paris in his early twenties and quickly took the intellectual community by storm. He ridiculed the established teachers, bested them in open debate, and established his own school, which drew the best minds of his day. Abelard's intellectual method combined the tools of legal analysis perfected in Bologna with Aristotelian logic and laid the foundation of what has been called the Scholastic method. Logical reasoning, Abelard believed, could be applied to all problems, even those concerning the mysteries of faith.

So great was Abelard's reputation that an ambitious local cleric engaged him to give private instructions to his brilliant niece, Heloise. Soon Abelard and Heloise were having an affair and all of Paris was singing the love song he composed for her. When Heloise became pregnant, the two were secretly married. Fearing to harm his clerical career, Abelard refused to make the marriage

public, preferring to protect his career rather than Heloise's honor. Her outraged uncle hired thugs who broke into Abelard's room and castrated him. After Abelard recovered from his mutilation, he and Heloise each entered monasteries, and Abelard spent years as the abbot of a small monastery in Brittany. In 1136 he returned to teach in Paris, where he quickly drew new attacks, this time led by Bernard of Clairvaux, who accused him of heresy. Abelard was convicted by a local council and forced to burn some of his own works. He sought protection from his persecutors in the monastery of Cluny, where he died in 1142.

Although Abelard himself met tragedy in his personal and professional life, the intellectual ferment he had begun in Paris continued long after him. By 1200 education had become so important in the city that the universitas, or corporation of professors, was granted a charter by King Philip Augustus, who guaranteed its rights and immunities from the control of the city. Unlike that at Bologna, the University of Paris remained a corporation of masters rather than of students. It was organized like other guilds into masters; bachelors, who were similar to journeymen in other trades; and students, who were analogous to apprentices.

Students began their studies at around age fourteen or fifteen in the faculty of arts. After approximately six years, they received a bachelor of arts degree, which was a prerequisite to enter the higher faculties of theology, medicine, or law. After additional years of reading and commenting on specific texts under the supervision of a master, they received the title of master of arts, which gave them the license to teach anywhere within Christian Europe.

Though these years were filled with study, students also enjoyed a spirited life that revolved around the taverns and brothels that filled the student district, or Latin Quarter. Drunken brawls were frequent and relationships between students and townspeople were often strained because students enjoyed legal immunity from city officials. In 1229 a fight between students and a tavern owner over their bill erupted into general rioting and street battles that left many students and citizens dead or injured. Furious at the government for having sent in soldiers to quell the riot, the masters dissolved the university for six years and threatened never to return to Paris. Masters and students migrated to Oxford, Reims, Orléans, and elsewhere, greatly aiding the development of these other intellectual centers. In 1231 most of the masters' demands were finally met and the teachers returned to Paris secure in their rights of self-governance.

The intellectual life of the universities was in its way as rough and tumble as any student brawl. Through the thirteenth and fourteenth centuries it was dominated by a pagan philosopher already dead for a thousand years. The introduction of the works of Aristotle into the West between 1150 and 1250 created an intellectual crisis every bit as profound as that of the Newtonian revolution of the seventeenth or the Einsteinian revolution of the twentieth century. For centuries, Western thinkers had depended on the Christianized Neoplatonic philosophy of Origen and Augustine. Aristotle was known in the West only through his basic logical treatises, which in the twelfth century, thanks in large part to the work of Peter Abelard, had become the foundation of intellectual work. Logic, or dialectic, was seen as the universal key to knowledge, and the university system was based on its rigorous application to traditional texts of law, philosophy, and Scripture.

Beginning in the late twelfth century, Christian and Jewish scholars began translating Aristotle's treatises on natural philosophy, ethics, and metaphysics into Latin. Suddenly Christian intellectuals who had already accepted the Aristotelian method were brought face to face with Aristotle's conclusions: a world without an active, conscious God; a world in which everything from the functioning of the mind to the nature of matter could be understood without reference to a divine creator. Further complicating matters, the texts arrived not from the original Greek, but normally through Latin translations of Arabic translations accompanied by learned commentaries by Muslim and Jewish scholars, especially by Averroës, the greatest Aristotelian philosopher of the twelfth century.

As the full impact of Aristotelian philosophy began to reach churchmen and scholars, reactions varied from condemnation to wholehearted acceptance. At one extreme, in 1210 Church authorities forbade the teaching of Aristotle's philosophy in Paris, a prohibition the professors ignored. At the other extreme, Parisian scholars such as Siger de Brabant (ca. 1235–ca. 1281) eagerly embraced Aristotelian philosophy as interpreted by Averroës, even when these teachings varied from Christian tradition. To many, it appeared that there were two irreconcilable kinds of truth, one knowable through divine revelation, the other through human reason.

One Parisian scholar who refused to accept this dichotomy was Thomas Aquinas (1225–74), a professor of theology and the most brilliant intellect of the High Middle Ages. Although an Aristotelian who recognized the genius of Averroës, Aquinas refused to accept the possibility that human reason, which was a gift from God, led necessarily to contradictions with divine revelation. Aquinas' great contribution, contained in his *Summa Against the Gentiles* (1259–64) and in his incomplete *Summa of Theology* (1266–73), was to defend the integrity of human reason and to reconcile it with divine revelation. Properly applied, the principles of Aristotelian philosophy could not lead to error, he argued. However, human reason unaided by revelation could not always lead to certain conclusions. Questions about such matters as the nature of God, creation, and the human soul could not be resolved by reason alone. In developing his thesis, Aquinas recast Christian doctrine and philosophy, replacing their Neoplatonic foundation with an Aristotelian base. Although not universally accepted in the thirteenth century (in 1277 the bishop of Paris condemned many of Aquinas' teachings as heretical), in time his synthesis came to dominate Christian intellectual life for centuries.

Aquinas was a member of a new religious order, the Dominicans, who along with the Franciscans appeared in response to the social and cultural needs of the new urbanized, monetized European culture. Benedictine monasticism was ideally suited to a rural, aristocratic world but had little place in the bustling cities of Italy, Flanders, and Germany. In these urban, commercial environments, Christians were more concerned with the problems of living in the world than escape from it. Lay persons and clerics alike were concerned with the growing wealth of ecclesiastical institutions, and across southern Europe especially individual reformers attacked the wealthy life-styles of monks and secular clergy as un-Christian. Individual monks might take vows of poverty, but monasteries themselves were often very wealthy. Torn between their own involvement in a commercial world and an inherited Christian-Roman tradition that looked upon commerce and capital as degrading, reformers called for a return to what they imagined to have been the life of the primitive Church, one that emphasized both individual and collective poverty. The poverty movement attracted great numbers of followers, many of whom added to their criticisms of traditional clergy a concern over clerical morality and challenges about the value of sacraments and the priesthood. Although many reformers were condemned as heretics and sporadically persecuted, the reform movement continued to grow and threatened to destroy the unity of western Christendom.

The people who preserved the Church's unity were inspired by the same impulses, but they channeled their enthusiasm into reforming the Church from within. Francis of Assisi (1182–1226), the son of a prosperous Italian merchant, rejected his luxurious life in favor of one of radical poverty, simplicity, and service to others. He was a man of extraordinary simplicity, humility, and joy, and his piety was in keeping with his character. As he wandered about preaching repentance he drew great numbers of followers from all ranks, especially from the urban communities of Italy. Convinced of the importance of obedience, Francis asked the pope to approve the way of life he had chosen for himself and his followers. The pope, recognizing that in Francis the impulses threatening the Church might be its salvation, granted his wish. The Order of Friars Minor, or Franciscans, grew by thousands, drawing members from as far away as England and Hungary.

Francis insisted that his followers observe strict poverty, both individually and collectively. The order could not own property, nor could its members even touch money. They were expected to beg food each day for their sustenance. They were to travel from town to town, preaching, performing manual labor, and serving the poor. In time the expansion of the order and its involvement in preaching against heresy and in education brought about compromises with Francis' original ideals. The Franciscans needed churches in which to preach, books with which to study, and protection from local bishops. Most of the friars accepted these changes. These, the so-called

conventuals, were bitterly opposed by the spirituals, or rigorists, who sought to maintain the radical poverty of their founder. In the fourteenth century this conflict led to a major split in the order and ultimately to the condemnation of the spirituals as heretics.

The order of friars founded by Dominic (1170–1221) also adopted a rule of strict poverty, but the primary focus of the Dominicans was on preaching to the society of the thirteenth century. This order, which emphasized intellectual activity, concentrated on preaching against heresies and on higher education. Thus the Dominicans too gravitated toward the cities of western Europe and especially toward its great universities. These new orders of preachers, highly educated, enthusiastic, and eloquent, began to formulate for the urban laity of Europe a new vision of Christian society, a society not only of peasants, lords, and monks, but also of merchants, craftsmen, and professionals. At the same time, their central organizations and their lack of direct ties to the rural aristocracies made them the favorite religious orders of the increasingly powerful centralized monarchies.

In this fifteenth-century terra cotta from Florence, Andrea della Robbia portrays an imaginary meeting between Saint Francis of Assisi and Saint Dominic, founders of the new orders of friars in the thirteenth century.

The Invention of the State

The disintegration of the Carolingian state in the tenth century left political power fragmented among a wide variety of political entities. In general these were of two types. The first, the papacy and the empire, were elective, traditional structures that claimed universal sovereignty over the Christian world, based on a sacred view of political power. The second, largely hereditary and less extravagant in their religious and political pretensions, were the limited kingdoms that arose within the old Carolingian world or on its borders.

The Universal States: Empire and Papacy

The Frankish world east of the Rhine had been less affected than the kingdom of the West Franks by the onslaught of Vikings, Magyars, and Saracens. The eastern Frankish kingdom, a loose confederacy of five great duchies—Saxony, Lorraine, Franconia, Swabia, and Bavaria—had preserved much of the Carolingian religious, cultural, and institutional traditions. In 919 Duke Henry I of Saxony (919–36) was elected king, and his son Otto I (936–73) laid the foundation for the revival of the empire. Otto inflicted a devastating defeat on the Magyars in 955, subdued the other dukes, and tightened his control over the kingdom. He accomplished this largely through the extensive use of bishops and abbots, whom he appointed as his agents and sources of loyal support. In 951, in order to prevent a southern German prince from establishing himself in northern Italy, Otto invaded and conquered Lombardy. Eleven years later he entered Rome, where he was crowned emperor by the pope.

Otto, known to history as "the Great," had established the main outlines of German imperial policy for the next three hundred years. These were conflict with the German aristocracy, reliance on bishops and abbots as imperial agents, and preoccupation with Italy. His successors, both in his own Saxon dynasty (919–1024) and in the succeeding dynasties, the Salians (1024–1125) and the Staufens (1138–1254), continued this tradition. Magnates elected the German kings, who were then consecrated as emperors by the pope. Royal fathers

The Empire of Otto the Great, ca. 963

generally were able to bring about the election of their sons, and in this manner they attempted to turn the kingship into a hereditary office. However, the royal families could not manage to produce male heirs in each generation, and thus the magnates continued to exercise real power in royal elections. Because of this elective tradition, German emperors were never able to establish effective control over the German magnates outside their own duchies.

The magnates' ability to expand their own power and autonomy at the expense of their Slavic neighbors to the east also contributed to the weakness of the German monarchy. In the 1150s for example, Henry the Lion (ca. 1130–95), Duke of Bavaria and Saxony, carved out an autonomous

THE SAXON, SALIAN, AND STAUFEN DYNASTIES

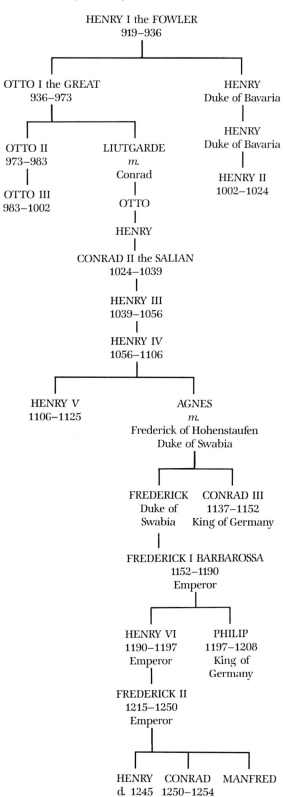

HENRY I the FOWLER
919–936

OTTO I the GREAT
936–973

HENRY
Duke of Bavaria

OTTO II
973–983

LIUTGARDE
m.
Conrad

HENRY
Duke of Bavaria

OTTO III
983–1002

OTTO

HENRY II
1002–1024

HENRY

CONRAD II the SALIAN
1024–1039

HENRY III
1039–1056

HENRY IV
1056–1106

HENRY V
1106–1125

AGNES
m.
Frederick of Hohenstaufen
Duke of Swabia

FREDERICK
Duke of
Swabia

CONRAD III
1137–1152
King of Germany

FREDERICK I BARBAROSSA
1152–1190
Emperor

HENRY VI
1190–1197
Emperor

PHILIP
1197–1208
King of
Germany

FREDERICK II
1215–1250
Emperor

HENRY
d. 1245

CONRAD
1250–1254

MANFRED

principality in the Slavic areas between the Elbe and the Vistula, founding the major trading towns of Lübeck and Rostock. It was the goal of every great aristocratic family to extend its own independent lordship.

In order to counter such aristocratic power, emperors looked to the Church both for the development of the religious cult of the emperor as "The Anointed of the Lord" and as a source of reliable military and political support. While the offices of count and duke had become hereditary within the great aristocracy, the offices of bishop and abbot remained public charges to which the emperor could appoint loyal supporters. Since these ecclesiastics had taken vows of celibacy, the emperor did not fear that they would attempt to pass their offices on to their children. Moreover, churchmen tended to be experienced, educated administrators who could assist the emperor in the administration of the empire. Like the Carolingians, the Saxon and Salian emperors needed a purified, reformed Church free of local aristocratic control to serve the interests of the emperor. This imperial church system·was the cornerstone of the empire.

Those laymen the emperor could count on, particularly from the eleventh century, were trusted household serfs whom the kings used as their agents. Although unfree, these ministerials were entrusted with important military commands and given strategic castles throughout the empire. Despised by the free-born nobility, they tended at first to be loyal supporters of the emperor. In the twelfth century, they took on the chivalric ideals of their aristocratic neighbors and benefited from conflicts between emperor and pope to acquire their autonomy. As old noble families died out, ministerial families replaced them as a new hereditary aristocracy.

Otto the Great had entered Italy to secure his southern flank. His successors became embroiled in Italian affairs until in the thirteenth century they abandoned Germany altogether. As emperors, they had to be crowned by the pope. This was possible only if they controlled Rome. Moreover, the growing wealth of northern Italian towns was an important source of financial support if Lombardy could be controlled. Finally, the preoccupation with Italy was a natural outcome of the nature of this empire. Imperial claims to universal sovereignty continued the Carolingian tradition of empire. An imperial office without Italy was unthinkable. Thus the emperors found themselves drawn into papal and Italian politics, frequently with disastrous results. Germany became merely a source of men and material with which to fight the Lombard towns and the pope. From the eleventh through the thirteenth centuries emperors granted German princes autonomy in return for this support.

The early successes of this imperial program created the seeds of its own destruction. Imperial efforts to reform the Church resulted in a second, competing claimant to universal authority, the papacy. In the later tenth and early eleventh centuries, emperors had intervened in papal elections, deposed and replaced corrupt popes, and worked to ensure that bishops and abbots within the empire would be educated, competent churchmen. The most effective reformer was Emperor Henry III (1039–56), an effective and devout emperor who took seriously his role as the anointed of the Lord to reform the Church both in Germany and in Rome. When three rivals claimed the papacy, Henry called a synod, or meeting of bishops, which deposed all three and installed the first of a series of German popes. The most effective was Henry's own cousin who, as Leo IX (1049–54), traveled widely in France, Germany, and Italy. He condemned simony, that is, the practice of buying Church offices, and fostered monastic reforms such as that of Cluny. He also encouraged the efforts of a group of young reformers drawn from across Europe.

In the next decades, these new, more radical reformers began to advocate a widespread renewal of the Christian world, led not by emperors but by popes. These reformers pursued an ambitious set of goals. They sought to reform the morals of the clergy and in particular to eliminate married priests. They tried to free churches and monasteries from lay control both by forbidding lay men and women from owning churches and monasteries and by eliminating simony. They particularly condemned "lay investiture," that is, the practice by which kings and emperors appointed bishops and invested them with the symbols of their office. Finally, they insisted that the pope, not the emperor, was the supreme representative of God on earth and as such had the right to exercise a universal sovereignty. Had not Christ said to Peter, the first bishop of Rome: "To you I shall give the keys of the kingdom of heaven; and whatsoever you shall bind on earth shall be bound also in heaven, and whatsoever you shall loose upon earth will be loosed also in heaven"?

Every aspect of the reform movement met with strong opposition throughout Europe. However, its effects were most dramatic in the empire because of the central importance there of the imperial church system. Henry III's son Henry IV (1056–1106) clashed head-on with the leading radical reformer and former protege of Leo IX, Pope Gregory VII (1073–85), over the emperor's right to appoint and to install or invest bishops in their offices. This investiture controversy changed the face of European political history. The contest was fought not simply with swords but with words. Legal scholars for both sides searched Roman and Church law for arguments to bolster their claims, thus encouraging the revival of legal studies at Bologna. For the first time, public opinion played a crucial role in politics, and both sides composed carefully worded propaganda tracts aimed at secular and religious audiences. Gradually, the idea of the separate spheres of church and state emerged for the first time in European political theory.

The actual course of the conflict was erratic and in the end weakened both the empire and the papacy. In 1075 the emperor, supported by many German bishops, attempted to depose Gregory. Gregory excommunicated and deposed Henry, freed the German nobility from their obligations to him, and encouraged them to rebel. As anti-imperial strength grew, Henry took a desperate gamble. Crossing the Alps in the dead of winter in 1077, he arrived before the castle of Canossa in northern Italy, where Gregory was staying. Dressed as a humble penitent, Henry stood in the snow asking the pope for forgiveness and reconciliation. As a priest, the pope could not refuse, and he lifted the excommunication. Once more in power, Henry began again to appoint bishops. Again in 1080 Gregory excommunicated and deposed him. This time the majority of the German nobles and bishops remained loyal to the emperor and Henry marched on Rome. Deserted by most of his clergy, Gregory had to flee to the Normans in southern Italy. He died in Salerno in 1085, his last words being "I have loved justice and hated iniquity, therefore I die in exile."

Henry did not long enjoy his victory. Gregory's successors rekindled the opposition to Henry and even convinced his own son to join in the revolt.

The conflict ended only in 1122, when Emperor Henry V (1106–25) and Pope Calixtus II (1119–24) reached an agreement known as the Concordat of Worms, which differentiated between the royal and the spiritual spheres of authority and allowed the emperors a limited role in episcopal election and investiture. This compromise changed the nature of royal rule in the empire, weakening the emperors and contributing to the long-term decline of royal government in Germany.

The decline that began with the investiture controversy continued as emperors abandoned political power north of the Alps in order to pursue their ambitions in Italy. Frederick I Barbarossa (1152–90) spent much of his reign attempting to reimpose imperial authority and to collect imperial incomes from the rich towns of northern Italy. For this he needed the support of the German princes, and he granted them extraordinary privileges in return for their cooperation south of the Alps. In 1156, for example, he gave Henry Jasomirgott (ca. 1114–77) virtual autonomy in the newly created duchy of Austria. Still, the combined efforts of the Lombard towns and the papacy were too much for Frederick and his armies to win a decisive victory. By the time of Frederick's death in 1190–he drowned crossing a river while on crusade–in Germany the emperor was more a feudal lord than a sovereign and in Italy his authority was disputed by the papacy and the towns. Frederick's successors continued his policy of focusing on Italy with no better success. In 1230 Frederick II (1215–50) conceded to each German prince sovereign rights in his own territory. From the thirteenth to the nineteenth century these princes ruled their territories as independent states, leaving the office of emperor a hollow title.

The investiture controversy ultimately compromised the authority of the pope as well as that of the emperor. First, the series of compromises beginning with the Concordat of Worms established a novel and potent tradition in Western political thought: the definition of separate spheres of authority for secular and religious government. Secondly, while in the short run popes were able to exercise enormous political influence, from the thirteenth century they were increasingly unable to make good their claims to absolute authority.

Papal power was based on more than Scripture. Over the centuries, the popes had acquired large amounts of land in central Italy and in the Rhone Valley, which formed the nucleus of the Papal States. Moreover, in every corner of Europe bishops and clergy were at least in theory agents of papal programs. The elaboration of systematic canon law encouraged by the papal reformers as a weapon in the investiture controversy created a system of courts and legal institutions more sophisticated than that of any secular monarch. Church courts claimed jurisdiction over all clerics regardless of the nature of the legal problem and over all baptized Christians in such fundamental issues as legitimacy of marriages, inheritances, and oaths. During the pontificate of Innocent III (1198–1216) the papacy reached the height of its powers. Innocent made and deposed emperors, excommunicated kings, summoned a crusade against heretics in the south of France, and placed whole countries such as England and France under interdict, that is, the suspension of all religious services when rulers dared to contradict him. Still, he found time to support Francis of Assisi and Dominic, and in 1215 to call the Fourth Lateran Council, which culminated the reforms of the past century and had a lasting effect on the spiritual life of clergy and laity alike. At the council, more than twelve hundred assembled bishops and abbots, joined by great nobles from across Europe, defined fundamental doctrines such as the nature of the eucharist, ordered annual confession of sins, and detailed procedures for the election of bishops. They also mandated a strict life-style for clergy and forbade their participation in judicial procedures in which accused persons had to undergo painful ordeals, such as grasping a piece of red-hot iron and carrying it a prescribed distance, to prove their innocence. More ominously, the council also mandated that Jews wear special identifying markings on their clothing—a sign of the increasing hostility Christians felt toward the Jews in their midst.

During the thirteenth century the papacy continued to perfect its legal system and its control over clergy throughout Europe. However, politically the popes were unable to assert their claims to universal supremacy. This was true both in Italy, where the communes in the north and the kingdom of Naples in the south resisted direct papal control, and in the emerging kingdoms north of the Alps, where monarchs successfully intervened in Church affairs. The old claims of papal authority rang increasingly hollow. When Pope Boniface VIII (1294–1303) attempted to prevent the French king Philip IV (1285–1314) from taxing the French clergy, boasting that he could depose kings "like servants" if necessary, Philip proved him wrong. Philip's agents hired a gang of adventurers who kidnapped the pope, plundered his treasury, and released him a broken, humiliated wreck. He died three weeks later. The French king who had engineered Boniface's humiliation represented a new political tradition much more limited but ultimately more successful than either the empire or the papacy—the medieval nation-state.

The Nation-States: France and England

King was a less pretentious and more familiar office than that of emperor. As the Carolingian world disintegrated, a variety of kingdoms had appeared in France, Italy, Burgundy, and Provence. Beyond the confines of the old Carolingian world, kingship was well established in England and northern Spain. In Scandinavia, Poland, Bohemia, and Hungary powerful chieftains were consolidating royal power at the expense of their aristocracies. The claims of kings were much more modest than those of emperors or popes. Kings lay claim to a limited territory and, while the king was anointed, and thus a "Christus" (from the Greek word for sacred oil), kings were only one of many representatives of God on earth. Finally, kings were far from absolute rulers. During the tenth and eleventh centuries, the powers of justice, coinage, taxation, and military command, once considered public, had been usurped by aristocrats and nobles. Kings needed the support of these magnates and often—as in the case of France—these dukes and counts were wealthier and more powerful than the kings. Still, between the tenth and fourteenth centuries some monarchies, especially those of France and England, developed into powerful, centralized, and vigorous kingdoms. In the process they gave birth to what has become the modern state.

In 987, when Hugh Capet was elected king of the West Franks, no one suspected that his successors would become the most powerful rulers of

Prominent Popes and Religious Figures of the High Middle Ages

1049–54*	Pope Leo IX
1073–85	Pope Gregory VII
1088–99	Pope Urban II
1119–24	Pope Calixtus II
1170–1221	Saint Dominic
1182–1226	Saint Francis of Assisi
1198–1216	Pope Innocent III
1225–74	Saint Thomas Aquinas
1294–1303	Pope Boniface VIII

*Dates for popes are dates of reign.

Europe, for they were relatively weak magnates whose only real power lay in the region between Paris and Orléans. The dukes of Normandy, descendants of Vikings whose settlement had been recognized by Frankish kings, ruled their duchy with an authority of which the kings could only dream. Less than a century later Duke William of Normandy expanded his power even more by conquering England. In the twelfth century, the English kings ruled a vast collection of hereditary lands on both sides of the English Channel termed the "Angevin Empire," territories much richer than those ruled by the French king. The counts of Flanders, too, ruled a prosperous region much better unified than the French king's small territory in the Parisian area. In the south, the counts of Poitou, who were also dukes of Aquitaine, were building up a powerful territorial principality in this most Romanized region of the kingdom, while in Anjou an ambitious aristocratic family was consolidating itself as a virtually independent principality.

Biology and bureaucracy created the medieval French monarchy. Between 987 and 1314, every royal descendant of Hugh Capet (after whom the dynasty was called the Capetian) left a male heir—an extraordinary record for a medieval family. During the same period, by comparison, the office of emperor was occupied by men from no less than nine families. By simply outlasting the families of their great barons, the Capetian kings were able to absorb lands when other families became extinct. This success was not just the result of luck. Kings such as Robert the Pious (996–1031) and Louis VII (1137–80) risked excommunication in order to divorce wives who had not produced male heirs. In 1152 Louis had his marriage with the richest heiress of the twelfth century, Eleanor of Aquitaine (1122–1204), annulled in part because she had given him no sons. With the annulment he also lost the chance to absorb her territories of Aquitaine and Poitou. A few months later Eleanor married Count Henry of Anjou (1133–89), who two years later became King Henry II of England. Imagine Louis' chagrin when with Henry Eleanor produced four sons, in the process making the English kings the greatest magnates in France.

The Capetians' long run of biological luck, combined with the practice of having a son crowned during his father's lifetime and thus being firmly established before his father's death, was only part of the explanation for the Capetian success. The Capetians also wisely used their position as consecrated sovereign to build a power base in the Ile de France (the region around Paris) and among the bishops and abbots of the kingdom, and then to insist on their feudal rights as the lords of the great dukes and counts of France. It was this foundation that Philip II (1180–1223), the son of Louis VII by his third wife, used to create the French monarchy.

Philip II was known to posterity as Augustus or the aggrandizer, because through his ruthless political intrigue and brilliant organizational sense he more than doubled the territory he controlled and more than quadrupled the revenue of the French crown. (See Special Feature, "The Paris of Philip Augustus," pp. 286–87.) Through marriage he acquired Vermandois, the Amiénois, Artois, and Valois. He later absorbed Flanders and set the stage for the absorption of the great county of Toulouse by his son Louis VIII (1223–26) in the aftermath of the Albigensian Crusade launched by Pope Innocent III. Philip's greatest coup, however, was the confiscation of all the continental possessions of the English king John (1199–1216), the son of Henry II and Eleanor of Aquitaine. Although sovereign in England, as lord of Normandy, Anjou, Maine, and Touraine, John was technically a vassal of King Philip. When John married the fiancée of one of his continental vassals, the outraged vassal appealed to Philip in his capacity as John's lord. Philip summoned John to appear before the royal court, and when he refused to do so, Philip ordered him to surrender all of his continental fiefs. This meant war, and one by one John's continental possessions fell to the French king. Philip's victory over John's ally the emperor Otto IV (1198–1215) at Bouvines in 1214 sealed the English loss of Normandy, Maine, Anjou, Poitou, and Touraine (see map, p. 285).

As important as the absorption of these vast regions was the administrative system Philip organized to govern them. Using members of families from the old royal demesne, he set up administrative officials called *baillis* and *seneschals*, nonfeudal, salaried agents who collected

THE CAPETIAN DYNASTY OF FRANCE (to 1314)

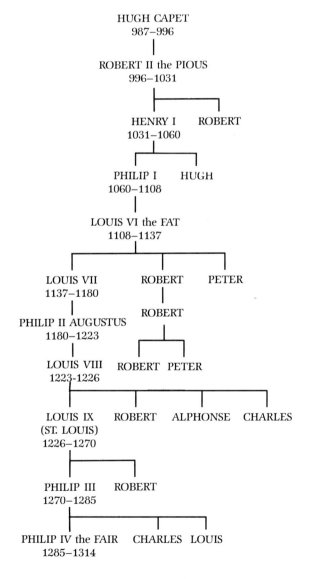

his revenues and represented his interests. The baillis in particular, who were drawn from non-noble families and who often had received their education at the University of Paris, were the foundation of the French bureaucracy, which grew in strength and importance through the thirteenth century. By governing the regions of France according to local traditions but always with an eye to the king's interests, these bureaucrats did more than anyone else to create a stable, enduring political system.

Philip's grandson Louis IX (1226–70) fine-tuned this administrative machine and endowed it with the aura of sanctity. Louis was as perfect an embodiment of medieval Christian virtue as Saint Francis of Assisi, who died in the year of Louis' coronation. Generous and pious, but also brave and capable, Louis took seriously his obligation to provide justice for the poor and protection for the weak. A disastrous Crusade in 1248, which ended in his capture and ransom in Egypt, convinced Louis that his failure was punishment for his sins and those of his government. When he returned to France, he dispatched investigators to correct abuses by baillis and other royal officials and restored property unjustly confiscated by his father's agents during the Albigensian Crusade. In addition he established a permanent central court in Paris to hear appeals from throughout the kingdom. Although much of the work was handled by a growing staff of professional jurists, Louis often became involved personally. One of his advisors recalled years later, "In summer, after hearing mass, the king often went to the wood of Vincennes, where he would sit down with his back against an oak, and make us all sit round him. Those who had any suit to present could come to speak to him without hindrance from an usher or any other person."

In 1270, Louis attempted another crusade and died in an epidemic in Tunis. The good will and devotion that Louis won from his subjects was a precious heritage that his successors were able to exploit for centuries. When his grandson Philip the Fair (1285–1314) faced the threat of Boniface VIII (see p. 283), he could rely on subjects and agents for whom the king of France and not the pope was sovereign.

The growth of royal power transformed the traditional role of the aristocracy. As the power and wealth of kings increased, the ability of

England and France in mid-1200s

the nobility to maintain their independence decreased. Royal judges undermined lords' control over the peasantry. Royal revenues enabled kings to hire warriors rather than relying on traditional feudal levies. At the same time, the increasing expenses of the noble life-style forced all but the wealthiest aristocrats to look for sources of income beyond their traditional estates. Increasingly they found this in royal service. Thus in the thirteenth century the nobility began to lose some of its independence to the state.

By a quite different path the English monarchy reached a level of power similar to that of the French kings by the end of the thirteenth century. France was made by a family and its bureaucracy. The kingdom originally forged by Alfred and his descendants was transformed by the successors of William the Conqueror, using its judges and its people, often in spite of themselves.

In 1066 the Norman conquerors of England acquired a small insular kingdom that had been united by Viking raids little more than a century before. Hostile Celtic societies bordered it to the north and west. Still, it had important strengths. First, the king of the English was not simply a feudal lord, a first among equals—he was a sovereign.

The Paris of Philip Augustus

Returning to Paris after his victory over the emperor Otto IV at Bouvines in July 1214, Philip Augustus was met before the city walls by crowds of townspeople, who spread flowers in his path and led him in triumph into his city. The people danced, clergy and students chanted, bells rang, and the homes and churches of the city overflowed with flowers. The rejoicing, which continued for seven days and nights, was a celebration of the king and the city that he had created.

Prior to his reign, Paris had been just one of several royal residences; Philip made it his capital, enriched it, and transformed it. During his reign the population of the city doubled, from approximately 25,000 to over 50,000 inhabitants, making it the most populous city north of the Alps. Philip paved the city's principal streets and built aqueducts to replace those built by the Romans, which were long in ruins. Shortly before leaving on crusade in 1192, he ordered construction of a new city wall, protected by seventy-six towers and pierced by fourteen gates. To guard against the English down the river, Philip also constructed a fortification, the Louvre, just outside the new walls. Within these walls, which eventually enclosed some 618 acres, developed a complex combination of commercial, political, and cultural life unique in Europe.

Paris was actually three cities in 1214: the ancient island of the *cité* with its royal and episcopal functions; the *ville*, the commercial center of Paris on the right bank; and the *université*, the intellectual center of Europe, on the left. Philip left his mark on each.

The cité continued its ancient function as the religious and political center of Paris. The island was divided between the two lords of the city, the king and the bishop. At the eastern end, surrounded by a rabbit warren of smaller churches and clerical residences, stood the cathedral. Notre Dame had been in the process of reconstruction since 1163, its soaring Gothic vaulting rising from its older Romanesque pillars. By the first quarter of the thirteenth century, work had begun on the west facade, and the great rose window was under way. Across the entire facade stretched the gallery of the kings—twenty-eight imposing statues of biblical rulers who looked across the cathedral square to the western end of the island and the palace of the king of France.

The palace itself consisted of a round stone tower and a chapel dedicated to Saint Nicholas, both of which dated to the early eleventh century. Here Philip had established the royal court and permanently fixed his archives and accounting office. Here he resided when in Paris, and here he housed his family, retainers, chaplains, and chancery personnel. To the palace came Philip's baillis to report on their annual activities. For the first time, the French monarchy had a fixed seat of government.

The royal precincts on the cité were linked with the ville on the right bank by the Grand-Pont, a bridge covered with the houses of money changers. At the end of the bridge stood a small tower, or *Châtelet*, protecting access to the cité. It was in the ville that in 1183 Philip constructed the first permanent Paris market, *Les Halles*, which remained the principal Paris market until the 1960s. The buildings consisted of two large sheds surrounded by walls pierced with great doors out of which merchants and craftsmen sold their products. Around Les Halles rose the residences and workshops of the tailors, blacksmiths, goldsmiths, shoemakers, coopers, tanners, cartwrights, furriers, potters, carpenters, and other tradespeople. With few exceptions these craftsmen occupied post-and-beam structures, crowded together so closely that often their upper stories touched, forming arches over the narrow, twisting streets. Near Les Halles was the great cemetery of the Saints-Innocents, the most squalid and bizarre quarter of Paris. The primary cemetery of Paris for centuries, the site was used as an informal market, the favorite meeting place for thieves, charlatans, and prostitutes. Here dogs tore at half-buried corpses while lovers met for a few moments of pleasure. Philip had walled the cemetery in their servants (the latter "nearly all thieves" as one alumnus later recalled), and wandering clerics, or goliards, who lived by their wits on the fringe of the university. Prosperous students rented rooms from local landlords and amused themselves in the numerous taverns. Generous benefactors were beginning to establish charitable foundations, or colleges in which poor clerics might find room and board. Already in existence were the colleges of *Dix-huit*, Saint-Honoré, and Saint-Thomas du Louvre. The most famous, founded by Louis IX's chaplain Robert de Sorbon, would not be established until 1257.

A great and vibrant capital, Philip's Paris was also dangerous, filthy, and smelly. Twice during Philip's reign flooding destroyed both the Grand-Pont and the Petit-Pont. In 1196 Philip had had to seek refuge from rising water on Mount Saint Geneviève. Although Philip had paved the principal streets, the others remained virtually open sewers. Crowded conditions were ideal breeding grounds for infectious diseases of all sorts, and hospitals such as the Hotel Dieu probably did more to incubate and spread disease than to contain it.

Despite its dangers, crime, and lack of sanitation, Paris was alive, exciting, teeming with new people and new ideas. In the thirteenth century Paris became what it would continue to be   the vibrant heart of the French nation.

1187, but the walls had accomplished little more than providing security for clandestine activities.

The episcopal quarter of the cité was connected to the predominantly clerical left bank by the Petit-Pont. At the end of this bridge stood another *Châtelet*, which protected access to the cité and which also served as a prison. In the previous century the left bank had become the intellectual center of Europe. Its schools, those of the monasteries of Saint-Germain-des-Prés and Saint-Victor, and especially the school established by Peter Abelard on Mont Sainte Geneviève, attracted students from as far away as Germany, England, Italy, Hungary, and Scandinavia. Philip's new wall enclosed only Mont Sainte Geneviève, which had become the nucleus of the corporation of masters that formed the University of Paris. Students and masters, reassured by the physical security of the new walls and the political security afforded by Philip's charters for the university, flocked to the area. By 1219 they were so numerous that they grouped themselves into four "nations," divisions of the university population according to their countries of origin.

The crowding, jostling atmosphere in the university was similar to that in the ville, but on the left bank the crowds consisted of students, teachers,

Secondly, Anglo-Saxon government had been participatory, with the free men of each shire taking part in court sessions and sharing the responsibilities of government. Finally, the king had agents, or *reeves*, in each shire (shire reeves, or sheriffs) who were responsible for representing the king's interests, presiding over the local court, and collecting royal taxes and incomes. This ability to raise money was the most important aspect of the English kingship for William the Conqueror and his immediate successors, who remained thoroughly Continental in interest, culture, and language—the first English king to speak English fluently was probably King John. England was seen primarily as a source of revenue. To tap this wealth, the Norman kings transformed rather than abolished Anglo-Saxon governmental traditions, adding Norman feudalism and administrative control to Anglo-Saxon kingship.

William preserved English government while replacing Anglo-Saxon officers with his continental vassals, chiefly Normans and Flemings. He rewarded his supporters with land confiscated from the defeated Anglo-Saxons, but he was careful to give out land only in fief. In contrast to continental practice, where many lords owned vast estates outright, in England all land was held directly or indirectly of the king. Because he wanted to know the extent of his new kingdom and its wealth, William ordered a comprehensive survey of all royal rights. The recorded account, known as the Domesday Book, was the most extensive investigation of economic rights since the late Roman tax rolls had been abandoned by the Merovingians.

Since William and his successors concentrated on their continental possessions and spent little time in England, they needed an efficient system of controlling the kingdom in their absence. To this end they developed the royal court, an institution inherited from their Anglo-Saxon predecessors, into an efficient system of fiscal and administrative supervision. The most important innovation was the use of a large checkerboard, or exchequer, which functioned like a primitive computer to audit the returns of their sheriffs. Annual payments were recorded on long rolls of parchment called pipe rolls, the first continuous accounting system in Europe. The use of extensive written records and strict accounting produced the most efficient and prosperous royal administration in Europe.

Almost two decades of warfare over the succession in the first half of the twelfth century greatly weakened royal authority, but Henry II (1154–89), reestablished central power by reasserting his authority over the nobility and through his legal reforms. Using his continental wealth and armies, he brought the English barons into line, destroyed private castles, and reasserted his rights to traditional royal incomes. He strengthened royal courts by expanding royal jurisdiction at the expense of Church tribunals and of the courts owned by feudal lords.

Henry's efforts to control the clergy led to one of the epic clashes of the investiture controversy. The archbishop of Canterbury, Thomas Becket (ca. 1118–70), although a personal friend of Henry, who had made him first chancellor and then archbishop, refused to accept the king's claim to jurisdiction over clergy. In spite of his friendship with the king, Becket, who had been educated at Paris, was deeply influenced by the papal reform movement and had a great sense of the dignity of his office. For six years Becket lived in exile on the Continent and infuriated Henry by his stubborn adherence to the letter of Church law. He was allowed to return to England in 1170, but that same year he was struck down in his own cathedral by four knights eager for royal favor. The king did penance but, unlike the German emperors, ultimately preserved royal authority over the Church.

Henry's program to assert royal courts over local and feudal ones was even more successful, laying the foundation for a system of uniform judicial procedures through which royal justice reached throughout the kingdom—the common law. In France, royal agents observed local legal traditions but sought always to turn them to the king's advantage. In contrast, Henry's legal system simplified and cut through the complex tangle of local and feudal jurisdictions concerning land law. Any free person could purchase, for a modest price, a letter, or *writ*, from the king ordering the local sheriff to impanel a jury to determine if that person had been recently dispossessed of an estate, regardless of that person's legal right to the property. The procedure was swift and efficient. If the jury found for the plaintiff, the sheriff immediately restored the property, by force if necessary. While juries may not have meted out justice, they did resolve conflicts, and they did so in a way that protected landholders. These writs became enormously successful and expanded the jurisdiction of royal courts into areas previously outside royal jurisdiction.

Henry's son John may have made the greatest contribution to the development of the English state by losing Normandy and most of his other continental lands. Loss of these territories forced English kings to concentrate on ruling England, not on their continental territories. Moreover, John's financial difficulties, brought about by his

THE NORMAN AND EARLY PLANTAGENET KINGS OF ENGLAND

WILLIAM I the CONQUEROR 1066–1087

ROBERT — WILLIAM II 1087–1100 — HENRY I 1100–1135 — ADELE *m.* Stephen Count of Blois

WILLIAM (son of Robert)

WILLIAM — MATILDA *m.* Geoffrey Plantagenet Count of Anjou

STEPHEN 1135–1154

HENRY II 1154–1189

HENRY — RICHARD I 1189–1199 — GEOFFREY — JOHN 1199–1216 — MATILDA *m.* HENRY the LION Duke of Saxony and Bavaria

HENRY III 1216–1272 — RICHARD

OTTO IV Emperor

EDWARD I 1272–1307 — EDMUND

EDWARD II 1307–1327

EDWARD III 1327–1377

unsuccessful wars to recover his continental holdings, led him to such extremes of fiscal extortion that his barons, prelates, and the townspeople of London revolted. In June 1215 he was forced to accept the "great charter of liberties," or *Magna Carta*, a conservative, feudal document demanding that he respect the rights of his vassals and of the burghers of London. The great significance of the document was its acknowledgment that the king was not above the law.

John and his weak, ineffective son Henry III (1216–72), although ably served by royal judges, were forced by their failures to cede considerable influence to the great barons of the realm. Henry's son Edward I (1272–1307), a strong and effective king who conquered Wales, defended the remaining continental possessions against France, and expanded the common law, found that he could turn baronial involvement in government to his own advantage. By summoning his barons, bishops, and representatives of the towns and shires to participate in a "parley" or "parliament," he could raise more funds for his wars. Like similar Spanish, Hungarian, and German assemblies of the thirteenth century, these assemblies were occasions to consult, to present royal programs, and to extract extraordinary taxes for specific projects. They were also opportunities for those summoned to petition the king for redress of grievances. Initially, representatives of the shires and towns attended only sporadically. However, since the growing wealth of the towns and countryside made their financial support essential, these groups came to anticipate that they had a right to be consulted and to consent to taxation.

This forced self-government through a system of royal courts and justices employing local juries and through a tradition of representative parliaments, coupled with an exacting system of accounting, increased the power of the English monarchy. By 1300, France with its powerful royal bureaucracy and England with its courts and accountants, were the most powerful states in the West.

In 1300 Pope Boniface VIII extended a plenary indulgence, the remission of all punishment due people's sins, to those who visited the churches of Rome during that year. It was a Jubilee Year, an extraordinary celebration to occur once every century. There was much to celebrate. By 1300 Europe had achieved a level of population density, economic prosperity, cultural sophistication, and political organization greater than at any time since the Roman Empire. Across Europe, a largely free peasantry cultivated a wide variety of crops both for local consumption and for growing commercial markets, while landlords sought increasingly rational approaches to estate management and investment. In cities and ports, merchants, manufacturers, and bankers presided over an international commercial and manufacturing economy that connected Scandinavia to the Mediterranean Sea. In schools and universities, students learned the skills of logical thinking and disputation while absorbing the traditions of Greece and Rome to prepare themselves for careers in law, medicine, and government. In courts and palaces, nascent bureaucracies worked to expand the rule of law over recalcitrant nobles, to keep the peace, and to preserve justice. Finally, after almost a thousand years of political, economic, and intellectual isolation, western Europe had become once more a dominant force in world civilization.

Suggestions for Further Reading

The Countryside

* Georges Duby, *Rural Economy and Country Life in the Medieval West* (Columbia, SC: University of South Carolina Press, 1968). An authoritative survey of medieval agriculture and society.

* Lynn White, Jr., *Medieval Technology and Social Change* (New York: Oxford University Press, 1966). Imaginative essays on the social impact of technology in the Middle Ages.

Georges Duby, *The Knight, the Lady, and the Priest: The Making of Modern Marriage in Medieval France* (New York: Pantheon Books, 1984). A short study of the conflict between lay and religious social values in medieval France.

* Indicates paperback edition available

* Georges Duby, *The Chivalrous Society* (Berkeley, CA: University of California Press, 1978). Essays on the French aristocracy by the leading medieval historian.

Ronald C. Finucane, *Soldiers of the Faith: Crusaders and Moslems at War* (New York: St. Martin's Press, 1984). A critical reappraisal of the Crusades for general readers.

Medieval Towns

* Robert S. Lopez, *The Commercial Revolution of the Middle Ages, 950–1350* (New York: Cambridge University Press, 1971). An excellent survey of medieval commercial history.

* Daniel Waley, *The Italian City-Republics* (New York: McGraw-Hill, 1969). A brief and highly readable account of Italian towns.

* Helene Wieruszowski, *The Medieval University* (Princeton, NJ: Van Nostrand, 1966). A short history of medieval universities.

* R. W. Southern, *Western Society and the Church in the Middle Ages* (New York: Penguin Books, 1990). A well-written account of the medieval Church for a general public.

The Invention of the State

* Joseph R. Strayer, *On the Medieval Origins of the Modern State* (Princeton, NJ: Princeton University Press, 1970). A very brief but imaginative account of medieval statecraft by a leading French institutional historian.

John W. Baldwin, *The Government of Philip Augustus: Foundations of French Royal Power in the Middle Ages* (Berkeley, CA: University of California Press, 1986). A detailed but important study of the crucial reign of Philip II.

* Horst Fuhrmann, *Germany in the High Middle Ages, c. 1050–1200* (New York: Cambridge University Press, 1986). A fresh synthesis of German history by a leading German historian.

Bryce Lyon, *A Constitutional and Legal History of Medieval England*, 2d ed. (New York: W. W. Norton, 1980). A detailed account of the making of the medieval English constitution.

M. T. Clanchy, *England and Its Rulers, 1066–1272* (New York: B & N Imports, 1983). A good, recent survey of English political history.

10

The Later Middle Ages

Webs of Stone and Blood

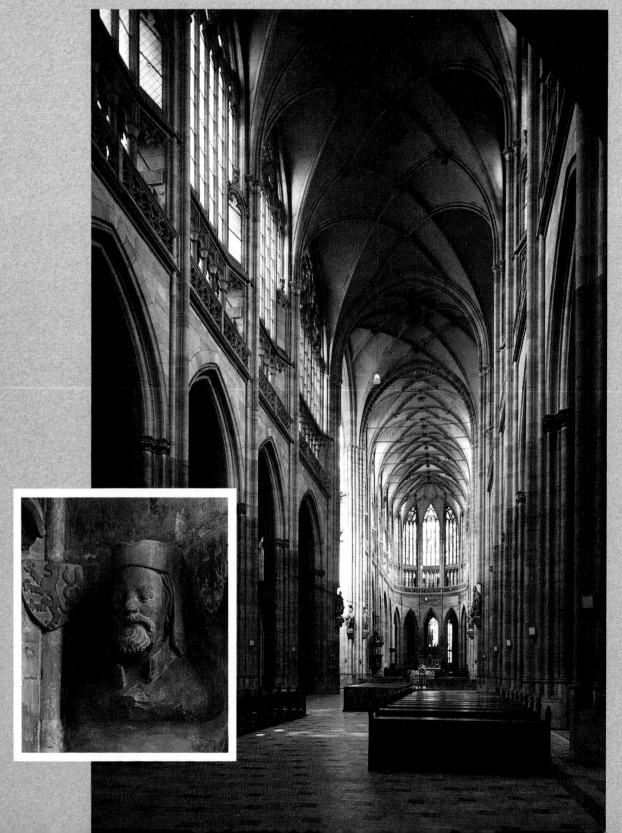

Like a delicate basket of woven stone, the Gothic vaulting in the choir of Saint Vitus Cathedral in Prague encloses and unifies the sacred space over which it floats. In a similar manner, the great aristocratic families of the fourteenth and fifteenth centuries spun webs of estates, hereditary principalities, and fiefs across Europe. In art as in life, dynamic individuals reshaped the legacy of the past into new and unexpected forms.

In France, where Gothic architecture originated in the twelfth century, architects had long used stone springers and vaults, but only to emphasize verticality and lift the eyes of the faithful to the heavens. Through the thirteenth and fourteenth centuries, French architects vied with one another to raise their vaults ever higher but never rethought the basic premise of their design. Peter Parler (1330–99), the architect of Saint Vitus, approached the design of his cathedral in a novel way. He used intersecting vaults not simply for height but to bind together the interior space of the edifice in a net of intersecting stone arches. This ability to rethink the architectural heritage of the past marked Peter Parler as the greatest architectural genius of the fourteenth century. Emperor Charles IV (1355–78), the head of the most successful web-spinning aristocratic family of the late Middle Ages, recognized Parler's talent and enlisted him in making his Bohemian capital one of the most splendid cities of Europe.

Along with his innovations in architecture, Peter Parler also opened new directions in sculpture. Again breaking with French tradition, in which sculptors sought to present their subjects as ideal types, Parler concentrated on realism and individual portraiture in his work. The carved heads of Bohemia's kings, queens, prelates, and princes that peer down from the ambulatory of Saint Vitus are real people, with their blemishes, their virtues, and their vices marked in their faces. This interest in the individual was entirely appropriate in the late fourteenth century, a time when kings and peasants, saints and heretics, lords and merchants sought to make their mark by stepping out of their traditional roles. The characters of the age had personalities as marked as Parler's individualistic sculptures. Their epithets tell much:

John "the Valiant" of Brittany; Philip "the Bold" of Burgundy; his son John "the Fearless"; the Habsburg John "the Parricide"; Charles II "the Bad" of Navarre; Pedro IV "the Cruel" of Aragon; Charles VI "the Mad" of France. Powerful and ambitious men and women fought for political dominance, religious visionaries and preachers announced new and daring revelations, and thinkers and artists broke with hallowed philosophical and literary traditions. Parler had no doubt about his own importance in this age of individuals. His own portrait bust looks down from the cathedral beside those of kings and queens.

Parler was born into a well-known family of stonemasons near the German town of Württemberg. He learned his craft from his father, but at a young age surpassed the elder Parler not simply in the execution of stone constructions, but in their design. A century earlier, a young man of such recognized talent would almost certainly have gravitated from his native Swabia to France, then the cultural center of Europe. However, although through the fourteenth century French language, styles, and tradition continued to inspire Europeans everywhere, by mid-century France was increasingly troubled by dynastic problems, war, economic decline, and the ravages of disease. It was no longer the magnet that drew the greatest artists, architects, and thinkers. Thus at the age of twenty-three the brilliant and ambitious young architect looked east rather than west and cast his lot with the splendid court of Charles IV, king of Bohemia and soon to be Holy Roman Emperor. Charles invited Parler to complete his great Prague cathedral, which had been begun by a French architect and modeled on the great cathedrals of France. With Charles' patronage, Parler modified the building program to incorporate his original vision of architecture and portraiture. He went on to direct the construction of churches, bridges, and towers in Prague and throughout Bohemia. Within a generation Parler's students spread his refinement of Gothic architecture and sculpture throughout the Holy Roman Empire, to Austria, Bavaria, Swabia, Alsace, Poland, and Italy. Parler, the weaver of stone, and Charles, the weaver of politics, were emblematic of their age.

Politics as a Family Affair

Like those of his architect, Charles' roots were in the Rhineland and his cultural inspiration in France. The ancestral estates of his family, the house of Luxembourg, lay on the banks of the Moselle River. Between 1250 and 1350, the Luxembourg family greatly expanded its political and geographical powers by involving itself in the dynastic politics of the decaying Holy Roman Empire. At the height of his power, Charles controlled a patchwork of lands that included Luxembourg, Brabant, Lusatia, Silesia, Moravia, Meissen, and Brandenburg. His daughter married Richard II of England. A son succeeded him in Bohemia and another obtained the Hungarian crown.

Such fragmented and shifting territorial bases were typical of the great families of the fourteenth and fifteenth centuries. Everywhere, family politics threatened the fragile institutional developments of the thirteenth century. Aristocrats competed for personal power and used public office, military command, and taxing power for private ends. What mattered was neither territorial boundaries nor political divisions but marriage alliances, kinship, and dynastic ambitions.

The Struggle for Central Europe

In addition to the Luxembourgs, four other similarly ambitious families competed for dominance in the empire. First were the Wittelsbachs, the chief competitors of the Luxembourgs. The Wittelsbachs had originated in Bavaria but had since spread across Europe. In the west the Wittelsbachs had acquired Holland, Hainaut, and Frisia, while in the east they temporarily held Tyrol and Brandenburg. Next were the Habsburgs, allies of the Luxembourgs, who had begun as a minor comital family in the region of the Black Forest. They expanded east, acquiring Austria, Tyrol, Carinthia, and Carniola. When Rudolf I of Habsburg (1273–91) was elected emperor in 1273, Otakar II, king of Bohemia (1253–78) and head of the powerful Premysl family, dismissed Rudolf as

"poor." Compared with the Premysls perhaps he was. The Premysl family controlled at its height not only Bohemia but also Moravia, Austria, and a miscellany of lands stretching from Silesia in the north to the Adriatic Sea. Finally, the house of Anjou, descendants of Charles of Anjou, the younger brother of the French king Louis IX, who had become king of Naples, created a similar eastern network. Charles' son Charles Robert secured election as king of Hungary in 1310. His son Louis (1342–82) added the crown of Poland (1370–82) to the Hungarian crown of Saint Stephen. The protracted wars and maneuvers that these families conducted for dominance in the empire resembled nothing so much as the competition that had taken place three centuries earlier for dominance in feudal France.

For over a century, not only great princes but also monks, adventurers, and simple peasants streamed into the kingdoms and principalities of eastern Europe. Since the early thirteenth century the Teutonic orders had used the sword to spread Christianity along the Baltic coast. By the early fourteenth century these knight-monks had conquered Prussia and the coast as far east as the Narva River, now well within Russia, where they reached the borders of the Christian principality of Novgorod. The pagan inhabitants of these regions had to choose between conversion and expulsion. When they fled, their fields were turned over to land-hungry German peasants. Long wagon trains of pioneers snaked their way across Germany from the Rhineland, Westphalia, and Saxony to this new frontier. There they were able to negotiate advantageous contracts with their new lords, guaranteeing them greater freedom than they had known at home.

By the fifteenth century religious and secular German lords had established a new agrarian economy, modeled on western European estates, in regions previously unoccupied or sparsely settled by the indigenous Slavic peoples. This economy specialized in the cultivation of grain for export to the west. Each fall fleets of hundreds of ships sailed from Gdansk and Riga to the ports of the Netherlands, England, and France. Returning flotillas carried Flemish cloth and tons of salt for preserving food as far as Novgorod. The influx of Baltic grain into Europe caused a decline in domestic grain prices and a corresponding economic slump for landlords throughout the fourteenth and fifteenth centuries.

Farther south, the Christian kingdoms of Poland, Bohemia, and Hungary beckoned different sorts of westerners. Newly opened silver and copper mines in Bohemia, Silesia, southern Poland, and Hungarian Transylvania needed skilled miners, smelters, and artisans. Many were recruited from the overpopulated regions of western Germany. East-west trade routes developed to export these metals, giving new life to the Bohemian towns of Prague and Brno, the Polish cities of Kracow and Lwow, and Hungarian Buda and Bratislava. Trade networks reached south to the

An illustration from Charles V's Grandes Chroniques de France. *The scene is a highlight from the visit to Paris in 1378 of Emperor Charles IV, the maternal uncle of the French king. The rulers are at table with three prelates.*

Mediterranean via Vienna, the Brenner Pass, and Venice. To the north, trade routes extended to the Elbe River and the trading towns of Lübeck and Bremen. The Bavarian towns of Augsburg, Rothenburg, and Nuremberg flourished at the western end of this network. To the east, Lwow became a great trading center connecting southern Russia with the west.

The wealth of eastern Europe, its abundant land, and its relative freedom attracted both peasants and merchants. The promise of profitable marriages with eastern royalty drew ambitious aristocrats. Continually menaced by one another and by the aggressive German aristocracy to the west, the royal families of Poland, Hungary, and Bohemia were eager to make marriage alliances with powerful aristocratic families from farther afield. Through such a marriage, for example, Charles Robert of Anjou became king of Hungary after the extinction of that realm's ancient royal dynasty. Similarly Charles Robert's son Louis inherited the Polish crown in 1370 after the death of Casimir III, the last king of the Polish Piast dynasty. Nobles of the eastern European kingdoms were pleased to confirm the election of such outsiders. The elections prevented powerful German nobles from claiming succession to the Bohemian, Hungarian, and Polish thrones. At the same time, the families of the western European aristocracy did not have sufficiently strong local power bases to challenge the autonomy of the eastern nobility. For the outsiders, eastern alliances meant the expansion of family power and the promise of glory.

Charles IV (1347–78) was typical of these restless dynasts. His grandfather, Emperor Henry VII (1308–13), had arranged for his son John of Luxembourg to marry Elizabeth (d. 1330), the Premysl heiress of Bohemia, and thus acquire the Bohemian crown in 1310. John was king in name only. He spent most of his career fighting in the dynastic wars of the empire and of France. However, by mastering the intricate politics of the decaying Holy Roman Empire, he arranged the deposition of the Wittelsbach emperor Louis IV (1314–47) and secured the election of Charles as king of the Romans, that is, heir of the empire, in 1346. The following year the Bohemian crown passed to Charles.

Although born in Prague and deeply committed to what he called "the sweet soil of my native land," Charles had spent most of his youth in France, where he was deeply influenced by French culture. Upon his return to Prague in 1333, however, he rediscovered his Czech cultural roots. As king of Bohemia, he worked to make Prague a cultural center by combining French and Czech traditions. He imported craftsmen, architects, and artists such as Peter Parler to transform and beautify his capital. In 1348 he founded a university in Prague, the first in the empire, modeled on the University of Paris. Keenly interested in history, Charles provided court historians with the sources necessary to write their histories of the Bohemian kingdom. "It is to the great profit of the state that young princes be taught history," he wrote, "lest through ignorance they should become degenerate inheritors of an ancient greatness."

Charles took a more active role in this cultural renewal than perhaps any European king since Alfred of England, fostering a literary renaissance in both Latin and Czech. Although he had forgotten his native Czech during his long stay in France, he soon learned to read and write it as well as French, German, Italian, and Latin. He authored a number of religious texts, fostered the use of the Czech language in religious services, and initiated a Czech translation of the Bible. He even composed his own autobiography, perhaps the first lay person to do so in medieval Europe.

The effects of Charles' cultural policies were

Central and Eastern Europe, ca. 1378

far-reaching, but in directions he never antici-pated. His interests in Czech culture and religious reform bore unexpected fruit during the reign of his son Sigismund, king of Germany (1410–37), of Bohemia (1419–37), of Hungary (1387–1437), and Holy Roman Emperor (1433–37). During Sigis-mund's reign Czech religious and political re-formers came into open conflict with the power-ful German-speaking minority in the University of Prague. Led by the theologian Jan Hus (ca. 1372–1415), this reform movement ultimately challenged the authority of the Roman Church and became the direct predecessor of the great reformation of the sixteenth century.

Even while building up his beloved city of Prague, Charles was dismantling the Holy Roman Empire. By the fourteenth century, the title of emperor held little political importance, although as an honorific title it was still bitterly contested by the great families of the empire. Charles sought to end such disputes and at the same time to solidify the autonomy of the king-doms such as Bohemia against the threats of future imperial candidates. In 1356 he issued the "Golden Bull," an edict that officially recognized what had long been the reality, namely that the various German princes and kings were autono-mous rulers. The bull also established the pro-cedure by which future emperors would be elected. Thereafter, the emperor was chosen by seven great princes of the empire without the consultation or interference of the pope, a tradi-tion of interference that dated to the coronation of Charlemagne. The procedure made disputed elections less likely, but it acknowledged that the office itself was less significant.

The same process that sapped the power of the emperor also reduced the significance of the princes. The empire fragmented into a number of large kingdoms and duchies such as Bohemia, Hungary, Poland, Austria, and Bavaria in the east and over sixteen hundred autonomous prin-cipalities, free towns, and sovereign bishoprics in the west. The inhabitants of these territories, often ruled by foreigners who had inherited sov-ereign powers through marriage, organized themselves into estates—political units of knights, burghers, and clergy—to present a united front in dealing with their prince. The princes in turn did not enjoy any universally rec-ognized right to rule and were forced to negotiate with their estates for any powers they actually enjoyed.

The disintegration of the empire left political power east of the Rhine widely disbursed for over five hundred years. While this meant that Ger-many did not become a nation-state until the nineteenth century, decentralization left late medieval Germany as a fertile region of cultural and constitutional creativity. In this creative pro-cess the office of emperor played no role. After the Habsburg family definitively acquired the impe-rial office in 1440, the office of emperor ceased to have any role in Germany. Rather the office became one of the building blocks of the great multinational Habsburg empire of central Europe, an empire that survived until 1918.

A Hundred Years of War

The political map of western Europe was no less a patchwork quilt of family holdings than was the empire. On the Iberian peninsula, the gradual Christian reconquest bogged down as the three Christian monarchies of Castile, Aragon, and Portugal largely ignored the remaining Mus-lim kingdom of Granada. Instead, dynastic rival-ries, expansionist adventures in Sicily and Italy, internal revolts of nobility and peasants, and futile wars against one another commanded the energy and attention of the Christian kingdoms. Only when Ferdinand of Aragon married Isabella of Castile in 1469 did something like a unified Spain begin to emerge from this world of familial rivalries.

North of the Pyrenees, the situation was even more critical. The same kinds of familial rivalries that destroyed the empire as a political entity threatened to overwhelm the feudal monarchies of France and England in the fourteenth and fifteenth centuries. In both kingdoms, weakening economic climates and demographic catastrophe exacerbated dynastic crises and fierce competi-tion. The survival of the English and French monarchies was due to luck, to a longer tradition of bureaucratic government, and—in the minds of contemporaries—to the hand of God.

Three long-simmering disputes triggered the series of campaigns collectively termed the Hundred Years' War. The first issue was conflicting rights in Gascony in southern France. Since the mid-thirteenth century, the kings of England had held Gascony as a fief of the French king. Neither monarchy was content with this arrangement, and for the next seventy-five years kings quarreled constantly over sovereignty in the region.

The second point of contention was the close relationship between England and the Flemish cloth towns. These manufacturing centers were the primary customers for English wool. Early in the fourteenth century, Flemish artisans rose up in a series of bloody revolts against the aristocratic cloth dealers who had long monopolized power. The count of Flanders and the French king supported the wealthy merchants, while the English sided with the artisans.

The final dispute concerned the royal succession in France. Charles IV (1322–28), the son of Philip IV, the Fair, died without an heir. The closest descendant of a French king was the grandson of Philip the Fair, King Edward III of England (1327–77). However, Edward was the son of Philip's daughter Isabella. The French aristocracy, which did not want an English king to inherit the throne and unite the two kingdoms, pretended that according to ancient Frankish law, the crown could not pass through a woman. Instead, they preferred to give the crown to a cousin of the late king, Philip VI (1328–50), who became the first of the Valois kings of France. At first, the English voiced no objection to Philip's accession, but in 1337, when the dispute over Gascony again flared up and Philip attempted to confiscate the region from his English "vassal" Edward III, the English king declared war on Philip. Edward's stated goal was not only to recover Gascony but also to claim the crown of his maternal grandfather.

Though territorial and dynastic rivalry were the triggers that set off the war, its deeper cause was chivalry. The elites of Europe were both inspired by and trapped in a code of conduct that required them not only to maintain their honor by violence but also to cultivate violence to increase that honor. This code had been appropriate in a period of weak kingship, but by the late thirteenth century the growth of courts and royal power in France and in England left little room

In this scene from Thomas Malory's Morte d'Arthur, *Galahad, who will occupy the vacant seat at the Round Table, is introduced to King Arthur and his knights.*

for private vengeance and vendettas. Nobles were now more often royal retainers than knights errant traveling about the countryside righting wrongs. Government was increasingly an affair of lawyers and bureaucrats, war an affair of professionals. Yet kings and nobles alike still agreed with the sentiment expressed by a contemporary poet: "The glory of princes is in their pride and in undertaking great peril." By the fourteenth century only war provided sufficient peril.

Edward III of England and his rival Philip VI of France both epitomized the chivalrous knight. Both gloried in luxurious living and conspicuous consumption. Captivated by the romantic tales of King Arthur and the Round Table, in 1344 Edward organized a four-day-long round table celebration to which he invited the most outstanding nobles in England. A contemporary noted: "Among the knights continuous joustings took place for three days; the best melody was made by the minstrels, and various joyous things; to these were given changes of clothing; to these gifts abounded; these were enriched with plenty of gold and silver." A few years later Edward organized the Order of the Garter, a select group of nobles who were to embody the highest qualities of chivalry. For a ruler like Edward, obsessed with knightly glory, war with France was the ideal way to win honor and fame.

In spite of his chivalric ideals, Edward was practical when it came to organizing and financing his campaigns. Philip shared Edward's ideals but lacked his rival's practicality and self-assurance. Before his elevation to the throne, Philip had been a valiant and successful warrior, fond of jousting, tournaments, and lavish celebrations. After his coronation, he continued to act like a figure from a knightly romance, surrounding himself with aristocratic advisors who formed the most brilliant court of Europe, dispensing the royal treasure to his favorites, and dreaming of leading a great crusade to free the Holy Land. However, as the first French king in centuries elected rather than born into the right of succession, he treated the magnates from whose ranks he had come with excessive deference. He hesitated to press them for funds and deferred to them on matters of policy even while missing opportunities to raise other revenue from towns and merchants. Finally, although a competent warrior, Philip was no match in strategy or tactics for his English cousin.

Still, the sheer size and wealth of France should have made it the favorite in any war with England. Its population of roughly 16 million made it by far the largest and most densely populated kingdom in Europe. The north of France was a major cereal producer. Vineyards around Bordeaux, Paris, Beaune, and Auxerre produced wines sold throughout the west. Paris, the largest city north of the Alps, was a center of commerce as well as an intellectual capital. The Flemish cloth towns, subdued by Philip in 1328, were the most industrialized area of Europe. England, by contrast, was a relatively small, sparsely populated kingdom. Its total population was under 5 million and its economy much less tied into international trade, with only the beginnings of a cloth industry and little to export except wool. At the start of the war Philip could rely on an income roughly three to five times greater than that of

THE FRENCH AND ENGLISH SUCCESSIONS

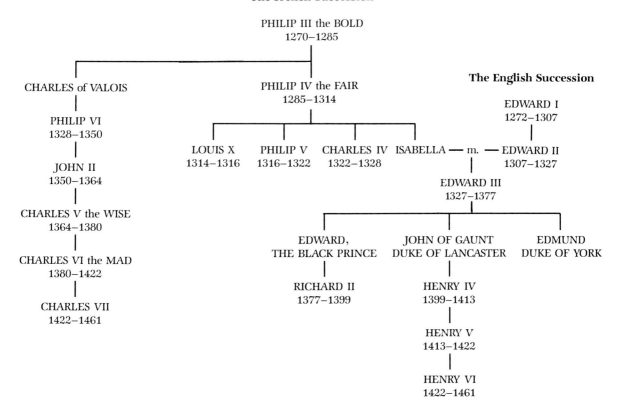

The French Succession

PHILIP III the BOLD
1270–1285

CHARLES of VALOIS

PHILIP VI
1328–1350

JOHN II
1350–1364

CHARLES V the WISE
1364–1380

CHARLES VI the MAD
1380–1422

CHARLES VII
1422–1461

PHILIP IV the FAIR
1285–1314

LOUIS X
1314–1316

PHILIP V
1316–1322

CHARLES IV
1322–1328

ISABELLA — m. — EDWARD II
1307–1327

The English Succession

EDWARD I
1272–1307

EDWARD III
1327–1377

EDWARD, THE BLACK PRINCE

JOHN OF GAUNT DUKE OF LANCASTER

EDMUND DUKE OF YORK

RICHARD II
1377–1399

HENRY IV
1399–1413

HENRY V
1413–1422

HENRY VI
1422–1461

Edward. However, these inequalities mattered little because the French king had no means of harnessing the resources of his kingdom. His greater income was matched by greater expenses, and he had no easy way to raise extraordinary funds for war. In contrast, the English king could use Parliament as an efficient source of war subsidies. Edward could also extract great sums from taxes on wool exports. Even after the invasion of France, Philip had to rely on manipulation of the coinage, confiscation of Italian bankers' property, and a whole range of nuisance taxes to finance his campaigns.

War was expensive. In spite of chivalrous ideals, nobles no longer fought as vassals of the king but as highly paid mercenaries. The nature of this service differed greatly on the two sides of the Channel. In France, the tactics and personnel had changed little since the twelfth century. The core of any army was the body of heavily armored nobles who rode into battle with their lords, supported by lightly armored knights. Behind them marched infantrymen recruited from towns and armed with pikes. Although the French also hired mercenary Italian crossbowmen, the nobles despised them and never used them effectively.

In contrast, centuries of fighting against Welsh and Scottish enemies had transformed and modernized the English armies and their tactics. The great nobles continued to serve as heavily armored horsemen, but professional companies of foot soldiers raised by individual knights made up the bulk of the army. These professional companies consisted largely of pikemen and, most importantly, of longbowmen. Although it was not as accurate as the crossbow, the English longbow had a greater range. Moreover, when massed archers fired volleys of arrows into enemy ranks, they proved extremely effective against enemy pikemen and even lightly armored cavalry.

The first real test of the two armies came at the Battle of Crécy in 1346. There an overwhelmingly superior French force surrounded the English army. Massing their archers on a hill, the English rained arrows down on the French cavalry, which attacked in glorious but suicidal manner. Typical of the French chivalric behavior was that of King John of Bohemia, father of Charles IV, both of whom were fighting as mercenaries of the French king. Although he was totally blind, John

requested and received the privilege of commanding the vanguard of the first French division. He had his men tie their horses together and lead him into battle so that he might strike a blow. The next day his body and those of all his men were found on the field, their mounts still bound together.

The English victory was total. By midnight they had repelled sixteen assaults, losing only one hundred men while killing over three thousand French. The survivors, including Philip VI, fled in disorder. Strangely enough, the French learned nothing from the debacle. In 1356 Philip's successor John II (1350–64) rashly attacked an English army at Poitiers and was captured. In 1415 the French blundered in a different way at Agincourt. This time most of the heavily armored French knights dismounted and attempted to charge the elevated English position across a soggy, muddy field. Barely able to walk and entirely unable to rise again if they fell, all were captured. Out of fear that his numerically inferior English army would be overwhelmed if the French recovered their breath, the English king ordered over fifteen hundred French nobles and three thousand ordinary soldiers killed. He kept over a thousand of the greatest nobles for ransom. English losses were less than one hundred.

Pitched battles were not the worst defeats for the French. More devastating were the constant raiding and systematic destruction of the French countryside by the English companies. The relief effort launched by Pope Benedict XII (1334–42) in 1339 gives some idea of the scale of destruction. Papal agents, sent to aid victims of the English invasion, paid out over 12,000 pounds, the equivalent of one-third of the English annual royal income, to peasants in just one region of northern France. The funds distributed were simple charity and far from adequate compensation. Villagers estimated that their actual losses were perhaps seven times greater than what they received.

Raiding and pillaging continued for decades, even during long truces between the French and English kings. During periods of truce unemployed free companies of French and English mercenaries roamed the countryside, supporting themselves by banditry while awaiting the renewal of more-formal hostilities. As one chronicler recalled, "From the Loire to the Seine and

The Hundred Years' War

(1396–1467) allied himself with England against France and profited from the war to form a far-flung lordship that included Flanders, Brabant, Luxembourg, and Hainaut. By the time of his death, he was the most powerful ruler in Europe. Much of the so-called Hundred Years' War was actually a French civil war.

During this century of war the French economy suffered even more than the French state. Trade routes were broken and commerce declined as credit disappeared. French kings repeatedly seized the assets of Italian merchant bankers in order to finance the war. Such actions made the Italians, who had been the backbone of French commercial credit, extremely wary about extending loans in the kingdom. The kings then turned to French and Flemish merchants, extorting from them forced loans that dried up capital that might otherwise have been returned to commerce and industry. Politically and economically, France seemed doomed.

The flower of French chivalry did not save France. Instead, at the darkest moment of the long and bloody struggle, salvation came at the hands of a simple peasant girl from the county of Champagne. By 1429 the English and their Burgundian allies held virtually all of northern France including Paris. Now they were besieging Orléans, the key to the south. The heir to the French throne, the dauphin, was the weak-willed and uncrowned Charles VII (1422–61). To him came Joan of Arc (1412–31), a simple, illiterate but deeply religious girl who bore an incredible message of hope. She claimed to have heard the voices of saints ordering her to save Orléans and have the dauphin crowned according to tradition at Reims.

Charles and his advisers were more than skeptical about this brash peasant girl who announced her divinely ordained mission to save France. Finally convinced of her sincerity if not of her ability, Charles allowed her to accompany a relief force to Orléans. The French army, its spirit buoyed by the belief that Joan's simple faith was the work of God, defeated the English and ended the siege. This victory led to others, and on 16 July 1429 Charles was crowned king at Reims.

After the coronation, Joan's luck began to fade. She failed to take Paris, and in 1431 she was captured by the Burgundians, who sold her to the English. Eager to get rid of this troublesome peas-

from there to the Somme, nearly all the fields were left for many years, not merely untended but without people capable of cultivating them, except for rare patches of soil, for the peasants had been killed or put to flight." Never had the ideals of chivalric conduct been so far distant from the brutal realities of warfare.

The French kings were powerless to prevent such destruction, just as they were unable to defeat the enemy in open battle. Since the kings were incapable of protecting their subjects or of leading their armies to victory, the "silken thread binding together the kingdom of France," as one observer put it, began to unravel, and the kingdom so painstakingly constructed by the Capetian monarchs began to fall apart. Not only did the English make significant territorial conquests, but the French nobles began behaving much as those in the Holy Roman Empire, carving out autonomous lordships. Private warfare and castle building, never entirely eradicated even by Louis IX and Philip IV, increased as royal government lost its ability to control the nobility. Whole regions of the kingdom slipped entirely from royal authority. Duke Philip the Good of Burgundy

A fifteenth-century portrait of Joan of Arc. The Maid of Orléans was tried for heresy and executed in 1431. Later, in 1456, Pope Calixtus III pronounced her innocent. Pope Benedict XV formally declared her a saint in 1920.

century, it was a hollow title. The continental warfare of more than a century was over.

Though war on the Continent had ended, warfare in England was just beginning. In some ways, the English monarchy had suffered even more from the Hundred Years' War than had the French. At the outset, English royal administration had been more advanced than the French. The system of royal agents, courts, and parliaments had created the expectation that the king could preserve peace and provide justice at home while waging successful and profitable wars abroad. As the decades dragged on without a decisive victory, the king came to rely on the aristocracy, enlisting its financial assistance by granting these magnates greater power at home. War created powerful and autonomous aristocratic families with their own armies. Under a series of weak kings these families fought among themselves. Ultimately they took sides in a civil war to determine the royal succession. For thirty years, from 1455 to 1485, supporters of the house of York, whose badge was the white rose, fought the rival house of Lancaster, whose symbol was the red rose, in the sort of dynastic struggle that would not have seemed out of place in the disintegrating German empire. The English Wars of the Roses, as the conflict came to be called, finally ended in 1485, when Henry Tudor of the Lancasterian faction defeated his opponents. He inaugurated a new era as Henry VII (1485–1509), the first king of the Tudor dynasty.

ant girl, the English had her tried as a heretic. Charles did nothing to save his savior. After all, the code of chivalry did not demand that a king intervene on behalf of a mere peasant girl, even if she had saved his kingdom. She was burned at the stake in Rouen on 30 May 1431.

Despite Joan's inglorious end, the tide had turned. The French pushed the English back toward the coast. In the final major battle of the war, fought at Formigny in 1450, the French used a new and telling weapon to defeat the English—gunpowder. Rather than charging the English directly as they had done so often before, they mounted cannon and pounded the English to bits. Gunpowder completed the destruction of the chivalric traditions of warfare begun by archers and pikemen. By 1452 English continental holdings had been reduced to the town of Calais. Although the English kings continued to call themselves kings of France until the eighteenth

Life and Death in the Later Middle Ages

The violence and pageantry of late medieval warfare played out against a backdrop of extraordinary social upheaval. By the end of the thirteenth century, population growth in the West had strained available resources to the breaking point. All arable land was under cultivation, and even marginal moorland, rocky mountainsides, and arid plains were being pressed into service to feed a growing population. At the same time, kings and nobles demanded ever higher taxes and rents to finance their wars and extravagant life-styles. The result was a precarious balance in which a late frost, a bad harvest, or hungry mercenaries could mean disaster. Part of the problem could be alleviated by importing grain from the Baltic or from Sicily, but this solution carried risks of its own. Transportation systems were too fragile to ensure regular supplies, and their rupture could initiate a cycle of famine, disease, and demographic collapse. Population began to decline slowly around 1300 and the downturn became catastrophic within fifty years. Between 1300 and 1450 Europe's population fell by more than 30 percent. It did not recover until the seventeenth century.

Dancing With Death

Between 1315 and 1317 the first great famine of the fourteenth century, triggered by crop failures and war, struck Europe. People died by the thousands. Urban workers, because they were chronically undernourished, were particularly hard hit. In the Flemish cloth town of Ypres, whose total population was less than twenty thousand, the town ordered the burial of 2,794 paupers' corpses within a five-month period. Although this was the greatest famine in medieval memory, it was not the last. The relatively prosperous Italian city of Pistoia, for example, recorded sixteen different famines and food shortages in the fourteenth and fifteenth centuries.

Disease accompanied famine. Crowded and filthy towns, opposing armies with their massed troops, and overpopulated countrysides provided fertile ground for the spread of infectious disease. Moreover, the greatly expanded trade routes of the thirteenth and fourteenth centuries that carried goods and grain between East and West also provided highways for deadly microbes. At Pistoia again, local chroniclers of the fourteenth and fifteenth centuries reported fourteen years of sickness, fevers, epidemic, and plague.

Between 1347 and 1352 from one-half to one-third of Europe's population died from a virulent combination of bubonic, septicemic, and pneumonic plague known to history as the Black Death. The disease, carried by the fleas of infected rats, traveled the caravan routes from central Asia. It arrived in Messina, Sicily, aboard a merchant vessel in October 1347. From there the Black Death spread up the boot of Italy and then into southern France, England, and Spain. By 1349 it had reached northern Germany, Portugal, and Ireland. The following year the Low Countries, Scotland, Scandinavia, and Russia fell victim.

Plague victims died horribly. Soon after being bitten by an infected flea, they developed high fever, began coughing, and suffered excruciatingly painful swellings in the lymph nodes of the groin or armpits. These swellings were known as buboes, from which the disease took its name. In the final stages the victims began to vomit blood. The bubonic form of the disease usually killed within five days. The septicemic form, which attacked the blood, was more swift and deadly. Those infected by the airborne, pneumonic form usually died in less than three days; in some cases, within a matter of hours.

A page from the fourteenth-century psalter and prayer book of Bonne of Luxembourg, Duchess of Normandy. The three figures of the dead contrast with three living figures on the facing page to illustrate a moral fable.

Plague was all the more terrifying because its cause, its manner of transmission, and its cure were totally unknown until the end of the nineteenth century. Preachers saw the plague as divine punishment for sin. Ordinary people frequently accused Jews of causing it by poisoning drinking water. The medical faculty of Paris announced that it was the result of the conjunction of the planets Saturn, Jupiter, and Mars, which caused a corruption of the surrounding air.

Responses to the plague were equally varied. Across Europe terrified people thought that by joining penitential groups that prayed, fasted, and even whipped themselves, they could turn away divine wrath through self-mortification. Others thought it best to abandon themselves to pleasure, either out of despair or in the hope that a pleasant life of eating and drinking would in some way ward off the terror of the plague. In many German towns terrified Christian citizens looked for outside scapegoats and slaughtered the Jewish community. Cities, aware of the risk of infection although ignorant of its process, closed their gates and turned away outsiders. Individuals with means fled to country houses or locked themselves in their homes to avoid contact with others. (See Special Feature, "A Room of One's Own," pp. 310–311.) Nothing worked. The Italian author Giovanni Boccaccio (1313–75) remarked on the wide range of opinions on how to deal with the plague, "Of the people who held these various opinions, not all of them died. Nor, however, did they all survive."

As devastating as the first outbreak of the plague was, its aftershocks were even more catastrophic. Once established in Europe, the disease continued to return roughly once each generation. Pistoia, for example, which probably lost roughly two-thirds of its population in 1348, suffered recurrences in 1389, in 1393, in 1399 when one-half of the population died, and again in 1410, 1416, 1418, 1423, 1436, and 1457. The rueful call, "Bring out your dead," resounded for centuries in European cities. The last outbreak of the plague in Europe was the 1771 epidemic in Moscow that killed 60,000.

The Black Death, along with other epidemics, famines, and war-induced shortages, affected western much more than eastern Europe. The culminating effect of these disasters was a darker, more somber vision of life than that of the previous centuries. This vision found its expression in the Dance of Death, an increasingly popular image in art. Naked, rotting corpses dance with great animation before the living. The latter, depicted in the dress of all social orders, are immobile, surprised by death, reluctant but resigned.

Although no solid statistics exist from the fourteenth century, the plague certainly killed more people than all of the wars and famines of the century. It was the greatest disaster ever to befall Europe. The Black Death touched every aspect of life, hastening a process of social, economic, and cultural transformation already under way. The initial outbreak shattered social and economic structures. Fields were abandoned, workplaces stood idle, international trade was suspended. Traditional bonds of kinship, village, and even religion were broken by the horrors of death, flight, and failed expectations. "People cared no more for dead men than we care for dead goats," wrote one survivor. Brothers abandoned brothers, wives deserted husbands, and terror-stricken parents refused to nurse their own children. Nothing had prepared Europe for this catastrophe, no teaching of the Church or its leaders could adequately explain it, and in spite of desperate attempts to fix the blame on Jews or strangers, no one but God could be held responsible. Survivors stood alone and uncertain before a new world. Across Europe, moralists reported a general lapse in traditional ethics, a breakdown in the moral codes. The most troubling aspect of this breakdown was what one defender of the old order termed "the plague of insurrection" that spread across Europe. This plague was brought on by the dimming of the hopes held by the survivors of the Black Death.

The Plague of Insurrection

Initially, even this darkest cloud had a silver lining. Lucky survivors of the plague soon found other reasons to rejoice. Property owners, when they finished burying their dead, discovered that they were far richer in land and goods. At the other end of the social spectrum, the plague had eliminated the labor surplus. Peasants were suddenly in great demand. For a time at least, they were able to negotiate substantially higher wages and an improved relationship with landlords. An

Spread of the Black Death

English thresher who before 1349 had been paid around three pence a day could hope to earn 25 percent more after the plague.

These hopes were short-lived. The rise in expectations produced by the redistribution of wealth and the labor shortage created new tensions. Landlords sought laws forcing peasants to accept preplague wages and tightened their control over serfs in order to prevent them from fleeing to cities or other lords. At the same time governments attempted to benefit from laborers' greater prosperity by imposing new taxes. In cities, where the plague had been particularly devastating, the demographic decline sharply lowered demand for goods and thus lowered the need for manufacturing and production of all kinds. Like rural landowners, master craftsmen sought legislation to protect their incomes. New laws reduced production by restricting access to trades and increased masters' control over the surviving urban laborers. Social mobility, once a characteristic of urban life, slowed to a halt. Membership in guilds became hereditary, and young apprentices or journeymen had little hope of ever rising to the level of independent master craftsmen.

These new tensions led to violence when kings added their demands for new war taxes to the landlords' and masters' attempts to erase the peasants' and workers' recent gains. The first revolts took place in France, where peasants and townspeople, disgusted with the incompetence of the nobility in their conduct of the war against England, feared that their new wealth would be stolen from them by corrupt and incompetent aristocrats.

In 1358, in order to ransom King John II from the English, the French government attempted to increase taxes on the peasantry. At the same time, local nobles increased their rents and demands. Peasants in the area of Beauvais, north of Paris, fearing they would lose the modest level of prosperity they had gained over the previous ten years, rebelled against their landlords. The revolt, known as the Jacquerie for the archetypical French peasant, Jacques Bonnehomme, was a spontaneous outburst directed against the nobility, whom the peasants saw as responsible for all their ills. Without real leadership or program, peasants attacked as many nobles as they could find, killing them along with their wives and children and burning their homes and castles. The peasants' brutality deeply shocked the upper classes, whose own violence was constrained within the bounds of the chivalric code. One chronicler reported in horror, "Among other evil deeds, they killed a knight and quickly began to roast him before the eyes of his wife and children. After ten or twelve had raped the noble lady, they wanted to force her to eat her husband's flesh. They then put her to death horribly." Because the Church largely supported the power structure, the uprising was also strongly anticlerical. Churches were burned and priests killed. Success bred further attacks, and the disorganized army of peasants began to march south toward Paris, killing, looting, and burning everything associated with the despised nobility.

In the midst of this peasant revolt, Etienne Marcel (ca. 1316–58), a wealthy Parisian cloth merchant, led an uprising of Parisian merchants, which sought to take control of royal finances and force fiscal reforms on the dauphin, the future Charles V. Although initially the rebels were primarily members of the merchant and guild elite, Marcel soon enlisted the support of the radical townspeople against the aristocracy. He even made overtures to the leaders of the Jacquerie to join forces. For a brief time it appeared that the aristocratic order in France might succumb. However, in the end peasant and merchant rebels were no match for professional armies. The Jacquerie met its end at Meaux, outside Paris, where an aristocratic force cut the peasants to pieces. Survivors were systematically hunted down and hung or burned alive. The Parisian revolt met a similar fate. Aristocratic armies surrounded the city and cut off its food supply. Marcel was assassinated and the dauphin Charles regained the city.

The French revolts set the pattern for similar uprisings across Europe. Rebels were usually relatively prosperous peasants or townspeople whose economic situations were threatened by aristocratic attempts to turn back the clock to the period before the Black Death. In 1381 English peasants, reacting to new and hated taxes, rose in a less violent but more coordinated revolt known as the Great Rebellion. Peasant revolts took place in the northern Spanish region of Catalonia in 1395 and in Germany throughout the fourteenth and fifteenth centuries. The largest was the great Peasant's Revolt of 1524. Although always ruthlessly suppressed, European peasant uprisings continued until the peasant rebellion of 1626 in upper Austria. These outbursts indicated not necessarily the desperation of Europe's peasantry, but the new belief that they could change their lives for the better through united action.

Urban artisans imitated the example of their rural cousins. Although there had been some uprisings in the Flemish towns before the Black Death, revolts of townspeople picked up momentum in the second half of the fourteenth century. In general the town rebels were not the destitute urban poor any more than the peasant rebels had been the landless rural poor. Instead they were generally independent artisans and small tradesmen who wanted to break the control of the powerful guilds. The one exception to this pattern was the Ciompi revolt of 1378 in Florence. There the wool workers rioted and forced recognition of two guilds of laborers alongside the powerful guilds of masters. The workers and artisans controlled city government until 1382, when mercenaries hired by the elite surrounded the workers' slums and crushed them in bloody house-to-house fighting. In spite of the brutal suppression and ultimate failure of popular revolts, they became permanent if intermittent features on

Jacquerie rebellion, from a fifteenth-century manuscript. The well-armed soldiers have won the day, and the unarmed rebels are consigned to the river to sink or swim. Such rebellions were put down with great ruthlessness.

the European social landscape. The line from the Jacquerie runs to the storming of the Bastille 431 years later, and beyond.

Living and Dying in Medieval Towns

Population decline, war, and class conflict in France and the Low Countries fatally weakened the vitality of the commercial and manufacturing system of northwestern Europe. These same events reduced the market for Italian goods and undermined the economic strength of the great Italian cities. The Hundred Years' War bankrupted many of Florence's greatest banking houses such as the Bardi and Peruzzi, who lent to both French and English kings. Commercial activity declined as well. While in the 1330s Venice had sent between four and nine trading galleys to Flanders each year, by the 1390s the city was sending only three to five. Genoa, which earlier had led in the trade with the cloth towns of the north, saw the economic activity of its port decline by roughly one-third to one-half during the same period. While Italians did not disappear from northern cities, they no longer held a near monopoly on northern trade.

These setbacks for the Italians worked to the advantage of German towns in the disintegrating empire. Along the Baltic Sea, in Scandinavia, and in northern Germany, towns such as Lübeck, Lüneburg, Visby, Bremen, and Cologne formed a commercial and political alliance to control northern trade. During the second half of the fourteenth century, this Hanseatic League—the word *Hansa* means "company"—monopolized the northern grain trade and forced Denmark to grant its members exclusive rights to export Scandinavian fish throughout Europe. Hanseatic merchants established colonies from Novgorod to London to Bruges and even in Venice. They carried dried and salted fish to Prague and supplied grain from Riga to England and France.

English towns also profited from the decline of Flanders and France. The population decline of the fourteenth century led many English landowners to switch from traditional farming to sheep raising, since pasturing sheep required few workers and promised cash profits. While surviving peasants were driven off the land and forced

The Hanseatic League

to beg for a living, lords produced more wool than ever before. However, instead of exporting the wool to Flanders to be made into cloth, the English began to make cloth themselves. Protected by high tariffs on imports and low duties on exports, England had become a major exporter of finished cloth by the middle of the fifteenth century.

The new social and economic circumstances of European towns accentuated the gulf between rich and poor. The streets and markets of fifteenth-century towns bustled with the sights and sounds of rich Hanseatic merchants, Italian bankers, and prosperous local tradesmen. The back alleys and squatter settlements on the edges of these towns teemed with a growing mass of desperate and despairing workers and their families. The combination of economic depression, plague, and rural crisis deepened the misery of the growing population of urban poor. Driven both by mounting compassion for the urban poor and by a growing fear of the violent potential of this ever increasing population, medieval towns developed novel systems to deal with poverty. The first was public assistance, the second social control and repression.

Traditionally, charity had been a religious act that focused more on the soul of the giver than on the effect on the life of the recipient. The same had been true of charitable organizations such as confraternities and hospitals. Confraternities were pious religious organizations of lay people and clergy who ministered to the poor and sick. Hospitals were all-purpose religious institutions providing lodging for pilgrims, the elderly, and the ill. By the fourteenth century, such pious institutions had become inadequate to deal with the growing numbers of poor and ill. Towns began to assume control over a centralized system of public assistance. New, specialized institutions appeared for the care of different categories of the poor, including the ill, women in childbirth, the aged, orphans, and travelers. Pest houses were founded in which plague victims could be isolated. Hospitals also distributed food to the poor. In 1403 the hospital of the Holy Spirit in Cologne supported over fourteen hundred paupers per week. Seventy years later that number had grown to almost five thousand.

Although men and women who had taken religious vows staffed these institutions, city governments contributed to their budgets and oversaw their finances. Cities also attempted to rationalize the distribution of charity according to need and merit. Antwerp, for example, established a centralized relief service, which distributed badges to those deemed worthy of public assistance. Only those who presented their badges could receive food. This system spread throughout Europe in the fourteenth century.

At the same time that towns began to organize public assistance, they attempted to control more strictly the activities of the urban poor. In the fourteenth century, Nuremberg forbade begging to everyone except those who had received a special license. In Strasbourg, blind beggars organized an official "Confraternity of Strasbourg Beggars" on the model of other professional guilds, with its own officers, regulations, and membership requirements. Many towns, fearing wandering, professional beggars and landless peasants, allowed them to remain only three days before being expelled.

One consequence of poverty was increased crime. Fear of the poor led to repressive measures and harsh punishments. Traditionally, in much of Europe crimes such as robbery, larceny, and even manslaughter had been punishable by fines and payments to the victim or the victim's heirs. Elsewhere, as in France and England, where corporal punishment had been the normal penalty for major crimes, hanging, blinding, and the loss of a hand or foot had been the most common punishments. During the later Middle Ages, gruesome forms of mutilation and execution became common for a long list of offenses. Petty larceny was punished with whipping, cutting off ears or thumbs, branding, or expulsion. In some towns, robbery of an amount over three pence was punished with death. Death by hanging might be replaced by more savage punishments such as breaking on the wheel. In this particularly brutal torture the prisoner's limbs and back were first broken with a wagon wheel. Then the criminal was tied to the wheel and left on a pole to die. Drowning, boiling, burning, and burial alive, a particularly common punishment for women, were other frequently used methods of execution.

The frequency of such punishments increased with their severity. In Augsburg until the middle of the thirteenth century executions were so rare that the city did not even have a public executioner before 1276. However, in the following two centuries, the city fathers increased executions in an attempt to control what they perceived as an ever rising crime rate, largely attributed to the growing masses of the poor. In 1452 the skulls of 250 hanged persons were found in pits on the gallows hill. At the same time the bodies of 32 thieves twisted in the wind above.

The Spirit of the Later Middle Ages

The Dance of Death and the gallows were not the only images of later medieval life. The constant presence of death made life more precious. Europeans celebrated life with a vigor and creativity characterized by a growing sense of individuality, independence, and variety. During the fourteenth century, the Church failed to provide unified spiritual and cultural leadership to Europe. The institutional division of the Church was paralleled by divisions over how to lead the proper Christian life. Many devout Christians developed independent life-styles intended to bring them closer to God without reliance on the Church hierarchy. They elaborated beliefs branded by the Church as heresy. Others called into question the philosophical bases of theological speculation developed since the time of Abelard and Aquinas. Finally, the increasing pluralism of European culture gave rise to new literary traditions that both celebrated and criticized the medieval legacy of Christianity, chivalry, and social order.

Christendom Divided

The universal empire as well as its traditional competitor, the universal Church, declined in the later Middle Ages. The papacy never recovered from the humiliating defeat Pope Boniface VIII suffered at the hands of King Philip the Fair in 1303. The ecclesiastical edifice created by the thirteenth-century popes was shaken to its foundations, first by becoming a virtual appendage of the French monarchy, and then by a dispute that for over forty years gave European Christians a choice between two, and finally three, claimants to the chair of Saint Peter.

In 1305 the College of Cardinals elected as pope the bishop of Bordeaux. The new pope, who took the name Clement V (1305–14), was close to Philip IV of France and had no desire to meet the fate of his predecessor, Pope Boniface VIII. Thus Clement took up residence not in Rome but in the papal city of Avignon on the east bank of the Rhone River. Technically, Avignon was a papal estate within the Holy Roman Empire. Actually, with France just across the river, the pope at Avignon was under French control.

For the next seventy years French popes and French cardinals ruled the Church. The traditional enemies of France as well as religious reformers who expected leadership from the papacy looked on this situation with disgust. The Italian poet Petrarch (1304–74) denounced what he termed the "Babylonian captivity" of the papacy in especially bitter tones:

> Now I am living in France, in the Babylon of the West. The sun in its travels sees nothing more hideous than this place on the shores of the wild Rhone. Here reign the successors of the poor fishermen of Galilee; they have strangely forgotten their origin.

Although Petrarch went on to accuse the popes and their courtiers of every possible crime and sin, the Avignon popes were no worse than any other great lords of the fourteenth century. In pursuit of political and financial rewards, they had simply lost sight of their roles as religious leaders.

The popes of Avignon were more successful in achieving their financial goals than in winning political power. Although they attempted to follow an independent course in international affairs, their French orientation eroded their influence in European politics, especially in the Holy Roman Empire. Pope John XXII (1316–34), one of the most unpleasant and argumentative persons ever to hold the chair of Peter, tried to block the election of the Wittelsbach Louis of Bavaria as emperor. Louis ignored the pope, invaded Italy, and was proclaimed emperor by the people of Rome. In 1338 the German electors solemnly declared that the imperial office was held directly from God and did not require papal confirmation—a declaration later upheld in the Golden Bull. No longer could the popes exert any direct influence in the internal affairs of Europe's states.

Frustrated politically, the Avignon popes concentrated on perfecting the legal and fiscal system of the Church and were enormously successful in concentrating the vast financial and legal power of the Church in the papal office. From the papal court, or curia, they created a vast and efficient central bureaucracy whose primary role was to increase papal revenues.

Revenues came from two main sources. The less lucrative but ultimately more critical source was the sale of indulgences. The Church had long taught that sinners who repented might be absolved of their sins and escape the fires of hell. However, they still had to suffer temporary punishment. This punishment, called penance, could take the form of fasting, prayer, or performance of some good deed. Failing to do penance on earth, absolved sinners would have to endure a period in purgatory before they could be admitted to heaven. However, since the saints had done more penance than was required to make up for the temporal punishments due them, they had established a treasury of merit, a sort of spiritual bank account. The pope was the "banker" and could transfer some of this positive balance to

A Room of One's Own

Through most of history, men and women lived and died in public, under the scrutiny of family, friends, and neighbors. Solitude and privacy, far from being considered desirable privileges, were dire punishments self-inflicted by ascetic hermits or imposed by society on its outcasts. Nowhere is this rejection of isolation more obvious than in the arrangement of physical space within which people lived. Through the Middle Ages, peasant families crowded into single-room cottages not only out of financial necessity but also out of a desire for intimacy. Lords resided in castles whose living quarters were no more private. Monks shared communal dormitories, and even bishops and abbots slept surrounded by their clerics.

Living in such a corporate world, medieval people thought of themselves first as members of a group, a *familia*, whether of kin, of members of a household, of a religious order, of a merchant society, or of a warrior band. People aspired less to self-expression and personal fulfillment than to conformity to a model, that of the ideal knight, monk, merchant, or Christian.

If life meant playing a role, then success demanded a constant audience. Medieval homes reflected the different types of audiences and the different degrees of intimacy to which they were admitted. Typically, houses in fourteenth-century towns had three types of space corresponding to three levels of intimacy. The ground-floor vestibule served as workshop or salesroom for artisans. For wealthy families it was where the public was received. Beyond or above the vestibule were the rooms devoted to family activities to which friends and intimates were invited. On the third level was the bedroom or bedrooms.

The center of privacy and intimacy was the bedroom, a place of repose and sleep, but also the space where one's most intimate guests might be entertained and where the family's most valued treasures were kept. The distinction between bedroom and public room might be fairly arbitrary. Often private portions of a wealthy house or castle consisted of a large room that could be divided by movable wooden partitions into a public hall and a more intimate chamber. Both

spaces were used for banquets and entertaining, the latter reserved for honored guests. At night the chamber might serve as the bedroom of the master and mistress of the house, but in some castles it was the sleeping room only for the lord, his warriors, and their concubines. Wives and children slept in communal chambers of their own.

Dominating the bedroom was the bed, and it was a poor family indeed that did not own at least a bed frame and a straw mattress. Beds were often huge by modern standards, ranging from five to twelve feet in width. The bed consisted of three parts. First was the frame, made of oak or pine. Often the frame was high enough for a small cot to be stored under it. The mattress, made of cloth and stuffed with straw or wool, was placed on top of straw piled up in the frame. The wealthy might be able to afford a mattress stuffed with feathers. Finally, the bed had a variety of cushions and pillows, sheets, and a canopy that could be drawn, making the bed virtually a room within a room.

The size of the bed was not just for display. Often, it was occupied by the whole family. One prosperous Italian peasant who died in 1406 shared his vast bed with his wife and three children. In fifteenth-century France, all the children of a family often shared a single bed. A French theologian, wor-

ried about the potential for incest, prayed that it would "please God that it should be the custom in France for children to sleep alone in small beds, or at worst brothers together and sisters or others together, as is the custom in Flanders."

Even if people did chose to sleep in their beds alone or only with their spouses, they normally kept one or more servants in their bedchambers, both to have help readily at hand and to keep an eye on them.

Only gradually, beginning around the fourteenth century, as states and communal governments sought greater control over subjects and citizens, did first families and then individuals begin to carve out their own space away from the prying eyes of outsiders or even more intimate companions. The number of bedrooms in houses and castles increased. Monasteries were renovated so that each monk or nun could occupy a single cell. Intellectuals added "thinking rooms" to their homes, where they might read, write, and meditate in solitude. This creation of private space within which a person could be truly alone with his or her own activities, thoughts, and emotions was an essential component of the development of a sense of the individual. Isolated within the confines of a room of their own, people could begin to explore the ultimate privacy— the interior of their own minds.

repentant sinners in return for some pious act such as contributing money to build a new church. These so-called indulgences could be purchased for one's own use or to assist the souls of family members already in purgatory. Papal "pardoners" working on commission used high-pressure sales pitches to sell indulgences across Europe.

The second and major source of papal income was the sale of Church offices, or benefices. Popes claimed the right to appoint bishops and abbots to all benefices and to collect a hefty tax for the appointment. The system encouraged pluralism, that is, individuals could acquire numerous ecclesiastical benefices scattered across Europe in the same way that lay lords held multiple fiefs and territories from France to Poland. Like the pope, papal appointees often viewed their offices merely as sources of income, leaving pastoral duties, when they were performed at all, to hired local clergy.

In 1377 Pope Gregory XI (1370–78) returned from Avignon to Rome but died almost immediately upon arrival. Thousands of Italians, afraid that the cardinals would elect another Frenchman, surrounded the church where they were meeting and demanded an Italian pope. The terrified cardinals elected an Italian, who took the name of Urban VI (1378–89). Once elected, Urban attempted to reform the curia, but he did so in a most undiplomatic way, insulting the cardinals and threatening to appoint sufficient non-French bishops to their number to end French control of the curia. The cardinals soon left Rome and announced that because the election had been made under duress it was invalid and that Urban should resign. When he refused they held a second election and chose a Frenchman, Clement VII (1378–94), who took up residence in Avignon. The Church now had two heads, both with reasonable claims to the office.

The chaos created by this so-called Great Schism divided western Christendom. In every diocese, when a bishop died his successor had to be appointed by the pope. But by which pope? To whom did taxes go? Who received the income from the sale of indulgences or benefices? Did appeals in the Church courts go to Rome or to Avignon? More significantly, since each pope excommunicated the supporters of his opponent,

The Great Schism

everyone in the West was under a sentence of excommunication. Could anyone be saved?

Communities were divided. When the city of Bruges officially accepted the Avignon pope, many citizens left their homes and professions to live in cities loyal to Rome. Not surprisingly, countries tended to side with one or the other contender for political reasons. France recognized Clement. France's traditional enemies, England and the empire, recognized Urban. England's traditional enemy Scotland accepted Clement. Most of Italy sided with Urban, but the Angevin kingdom of Naples and Sicily recognized Clement, as did most of Spain.

Nothing in Church law or tradition offered a solution to this crisis. Nor did unilateral efforts to settle the crisis succeed. Twice France invaded Italy in an attempt to eliminate Urban but failed both times. Professors at the University of Paris argued that both popes should abdicate, but neither was willing to do so. Moreover, the situation perpetuated itself. When Urban and Clement died, cardinals on both sides elected successors. By the end of the fourteenth century, France and the empire were exasperated with their popes and even the cardinals were determined to end the stalemate.

Church lawyers argued that a general council alone could end the schism. Both popes opposed this "conciliarist" argument because it suggested that an assembly of the Church rather than the pope held supreme authority. However, in 1408 cardinals from both sides summoned a council in the Italian city of Pisa. The council deposed both rivals and elected a new pope. But this solution only made matters worse, since neither pope accepted the decision of the council. Europe now had to contend with not two but three popes, each claiming to be the true successor of Saint Peter.

Six years later the Council of Constance managed a final solution. There under the patronage of the emperor-elect Sigismund (1410–37), cardinals, bishops, abbots, and theologians from across Europe met to resolve the crisis. Their goal was not only to settle the schism but also to reform the Church to prevent a recurrence of such a scandal. The participants at Constance hoped to restructure the Church as a limited monarchy in which the powers of the pope would be controlled through frequent councils. The Pisan and Avignon popes were deposed. The Roman pope, abandoned by all of his supporters, abdicated. Before doing so, however, he formally convoked the council in order to preserve the tradition that a general council had to be called by the pope. Finally, the council elected as pope an Italian cardinal not aligned with any of the claimants. The election of the cardinal, who took the name Martin V (1417–31), ended the schism.

The relief at the end of the Great Schism could not hide the very real problems left by over a century of papal weakness. The prestige of the papacy had been permanently compromised. Everywhere the Church had become more national in character. The conciliarist demand for control of the Church, which had ended the schism, lessened the power of the pope. Finally, during the century between Boniface VIII and Martin V, new religious movements had taken root across Europe, movements which the political creatures who had occupied the papal office could neither understand nor control. The Council of Constance, which brought an end to the schism, also condemned Jan Hus, the leader of the Czech reform movement and the spiritual founder of the Protestant reformation of the sixteenth century. The disintegration of the Church loomed ever closer as pious individuals turned away from the organized Church and sought divine help in personal piety, mysticism, or even magic.

Discerning the Spirit of God

When Joan of Arc first appeared before the dauphin in 1429, he feared that she was a witch. Only a physical examination by matrons, which determined that she was a virgin, persuaded him otherwise—witches were believed to have had intercourse with the devil. In 1431 the English burned Joan as a heretic. For the two years between 1429 and 1431 and long after, many venerated her as a saint. Everyone in the late Middle Ages was familiar with witches, saints, and heretics. Distinguishing among them was often a matter of perspective.

Accusations of witchcraft were relatively rare in the Middle Ages. The age of witch-hunts occurred in the sixteenth and seventeenth centuries. During the Middle Ages magic existed in a wide variety of forms, but its definition was fluid and its practitioners were not always considered witches. Alchemists and astrologers held honored places in society, while simple practitioners of folk religion, medicine, and superstition were condemned, particularly when they were poor women.

Witches, believed to have made a contract with the devil, were condemned as one type of heretic and were persecuted like other heretics. Only at the end of the fifteenth century, with the publication of the *Witches' Hammer,* a great handbook for inquisitors, did the European witch craze begin in earnest. Earlier, authorities feared more those people who sought their own pacts not with the devil but with God.

Even as Europeans were losing respect for the institutional Church, people everywhere were seeking closer and more intimate relationships with God. Distrusting the formal institutions of the Church, lay persons and clerics turned to private devotions and to mysticism to achieve union with the divine. They developed their own forms of devotion based on translations of the Bible into their native languages. They looked for a direct relationship with God, thus minimizing the importance of the Church hierarchy. Most of these, like the Beguines and Beghards of northern Europe, stayed within the Church. Others, among them many female mystics, maintained an ambiguous relationship with the traditional institutions of Christianity. A few, such as the Brethren of the Free Spirit, broke sharply with it.

In the fourteenth and fifteenth centuries, a great many pious laymen and women chose to live together to strive for spiritual perfection without entering established religious orders. The female Beguines and male Beghards of northern cities often formed miniature towns-within-towns. The Brethren of the Common life in the Rhineland and Low Countries dedicated themselves to preaching, charity, and a pious life. In the early fifteenth century an unknown member of the Brethren wrote the *Imitation of Christ*, a book of spiritual direction that remains today the most widely read religious text after the Bible.

Christians of the later Middle Ages sought to imitate Christ and venerated the Eucharist, or communion wafer, which the Church taught was the actual body of Jesus. Male mystics focused on imitating Jesus in his poverty, his suffering, and his humility. The Spiritual Franciscans made radical poverty the cornerstone of their belief and the yardstick by which to judge Christian action. The furor between the Spiritual Franciscans and the more moderate Conventuals led Pope John XXII to condemn radical poverty in 1323 and to begin persecuting the Spirituals as heretics. As the wealth and luxury of the Church hierarchy increased, so did the spiritual reaction against it.

Women developed their own form of piety, which focused not on wealth and power but on spiritual nourishment, particularly as provided by the Eucharist. For women mystics, radical fasting became preparation for the reception of the Eucharist, often described in highly emotional and erotic terms. After a long period of fasting, Lukardis of Obverweimar (d. 1309) had a vision in which Jesus appeared to her as a handsome youth and blew into her mouth. In the words of her biographer, "She was infused with such sweetness and such inner fruition that she felt as if drunk." From the age of twenty-three, Catherine of Sienna (d. 1380) subsisted entirely on the Eucharist, cold water, and bitter herbs that she sucked and then spat out. She wrote of the importance of the Eucharist, "We must attach ourselves to the breast of Christ crucified, which is the source of charity, and by means of that flesh we draw milk." For these and other pious women, fasting and devotion to the Eucharist did not mean rejection of the body. Rather these were attempts to use their senses to approach perfect union with God, who was for them both food and drink.

Only a thin line separated the saint's heroic search for union with God from the heretic's identification with God. The radical Brethren of the Free Spirit believed that God was all things and that all things would return to God. Such pantheism denied the possibility of sin, punishment, and the need for salvation. Members of the sect were hunted down and many were burned as heretics. Local bishops and clergy often confused Beguines, Beghards, and Brethren of the Common Life with adherents of the Free Spirit movement. The specter of the Inquisition, the ecclesiastical court system charged with ferreting out heretics, hung over all such communities.

When unorthodox Christians were protected by secular lords, the ecclesiastical courts were powerless. This was the case with John Wycliffe (ca. 1330–84), an Oxford theologian who attacked the doctrinal and political bases of the Church. He taught that the value of the sacraments depended on the worthiness of the priest administering them, that Jesus was present in the Eucharist only in spirit, that indulgences were useless, and that salvation depended on divine predestination rather than individual merit. Normally these teachings would have led him to the stake. But he had also attacked the Church's right to wealth and luxury, an idea whose political implications pleased the English monarchy and nobility. Wycliffe's own exemplary manner of life and his teaching that the Church's role in temporal affairs should be severely limited made him an extremely popular figure in England. Thus he was allowed to live and teach in peace. Only under Henry V (1413–22) were Wycliffe's followers, known as Lollards, vigorously suppressed by the state.

Before this condemnation took place, however, Wycliffe's teachings reached the kingdom of Bohemia through the marriage of Charles IV's daughter Anne of Bohemia to the English King Richard II. Anne took with her to England a number of Bohemian clerics, some of whom studied at Oxford and absorbed the political and religious teachings of Wycliffe, which they then took back to Bohemia. In Prague some of Wycliffe's less radical teachings took root among the theology faculty of the new university. Wycliffe's ideas were particularly popular with Czech professors of theology, who were demanding not only a reform of religious teaching and practice but also a reduction of the influence of German professors in the University of Prague. The leading proponent of Wycliffe's teachings in Prague was Jan Hus (1373–1415), an immensely popular young master and preacher. Although Hus rejected Wycliffe's ideas about the priesthood and the sacraments, he and other Czech preachers attacked indulgences and demanded a reform of Church liturgy and morals. They grafted these religious demands onto an attack on German dominance of the Bohemian kingdom. These attacks outraged both the Pisan pope John XXIII (1410–15) and the Bohemian king Wenceslas IV (1378–1419), who favored the German faction. The pope excommunicated Hus, and the king expelled the Czech faculty from the university. Hus was convinced that he was no heretic and that a fair hearing would clear him. He therefore agreed to travel to the Council of Constance under promise of safe conduct from the emperor-elect Sigismund to defend his position. There he was tried on a charge of heresy, convicted, and burned at the stake.

News of Hus' execution touched off a revolt in Bohemia. Unlike the peasant revolts of the past, however, this revolt had broad popular support throughout all levels of Czech society. Peasants, nobles, and townspeople saw the attack on Hus and his followers as an attack on Czech independence and national interest by a Church and an empire controlled by Germans. The rebels slaughtered the largely German city council and defeated an army sent by emperor-elect Sigismund to crush the revolt. Soon a radical faction known as the Taborites was demanding the abolition of private property and the institution of a communal state. Although moderate Hussites and Bohemian Catholics combined to defeat the radicals in 1434, most of Bohemia remained Hussite through the fifteenth century. The sixteenth-century reformer Martin Luther declared himself a follower of Jan Hus.

William of Ockham and the Spirit of Truth

The critical and individualistic approach that characterized religion during the later Middle Ages was also typical of the philosophical thought of the period. The delicate balance between faith and reason taught by Aquinas and other intellectuals in the thirteenth century disintegrated in the fourteenth. As in other areas of life, intellectuals questioned the basic suppositions of their predecessors, directing intellectual activity away from general speculations and toward particular, observable reality.

The person primarily responsible for this new intellectual climate was the English Franciscan William of Ockham (ca. 1300–49). Ockham was

Illustration from the sixteenth-century Bohemian Gradual of Malá Strana. *Jan Hus, wearing the traditional heretic's cap adorned with devils, is burned at the stake.*

no ivory-tower intellectual. He was a dedicated Spiritual Franciscan, whose defense of radical poverty led to his excommunication by the cantankerous John XXII. Excommunication drove Ockham to the court of John's enemy, the Emperor Louis IV, where he became a dedicated propagandist for the imperial cause. There he developed a truly radical political philosophy. Imperial power, Ockham argued, derived not from the pope but from the people. People are free to determine their own form of government and to elect rulers. They can make their choice directly, as in the election of the emperor by electors who represent the people, or implicitly, through continuing forms of government. In either case, government is entirely secular. Neither popes, nor bishops, nor priests have any role.

Ockham went still further. He denied the absolute authority of the pope, even in spiritual matters. Rather, Ockham argued, parishes, religious orders, and monasteries should send representatives to regional synods, which in turn would elect representatives to general councils. Both laypersons and clergy would serve on these councils, which were to act rather like parliaments, tempering papal absolutism.

As radical as Ockham's political ideas were, his philosophical outlook was even more extreme and exerted a more direct and lasting influence. The Christian Aristotelianism that developed in the thirteenth century had depended on the validity of general concepts, called universals, which could be analyzed through the use of logic. Aquinas and others who studied the eternity of the world, the existence of God, the nature of the soul, and other philosophical questions believed that people could reach general truths by abstracting universals from particular, individual cases. Ockham argued that universals were merely names, no more than convenient tags for discussing individual things. Universals had no connection with reality and could not be used to reason from particular observations to general truths. This radical nominalism (from the Latin *nomen*, "name") thus denied that human reason could aspire to certain truth. For Ockham and his followers, philosophical speculation was essentially a logical, linguistic exercise, not a way to certain knowledge. Ockham died in 1349, a victim of the plague, but his political and philosophical teach-

The Later Middle Ages, 1300–1500

1305–1377	Babylonian Captivity (Avignon papacy)
1337–1452	Hundred Years' War
1347–1352	Black Death spreads through Europe
1358	Jacquerie revolt of French peasants Etienne Marcel leads revolt of Parisian merchants
1378	Ciompi revolt in Florence
1378–1417	Great Schism divides Christianity
1381	Great Rebellion of English peasants
1409–1410	Council of Pisa
1414–1417	Council of Constance ends Great Schism
1415	Jan Hus executed
1455–1485	English Wars of the Roses

ings lived on. His ideas on Church governance by a general council representing the whole Christian community offered the one hope for a solution to the Great Schism that erupted shortly after his death. Conciliarists like Pierre d'Ailly (1350–1420) and Jean de Gerson (1363–1429) drew on Ockham's attack on papal absolutism to propose an alternative church. The Council of Constance, which ended the schism, was the fruit of Ockham's political theory, as were the various organizational structures of the Protestant churches of the sixteenth century.

Just as Ockham's political theory dominated the later fourteenth century, his nominalist philosophy won over the philosophical faculties of Europe. Since he had discredited the value of Aristotelian logic to increase knowledge, the result was, on the one hand, a decline in abstract speculation and on the other, a greater interest in scientific observation of individual phenomena. In the next generation Parisian professors, trained in the tradition of Ockham, laid the foundation for scientific studies of motion and the universe that led to the scientific discoveries of the sixteenth and seventeenth centuries.

Vernacular Literature and the Individual

Just as the religious and philosophical concerns of the later Middle Ages developed within national frameworks and criticized accepted authority from the perspective of individual experience, so too did the vernacular (as opposed to Latin) literatures of the age begin to explore the place of the individual within an increasingly complex society. Across Europe, authors reviewed the traditional values of society with a critical eye, reworking and transforming traditional literary genres into statements both personal and profound.

In Italy, a trio of Tuscan poets, Dante Alighieri (1265–1321), Petrarch (1304–74), and Boccaccio (1313–75), not only made Italian a literary language but composed in it some of the greatest literature of all time. Dante, the first and greatest of the three, was born into a modest but respectable Florentine family and after receiving an excellent education entered the public life of his city. At the same time he began writing poetry and quickly acquired a reputation for his ability to express in love lyrics a new sensitivity and individual expression. In 1301 he fell victim to the viciousness of Florentine politics and was exiled from his beloved city for the remainder of his life. For two decades he traveled through Italy, residing in the courts of friendly princes and writing philosophical treatises and literary works, which culminated in his *Divine Comedy*, written during the last years of his life.

The *Divine Comedy* is a view of the whole Christian universe, populated with people from antiquity and from Dante's own day. The poem is both a sophisticated summary of philosophical and theological thought at the beginning of the fourteenth century and an astute political commentary on his times. The poet sets this vision within a three-part poetic journey through hell (*Inferno*), purgatory (*Purgatorio*), and heaven (*Paradiso*). In each part Dante adopts a poetic style appropriate to the subject matter. His journey through hell to witness the sufferings of the damned is described in brutal, immediate language that makes one almost feel the agony of the condemned, each of whom receives an eternal punishment appropriate to his or her sins. The

violent conquerors Alexander the Great and Attila the Hun, for example, wallow for all eternity in boiling blood as punishment for spilling the blood of so many others. In purgatory, Dante meets sinners whose punishments will someday end. These he describes in a language of dreams and imagination, of nostalgic recollections cast in a misty landscape of the memory. On a ledge populated by hoarders and wasters, for example, the poet hears but does not see Hugh Capet, founder of the French Capetian dynasty, who describes a vision of his greedy descendants who devastate Italy to gain riches. Dante describes paradise in a symbolic language that is nonphysical and nonrepresentational. In the face of transcendent perfection, human imagery and poetry fail. In his final vision, he sees the reflected light of a mystical rose in which the saints are ranked. These include both religious leaders such as Bernard of Clairvaux and political leaders such as Emperor Henry VII, grandfather of Charles IV. The *Divine Comedy* is Dante's personal summary of all that is good and bad in medieval culture and politics.

English literature emerged from over two centuries of French cultural domination with the writings of William Langland (ca. 1330–95) and Geoffrey Chaucer (ca. 1343–1400). Both presented images of contemporary society with a critical and often ironic view. In *Piers Plowman* Langland presents society from the perspective of the peasantry. Chaucer's work is much more sophisticated and wide ranging, weaving together the whole spectrum of late medieval literature and life.

Chaucer was born into a London merchant family and spent a long and successful career as a courtier, serving English aristocrats and finally the king both in England and on the Continent. His travels brought him into contact with the literary and philosophical traditions of all of Europe, and he mastered every genre, always molding them with wit and imagination into something new.

Dante had set his great poem within a vision of the other world. Chaucer placed his tales in the mouths of a group of thirty pilgrims traveling to the tomb of Thomas Becket at Canterbury. The pilgrims represent every walk of life and spectrum of society: a simple knight, a vulgar miller, a lawyer, a lusty widow, a merchant, a squire, a physician, a nun, her chaplain, and a monk, among others. Each pilgrim is at once strikingly individual and representative of his or her profession or station in life. The tales that they tell are drawn from folklore, Italian literature, the lives of the saints, courtly romance, and religious sermons. However, Chaucer plays with the tales and their genres in the retelling. He uses them to contrast or illuminate the persons and characters of their tellers as well as to comment in subtle and complex ways on the literary, religious, and cultural traditions of which they are part. His knight, for example, tells a tale of chivalric love taken from Boccaccio. However, in Chaucer's version, the tale becomes both more real and vivid and more humorous as he plays with the traditional genre of courtly love poetry. The Wife of Bath, a forceful woman who has survived five husbands, argues for the superiority of married life over celibacy, particularly when the wife controls the marriage. Her tale, which takes a form common in religious sermons, continues her argument. It is a retelling of a fairy tale in which a woman is released from a spell by a knight, to whom she offers the choice of having her ugly and faithful or beautiful and free to bestow her favors where she will. The knight courteously leaves the decision to her and is rewarded by her promise to be both fair and faithful. In his mastery of the whole heritage of medieval culture and his independent use of this heritage, Chaucer proved himself the greatest English writer before Shakespeare.

Much of Italian and English literature drew material and inspiration from French, which continued into the fifteenth century to be the language of courtly romance. In France, literature continued to project an unreal world of allegory and nostalgia for a glorious if imaginary past. Popular literature, developed largely in the towns, often dealt with courtly themes, but with a critical and more realistic eye.

In this literary world appeared a new and extraordinary type of poet, a woman who earned her living with her pen, Christine de Pisan (1364– ca. 1430). Married at sixteen and widowed at twenty-five, Christine was left virtually impoverished with the responsibility for supporting herself, her three children, her mother, and a niece. Rather than remarrying, she decided to earn her way as an author, an unheard-of decision

This picture from an illuminated manuscript of Geoffrey Chaucer's The Canterbury Tales *illustrates the Prologue to the poem. The pilgrims are on their way to the shrine of Saint Thomas à Becket at Canterbury.*

for a woman of the fourteenth century. Beginning her education from scratch, she absorbed history and literature and began writing the sorts of conventional love poems popular with the French aristocracy. From there she moved to autobiographical poetry in which she described how fortune had changed her life. Her success was immediate and tremendous. Kings, princes, and aristocrats from England to Italy bought copies of her works and tried to attract her to their courts.

As a professional woman of letters, Christine fought the stereotypical medieval image of women as weak, sexually aggressive temptresses. With wit and reason she argued that women could be virtuous and showed the fallacies of traditional antifeminist preaching, poetry, and belief. She appealed to women to develop their own sense of self-worth directly from experience and not to rely on the advice of men who, no matter how well read, could not have any direct, accurate knowledge of the meaning of being a woman. In her *Hymn to Joan of Arc*, she saluted her famous contemporary for her accomplishments, bringing dignity to women, striving for justice, and working for peace in France.

Though Christine de Pisan was the exception rather than the rule, her life and writing epitomized the new possibilities and new interests of the fifteenth century. They included an acute sense of individuality, a willingness to look for truth not in the clichés of the past but in actual experience, and a readiness to defend one's views with tenacity. Although an heir of the medieval world, Christine, like her contemporaries, already embodied the attitudes of a new age.

That new age was reflected in a second tradition in fifteenth-century France, that of realist poetry. Around 1453, just as the English troops were enduring a final battering from the French artillery, Duke Charles of Orléans (1394–1465) organized a poetry contest. Each contestant was to write a ballad that began with the contradictory line, "I die of thirst beside the fountain." The duke, himself an outstanding poet, wrote an entry that embodied the traditional courtly themes of love and fortune:

> I die of thirst beside the fountain,
> Shaking from cold and the fire of love;
> I am blind and yet guide the others;
> I am weak of mind, a man of wisdom;
> Too negligent, often cautious in vain,
> I have been made a spirit,
> Led by fortune for better or for worse.

An unexpected and very different entry came from the duke's prison. The prisoner-poet, François Villon (1432–ca. 1464), was a child of the Paris streets, an impoverished student, a barroom brawler, a killer, and a thief who spent much of his life trying to escape the gallows. He was also the greatest realist poet of the Middle Ages. His entry read:

> I die of thirst beside the fountain,
> Hot as fire, my teeth clattering,
> At home I am in an alien land;
> I shudder beside a glowing brazier,
> Naked as a worm, gloriously dressed,
> I laugh and cry and wait without hope,
> I take comfort and sad despair,
> I rejoice and have no joy,
> Powerful, I have no force and no strength,
> Well received, I am expelled by all.

The duke focused on the sufferings of love; the thief on the physical sufferings of the downtrodden. The two poets represent the contradictory tendencies of literature in the later Middle Ages. From Prague to Paris, everywhere vernacular languages had come into their own. Poets used their native tongues to express a spectrum of sentiments and to describe a spectrum of emotions and values. The themes and ideas expressed ranged from the polished, traditional values of the aristocracy trying to maintain the ideals of chivalry in a new and changed world to the views of ordinary people, by turns reverent or sarcastic, joyful or despondent.

Late in life, Christine de Pisan relinquished her independence to enter a convent. Charles of Orléans was so moved by Villon's poetry that he released him from prison. The pope and the Hussites came to terms. King Charles VII ordered a new investigation into Joan of Arc, which absolved her—posthumously—of the charge of heresy. The religious, political, and cultural systems of the late Middle Ages remained sufficiently flexible to absorb the contradictory tendencies that they had created. This flexibility would not last. In the next century the political, religious, and cultural landscapes of Europe would be transformed by the new impulses born in the later Middle Ages.

The fourteenth and fifteenth centuries saw demographic collapse brought on by plague and accentuated by overpopulation and the ravages of warfare. They saw the transformation of the masses of the poor from the objects of Christian charity to the objects of fear and mistrust. During these centuries warfare in France, England, Italy, and elsewhere evolved from elite battles to devastating, professional campaigns of mass destruction capable of leaving whole countries in ruins for decades. Peasants fought for survival; aristocrats and wealthy merchants fought for greater power, prestige, and wealth on an international scale. Family alliances and merchant companies bound Europe together in a web of blood and money.

As the inherited forms of social and political organization strained to absorb these new conditions, individuals sought their own answers to the problems of life and death, using the legacy of the past, but using it in novel and creative ways. Dynasts created new principalities without regard for ancient allegiances. Mystics and heretics sought God without benefit of traditional religious hierarchies, and poets and philosophers sought personal expression outside the confines of inherited tradition.

The legacy of the later Middle Ages was a complex and ambiguous one. The thousand years of synthesis of classical, barbarian, and Christian traditions did not disappear. The bonds holding this world together were not yet broken. But the last centuries of the Middle Ages bequeathed a critical detachment from this heritage, expressed in the revolts of peasants and workers, the preaching of radical religious reformers, and the poems of mystics and visionaries.

Suggestions for Further Reading

General Reading

Daniel Waley, *Later Medieval Europe* (London: Longman, 1975). A brief introduction with a focus on Italy.

Margaret Aston, *The Fifteenth Century: The Prospect of Europe* (New York: W. W. Norton, 1968). A general survey of the fifteenth century.

* Johan Huizinga, *The Waning of the Middle Ages* (New York: St. Martin's Press, 1954). An old but still powerful interpretation of culture and society in the Burgundian court in the late Middle Ages.

Politics as a Family Affair

Francis Dvornik, *The Slavs in European History and Civilization* (New Brunswick, NJ: Rutgers University Press, 1962). A masterful introduction to the history of eastern Europe.

* Geoffrey Barraclough, ed., *Eastern and Western Europe in the Middle Ages* (New York: 1970). An excellent collection of essays on various aspects of eastern European history.

Joachim Leuschner, *Germany in the Late Middle Ages* (Amsterdam: Elsevier, 1980). An introduction to late medieval German history.

Richard W. Kaeuper, *War, Justice and Public Order: England and France in the Later Middle Ages* (Oxford: Oxford University Press, 1988). A fine analysis of the effects of war on England and France.

* C. T. Allmand, *The Hundred Years War: England and France at War c. 1300–c. 1450* (New York: Cambridge University Press, 1988). A recent, brief introduction to the Hundred Years' War by a British historian.

* Régine Pernoud, *Joan of Arc, by Herself and Her Witnesses* (New York: Stein & Day, 1966). Contemporary writings by and about Joan of Arc.

Life and Death in the Later Middle Ages

* Philip Zieger, *The Black Death* (New York: Harper & Row, 1969). A reliable introduction to the plague in the fourteenth century.

H. A. Miskimin, *The Economy of Early Renaissance Europe, 1300–1460* (New York: Cambridge University

Press, 1975). An accessible introduction to the economic history of the later Middle Ages.

* P. Dollinger, *The German Hansa* (Stanford, CA: Stanford University Press, 1970). A brief history of the Hansa intended for the nonspecialist.

* Edith Ennen, *The Medieval Town* (New York: 1979). A brief history of medieval cities by a German specialist.

Georges Duby, ed., *A History of Private Life. Volume 2. Revelations of the Medieval World* (Cambridge, MA: Harvard University Press, 1988). A series of provocative essays on the origins of privacy and the individual.

Bronislaw Geremek, *Power or Pity: Europe and the Poor From the Middle Ages to the Present* (forthcoming). A history of the origins of public welfare, focusing on the late Middle Ages.

* Michel Mollat and Philippe Wolff, *The Popular Revolutions of the Late Middle Ages* (London: 1973). An accessible history of late medieval revolts, focusing on those of medieval cities.

The Spirit of the Later Middle Ages

* Geoffrey Barraclough, *The Medieval Papacy* (New York: W. W. Norton, 1968). A brief overview of the papacy.

Yves Renouard, *The Avignon Papacy (1305–1403)* (Hamden, CT: Archon Books, 1970). A readable account of the Avignon popes.

* Heiko A. Oberman, *The Harvest of Medieval Theology* (Cambridge, MA: Labyrinth Press, 1963). A technical but rewarding account of late medieval theology.

Howard Kaminsky, *A History of the Hussite Revolution* (Berkeley, CA: University of California Press, 1967). The best account of the Hussite movement.

Gordon Leff, *Heresy in the Later Middle Ages* (Manchester: Manchester University Press, 1967). A survey of heretical movements in the fourteenth and fifteenth centuries.

* Caroline Walker Bynum, *Holy Feast and Holy Fast: The Religious Significance of Food to Medieval Women* (Berkeley, CA: University of California Press, 1987). An imaginative and scholarly examination of the role of food in the spirituality of medieval women.

E. F. Chaney, *François Villon in His Environment* (Oxford: Oxford University Press, 1946). An old but still valuable study of Villon and his world.

H. S. Bennett, *Chaucer and the Fifteenth Century* (Oxford: Oxford University Press, 1961). An accessible historical introduction to Chaucer.

John Freccero, *Dante and the Poetics of Conversion* (Cambridge, MA: Harvard University Press, 1986). A serious and rewarding study of Dante by an acknowledged master.

* Indicates paperback edition available.

11

The Italian Revival

A Civic Procession

It is 25 April 1444. On this day each year the city of Venice celebrates its patron, Saint Mark, with a procession around the square that bears his name. Processions are a common form of civic ritual through which a community defines itself. The special features that identify Venice for its citizens are all on display. Flags and emblems of the city are mounted on poles, and clothes bear the insignia of various orders and groups. The procession re-creates all forms of communal life. Here are the religious orders (the white-clad brothers of the Confraternity of Saint John are passing before us now), and the civic leaders can be seen just behind them. Musicians entertain both marchers and onlookers. An entire band files by on the right. The procession is orderly, but it is by no means contrived. It is not staged, as would be a modern ceremony, and this difference is evident in the relaxed attitude of the ordinary citizens who stand in groups in the middle of the square. There is no apparent drama to observe, and they walk and talk quite naturally. So, too, do the participants. In the lower left-hand corner, some friars are reading music; at the lower right, members of the confraternity carry their candles negligently.

Yet the painting, *The Procession of the Relic of the Holy Cross* (1496) by Gentile Bellini (ca. 1429–

the line of brothers breaks. The next day, the boy revived and his injury healed.

The Brothers of Saint John commissioned Bellini to commemorate this event. Bellini came from the most distinguished family of painters in Venice. His father Jacopo had studied in Florence and had brought both of his sons into his workshop when they were young boys. Until the age of thirty Gentile and his younger and more famous brother, Giovanni, worked on their father's commissions, learning the difficult craft of painting. Art was very much a family business in fifteenth-century Italy. The large workshops with their master and hordes of apprentices turned out vast canvasses with almost assembly-line precision. The master created the composition and sketched it out; his skilled assistants, like the Bellini brothers, worked on the more complex parts; and young apprentices painted backgrounds and indistinct faces. The master was first and foremost a businessman, gaining commissions to sustain his family and his workers. The Bellinis were well connected to the Confraternity of Saint John, and it was only natural that Gentile would receive this lucrative contract.

Though *The Procession of the Relic of the Holy Cross* was designed to re-create a central moment in the history of the confraternity, it is not the confraternity that dominates the picture. Miracles were part of civic life, and each town took pride in the special manifestations of heavenly care that had taken place within it. And it is very much Venice that is the centerpiece of Bellini's canvas. Dominating the painting is the Basilica of San Marco, with its four great horses over the center portico and the winged lion, the city's symbol, on the canopy above the horses. The procession emanates from the duke's palace to the right of the church, and the great flags of the city are seen everywhere. By the end of the fifteenth century, Venice was one of the greatest powers on earth, the center for international trade and finance. Home to the largest concentration of wealthy families anywhere in Europe, it could well afford the pomp and splendor of its processions. The achievements of God and the achievements of humans blend together in this painting as they blended together in that era of remarkable accomplishments that historians call the Renaissance.

1507), was commissioned to commemorate a miracle rather than a civic procession. On the evening before Saint Mark's day, a visiting merchant and his son were touring the square when the boy accidentally fell and cracked his skull. The doctors who were called to treat him regarded the case as hopeless and advised the father to prepare for his son's death. The next morning, the Brothers of the Confraternity of Saint John carried the relic of a piece of the true cross beneath an embroidered canopy. The merchant approached the golden altarpiece that contained the relic, dropped to his knees, and prayed that Saint Mark would miraculously cure his son. He is the red-clad figure kneeling just to the right of center where

Renaissance Society

Perhaps the most surprising result of the Black Death was the way in which European society revived itself in the succeeding centuries. Even at the height of the plague a spirit of revitalization was evident in the works of artists and writers. Petrarch (1304–74), the great humanist poet and scholar, was among the first to differentiate the new age in which he was living from two earlier ones: the classical world of Greece and Rome, which he admired, and the subsequent Dark Ages, which he detested. This spirit of self-awareness is one of the defining characteristics of the Renaissance. "It is but in our own day that men dare boast that they see the dawn of better things," wrote Matteo Palmieri (1406–75). Like many others, Marsilio Ficino (1433–99), a Florentine physician and philosopher who translated Plato and dabbled in astrology, dubbed his times a golden age. "This century, like a golden age, has restored to light the liberal arts, which were almost extinct: grammar, poetry, rhetoric, painting, sculpture, architecture, and music." The Renaissance was a new age by self-assertion. In that self-assertion wave after wave of artistic celebration of the human spirit found its wellspring and created a legacy that is still vibrant five hundred years later.

What was the Renaissance? A French word for an Italian phenomenon, *Renaissance* literally means "rebirth." The word captures both the emphasis on humanity that characterized Renaissance thinking and the renewed fascination with the classical world. But the Renaissance was an age rather than an event. There is no moment at which the Middle Ages ended and, as we have seen, late medieval society was artistically creative, socially well developed, and economically diverse. Early Renaissance and late medieval are all but indistinguishable. Yet eventually the pace of change accelerated, and it is best to think of the Renaissance as an era of rapid transitions. Encompassing the two centuries between 1350 and 1550, it passed through three distinct phases. The first, from 1350 to 1400, was characterized by a declining population, the uncovering of classical texts, and experimentation in a variety of art forms. The creation of a set of cultural values and artistic and literary achievements that defined Renaissance style distinguished the second phase, from 1400 to 1500. The large Italian city-states developed stable and coherent forms of government and the warfare between them gradually ended. In the final period, from 1500 to 1550, invasions from France and Spain transformed Italian political life, and the ideas and techniques of Italian writers and artists radiated to all points of the Continent. Though Renaissance ideas and achievements did spread throughout western Europe, they are best studied where they first developed, on the Italian peninsula.

The Environment

The Italian peninsula differed sharply from other areas of Europe in the extent to which it was urban. By the late Middle Ages nearly one in four Italians lived in a town, in contrast to one in ten elsewhere. Not even the plague did much to change this ratio. There were more Italian cities and more people in them. By 1500 seven of the ten largest cities in the West were in Italy. Naples, Venice, and Milan, each with a population of more than one hundred thousand, led the rest. But not every city was a great metropolis, and it was the numerous smaller towns, with populations nearer to one thousand, that gave the Italian peninsula its urban character. Cities were still the wonder of the world, dominating their regions economically, politically, and culturally. The diversified economic activities in which the inhabitants engaged created vast concentrations of wealth. Cities also served as convenient centers of judicial and ecclesiastical power. Moreover, they attracted to their regions the novelties of life, whether new products or new ideas.

Though cities served as regional centers, they cannot be viewed in isolation from their rural surroundings. Cities acted as central places around which a cluster of large and small villages was organized. Urban areas, especially the small towns, provided markets for the agricultural produce of the countryside and for the manufactured goods of the urban craftsmen. It was in the cities that goods and services changed hands. This allowed for the specialization in agricultural and industrial life that increased both productivity and wages. Cities also caught the runoff of rural population, especially the shower of younger sons

Europe, ca. 1500

and daughters who could not be accommodated on the farms. Cities grew by migration rather than by natural increase, and immigrants flooded into them. Thus the areas surrounding a city were critical to its prosperity and survival. The urban system was a network of cities encompassed by towns encircled by rural villages. Florence, the dominant city in the region of Tuscany, exemplifies this relationship. Though it possessed two-thirds of its region's wealth, Florence contained only 14 percent of the regional population. The surrounding countryside was agriculturally rich, for marketing costs were low and demand for foodstuffs high. A number of smaller cities like Prato and Pistoia to the north and Pisa to the west channeled their local produce and trade to Florence.

Though cities may have dominated Renaissance Italy, by present standards they were small

in both area and population. Despite the city's wealth, great banks, magnificent palaces and piazzas, a person could walk across fifteenth-century Florence in less than half an hour. In 1427 its population was thirty-seven thousand, only half its pre-plague size. Most Italian cities contained large fields for agricultural production, and within the outer walls of Florence were gardens and grain fields. Inside the inner city walls the people crowded together into tightly packed quarters. Streets were narrow and dark, with an incredible jumble of buildings in all sizes, shapes, and states of repair, though with the exception of churches and the "towers" of the rich, few were taller than three stories. The intensity of the stench from raw sewage, rotting foodstuffs, and animals being brought to slaughter was equaled only by the din made by hoofs and wooden cartwheels on paving stones and roaring open fires around which people plied their crafts, cooked their food, or huddled for warmth.

Urban populations were organized far differently from rural ones. On the farms the central distinctions involved ownership of land. Some farmers owned their estates outright and left them intact to their heirs. Others were involved in a sharecropping system by which absentee owners of land supplied working capital in return for half of the farm's produce. A great gulf in wealth separated owners from sharecroppers. Those who owned their land normally lived with surplus, those who sharecropped always lived on the margin of subsistence. But within the groups the gaps were not as great. There were gradations, but these were ordinarily temporary conditions that bad harvests, generous dowries, or divided inheritances balanced out over time.

Sheltering Pilgrims, by Francisco Hubertini Bacchiacca. Oil on wood. Pilgrims are looking for lodging on a street in Florence. All public inns in Florence were on a single street, and their management was strictly regulated.

In the city, however, distinctions were based first on occupation, which largely corresponded to social position and wealth. Cities began as markets and it was the privilege to participate in the market that defined citizens. As the trades and crafts expanded, city governments provided protection for consumers and producers by creating monopolies through which standards for craftsmanship were maintained and profits for craftsmen were guaranteed. These monopolies were called guilds or companies. Each large city had its own hierarchy of guilds, and membership in a major guild ensured a successful career. At the top were the important manufacturing groups—clothiers, metalworkers, and the like. Just below them were bankers, merchants, and the administrators of civic and Church holdings. At the bottom were grocers, masons, and other skilled workers. Roughly speaking, all of those within the guild structure, from bottom to top, lived comfortably, though throughout their lifecycle they might experience want as well as plenty. Yet the majority of urban inhabitants were not members of guilds. Many managed to eke out a living as wage laborers; many more were simply destitute. As a group these poor constituted as much as half of the entire population. Most were dependent upon civic and private charity for their very survival, but the continued migration of the destitute into cities suggests that opportunities were greater there than in the countryside.

The disparities between rich and poor were overwhelming. The concentration of wealth in the hands of an ever narrowing group of families and favored guilds characterized every large city. One reason for this was the extreme instability of economic life. Prices and wages fluctuated wildly in response to local circumstance. After an epidemic of plague, wages climbed and the prices of consumer goods tumbled. A bad harvest sent food prices skyrocketing. Only those able to even out these extreme swings by stockpiling goods in times of plenty and consuming them in times of want were safe. Capital, however initially accumulated, was the key to continued wealth. Monopolies ensured the profitability of trade and manufacturing, but only those with sufficient capital could engage in either. In Florence, for example, 10 percent of the families controlled 90 percent of the wealth, with an even more extreme

Cloth making was a major contributor to European economic growth during the Middle Ages. In this 1470 portrait of Cloth Merchants' Street, Bologna, a tailor (center) measures a prospective client.

concentration at the top. The combined wealth of the richest one hundred Florentine families was greater than the combined wealth of 87 percent of the city's population.

Production and Consumption

This concentration of wealth and the way in which it was used defined Renaissance economy. Economic life is bound up in the relationship between resources and desires, or, as economists would have it, supply and demand. The late medieval economy, despite the development of international banking and long-distance trade, was still an economy of primary producers: between 70 and 90 percent of Europe's population was involved in subsistence agriculture. Even in Italy, which contained the greatest concentration of urban areas in the world, agriculture predominated. The manufacture of clothing was the only other significant economic activity, and it was dwarfed in comparison to farming. Moreover, most of what was produced was for local consumption rather than for the marketplace. The relationship between supply and demand was precisely measured by the full or empty stomach. Even in good times more than 80 percent of the population lived at subsistence level with food, clothing, and shelter their only expenses. Thus when we discuss the market economy of the Renaissance, we are discussing the circumstances of the few rather than the many.

The defining characteristic of the early Renaissance economy was change in population. Recurring waves of plague kept population levels low for more than a century. The first shocks of the 1340s and 1350s carried away between one-third and one-half of the European population. Tremors, which curtailed recovery, followed. For example, Florence lost well over one-half of its citizens in the mid-fourteenth century. Population growth began immediately after the first series of plagues, but an epidemic in 1400, which carried away one-fourth of the city's residents, arrested it. Thereafter the population stabilized and recurrences of infectious disease checked each tiny spurt of growth. In the century between 1350 and 1450 one in every six years was characterized by an unusually high mortality rate. At the end of this period Florence's population was only a quarter of what it had been at the beginning.

This dramatic reduction in population depressed economic growth. Until 1460 the major sectors of the economy were stagnant. The general economy did not revive until the sustained population increase toward the end of the fifteenth century. Until then, in both agriculture and manufacturing, supply outstripped demand. On the farms overabundance resulted from two related developments, the concentration of surviving farmers on the best land and the enlargement of their holdings. In the shops finished products outnumbered the consumers who survived the epidemics. Overproduction meant lower prices for basic commodities, and the decline in population meant higher wages for labor. The result was that at the lowest levels of society survivors found it easier to earn their living and even to create a surplus than had their parents. For a time the lot of the masses improved.

But for investors, such economic conditions meant that neither agriculture nor cloth making were particularly attractive. Expensive investments in land or equipment for sharecropping were paid off in inexpensive grain; high wages for the few surviving skilled workers brought a return in cheap cloth. In such circumstances, consumption was more attractive than investment and luxury became more alluring than ever. It was not merely the perceived shortage in profitable investments that brought on the increase in conspicuous consumption during the fifteenth century. In the psychological atmosphere created by unpredictable, swift, and deadly epidemics, people who were interested in life on earth became more concerned with the present than the future. Secondly, in order to pay for wars, both offensive and defensive, rates of taxation increased. Since both houses and personal property were normally exempt from the calculations of wealth upon which taxation was based, the richest members of the community could escape this additional burden by purchasing luxury goods. Even those at the lowest levels of society eagerly purchased whatever their meager means permitted.

For whatever reasons, the production and consumption of luxuries soared. By the middle of the fourteenth century Florence was known for its silks and jewelry as much as for its cloth. Venice became a European center for the glass industry, especially for the finely ground glass that was used in eyeglasses. Production of specialty crops like sugar, saffron, fruits, and high-quality wine expanded. International trade centered more than ever on bringing into western Europe the exotic goods of the East, resulting in the serious outflow of gold and silver that enriched first the Byzantine and then the Ottoman emperors. Both public and private building projects increased, spurring the demand for architects, sculptors, and painters. Centers of government, even in the so-called republican cities, were richly appointed in a new style of conspicuous display. At the courts of the hereditary nobility and of the pope the

Scene From the Life of Saint Nicholas of Bari, *by Fra Angelico (Angelic Brother). The workmen in the foreground are unloading wheat. Fra Angelico, a Dominican monk, helped to pioneer the Renaissance methods of art in Florence.*

ceremonies of state were lavish beyond compare. The rise in the consumption of luxuries was everywhere apparent, taken by some as a sign of the vitality of the age, by others as an indication of its decay.

The Experience of Life

Luxury helped improve a life that for rich and poor alike was short and uncertain. Nature was still people's most potent enemy. Renaissance children who survived infancy found their lives governed by parentage and by sex. In parentage the great divide was between those who lived with surplus and those who lived at subsistence. The first category encompassed the wealthiest bankers and merchants down to those who owned their own farms or engaged in small urban crafts. The vast majority of urban and rural dwellers comprised the second category. About the children of the poor we know very little other than that their survival was unlikely. If they did not die at birth or shortly afterward, they might be abandoned—especially if female—to the growing number of orphanages in the cities, waste away from lack of nutrition, or fall prey to ordinary childhood diseases for which there were no treatments. Eldest sons were favored, younger daughters were disadvantaged. But in poor families this favoritism meant little more than early apprenticeship to day labor in the city or farm labor in the countryside. Girls were frequently sent out as domestic servants far from the family home. The economic necessities of family survival dictated this course of childhood, which made it difficult for Renaissance parents to develop a strong emotional attachment to individual children.

Children of the wealthy had better chances for survival than did children of the poor. For the better off, childhood might begin with "milk parents," life in the home of the family of a wet nurse who would breast-feed the baby through infancy. Only the very wealthy could afford a live-in wet nurse, which would increase the child's chances of survival. Again, daughters were more likely to be sent far from home and least likely to have their nursing supervised. The use of wet nurses not only emancipated parents from the daily care of infants, it also allowed them to resume sexual relations. Nursing women refrained from sex in the belief that it affected their milk, and wet nurses were hired with the stipulation that they remain celibate during their employment.

During the period between weaning and apprenticeship Renaissance children lived with their families. There was no typical Renaissance family. Nuclear families—that is, parents and their children under one roof—were probably more common than extended families, which might include grandparents and other relatives. But the composition of the family changed over the course of the life-cycle and included times in which married children or grandparents were present and others when a single parent and small children were the only members. Moreover, even nuclear families commonly contained stepparents and stepchildren as well as domestic servants or apprentices. Thus a child returning to the parental household was as likely to form emotional bonds with older siblings as with parents.

The family was an economic unit as well as a grouping of relatives. Decisions to abandon children, to send them away from the household when very young, or to take in domestic servants were based on economic calculations. In the competition for scarce resources, the way in which children were managed might determine the survival of the family unit. Sons could expect to be apprenticed to a trade probably between the ages of ten and thirteen. Most, of course, learned the

crafts of their fathers, but not necessarily in their father's shop. By adolescence these fortunate boys, who might have had some rudimentary schooling, were earning token wages that contributed to family income. Sons inherited the family business and its most important possessions, tools of the trade or beasts of labor for the farm. Inheritance customs varied. In some places only the eldest son received the equipment of the family occupation; in others, like Tuscany, all the sons shared it. Still, in the first fifteen years of life, these most favored children would have spent between one-third and one-half of their time outside the household in which they had been born.

Expectations for daughters centered on their chances of marriage. For a girl, dowry was everything. If a girl's father could provide a handsome one, her future was secure; if not, the alternatives were a convent, which would take a small bequest, or a match lower down the social scale, where the quality of life deteriorated rapidly. Daughters of poor families entered domestic service in order to have a dowry provided by their masters. The dowry was taken to the household of their husband. There the couple resided until they established their own separate family. If the husband died, it was to his parental household that the widow returned. After marriage the Renaissance woman was permanently separated from her childhood home.

Women married in late adolescence, usually around the age of twenty. Among the wealthy, marriages were perceived as familial alliances and business transactions rather than love matches. The dowry was an investment on which fathers expected a return, and while the bride might have some choice, it was severely limited. Compatibility was not a central feature in matchmaking. Husbands were, on average, ten years older than their wives and likely to leave them widows. In the early fifteenth century about one-fourth of all adult women in Florence were widows, many without prospects of remarriage.

Married women lived in a state of nearly constant pregnancy. Alessandra Strozzi, whose father was one of the wealthiest citizens of Florence, married at the age of sixteen, gave birth to eight children in ten years, and was widowed at the age of twenty-five. Not all pregnancies produced children. The rates of miscarriages and stillbirths were very high, and abortions and infanticide were not unknown. Only among the families who hovered between surplus and subsistence is there any evidence of attempts to control pregnancies. These efforts, which relied upon techniques like the rhythm method and withdrawal, were not particularly effective. The rhythm method was especially futile because of the misunderstanding of the role of women in conception. It was not yet known that the woman contained an egg that was fertilized during conception. Without this knowledge it was impossible to understand the cycle of ovulation. Practically speaking, family size was limited on the one end by late marriages and on the other by early deaths.

Life experiences differed for males. Men married later, near the age of twenty-five on the farms, nearer thirty in the cities because of the cost of setting up in trade or on the land. Late marriage meant long supervision under the watchful eye of father or master, an extended period between adolescence and adulthood. The reputation that Renaissance cities gained for homosexuality and licentiousness must be viewed in light of the advanced age at which males married. The level of sexual frustration was high and its outlet in ritual violence and rape was also high.

The establishment of one's own household through marriage was a late rite of passage considering the expectations of early death. Many men, even with families, never succeeded in setting up separately from their fathers or elder brothers. Men came of age at thirty but were thought to be old by fifty. Thus for men marriage and parenthood took place in middle age rather than in youth. Valued all their lives more highly than their sisters, male heads of households were the source of all power in their domicile, in their shops, and in the state. They were responsible for overseeing every aspect of the upbringing of their children, even choosing wet nurses for their infants and spouses for their daughters. But their wives were essential partners who governed domestic life. Women labored not only at the hearth, but in the fields and shops as well. Their economic contribution to the well-being of the family was critical, both in the dowry they brought at marriage and in the labor they contributed to the household. If their wives died, men with young children remarried quickly. While there were many bachelors in Renaissance society, there were few widowers.

In most cases death came suddenly. Epidemic diseases, of which plague was the most virulent, struck fifteenth-century Italians with fearful regularity. Even in the absence of a serious outbreak, there were always deaths in town and country attributable to the plague. Epidemics struck harder at the young—children and adolescents who were the majority of the population—and hardest in the summer months when other viruses and bacteria weakened the population. Influenza must have been the second largest cause of death, though in the absence of proper records we can only guess. Medical treatment was more likely to hasten death than to prolong life. Lorenzo de Medici's physician prescribed powdered pearls for the Florentine ruler's gout. After that Lorenzo complained more of stomach pains than of gout. Marsilio Ficino, in his popular medical tract "How to Prolong Your Life," recommended drinking liquefied gold during certain phases of the moon. Such remedies revealed a belief in the harmony of nature and the healing power of rare substances. They were not silly or superstitious; but they were not effective either. Starvation was rare, less because of food shortage than because the seriously undernourished were more likely to succumb to disease than to famine. In urban areas, the government would intervene to provide grain from public storehouses at times of extreme shortage; in the countryside large landholders commonly exercised the same function.

The Quality of Life

Though life may have been difficult during the Renaissance, it was not unfulfilling. Despite constant toil and frequent hardship, people of the Renaissance had reason to believe that their lives were better than those of their ancestors and that their children's lives would be better still. On the most basic level, health improved and, for those who survived plague, life expectancy increased. Better health was related to better diet. Improvement came from two sources, the relative surplus of grain throughout the fifteenth century and the wider variety of foods consumed. Bread remained the most widely consumed foodstuff, but even subsistence consumers were beginning to supplement their diet with meat and dairy products. There was more pork and lamb in the diet of ordinary people in the fifteenth century than there would be for the next four hundred years. At the upper levels of society, sweet wine and citrus fruits helped offset the lack of vegetables. This diversification of diet resulted from improvements in transportation and communication, which brought more goods and services to a growing number of towns in the chain that linked the regional centers to the rural countryside.

But the towns and cities contributed more than consumer goods to Renaissance society. They also introduced a new sense of social and political cohesiveness. The city was something to which people belonged. In urban areas they could join social groups of their own choosing and develop networks of support not possible in rural environments. Blood relations remained the primary social group. Kin were the most likely source of aid in times of need, and charity began at home. Kin groups extended well beyond the immediate family, with both cousins and in-laws laying claim to the privileges of blood. The urban family could also depend upon the connections of neighborhood. In some Italian cities wealth or occupation determined housing patterns. In others, like Florence, rich and poor lived side by side and identified themselves with their small administrative unit and with their local church. Thus they could participate in relationships with others both above and below them in the social scale. From their superiors they gained connections that helped their families; from their inferiors they gained devoted clients. The use of both in such important functions as godparenting demonstrates how the urban family built a complex set of social relations.

As in the Middle Ages, the Church remained the spatial, spiritual, and social center of people's lives. Though the Renaissance is singled out as a time when people became more worldly in their outlook, this worldliness took place within the context of an absorbing devotional life. There was not yet any separation between faith and reason. The Church provided explanations for both the mysterious and the mundane. It offered comfort in this life and in the life to come. In it were performed the rituals of baptism, marriage, and burial that measured the passage of life. The Church was also the source of the key symbols of urban society. The flags of militia troops, the emblems of guilds, the regalia of the city itself were all adorned by recognizably religious symbols. The Church preserved holy relics, like the piece of the true cross in Venice, that were venerated for their power to protect the city or to endow it with particular skills and resources. Churches were the most prominent sites of the urban area, towering above all other buildings. They provided the spatial reference points for where people lived or worked and even the formal geographical divisions into which the city might be divided. Through its holy days, as much as through its rituals, the Church helped channel leisure activities into community celebrations.

A growing sense of civic pride and individual accomplishment were underlying characteristics of the Italian Renaissance, enhanced by the development of social cohesion and community solidarity that both Church and city-state fostered. It is commonly held that the Renaissance was both elitist and male dominated, that it was an experience separate from that of the society at large. There can be no question that it was the rich who commissioned works of art or that it was the highly skilled male craftsmen who executed them. But neither lived in a social vacuum. The Renaissance was not an event whose causes were the result of the efforts of the few or whose consequences were limited to the privileged. In fact, the Renaissance was not an event at all. Family values that permitted early apprenticeships in surrogate households and that emphasized the continuity of crafts from one generation to the next made possible the skilled artists of the Renaissance cities. The stress on the production of luxury goods placed higher value upon individual skills and therefore upon excellence in workmanship. Church and state sought to express social values through representational art. One of the chief purposes of wall murals was to instruct the unlettered in religion, to help them visualize the central episodes in Christian history and thus increase the pleasure they derived from their faith. The grandiose architecture and statuary that adorned central places was designed to enhance civic pride and communicate the protective power of public institutions.

Renaissance Art

In every age, artistic achievement represents a combination of individual talent and predominant social ideals. Artists may be at the leading edge of the society in which they live, but it is the spirit of that society that they capture in word or song or image. Artistic disciplines also have their own technical development. Individually, Renaissance artists were attempting to solve problems about perspective and three-dimensionality that had defeated their predecessors. But the particular techniques or experiments that interested them owed as much to the social context as they did to the artistic one. For example, the urban character of Italian government led to the need for civic architecture, public buildings on a grand scale. The celebration of individual achievement led to the explosive growth of portraiture. Not surprisingly, major technological breakthroughs were achieved in both areas. Nor should we underestimate the brilliance of the artists themselves. To deny genius is to deprecate humanity. What we need to explain is not the existence of a Leonardo or a Michelangelo but their co-existence.

This relationship between artist and social context was all the more important in the Renaissance, when artists were closely tied to the crafts and trades of urban society and to the demands of clients who commissioned their work. Although it was the elite who patronized art, it was skilled tradesmen who produced it. Artists normally followed the pattern of any craftsman, an apprenticeship begun as a teenager and a long period of training and work in a master's shop. This form of education gave the aspiring artist a practical rather than a theoretical bent and a keen appreciation for the business side of art. Studios were identified with particular styles and competed for commissions from clients, especially the Church. Wealthy individuals commissioned art as investments, as marks of personal distinction, and as displays of public piety. They got what they paid for, usually entering into detailed contracts that stipulated the quality of materials and the amount of work done by the master himself. Isabella d'Este (1474–1539), one of the great patrons of Renaissance artists, wrote hundreds of letters specifying the details of the works she commissioned. She once sent an artist a thread of the exact dimensions of the pictures she had ordered. Demand for art was high. The vast public-works projects needed buildings, the new piazzas (public squares) and palazzos (private houses) needed statuary, and the long walls of churches needed murals.

The survival of so many Renaissance masterpieces allows us to reconstruct the stages by which the remarkable artistic achievements of this era took place. Although advances were made in a variety of fields during the Renaissance, the three outstanding areas were architecture, sculpture, and painting. While modern artists would consider each a separate discipline, Renaissance artists crossed their boundaries without hesitation. Not only could these artists work with a variety of materials, their intensive and varied apprenticeships taught them to apply the technical solutions of one field to the problems of another. Few Renaissance artists confined themselves to one area of artistic expression, and many created works of enduring beauty in more than one medium. Was the greatest achievement of Michelangelo his sculpture of David, his paintings on the ceiling of the Sistine Chapel, or his design for the dome of Saint Peter's? Only a century of interdisciplinary cross-fertilization could have prepared the artistic world for such a feat.

Three Masters

That century began with the work of three Florentine masters who deeply influenced one another's development, Brunelleschi (1377–1446), Donatello (1386–1466), and Masaccio (1401–28). In the Renaissance the dominant artistic discipline was architecture. Buildings were the most expensive investment patrons could make and the technical knowledge necessary for their successful construction was immense. The architect not only designed a building, he served as its general contractor, its construction supervisor, and its inspector. Moreover, the architect's design determined the amount and the scale of the statuary and decorative paintings to be incorporated. By 1400 the Gothic style of building had dominated western Europe for over two centuries. Its characteristic pointed arches, vaulted ceilings, and slender spires had simplified building by removing the heavy walls formerly thought necessary to support great structures. Gothic construction permitted greater height, a characteristic especially desirable in cathedrals, which stretched toward the heavens. The thinner walls did not have to support the structure, so they could be pierced by more and larger windows, admitting more light and air. But though the buildings themselves were simplified, the techniques for erecting them became more complex. By the fifteenth century architects had turned their techniques into an intricate style. They became obsessed by angular arches, elaborate vaultings and buttresses, and long, pointed spires. Each element competed with the others for prominence.

It was Brunelleschi who decisively challenged the principles of Gothic architecture by recombining its basic elements with those of classical structures. His achievement was less an innovation than a radical synthesis of old and new. Basing his designs on geometric principles, Brunelleschi reintroduced planes and spheres as dominant motifs. His greatest work was the dome on the cathedral in Florence, begun in 1420. He won the commission by challenging his competitors to make an egg stand on a flat piece of marble, a feat, he claimed, as difficult as designing the dome. When they all failed, Brunelleschi "taking the egg graciously, cracked its bottom on the marble and made it stay upright." The solution was simple but bold. So was his design for the dome. The windows at the base of the dome of the cathedral illustrate the simplicity of Brunelleschi's geometric technique. Circular windows are set inside a square of panels, which in turn are set inside a rectangle. The facades are dominated by columns and rounded arches, proportionally spaced from a central perspective. Brunelleschi is generally credited with having been the first Renaissance artist to have understood and made use of perspective, though it was immediately put to more dramatic effect in sculpture and painting.

The sculptor's study was the human form in all of its three-dimensional complexity. The survival of Roman and Hellenistic pieces, mostly bold and muscular torsos, meant that the influence of

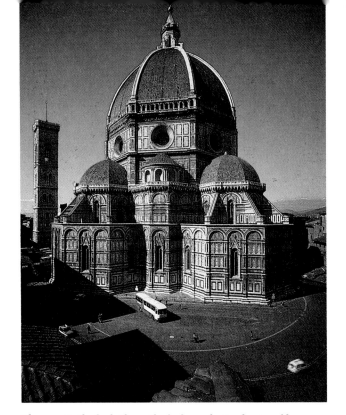

Florence Cathedral. The cathedral was begun by Arnolfo di Cambio in 1296. This view shows the dome and the apse end of the cathedral. The free-standing campanile, or bell tower, at the left recalls early Christian church architecture.

classical art was most direct in sculpture. Donatello translated these classical styles into more naturalistic forms. His technique is evident in the long flowing robes that form the bulk of most of his works. Donatello sculpted the cloth, not in the stylized angularity of the past in which the creases were as sharp as sword blades, but in the natural fashion in which cloth hung. Donatello also revived the free-standing statue, which demanded greater attention to human anatomy because it was viewed from many angles. *Judith Slaying Holofernes* (1455) is an outstanding example of Donatello's use of geometric proportion and perspective. Each side of the piece captures a different vision of Judith in action. In addition Donatello led the revival of the equestrian statue, sculpting the Venetian captain-general *Gattamelata* (1445–50) for a public square in Padua. This enormous bronze horse and rider borrowed from surviving first- and second-century Roman models but relied upon the standpoint of the viewer to achieve its overpowering effect. This use of linear perspective was also a characteristic of Donatello's dramatic works, like the breathtaking altar scenes of the miracles of Saint Anthony in Padua, which resemble nothing so much as a canvas cast in bronze.

These altar scenes clearly evince the unmistakable influence of the paintings of Masaccio. Although he lived less than thirty years, Masaccio created an enduring legacy. His frescoes in the Brancacci Chapel in Florence were studied and sketched by all of the great artists of the next generation, who unreservedly praised his naturalism. What most claims the attention of the modern viewer is Masaccio's shading of light and shadow and his brilliant use of linear perspective to create the illusion that a flat surface has three dimensions. Masaccio's work was on standard Christian themes, but he brought an entirely novel approach to them all. In an adoration scene he portrayed a middle-aged Madonna and a dwarfish baby Jesus; in a painting of Saint Peter paying tribute money, he used his own likeness as the face of one of the Apostles. His two best known works are the *Expulsion of Adam and Eve*

In this fresco, called The Expulsion of Adam and Eve, *Masacchio's mastery of perspective helps create the illusion of movement, as an angel drives the grieving Adam and Eve into the world.*

(ca. 1427) and the *Holy Trinity* (1425). In the *Expulsion of Adam and Eve*, Masaccio has left an unforgettable image of the fall from grace in Eve's primeval anguish. Her deep eyes and hollow mouth are accentuated by casting the source of light downward and shading what otherwise would be lit. In the *Holy Trinity*, Masaccio provides the classic example of the use of linear perspective in painting. The ceiling of a Brunelleschi-designed temple recedes to a vanishing point beyond the head of God, creating the simultaneous illusion of height and depth.

Renaissance Style

By the middle of the fifteenth century a recognizable Renaissance style had triumphed. Florence continued to lead the way although ideas, techniques, and influences had spread throughout the Italian peninsula and even to the north and west. The outstanding architect of this period was Leon Battista Alberti (1404–72), whose treatise *On Building* (1452) remained the most influential work on the subject until the eighteenth century. Alberti consecrated the geometric principles laid down by Brunelleschi and infused them with a humanist spirit. He revived the classical dictum that a building, like a body, should have an even number of supports and, like a head, an odd number of openings. This furthered precise geometric calculations in scale and design. To Brunelleschi's circles and squares Alberti added triangles, reviving another of the classical forms of construction. But it was in civic architecture that Alberti made his most significant contributions. Here he demonstrated how classical forms could be applied to traditional living space by being made purely decorative. His facade of the Palazzo Rucellai uses columns and arches not as building supports, but as embellishments that give geometric harmony to the building's appearance.

No sculptor challenged the preeminence of Donatello for another fifty years, but in painting there were many contenders for the garlands worn by Masaccio. The first was Piero della Francesca (ca. 1420–92) who, though trained in the tradition of Masaccio, broke new ground in his concern for the visual unity of his paintings. From portraits to processions to his stunning

Botticelli's Primavera (Spring)*, also called* Garden of Venus. *Venus, in the center, is attended by the three Graces and by Cupid, Flora, Chloris, and Zephyr. With its lack of attention to perspective and elongated figures, the style has more in common with medieval tapestries than with Renaissance art.*

fresco *The Resurrection* (ca. 1463) Piero concentrated upon the most technical aspects of composition. He was influenced by Alberti's ideas about the geometry of form and it is said that his measurements and calculations for various parts of *The Resurrection* took more time than the painting itself. Another challenger was Sandro Botticelli (1445–1510), whose classical themes, sensitive portraits, and bright colors set him apart from the line of Florentine painters with whom he studied. His mythologies of the *Birth of Venus* and *Spring* (ca. 1478) depart markedly from the naturalism inspired by Masaccio. Botticelli's paintings have a dreamlike quality, an unreality highlighted by the beautiful faces and lithe figures of his characters.

Botticelli's concern with beauty and personality is also seen in the paintings of Leonardo da Vinci (1452–1519), whose creative genius embodied the Renaissance ideal of the "universal man."

Leonardo's achievements in scientific, technical, and artistic endeavors read like a list of all of the subjects known during the Renaissance. His detailed anatomical drawings and the method he devised for rendering them, his botanical observations, and his engineering inventions (including models for the tank and the airplane) testify to his unrestrained curiosity. His paintings reveal a continuation of the scientific application of mathematics to matters of proportion and perspective. The dramatic fresco *The Last Supper* (ca. 1495–98), for example, takes the traditional scene of Christ and his disciples at a long table and divides it into four groups of three, each with its own separate action, leaving Jesus to dominate the center of the picture by balancing its two sides. Leonardo's psychological portrait *La Gioconda* (1503–06), popularly called the Mona Lisa, is quite possibly the best-known picture in the Western world.

Michelangelo

The artistic achievements of the Renaissance culminated in the creative outpourings of Michelangelo Buonarroti (1475–1564). It is almost as if the age itself had produced a summation of how it wished to be remembered. Poet, sculptor, painter, and architect, Michelangelo imparted his genius to everything he touched. He was the first Renaissance artist to be publicly recognized as the master he was. His works drew vast crowds and were studied and copied by his competitors. Unlike the early fifteenth-century artists who enjoyed fruitful cooperation, Michelangelo detested his rivals, especially Bramante, the leading architect of Rome, and Raphael, one of its leading painters.

Uncharacteristically, Michelangelo came from a family of standing in Florentine society and gained his apprenticeship over the opposition of his father. He claimed to have imbibed his love of sculpture from the milk of his wet nurse, who was the wife of a stonecutter. At the age of fourteen he was apprenticed to a leading painter, Ghirlandaio, and spent his spare time in Florentine churches copying the works of Masaccio among others. In 1490 Michelangelo gained a place in the household of Lorenzo de' Medici, which was adorned by the presence of a number of gifted artists and philosophers. There he studied art and architecture under a student of Donatello. During this two-year period he claimed to have taught himself sculpturing, a remarkable feat considering the skills required. In fact, what was unusual about Michelangelo's early development was that he avoided the long years of apprenticeship during which someone else's style was implanted upon the young artist. He may well have learned more about philosophy than art in the Medici household, for there he came into contact with leading Neoplatonists, who taught that man was on an ascending journey of perfectability toward God. The human capacity for self-improvement was one of the central ideas of Renaissance thinkers and one that the Neoplatonists forcefully emphasized. Whether these ideas did anything other than fortify Michelangelo's own temperament is questionable, but they can be seen as one source of the heroic concept of humanity that he brought to his work.

In 1496 Michelangelo moved to Rome. There his abilities as a sculptor quickly brought him to the attention of Jacopo Galli, a Roman banker who was interested in art and learning. Galli commissioned a classical work for himself and procured another for a French cardinal, which became the *Pietà*. Although this was his first attempt at sculpting a work of religious art, Michelangelo would never surpass it in beauty or composition. The *Pietà* created a sensation in Rome and by the time that Michelangelo returned to Florence in 1501, at the age of twenty-six, he was already acknowledged as one of the great sculptors of his day. He was immediately commissioned to work on an enormous block of marble that had been quarried nearly a half-century before and had defeated the talents of a series of carvers. He worked continuously for three years on his *David* (1501–04), a piece that completed the union between classical and Renaissance styles. Michelangelo's giant nude gives eloquent expression to his belief that the human body is the "mortal veil" of the soul. The *David* replaced Donatello's *Judith* outside the Palazzo Vecchio.

Though Michelangelo always believed himself to be primarily a sculptor, his next outstanding work was in the field of painting. In 1508 Pope Julius II summoned Michelangelo to Rome and commissioned him to decorate the small ceremonial chapel that had been built next to the new papal residence. The initial plan called for figures of the twelve apostles to adorn the ceiling, but Michelangelo soon launched a more ambitious scheme: to portray, in an extended narrative, man's creation and those Old Testament events that foreshadowed the birth of the Savior. Everything about the execution of the Sistine Chapel paintings was extraordinary. First Michelangelo framed his scenes within the architecture of a massive classical temple. In this way he was able to give the impression of having flattened the rounded surface on which he worked. Then, on the two sides of the central panels, he represented figures of Hebrew prophets and pagan Sybils as sculptured marble statues. Finally, within the center panels came his fresco scenes of the events of the creation and of human history from the Fall to the Flood. His representations were simple and compelling: the fingers of God and Adam nearly touching; Eve with one leg still emerging from

Adam's side; the half-human snake in the temptation are all majestically evocative.

The *Pietà*, the *David*, and the paintings of the Sistine Chapel were the work of youth. Michelangelo's crowning achievement, the building of Saint Peter's, was the work of age. The intervening years saw the production of masterpiece after masterpiece, enough completed and unfinished work to have established his genius. Yet at the age of seventy-one Michelangelo undertook to finish a project that, like the marble block that had become the *David*, had defeated others for decades. The purpose of the church was to provide a suitable monument for the grave of Saint Peter. The basework had already been laid and drawings for its completion had been made thirty years earlier by Bramante. Michelangelo altered these plans in an effort to bring more light within the church and provide a more majestic facade outside. His main contribution, however, was the design of the great dome, which centered the interior of the church on Saint Peter's grave. He integrated the exterior of the dome so that its facade completed the themes of the building itself. The paired ribs on the dome imitate the paired columns on its base and the paired mock columns on the face of the building. More than the height, it is the harmony of Michelangelo's design that creates the sense of the building thrusting upward like a Gothic cathedral of old. The dome on Saint Peter's was the largest then known and provided the model, in succeeding generations, for Saint Paul's Cathedral in London and the U.S. Capitol building in Washington, D.C. Michelangelo did not live to see the dome of Saint Peter's completed.

Renaissance art served Renaissance society. It reflected both its concrete achievements and its visionary ideals. It was a synthesis of old and new, building upon classical models, particularly in sculpture and architecture, but adding newly discovered techniques and skills. Demanding patrons, like Pope Julius II, who commonly interrupted Michelangelo's work on the Sistine Chapel with criticisms and suggestions, fueled the remarkable growth in both the quantity and quality of Renaissance art. When Giorgio Vasari (1511–74) came to write his *Lives of the Great Painters, Sculptors, and Architects* (1550) he found over two hundred artists worthy of distinction. But Renaissance artists did more than construct and adorn buildings or celebrate and beautify spiritual life. Inevitably their work expressed the ideals and aspirations of the society in which they lived, the new emphasis upon learning and knowledge; upon the here and now rather than the hereafter; and most importantly, upon humanity and its capacity for growth and perfection.

The creation of Adam and Eve. Detail from Michelangelo's frescoes on the ceiling of the Sistine Chapel. The Michelangelo frescoes had become obscured by dirt and layers of varnish and glue applied at various times over the years. In the 1980s they were cleaned to reveal their original colors.

Renaissance Ideals

Renaissance thought went hand in glove with Renaissance art. Scholars and philosophers searched the works of the ancients to find the principles on which to build a better life. They scoured monastic libraries for forgotten manuscripts, discovering among other things, Greek poetry, history, the works of Homer and Plato, and Aristotle's *Poetics*. Their rigorous application of scholarly procedures for the collection and collation of these texts was one of the most important contributions of those Renaissance intellectuals who came to be known as humanists. Humanism developed in reaction to an intellectual world that was centered on the Church and dominated by otherworldly concerns. Humanism was secular in outlook, though by no means was it antireligious.

Humanists celebrated worldly achievements. Pico della Mirandola's *Oration on the Dignity of Man* (1486) is the best known of a multitude of Renaissance writings influenced by the discovery of the works of Plato. Pico believed that people could perfect their existence on earth because God had endowed humans with the capacity to determine their own fate. "O highest and most marvelous felicity of man! To him it is granted to have whatever he chooses, to be whatever he wills." A century later Shakespeare echoed these same themes in *Hamlet* (1603): "What a piece of work is a man. How noble in reason, how infinite in faculties, in form and moving how express and admirable, in action how like an angel, in apprehension how like a God! The beauty of the world, the paragon of animals!" This emphasis on human potential finds expression in the celebration of human achievement. Autobiographers like the artist Benvenuto Cellini (1500–71) marveled at their own accomplishments and held them up as a mirror to others. With the symbols of human achievement everywhere apparent, from public art and architecture to the vast accumulations of private riches, the Renaissance emphasized the significance of worldly attainments.

Humanism was neither a set of philosophical principles nor a program for social action. There were no antihumanists to give it form and whatever coherence Italian humanism may have had, it was quickly diluted as it rapidly spread across Europe. Quite simply, humanists studied and taught the humanities, the skills of disciplines like philology, the art of language, and rhetoric, the art of expression. Though they were mostly laymen, humanists applied their learning to both religious and secular studies. We must not think of humanists as antireligious. Although they reacted strongly against Scholasticism, they were heavily indebted to the work of medieval churchmen. Nor were they hostile to the Church. Petrarch, Bruni, and Alberti were all employed by the papal court at some time in their careers, as was Lorenzo Valla, the most influential of the humanists. Their interest in human achievement and human potential must be set beside their religious beliefs. As Petrarch stated quite succinctly: "Christ is my God; Cicero is the prince of the language I use."

The Humanists

The most important achievements of humanist scholars centered upon ancient texts. It was the humanists' goal to discover as much as had survived from the ancient world and to provide as full and accurate as possible texts of classical authors. Though much was already known of the Latin classics, few of the central works of ancient Greece had been uncovered. Humanists preserved this heritage by reviving the study of the Greek language and by translating Greek authors into Latin. After the fall of Constantinople in 1453, Italy became the center for Greek studies as scholars fled the Ottoman conquerors. Humanists also introduced historical methods in studying texts, establishing principles for determining which of many manuscript copies of an ancient text was the oldest and which had been least corrupted by their copyists. This was of immense importance in studying the writings of the ancient Fathers of the Church, many of whose manuscripts had not been examined for centuries. Humanists even introduced a new form of handwriting, the italic that we still use today, which made transcription easier. Their emphasis upon the humanistic disciplines fostered new educational ideals. Along with the study of theology, logic, and natural philosophy which had dominated the medieval university, humanist scholars stressed the importance of grammar, rhetoric, moral philosophy,

A miniature portrait of Petrarch is seen within the illuminated initial A in a manuscript of the poet's treatise De remediis utriusque fortunae *(Remedies Against Fortune).*

and history. They believed that the study of these "liberal arts" should be undertaken for its own sake. This gave a powerful boost to the ideal of the perfectability of the individual that appeared in so many other aspects of Renaissance culture.

Humanists furthered the secularization of Renaissance society through their emphasis on the study of the classical world. The rediscovery of Latin texts during the late Middle Ages spurred interest in all things ancient. Petrarch, who is rightly called the father of humanism, revered the great Roman rhetorician Cicero above all others. "If to admire Cicero means to be a Ciceronian, I am a Ciceronian. I admire him so much that I wonder at people who do not admire him." Petrarch imitated Cicero's style in long imaginary letters to ancient Romans and early Fathers of the Church. For Petrarch, Cicero's legacy was eloquence. He stressed this in his correspondence with the leading scholars of his day and taught it to those who would succeed him. From 1350 to 1450 Cicero was the dominant model for Renaissance poets and orators. Petrarch's emphasis upon language led to efforts to recapture the purity of ancient Latin and Greek, languages that had become corrupted over the centuries. Philology became one of the most celebrated humanist skills and the study of ancient manuscripts one of the most common humanist activities. The leading humanist in the generation after Petrarch was Leonardo Bruni (1370–1444), who was reputed to be the greatest Greek scholar of his day. He translated both Plato and Aristotle and laid the foundation for the Florentine Platonic Academy, which did so much to advance mastery of classical Greek and foster the ideas of Plato in the late fifteenth century.

The study of the origins of words, their meaning, and their proper grammatical usage may seem an unusual foundation for one of the most vital of all European intellectual movements. But philology was the humanists' chief concern. This can best be illustrated by the work of Lorenzo Valla (1407–57). Valla was brought up in Rome, where he was largely self-educated, though according to the prescriptions of the Florentine humanists. After failing to obtain a post at the papal court, he took a job as a lecturer in rhetoric at the university of Pavia. He was forced to leave the city when the supporters of a scholar he had criticized threatened to murder him. Soon he entered the service of Alfonso I, king of Naples, and applied his humanistic training to affairs of state. The kingdom of Naples bordered on the Papal States, and its kings were in continual conflict with the papacy. The pope asserted the right to withhold recognition of the king, a right that was based upon the jurisdictional authority supposedly ceded to the papacy by the Emperor Constantine in the fourth century. This so-called Donation of Constantine had long been a matter of dispute and its authenticity had been challenged frequently in the Middle Ages. But those challenges were made on political grounds and the arguments of papal supporters were as strenuous as those of papal opponents. Valla settled the matter definitively. Applying historical and philological critiques to the text of the Donation, Valla proved that it could not have been written earlier than the eighth century, four hundred years after Constantine's death. He mercilessly exposed words and terms that had not existed in Roman times, like *fief* and *satrap*, and thus proved beyond doubt that the Donation was a forgery and papal claims based upon it were without merit. Interestingly, Valla finally did receive an appointment as a papal secretary and his reputation as the outstanding humanist of his generation was secured.

Valla's career demonstrates the impact of humanist values on practical affairs. Although humanists were scholars, they made no distinction between an active and a contemplative life. A life of scholarship was a life of public service. They saw their studies as means of improving themselves and their society—"man is born in order to be useful to man." Many, like Valla, were active as political councillors. Others like Bruni, who served as Chancellor of Florence, accepted high office. This civic humanism is best expressed in the writings of Leon Battista Alberti (1404–72), whose treatise *On the Family* (1443) is a classic study of the new urban values, especially prudence and thrift. Alberti extolled the virtues of "the fatherland, the public good, and the benefit of all citizens." An architect, a mathematician, a poet, a playwright, a musician, and an inventor, Alberti was one of the great virtuosi of the Renaissance.

Alberti's own life might have served as a model for the most influential of all Renaissance tracts, Castiglione's *The Courtier* (1528). While Alberti directed his lessons to the private lives of successful urban families, Baldesar Castiglione (1478–1529) directed his to the public life of the aspiring elite. It was Castiglione's purpose to prescribe those characteristics that would make the ideal courtier, a man of such charm and accomplishment that he would be able to influence the good government of his state. In Castiglione's view the perfect courtier was as much born as made: "Besides his noble birth I would have the Courtier endowed by nature not only with talent and beauty of person and feature, but with a certain grace and air that shall make him at first sight pleasing." Everything that the courtier did was to maintain his pleasing grace and his public reputation. *The Courtier* was an etiquette book, and in it Castiglione prescribed every detail of the education necessary for the ideal state servant from table manners to artistic attainments. Though each talent was to be acquired through careful study and application, it was to be manifested with *sprezzatura*, a natural ease and superiority that was the essence of the gentleman. Castiglione's perfect courtier was an amalgam of all that the elite of Renaissance society held dear. He was to be educated as a scholar, he was to be occupied as a soldier, and he was to serve his state as an advisor.

Machiavelli

At the same time that Castiglione was drafting a blueprint for the idealized courtier, Niccolo Machiavelli (1469–1527) was laying the foundation for the realistic sixteenth-century ruler. No Renaissance work has been more important or more controversial than Machiavelli's *The Prince*

(1513). Its vivid prose, its epigrammatic advice—"men must either be pampered or crushed"—and its clinical dissection of power politics have attracted generation after generation of readers. With Machiavelli, for better or worse, begins the science of politics. Machiavellianism has passed into the language as a label for the ruthless, amoral pursuit of power, though the fact that subsequent generations needed a word to describe such behavior is as interesting as the one they chose. Machiavelli himself has been depicted as everything from an evil genius to a champion of republicanism. He could hardly have imagined himself one or the other.

Machiavelli's early life gave no promise of his distinguished career or his far-reaching and long-lasting reputation. Though he came from an established Florentine family, his father was a struggling lawyer who could provide his son with little more than a good humanist education, especially in the Latin classics. Machiavelli entered state service as an assistant to one of his teachers and unexpectedly rode those coattails into the relatively important office of secretary to the Council of Ten, the organ of Florentine government that had responsibility for war and diplomacy. Here Machiavelli received his education in practical affairs. His special interest was in the militia, and he was an early advocate of organizing and training Florentine citizens to defend the city rather than hiring Swiss or French mercenaries. He drafted position papers on the tense international situation that followed the French invasion of Italy in 1494 and was soon used as an envoy in diplomatic missions. He was an emissary to Cesare Borgia during his consolidation of the Papal States at the turn of the century and carefully studied Borgia's methods. Clearly Machiavelli devoted all his energies and his entire intellect to his career. He was a tireless correspondent and he began to collect materials for various tracts on military matters. He also planned out a prospective history in which to celebrate the greatness of the Florentine republic that he served.

But as suddenly as he rose to his position of power and influence he fell from it. The militia that he had advocated and in part organized was soundly defeated by the Spaniards, and the Florentine republic fell. Machiavelli was summarily dismissed from office in 1512 and was imprisoned and tortured the following year. Released and banished from the city, he retired to a small country estate and turned his restless energies to writing. Immediately he began writing what became his two greatest works, *The Prince* (1513) and *The Discourses on Livy* (1519). He followed these with the comic play *Mandragola* (1518), the treatise *The Art of War* (1520), and the massive *History of Florence* (1525). He died in 1527.

Machiavelli has left a haunting portrait of his life in exile, and it is important to understand how intertwined his studies of ancient and modern politics were.

> On the coming of evening, I return to my house and enter my study; and at the door I take off the day's clothing, covered with mud and dust, and put on garments regal and courtly; and reclothed appropriately, I enter the ancient courts of ancient men, where, received by them with affection, I feed on that food which only is mine and which I was born for. For four hours of time I do not feel boredom, I forget every trouble, I do not dread poverty, I am not frightened by death; entirely I give myself over to them.

In this state of mind *The Prince* was composed.

The Prince is a handbook for a ruler who would establish a lasting government. It attempts to set down principles culled from historical examples and contemporary events to aid the prince in attaining and maintaining power. By study of these precepts and by their swift and forceful application Machiavelli believed that the prince might even control fortune itself. *The Prince* is purely secular in content and philosophy. Where the medieval writer of a manual for princes would stress the divine foundations of the state, Machiavelli asserted the human bases: "The chief foundations on which all states rest are good laws and good arms." What made *The Prince* so remarkable in its day, and what continues to enliven debate over it, is that Machiavelli was able to separate all ethical considerations from his analysis. Whether this resulted from cynicism or from his own expressed desire for realism, Machiavelli uncompromisingly instructed the would-be ruler to be half man and half beast—to conquer neighbors, to murder enemies, and to deceive friends. Nothing better illustrates the principle that humanists were not necessarily humanitarians.

Terra-cotta bust of Niccolò Machiavelli by an unknown artist. Because of the ideas set forth in The Prince, *the name of Machiavelli has long stood for treachery, duplicity, and bad faith in statesmanship.*

Machiavelli combines admiration for the ancient world with the duty of the humanist citizen to perfect the present. Unlike most Renaissance thinkers, Machiavelli preferred change to stability. The great princes were all innovators rather than conservators. They joined with the warrior citizens to make their own fortune and that of their state. Taken as a whole, Machiavelli's writings aspire to the restoration of the glory of Rome, the establishment of an empire that is a good in itself. "I believe that the finest deed man can achieve, and the one most precious to God, is what he does for his Fatherland." A life bounded by a half-century of destructive warfare might have taught no other lesson than the sweetness of peace. But Machiavelli's thought transcended the immediacy of his historical context. Steeped in the humanist ideals of fame and *virtù*—a combination of virtue and virtuosity, of valor, character, and ability—he sought to reestablish Italian rule and place government upon a stable, scientific basis that would end the perpetual conflict among the Italian city-states.

The Politics of the Italian City-States

Like studs on a leather boot, city-states dotted the Italian peninsula. They differed in size, shape, and form. Some were large seaports, others small inland villages; some cut wide swaths across the plains, others were tiny islands. The absence of a unifying central authority in Italy, resulting from the collapse of the Holy Roman Empire and the papal schism, allowed ancient guilds and confraternities to transform themselves into self-governing societies. By the beginning of the fifteenth century the Italian city-states were the center of power, wealth, and culture in the Christian world.

This dominion rested on several conditions. First, their geographical position favored the exchange of resources and goods between East and West. Until the fifteenth century, and despite the crusading efforts of medieval popes, East and West fortified each other. A great circular trade had developed, encompassing the Byzantine Empire, the North African coastal states, and the Mediterranean nations of western Europe. The Italian peninsula dominated the circumference of that circle. Its port cities, Genoa and Venice especially, became great maritime powers through their trade in spices and minerals. Second, just beyond the peninsula to the north lay the vast and populous territories of the Holy Roman Empire. There the continuous need for manufactured goods, especially cloths and metals, was filled by long caravans that traveled from Italy through the Alps. Milan specialized in metal crafts and was, for a time, the armory of Europe. Florence, which originally founded its wealth on the woolen cloth trade, was now a financial capital as well as a center for the manufacture of fine luxury goods. Finally, the city-states and their surrounding areas were agriculturally self-sufficient. This is all the more remarkable in that most were entirely urban and held large concentrations of people who were not engaged in growing food. But in the south were great breadbaskets, like Naples and Sicily, which could feed not only Italians, but northern and eastern Europeans as well.

Because of their accomplishments we tend to think of these Italian city-states as small nations.

Even the term *city-state* implies national identity. Inhabitants, like the Roman citizens of old, identified themselves with their city, as Milanese or Florentines or Venetians. Each city-state governed itself according to its own rules and customs and each defined itself in isolation from the larger regional or tribal associations that once prevailed. Indeed, their struggles against one another speak eloquently of their local self-identification. Italy was neither a nation nor a people.

The Five Powers

Although there were dozens of Italian city-states, by the early fifteenth century five had emerged to dominate the politics of the peninsula. In the south was the kingdom of Naples, the only city-state governed by a hereditary monarchy. Its politics were mired by conflicts over its succession. During the fourteenth century Naples was successively ruled by French and Hungarian princes. The fifteenth century began with civil warfare between rival claimants of both nations and it was not until the Spaniard Alfonso I of Aragon (1442–58) secured the throne in 1443 that peace was restored and Naples and Sicily were reunited. Bordering Naples were the Papal States, whose capital was Rome but whose territories stretched far to the north and lay on both sides of the spiny Apennine mountain chain that extends down the center of the peninsula. Throughout the fourteenth and early fifteenth centuries, the territories under the nominal control of the Church were largely independent and included such thriving city-states as Bologna, Ferrara, and Urbino. Even in Rome the weakened papacy had to contend with noble families for control of the city.

The three remaining dominant city-states were bunched together in the north. Florence, center of Renaissance culture, was one of the wealthiest cities of Europe before the devastations of the plague and the sustained economic downturn of the late fourteenth century. The city itself was inland and its main waterway, the Arno, ran to the sea through Pisa, whose subjugation in 1406 was a turning point in Florentine history. Nominally Florence was a republic, but during the fifteenth century it was ruled in effect by its principal banking family, the Medici.

To the north of Florence was the duchy of Milan, the major city in Lombardy. It too was landlocked, cut off from the sea by Genoa. But Milan's economic life was oriented northward to the Swiss and German towns beyond the Alps, and its major concern was preventing foreign invasions. The most warlike of the Italian cities, Milan was a despotism, ruled for nearly two centuries by the Visconti family.

The last of the five powers was the republic of Venice. Ideally situated at the head of the Adriatic Sea, Venice became the leading maritime power of the age. Until the fifteenth century, Venice was less interested in securing a landed empire than in dominating a seaborne one. Its outposts along the Grecian and Dalmatian coasts, and its favored position in Constantinople, were the source of vast mercantile wealth. The republic was ruled by a hereditary elite, headed by an elected doge, who was the chief magistrate of Venice, and a variety of small elected councils.

The political history of the peninsula during the late fourteenth and early fifteenth centuries is one of unrelieved turmoil. Wherever we look, the governments of the city-states were threatened by foreign invaders, internal conspiracies, or popular revolts. In the 1370s the Genoese and Venetians fought their fourth war in little more than a century, this one so bitter that the Genoese risked much of their fleet in an unsuccessful effort to conquer Venice itself. At the turn of the century, the Hungarian occupant of the throne of Naples invaded both Rome and Florence. Florence and Milan were constantly at war with each other. Nor were foreign threats the only dangers. In Milan three Visconti brothers inherited power. Two murdered the third, and then the son of one murdered the other to reunite the inheritance. The Venetians executed one of their military leaders who was plotting treachery. One or another Florentine family usually faced exile when governments there changed hands. Popular revolts channeled social and economic discontent against the ruling elites in Rome, Milan, and Florence. The revolt of the "Ciompi" (the wooden shoes) in Florence in 1378 was an attempt by poorly paid wool workers to reform the city's exclusive guild system and give guild protection to the wage laborers lower down the social scale. In Milan an abortive republic was established in reaction against strong-arm Visconti rule.

By the middle of the fifteenth century, however, two trends were apparent amid this political chaos. The first was the consolidation of strong centralized governments within the large city-states. These took different forms but yielded a similar result—internal political stability. The return of the popes to Rome after the Great Schism restored the pope to the head of his temporal estates and began a long period of papal dominance over Rome and its satellite territories. In Milan, one of the great military leaders of the day, Francesco Sforza (1401–66), seized the reins of power after the failure of the Visconti line. The succession of King Alfonso I in Naples ended a half-century of civil war. In both Florence and Venice the grip that the political elite held over high offices was tightened by placing greater power in small advisory councils and, in Florence, by the ascent to power of the Medici family. In sum, this process is known as the rise of signorial rule. Whether the signories usurped power or had it thrust upon them in the hope that they might relieve the sustained economic and political crises is difficult to determine. But their rise made possible the second development of this period, the establishment of a balance of power within the peninsula.

It was the leaders of the Italian city-states who first perfected the art of diplomacy. Constant warfare necessitated continual alliances, and by the end of the fourteenth century the large city-states had begun the practice of keeping resident ambassadors at the major seats of power. This enhanced communication, a principal challenge in Renaissance diplomacy, and also provided leaders with accurate information about the conditions of potential allies and enemies. Diplomacy was both an offensive and defensive weapon. This was especially so because the city-states hired their soldiers as contract labor. These mercenary armies, whose leaders were known as *condottieri* from the name of their contract, were both expensive and dangerous to maintain. If they did not bankrupt their employers, they might desert them or, even worse, turn on them. Thus Francesco Sforza, the greatest *condottiere* of the fifteenth century, gained power in Milan. Before serving the Milanese, Sforza had been in the pay of the Florentines in a war against Milan. Sforza's consolidation of power in Milan initially led to warfare, but ultimately it formed the basis of the

Peace of Lodi (1454). This established two balanced alliances, one between Florence and Milan, the other between Venice and Naples. These states, along with the papacy, pledged mutual nonaggression, a policy that lasted for nearly forty years.

The Peace of Lodi did not bring peace. It only halted the long period in which the major city-states struggled against one another. Under cover of the peace, the large states continued the process of swallowing up their smaller neighbors and creating quasi-empires. This was a policy of imperialism as aggressive as that of any in the modern era. Civilian populations were overrun, local leaders exiled or exterminated, tribute money taken, and taxes levied. Each of the five states either increased its mainland territories or strengthened its hold upon them. Venice and Florence especially prospered.

Venice

Water was the source of the prosperity of Venice. Located at the head of the Adriatic Sea, the city is formed by a web of lagoons. Through its center snakes the Grand Canal, whose banks were lined with large and small buildings that celebrated its civic and mercantile power. At the Piazza San Marco stood the vast palace of the doge, elected leader of the republic, and the Basilica of Saint Mark, a domed church built in the Byzantine style. At the Rialto were the stalls of the bankers and moneylenders, less grand perhaps but no less important. Here, too, were the auction blocks for the profitable trade in European slaves, east European serfs, and battlefield captives who were sold into service to Egypt or Byzantium. On the eastern edge of the island city was the Arsenal, erected in the twelfth century to house the shipbuilding and arms manufacturing industries. Three centuries later it was the industrial marvel of the world, where the Venetian great galleys were constructed with assembly-line precision.

Its prosperity based on trade rather than conquest, Venice enjoyed many natural advantages. Its position at the head of the Adriatic permitted access to the raw materials of both East and West. The rich Alpine timberland behind the city

provided the hardwoods necessary for shipbuilding. The hinterland population were steady consumers of grain, cloth, and the new manufactured goods—glass, silk, jewelry, and cottons—that came pouring onto the market in the late Middle Ages. The winged lion of Saint Mark, the city's emblem, could be seen up and down the Italian and Dalmatian coasts, on the Greek islands, and in the ports of the Black Sea.

But the success of Venice owed more to its own achievements than to these rich inheritances. "It is the most triumphant city I have ever seen," wrote the Frenchman Philippe de Commynes at the end of the fifteenth century. The triumph of the Venetian state was the triumph of dedicated efficiency. The heart of its success lay in the way in which it organized its trade and its government. The key to Venetian trade was its privileged position with the Byzantine Empire. Venice had exchanged with the Byzantines military support for tax concessions that gave Venetian traders a competitive edge in the spice trade with the East. Venetians were the largest group of resident Europeans in Constantinople, and their personal contacts with eastern traders were an important part of their success. The spice trade was so lucrative that special ships were built to accommodate it. These galleys were constructed at public expense and doubled as the Venetian navy in times of war. By controlling these ships, the government strictly regulated the spice trade. Goods imported into or exported from Venice had to be carried in Venetian ships and be consigned by Venetian merchants. The trade in spices was carefully organized in other ways as well. Rather than allow the wealthiest merchants to dominate it, as they did in other cities, Venice specified the number of annual voyages and sold shares in them at auction based on a fixed price. This practice allowed big and small merchants to gain from the trade and encouraged all merchants to find other trading outlets. In the fourteenth century the Venetian empire included all of the most important trading ports on the coast of Dalmatia and in the Aegean Sea.

Like its trade, Venetian government was also designed to disperse power. Although it was known as "the most serene republic," Venice was not a republic in the sense that we use the word; it was rather an oligarchy—a government by a restricted group. Political power was vested in a Great Council whose membership had been fixed at the end of the thirteenth century. All males whose fathers enjoyed the privilege of membership in the Great Council were registered at birth in the Book of Gold and became members of the Great Council when adults. There were no further distinctions of rank within this nobility, whose members varied widely in wealth and intermarried freely with other groups in the society. From the body of the Great Council, which numbered about twenty-five hundred at the end of the fifteenth century, was chosen the Senate, a council about one-tenth the size, whose members served a one-year term. It was from the Senate that the true officers of government were selected: the doge, who was chosen for life, and members of a number of small councils, who administered affairs and advised the doge. Members of these councils were chosen by secret ballot in an elaborate process by which nominators were selected at random. Terms of office on the councils were extremely short in order to limit factionalism and to prevent any individual from gaining too much power. Though small groups exercised more power in practice than they should have in theory, the Venetian oligarchy was never troubled by either civil war or popular rebellion. "Venice governs itself with the greatest wisdom," Commynes declared, and Venetian-style republicanism was much admired throughout Europe.

With its mercantile families firmly in control of government and trade, Venice created a vast overseas empire in the East during the thirteenth and fourteenth centuries. Naval supremacy, based largely on technological advances that made long-distance and winter voyages possible, allowed the Venetians to offer protection to strategic outposts in return for either privileges or tribute. But in the fifteenth century Venice turned west. In a dramatic reversal of its centuries-old policy, it began a process of conquest in Italy itself, an empire on "terra firma," as Venetian islanders called it. There were several reasons for this new policy. First, the Venetian navy was no longer the unsurpassed power that it once had been. The Genoese wars had drained resources, and the revival of

the Ottoman Turks in the east posed a growing threat that ultimately resulted in the fall of Constantinople (1453) and the end of Venetian trading privileges. Outposts in Dalmatia and the Aegean came under assault from both the Turks and the king of Hungary, cutting heavily into the complicated system by which goods were circulated by Venetian merchants. Additionally, the trade in both sweet wine and sugar that the Venetians dominated through control of the Greek islands was now challenged by the Portuguese. It was not long before Portuguese competition affected the most lucrative of all the commodities traded by the Venetians—pepper. Perhaps most importantly, mainland expansion offered new opportunities for Venice. Not all Venetians were traders, and the new industries that were being developed in the city could readily benefit from control of mainland markets. So could those Venetian nobles employed to administer the conquered lands. They argued persuasively that the supply of raw materials and foodstuffs on which Venetian trade ultimately depended should be secured by the republic itself. Most decisively of all, opportunity was knocking. In Milan Visconti rule was weakening and the Milanese territories were ripe for picking.

Venice reaped a rich harvest. From the beginning of the fifteenth century to the Peace of Lodi, the Most Serene Republic engaged in unremitting warfare. Its successes were remarkable. It pushed out to the north to occupy all the lands between the city and the Habsburg territories; it pushed to the east until it straddled the entire head of the Adriatic; and it pushed to the west almost as far as Milan itself. Venetian victories resulted from both the traditional use of hired mercenaries and from the Venetians' own ingenuity at naval warfare. Although Venice was creating a landed empire, the course of expansion, especially in Lombardy, was along river routes. At the Arsenal were built new oared vessels armed with artillery for river sieges. Soon the captured territories were paying for continued expansion. The western conquests in particular brought large populations under Venetian control which, along with their potential as a market, provided a ready source of taxation. By the end of the fifteenth century the mainland dominions of Venice were contributing nearly 40 percent of the city's revenue at a cost far smaller than that of the naval empire a century earlier. Venice had become the most powerful city-state in Italy.

Florence

"What city, not merely in Italy, but in all the world...is more proud in its palazzi, more bedecked with churches, more beautiful in its architecture, more imposing in its gates, richer in piazzas, happier in its wide streets, greater in its people, more glorious in its citizenry, more inexhaustible in wealth, more fertile in its fields?" So boasted the humanist Coluccio Salutati (1331–1406) in 1403 during one of the most calamitous periods in Florentine history. Salutati's boastings were not unusual; the Florentines' mythical view of their homeland, as savior of Christianity and as heir to the republican greatness of Rome, was everywhere apparent. And it seemed to be most vigorously expressed in the city's darkest moments. There is much in the belief that the artistic genius of Florence flowed from the turmoil of its economic and political life.

Florentine prosperity was built on two foundations: money and wool. Beginning in the thirteenth century, Florentine bankers were among the wealthiest and most powerful in the world. Initially their position was established through support of the papacy in its long struggle with the Holy Roman Empire. Florentine financiers established banks in all the capitals of Europe and the East, though their seats in Rome and Naples were probably most important. In the Middle Ages, bankers served more functions than simply handling and exchanging money. Most were also tied to mercantile adventures and underwrote industrial activity. So it was in Florence where international bankers purchased high-quality wool to be manufactured into the world's finest woven cloth. At its height before the plague, the cloth industry employed nearly thirty thousand workers, providing jobs at all levels of society, from the rural women who spun the wool into yarn at piecework wages, to the highly paid weavers and dyers whose skills made Florentine cloth so highly prized.

The activities of both commerce and cloth manufacture depended on external conditions, and thus the wealth of Florence was potentially unstable. In the mid-fourteenth century instability came with the plague that devastated the city. Nearly 40 percent of the entire population was lost in the single year 1348, and recurring outbreaks continued to ravage the already weakened survivors. Loss of workers and loss of markets seriously disrupted manufacturing. By 1380 cloth production had fallen to less than a quarter of preplague levels. On the heels of plague came wars. The property of Florentine bankers and merchants abroad was an easy target, and in this respect the wars with Naples at the end of the fourteenth century were particularly disastrous. Thirty years of warfare with Milan, interrupted by only a single decade of peace (1413–23), resulted in total bankruptcy for many of the city's leading commercial families. More significantly, the costs of warfare, offensive and defensive, created a massive public debt. Every Florentine of means owned shares in this debt, and the republic was continually devising new methods for borrowing and staving off crises of repayment. Small wonder that the republic turned for aid to the wealthiest banking family in Europe, the Medici.

As befitted a city whose prosperity was based on manufacturing, Florence had a strong guild tradition. The most important guilds were associated with banking and cloth manufacture but they included the crafts and food-processing trades as well. Only guild members could participate in government, electing the nine *Signoria* who administered laws, set tax rates, and directed foreign and domestic policy. Like that of Venice, Florentine government was a republican oligarchy and like Venice, it depended upon rotated short periods in office and selections by lot to avoid factionalism. But Florence had a history of factionalism longer than its history of republican government. Its formal structures were occasionally altered so that powerful families could gain control of the real centers of political power, the small councils and emergency assemblies through which the *Signoria* governed. This was especially the case following the revolt of the Ciompi (1378) in which the workers in the severely depressed cloth industry rioted and briefly gained control of the city. After that the merchant elite gripped the reins of government tightly, even establishing a kind of secret police to quash conspiracies. Conservative leadership drawn from the upper ranks of Florentine society guided the city through the wars of the early fourteenth century. But soon afterward the leaders of its greatest families, the Albizzi, the Pazzi, and the Medici, again divided Florentine politics into factions.

The ability of the Medici to secure a century-long dynasty in a government that did not have a head of state is just one of the mysteries surrounding the history of this remarkable family. Cosimo de' Medici (1389–1464) was one of the richest men in Christendom when he returned to the city in 1434 after a brief exile. His leading position in government rested upon supporters who were able to gain a controlling influence on the *Signoria*. Cosimo built his party carefully, banishing his Albizzi enemies, recruiting followers among the craftsmen whom he employed, and even paying delinquent taxes to maintain the eligibility of his voters. Most importantly, emergency powers were invoked to reduce the number of citizens qualified to vote for the *Signoria* until the majority were Medici backers.

Cosimo was a practical man. He raised his children along humanist principles and was a great patron of artists and intellectuals. He collected books and paintings, endowed libraries, and spent lavishly on his own palace, the Palazzo Medici, which after his death was transformed into the very center of Florentine cultural life. Cosimo's position as an international banker brought him into contact with the heads of other Italian city-states and it was his personal relationship with Francesco Sforza that finally ended the Milanese wars and brought about the Peace of Lodi.

It was Cosimo's grandson, Lorenzo (1449–92), who linked the family's name to that of the age. Lorenzo was trained to office as if he had been a prince rather than a citizen of a republic. His own father ruled for five years and used his son as a diplomat in order to acquaint him with the leaders of Europe. Diplomacy was Lorenzo's greatest achievement. He held strong humanist values instilled in him by his mother, Lucrezia Tornabuoni, who organized his education. He wrote poetry and drama and even entered competitions for architectural designs. But Lorenzo's chief contri-

bution to artistic life as it reached its height in Florence was to facilitate its production. He brought Michelangelo and other leading artists to his garden; he brought Pico della Mirandola and other leading humanists to his table. He secured commissions for Florentine artists throughout the peninsula, ensuring the spread of their influence and the continued regeneration of artistic creativity in Florence itself.

Lorenzo was generally regarded as the leading citizen of Florence and this was true both in terms of his wealth and his influence. He did not rule from high office, though he maintained the party that his grandfather had built and even extended it through wartime emergency measures. His power was based on his personality and reputation, a charisma enhanced when he survived an assassination attempt in which his brother was killed. His diplomatic abilities were the key to his survival. Almost immediately after Lorenzo came to power, Naples and the papacy began a war with Florence, a war that was costly to the Florentines in both taxation and lost territory. In 1479 Lorenzo traveled to Naples and personally convinced the Neapolitan king to sign a separate treaty. This restored the Italian balance of power and ensured continued Medici rule in Florence. Soon Lorenzo even had a treaty with the pope that allowed for the recovery of lost territories and the expansion of Florentine influence.

There is some doubt whether Lorenzo should be remembered by the title "the Magnificent" that was bestowed upon him. His absorption in politics came at the expense of the family's commercial enterprises, which were nearly ruined during his lifetime. Branch after branch of the Medici bank closed as conditions for international finance deteriorated. Though his children were all to enjoy successful careers, one as ruler of Florence, one as Pope Leo X, and the third as duke of Nemours, to whom Machiavelli originally dedicated *The Prince*, the family fortune was dwindling. Moreover, the emergency powers that Lorenzo invoked to restrict participation in government changed forever the character of Florentine republicanism, irredeemably corrupting it. There is no reason to accept the judgment of his enemies that Lorenzo was a tyrant, but the negative consequences of his rule cannot be ignored. Yet Lorenzo was celebrated because he stood for all that Florentines believed about their city during the last moments that its splendor was unquestionable. It was the city more than the man that was being dubbed "magnificent." In 1494, two years after Lorenzo's death, the peninsula was plunged into those wars that turned it from the center of European civilization into one of its lesser satellites.

The End of Italian Hegemony

In the course of the Renaissance western Europe was Italianized. For a century the city-states dominated the trade routes that connected East and West. Venetian and Genoese merchants exchanged spices and minerals from the Black Sea to the North Sea, enriching the material life of three continents. They brought wool from England and Spain to the skilled craftsmen in the Low Countries and Florence. Italian manufactures, such as Milanese artillery, Florentine silk, and Venetian glass, were prized above all others. The ducat and the florin, two Italian coins, were universally accepted in an age when every petty prince minted his own. The peninsula exported culture in the same way that it exported goods. Humanism quickly spread across the Alps, aided by the recent invention of printing (which the Venetians soon dominated), while Renaissance standards of artistic achievement were known worldwide and everywhere imitated. The city-states shared their technology as well. The compass and the navigational chart, projection maps, double-entry bookkeeping, eyeglasses, the telescope—all profoundly influenced what could be achieved and what could be hoped for. In this spirit Christopher Columbus, a Genoese seaman, successfully crossed the Atlantic under the Spanish flag, and Amerigo Vespucci, a Florentine merchant, gave his name to the newly discovered continents.

But it was not in Italy that the rewards of innovation or the satisfactions of achievement were enjoyed. There the seeds of political turmoil and military imperialism, combined with the rise of the Ottoman Turks, were to reap a not-unexpected harvest. Under the cover of the Peace of Lodi, the major city-states had scrambled to enlarge their mainland empires. By the end of the fifteenth century they eyed one another greedily and warily. Each expected the others to begin a

Italy, 1494

peninsula-wide war for hegemony and took the steps that ultimately ensured the contest. Perhaps the most unusual aspect of the imperialism of the city-states was that it had been restricted to the peninsula itself. Each of the major powers shared the dream of recapturing the glory that was Rome. Though the Venetians had expanded abroad, their acquisitions had not come through conquest or occupation. In their Greek and Dalmatian territories local law and custom continued to govern under the benevolent eye of Venetian administrators. But in their mainland territories the Venetians were as ruthless as were the Florentines in Pisa or as was Cesare Borgia in Romagna when he consolidated the Papal States by fire and sword. Long years of siege and occupation had militarized the Italian city-states. Venice and Florence balanced their budgets on the backs of their captured territories. Milan had been engaged in constant war for decades and even the papacy was militarily aggressive.

And the Italians were no longer alone. The most remarkable military leader of the age was not a Renaissance *condottiere* but an Ottoman prince, Mehmed II (1451–81), who conquered Constantinople and Athens and threatened

Rome itself. The rise of the Ottomans, whose name is derived from Osman, their original tribal leader, is one of the most compelling stories in world history. Little more than a warrior tribe at the beginning of the fourteenth century, a hundred and fifty years later the Ottomans had replaced stagnant Byzantine rule with a virile and potent empire. First they gobbled up the towns and cities in a wide arc around Constantinople. Then they fed upon the Balkans and the eastern kingdoms of Hungary and Poland. By 1400 they were a presence in all the territory that stretched from the Black Sea to the Aegean. By 1450 they were its master. (See Special Feature, "The Fall of Constantinople," pp. 350–351.)

Venice was most directly affected by the Ottoman advance. Not only was its favored position in eastern trade threatened, but during a prolonged war at the end of the fifteenth century the Venetians lost many of their most important commercial outposts. Ottoman might closed off the markets of eastern Europe. Islands in the Aegean and seaports along the Dalmatian coast fell to the Turks in alarming succession. By 1480 Venetian naval supremacy was a thing of the past.

The Italian city-states might have met this challenge from the east had they been able to unite in opposing it. Successive popes pleaded for holy wars to halt the advance of the Turks, which was compared in officially inspired propaganda to an outbreak of plague. The fall of Constantinople in 1453 was an event of epochal proportions for Europeans, many believing that it foreshadowed the end of the world. "A thing terrible to relate and to be deplored by all who have in them any spark of humanity. The splendor and glory of the East has been captured, despoiled, ravaged and completely sacked by the most inhuman barbarians," the Venetian doge was informed. Yet it was Italians rather than Ottomans who plunged the peninsula into those wars from which it never recovered.

The Wars of Italy (1494–1529) began when Naples, Florence, and the Papal States united against Milan. At first this alliance seemed little more than another shift in the balance of power. But rather than call upon Venice to redress the situation, the Milanese leader, Ludovico il Moro, sought help from the French. An army of French cavalry and Swiss mercenaries, led by Charles VIII of France (1483–98) invaded the peninsula in 1494. With Milanese support the French swept all before them. Florence was forced to surrender Pisa, a humiliation that led to the overthrow of the Medici and the establishment of French sovereignty. The Papal States were next to be occupied, and within a year Charles had conquered Naples without engaging the Italians in a single significant battle. Unfortunately, the Milanese were not the only ones who could play at the game of foreign alliances. Next it was the turn of the Venetians and the pope to unite and call upon the services of King Ferdinand of Aragon and the Holy Roman Emperor. Italy was now a battleground in what became a total European war for dynastic supremacy. The city-states used their foreign allies to settle old scores and to extend their own mainland empires. At the turn of the century Naples was dismembered. In 1509 the pope conspired to organize the most powerful combination of forces yet known against Venice. All of the "terra firma" possessions of the Most Serene Republic were lost, but by a combination of good fortune and skilled diplomacy Venice itself survived. Florence was less fortunate, becoming a pawn first of the French and then of the Spanish. The final blow to Italian hegemony was the sack of Rome in 1527, when German mercenaries fulfilled the fears of what the "infidels" would do to the Holy City.

Surveying the wreckage of the Italian wars Machiavelli ended *The Prince* with a plea for a leader to emerge to restore Italian freedom and re-create the unity of the ancient Roman republic. He concluded with these lines from Petrarch:

> Then virtue boldly shall engage
> And swiftly vanquish barbarous rage,
> Proving that ancient and heroic pride
> In true Italian hearts had never died.

The revival of "ancient and heroic pride" fueled the Italian revival. The sense of living in a new age, the spirit of human achievement, and the curiosity and wonderment of writers and artists all characterized the Renaissance. The desire to re-create the glories of Rome was not Machiavelli's alone. It could be seen in the palaces of the Italian aristocracy; in the papal rebuilding of the Holy City; and in the military ambitions of princes. But the legacy of empire, of "ancient and heroic pride," had passed out of Italian hands.

The Fall of Constantinople

The prayers of the devout were more fervent than ever on Easter Sunday, 1453. The Christians of Constantinople knew that it was only a matter of time before the last remaining stronghold of the Byzantine Empire came under siege. For decades the ring of Ottoman conquests had narrowed around this holy city until it alone stood out against the Turkish sultan. Constantinople, the bridge between Europe and Asia, was tottering. The once teeming center of Eastern Christianity had never recovered from the epidemics of the fourteenth century. Dwindling revenues matched the dwindling population. Concessions to Venetian and Genoese traders reduced customs while Ottoman conquests eliminated tribute money.

Perhaps it was this impoverishment that had kept the Turks at bay. Constantinople was still the best-fortified city in the world. Two of its three sides faced the sea, and the third was protected by two stout rings of walls and a trench lined with stones. No cannon forged in the West could dent these battlements and no navy could hope to force its way through the narrow mouth of the Golden Horn. A siege of Constantinople hardly seemed worthwhile as long as there were conquests to be made in eastern Europe and Asia Minor. Thus an uneasy peace existed between sultan and emperor. It

was shattered in 1451 when a new sultan, the nineteen-year-old Mehmed II, came to the throne. Mehmed's imagination was fired by the ancient prophecies that a Muslim would rule in all of the territories of the east. Only Constantinople was a fitting capital for such an empire, and Mehmed immediately began preparations for its conquest.

In 1452 Mehmed had constructed a fortress at the narrow mouth of the Bosporus and demanded tribute from all ships that entered the Golden Horn. The Byzantine emperor sent ambassadors to Mehmed to protest this aggression. Mehmed returned their severed heads. When the first Venetian convoy refused to lower its sails, Mehmed's artillery efficiently sank one of the galleys with a single shot. The Turks now controlled access to the city for trade and supplies. An attack the following spring seemed certain.

The emperor appealed far and wide for aid for his beleaguered city. Many had reasons for preserving Constantinople—the Venetians and Genoese to protect their trade; the pope to defend Christianity. Reluctantly, they agreed to act. But the Europeans were in no hurry to pledge their support, as it was inconceivable that the Ottomans could assemble the army necessary to besiege Constantinople before summer. By then, the Europeans assumed, an Italian armada could easily dislodge the Ottoman fortress and reinforce the city with trained fighting men.

But in this they reckoned

without Mehmed. While the Italians bickered over their share of the expedition and Christians everywhere made ready to celebrate Holy Week, the Ottomans assembled a vast army of fighters and laborers and a huge train of weapons and supplies. Among this was the largest cannon ever cast, with a twenty-six-foot barrel that shot a twelve-hundred-pound ball. Fifty teams of oxen and two hundred men took two months to pull it in place.

Mehmed's forces, which eventually numbered more than 150,000, of which 60,000 were soldiers, assembled around the walls of Constantinople on April 5. During the next week a great flotilla sailed up the Bosporus and anchored just out of reach of the Byzantine warships in the Golden Horn. A census taken inside the city revealed that there were only 7,000 able-bodied defenders, about 5,000 Greek residents and 2,000 foreigners, mostly Genoese and Venetians. The Italians were the only true soldiers among them.

Though the defenders were vastly outnumbered, they still held the military advantage. As long as their ships controlled the entrance to the Golden Horn, they could limit the Ottoman attack to only one side, where all of the best defenders could be massed. The Byzantines cast a boom—an iron chain supported by wooden floats—across the mouth of the bay to forestall a naval attack. By the middle of April the Turks had begun their land assault. Each day great guns pounded the walls of the city and each night residents worked frantically to repair the damage. Everyone contributed. Old women wove baskets in which children carried stones, monks and nuns packed mud and cut branches to shore up the breaches in the wall. The Turks suffered heavily for each attempt to follow a cannon shot with a massed charge. But the attack took its toll among the defenders as well. No one was safe from the flaming arrows and catapulted stones flung over the city's walls. Choking black smoke filled the air as the huge cannon shook the foundations of the city and treated its stout stone walls as if they were plaster. Nevertheless, in the first month of siege the defenders held their own.

The vigorous defense of the city infuriated Mehmed. As long as there was only one point of attack, the defenders could resist indefinitely. The line of assault had to be extended, and this could only be done by sea. With the boom effectively impregnable and with Italian seamen superior to the Turks, the prospects seemed dim. But what could not be achieved by force might be achieved by cunning. A plan was devised to carry a number of smaller ships across land and then to float them behind the Christian fleet. Protected by land forces, the ships could be used as a staging point for another line of attack. Thousands of workmen were set the task of building huge wooden rollers, which were greased with animal fat. Under cover of darkness and the smoke of cannon fire, seventy-two ships were pulled up the steep hills and pushed down into the sea. Once they were safely anchored, a pontoon bridge was built and cannon were trained on the seaward walls of the city.

The crafty plan succeeded, but moving ships across dry land was not the only engineering feat that sapped the defenders. One night a tower higher than the city's battlements was assembled in front of the landward walls. From there archers pelted the city and sorties of attackers sallied forth. In May, the defenders discovered the tunnels the Turks had built underneath the city, one of which had reached beyond the second ring of protective walls. The attacks and bombardments were now relentless. The city had withstood siege for nearly six weeks without any significant reinforcement. At the end of the month there was a sudden lull. A messenger from the sultan arrived to demand surrender. The choice was clear. If the city was taken by force the customary three days of unrestricted pillage would be allowed, but if it yielded, the sultan pledged to protect the property of all who desired to remain under his rule. The emperor replied feebly that no one who had ever laid siege to Constantinople had enjoyed a long life. He was ready to die in defense of the city.

On May 30 the final assault began. Mehmed knew that his advantage lay in numbers. First he sent in waves of irregular troops, mostly captured slaves and Christians, who suffered great losses and were finally driven back by the weakened defenders. Next, better-trained warriors attacked and widened the breaches made by the irregulars. Finally came the crack Janissaries, the sultan's elite warriors, disciplined from birth to fight. It was the Janissaries who found a small door left open at the base of the wall. In they rushed, quickly overwhelming the first line of defenders and battering their way through the weaker second walls. By dawn the Ottoman flag was raised over the battlements and the sack of Constantinople had begun.

There was no need for the customary three days of pillage. By the end of the first day there was nothing left worth taking. The churches and monasteries had been looted and defaced, the priests and nuns murdered or defiled, and thousands of civilians had been captured to be sold into slavery. Large areas of the city smoldered from countless fires. The desolation was so complete that not even Mehmed could take joy in the ceremonial procession into the new capital of his empire. The bastion of Eastern Christendom was no more.

Suggestions for Further Reading

General Reading

Ernst Breisach, *Renaissance Europe 1300–1517* (New York: Macmillan, 1973). A solid survey of the political history of the age.

* Denys Hay, *The Italian Renaissance* (Cambridge: Cambridge University Press, 1977). An elegant interpretive essay. The best first book to read.

J. R. Hale, ed., *A Concise Encyclopedia of the Italian Renaissance* (Oxford: Oxford University Press, 1981). A treasure trove of facts about the major figures and events of the era.

* P. Burke, *Culture and Society in Renaissance Italy* (Princeton, NJ: Princeton University Press, 1987). A good introduction to social and intellectual developments.

Renaissance Society

* M. Aston, *The Fifteenth Century: The Prospect of Europe* (London: Thames and Hudson, 1968). A concise survey of Continental history; well written and illustrated.

* J. R. Hale, *Renaissance Europe: The Individual and Society* (Berkeley, CA: University of California Press, 1978). A lively study that places the great figures of the Renaissance in their social context.

* Carlo Cipolla, *Before the Industrial Revolution: European Society and Economy, 1000–1700* (New York: Norton, 1976). A sweeping survey of social and economic developments across the centuries.

* Harry Miskimin, *The Economy of Early Renaissance Europe 1300–1460* (Englewood Cliffs, NJ: Prentice Hall, 1969). A detailed scholarly study of economic development.

D. Herlihy and C. Klapiche-Zuber, *The Tuscans and Their Families* (New Haven, CT: Yale University Press, 1985). Difficult but rewarding study of the social and demographic history of Florence and its environs.

* Christiane Klapiche-Zuber, *Women, Family, and Ritual in Renaissance Italy* (Chicago: University of Chicago Press, 1985). A sparkling collection of essays on diverse topics in social history from wet-nursing to family life.

Renaissance Art

* Michael Baxandall, *Painting and Experience in Fifteenth Century Italy* (Oxford: Oxford University Press, 1972). A study of the relationship between painters and their patrons, of how and why art was produced.

Frederick Hartt, *History of Italian Renaissance Art* (Englewood Cliffs, NJ: Prentice Hall, 1974). The most comprehensive survey, with hundreds of plates.

* Michael Levey, *Early Renaissance* (London: Penguin Books, 1967). A concise survey of art; clearly written and authoritative.

* Rudolph Wittkower, *Architectural Principles in the Age of Humanism* (New York: Norton, 1971). A difficult but rewarding study of Renaissance architecture.

John Pope-Hennessy, *Introduction to Italian Sculpture* (New York: Phaidon, 1972). A thorough analysis of the development of sculpture; carefully illustrated.

* Linda Murray, *High Renaissance and Mannerism* (London: Thames and Hudson, 1985). The best introduction to late Renaissance art.

* Howard Hibbard, *Michelangelo* (New York: Harper & Row, 1974). A compelling biography of an obsessed genius.

Renaissance Ideals

* Hans Baron, *The Crisis of the Early Italian Renaissance* (Princeton, NJ: Princeton University Press, 1966). One of the most influential intellectual histories of the period.

* Ernst Cassirer, ed., *The Renaissance Philosophy of Man* (Chicago: University of Chicago Press, 1948). Translations of the works of Petrarch, Valla, and Pico della Mirandola, among others, with excellent introductions.

George Holmes, *The Florentine Enlightenment* (New York: Pegasus, 1969). The best work on the successive generations of Florentine humanists.

Albert Rabil, ed., *Renaissance Humanism* (Philadelphia: University of Pennsylvania Press, 1988). A multi-authored, multi-volume collection of essays on humanism, with all of the latest scholarship.

* Quentin Skinner, *Machiavelli* (Oxford: Oxford University Press, 1981). A brief but brilliant life.

The Politics of the Italian City-States

* Lauro Martines, *Power and Imagination: City-States in Renaissance Italy* (New York: Alfred A. Knopf, 1979). An important interpretation of the politics of the Italian powers.

* Frederic C. Lane, *Venice: A Maritime Republic* (Baltimore: Johns Hopkins University Press, 1973). A complete history of Venice, which stresses its naval and mercantile developments.

* Gene Brucker, *Renaissance Florence*, 2d ed. (Berkeley, CA: University of California Press, 1983). The best single volume introduction to Florentine history.

* J. R. Hale, *Florence and the Medici* (London: Thames and Hudson, 1977). A compelling account of the relationship between a city and its most powerful citizens.

* Eugene F. Rice, Jr., *The Foundations of Early Modern Europe 1460–1559* (New York: Norton, 1970). The best short, synthetic work.

*Indicates paperback edition available.

MAP CREDITS
325 Europe, ca. 1500 Based on information from Jan de Vries, *European Urbanization, 1500-1800* (Cambridge, MA: Harvard University Press, 1984).

PHOTOGRAPH CREDITS
Positions of the photographs are indicated in the abbreviated form as follows; top (t), bottom (b), center (c), left (1), right (r). Unless otherwise acknowledged, all photographs are the property of Scott, Foresman.

TABLE OF CONTENTS
v (t) Hirmer Fotoarchiv, Munich (b) Courtesy of The Oriental Institute of The University of Chicago
vi Hirmer Fotoarchiv, Munich
vii Bibliothèque Nationale, Paris
viii(t) Giraudon/Art Resource, NY (b) Scala/Art Resource, NY

CHAPTER OPENERS
Chapter 1, p. 2 Europe photographed from space. European Space Agency
Chapter 2, p. 34 *Achilles Dragging the Body of Hector around the Walls of Troy*, Attic black-figured water jar, c. 510 B. C. William Francis Warden Fund. Courtesy, Museum of Fine Arts, Boston
Chapter 3, p. 66-67 *Battle of Issus* and a detail showing Alexander the Great. Mosaic copy of a Hellenistic painting. (both) Scala/Art Resource, NY
Chapter 4, p. 102 The Roman Forum. Istituto Geografico de Agostini, Milan. Photo: A. De Gregorio
Chapter 5, p. 134 Fully excavated street (Cardo IV) in Herculaneum. Scala/Art Resource, NY
Chapter 6, p. 166-167 Barbarian medallion (front and back) of Valentinian I and Valens. (both) Hirmer Fotoarchiv, Munich
Chapter 7, p. 192-193 Doorway and courtyard, the Great Mosque, Damascus. (192) Shostal/SuperStock (193) Hubertus Kanus/SuperStock
Chapter 8, p. 224 Interior of the Palatine Chapel, Aachen. Domkapitel Aachen. Photo: Ann Münchow
Chapter 9, p. 258-259 Details of the *Bayeux Tapestry*, c. 1073-83 (all) Giraudon/Art Resource, NY
Chapter 10, p. 292 Chevet and portrait bust of Emperor Charles IV by Peter Parler, Saint Vitus Cathedral, Prague. (both) Michael Wolgensinger
Chapter 11, p. 322-323 *The Procession of the Relic of the Holy Cross* by Gentile Bellini, 1496. Scala/Art Resource, NY

CHAPTER 1
4 The Cleveland Museum of National History 5 © Kazuyoshi Nomachi/pacific Press Service 6 Aldo Durazzi 7 Kathleen M. Kenyon/Jericho Excavations 10 Reproduced by Courtesy of the Trustees of the British Museum 11 Cliché des Musées Nationaux, Paris 12 Hirmer Fotoarchiv, Munich 13 Courtesy of The Oriental Institute of the University of Chicago 15 Hirmer Fotoarchiv, Munich 16 Hirmer Fotoarchiv, Munich 19 John Stevens/Ancient Art & Architecture Collection 20 Reproduced by Courtesy of the Trustees of the British Museum 22 The Metropolitan Museum of Art, Rogers Fund 1931 23 Hirmer Fotoarchiv, Munich 24 The Metropolitan Museum of Art, Photograph by Harry Burton 25 Lee Boltin 28 Erich Lessing/Magnum 30 Reproduced by Courtesy of the Trustees of the British Museum

CHAPTER 2
36 The Metropolitan Museum of Art, Rogers Fund, 1947 38 Hirmer Fotoarchiv, Munich 39 (t) Scala/Art Resource, NY (b) Hirmer Fotoarchiv, Munich 40 Hirmer Fotoarchiv, Munich 41 Ronald Sheridan/Ancient Art & Architecture Collection 42 Deutsches Archäologisches Institut, Athens 43 Reproduced by Courtesy of the Trustees of the British Museum 45 Reproduced by Courtesy of the Trustees of the British Museum 47 Bibliothèque Nationale, Paris 48 Scala/Art Resource, NY 50 Alexander Tsiaras/Stock, Boston 52 Staatliche Museen Preussischer Kulturbesitz, Antikenmuseum, Berlin 53 Reproduced by Courtesy of the Trustees of the British Museum 54 Scala/Art Resource, NY 55 (tl, b) Hirmer Fotoarchiv, Munich (tr) The Metropolitan Museum of Art, Fletcher Fund, 1932 56 Hirmer Fotoarchiv, Munich 59 Wadsworth Atheneum, Hartford. J. Pierpont Morgan Collection. © Wadsworth Atheneum 62 Lee Boltin

CHAPTER 3
68 Raymond V. Schoder, S. J. © 1989 Loyola University of Chicago 69 American School of Classical Studies at Athens: Agora Excavations 72 Staatliche Museen Preussischer Kulturbesitz, Antikenmuseum, Berlin 74 William Francis Warden Fund. Courtesy, Museum of Fine Arts, Boston 79 Reproduced by Courtesy of the Trustees of the British Museum 80 Staatliche Antikensammlungen und Glyptothek, Munich 81 Martin-von-Wagner Museum, University of Wurzburg 83 The Metropolitan Museum of Art, Rogers Fund, 1952 84 (t) Ronald Sheridan/Ancient Art & Architecture Collection (bl, br) Robert Frerck/Odyssey Productions, Chicago 87 Alinari/Art Resource, NY 88 Scala/Art Resource, NY 92 Reproduced by Courtesy of the Trustees of the British Museum 96 Scala/Art Resource, NY 97 The Metropolitan Museum of Art, Bequest of Walter C. Baker, 1971

CHAPTER 4
104 Hirmer Fotoarchiv, Munich 106 Arxiu Mas, Barcelona 107 Hirmer Fotoarchiv, Munich 109 Hirmer Fotoarchiv, Munich 114 Bibliothèque Nationale, Paris 115 Alinari/Art Resource, NY 119 Museo Nazionale, Naples 123 (both) Giraudon/Art Resource, NY 124 Giraudon/Art Resource, NY 125 Alinari/Art Resource, NY 127 The Metropolitan Museum of Art 128 Scala/Art Resource, NY 129 Alinari/Art Resource, NY

CHAPTER 5
136 Römisch-Germanisches Zentralmuseum, Mainz 137 Reproduced by Courtesy of the Trustees of the British Museum 139 Erich Lessing/Magnum 143 H. Roger-Viollet 146 Alinari/Art Resource, NY 147 Scala/Art Resource, NY 149 Scala/Art Resource, NY 152 Museo Torlonia, Rome 153 Staatliche Skulpturensammlung, Dresden 155 Ronald Sheridan/Ancient Art & Architecture Collection 156 Alinari/Art Resource, NY 163 Alinari/Art Resource, NY

CHAPTER 6
169 Bibliothèque Nationale, Paris 170 Alinari/Art Resource, NY 172 Alinari/Art Resource, NY 174 Scala/Art Resource, NY 176 André Held 177 Hirmer Fotoarchiv, Munich 181 Reproduced by Courtesy of the Trustees of the British Museum 182 Vatican Museums 186 (1) Worcester Art Museum, Worcester, Massachusetts (c) Hirmer Fotoarchiv, Munich (r) Scala/Art Resource, NY 187 (1) The Virginia Museum of Fine Arts, Richmond. Museum Purchase: The Adolph D. and Wilkins C. Williams Fund (c) After A. Grabar, *Byzantium* (r) Staatliche Museen Preussischer Kulturbesitz, Antikenmuseum, Berlin 189 Cliché des Musées Nationaux, Paris

CHAPTER 7
195 Giraudon/Art Resource, NY 196 Erich Lessing/Magnum 197 Reproduced by Courtesy of the Trustees of the British Museum 198 Giraudon/Art Resource, NY 199 Bibliothèque Nationale, Paris 202 Roger Wood 205 Courtesy of the Freer Gallery of Art, Smithsonian Institution, Washington, D. C. (30.60) 206 Bibliothèque Nationale, Paris 207 Bibliothèque Nationale, Paris 210 The Metropolitan Museum of Art, The Cloisters Collection, 1966 213 Arxiu Mas, Barcelona 216 The Metropolitan Museum of Art, Rogers Fund, 1918 217 The Metropolitan Museum of Art, Bequest of Edward C. Moore, 1891. The Edward C. Moore Collection

CHAPTER 8
226 Fototeca Unione, Rome 229 Ann Münchow 231 Bodleian Library, Oxford. MS. OPP. 154, fol, 39v 232 Reproduced by Courtesy of the Trustees of the British Museum 233 The British Library 234 Foto Marburg 237 Österreichische Nationalbibliothek, Vienna 239 Reproduced by Courtesy of the Trustees of the British Museum 243 Giraudon/Art Resource, NY 245 Bibliothèque Nationale, Paris 246 The Board of Trinity College Dublin 247 Bibliotheek der Rijksuniversiteit, Utrecht

CHAPTER 9
260 Bridgeman/Art Resource, NY 263 Giraudon/Art Resource, NY

264 Giraudon/Art Resource, NY 265 The British Library 267 Giraudon/Art Resource, NY 271 Bodleian Library, Oxford. MS. Bodley 264, fol. 218r 274 The British Library 278 Alinari/Art Resource, NY

CHAPTER 10
295 Bibliothèque Nationale, Paris 298 Bibliothèque Nationale, Paris 302 Giraudon/Art Resource, NY 303 The Metropolitan Museum of Art, The Cloisters Collection, 1969 306 Bibliothèque Nationale, Paris 310 Copyright Bibliothèque royale Albert Ier,

Bruxelles. MS. 9392, fol. 6lv 315 State Library of the Czechoslovak Socialist Republic, Prague: University Library 318 The British Library

CHAPTER 11
326 Rijksmuseum Amsterdam 327 Scala/Art Resource, NY 328 Scala/Art Resource, NY 333 Scala/Art Resource, NY 334 Scala/Art Resource, NY 335 Scala/Art Resource, NY 337 Scala/Art Resource, NY 339 Biblioteca Nazionale Marciana, Venice 341 Scala/Art Resource, NY

INDEX